# Additional Toolbar Features and Functions

W9-CEQ-582

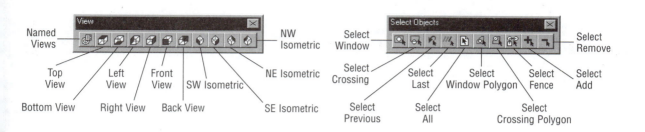

View toolbar:
- Named Views
- Top View
- Bottom View
- Left View
- Right View
- Front View
- Back View
- SW Isometric
- NW Isometric
- NE Isometric
- SE Isometric

Select Objects toolbar:
- Select Window
- Select Crossing
- Select Previous
- Select Last
- Select All
- Select Window Polygon
- Select Crossing Polygon
- Select Fence
- Select Add
- Select Remove

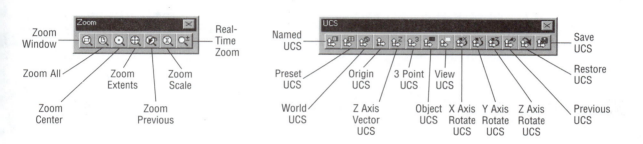

Zoom toolbar:
- Zoom Window
- Zoom All
- Zoom Center
- Zoom Extents
- Zoom Previous
- Zoom Scale
- Real-Time Zoom

UCS toolbar:
- Named UCS
- Preset UCS
- World UCS
- Origin UCS
- Z Axis Vector UCS
- 3 Point UCS
- Object UCS
- View UCS
- X Axis Rotate UCS
- Y Axis Rotate UCS
- Z Axis Rotate UCS
- Previous UCS
- Save UCS
- Restore UCS

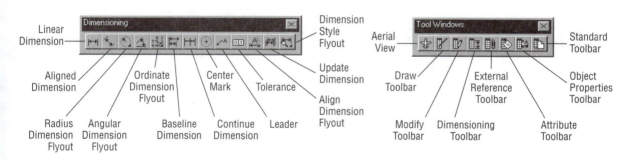

Dimensioning toolbar:
- Linear Dimension
- Aligned Dimension
- Radius Dimension Flyout
- Angular Dimension Flyout
- Ordinate Dimension Flyout
- Baseline Dimension
- Continue Dimension
- Center Mark
- Leader
- Tolerance
- Align Dimension Flyout
- Update Dimension
- Dimension Style Flyout

Tool Windows toolbar:
- Aerial View
- Draw Toolbar
- Modify Toolbar
- Dimensioning Toolbar
- External Reference Toolbar
- Attribute Toolbar
- Standard Toolbar
- Object Properties Toolbar

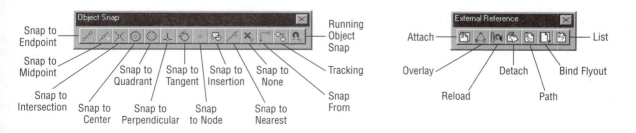

Object Snap toolbar:
- Snap to Endpoint
- Snap to Midpoint
- Snap to Intersection
- Snap to Center
- Snap to Quadrant
- Snap to Perpendicular
- Snap to Tangent
- Snap to Node
- Snap to Insertion
- Snap to Nearest
- Snap to None
- Snap From
- Tracking
- Running Object Snap

External Reference toolbar:
- Attach
- Overlay
- Reload
- Detach
- Path
- Bind Flyout
- List

# Mastering™ AutoCAD® LT

## George Omura

SYBEX®

San Francisco • Paris • Düsseldorf • Soest

Associate Publisher: Amy Romanoff

Acquisitions Manager: Kristine Plachy

Developmental Editor: Melanie Spiller

Editor: Kristen Vanberg-Wolff

Project Editors: Kim Wimpsett and Lee Ann Pickrell

Technical Editor: Robin Hansen

Book Designer: London Road Design

Electronic Publishing Specialists: Kate Kaminski and London Road Design

Production Coordinator: Alexa Riggs

Indexer: Nancy Guenther

Cover Designer: Design Site

Cover Photographer: Mark Johann

Screen reproductions produced with Collage Complete.

Collage Complete is a trademark of Inner Media Inc.

SYBEX is a registered trademark of SYBEX Inc.

Mastering is a trademark of SYBEX Inc.

TRADEMARKS: SYBEX has attempted throughout this book to distinguish proprietary trademarks from descriptive terms by following the capitalization style used by the manufacturer.

Every effort has been made to supply complete and accurate information. However, SYBEX assumes no responsibility for its use, nor for any infringement of the intellectual property rights of third parties which would result from such use.

Library of Congress Card Number: 96-69282

ISBN: 0-7821-1855-0

Manufactured in the United States of America

10 9 8 7 6 5 4 3 2 1

## Warranty

SYBEX warrants the enclosed CD-ROM to be free of physical defects for a period of ninety (90) days after purchase. If you discover a defect in the CD during this warranty period, you can obtain a replacement CD at no charge by sending the defective CD, postage prepaid, with proof of purchase to:

SYBEX Inc.
Customer Service Department
1151 Marina Village Parkway
Alameda, CA 94501
(800) 227-2346
Fax: (510) 523-2373

After the 90-day period, you can obtain a replacement by sending us the defective CD, proof of purchase, and a check or money order for $10, payable to SYBEX.

## Disclaimer

SYBEX makes no warranty or representation, either express or implied, with respect to this medium or its contexts, its quality, performance, merchantability, or fitness for a particular purpose. In no event will SYBEX, its distributors, or dealers be liable for direct, indirect, special, incidental, or consequential damages arising out of the use of or inability to use the software even if advised of the possibility of such damage.

The exclusion of implied warranties is not permitted by some states. Therefore, the above exclusion may not apply to you. This warranty provides you with specific legal rights; there may be other rights that you may have that vary from state to state.

## Copy Protection

None of the files on the CD are copy-protected. However, in all cases, reselling or redistribution of these files, except as specifically provided for by the copyright owners, is prohibited.

*To all my teachers*

# Acknowledgments

Thanks and much gratitude go to everyone who helped create this book. I'd like to thank developmental editors Richard Mills and Melanie Spiller and also associate publisher Amy Romanoff, who started things off and gave encouragement along the way; project editors Kim Wimpsett and Lee Ann Pickrell for expertly managing this project; editor Kristen Vanberg-Wolff, whose editorial skills contributed much to the quality and consistency of this book; and Robin Hansen, technical reviewer, for her comments, tips, and advice.

Many thanks go to the Sybex production staff for its efforts to get this book out on the usual impossible schedule: production coordinator Alexa Riggs, electronic publishing specialists Kate Kaminski and Bob Bihlmayer, and everyone else who lent a hand during the process.

At Autodesk, Art Cooney, technical support, gave invaluable advice, and Lisa Senauke and Jeffrey Allen provided the greatly needed prerelease software.

I must also thank my colleagues, Paul Richardson and Christine Meredith at Technical Publications, for their invaluable assistance in the preparation of this edition.

And finally, as ever, thanks to my family—Cynthia, Arthur, and Charles —for their ongoing encouragement and support.

# Contents at a Glance

# Table of Contents

## *Appendices*    **693**

# Introduction

Welcome to *Mastering AutoCAD LT*. As many readers have already discovered, this book is a unique blend of tutorial and source book, which offers everything you need to get started and stay ahead with AutoCAD LT.

## How to Use This Book

Rather than just showing you how each command works, *Mastering AutoCAD LT* shows you AutoCAD LT in the context of a meaningful activity: you will learn how to use commands to reach a goal. It also provides a foundation on which you can build your own methods for using AutoCAD LT and become an AutoCAD LT expert yourself. For this reason, I haven't covered every single command or every permutation of a command response. The AutoCAD LT help system (described in *Chapter 2*) and the AutoCAD LT User's Guide are quite adequate for this purpose. You should think of this book as a way to get a detailed look at AutoCAD LT as it is used on a real project. As you follow the exercises, I encourage you to also explore AutoCAD LT on your own, applying the techniques you learn to your own work.

If you are not an experienced user, you may want to read *Mastering AutoCAD LT* as a tutorial from front to back because later chapters rely on the skills and information you learned in earlier ones. To help you navigate, the exercises are shown in numbered steps. *Mastering AutoCAD LT* can also be used as a ready reference for your day-to-day problems and questions about commands. Optional exercises at the end of each chapter will help you review what you have learned.

## Getting Information Fast

If you are already familiar with AutoCAD LT, you will appreciate the Fast Tracks at the beginning of each chapter. Fast Tracks are highly encapsulated instructions on the use of commands and functions found in the chapter. They include the page number in the chapter where you can find a more detailed description of the function or command. If you only need to refresh your memory on how to do something, check the Fast Tracks first.

I've also included comments labeled as *Notes*, *Tips*, and *Warnings*. Notes supplement the main text, Tips are designed to make practice easier, and Warnings steer you away from pitfalls. Also, in each chapter you will find more extensive tips and discussions in the form of specially screened *sidebars*. Together they provide a wealth of information gathered by using AutoCAD LT on a variety of projects in different office environments. You may want to browse through the book, just reading the margin notes and sidebars, to get an idea of how they might be useful to you.

In *Appendices D* and *E*, I provide tables of all the system variables and commands with comments on their use and options. And inside the front cover of the book, you'll find labeled illustrations of the many toolbars available with AutoCAD LT for Windows.

## What to Expect

*Mastering AutoCAD LT* is divided into five parts, each representing a milestone in your progress toward becoming an expert AutoCAD LT user. Here is a description of those parts and what they will show you.

### Part 1: The Basics

As with any major endeavor, you must begin by tackling small, manageable tasks. In this first part, you will get familiar with the way Auto-CAD LT looks and feels. *Chapter 1: This Is AutoCAD LT* shows you how to get around the AutoCAD LT window. In *Chapter 2: Creating Your First Drawing*, you will learn how to start and exit the program and how to respond to AutoCAD LT commands. *Chapter 3: Learning the Tools of the Trade* tells you how to set up a work area, edit objects, and lay out a drawing. In *Chapter 4: Organizing Your Work*, you will explore some tools unique to CAD: symbols, blocks, and layers. As you are introduced to AutoCAD LT, you will also get a chance to make some drawings you can use later in the book and perhaps even in future projects of your own.

## Part 2: Building on the Basics

Once you have the basics down, you will begin to explore some of AutoCAD LT's more subtle qualities. *Chapter 5: Editing for Productivity* tells you how to reuse drawing setup information and parts of an existing drawing. In *Chapter 6: Enhancing Your Drawing Skills*, you will learn how to assemble and edit a large drawing file. *Chapter 7: Printing and Plotting* shows you how to get your drawing onto hard copy. *Chapter 8: Adding Text to Drawings* tells you how to annotate your drawing and edit your notes. *Chapter 9: Using Dimensions* gives you practice in using automatic dimensioning, another unique AutoCAD capability. Along the way, I will be giving you tips on editing and problems you may encounter as you begin to use AutoCAD LT for more complex tasks.

## Part 3: Becoming an Expert

At this point, you will be on the verge of becoming a real expert. The third part is designed to help you polish your existing skills and give you a few new ones. *Chapter 10: Attributes—Storing Data with Graphics* tells you how to attach information to drawing objects and how to link your drawing to database files. In *Chapter 11: Copying Pre-existing Drawings into AutoCAD LT*, you will learn some techniques for transferring paper drawings to AutoCAD LT. In *Chapter 12: Power Editing*, you will complete the apartment building tutorial, and in the process, you will learn how to integrate what you've learned so far and gain some tips on working in groups. *Chapter 13: Drawing Curves and Solid Fills* gives you an in-depth look at some special drawing objects, such as spline and fitted curves. In *Chapter 14: Getting and Exchanging Data from Drawings*, you will practice getting information about a drawing, and you will learn how AutoCAD LT can interact with other applications, such as spreadsheets, word processors, and desktop-publishing programs. You'll also learn how to copy and paste data.

## Part 4: Working in Three Dimensions

While 2D drafting is AutoCAD LT's workhorse application, AutoCAD LT's 3D capabilities give you a chance to expand your ideas and look at them in a new light. *Chapter 15: Creating 3D Models* covers AutoCAD LT's basic features for creating three-dimensional drawings. *Chapter 16: Navigating in 3D Space* introduces you to two different ways to orient and view your 3D objects.

## Part 5: Customizing AutoCAD LT

In the last part of the book, you will learn how you can take control of AutoCAD LT. *Chapter 17: Integrating AutoCAD LT into Your Projects and Organization* shows you how you can create menus and toolbars which adapt AutoCAD LT to your own work style.

## The Appendices

Finally, this book has five appendices. *Appendix A: Hardware and Software Tips* should give you a start on selecting hardware appropriate for AutoCAD LT. It also provides tips on improving AutoCAD LT's performance and troubleshooting. *Appendix B: Installing and Setting Up AutoCAD LT* contains an installation and configuration tutorial that you should follow before starting *Chapter 1* if AutoCAD LT is not already installed on your system. *Appendix C* describes the bonus software available on the CD-ROM. *Appendix D: System and Dimension Variables* will illuminate the references to the system variables scattered throughout the book. *Appendix D* also discusses the many dimension settings and system features AutoCAD LT has to offer. Finally, *Appendix E: Standard AutoCAD LT Commands* provides a listing of all the AutoCAD LT commands, with a brief description of their function and options.

# The Minimum System Requirements

This book assumes you have an IBM-compatible 80486 computer that will run AutoCAD LT and support a mouse. Your computer should have at least one disk drive capable of reading a 3″ 1.44MB disk and a hard disk with about 150MB or more free space (about 70MB for the AutoCAD LT program and at least another 64MB available for drawing files and work space for AutoCAD LT). A CD-ROM is a preferred option as it makes installation easier, and it allows you to take advantage of AutoCAD LT's online documentation. In addition to these requirements, you should also have enough space for a permanent swap file. Consult *Appendix A* of this book for more information on this. AutoCAD LT Release 3 runs best on systems with at least 16MB or more of RAM, though you can get by with 12MB.

Your computer should also have a high-resolution monitor and a color display card. The current standard is the Super VGA. This is adequate for most AutoCAD LT work. The computer should also have at least one serial port. I also assume you are using a mouse and have the use of a printer or a plotter.

If you want a more detailed explanation of hardware options with AutoCAD LT, look at *Appendix A*. You will find a general description of the available hardware options and their significance to AutoCAD LT.

## Doing Things in Style

Much care has been taken to see that the stylistic conventions in this book—the use of upper- or lowercase letters, italic or boldface type, and so on—will be the ones most likely to help you learn AutoCAD LT. On the whole, their effect should be subliminal. You may find it useful, however, to be conscious of the following rules that we have followed:

1. Pull-down menu selections are shown by a series of menu options separated by the ➤ symbol.

2. Keyboard entries are shown in boldface (e.g. enter **Rotate** ↵).

3. Command line prompts are shown in a different font (e.g. Array).

For most functions, we describe how to select options from toolbar buttons and flyouts. In addition, where applicable, we include related command names in parentheses. By providing command names, we have a way of providing continuity for those readers already familiar with the earlier versions of AutoCAD LT.

## All This and Software, Too

Finally, we have included a CD-ROM containing bonus utilities, as well as symbol and custom linetype libraries that can greatly enhance your use of AutoCAD LT. *Appendix C* gives you detailed information about the CD. Here's a brief rundown of what's available. Check it out!

## *Finding What You Want in the Third-Party World*

When you're ready to expand into third-party products, we've included the latest Autodesk Resource Guide. This is a comprehensive online database of nearly every third-party hardware and software product available for AutoCAD and AutoCAD LT. Many of the programs in the Resource Guide include demos and screen shots, so you can get a better idea of what is offered.

## *Drawing Files for the Exercises*

We've even included drawing files from the exercises in this book. These are provided so that you can pick up an exercise anywhere in the book, without having to work through the book from front to back.

# New Features of Release 3

AutoCAD LT Release 3 offers a higher level of speed, accuracy, and ease of use. It has always provided drawing accuracy to 16 decimal places. With this kind of accuracy, you can create a computer model of the earth and include details down to submicron levels. It also means that no matter how often you edit an AutoCAD LT drawing, its dimensions will remain true. And AutoCAD LT Release 3 has improved its display speed and other operations, so learning and using AutoCAD LT is easier than ever.

Other new features include:

▶ Windows 95 user interface ISO-compliant linetypes, dimensions, and hatching

▶ File Preview when opening files (see *Chapter 1*)

▶ ZoomIn/Out single-click options and also Real-Time Pan and Zoom (see *Chapter 1*)

▶ Object selection cycling for easier selection of objects close together (see *Chapter 3*)

▶ Improved Object Snaps with Snap From: and Tracking (see *Chapter 3*)

▶ Improvements to many existing commands, such as Extend and Trim to apparent objects (see *Chapter 3*)

▶ New construction geometry (Rays and Xlines), similar to manual drafting construction lines (see *Chapter 5*)

▶ Complex linetypes that can include text or multiple lines (see *Chapters 4* and *5*)

▶ Associative hatching and easier hatch editing (see *Chapter 6*)

▶ Multiple-line text objects (Paragraph text) for easy creation and editing of multiple lines of text (see *Chapter 8*)

▶ Spell checking with customizing capability (see *Chapter 8*)

▶ Streamlined dimensioning commands (see *Chapter 9*)

▶ Tolerance Notation tools for mechanical drafting (see *Chapter 9*)

▶ Curved leader tool (see *Chapter 9*)

▶ True ellipses and elliptical arcs and curves (NURBS) (see *Chapter 13*)

▶ Support for OLE as both client and server, allowing you to cut and paste spreadsheets, text, bitmaps, video clips, and sound into Auto-CAD LT (see *Chapter 14*)

▶ Customizable toolbars and toolbar icons (see *Chapter 17*)

▶ Individual pull-down menu groups can be added without replacing the entire menu file (see *Chapter 17*)

▶ Linetypes can now include text or complex shapes (see *Chapter 17*)

# The AutoCAD LT Package

This book assumes you are using AutoCAD LT Release 3.

## The User's Guide

The AutoCAD LT User's Guide consists of three main sections plus some useful Appendices. The sections are as follows:

▶ Drawing with AutoCAD LT (which includes a chapter on installing the software)

▶ Completing Your Drawings

▶ Customizing AutoCAD LT

You'll probably want to read the installation guide for Windows 95 first, then browse through the first two sections to get a feel for the kind of information available there. You may want to save Customizing AutoCAD LT for later when you've become more familiar with AutoCAD LT.

## The Disks

AutoCAD LT comes on a single disk and CD-ROM combination. Optionally, you can get AutoCAD LT on a set of diskettes. Before you do anything else, make copies of your disks and put the originals in a safe place.

## The Digitizer Template

If you intend to use a digitizer tablet in place of a mouse, Autodesk also provides you with a digitizer template. Commands can be selected directly from the template by pointing at the command on the template and pressing the pick button. Each command is shown clearly by name and a simple icon. Commands are grouped on the template by the type of operation the command performs. Before you can use the digitizer template, you must configure the digitizer. See *Appendix A: Hardware and Software Tips* for a more detailed description of digitizing tablets and *Appendix B* for instructions on configuring the digitizer.

# The Basics

As with any major endeavor, you must begin by tackling small, manageable tasks. In this first part, you will get familiar with the way AutoCAD LT looks and feels. *Chapter 1: This is AutoCAD LT* shows you how to get around the AutoCAD LT window. In *Chapter 2: Creating Your First Drawing*, you will learn how to start and exit the program and how to respond to AutoCAD LT commands. *Chapter 3: Learning the Tools of the Trade* tells you how to set up a work area, edit objects, and lay out a drawing. In *Chapter 4: Organizing Your Work*, you will explore some tools unique to CAD: symbols, blocks, and layers.

# Chapter 1
# This Is AutoCAD LT

## FAST TRACKS

**A**UTO**CAD LT** has undergone a major facelift for Version 3.0. With AutoCAD LT's new Windows 95 and Windows NT user interface, you have the freedom to arrange the screen by clicking and dragging its components. AutoCAD LT offers many time-saving tools such as a drop-down list for layer settings and line types, toolbars for easy access to all of AutoCAD LT's commands, and flyout menus that remember the last item you've selected. You have an expanded help system, with online tutorials and full documentation.

If you have already been using the Windows 3.1 version of AutoCAD LT, you will notice an impressive improvement in performance in Windows 95 and Windows NT.

If you are new to AutoCAD LT, this is the version you may have been waiting for before purchasing the software. Even with its many new features, the programmers at Autodesk have managed to make AutoCAD LT easier to use. Version 3.0 is fully compliant with the Windows interface guidelines, and is especially designed to conform with the Microsoft Office standard interface. So if you are familiar with the Microsoft Office suite of programs, you will feel right at home with AutoCAD LT.

In this first chapter, you will look at many of AutoCAD LT's basic operations, such as opening and closing files, getting a close-up look at part of a drawing, and making changes to a drawing.

## Taking a Guided Tour

First, you will get a chance to familiarize yourself with the AutoCAD LT screen and how you communicate with AutoCAD LT. Along the way, you will also get a feel for how to work with this book. Don't worry about understanding or remembering everything that you see in this chapter. You will get plenty of opportunities to probe the finer details of the program as you work through the later tutorials. If you are already familiar with earlier versions of AutoCAD LT, you may want to read through this chapter anyway, to get acquainted with new features and the graphical interface. To help you remember the material, you will find a brief exercise at the end of each chapter. For now, just enjoy your first excursion into AutoCAD LT.

1. Start your computer, and if you are using Windows 95 on a network, enter your login password.

2. From the Start button on the Windows 95 taskbar, select Programs ➤ AutoCAD LT, then select the program AutoCAD LT.

**TIP  You can create a shortcut for AutoCAD LT, as follows. Right-click your mouse on the Start button to open the Start Menu folder. Choose Open ➤ Programs Folder ➤ AutoCAD LT Folder. Ctrl-drag the AutoCAD LT icon to the desktop or to the start view for easy access. From here you can drag shortcuts to the desktop for rapid access. Use the control key while dragging to copy a shortcut and leave the original.**

The AutoCAD LT Start Up screen will be displayed while the program is loading. Next, the Start Up dialog box will appear.

3. For now, press Cancel. The AutoCAD LT program window will appear.

**NOTE  The AutoCAD LT Start Up screen is identical to the Create New Drawing screen. We will review the elements of the Create New Drawing screen in *Chapters 3* and *5*.**

### The AutoCAD LT Window

The AutoCAD LT program window is divided into six parts:

▶   Pull-down menus

- ▶ Toolbars
- ▶ Drawing area
- ▶ Command window
- ▶ Text window
- ▶ Status bar

> **NOTE** A seventh hidden component, the Aerial View window, displays your entire drawing and lets you select close-up views of parts of your drawing. After you're more familiar with AutoCAD LT, consult *Appendix B* for more on this feature.

Figure 1.1 shows a typical layout of the AutoCAD LT program window. Along the top is the *menu bar*, and at the bottom is the *command window* and the *status bar*. Just below the menu bar are the *toolbars*. The rest of the screen is occupied by the *drawing area*. When you start

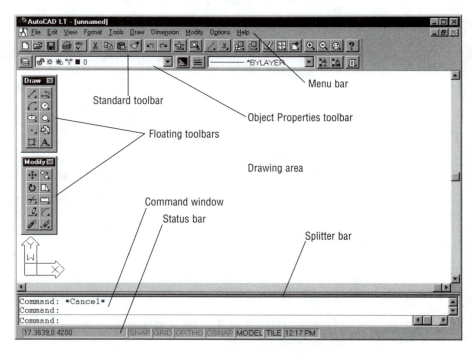

*Figure 1.1:    A typical arrangement of the elements of the AutoCAD window*

AutoCAD LT, the drawing area will typically contain two floating tool-bars, the Draw and Modify toolbars. The position of toolbars is adjustable, and they can be dragged, opened or closed, docked or floated like any standard Windows application. Similarly, the command window, text screen, and drawing area may be dragged and resized, docked or floated.

Many of the elements within the AutoCAD LT window can be easily moved and reshaped. Figure 1.2 demonstrates how different AutoCAD LT can look after some simple rearranging of window components.

*Figure 1.2:* **An alternative arrangement of the elements of the AutoCAD LT window**

 **NOTE** All of the AutoCAD LT toolbars can be "docked" to any side of the drawing window, or left to float in the drawing editor's workspace. To dock a floating toolbar, click on the name of the toolbar and then drag the toolbar to the top, bottom, or either side of the drawing window. When the outline of the toolbar appears in the docking area (at the edge of the graphics area), release the toolbar. A docked toolbar does not overlap the drawing window.

The menu bar at the top of the drawing area (see Figure 1.3) offers pull-down menus from which you select commands in a typical Windows fashion. The toolbars offer a variety of commands through icon buttons and drop-down lists. For example, the *layer* name or number you are presently working on is displayed in a drop-down list in the standard toolbar. The layer name is preceded by icons that inform you of the status of the layer. The tools, icons, and lists on the toolbars are plentiful, and you'll learn more about all of them later in this chapter and as you work through this book.

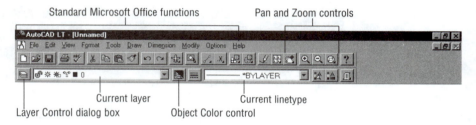

Figure 1.3:    **The components of the menu bar and toolbar**

  **NOTE** A *layer* is like an overlay that allows you to separate different types of information. AutoCAD LT allows an unlimited number of layers. On new drawings the default layer is 0. You'll get a detailed look at layers and the meaning of the icons in *Chapter 4*.

The floating toolbars (see Figure 1.4) offer commands that create new objects and edit existing ones. These are just two of many toolbars available to you.

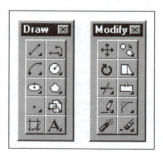

Figure 1.4:    **The floating toolbars**

The drawing area—your workspace—occupies most of the screen. Everything you draw appears in this area. As you move your mouse around, you will see crosshairs appear to move within the drawing area. This is your drawing cursor. It lets you point to locations in the drawing area.

> **NOTE** If you have the Windows 95 taskbar "Autohide" option set to ON, you will notice that the AutoCAD LT status bar is sometimes overlaid by the Win 95 taskbar. This arrangement allows access to both bars, while giving a larger workspace. To toggle between the status bar and the Win 95 taskbar, glide your mouse cursor vertically across the visible bar. To adjust the Windows 95 Autohide setting, do a right mouse-click on the taskbar, and select Properties from the menu. Then select or de-select the Autohide option.

At the bottom of the drawing area, the status bar (see Figure 1.5) gives you information at a glance about the drawing. For example, the *coordinate readout* toward the far left of the status bar tells you the location of your cursor. Let's practice using the coordinate readout and drawing cursor.

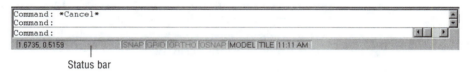

Status bar

*Figure 1.5:* **The status bar and command window**

## Picking Points

1. Move the cursor around in the drawing area, and note how the coordinate readout changes as you move to tell you the cursor's location. It shows the coordinates in an X,Y format.

2. Now place the cursor in the middle of the drawing area, and press the mouse/pick button and immediately let it go. Move the cursor, and a rectangle follows. This is a *selection window*; you'll learn more about this window in *Chapter 2*.

> NOTE The operation you perform in steps 1 and 2—placing the cursor on a specific point and pressing the mouse (pick) button—is referred to as *clicking on* a point. From now on, we will use the expression "click on" to describe the process of placing the cursor on an item or in an area and pressing the mouse/pick button.

3. Move the cursor a bit in any direction; then press and let go of the mouse/pick button again. Notice that the rectangle disappears. You have just picked a point.

4. Try picking several more points in the drawing area.

   You will notice that tiny crosses appear where you picked points. These are called *blips*—markers that show where you've selected points. They do not become a permanent part of your drawing, nor do they print onto hardcopy output.

### UCS Icon

In the lower-left corner of the drawing area, you should see a thick, L-shaped arrow outline. If not, type **UCSICON** in your command window, then type **ON**. You should now be able to see the UCS icon, or the *user coordinate system* (UCS) icon, which tells you your orientation in the drawing. This icon becomes helpful as you start to work with complex 2D drawings or edit 3D models. The X and Y inside the icon indicate the x- and y-axes of your drawing. The W tells you that you are in what is called the *world coordinate system*. We will discuss this icon in detail in *Chapter 16*. For now, you can use it as a reference to tell you the direction of the axes.

### The Command Window

At the bottom of the screen, just above the status bar, is a small horizontal window, called the *command window*. Here you'll see displayed AutoCAD LT's responses to your input. Right now, it shows the word Command: which tells you that AutoCAD LT is waiting for your instructions. As you click on a point in the drawing area, you'll see the message "Other corner."

It is important to pay special attention to messages displayed in the command window, because this is how AutoCAD LT communicates with you. Besides giving you messages, the command window records your activity in AutoCAD LT. You can use the scroll bar to the right of the command window to review previous messages. You can also enlarge the command window to a full-size text window. (We'll discuss this in more detail in *Chapter 2.*)

Now let's look at the window components in detail.

## The Pull-down Menus

Like many Windows programs, the pull-down menus available on the menu bar offer a quicker way to access the general controls and settings for AutoCAD LT. Within these menus you'll find the commands and functions that are the heart of AutoCAD LT. By clicking on menu items, you can cut and paste items to and from AutoCAD LT, change the settings that make AutoCAD LT work the way you want it to, set up the general organization of components within the AutoCAD LT window, access the help system, and much more.

**TIP**  To close a pull-down menu without selecting anything, press the Esc (Escape) key. Or you can click on any other part of the AutoCAD LT window or on another pull-down menu.

The pull-down menu options perform three basic functions:

▶ Display additional menu choices

▶ Display a dialog box that contains settings you can change

▶ Issue a command that requires keyboard or drawing input. As you select commands and options, AutoCAD LT provides additional help for you, in the form of brief descriptions of each menu option, which appear in the status bar.

Here's an exercise to let you practice with the pull-down menus and get acquainted with AutoCAD LT's interface:

1. Place your arrow cursor on Options on the pull-down menu bar. Press the mouse/pick button and hold it down. The list of items that appear are the commands and settings that let you set up your AutoCAD LT environment. Don't worry if you don't understand them; you'll get to know them in later chapters.

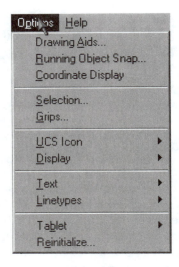

2. While still holding down the mouse/pick button, move the highlight cursor slowly down the list of menu items. As you highlight each item, notice that a description of it appears in the status bar at the bottom of the AutoCAD LT window. These descriptions help you choose the menu option you need.

3. Some of the menu items have triangular pointers to their right. This means the command has additional choices. Highlight the Display item, and you'll see another set of options appear to the right of the menu.

   This second set of options is called a *cascading menu*. Whenever you see a pull-down menu item with the triangular pointer, you know that this item opens a cascading menu offering a more detailed set of options.

   You might have noticed that other pull-down menu options are followed by three periods, or an ellipsis (…). This indicates that the option brings up a dialog box, as the following exercise demonstrates:

4. On the menu bar, this time click on Tools, but don't hold down the mouse/pick button.

NOTE You can either click and drag the highlight cursor over the pull-down menu to select an option, as shown in the previous steps, or click once on the menu bar command to open the menu, then once on the option you desire. This second method, demonstrated here in steps 4 and 5, does not display the option descriptions in the status bar.

**5.** Click on the Preferences... item. The Preferences dialog box will appear:

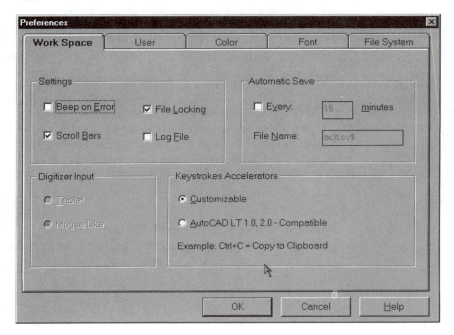

This dialog box contains several "pages," indicated by the tabs across the top, that contain settings for controlling what AutoCAD LT shows you on its screens, where you want it to look for special files, and other "housekeeping" settings. *Appendix B* describes this dialog box in more detail. You may also access the Preferences dialog box by right-clicking the command window and selecting preferences.

**6.** Click on the Cancel button on the lower-right side of the dialog box.

The third type of item you'll find on pull-down menus is a command that directly executes an AutoCAD LT operation.

**7.** Click on Options again on the menu bar.

**8.** In the Options menu, click on Text ➤ Text Quality. The Options menu will close, and the following message will appear in the command line:

        New value for TXTQLTY <50>:

This message is asking you to enter a new value for the Txtqlty setting, which controls the resolution of certain text fonts used by AutoCAD LT (Bitstream, Truetype, and Adobe Type 1 fonts). Lower values decrease resolution and increase display and plotting speed. Valid values are 0 to 100.0. The item between the < > brackets is the current setting: a value of 50. You will often be asked to enter or change settings via the command window.

> **TIP**  Txtqlty is an AutoCAD LT setting called a *system variable*. You'll learn more about these variables as you work through the tutorial. For a full list and description of all the variables, consult *Appendix D*. Text fonts used by AutoCAD LT are described in more detail in *Chapter 8*.

9.  Type **20** ↵. When you type your response, it, too, will appear in the command line. Then the word Command: returns to the command line. You have just changed AutoCAD LT's text quality setting to a very low value. This will speed up screen response and plotting time for the display fonts listed above. The output *quality* of the text may be lower than you desire, however.

At this point you've seen how most of AutoCAD LT's commands work.

## COMMUNICATING WITH AUTOCAD LT

AutoCAD LT is the perfect servant: it does everything you tell it to, and no more. You communicate with AutoCAD LT using the pull-down menus, and the buttons on toolbars and flyouts. These devices invoke AutoCAD LT commands. A command is a single-word instruction you give to AutoCAD LT telling it to do something, such as draw a line (the Line button on the Draw toolbar) or erase an object (the Erase button on the Modify toolbar). Whenever you invoke a command, either by typing it in or selecting a menu or toolbar item, AutoCAD LT responds by presenting messages to you in the command window area, or by displaying a dialog box.

The messages in the command window area often tell you what to do next, or offer a list of options. A single command will often present several messages, which you answer to complete the command.

A dialog box is like a form you fill out on the computer screen. It lets you adjust settings or make selections from a set of options pertaining to a command. Dialog boxes typically allow you to enter information in any order you prefer, to change your mind, and finally to accept or cancel your choices. You'll get a chance to work with commands and dialog boxes later in this chapter.

## *The AutoCAD LT Toolbars*

Just as the pull-down menus give you control over the general operation of AutoCAD LT, the commands in the toolbars do the nitty-gritty work of creating new objects and editing existing ones. These commands are grouped by type of action. For example, the Modify toolbar contains functions that modify existing objects in a drawing. The Draw toolbar contains tools needed to create new objects. And so on.

The icon buttons in the toolbars perform three types of actions, just like the pull-down menu commands: They display further options, open dialog boxes, and issue commands that require keyboard or cursor input.

### *How Toolbars Work*

AutoCAD LT's toolbars contain icons that represent commands. To help you understand each icon, a *tool tip* appears just below the arrow cursor when you rest the cursor on an icon. Each tool tip helps you identify the icon with its function. A longer help description is displayed in the status bar when tool tips are displayed.

NOTE Tool tips are available for the flyout buttons as well as the toolbar icons.

1. Move the cursor onto one of the toolbar icons and leave it there for a second or two. Notice that the command's name appears nearby—this is the tool tip. In the status bar, a brief description of the button's purpose appears. See Figure 1.6.

2. Move the cursor across the toolbar. As you do, notice that the tool tips and status-line descriptions change to describe each button.

NOTE When you install AutoCAD LT for the first time, the Draw and Modify toolbars are loaded automatically. The default drawing screen looks just like Figure 1.6. If these two toolbars are *not* visible on your screen, you will need to reload them, using the View ➤ Toolbars option.

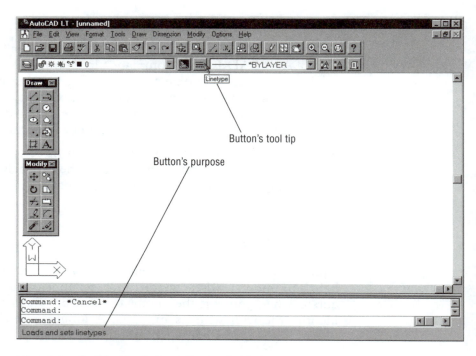

*Figure 1.6:    Each toolbar button tells you what it does.*

If the two toolbars in Figure 1.6 are not visible, click on the View menu and then on the Toolbars option at the bottom of the menu. The Toolbars dialog box will appear, with a list of all of the AutoCAD LT toolbars, in alphabetical order. Use the slider bar to browse down the list, and click on the check box beside the Draw and Modify toolbars, if required. If the toolbars already have a check mark in the dialog box, and you *still* cannot see them on the screen, you should look at the screen edges. Make sure that the toolbars have not been "docked" there. A docked toolbar can look quite different from a floating toolbar.

### Flyouts

Most toolbar icons start a command as soon as you click on them, but other icons will display a set of additional icons (similar to the cascading menus) that are related to the tool you have selected. This set of additional icons is called a *flyout*. If you've used other Windows graphics programs, chances are you've seen flyouts. Look closely at the toolbars on your screen or in Figure 1.6 and you'll be able to identify which toolbar icons have flyouts; they'll have a small right-pointing arrow in the lower-right corner of the toolbar button.

> **TIP**   Remember, when an instruction says "click on," you should lightly press the mouse/pick button until you hear a click, and then immediately let it go. Don't hold it down.

Let's see how a flyout works:

1.  Move the cursor to the Circle tool button in the Draw toolbar. Click and hold the left mouse button to display the flyout. Don't release the mouse button. (If you do not seem to have the Draw and Modify toolbars on your screen, read the Note before Figure 1.6.)

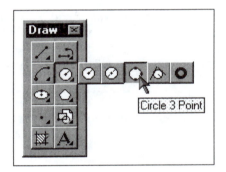

2.  Still holding down the left mouse button down, move the cursor over the flyout, and notice that the tool tips appear here, as well. Also, notice the description at the bottom of the AutoCAD LT window on the status bar.

As you can see from this exercise, you get a lot of feedback from AutoCAD LT!

### Moving Toolbars

One unique characteristic of AutoCAD LT's toolbars is their mobility. In fact, a toolbar in its standard location is really a *floating* toolbar in its *docked* position. This means it is placed against the top and side borders of the AutoCAD LT window, so that the toolbar occupies a minimal amount of space. If you want to, you can move the toolbar to any location on your desktop, thus turning it into a floating toolbar.

Later in this section you'll find descriptions of all of AutoCAD LT's toolbars, but first try the following exercise to move the Object Properties toolbar away from its current position in the AutoCAD LT window.

1. Move the arrow cursor so that it points to the border of the Object Properties toolbar, as shown here:

 **NOTE** The action you perform in steps 2 and 3 of this exercise—holding down the mouse/pick button while simultaneously moving the mouse—is called *click and drag*. (If you have used other Windows applications, you already know this.) From now on, we will use "click and drag" to describe this type of action.

2. Press and hold down the left mouse button. Notice that a gray rectangle appears by the cursor.

3. Still holding down the mouse button, move the mouse downward. The gray box follows the cursor.

4. When the gray box is over the drawing area, release the mouse button, and the Object Properties toolbar—now a floating toolbar—moves to its new location.

You can now move the Object Properties toolbar to any location on the screen that suits you. You can also change the shape of the toolbar; try this:

5. Place the cursor on the bottom-edge border of the Object Properties toolbar. The cursor becomes a double-headed arrow, as shown here:

6. Click and drag the border downward. The gray rectangle jumps to a new, taller rectangle as you move the cursor.

7.  When the gray rectangle changes to the shape you want, release the mouse button to reform the toolbar.

8.  To move the toolbar back into its docked position as a toolbar, place the arrow cursor on ("point to") the toolbar's title bar, and slowly click and drag the toolbar so the cursor is in position in the upper-left corner of the AutoCAD LT window. Notice how the gray outline of the toolbar changes as it approaches its docked position.

9.  When the outline of the Object properties toolbar is near its docked position, release the mouse button. The toolbar, once again a toolbar, moves back into its previous position in the AutoCAD LT window.

    Thus you can move and reshape any of AutoCAD LT's toolbars to place them out of the way yet still have them ready to give you quick access to commands. You can also put them away altogether when you don't need them and bring them back at will, as shown in these next steps:

10. Click on the Close button in the upper-left corner of the Draw floating toolbar. Like other Windows 95 applications, the Close button is the small square button with the "x" in it. The toolbar disappears.

> **NOTE** To show a menu/command combination, we will use the notation *Menu ➤ Command*—for example, View ➤ Toolbars. For commands/options from cascading menus, we will use *Menu ➤ Command ➤ Option ➤ Option...*—for example, View ➤ Toolbars.

11. To recover a toolbar, or to display a hidden toolbar, click on the View pull-down menu and then on Toolbars (View ➤ Toolbars) and click the check boxes for the toolbars you wish to display.

You can also use the Tool Windows flyout on the Standard toolbar to recover a closed toolbar. The Tool Windows flyout contains seven of the most commonly used AutoCAD LT toolbars, including Draw, Modify, the Standard toolbar, and the Object Properties toolbar. To open the flyout, click on the Tool Windows button. It is located in the middle of the Standard toolbar, beside the Undo/Redo buttons. Then click on the flyout button for the toolbar you want. The Tool Windows toolbar icons will toggle the specified toolbars ON and OFF.

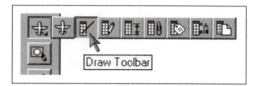

AutoCAD LT will remember your toolbar arrangement between sessions. When you exit and then reopen AutoCAD LT later, the AutoCAD LT window will appear just as you left it.

## MENUS VERSUS THE KEYBOARD

Throughout this book, you will be told to select commands and command options from the pull-down menus and toolbars. For new and experienced users alike, menus and toolbars offer an easy-to-remember method for accessing commands. You can also enter commands and command options through the keyboard, in the Command window.

Typing in commands via the keyboard can sometimes be faster than using the menu and toolbar options. All toolbar and menu items have Command line equivalents, some of which have two or three letter shortcuts. As you work through the tutorial, we'll show you the keyboard equivalents of pull-down menu options and toolbar icon buttons.

In addition to the traditional AutoCAD LT keyboard commands, you can use accelerator keys—special keystrokes that open and activate pull-down menu options. You might have noticed that the commands in the menu bar and the items in the pull-down menus each have an underlined character. By pressing the Alt key followed by the key corresponding to the underlined character, you activate that command or option, without having to engage the mouse. For example, to issue File ➤ Open, press Alt, then F, then finally O (Alt-F O).

Finally, if you are feeling adventurous, you can create your own single-key shortcuts for executing commands by adding them to the AutoCAD LT menu file. We'll discuss customization of the menus, icon toolbars, and keyboard shortcuts in *Chapter 17*.

You may have noticed several other toolbars listed in the Toolbars dialog box that don't appear in the AutoCAD LT window. To keep the screen from becoming cluttered, many of the toolbars are not placed on the screen. The toolbars you'll be using most are displayed first; others that are less frequently used can be kept out of sight until they are needed. Here are brief descriptions of the major toolbars available either from the View menu, or by typing **viewtoolbar** in the command window:

**Draw:** Commands for creating common objects, including lines, arcs, circles, curves, ellipses, and text. This toolbar appears in the AutoCAD LT window by default.

**Modify:** Commands for editing existing objects. You can Move, Copy, Rotate, Erase, Trim, Extend, and so on.

**Dimensioning:** Commands that help you dimension your drawings. See *Chapter 9*.

**External References:** Commands that control external referencing of drawings. See *Chapters 6 and 12*.

**Attribute:** Commands for creating and editing object attributes. See *Chapter 10*.

**Select Objects:** Tools for modifying the method used to select objects on the screen. See *Chapter 2*.

**Object Snap:** Tools to help you select specific points on objects, such as endpoints and midpoints. See *Chapter 3*.

**Point Filters:** Tools for fine-tuning the selection of coordinates. See *Chapter 15*.

**UCS:** Tools for setting up a plane on which to work. This is most useful for 3D modeling, but it can be helpful in 2D drafting, as well. See *Chapter 16*.

**View:** Tools for saving views of a drawing, and quickly obtaining standard orthogonal views of 3D objects. See *Chapter 6* for saving views and *Chapter 17* for orthogonal views of 3D objects.

**Object Properties:** Commands for manipulating the properties of objects. This toolbar is normally docked below the pull-down menu bar.

**Standard Toolbar:** The most frequently used commands for view control, file management, and editing. This toolbar is normally docked below the pull-down menu bar.

You'll get a chance to work with all of the toolbars as you work through this book. Or, if you plan to use the book as a reference rather than working through it as a chapter-by-chapter tutorial, any exercise you try will tell you which toolbar to use for performing a specific operation.

## Working with AutoCAD LT

Now that you've been introduced to the drawing editor, let's try using a few of AutoCAD LT's commands. First, you'll open a sample file and make a few simple modifications to it. In the process, you'll get familiar with some common methods of operation in AutoCAD LT.

### Opening an Existing File

In this exercise, you will get a chance to see and use a typical file dialog box. To start with, you will open an existing file.

1.  Click on the Open icon (the one that looks like an open folder) on the Standard toolbar. Or choose File ➤ Open from the menu bar. A file dialog box will appear. This is a typical Windows file dialog box, with an added twist. Notice the large Preview box on the right. When you click on a drawing name in the File Name list box, a preview of the drawing appears before you open it, thereby saving time while searching for files.

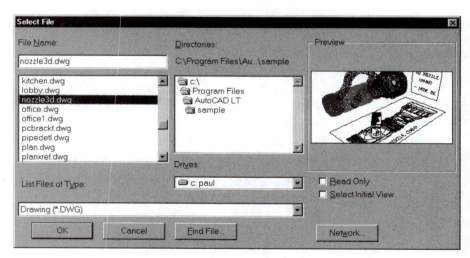

2. In the Directories list in the center, locate the directory named Sample (you may need to scroll down the list to find it). Point to it, and then double-click—press the mouse/pick button twice in rapid succession. (If you're having trouble opening files with a double-click, here's another way to do it until you are more proficient with the mouse: Click on the file once to highlight it, and then click on the OK button.) The file list on the left changes to show the contents of the Sample directory.

> **NOTE** The Nozzle3d drawing is included on the companion CD. If you cannot find this file, be sure you have installed the sample drawings from the companion CD. See *Appendix C* for installation instructions.

3. Move the arrow to the file named Nozzle3d, and click on it. Notice that the name now appears in the File Name input box above the file list. Also, the Preview box now shows a thumbnail image of the file.

4. Click on the OK button at the bottom of the dialog box. AutoCAD LT proceeds to open the Nozzle3d file, as shown in Figure 1.7.

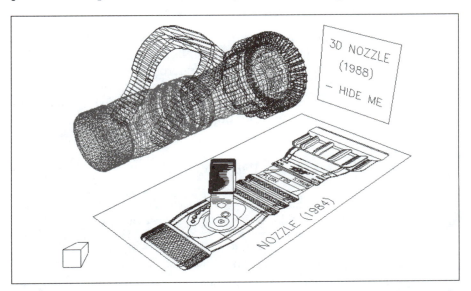

*Figure 1.7:* **The Nozzle drawing**

NOTE Pressing the mouse/pick button twice in rapid succession is called *double-clicking*. Double-clicking on an item in a list is a quick way of selecting it. If you prefer, you can double-click on a filename to open that file, instead of highlighting the name and clicking on the OK button.

The Nozzle3d file opens to display the entire drawing in the same state as when you last saved it. Also, the AutoCAD LT window's title bar displays the name of the drawing. This offers easy identification of the file.

### Getting a Closer Look

Usually, you will want to get a closer look at a part of your drawing. To do that in the nozzle drawing, use the Zoom command (View ➤ Zoom). To tell AutoCAD LT what area you wish to enlarge, you will use what is called a *window*.

1. Choose View ➤ 3D Viewpoint ➤ Plan View ➤ World. Your view changes to display a two-dimensional view looking down on the drawing.

2. Choose View ➤ Zoom ➤ Window.

3. The prompt area displays First corner:. Look at the dotted-line rectangle shown in panel 1 of Figure 1.8. Move the crosshair cursor on your screen to about where the lower-left corner of the square is in the figure; then press the mouse/pick button. Move the cursor, and you see the rectangle appear, one corner fixed on the point you just picked, while the other corner follows the cursor.

## THE AERIAL VIEW WINDOW

The Aerial View window is an optional AutoCAD LT display tool. It gives you an overall view of your drawing, no matter how much magnification you may be using for the drawing editor. Aerial View also makes it easier to get around in a large-scale drawing. You'll find that this feature is best suited to more complex drawings that cover great areas, such as site plans, topographical maps, or city planning documents.

We won't discuss this view much here in the first chapter, as it can be a bit confusing for the first-time AutoCAD LT user. As you become more comfortable with AutoCAD LT, however, you may want to try it out. You'll find a detailed description in *Chapter 6*.

**4.** The prompt area now displays First corner: Other corner:. Position the other corner of the window so it encloses the handle of the nozzle, as shown in the figure, and press the mouse/pick button. The handle enlarges to fill the screen (the bottom of Figure 1.8).

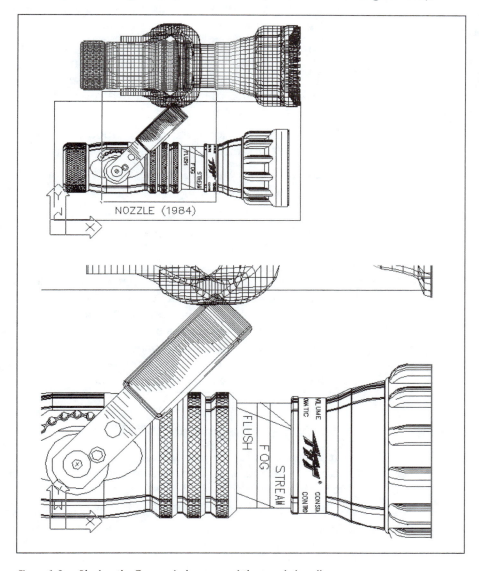

*Figure 1.8:* **Placing the Zoom window around the nozzle handle**

In this exercise, you used the Window option of the Zoom command to define an area to enlarge for your close-up view. You saw how AutoCAD LT prompts you to indicate first one corner of the window, then the other. These messages are helpful for first-time users of AutoCAD LT. You will be using the Window options frequently—not just to define views, but also to select objects for editing.

Getting a close-up view of your drawing is crucial to working accurately with a drawing, but you'll often want to return to a previous view to get the overall picture. To do so, choose View ➤ Zoom ➤ Previous. Do this now, and the previous view—one showing the entire nozzle—returns to the screen.

You can also quickly enlarge or reduce your view using Zoom In and Zoom Out buttons on the Standard toolbar, as follows:

1. Click the Zoom In icon on the Standard toolbar to magnify the view. (The icon looks like a magnifying glass with a plus sign.)

2. Click the Zoom Out icon on the Standard toolbar. (The Zoom Out icon looks like a magnifying glass with a minus sign.) The view changes back to include more of the drawing.

**NOTE** New to Release 3 of AutoCAD LT are Real-Time Pan and Real-Time Zoom found on the Pan flyout and the Zoom flyout of the Standard toolbar. Alternatively, you can type **Rtpan** or **Rtzoom** in the Command window. These tools will allow you to dynamically resize your view using your mouse. Real-Time Pan moves the entire image of your screen in the direction you move your mouse. Real-Time Zoom zooms out when you move your mouse upward and zooms in when you move your mouse downward.

## Saving a File as You Work

It is a good idea to periodically save your file as you work on it. You can save it under its current name, or under a different name, thereby creating a new file.

By default, AutoCAD LT automatically saves your work at 120-minute intervals under the name ACLT.SV$ as a safety precaution; this is known as the *autosave* feature. Two hours of work is a lot to lose, especially in a deadline situation. You should consider resetting the save interval to a much shorter time frame, say 15 or 30 minutes. Using system variables, you can change the name of the autosaved file and control the time between autosaves. See the sidebar, "Using AutoCAD LT's Automatic Save Feature," at the end of *Chapter 3* for details.

First try the Save command. This quickly saves the drawing in its current state without exiting the program.

**TIP** You can also issue the File ➤ Save command by entering **Qsave** ↵ in the command window.

Click on the Save icon on the Standard toolbar, or choose File ➤ Save. You will notice some disk activity while AutoCAD LT saves the Nozzle drawing file to the hard disk. As an alternative to picking File ➤ Save from the menus, you can type **Alt+F S**. This is the accelerator key, also called hotkey, for the File ➤ Save command.

Now try the Save As command. This command brings up a dialog box that allows you to save the current file under a new name.

1.  Choose File ➤ Save As or type **Saveas** ↵ at the command window. The Save Drawing As dialog box appears. Note that the current file name, Nozzle3d, is highlighted in the File Name input box at the bottom of the dialog box.

**NOTE** When you start a brand new drawing, rather than opening an existing drawing, AutoCAD LT assigns it the temporary file name "Unnamed." When you try to save an "Unnamed" file, AutoCAD LT automatically opens the Save Drawing As dialog box to remind you to give your drawing a proper name.

2.  Type **Myfirst**. As you type, the name Nozzle3d disappears from the input box and is replaced by Myfirst. You don't need to enter the .DWG filename extension. AutoCAD LT adds it to the filename automatically when it saves the file.

3.  Click on the OK button. The dialog box disappears, and you will notice some disk activity.

You now have a copy of the nozzle file under the name Myfirst.DWG, and the name of the file displayed in the AutoCAD LT window's title bar has changed to Myfirst. From now on, when you use the File ➤ Save option, your drawing will be saved under its new name. Saving files under a different name can be useful when you are creating alternatives or when you just want to save one of several ideas you are trying out.

## Making Changes

You will be making frequent changes to your drawings. In fact, one of AutoCAD LT's chief advantages is the ease with which you can make changes. The following exercise shows you a typical sequence of operations involved in making a change to a drawing.

1.  From the Modify toolbar, click on the Erase icon (the one with a pencil eraser touching paper). This activates the Erase command.

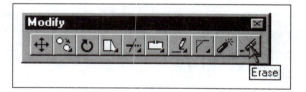

Notice that the cursor has turned into a small square; this square is called the *pickbox*. You also see Select object: in the command window.

2.  Place the pickbox on the diagonal pattern of the nozzle handle (see Figure 1.9) and click on it. The 2D image of the nozzle becomes highlighted. The pickbox and the Select object prompt remain, telling you that you can continue to select objects.

**TIP**  You can also issue the Erase command by typing **Erase** ↵ in the command window.

3.  Now press ↵. The nozzle and the rectangle disappear. You have just erased a part of the drawing.

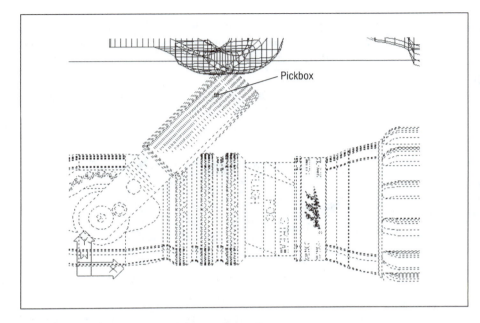

*Figure 1.9:* **Erasing a portion of the Nozzle handle**

## Pickbox

In this exercise, you first issued the Erase command, and then selected an object by clicking on it using a pickbox. The pickbox tells you that you must select items on the screen. Once you've done that, you press ↵ to move on to the next step. This sequence of steps is common to many of the commands you will work with in AutoCAD LT.

## Closing AutoCAD LT

When you are done with your work on one drawing, you can open another drawing, or temporarily leave AutoCAD LT, or close Auto-CAD LT entirely. To close a file and exit AutoCAD LT, use the Exit option on the File menu.

NOTE You can also issue the Exit command by typing **Quit** ↵ at the command window, or you can click on the Close button in the upper-right corner of the AutoCAD LT window.

1. Choose File ➤ Exit, the last item in the menu. A dialog box appears, asking you "Save changes to Myfirst?" and offering three buttons, labeled Yes, No, and Cancel.

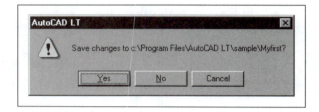

2. Click on the No button. AutoCAD LT exits the nozzle drawing and closes without saving your changes.

   Whenever you attempt to exit a drawing that has been changed, you will get this same inquiry box. This request for confirmation is a safety feature that lets you change your mind and save your changes before you exit AutoCAD LT. In the previous exercise, you discarded the changes you made, so the nozzle drawing reverted back to its state before you erased the handle.

   If you want to exit AutoCAD LT only temporarily, you can minimize it so it appears as a button on the Windows 95 taskbar. You do this by clicking on the Minimize button in the upper-right corner of the Auto-CAD LT window. Alternatively, you can use the taskbar to switch to another program.

## If You Want to Experiment...

Try opening and closing some of the sample drawing files.

1. Start AutoCAD LT by clicking on the Start button on the Windows 95 taskbar, and select Programs ➤ AutoCAD LT ➤ AutoCAD LT. Once again, click on Cancel when the Start Up screen appears.

2. Click on the Open icon on the Standard toolbar, or select File ➤ Open.

3. Use the dialog box to open the Myfirst file again. Notice that the drawing appears on the screen with the handle enlarged. This is the view you had on screen when you used the Save command in the earlier exercise.

4. Erase the handle, as you did in the earlier exercise.

5. Click on Open again. This time, open the Dhouse file. Notice that you get the Save Changes inquiry box you saw when you used the Exit option earlier. Open acts just like Exit, but instead of exiting AutoCAD LT altogether, it closes the current file and then opens a different one.

6. Click on the No button. The 3D Dhouse drawing opens.

7. Click on File ➤ Exit. Notice that this time you exit AutoCAD LT without getting the Save Changes dialog box. This is because you didn't make any changes to the Dhouse file.

# Chapter 2

# Creating Your First Drawing

## *Fast Tracks*

**I**N this chapter we'll examine some of AutoCAD LT's basic functions and practice with the drawing editor by creating a simple drawing to use in later exercises. We'll discuss giving input to AutoCAD LT, interpreting prompts, and getting help when you need it. We'll also cover the use of coordinate systems to give AutoCAD LT exact measurements for objects. You'll see how to select objects you've drawn, and how to specify base points for moving and copying.

If you're not a beginning AutoCAD LT user, you might want to move on to the more complex material in *Chapter 3*. You can use the files supplied on the companion disk of this book to continue the tutorials at that point.

## Getting to Know the Draw Toolbar

Your first task in learning how to draw in AutoCAD LT is to try to draw a line. But before you begin drawing, take a moment to familiarize yourself with the toolbar you'll be using more than any other to create objects with AutoCAD LT: the Draw toolbar.

1. Start AutoCAD LT just as you did in the first chapter. From the Windows 95 taskbar choose Start ➤ Programs ➤ AutoCAD LT ➤ AutoCAD LT.

2. In the Start Up dialog box, pick Start from Scratch, and select the English measurement system (feet and inches).

 **NOTE** Moving the arrow cursor onto an element on the screen is also referred to as "pointing to" that element.

3. Move the arrow cursor to the upper-left icon on the Draw toolbar, and rest it there so that the tool tip appears.

4. Slowly glide the arrow cursor over the other buttons on the Draw toolbar, and read each tool tip.

   In most cases, you'll be able to guess what each button does by looking at its icon. The icon with an arc, for instance, indicates that the button draws arcs; the one with the ellipse shows that the button draws ellipses; and so on. The tool tip gives you more information on the use of the button. For example, if you point to the Arc icon just below the Line icon, the tool tip reads "Arc Start Center End." This tells you the button draws an arc using 3 points that you supply by picking points in the drawing area. Remember also that the status bar provides additional information. When you point at the Arc Start Center End icon, the status bar reads "Creates an arc using the start point, center, and end point."

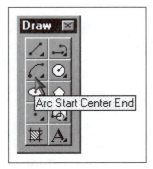

Figure 2.1 and Table 2.1 will aid you in navigating the two main toolbars (Draw and Modify), and you'll get experience with many of AutoCAD LT's tool buttons as you work through this book.

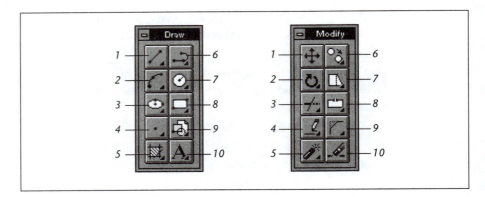

*Figure 2.1:*    **The Draw and Modify toolbars. The options available from each tool button are listed by number in Table 2.1.**

As you saw in Chapter 1, clicking on a button issues a command. Clicking *and dragging* a button, however, opens a flyout, which offers further options for that tool.

1.   Click and drag the Arc button. The Arc flyout appears. As you can see, there are a number of additional ways you can draw an arc. The arc flyout shows the seven arc options, which are listed in Table 2.1.

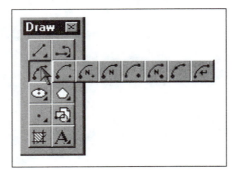

2.   Move the cursor across the flyout almost to the end, until the tool tip reads "Arc 3 Points," and then let go of the mouse button. Notice that the icon representing the Arc tool now changes and becomes the icon from the flyout that represents Arc 3 Points. By releasing the mouse you've also issued the Arc command with the 3 Points option.

*Table 2.1:* **The Options That Appear on the Draw and Modify Toolbars and Flyouts**

| Draw Toolbar | |
|---|---|
| 1 | Line    Construction Line    Ray |
| 2 (Arc) | 3 Point    Start Center End    Start Center Angle    Start End Angle    Center Start End    Center Start Angle    Continue |
| 3 (Ellipse) | Center    Axis End    Arc |
| 4 | Point    Divide    Measure |
| 5 | Boundary Hatch |
| 6 | Polyline    Double Line    Spline |
| 7 (Circle) | Center Radius    Center Diameter    3 Point    Tan Tan Radius    Donut |
| 8 | Rectangle    Polygon    2D Solid    Boundary |
| 9 | Insert Block    Make Block |
| 10 | Text    Paragraph text    Line Text |
| **Modify Toolbar** | |
| 1 | Move |
| 2 | Rotate |
| 3 | Trim    Extend |
| 4 | Edit Polyline    Edit Spline    Edit Text    Edit Hatch |
| 5 | Explode |
| 6 | Copy    Offset    Mirror    Rectangular Array    Polar Array |
| 7 | Stretch    Scale    Lengthen |
| 8 (Break) | 1 Point    1 Point Select    2 Point    2 Point Select |
| 9 | Chamfer    Fillet |
| 10 | Erase    Oops! |

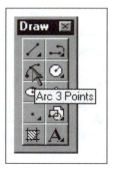

**3.** Press Esc twice to exit the Arc command.

 **TIP** If you find you are working a lot with one particular flyout, you can easily turn it into a stand-alone toolbar, so that all the flyout options are readily available with a single click. To create an Arc toolbar, choose View ➤ Toolbars, click on the check box next to Arc, and then press OK.

By making the most recently selected option on a flyout the default option for the toolbar button, AutoCAD LT gives you quick access to frequently used commands. The grouping of options on the flyout menus, however, is not always self-explanatory. Refer to Table 2.1 when you need help.

Don't be too concerned if you don't understand all the options you see in Table 2.1. You will get to know them as you work with AutoCAD LT and the tutorials in this book. Now let's get down to the business of drawing.

## WORKING WITH TOOLBARS

As you work through the exercises, this book will show you graphics of the icons to choose, along with the toolbar or flyout that contains the icon. Don't be alarmed if the toolbars you see in the examples don't look exactly like those on your screen. To save page space, the toolbars and flyouts have been adjusted horizontally for the illustrations; the ones on your screen may be oriented vertically, or in the case of the Draw and Modify toolbars, may be in a two-column setup. Although the shape of your toolbars and flyouts may differ from the ones you see in this book, the contents are the same. So when you see a graphic showing an icon, focus on the icon itself with its tool tip name, along with the name of the toolbar in which it is shown.

## Starting Your First Drawing

In *Chapter 1*, you looked at a pre-existing sample drawing. This time you will begin to draw on your own, by creating a door that will be used in later exercises. First, though, you must learn how to tell AutoCAD LT what you want and, even more importantly, to understand what AutoCAD LT wants from you.

1. Click on the New icon on the Standard toolbar. It's the blank page icon at the far left of the toolbar.

2. When the Create New Drawing dialog box appears, select the Start from Scratch option, and press OK. The AutoCAD LT opening message appears briefly and a new file is opened. AutoCAD LT gives the new file the temporary filename "Unnamed."

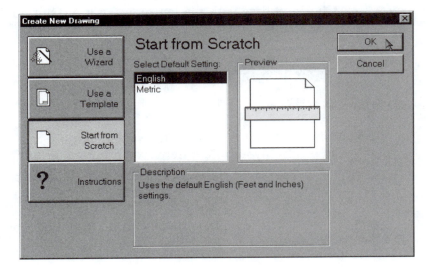

 **NOTE** When the Start from Scratch option in the Create New Drawing dialog box is selected, AutoCAD LT creates a new file using the standard AutoCAD LT default settings. For the sake of simplicity, the standard AutoCAD LT settings will be used throughout this book.

3. You should now save the new "Unnamed" file under a new name. Click on the Save icon on the Standard toolbar, or choose File ➤ Save/Save As. When the Save As dialog box appears type **Door** in the File Name edit box and press OK.

The new file shows a drawing area roughly 12 inches wide by 9 inches high. To check this for yourself, move the crosshair cursor to the upper-right corner of the screen, and observe the value shown in the coordinate readout. This is the standard AutoCAD LT default drawing area for new drawings.

4. Point to the Line icon on the Draw toolbar. (Remember, "point to" means "move the arrow cursor to.")

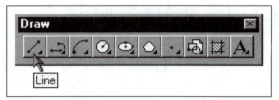

Click and drag with the left mouse button, but don't release the button. A flyout appears:

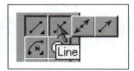

5. While still holding down the mouse button, move the arrow cursor across the flyout to a different icon button. Hold it there for a second until the tool tip appears. Continue to move the cursor, and watch the tool tips appear for each option.

 **NOTE** You can also type **Line** ↵ at the command prompt to start the Line command.

6. Point to the Line icon and release the mouse button. You've just issued the Line command. AutoCAD LT responds in two ways. First, you see the message

        From point:

in the command window at the bottom of your screen, asking you to select a point to begin your line. Also, the cursor has changed its appearance; it no longer has a square in the crosshairs. This is a clue telling you to pick a point to start a line.

7. Using the mouse/pick button, select a point on the screen near the center. As you select the point, AutoCAD LT adds

    `To point:`

    to the prompt in the command window.

    Now as you move the mouse around, you will notice a line with one end fixed on the point you just selected, and the other end following the cursor, as you move the mouse (see the top of Figure 2.2). This action is called *rubber-banding*.

    Now continue with the Line command.

8. Move the cursor to a point to the right of the first point you selected, and press the mouse/pick button again. The first rubber-band line is now fixed between the two points you selected, and a second rubber-band line appears (see the bottom of Figure 2.2).

9. If the line you drew isn't the exact length you want, you can back up during the Line command and change it. To do this, click on the Undo icon on the Standard toolbar, or type **U** from the keyboard and press ↵.

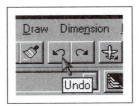

    Now the line you drew previously will rubber-band as if you hadn't selected the second point to fix its length.

 NOTE From now on, this crosshair cursor without the small box will be referred to as the *point selection mode* of the cursor. If you look ahead to Figure 2.8, you'll see all the different modes of the drawing cursor.

You've just drawn, and then undrawn, a line of an arbitrary length. The Line command is still active. There are two things that tell you that you are in the middle of a command, as mentioned in step 6. If you don't see the word `Command` in the command window, you know a command is still active. Also, the cursor will be the plain crosshair without the little box at its intersection.

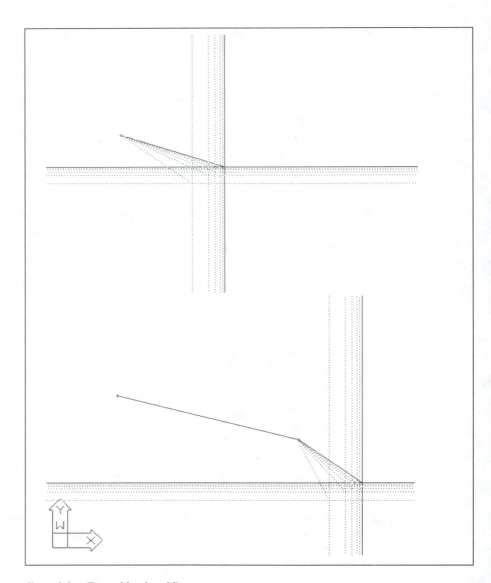

*Figure 2.2:* **Two rubber-band lines**

## Specifying Distances with Coordinates

Next, you will continue with the Line command to draw a *plan view* (an overhead view) of a door, to no particular scale. Later you will resize the drawing to use in future exercises. The door will be 3.0 units long and 0.15 units thick. To specify these exact distances in AutoCAD LT, you can use either *polar coordinates* (using angle and distance) or *Cartesian* (x,y) *coordinates*. Both types of coordinate can be specified as *relative* to another object or as *absolute* values.

## Specifying Polar Coordinates

To enter the exact distance of 3 units to the right of (or *relative* to) the last point you selected:

1. Type **@3<0**. As you type, the letters appear in the Command window.

2. Press ↵. A line appears, starting from the first point you picked and ending 3 units to the right of it (see Figure 2.3). You have just entered a relative polar coordinate.

---

### GETTING OUT OF TROUBLE

Beginners and experts alike are bound to make a few mistakes. Before you get too far into the tutorial, here are some powerful yet easy-to-use tools to help you recover from accidents.

**Backspace [←]**   If you make a typing error, you can use the Backspace key to back up to your error, and then retype your command or response. Backspace is located in the upper-right corner of the main keyboard area.

**Escape [Esc]**   This is perhaps the single most important key on your keyboard. When you need to quickly exit a command or dialog box without making changes, just press the Escape key in the upper-left corner of your keyboard. Press it twice if you want to make absolutely sure you've canceled a command.

Tip: Use the Escape key before editing with grips or issuing commands through the keyboard. You can also use it to clear grip selections.

**Undo** ↵   If you accidentally change something in the drawing and want to reverse that change, click on the Undo button in the Standard toolbar (the left-pointing curved arrow). Or type **Undo** ↵ at the command prompt. Each time you do this, AutoCAD LT will undo one operation at a time, in reverse order—so the last command performed will be undone first, then the next to last, and so on. The prompt will display the name of the command being undone, and the drawing will revert to its state prior to that command. You can undo everything back to the beginning of an editing session, if you need to.

**Redo** ↵   If you accidentally Undo one too many commands, you can redo the last undone command by clicking on the Redo button (the right-pointing curved arrow) on the Standard toolbar. Or type **Redo** ↵. Unfortunately, Redo only restores one command.

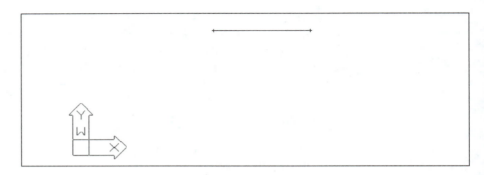

*Figure 2.3:* **A line three units long**

The at (@) sign you entered tells AutoCAD LT that the distance you are specifying is from the last point you selected. The 3 is the distance, and the less-than symbol (<) tells AutoCAD LT that you are designating the angle at which the line is to be drawn. The last part is the value for the angle, which in this case is 0. This is how to use *polar coordinates* to communicate distances and direction to AutoCAD LT.

---

**NOTE** If you prefer a different method for describing directions, you can set AutoCAD LT to use a vertical direction or downward direction as 0°. See *Chapter 3* for details.

---

Angles are given based on the system shown in Figure 2.4, where 0° is a horizontal direction from left to right, 90° is straight up, 180° is horizontal from right to left, and so on. You can specify degrees, minutes, and seconds of arc if you want to be that exact. We'll discuss angle formats in more detail in *Chapter 3*.

## Specifying Relative Cartesian Coordinates

For the next line segment, let's try another method of specifying exact distances.

1. Enter **@0,.15** ↵. A short line appears above the endpoint of the last line.

   Once again, the @ tells AutoCAD LT that the distance you specify is from the last point picked. But in this example, you give the distance in x and y values. The x distance, 0, is given first, followed by a comma, and then the y distance, 0.15. This is how to specify distances in relative Cartesian coordinates.

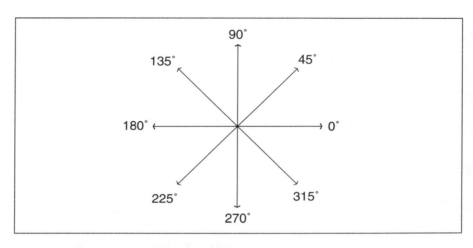

*Figure 2.4:* **AutoCAD LT's system for specifying angles**

**2.** Enter **@-3,0** ↵. The result is a drawing that looks like Figure 2.5.

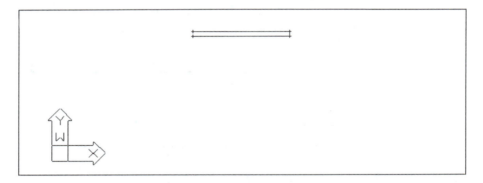

*Figure 2.5:* **Three sides of the door in the plan**

The distance you entered in step 2 was also in x,y values, but here you used a negative value to specify the x distance. Positive values in the Cartesian coordinate system are from left to right and from bottom to top (see Figure 2.6). If you want to draw a line from right to left, you must designate a negative value.

 **TIP** To finish drawing a series of lines without closing them, you can press Esc, ↵, or the Spacebar.

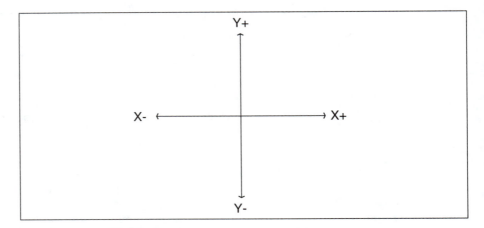

*Figure 2.6:   **Positive and negative Cartesian coordinate directions***

3.   Now type **C** ↵. A line connecting the first and last points of a sequence of lines is drawn (see Figure 2.7), and the Line command terminates.

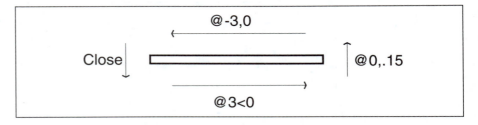

*Figure 2.7:   **Distance and direction input for the door***

## Cleaning Up the Screen

By now, with all the blips, the screen looks a bit messy. To clean up a screen image, use the Redraw command. Click on the Redraw View button on the Standard toolbar, choose View ➤ Redraw, or type **R** ↵. The screen quickly redraws the objects, clearing them of the blips.

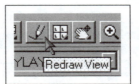

Another command, Regen, does the same thing as Redraw, but also updates the drawing database—which means it takes longer to restore the drawing.

## Interpreting the Cursor Modes and Understanding Prompts

The key to working with AutoCAD LT successfully is understanding the way it interacts with you. In this section you will become familiar with some of the ways AutoCAD LT prompts you for input. Understanding the format of the messages in the prompt area and recognizing other events on the screen will help you learn the program more easily.

As the command prompt aids you with messages, the cursor also gives you clues about what to do. Figure 2.8 illustrates the various modes of the cursor and gives a brief description of the role of each mode. Take a moment to study this figure.

### Using the Command Line

AutoCAD LT and this book are designed to allow you to work extensively from the toolbars. Most commands in AutoCAD LT, however, can be accessed in a variety of ways, including from the command line. You should be conversant with the command line option. Here, we'll use the Arc command, issued from the keyboard, to illustrate the format of AutoCAD LT's command window option.

In this exercise, you will draw the arc for the door you started in the previous exercise. Usually, in a floor-plan drawing, an arc is drawn to indicate the direction of a door swing. Figure 2.9 shows some of the other standard symbols used in architectural style drawings.

---

 **NOTE** The *default* is the option AutoCAD LT assumes you intend to use unless you tell it otherwise.

---

1.  Start the command by typing **Arc** ↵. The prompt Center/<Start point>: appears, and the cursor changes to point selection mode.

    Let's examine this Center/<Start point>: prompt. It contains two options. The *default* option always appears between angle brackets (< >), and all other options are separated by slashes (/). If you choose to take the default, Start point, you can input a point by clicking on a location on the screen or by entering a coordinate.

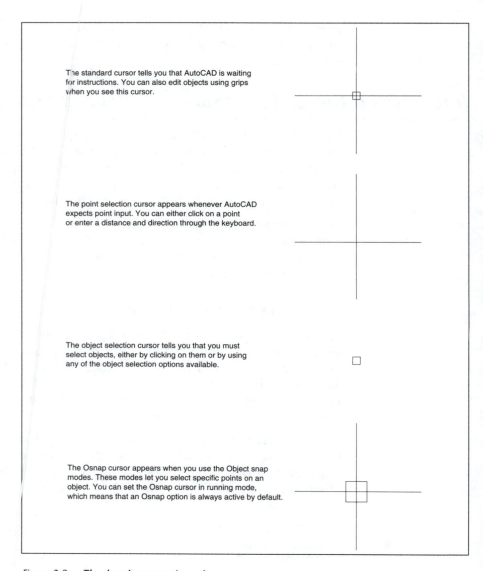

The standard cursor tells you that AutoCAD is waiting for instructions. You can also edit objects using grips when you see this cursor.

The point selection cursor appears whenever AutoCAD expects point input. You can either click on a point or enter a distance and direction through the keyboard.

The object selection cursor tells you that you must select objects, either by clicking on them or by using any of the object selection options available.

The Osnap cursor appears when you use the Object snap modes. These modes let you select specific points on an object. You can set the Osnap cursor in running mode, which means that an Osnap option is always active by default.

*Figure 2.8:*    ***The drawing cursor's modes***

**NOTE** When you see a set of options in the prompt, note their capitalization. If you choose to respond to prompts using the keyboard, these capitalized letters are all you need to enter to select that option. In some cases, the first two letters are capitalized to differentiate two options that begin with the same letter, such as **LAyer** and **LType**.

The Basics

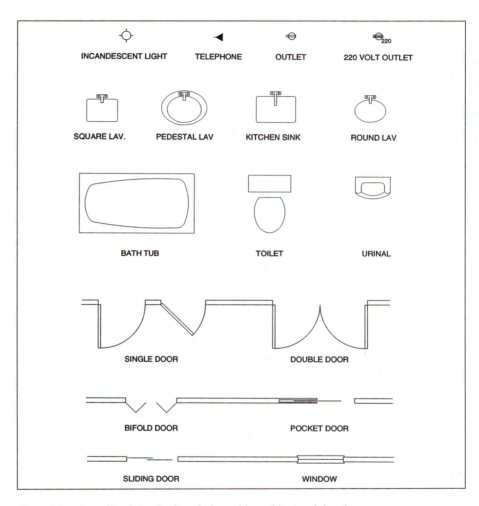

*Figure 2.9:    Samples of standard symbols used in architectural drawings*

2.  Type **C** ↵ to select the Center option. The prompt `Center:` appears.
    Notice that you only had to type in the C and not the whole word
    Center.

3.  Now pick a point representing the center of the arc near the upper-left
    corner of the door (see panel 1 of Figure 2.10). The prompt `Start`
    `point:` appears.

4.  Type **@3<0**. The prompt `Angle/Length  of  chord/<End  point>:`
    appears.

5. Move the mouse, and you will see a temporary arc originating from a point 3 units to the right of the center point you selected and rotating about that center, as in panel 2 of Figure 2.10.

As the prompt indicates, you now have three options. You can enter an angle, length of chord, or the endpoint of the arc. The default, indicated by <End point> in the prompt, is to pick the arc's endpoint. Again, the cursor is in a point selection mode, telling you it is waiting for point input. To select this default option, you need only pick a point on the screen indicating where you want the endpoint.

6. Pick a point directly vertical from the center of the arc. The arc is now fixed in place, as in panel 3 of Figure 2.10.

You could have selected the Center Start End icon from the Arc flyout of the Draw toolbar and obtained the same results as in the foregoing exercise. However, this exercise has given you some practice working with AutoCAD LT's prompts and entering keyboard commands.

As you can see, AutoCAD LT has a distinct structure in its prompt messages. When you first issue a command, AutoCAD LT offers options in the form of a prompt. Depending on the option you select, you will get another set of options or you will be prompted to take some action, such as picking a point, selecting objects, or entering a value.

As you work through the exercises, you will become very familiar with this routine. Once you understand the workings of the toolbars, command prompts, and dialog boxes, you can almost teach yourself the rest of the program!

# Selecting Objects

AutoCAD LT provides many options for selecting objects. This section covers two distinct approaches to object selection: The first part deals with object selection methods unique to AutoCAD LT. The second part deals with the more common selection method used in most popular graphic programs, the *Noun/Verb* method. It's a good idea to familiarize yourself with these two methods early on, since you will use them constantly when you are working with AutoCAD LT.

## Selecting Objects in AutoCAD LT

Many AutoCAD LT commands prompt you to Select objects:. Along with this prompt, the cursor will change from crosshairs to a small

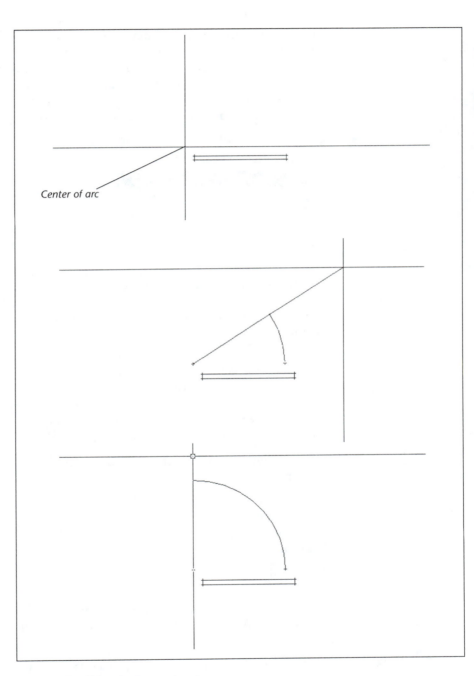

Center of arc

*Figure 2.10:* **Using the Arc command**

square (see Figure 2.8). Whenever you see this object-selection prompt and the square cursor, you have several options while making your selection. Often, as you select objects on the screen, you will change your mind about a selection or accidentally pick an object you do not want. Let's take a look at most of the selection options available in AutoCAD LT, and learn what to do when you make the wrong selection.

1. Choose Move from the Modify toolbar.

 **NOTE** *Highlighting* means an object changes from a solid image to one composed of dashes. When you see an object highlighted on the screen, you know that you have chosen that object to be acted upon by whatever command you are currently using.

2. At the `Select objects` prompt, click on the two horizontal lines that compose the door. As you saw in the last chapter, whenever AutoCAD LT wants you to select objects, the cursor turns into the small square pickbox. This tells you that you are in *object-selection mode*. As you pick an object, it is *highlighted,* as shown in Figure 2.11.

3. After making your selections, you may decide to deselect some items. Click on Undo on the Standard toolbar, or enter **U** ↵ from the keyboard.

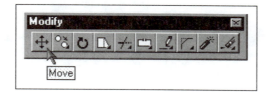

Notice that one line is no longer highlighted. The Undo option deselects objects, one at a time, in reverse order of selection.

 **TIP** You can also type **R** ↵ while you are in the selection process to remove selected objects. Then type **A** ↵ to exit "remove" mode and return to selecting objects.

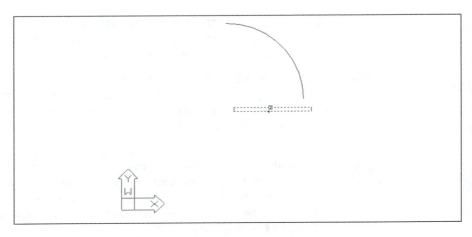

*Figure 2.11:* **Selecting the lines of the door and seeing them highlighted**

4. There is another way to deselect objects: Hold down the Shift key and click on the remaining highlighted line. It reverts to a solid line, showing you that it is no longer selected for editing.

   By now you have deselected both lines. Let's try using another method for selecting groups of objects.

 **NOTE** Do not confuse the *selection window* with the Zoom window you used in *Chapter 1*. That window option under the Zoom command does not *select* objects. Rather, it defines an area of the drawing you want to enlarge. The window option works differently under the Zoom command than it does for other editing commands.

5. Another option for selecting objects is to *window* them. Click and drag on the Select Objects button (on the Standard toolbar). Here is the flyout that appears (shown horizontally to conserve space):

6. Point to the Select Window icon, and release the mouse button. The cursor changes to a point-selection cursor, and the prompt changes to

   ```
   First corner:
   ```

7. Click on a point below and to the left of the rectangle representing the door. As you move your cursor across the screen, the window appears, and stretches across the drawing area.

8. Once the window completely encloses the door but not the arc, press the mouse/pick button and the entire door will be highlighted. This window selects only objects that are completely enclosed by the window, as shown in Figure 2.12.

> **WARNING** If you are using a mouse you're not familiar with, it's quite easy to accidentally click the button that triggers the ⏎ action when you really wanted to click the pick button, and vice versa. If you click the wrong button, you'll get the wrong results. On a two- or three-button mouse, the right button acts like the ⏎ key.

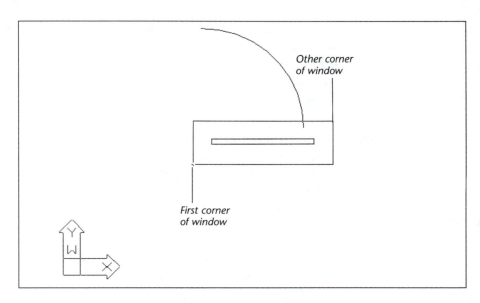

Figure 2.12: *Selecting the door within a window*

9. Now that you have selected the entire door but not the arc, press ⏎. *It is important to remember to press ⏎ as soon as you have finished selecting the objects you want to edit.* You must tell AutoCAD LT when you have finished selecting an object. A new prompt, `Base point or displacement:`, appears. The cursor changes to its point selection mode.

Now you have seen how the selection process works in AutoCAD LT—but we've left you in the middle of the Move command. In the next section, we'll discuss the prompt that's now on your screen, and see how to input base points and displacement distances.

### Providing Base Points

When you move or copy objects, AutoCAD LT prompts you for a *base point*. AutoCAD LT must be told specifically *from* where and *to* where the move occurs. The base point is the exact location from which you determine the distance and direction of the move. Once the base point is determined, you can tell AutoCAD LT where to move the object in relation to that point.

1. To select a base point, hold down the Shift key and press the right mouse button. A menu pops up on the screen. This is the Cursor menu. It contains the *object snap overrides* (or *Osnap overrides*), which allow you to select points with exact precision.

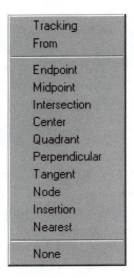

2. Pick Intersection from the Cursor menu. The Cursor menu disappears, and a square appears on the cursor (look back to Figure 2.8).

3. Pick the lower-right corner of the door. Whenever you see the square in the cursor, you don't have to point exactly at the intersection. Just get the intersection within the square, and AutoCAD LT will find the exact point where the two lines meet (see Figure 2.13).

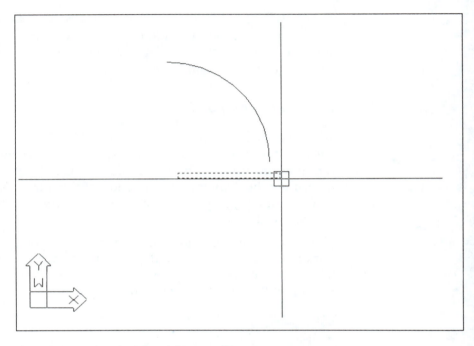

*Figure 2.13:* **Using the Osnap (object snap) cursor**

4.  At the Second point of displacement: prompt, hold down the Shift key and press the right mouse button again. In the Cursor menu, pick Endpoint.

5.  Now pick the lower-right end of the arc you drew earlier. (Remember, you need to place only the end of the arc within the square.) The door moves so that the intersection of the door connects exactly with the endpoint of the arc (see Figure 2.14).

    As you can see, the Osnap (*object snap*) overrides allow you to select specific points on an object. You used Endpoint and Intersect in this exercise, but other options are available. We will look at some of those later.

    If you want to specify an exact distance and direction by typing in a value, you can select any point on the screen as a base point. Or you can just type @ followed by ↵ at the base point prompt; then enter the second point's location in relative coordinates. Remember that @ means the last point selected. In this next exercise, you'll try moving the entire door an exact distance of 1 unit in a 45° angle.

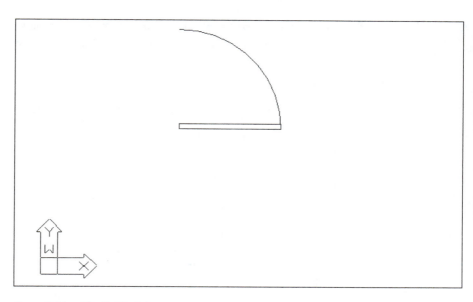

*Figure 2.14:* **The finished door**

1. Pick Move from the Modify toolbar again.

> **NOTE** You can activate most AutoCAD LT commands in a variety of ways: toolbar button, menu selection, and command line. The exercises in this book primarily show the toolbar options, since these demonstrate the new user interface for Release 3. At times you may find the command line alternatives more convenient. For example, you could accomplish the same results as steps 1 and 2 here, by typing **M** ↵ to start the Move command and then typing **P** ↵ to select the Previous selection set.

2. Click and drag to open the Select Objects flyout from the Standard toolbar, or type in **P** for previous, and click on the Select Previous icon. (The Select Previous icon is a backwards-pointing arrow, like the Undo button.) The set of objects you selected in the previous command is highlighted.

3. You're still in the object selection mode, so click on the arc to include it in the set of selected objects. Now the entire door, including the arc, is highlighted, as shown in Figure 2.15.

4. Now press ↵ to tell AutoCAD LT you have finished your selection. The cursor changes to point selection mode.

5. At the Base point of displacement prompt, pick a point on the screen between the door and the left side of the screen (see Figure 2.15).

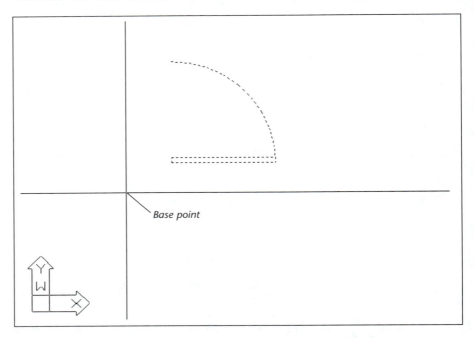

*Figure 2.15:* **The highlighted door and the base point just left of the door**

6. Move the cursor around slowly and notice that the door moves as if the base point you selected were attached to the door. The door moves with the cursor, at a fixed distance from it. This demonstrates how the base point relates to the objects you select.

7. Now type @1<45 ↵. The door will move to a new location on the screen at a distance of 1 unit from its previous location and at an angle of 45°.

This exercise illustrates that the base point does not have to be on the object you are manipulating—provided you enter specific distances with the keyboard. The base point can be virtually anywhere on your drawing. You also saw how you can reselect a group of objects that were selected previously, without having to duplicate the selection process.

## Selecting Objects Before the Command: Noun/Verb

Nearly all graphics programs today use the *noun/verb* method for selecting objects. This method requires you to select objects *before* you issue a command to edit them. The next set of exercises shows you how to use the noun/verb method in AutoCAD LT.

 **TIP** This chapter presents the standard AutoCAD LT method for object selection. AutoCAD LT also offers selection methods with which you may be more familiar. Refer to the section on the Object Selection Settings dialog box in *Appendix B* to learn how you can control object selection methods. This appendix also describes how you can change the size of the pickbox cursor.

You have seen that when AutoCAD LT is waiting for a command, it displays the crosshair cursor with the small square. This square is actually a pickbox superimposed on the cursor. It tells you that you can select objects, even while the command prompt appears at the bottom of the screen and no command is currently active. The square momentarily disappears when you are in a command that asks you to select points. From now on, we'll refer to this crosshair cursor with the small box as the *standard cursor*.

Now try moving objects by first selecting them and then using the Move command.

 **WARNING** If you find that this exercise does not work as described here, chances are the Noun/Verb setting has been turned off on your copy of AutoCAD LT. Refer to *Appendix B* to find out how to activate this setting.

1. First, press Esc to make sure AutoCAD LT isn't in the middle of a command you may have accidentally issued. Then click on the arc. The arc is highlighted, and you may also see squares appear at its endpoints and midpoint. These squares are called *grips*. You'll get a chance to work with them a bit later.

2. Choose Move from the Modify toolbar.

3. At the `Base point of displacement:` prompt, pick any point on the screen. The prompt `Second point of displacement:` appears, and the cursor changes to point selection mode.

4. Type **@1<0** ↵. The arc moves to a new location 1 unit to the right.

   In this exercise, you picked the arc *before* issuing the Move command. Then, when you clicked the Move button, you didn't see the object-selection prompt. Instead, AutoCAD LT assumed you wanted to move the arc you had selected and went directly to the base point prompt.

## OTHER SELECTION OPTIONS

There are several other selection options you haven't tried yet. The following describes these other options. You'll see how these options work in exercises later in this book. Or if you are adventurous, try them out now on your own. To use these options, type their keyboard abbreviations (shown in brackets in the following list) at any Select Objects prompt, or click on them in the Standard toolbar's Select Objects flyout.

**Select All [All ↵]** selects all the objects in a drawing except those in frozen or locked layers (see Chapter 4 for more on layers).

**Auto [Au ↵]** forces the standard automatic window or crossing window when a point is picked and no object is found. A standard window is produced when the two window corners are picked from left to right. A crossing window is produced when the two corners are picked from right to left. Once this option is selected, it remains active for the duration of the current command. Auto is intended for use on systems where the Automatic selection feature has been turned off. This has no menu equivalent.

**Box [BOX ↵]** allows you to use either a crossing or standard window, depending on which direction you draw the window. If your window is drawn from right to left, you will get a crossing window. If your window is drawn from left to right you will get a standard window.

**Select Crossing [C ↵]** is similar to the Select Window option but will select anything that crosses through the window you define.

**Select Crossing Polygon [Cp ↵]** acts exactly like WPolygon (see below) but, like the Select Crossing option, will select anything that crosses through a polygon boundary.

**Select Fence [F ↵]** selects objects that are crossed over by a temporary line called a fence. The operation is like crossing out the objects you want to select with a line. When you invoke this option, you can then pick points, as when you are drawing a series of line segments. When you are done drawing the fence, press ↵.

**Select Last [L ↵]** selects the last object you input.

**Multiple [M ↵]** lets you select several objects first, before AutoCAD LT highlights them. In a very large file, picking objects individually can cause AutoCAD LT to pause after each pick, while it locates and highlights each object. The Multiple option can speed things up by letting you first pick all the objects quickly, and then highlight them all by pressing ↵. This has no menu equivalent.

**Select Previous [P ↵]** selects the last object or set of objects that was edited or changed.

**Single [Si ↵]** forces the current command to select only a single object. If you use this option, you can pick a single object; then the current command will

## OTHER SELECTION OPTIONS (continued...)

act on that object as if you had pressed ↵ immediately after selecting the object. This has no menu equivalent.

**Select Window [W ↵]** forces a standard selection window. This option is useful when your drawing area is too crowded to place a window around a set of objects. It prevents you from accidentally selecting an object with a single pick when you are placing your window.

**Select Window Polygon [Wp ↵]** lets you select objects by enclosing them in an irregularly shaped polygon boundary. When you use this option, you see the prompt First polygon point. You then pick points to define the polygon boundary. As you pick points, the prompt Undo/<Endpoint of line> appears. Select as many points as you need to define the boundary. You can Undo boundary line segments as you go, by clicking on the Undo button on the Standard toolbar or by pressing the U key. With the boundary defined, press ↵. The bounded objects are highlighted and the Select Objects prompt returns, allowing you to use more selection options.

### Using Autoselect

Next you will move the rest of the door in the same direction by using the Autoselect feature.

1. Pick a point just above and to the left of the rectangle representing the door. Be sure not to pick the door itself. Now a window appears that you can drag across the screen as you move the cursor. If you move the cursor to the left of the last point selected, the window appears dotted (see the top of Figure 2.16). If you move the cursor to the right of that point, it appears solid (see the bottom of Figure 2.16).

> **TIP** In previous exercises, you were able to deselect objects by using the Undo selection options. With Noun/Verb selection turned on, you can only deselect objects by holding down the Shift key and simultaneously picking an object or using a window.

2. Now pick a point below and to the right of the door, so that the door is completely enclosed by the window, as shown in panel 2 of Figure 2.16. The door is highlighted (and again, you may see small squares appear at the line's endpoints and midpoints).

3. Start the Move command again. Just as in the last exercise, the base point prompt appears.

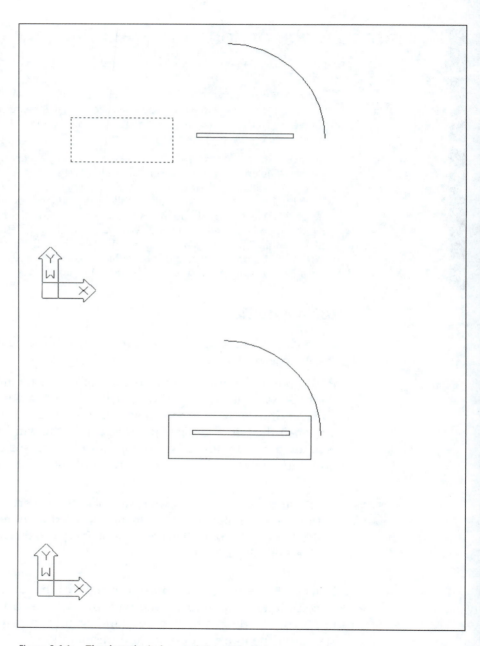

Figure 2.16: *The dotted window and the solid window*

4. Pick any point on the screen; then enter **@1<0** ↵. The door joins with the arc.

The two different windows you have just seen—the solid one and the dotted one—represent a *standard window* and a *crossing window*. If you use a standard window, anything that is completely contained within the window will be selected. If you use a crossing window, anything that crosses through the window will be selected. These two types of windows start automatically when you click on any blank portion of the drawing area with a standard cursor or point selection cursor; hence the name Autoselect.

Next, you will select objects with an automatic crossing window.

1. Pick a point below and to the right of the door. As you move the cursor to the left, the crossing (dotted) window appears.

2. Select the next point so that the window encloses the door and part of the arc (see Figure 2.17). The entire door, including the arc, highlights.

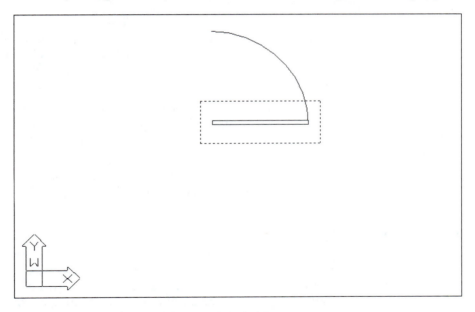

*Figure 2.17:*  **The door enclosed by a crossing window**

3. Start the Move command.

4.  Pick any point on the screen; then enter **@1<180**. The door moves back to its original location.

You'll find that the Autoselect standard and crossing windows are all you need when selecting objects. They will really save you time, so you'll want to get familiar with these features.

Before we continue, you need to click on the Save button on the Standard toolbar, or use File ➤ Save to save the Door file. You won't want to save the changes you make in the next section, so saving now will store the current condition of the file on your hard disk for safekeeping.

### Restrictions on Noun/Verb Object Selection

If you prefer to work with the Noun/Verb selection feature, you should know that its use is limited to the following subset of AutoCAD LT commands, listed here in no particular order.

| | | | |
|---|---|---|---|
| Array | Mirror | Wblock | Block |
| Dview | Move | Explode | Change |
| Erase | Rotate | Chprop | Hatch |
| Scale | Copy | List | Stretch |

For all other modifying or construction-oriented commands, the Noun/Verb selection method is inappropriate, because for those commands you must select more than one set of objects.

If you want to take a break, now is a good time to do it. If you wish, you can exit AutoCAD LT and return to this point in the tutorial later. When you return, start AutoCAD LT and open the Door file.

## Editing with Grips

Earlier, when you selected the door, little squares appeared at the endpoints and midpoints of the lines and arcs. These squares are called *grips*. Grips can be used to make direct changes to the shape of objects, or to quickly move and copy them.

WARNING  If you did not see small squares appear on the door in the previous exercise, your version of AutoCAD LT may have the Grips feature turned off. Before continuing with this section, refer to the information on grips in *Appendix B.*

So far, you have seen how operations in AutoCAD LT have a clear beginning and ending. For example, to draw an arc, you first issue the Arc command and then go through a series of operations, including answering prompts and picking points. When you are done, you have an arc and AutoCAD LT is ready for the next command.

The Grips feature, on the other hand, plays by a different set of rules. Grips offer a small yet powerful set of editing functions that don't conform to the lockstep command/prompt/input routine you have seen so far. As you work through the following exercises, it will be helpful to think of the Grips feature as a "subset" to the standard method of operation within AutoCAD LT.

To practice using the grips feature, you'll make some temporary modifications to the door drawing.

### Stretching Lines Using Grips

In this exercise, you'll stretch one corner of the door by grabbing the grip points of two lines.

1.  Press Esc to make sure AutoCAD LT is not in the middle of a command. Click on a point below and to the left of the door to start a selection window.

2.  Click above and to the right of the rectangular part of the door to select it.

3.  Place the cursor on the lower-left corner grip of the rectangle, *but don't press the pick button yet.* Notice that the cursor jumps to the grip point.

4.  Move the cursor to another grip point. Notice again how the cursor jumps to it. When the cursor is placed on a grip, the cursor moves to the exact center of the grip point. This means, for example, that if the cursor is placed on an endpoint grip, it is on the exact endpoint of the object.

NOTE When you select a grip by clicking on it, it turns a solid color and is known as a *hot grip*. You can control the size and color of grips using the Grips dialog box (see *Appendix B*).

5. Move the cursor to the upper-left corner grip of the rectangle and click on it. The grip becomes a solid color, and is now a *hot grip*. The prompt displays the following message:

   ```
   **STRETCH**

   <Stretch to point>/Base point/Copy/Undo/eXit:
   ```

   This prompt tells you that the Stretch mode is active. Notice the options shown in the prompt. As you move the cursor, the corner follows and the lines of the rectangle stretch (see Figure 2.18).

NOTE When you click on the corner grip point, AutoCAD LT selects the overlapping grips of two lines. When you stretch the corner away from its original location, the endpoints of both lines follow.

6. Move the cursor upward toward the top end of the arc and pick that point. The rectangle deforms, with the corner placed at your pick point (see Figure 2.18).

   Here you saw that a command called **Stretch** is issued simply by clicking on a grip point. As you will see, a handful of other hot-grip commands are also available.

1. Click on the grip point that you moved before.

2. Enter **B** ↵. The prompt changes to Base point:.

3. Click on a point to the right of the hot grip. Now as you move the cursor, the hot grip moves relative to the cursor.

TIP You can place multiple copies of an object at regularly spaced intervals by creating an *offset snap*. Do this by using the Shift key in conjunction with the Copy command. With Grips on, first select the object to copy and make an initial copy. The distance between the object and this first copy defines the *offset snap*. Now hold down the Shift key and position additional copies. These copies will appear at exactly the same offset distance. If the first copy was placed at an offset of 3 units, all subsequent copies will then be placed 3 units apart.

The Basics

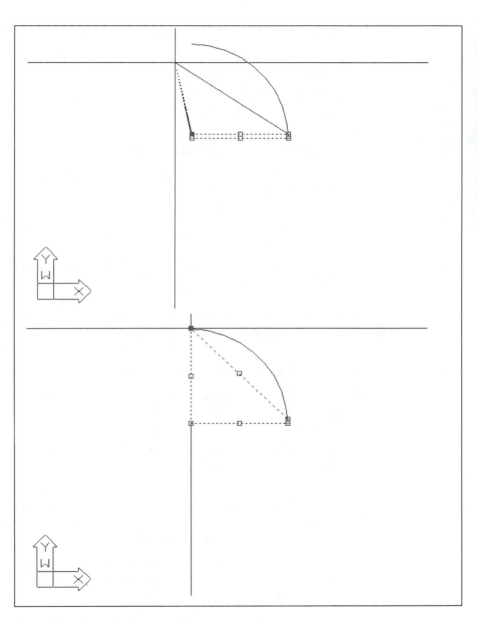

*Figure 2.18:* **Stretching lines using hot grips**

**4.** Type **C** ↵ to select the Copy option, and enter **@1<-90**. Instead of moving the hot grip and changing the lines, copies of the two lines are made, with their endpoints 1 unit below the first set of endpoints.

5. Pick another point just below the last. More copies are made.

6. Press ↵ or enter **X** ↵ to exit the Stretch mode.

   In this exercise, you were shown that you can select a base point other than the hot grip. You also saw how you can specify relative coordinates to move or copy a hot grip.

## Moving and Rotating with Grips

As you've just seen, the Grips feature offers an alternative method of editing your drawings. You've already seen how you can stretch end-points, but there is much more you can do with grips. The next exercise demonstrates some other options. You will start by undoing the modifications you made in the last exercise.

1. Click on the Undo button on the Standard toolbar, or type **U** ↵. The copies of the stretched lines disappear.

---

**TIP**  Pressing ↵ at the command prompt causes AutoCAD LT to repeat the last command entered—in this case, U.

---

2. Press ↵ again. The deformed door snaps back to its original form.

3. Click on the Redraw View button on the Standard toolbar, or choose View ➤ Redraw to clean up the display. Now you're ready to make a rotated copy of the door.

4. Select the entire door, including the door swing, by first clicking on a blank area below and to the right of the door.

5. Move the cursor to a location above and to the left of the rectangular portion of the door, and click. Since you went from right to left, you created a crossing window. Recall that this selects anything enclosed and crossing through the window.

6. Click on the lower-left grip of the rectangle to turn it into a hot grip. Now as you move your cursor, the corner stretches.

7. Press ↵ or the Spacebar. The prompt changes to

   ```
   **MOVE**

   <Move to point>/Base point/Copy/Undo/eXit:
   ```

   Now as you move the cursor, the entire door moves with it.

8.  Position the door near the center of the screen and click there. The door moves to the center of the screen. Notice that the command prompt returns, yet the door remains highlighted, telling you that it is still selected for the next operation.

9.  Click on the lower-left grip again, and press ↵ or the Spacebar twice. This time, the command prompt changes to

    ```
    **ROTATE** <Rotation angle>/Base point/copy/Undo/
    Reference/eXit:
    ```

    As you move the cursor, the door rotates about the grip point.

10. Position the cursor so that the door rotates 180° (see Figure 2.19). Then, while holding down the Shift key, press the mouse/pick button. A copy of the door appears in the new rotated position, leaving the original door in place.

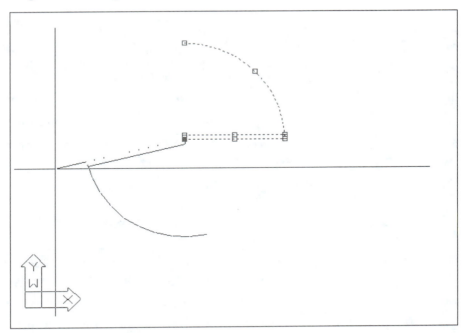

*Figure 2.19:* **Rotating and copying the door using a hot grip**

11. Press ↵ to exit the Rotate mode.

**NOTE** You've seen how the Move command is duplicated in a modified way as a hot-grip command. Other hot-grip commands (\*\*Stretch\*\*, \*\*Rotate\*\*, \*\*Scale\*\*, and \*\*Mirror\*\*) also have similar counterparts in the standard set of AutoCAD LT commands. You'll see how those work later in this book.

After you've completed any operation using grips, the objects are still highlighted with their grips still active. To clear the grip selection, press Esc twice.

In this exercise, you saw how new hot-grip commands appear as you press ↵. Two more commands, \*\*Scale\*\* and \*\*Mirror\*\*, are also available by continuing to press ↵ while a hot grip is selected. The commands then repeat if you continue to press ↵. The Shift key with the Copy option lets you set up an offset snap.

## A QUICK SUMMARY OF THE GRIP FEATURE

The exercises in this chapter using hot grips include only a few of the Grips options. You'll get a chance to use other hot-grip commands in later chapters. Meanwhile, here is a summary of Grips.

▶ Clicking on endpoint grips causes those endpoints to stretch.

▶ Clicking on midpoint grips of lines causes the entire line to move.

▶ If two objects meet end to end and you click on their overlapping grips, both grips are selected simultaneously.

▶ You can select multiple grips by holding down the Shift key and clicking on the desired grips.

▶ When a hot grip is selected, the Stretch, Move, Rotate, Scale, and Mirror commands are available to you.

▶ You can cycle through the Stretch, Move, Rotate, Scale, and Mirror commands by pressing ↵ or the Spacebar while a hot grip is selected.

▶ All the hot grip commands allow you to make copies of the selected objects.

▶ All the hot grip commands allow you to select a base point other than the originally selected hot grip.

The Basics

# Getting Help

Eventually, you will find yourself somewhere without documentation and you will have a question about an AutoCAD LT feature. AutoCAD LT provides online Help that will give you information on nearly any topic related to AutoCAD LT.

1. Click on the Help icon on the Standard toolbar, or on Help on the menu bar. A Help dialog box appears, with tabbed sub-dialog boxes: *Contents*, *Index*, and *Find*. This window shows the contents of the Help system at a glance.

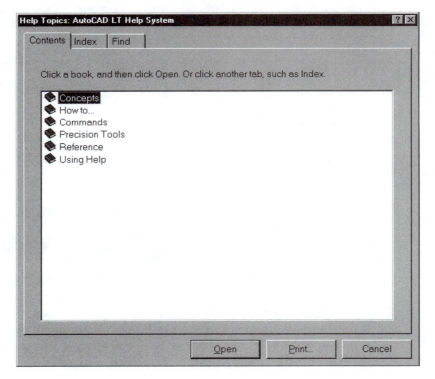

**NOTE** You can also press F1 to open the AutoCAD LT Help window. If you are in the middle of a command, you can click on the Help icon (the question mark) or type '**help** ↵ in the command window to get information about your current activity.

2.  First, select the Contents tab. From this dialog box you may ask for further information on *Concepts*, *How to* questions, and AutoCAD LT *Commands* and *System variables*. Double-click on Commands and then on the A-C listing. A list of AutoCAD LT commands appears.

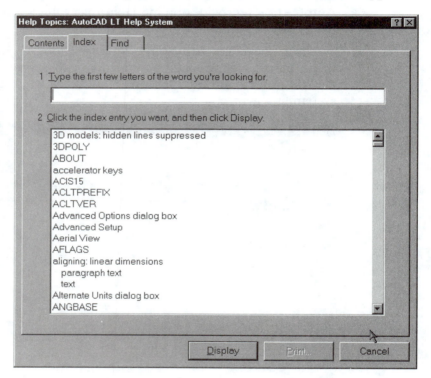

3.  At the top of the list is an abbreviated alphabet. Below, you see a list of commands that begin with the characters *A* through *C*. You can select alternative alphabetical ranges from the characters at the top to show more commands. For now, click on the word Copy. A detailed description of the Copy command appears. When you have reviewed the topic, press Esc to close the Help screen and return to the AutoCAD LT drawing editor.

You should take a moment now to experiment with the options available within the Online Help system. The *Concepts* includes everything from Drawing Set Up to Printing and Plotting. *How to…* includes practical topics such as how to Turn On a Grid or Use Grip Mode.

To use the *Index* option, click on the Index tab at the top of the window. The Index dialog box appears, with a list of topics in alphabetical order. You can enter a word to search for, or you can choose a topic in the Index list box.

1. Type the word **Change**. The list box immediately goes to Change in the list. Alternatively you may scroll down and then double-click on Change in the Index list box.

2. Click on the Display button. The Change command Help screen will appear.

3. When you have finished reviewing the Change command, press Esc to close the Help screen and return to the AutoCAD LT drawing editor.

AutoCAD LT also provides *context-sensitive help* to give you information related to the command you are currently using. To see how this works, try the following:

1. Click on the Move button in the Modify toolbar to start the Move command.

2. Click on the Help button on the Standard toolbar, or type **'Help** ↵. The Help screen appears, with a description of the Move command.

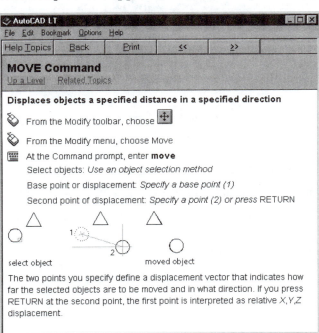

3. Press Esc to return to the drawing editor.

4. Press Esc to exit the Move command.

## Displaying More of the Prompt Text

At the bottom of the desktop is the AutoCAD LT Command Window. This window keeps a record of the most recent activity in AutoCAD LT. Some commands produce more information than will fit in the prompt area, which is typically only three lines. This frequently happens when you are trying to get information about your drawing. You can open the window at any time to view its contents. The following exercise shows how you can get an enlarged view of messages that have scrolled past the prompt area.

1. Click on the List button on the Object Properties toolbar. (It's the icon that's a piece of paper with writing on it.)

2. At the Select objects prompt, click on one of the arcs and press ↵. Information about the arc is displayed in the prompt area, but the information is too long to fit on the three lines.

3. The AutoCAD LT Text Window pops open. Toward the bottom is the list of the arc's properties (you'll get a detailed look at this information later in this book.)

4. To go back to the drawing editor, click on the Minimize button (the "-" button) in the upper-right corner of the Text Window, or press F2.

TIP  The F2 function key offers a quick way to toggle between the drawing editor and the Text Window.

5. Press the F2 key a few times and see what happens.

6. Now you are done with the door drawing, so choose File ➤ Exit.

7. At the Save Changes? dialog box, click on the No button. (You've already saved this file in the condition you want it in, so you need not save it again at this time.)

## If You Want to Experiment...

Try drawing the latch shown in Figure 2.20.

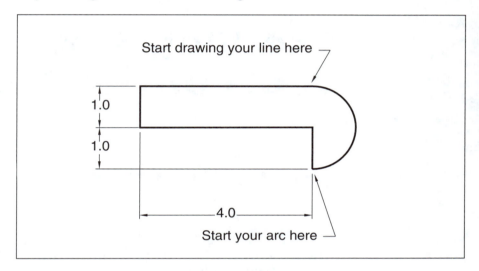

*Figure 2.20:   **Try drawing this latch. Dimensions are provided for your reference.***

1.  Start AutoCAD LT, open a new file, and Save it as Latch.

2.  When you get to the drawing editor, use the Line command to draw the straight portions of the latch. Start a line as indicated in the figure; then enter relative coordinates from the keyboard. For example, for the first line segment, enter **@4<180** to draw a line segment 4 units long from right to left.

3.  Draw an arc for the curved part. To do this, click on the Arc flyout on the Draw toolbar, and then click on Arc Start End Angle.

4.  Use the Endpoint Osnap override, and pick the endpoint indicated in the figure to start your arc.

5.  Using the Endpoint Osnap override again, click on the endpoint above where you started your line. A rubber-band line and a temporary arc appear.

6.  Position your cursor so the ghosted arc looks like the one in the figure, and press the mouse/pick button to draw in the arc.

# Chapter 3

# Learning the Tools of the Trade

## FAST TRACKS

**S**O far we have covered the most basic information you need to understand the workings of AutoCAD LT. Now you will put your knowledge to work. In this architectural tutorial, which begins here and continues through Chapter 12, you will draw a studio apartment building. The tutorial illustrates how to use AutoCAD LT commands and will give you a solid understanding of the basic AutoCAD LT package. With these fundamentals, you can use AutoCAD LT to its fullest potential, regardless of the kinds of drawings you intend to create or the enhancement products you may use in the future.

In this chapter, you will start drawing an apartment's bathroom fixtures. In the process, you will learn how to use AutoCAD LT's basic tools.

## Setting Up a Work Area

Before beginning most drawings, you will want to set up your work area. To do this you must determine the *measurement system,* the *drawing sheet size,* and the *scale* you want to use. The default work area is roughly 9″×12″ at full scale, given a decimal measurement system where one unit equals one inch. If these are appropriate settings for your drawing, then you don't have to do any setting up. It is more likely, however, that you will be doing drawings of various sizes and scales. For example, you may want to create a drawing in a measurement system where you can specify feet, inches, and fractions of inches, at 1″=1′

scale, and print the drawing on an 8½″×11″ sheet of paper. In this section, you will learn how to set up a drawing.

## Specifying Units

When you start up a new drawing, the first thing you will want to tell AutoCAD LT is the *unit style* you intend to use. So far, you've been using the default, which is decimal inches. In this style, whole units represent inches, and decimal units are decimal inches. If you want to be able to enter distances in feet, then you must change the unit style to one that accepts feet as input.

Drawing units can be specified in two ways. In the next two exercises we will review each of these methods. You can set drawing units as you open any new drawing by using the AutoCAD LT Drawing Setup Wizard. AutoCAD LT will guide you through the steps required to precisely specify the drawing units. Alternatively you may use the Units Control dialog box.

**TIP**  The Units Control settings can also be changed while another command is in progress. To change the unit style, you can type ´**lunits** ↵ at the command prompt. (The apostrophe lets you enter this command while in the middle of other commands.)

Start by creating a new file. Once you have set it up you will save it under the name Bath.

**NOTE** When you start a new drawing in AutoCAD LT, the default drawing name is "Unnamed." When you have completed setting up your new drawing, you should use the Save command to give your drawing a name. Click on the Save button on the Standard toolbar, and specify the name you want to give it in the Save As dialog box.

1.  Start up AutoCAD LT; then click on the New button on the Standard toolbar.

2.  In the Create New Drawing dialog box, click on the Use a Wizard option, select Advanced Setup, and press OK. The Advanced Setup dialog box appears.

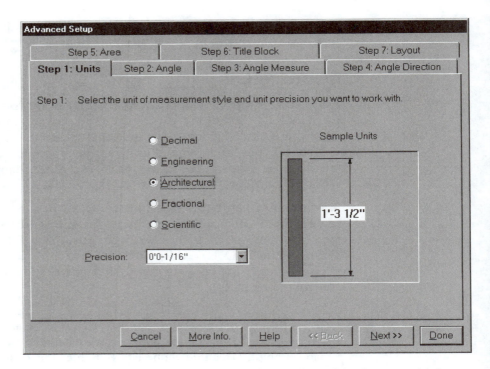

The Advanced Setup Wizard shows you seven tabbed steps which you can follow to set up a drawing. We are not going to complete all of these in this exercise; we will simply review Steps 1, 2, 3, and 4.

3. Take a look at Step 1: of the Wizard. Notice the unit styles listed in the Units group. Click on the Architectural button. The units change to Architectural units.

4. Click on the down-pointing arrow in the Precision drop-down list at the bottom of the Units group. Notice the options available. You can set the smallest unit AutoCAD LT will display in this drawing.

5. For now, click on Decimal Units again, and leave the precision setting at its default value of 0.0000.

6. Click on the Next button at the bottom of the Wizard, or on the Step 2: tab. This option allows you to select the angle of measurement system you want to use for this drawing—for example, decimal degrees or degrees/minutes/seconds. Click on the various options to review them, but return to the default setting of decimal degrees.

7. Click on the Next button at the bottom of the Wizard, or on the Step 3: tab. This option, Angle Measure, lets you set the direction for the 0° angle, or the direction *from* which AutoCAD LT measures angles. When you select different options (East/North/West/South), the screen graphic changes to show the changed positions of 90°, 180°, and 270°. Return to the default setting of East equals 0°.

8. Click on the Next button at the bottom of the Wizard, or on the Step 4: tab. This dialog box lets you set the direction for positive degrees, clockwise or counter-clockwise. For now, don't change the default setting—you'll read more about these settings in a moment. Click on the Cancel button.

9. When you return to the AutoCAD LT drawing editor, save your drawing with the name Bath. To do this, click on the Save button on the Standard toolbar. Type **Bath** in the File Name: list box in the Save As dialog box.

In the previous exercise, you had a chance to explore the Setup Wizard, but you did not actually change any of the Unit Settings. Now let's take a look at unit settings in more detail using the Units Control dialog box.

1. Choose Format ➤ Units .... The Units Control dialog box appears. It presents essentially the same choices as the Setup Wizard, but they are organized differently within the dialog box. Let's look at a few of the options available.

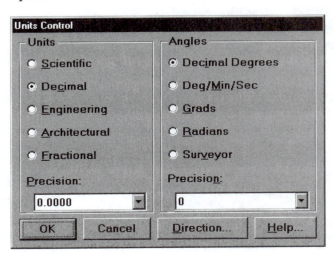

NOTE This dialog box has two button groups: Units and Angles. Both groups contain Precision settings in drop-down lists near the bottom of the dialog box. These lists operate in exactly the same way as the first two steps of the Setup Wizard. The Units group lets you select the type of measurement unit you want to use; in the Angles group you select the angle type.

2. The unit styles are listed in the Units group. Click on the Architectural button.

3. Click on the down-pointing arrow in the Precision drop-down list at the bottom of the Units group, and review the options available once again. Leave this setting at its default value of $\frac{1}{16}$".

4. Click on the Direction... button at the bottom of the dialog box. The Direction Control dialog box appears. This dialog box offers the same options as Steps 3 and 4 on the Setup Wizard. The default settings do not need to be changed for this particular exercise. Click on the Cancel button.

 NOTE The Direction Control dialog box lets you set the direction for the 0° angle. It also lets you determine the positive and negative direction for angles.

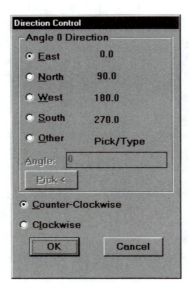

5.  Click on OK in the main Units Control dialog box to return to the drawing.

You picked Architectural measurement units for this tutorial, but your own work may require a different unit style. You saw the unit styles available in the Units Control dialog box. Table 3.1 shows examples of how the distance 15.5 is entered in each of these styles.

*Table 3.1:* **Measurement Systems Available in AutoCAD LT**

| Measurement System | AutoCAD LT's Display of Measurement |
|---|---|
| Scientific | 1.55E+01 (inches) |
| Decimal | 15.5000 (inches) |
| Engineering | 1'-3.5" (input as 1'3.5") |
| Architectural | 1'-3½" (input as 1'3-1/2") |
| Metric | 15.5000 (converted to metric at plot) |
| Fractional | 15½" (input as 15½") |

Let's take a look at the Units Control settings in more detail. As you read, you may want to refer to the illustration of the Units Control dialog box.

## Fine-Tuning the Measurement System

Most of the time, you will be concerned only with the Units and Angles setting groups of the Units Control dialog box. But as you saw from the exercise, you can control many other settings related to the input and display of units.

The Precision drop-down list in the Units group lets you specify the smallest unit value that you want AutoCAD LT to display in the status line and in the prompts. If you choose a measurement system that uses fractions, the Precision list will include fractional units. This setting can also be controlled with Lunits and Luprec system variables.

AutoCAD LT's *system variables* are settings which control the operating environment, for example the degree of precision for measurement units. Some variables are read-only, and cannot be changed. Most system variables, however, can be set by the individual user. For a fuller review of all of the AutoCAD LT system variables, see *Appendix D.*

**TIP** To find the distance between two points, choose Distance from the Inquiry flyout on the Object Properties toolbar, or type **Dist** ↵ and then click on the two points. But if you find that this command doesn't give you an accurate distance measurement, examine the Units/Precision option in the Units Control dialog box. If it is set too high, the value returned by Distance may be rounded to a value greater than your tolerances allow, even though the distance is drawn accurately.

The Angles group lets you set the style for displaying angles. You have a choice of five angle styles: decimal degrees, degrees/minutes/seconds, grads, radians, and surveyor's units. In the Angles group's Precision drop-down list, you can determine the degree of accuracy you want AutoCAD LT to display for angles. These settings can also be controlled with the Aunits and Auprec system variables.

**NOTE** You can find out more about system variables in *Appendix D.*

The Direction Control dialog box lets you set the direction of the base angle, 0°. The default base angle (and the one used throughout this book) is a direction from left to right. However, there may be times when you will want to designate another direction as the 0° base angle. You can also tell AutoCAD LT which direction is positive, either clockwise or counterclockwise. In this book we use the default, counterclockwise. These settings can also be controlled with the Angbase and Angdir system variables.

## Setting Up the Drawing Limits

One of the big advantages in using AutoCAD LT is that you can draw at full scale; you aren't limited to the edges of a piece of paper the way you are in manual drawing. But you still have to consider what will happen when you want a printout of your drawing. If you're not careful, you may create a drawing that won't fit on the paper size you want

# THINGS TO WATCH OUT FOR WHEN ENTERING DISTANCES

When you are using Architectural units, there are two points you should be aware of:

▶ Hyphens are used only to distinguish fractions from whole inches.

▶ You cannot use spaces while giving a dimension. For example, you can specify eight feet, four and one-half inches as 8′4–½″ or 8′4.5, but not as 8′–4½″.

These idiosyncrasies are a source of confusion to many architects and engineers new to AutoCAD LT, since the program often displays architectural dimensions in the standard architectural format but does not allow you to enter dimensions that way.

When inputting distances and angles in unusual situations, here are some tips:

▶ When entering distances in inches and feet, you can omit the inch (″) sign.

▶ You can enter fractional distances and angles in any format you like, regardless of the current unit system. For example, you can enter a distance as @1/2< 1.5708r even if your current unit system is set for decimal units and decimal degrees (1.5708r is the radian equivalent of 90°).

▶ If you have your angle units set to degrees, grads, or radians, you do not need to specify g, r, or d after the angle. You do have to specify g, r, or d, however, if you want to use these units when they are not the current default angle system.

▶ If your current angle system is set to something other than degrees, but you want to input angles in degrees, you can use a double less-than symbol (<<) in place of the single less-than symbol (<) to override the current angle system of measure. The << also assumes the base angle of 0° to be a direction from left to right and the positive direction to be counterclockwise.

▶ If your current angle system uses a different base angle and direction (other than left to right for 0° and a counterclockwise direction for positive angles), and you want to specify an angle in the standard base direction, you can use a triple less-than symbol (<<<) to indicate angle.

▶ You can specify a denominator of any size when specifying fractions. However, you should be aware that the value you have set for the maximum number of digits to the right of decimal points (under the Units setting) will restrict the actual fractional value AutoCAD LT will use. For example, if your units are set for a maximum of two digits of decimals and you give a fractional value of 5/32, AutoCAD LT will round it out to 3/16 or 0.16.

▶ You are allowed to enter decimal feet for distances in the architectural unit style.

at the scale you want. You must limit your drawing area to one that can be scaled down to fit on a standard sheet size.

In order to set up the drawing work area, you need to understand how standard sheet sizes translate into full-scale drawing sizes. Tables 3.2 and 3.3 list widths and heights of drawing areas in inches, according to scales and final printout sizes. The scales are listed in the far left column; the output sheet sizes are listed across the top.

Let's take an example: To find the area needed in AutoCAD LT for your Bath drawing, for instance, look across from the scale 1″=1′ to the column that reads 8½″×11″ at the top. You'll find the value 102×132. This means the drawing area needs to fit within an area 102″ by 132″ (8.5 feet by 11 feet) in AutoCAD LT in order to fit a printout of a 1″=1′-0″ scale drawing on an 8½″×11″ sheet of paper. You will want the drawing area to be oriented horizontally, so that the 11 feet will be in the x-axis and the 8.5 feet will be in the y-axis.

Now that you know the area you need, you can use the Limits command to set up the area.

It's a good idea to let the origin (0,0) of the drawing be the lower-left corner, because it gives you a point of reference when using absolute coordinates. Also, you will want to set reasonable limits for your drawings. If the limits cover too great an area, AutoCAD LT will take longer to redraw.

1. Choose Format ➤ Drawing Limits or type **Limits** ↵ at the command prompt.

2. At the ON/OFF/<Lower left corner> <0′−0″,0′−0″>: prompt, specify the lower-left corner of your work area. Press ↵ to accept the default.

3. At the Upper right corner <1′0″,0′9″>: prompt, specify the upper-right corner of your work area. (The default is shown in brackets.) Enter **132,102**. Or if you prefer, you can enter **11′,8′6**.

NOTE You can set the drawing limits (just as you can set drawing units) before you open any new drawing. Use the AutoCAD LT Setup Wizard. When the Create New Drawing dialog box appears, select Use a Wizard, then select Quick setup; and choose OK. When the Wizard opens, click on the second tabbed heading, Step 2: Area. The Wizard will show the current default drawing limits. Double-click on the default values and type in the limits which you require for your new drawing. Click on the Done button to set the drawing limits and exit Setup.

4. Next, click on Zoom All on the Zoom flyout on the Standard toolbar, or choose View ➤ Zoom ➤ All. Though it appears that nothing has changed, your drawing area is now set to a size that will allow you to draw your bathroom at full scale.

   You can toggle through the different coordinate readout modes by pressing F6 or clicking on the coordinate readout on the status bar. For more on the coordinate readout modes, see *Chapter 1* and "Using the Coordinate Readout as Your Scale" later in this chapter.

5. Move the cursor to the upper-right corner of the drawing area and watch the coordinate readout. You will see that now the upper-right corner has a Y coordinate of 8´6. The X coordinate will vary depending on the proportion of your AutoCAD LT window. The coordinate readout also displays distances in feet and inches.

   In step 5 above, the coordinate readout shows you that your drawing area is larger than before, but there are no visual clues to tell you where you are or what distances you are dealing with. To help you get your bearings, you can use the Grid mode, which you will learn about shortly. But first, let's take a closer look at scale factors and how they work.

## Understanding Scale Factors

All the drawing sizes in Tables 3.2 and 3.3 were derived by using scale factors. Table 3.4 shows scale factors as they relate to standard drawing scales. These scale factors are the values by which you multiply the desired final printout size to get the equivalent full-scale size. For example, if you have a sheet size of 11×17″, and you want to know the equivalent full-scale size for a ¼″-scale drawing, you multiply the sheet measurements by 48. In this way, 11″ becomes 528″ (48×11) and 17″ becomes 816″ (48×17). Your work area must be 528″ by 816″ if you intend to have a final output of 11″ by 17″ at ¼″=1´. You can divide these inch measurements by 12″ to get 44´×68´.

**TIP** If you get the message **Outside limits**, it means you have selected a point outside the area defined by the limits of your drawing and the Limits command's limits-checking feature is on. (Some third-party programs may use the limits-checking feature.) If you must select a point outside the limits, issue the Limits command and then enter **off** at the ON/OFF <Lower left corner>... prompt to turn off the limits-checking feature.

Table 3.2:   Work Area in Drawing Units (Inches) by Scale and Plotted Sheet Size

| Scale | 8½"x11" | 11"x17" | 17"x22" | 18"x24" | 22"x34" | 24"x36" | 30"x42" | 36"x48" |
|---|---|---|---|---|---|---|---|---|
| 3"=1' | 34×44 | 44×68 | 68×88 | 72×96 | 88×136 | 96×144 | 120×168 | 144×192 |
| 1½"=1' | 68×88 | 88×136 | 136×176 | 144×192 | 176×272 | 192×288 | 240×336 | 288×384 |
| 1"=1' | 102×132 | 132×204 | 204×264 | 216×288 | 264×408 | 288×432 | 360×504 | 432×576 |
| ¾"=1' | 136×176 | 176×272 | 272×352 | 288×384 | 352×544 | 384×576 | 480×672 | 576×768 |
| ½"=1' | 204×264 | 264×408 | 408×528 | 432×576 | 528×816 | 576×864 | 720×1008 | 864×1152 |
| ¼"=1' | 408×528 | 528×816 | 816×1056 | 864×1152 | 1056×1632 | 1152×1728 | 1440×2016 | 1728×2304 |
| ⅛"=1' | 816×1056 | 1056×1632 | 1632×2112 | 1728×2304 | 2112×3264 | 2304×3456 | 2880×4032 | 3456×4608 |
| 1/16"=1' | 1632×211 | 2112×3264 | 3264×4224 | 3456×4608 | 4224×6528 | 4608×6912 | 5760×8064 | 6912×9216 |
| 1/32"=1' | 3264×4224 | 224×6528 | 6528×8448 | 6912×9216 | 8448×13056 | 9216×13824 | 11520×16128 | 13824×18432 |
| 1"=10' | 1020×1320 | 1320×2040 | 2040×2640 | 2160×2880 | 2640×4080 | 2880×4320 | 3600×5040 | 4320×5760 |
| 1"=20' | 2040×2640 | 2640×4080 | 4080×5280 | 4320×5760 | 5280×8160 | 5760×8640 | 7200×10080 | 8640×11520 |
| 1"=30' | 3060×396 | 3960×612 | 6120×7920 | 6480×8640 | 7920×12240 | 8640×12960 | 10800×15120 | 12960×17280 |
| 1"=40' | 4080×5280 | 5280×8160 | 8160×10560 | 8640×11520 | 10560×16320 | 11520×17280 | 14400×20160 | 17280×23040 |
| 1"=50' | 5100×6600 | 6600×10200 | 10200×13200 | 10800×14400 | 13200×20400 | 14400×21600 | 18000×25200 | 21600×28800 |
| 1"=60' | 6120×7920 | 7920×12240 | 12240×15840 | 12960×17280 | 15840×24480 | 17280×25920 | 21600×30240 | 25920×34560 |

Table 3.3:    *Work Area in Metric Units (Millimeters) by Scale and Plotted Sheet Size*

| Scale | A0 | A1 | A2 | A3 | A4 |
|---|---|---|---|---|---|
| | 841mm×<br>1189mm | 594mm×<br>841mm | 420mm×<br>594mm | 297mm×<br>420mm | 210mm×<br>297mm |
| | (33.11″×<br>46.81″) | (23.39″×<br>33.11″) | (16.54″×<br>23.39″) | (11.70″×<br>16.54″) | (8.27″×<br>11.70″) |
| 1:2 | 1682mm×<br>2378mm | 1188mm×<br>1682mm | 840mm×<br>1188mm | 594mm×<br>840mm | 420mm×<br>594mm |
| 1:5 | 4205mm×<br>5945mm | 2970mm×<br>4205mm | 2100mm×<br>2970mm | 1485mm×<br>2100mm | 1050mm×<br>1485mm |
| 1:10 | 8410mm×<br>11890mm | 5940mm×<br>8410mm | 4200mm×<br>5940mm | 2970mm×<br>4200mm | 2100mm×<br>2970mm |

The scale factor for fractional inch scales is derived by multiplying the denominator of the scale by 12, then dividing by the numerator. For example, the scale factor for ¼″=1′–0″ is (4×12)/1, or 48/1. For whole-foot scales like 1″=10′, multiply the feet side of the equation by 12. Metric scales require simple decimal conversions.

If you are using the metric system, or are working in decimal feet, the drawing scale can be used directly as the scale factor. For example, a drawing scale of 1:10 would have a scale factor of 10; a drawing scale of 1:50 would have a scale factor of 50, and so on.

Table 3.4:    *Scale Conversion Factors*

| Scale Factors for Engineering Drawing Scales | | | | | | | | |
|---|---|---|---|---|---|---|---|---|
| 1″ = n | 10′ | 20′ | 30′ | 40′ | 50′ | 60′ | 100′ | 200′ |
| Scale factor | 120 | 240 | 360 | 480 | 600 | 720 | 1200 | 2400 |
| **Scale Factors for Architectural Drawing Scales** | | | | | | | | |
| n = 1′-0″ | ¹⁄₁₆″ | ⅛″ | ¼″ | ½″ | ¾″ | 1″ | 1½″ | 3″ |
| Scale factor | 192 | 96 | 48 | 24 | 16 | 12 | 8 | 4 |

You will be using scale factors to determine text height and dimension scaling and viewport scaling, so getting to understand them now will pay off later.

# Using the AutoCAD LT Modes as Drafting Tools

After you have set up your work area, you can begin the plan of a typical bathroom in your studio. We will use this example to show you some of AutoCAD LT's drawing aids. These tools might be compared to a background grid (the *grid mode*), scale (the *coordinate readout*), and a T square and triangle (the *ortho mode*). The drawing modes can be indispensable tools when used properly. The Drawing Aids dialog box helps you visualize the modes in an organized manner and simplifies their management.

**TIP** You can use the Gridunit system variable to set the grid spacing. Enter ´**Gridunit** ↵, and at the New value for GRIDUNIT <0'0″,0'0″>: prompt, enter **10,10**. Note that the Gridunit value must be entered as an x,y coordinate.

## Using the Grid Mode as a Background Grid

Using the *grid mode* is like having a grid under your drawing to help you with layout. In AutoCAD LT, the grid mode also lets you see the limits of your drawing and helps you visually determine the distances you are working with in any given view. In this section, you will learn how to control the grid's appearance. Double-click on GRID on the status bar to turn the grid on or off. The F7 key also toggles the grid mode on and off.

1. Double-click on GRID on the status bar, or press F7, or hold down the Ctrl key and press **G**. An array of dots appears. These dots are the *grid points*. They will not print or plot with your drawing. If the grid seems a bit too dense, you can alter the grid spacing by using the Grid command.

**TIP** When you turn on the Grid, you may get a message "Grid too dense to display." If so, click on the Zoom In button on the Standard toolbar until the grid dots appear. If the grid setting is very close, and you are zoomed out too far, AutoCAD LT cannot display the grid.

2. Choose Options ➤ Drawing Aids… to display the Drawing Aids dialog box, showing all the mode settings. You see four button groups: Modes, Snap, Grid, and Isometric Snap/Grid. Let's start with the Grid group.

**Drawing Aids**

| Modes | Snap | | Grid | |
|---|---|---|---|---|
| ☐ Ortho | ☐ On | | ☑ On | |
| ☑ Solid Fill | X Spacing | 0'1" | X Spacing | 0'0" |
| ☐ Quick Text | Y Spacing | 0'1" | Y Spacing | 0'0" |
| ☑ Blips | Snap Angle | 0 | **Isometric Snap/Grid** | |
| ☑ Highlight | X Base | 0'0" | ☐ On | |
| | Y Base | 0'0" | ◉ Left  ○ Top  ○ Right | |

|  OK  |  Cancel  |  Help…  |

3. Notice that the X Spacing edit box contains a value of 0'0". Above that, the On check box contains a check mark, telling you that the grid is turned on.

> **TIP**  If you want to change an entry in an input box, you can double-click on it to highlight the whole entry, and then replace the entry by simply typing in a new one.

4. Double-click on the X Spacing input box. The 0'0" highlights. You can now type in a new value for this setting.

5. Enter **10** ↵ for 10". Notice that the Y Spacing input box automatically changes to 0'10". AutoCAD LT assumes you want the X and Y grid spacing to be the same, unless you specifically ask for a different Y setting.

6. Click on OK. The grid now appears with a 10" spacing in your drawing area.

   With the grid at a 10-unit spacing, the grid doesn't clutter the screen. Since the grid will appear only within the drawing limits, you are better able to see your work area. Next, you'll see how the snap mode works.

## Using the Snap Mode

The *snap mode* has no equivalent in hand drafting. This mode forces the cursor to step a specific distance. It is useful if you want to maintain accuracy while entering distances with the cursor. Like in grid mode, there is a SNAP button in the status bar that you can double-click to turn snap mode on or off. The F9 key also toggles the snap mode on and off.

> **TIP** You can use the Snapunit system variable to set the snap spacing. Enter **'Snapunit** ↵, then at the `New value for SNAPUNIT <0'0",0'0">:` prompt, enter **4,4**. Note that the Snapunit value must be entered as an x,y coordinate.

1.  Double click on SNAP on the status bar, or press F9, or hold down the Ctrl key and press **B**; then move the cursor slowly around the drawing area. Notice how the cursor seems to move in "steps" rather than in a smooth motion. Also note that the prompt in the command window reads `Snap On`, which tells you that the snap mode is on.

2.  Choose Options ➤ Drawing Aids. The Drawing Aids dialog box appears again.

3.  In the Snap group of the dialog box, double-click on the X Spacing input box, and enter **4** ↵. As with the Grid setting, AutoCAD LT assumes you want the X and Y snap spacing to be the same, unless you specifically ask for a different Y setting.

4.  Click on OK, and start moving the cursor around. Notice how it steps at a greater distance than before—4″ to be exact.

    The other options in the Snap group of the Drawing Aids dialog box allow you to set the snap origin point (X Base and Y Base), rotate the cursor to an angle other than its current 0—90° (Snap angle), and set the horizontal snap spacing to a value different from the vertical spacing (X Spacing and Y Spacing). You can also adjust other settings, such as the grid/snap orientation that allow isometric-style drawings (Isometric Snap/Grid). We will look at these features in *Chapters 6* and *15*.

## Using Grid and Snap Together

You can set the grid spacing to be the same as the snap setting, allowing you to see every snap point. Let's take a look at how grid and snap work together.

1. Open the Drawing Aids dialog box.

2. Double-click on the X Spacing input box in the Grid group, and enter **0** ↵.

3. Click on OK. Now the grid display spacing has changed to reflect the 4″ snap interval. Move the cursor, and watch it snap to the grid points.

4. Open the Drawing Aids dialog box again.

5. Double-click on the X Spacing input box in the Snap group, and enter **1** ↵.

6. Click on OK. The grid automatically changes to conform to the new snap setting. When the grid spacing is set to 0, the grid then aligns with the snap points. At this density, the grid is overwhelming.

7. Open the Drawing Aids dialog box again.

8. Double-click on the X Spacing input box in the Grid group, and enter **10** ↵.

9. Click on OK. The grid spacing is now at 10 again, a more reasonable spacing for the current drawing scale.

## Using the Coordinate Readout as Your Scale

Now you will draw the first item in the bathroom: the toilet. It is composed of a rectangle representing the tank, and a truncated ellipse representing the seat.

As you move the cursor over the drawing area, the coordinate readout dynamically displays its position in absolute Cartesian coordinates. This allows you to find a position on your drawing by locating it in reference to the drawing origin—0,0—which is in the lower-left corner of the sheet. You can also set the coordinate readout to display relative coordinates. Throughout these exercises, coordinates will be provided to enable you to select points using the dynamic coordinate readout. (If you want to review the discussion of AutoCAD LT's coordinates display, see *Chapter 1.*)

**NOTE** Ortho mode (also available under Modes in the Drawing Aids dialog box) restricts the cursor to horizontal and vertical movement. ORTHO appears on the status bar to tell you that Ortho mode is on. You can toggle ORTHO On or Off in the same way as SNAP and GRID.

1. Click on the Line flyout on the Draw toolbar.

2. Using your coordinate readout for guidance, start your line at the coordinate 5′–7″, 6′–3″.

3. Double-click on the coordinate readout on the status bar, or choose Option ➤ Coordinate Display, or press F6 until you see the relative polar coordinates appear in the coordinate readout at the bottom of the AutoCAD LT window. Polar coordinates allow you to see your current location in reference to the last point selected. This is helpful when you are using a command that requires distance and direction input.

4. Move the cursor until the coordinate readout lists 1′–10″< 0, and pick this point. As you move the cursor around, the rubber-banding line follows it at any angle.

5. You can also force the line to be orthogonal. Double-click ORTHO on the status bar, or press F8, or hold down the Ctrl key and press **O** to toggle on the ortho mode, and move the cursor around. Now the rubber-band line will move only vertically or horizontally.

6. Move the cursor down until the coordinate readout lists 0′–9″< 270.

7. Continue drawing the other two sides of the rectangle by using the coordinate readout. You should have a drawing that looks like Figure 3.1.

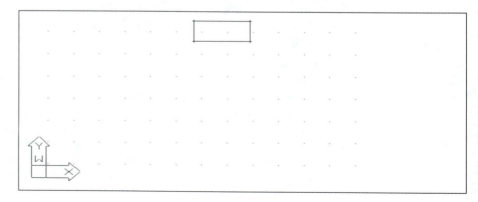

*Figure 3.1:* ***A plan view of the toilet tank***

By using the snap mode in conjunction with the coordinate readout, you can measure distances as you draw lines. This is similar to the way you would draw using a scale. Be aware that the smallest distance the coordinate readout will register depends on the area you have displayed in your drawing area. For example, if you are displaying an area the size of a football field, the smallest distance you can indicate with your cursor may be 6″. On the other hand, if your view shows an area of only one square inch, you can indicate distances as small as $\frac{1}{1000}''$ using your cursor.

## Exploring the Drawing Process

In this section, you will look at some of the more common commands and use them to complete this simple drawing. As you draw, watch the prompts and notice how your responses affect them. Also note how you use existing drawing elements as reference points.

NOTE In essence, you alternately create and edit objects to build your drawing.

While drawing with AutoCAD LT, you create gross geometric forms to determine the basic shapes of objects, and then modify the shapes to fill in detail. This is where the differences between drawing with AutoCAD LT and manual drafting become more apparent.

AutoCAD LT offers many basic types of drawing objects, a number of which are new in Release 3. The object types from earlier versions of AutoCAD LT are lines, arcs, circles, text, polylines, polygons, points and solids. The new object types are true ellipses, elliptical arcs, spline curves, x-lines, rays, and multiline text. All drawings are built on these objects. In addition, in AutoCAD LT you may *edit* 3D meshes, 3D faces, and other 3D objects which have been created in AutoCAD Release 13.

You are familiar with lines and arcs; these, along with circles, are the most commonly used objects. As you progress through the book, we will introduce you to the other objects and how they are used.

## Locating an Object in Reference to Others

To date, AutoCAD LT has been sorely lacking an accurate representation of ellipses and spline curves. Release 3 fills this gap with true ellipses and curves, or NURBS. NURBS stands for Non-Uniform Rational B-Splines. This means that curved objects in AutoCAD LT are now based on accurate mathematical models. When you trim the ellipse in a later exercise, it will become a NURBS curve, not a segmented polyline as in earlier versions of AutoCAD LT. You'll learn more about curves in *Chapter 13*.

To define the toilet seat, you will use an ellipse.

1.  Click and drag the Ellipse icon on the Draw toolbar. You can also type **Ellipse** ↵ to start the Ellipse command

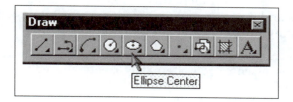

    and then select Ellipse Axis Endpoint from the flyout.

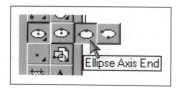

2.  At the `Arc/Center/<Axis endpoint 1>:` prompt, pick the midpoint of the bottom horizontal line of the rectangle. Do this by bringing up the Osnap overrides and selecting Midpoint; then pick the bottom line. (Remember, to bring up the Cursor menu, Shift-click the right mouse button.)

3.  At the `Axis endpoint 2:` prompt, move the cursor down until the coordinate readout lists 1′–10″<270. Alternatively, you may type in **@1′–10″< 270** ↵.

4.  Pick this as the second axis endpoint.

5. At the <Other axis distance>/Rotation: prompt, move the cursor horizontally from the center of the ellipse until the coordinate readout lists 0′–8″< 180 (or type in **@0′–8″< 180** ↵).

6. Pick this as the axis distance defining the width of the ellipse. Your drawing should look like Figure 3.2.

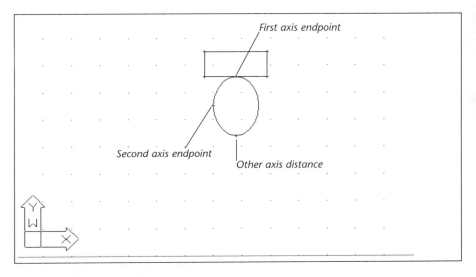

First axis endpoint

Second axis endpoint

Other axis distance

Figure 3.2:    **The ellipse added to the tank**

## Getting a Closer Look

During the drawing process, you will want to enlarge areas of a drawing to more easily edit its objects. In *Chapter 1*, you already saw how the Zoom command is used for this purpose.

1. Click on the Zoom Window button on the Zoom flyout on the Standard toolbar, or choose View ➤ Zoom ➤ Window. You can also enter **Zoom** ↵. The Zoom Window icon shows a magnifying glass with a rectangle (or "window") in it.

2. At the First corner: prompt, pick a point below and to the left of your drawing at coordinate 5′–0″, 3′–6″.

3. At the Other corner: prompt, pick a point above and to the right of the drawing at coordinate 8′–3″, 6′–8″, so that the toilet is completely

enclosed by the view window. The toilet enlarges to fill more of the screen (see Figure 3.3).

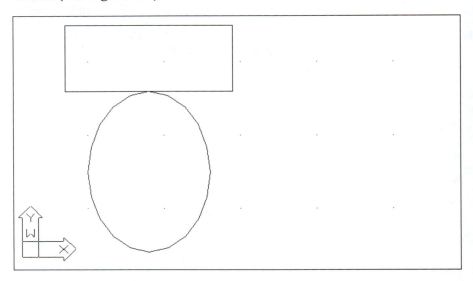

*Figure 3.3:    A close-up of the toilet drawing*

 **NOTE** You should also know about the Real-time Zoom option. Real-time Zoom is available on the Zoom Flyout on the Standard toolbar. When Real-time Zoom is turned on, your cursor changes to a magnifying glass icon with a plus/minus sign. In Real-time Zoom mode, simple cursor movement will zoom you in or out of your drawing. Moving the cursor *up* the screen will *enlarge* your drawing; moving the cursor *down* the screen will *reduce* your drawing.

## Modifying an Object

Now let's see how editing commands are used to construct an object. To define the back edge of the seat, let's put a copy of the line defining the front of the toilet tank, about 3″ toward the center of the ellipse.

1. Click on Duplicate Object on the Modify toolbar to activate the Copy command. You can also type **Copy** ↵, or you can use grips to copy the line (see *Chapter 2*).

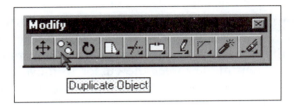

2. At the Select object: prompt, pick the horizontal line that touches the top of the ellipse. The line is highlighted. Press ↵ to confirm your selection.

3. At the <Base point or displacement>/Multiple: prompt, pick a base point near the line. Then move the cursor down until the coordinate readout lists 0′–3″< 270.

4. Pick this point. Your drawing should look like Figure 3.4.

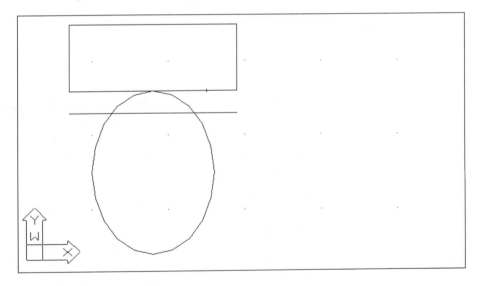

Figure 3.4: *The line copied down*

You will have noticed that the Copy command acts exactly like the Move command you used in *Chapter 2*, except that Copy does not alter the position of the objects you select.

### Trimming an Object

Now you must delete the part of the ellipse that is not needed. You will use the Trim command to trim off parts of the ellipse.

1. First, turn the snap mode off by clicking on the SNAP button on the status bar, or pressing F9. Snap may be a hindrance at this point in your editing session, because it may keep you from picking the points you want. Snap mode forces the cursor to move to points at a given interval, so you will have difficulty selecting a point that doesn't fall exactly at one of those intervals.

2. Click on Trim on the Modify toolbar. You can also type **Trim** ↵ to start the Trim command.

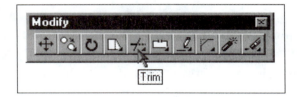

▶ You will see this prompt:

        Select cutting edges: (Projmode=UCS, Edgemode=No extend)

        Select objects:

3. Click on the line you just created—the one that crosses through the ellipse—and press ↵ to finish your selection.

4. At the <Select object to trim>/Project/Edge/Undo: prompt, pick the topmost portion of the ellipse above the line. This trims the ellipse back to the line.

In step 2 of the foregoing exercise, the Trim command produces two messages in the prompt. The first message, Select cutting edges…, tells you that you must first select objects to define *the edge to which you wish to trim*. In step 4, you are again prompted to select objects, this time to select the *objects to trim*. Trim is one of a handful of AutoCAD LT commands that asks you to select two sets of objects: The first set defines a boundary, and the second is the set of objects you want to edit. The two sets of objects are not mutually exclusive. You can, for example, select the cutting edge objects as objects to trim. The next exercise shows how this works.

The Basics

## SELECTING CLOSE OR OVERLAPPING OBJECTS

At times, you will want to select an object that is in close proximity to or lying underneath another object, and AutoCAD LT won't obey your mouse click. It's frustrating when you click on the object you want to select but AutoCAD LT selects the one next to it instead. To help you make your selections in these situations, AutoCAD LT provides Object Selection Cycling, which is new with Release 3. To use it, you hold down the Ctrl key while simultaneously clicking on the object you want to select. If the wrong object is highlighted, press the mouse/pick button again (you needn't hold down the Ctrl key for the second pick), and the next object in close proximity will be highlighted. If several objects are overlapping or close together, just continue to press the mouse/pick button until the correct object is highlighted.

First you will undo the Trim you just did. Then you will use the Trim command again in a slightly different way to finish off the toilet.

1.  Click on the Undo button on the Standard toolbar, or enter **U** ↵ at the command prompt. The top of the ellipse reappears.

2.  Start the Trim command again by clicking on it on the Modify toolbar.

3.  At the `Select cutting edges… Select objects` prompt, click on the ellipse and the line crossing the ellipse (see panel 1 of Figure 3.5).

4.  Press ↵ to finish your selection and move to the next step.

5.  At the `<Select object to trim>/Project/Edge/Undo:` prompt, click on the top portion of the ellipse, as you did in the previous exercise. The ellipse trims back.

**NOTE** The Trim options—Project, Edge, and Undo—are described in the next section.

6.  Click on a point near the left end of the trim line, past the ellipse. The line trims back to the ellipse.

7.  Click on the other end of the line. The right side of the line trims back to meet the ellipse. Your drawing should look like panel 2 of Figure 3.5.

8.  Press ↵ to exit the Trim command.

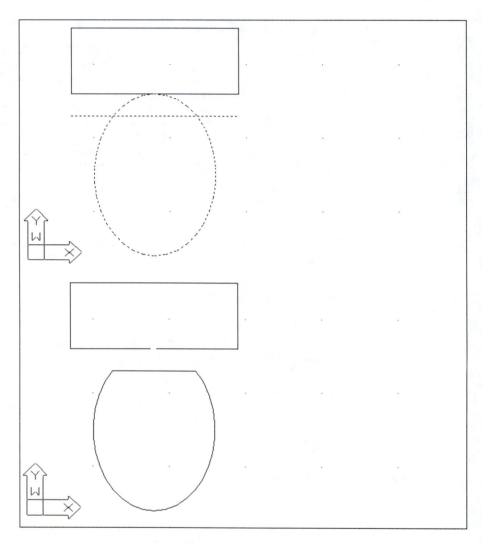

Figure 3.5:   *Trimming the ellipse and the line*

**9.** If there are any remnants of the Ellipse left on your screen, you should Erase them now.

Here you saw how the ellipse and the line are both used as trim objects, as well as the objects to be trimmed.

### The Trim Options

AutoCAD LT Release 3 offers three options for the Trim command: Edge, Project, and Undo. As described in the following paragraphs, these options give you a higher degree of control over how objects are trimmed.

**Edge** [E] allows you to trim an object to an apparent intersection, even if the cutting-edge object does not intersect the object to be trimmed (see the top of Figure 3.6). Edge offers two options, Extend and No Extend. These can also be set using the Edgemode system variable.

**Project** [P] is useful when working on 3D drawings. It controls how AutoCAD LT trims objects that are not coplanar. Project offers three options: None, UCS, and View. None causes Trim to ignore objects that are on different planes, so that only coplanar objects will be trimmed. If you choose UCS, the Trim command trims objects based on a plan view of the current UCS and then disregards whether the objects are coplanar or not (see the middle of Figure 3.6). View is similar to UCS but uses the current view's "line of sight" to determine how non-coplanar objects are trimmed (see the bottom of Figure 3.6).

**Undo** [U] causes the last trimmed object to revert to its original length.

You've just seen one way to construct the toilet. However, there are many ways to construct objects. For example, you could have just trimmed the top of the ellipse, as you did in the first Trim exercise, then used the Grips feature to move the endpoints of the line to meet the endpoints of the ellipse. As you become familiar with AutoCAD LT, you will start to develop your own ways of working, using the tools best suited to your style.

---

**TIP**   To draw the toilet tank, or any other rectangular object, you can use the Rectang command. Choose Draw toolbar ➤ Polygon flyout ➤ Rectang, or type **rectang** ↵. Using the coordinate readouts as you did above, click on the coordinate points that mark the diagonal corners of the rectangle.

---

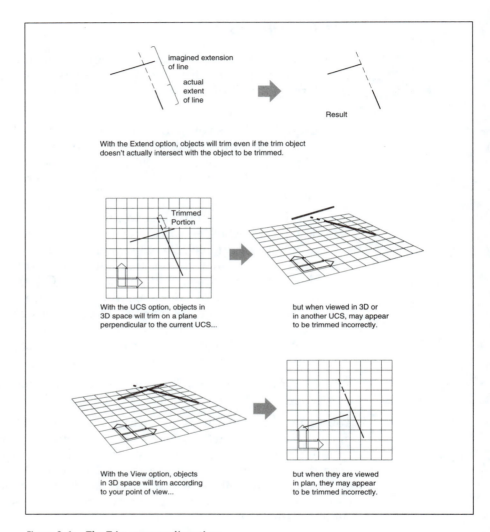

Figure 3.6:    **The Trim command's options**

## Planning and Laying Out a Drawing

For the next object, the bathtub, you will use some new commands to lay out parts of the drawing. This will help you get a feel for the kind of planning you must do to use AutoCAD LT effectively. You'll also get a chance to use some of the keyboard shortcuts built into AutoCAD LT. First, though, go back to the previous view of your drawing, and arrange some more room to work.

1.  Click on the Zoom Previous button on the Zoom flyout on the Standard toolbar, or choose View ➤ Zoom ➤ Previous. Your view will return to the one you had before the last Zoom command (Figure 3.7).

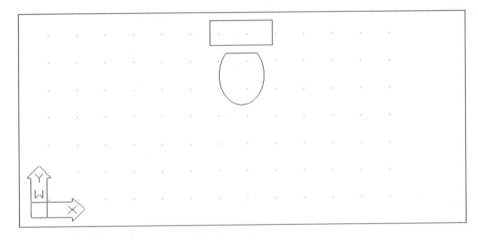

Figure 3.7:   *The finished toilet*

You'll begin the bathtub by using the Line command to draw a rectangle 2′–8″×5′–0″ on the left side of the drawing area. This time, you'll use the Line command's keyboard shortcut.

2.  Turn Snap mode on by pressing F9.

3.  Type **L** ↵, and at the From point prompt, pick the coordinate location 0′–9″, 0′–10″.

4.  Type **@2′8″<0** ↵ for the first side of the tub.

5.  Type **@5′<90** ↵ for the next side.

6.  Type **@2′8″<180** ↵ for the next side.

7. Type **C** ↵ to close the rectangle.

Now you have the outline of the tub. Notice that when you enter feet and inches through the keyboard, you must avoid hyphens or spaces. Thus *2 feet 8 inches* is typed as *2'8"*.

## Making a Preliminary Sketch

The following exercise will show you how planning ahead will make your use of AutoCAD LT more efficient. When drawing a complex object, you will often have to do some layout before you do the actual drawing. This is similar to drawing an accurate pencil sketch using construction lines that you later trace over to produce a finished drawing. The advantage of doing this in AutoCAD LT is that your drawing doesn't lose any accuracy between the sketch and the final product. Also, AutoCAD LT allows you to use the geometry of your sketch to aid you in drawing. While planning your drawing, think about what it is you want to draw, and then decide what drawing elements will help you create that object.

You will use the Offset command to establish reference lines to help you draw the inside of the tub. This is where the Osnap overrides are quite useful. See the sidebar, "The Osnap Options."

### THE OSNAP OPTIONS

Here is a summary of all the available Osnap options. You've already used many of these options in this and the previous chapter. Pay special attention here to those options you haven't yet used in the exercises but may find useful to your style of work. The full name of each option is followed by its keyboard shortcut name in brackets. To use these options, you can enter either the full name or abbreviation at any point prompt. You can also pick these options from the pop-up Cursor menu obtained by Shift-clicking on the right mouse button.

Tip: Sometimes you'll want to have one or more of these Osnap options available as the default selection. You can set Osnaps to be on at all times (called a running Osnap). Use the Running Osnap option on the Object Snap flyout on the Standard toolbar. Or you can click on Options ➤ Running Object Snaps from the pull-down menu. When the dialog box opens, you may turn on as many Osnap options as you require.

**Center [cen]** selects the center of an arc or circle. You must click on the arc or circle itself, not its apparent center.

## THE OSNAP OPTIONS (continued...)

**Endpoint [endp]** selects all the endpoints of lines, polylines, arcs, curves, and 3dface vertices.

**Insertion [ins]** selects the insertion point of text, blocks, xrefs, and overlays.

**Intersection [int]** selects the intersection of objects.

**Midpoint [mid]** selects the midpoint of a line or arc. In the case of a polyline, it selects the midpoint of the polyline segment.

**Nearest [nea]** selects a point on an object nearest the pick point.

**Node [nod]** selects a point object.

**None [non]** temporarily turns off running Osnaps.

**Perpendicular [per]** selects a position on an object that is perpendicular to the last point selected. Normally, this option is not valid for the first point selected in a string of points.

**Quadpoint [qua]** selects the nearest cardinal (north, south, east, or west) point on an arc or circle.

**Quick [qui]**, by sacrificing accuracy, improves the speed at which AutoCAD LT selects geometry. You use Quick in conjunction with one of the other Osnap options. For example, to speed up the selection of an intersection, you would enter QUICK,INT ↵ at a point prompt, and then select the intersection of two objects.

**Tangent [tan]** selects a point on an arc or circle that represents the tangent from the last point selected. Like the Perpendicular option, Tangent is not valid for the first point in a string of points.

Two additional options are available at the top of the Cursor menu, which are not Object Snap modes: From and Tracking. Both of these options allow you select points relative to other points or objects.

**From [fro]** allows you to select a point relative to a picked point. For example, you can select a point that is two units to the left and four units to the right of a circle's center.

**Tracking [tk]** lets you select a series of temporary points, each offset orthogonally from the previous one. Tracking is like a series of sequential From: commands. Using tracking you can determine a new point location from a series of directions and distances.

### Setting Up a Layout

The Offset option on the Duplicate Objects flyout of the Modify tool-bar allows you to make parallel copies of a set of objects, such as the lines forming the outside of your tub. Offset is different from the Copy command; Offset allows only one object to be copied at a time, but it can remember the distance you specify. The Offset option does not work with all types of objects. Only lines, arcs, circles, and 2D polylines can be offset.

In this exercise, you will use standard lines to layout your drawing. Lines are best suited for the layout of the bathtub in this situation. In Chapter 5 you will learn about two other objects, Xlines and Rays, which are specifically designed to help you layout a drawing.

1. From the Modify toolbar, click and drag the Duplicate Objects button to display the flyout, and select Offset.

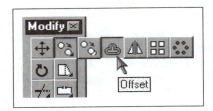

2. At the Offset distance or Through <Through>: prompt, enter **3** ↵. This enters the distance of 3″ as the offset distance.

3. At the Select object to offset: prompt, click on the bottom line of the rectangle you just drew.

4. At the Side to offset? prompt, pick a point inside the rectangle. A copy of the line appears. You don't have to be exact about where you pick the side to offset; AutoCAD LT only wants to know on which side of the line you want to make the offset copy.

5. The prompt Select an object to offset: appears again. Click on another side to offset; then click again on a point inside the rectangle.

**NOTE** Notice that Offset is now the default button on the Modify toolbar, where Duplicate Object was when you first opened AutoCAD LT.

6. Continue to offset the other two sides. then offset these four new lines inside the rectangle toward the center. You will have a drawing that looks like Figure 3.8.

7. When you are done, exit the Offset command by pressing ↵.

### Using the Layout

Now you will begin to draw the inside of the tub, starting with the narrow end. You will use your offset lines as references to construct the arcs that make up the tub.

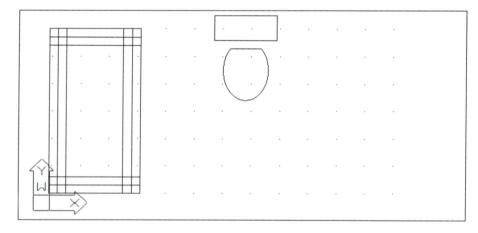

Figure 3.8:  **The completed layout**

 **TIP  Remember that you bring up the Cursor menu by Shift-clicking the right mouse button.**

1. From the Draw toolbar, click and drag the Arc button to open the flyout, and select 3 Points. (See Figure 3.9 for an explanation of 3 Points and the other Arc options.)

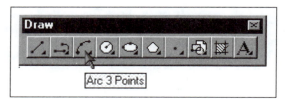

2. Using the Intersection Osnap override on the cursor menu, click on the intersection of the two lines located at coordinate 2′–11″, 5′–4″.

3. Using the Midpoint Osnap override, pick the midpoint of the second horizontal line near the top.

4. Finally, pick the intersection of the two lines at coordinate 1′–3″, 5′–4″. An arc appears. Panel 1 of Figure 3.10 shows the sequence we've just described.

Next you will draw an arc for the left side of the tub.

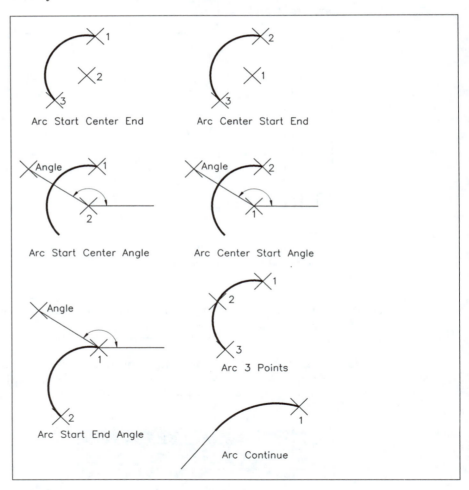

*Figure 3.9:*  **The Arc options and what they mean**

5. From the Draw toolbar, click and drag the Arc button and select Start End Angle from the flyout:

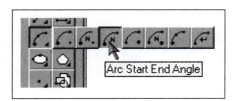

and then type @ ↵. This selects the last point you picked as the start of the next arc.

6. At the End point prompt, use the Intersection Osnap override to pick the intersection of the two lines at coordinate 1′–0″, 1′–4″ in the lower-left corner of the tub. See panel 2 of Figure 3.10 for the location of this point.

---

**TIP**  In step 7, the rubber-band line indicates the direction of the arc. Be sure ortho mode is off, because ortho will force the rubber-band line and the arc in a direction you don't want. Check the status line; if "ORTHO" appears as solid black, not gray, double-click on it, or press F8 to turn ortho off.

---

7. You will see the arc drag as you move the cursor, along with a rubber-band line from the starting point of the arc. At the Included Angle: prompt, type **10** ↵. This will position the arc as shown in panel 2 of Figure 3.10.

Now you will draw the bottom of the tub.

8. Click and drag the Arc button in the Draw toolbar, and select 3 Points from the flyout.

9. Using the Osnap overrides, pick the endpoint of the bottom of the arc just drawn.

10. Using the Osnap overrides, pick the midpoint of the middle horizontal line at the bottom of the tub.

11. Finally, pick the intersection of the two lines at coordinate 3′–2″, 2′–1″ (see panel 3 of Figure 3.10).

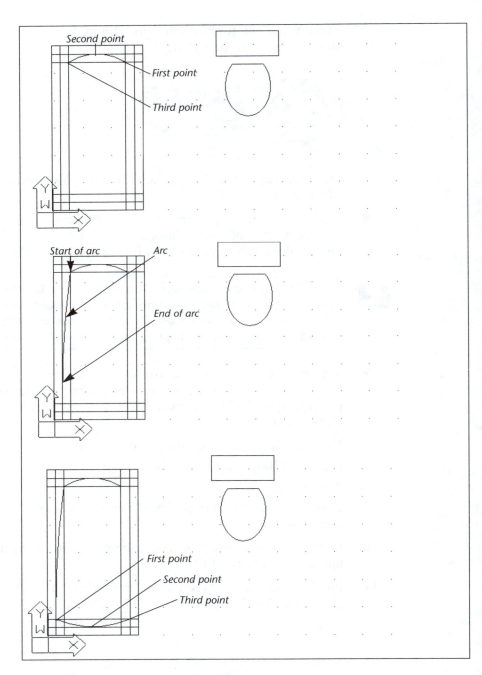

*Figure 3.10:*    **The top, left side, and bottom of the tub**

Now create the right side of the tub by mirroring the left side.

**12.** Click and drag the Offset button on the Modify toolbar, and select Mirror from the Duplicate Objects flyout.

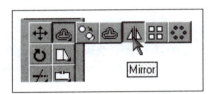

**13.** At the object-selection prompt, pick the long arc on the left side of the tub. The arc highlights. Press ↵ to indicate that you've finished your selection.

**14.** At the `First point of mirror line:` prompt, pick the midpoint of the top horizontal line.

**15.** At the `Second point:` prompt, turn on the ORTHO mode and pick a point directly below the last point selected.

**16.** At the `Delete old objects?<N>` prompt, press ↵ to accept the default, No. A mirror image of the arc you picked appears on the right side of the tub. Your drawing should look like Figure 3.11.

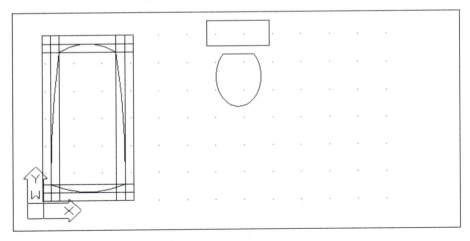

*Figure 3.11:* **The inside of the tub completed**

### Erasing the Layout Lines

For the next step, you will erase the layout lines you created using the Offset command. But this time, try selecting the lines *before* issuing the Erase command.

 **NOTE** If the following exercise doesn't work as described, be sure you have the Noun/Verb selection setting turned on. See *Appendix B* for details.

1. Click on each internal layout line individually.

 If you have problems selecting just the lines, try using a window to select single lines. (Remember, a window selects only objects that are completely within the window.) You might also try the Object Selection Cycling option, as explained in the sidebar, "Selecting Close or Overlapping Objects."

2. Once all the layout lines are highlighted, click on the Erase button on the Modify toolbar. You may also simply enter **E** ↵. This is a keyboard shortcut for entering the Erase command.

 **TIP** When preparing to erase an object that is close to other objects, you may want to select the object first, using the Noun/Verb method. This way you can carefully select objects you want to erase before you actually invoke the Erase command. You can also use Object Selection Cycling, as described in the sidebar, "Selecting Close or Overlapping Objects."

You will notice that parts of the arcs you drew are missing. Don't be alarmed; they are still there. When an object that overlaps another object is changed or moved in any way, the overlapped object seems to disappear. This frequently occurs while you are using the Change, Fillet, Move, Mirror, and Erase options on the Modify toolbar or menu.

To correct this, enter **R** ↵. The screen redraws, and your drawing should look like Figure 3.12.

## Putting on the Finishing Touches

The inside of the tub still has some sharp corners. To round out these corners, you can use the versatile Fillet command (on the Modify toolbar). Fillet allows you to join lines and arcs end to end, and it can add a radius where they join, so there is a smooth transition from arc to arc or line to line. Fillet can join two lines that do not intersect, and it can trim two crossing lines back to their point of intersection.

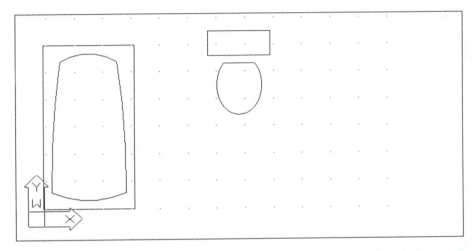

Figure 3.12:  **The redisplayed drawing**

1.  Select Fillet from the Feature flyout on the Modify toolbar. You can also type **Fillet** ⏎ at the command prompt to start the Fillet command.

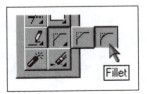

2.  At the Polyline/Radius/Trim/<Select first object>: prompt, enter **R** ⏎.

3.  At the Enter fillet radius <0´0″>: prompt, enter 4 ⏎. This tells AutoCAD LT that you want a 4″ radius for your fillet.

4. Press ↵ to invoke the Fillet command again; this time, pick two adjacent arcs. The fillet arc joins the two larger arcs.

5. Press ↵ again and fillet another corner. Repeat until all four corners are filleted. Your drawing should look like Figure 3.13.

6. Save the Bath file and exit AutoCAD LT.

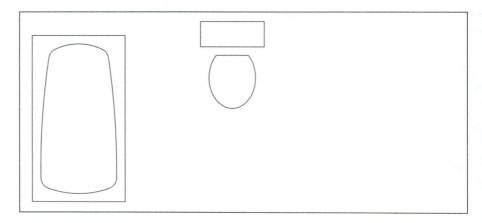

*Figure 3.13:* **A plot of the finished toilet and tub**

## USING AUTOCAD LT'S AUTOMATIC SAVE FEATURE

As you work with AutoCAD LT, you may notice that AutoCAD LT periodically saves your work for you. Your file is saved not as its current file name, but as a file called ACLT.SV$. The default time interval between automatic saves is 120 minutes. You can change this interval by doing the following:

1. Enter **Savetime** ↵ at the command prompt.

2. At the New value for SAVETIME < 120 >: prompt, enter the desired interval, in minutes. Or, to disable the automatic save feature entirely, enter 0 at the prompt.

## *If You Want to Experiment...*

As you draw, you will notice that you are alternately creating objects, then copying and editing them. This is where the difference between hand-drafting and CAD really begins to show.

Try drawing the part shown in Figure 3.14. The figure shows you what to do, step by step. Take particular note of how you are applying the concepts of layout and editing to this drawing.

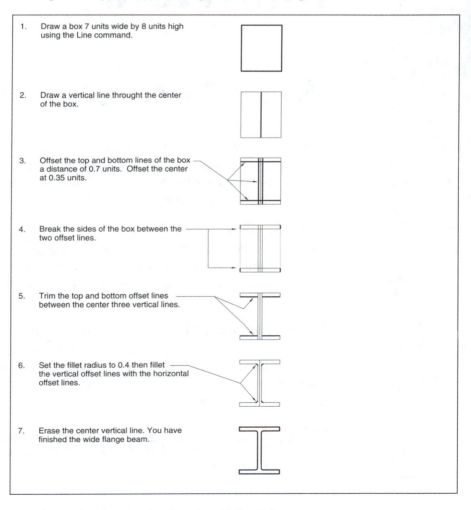

1.  Draw a box 7 units wide by 8 units high using the Line command.

2.  Draw a vertical line throught the center of the box.

3.  Offset the top and bottom lines of the box a distance of 0.7 units.  Offset the center at 0.35 units.

4.  Break the sides of the box between the two offset lines.

5.  Trim the top and bottom offset lines between the center three vertical lines.

6.  Set the fillet radius to 0.4 then fillet the vertical offset lines with the horizontal offset lines.

7.  Erase the center vertical line. You have finished the wide flange beam.

*Figure 3.14:   **Drawing a section view of a wide flange beam***

# Chapter 4

# Organizing Your Work

## *FAST TRACKS*

**D**RAWING the tub and toilet in Chapter 3 may have taken what seemed to you an inordinate amount of time. As you continue to use AutoCAD LT, however, you will learn to draw objects more quickly. You will also need to draw fewer of them, because you can save drawings as symbols to be used like rubber stamps, duplicating drawings instantaneously wherever they are needed. This will save you a lot of time when you're composing drawings.

To make effective use of AutoCAD LT, you should begin a *symbols library* of drawings you use frequently. A mechanical designer might have a library of symbols for fasteners, cams, valves, or any type of parts for his or her application. An electrical engineer might have a symbols library of capacitors, resistors, switches, and the like. And a circuit designer will have yet another unique set of frequently used symbols.

In Chapter 3 you drew two objects, a bathtub and a toilet, that architects often use. In this chapter, you will see how to create symbols from those drawings. You will also learn about layers and how you can use them to organize information.

# Creating a Symbol

To save drawn objects within a drawing as a symbol, you can use the Bmake or Block command. This symbol may then be used as many times as required at any required location, size, or rotation throughout the drawing.

1. Start AutoCAD LT and open the existing Bath file. Use the one you created in *Chapter 3*, or open 04-BATH.DWG on the companion CD. (If you have installed the tutorial drawings per the instructions in *Appendix C*, 04-BATH.DWG will be in the Sample directory.) The Bath drawing will appear just as you left it in the last session.

2. From the Draw toolbar, click and drag Insert Block, and choose Make Block from the flyout. (Or type ↵ at the command prompt to start the **Bmake** command.)

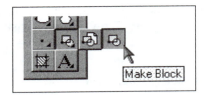

3. The Block Definition dialog box appears, asking you to supply a name for the block you are about to define. Type **Toilet** in the Block Name edit box.

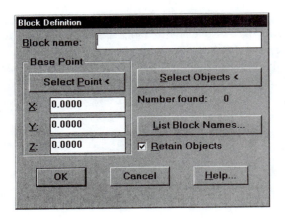

4.  The dialog box asks you to type in an insertion base point, or absolute coordinates, for the block in the X, Y, and Z input boxes. In this exercise, you should click the Select Point < button to exit to the drawing editor and *pick* an insertion base point.

NOTE The *insertion base point* of a block is similar to the base point you used as a handle on an object in *Chapter 2*.

5.  Once you are back in the drawing editor, use the Osnap overrides to pick the midpoint of the back of the toilet.

6.  You should now see the coordinates of the point you picked displayed in the Base Point dialog box. Next click the Select Objects button to obtain the object-selection prompt. Click on a point below and to the left of the toilet. Then window the entire toilet; it will be highlighted.

7.  Press ↵ to confirm your selection. If you are satisfied with your selection, press the OK button; press Cancel if you wish to start over. You now have a block with the name Toilet.

TIP  You can press ↵ to start Bmake again.

8.  Repeat the blocking process for the tub, but this time use the upper-left corner of the tub as the insertion base point and give the block the name **Tub**.

NOTE You may also use the Block command to create a block. Whereas Bmake opens a dialog box, Block prompts you through the steps in the command window.

### Recalling Blocked or Erased Objects

When you turn an object into a block, it is stored within the drawing file, ready to be recalled at any time. The block remains part of the drawing file even when you end the editing session. When you open the file again, the block will be available for your use. A block acts like a single object, even though it can be made up of several objects. Its components can be modified only by unblocking it using the Explode command. You can then edit it and turn it back into a block. We will look at the block-editing process later in this chapter.

If you want to retain the original objects you just turned into a block, make sure that the Retain Objects check box is highlighted in the Block Definition dialog box.

Retain Objects is also useful when you want to create several blocks that are only slightly different. For example, suppose you want several versions of the tub. You can save the tub as a block, say, Tub1, modify the original object to a different shape, and then save this new tub as a different block—Tub2 this time.

## Inserting a Symbol

In the following exercise you'll first draw the interior walls of the bathroom and then insert the tub and toilet. The original tub and toilet still remain on the screen. These are not the blocks you have just created. Erase them before you start the exercise.

**TIP**   If you're in a hurry, enter **Insert** ⏎ at the command prompt, then enter **Tub** ⏎, and then go to step 6.

1. Draw a rectangle 5′×7′. Orient the rectangle so the long sides go from left to right and the lower-left corner is at coordinate 1′-10″, 1′-10″. Your drawing will look like Figure 4.1.

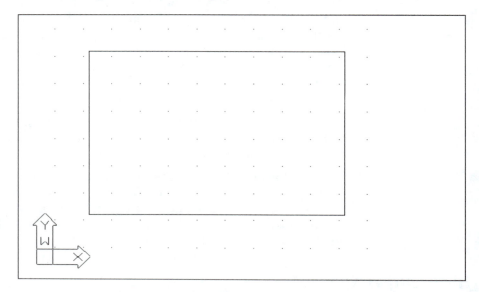

*Figure 4.1:* **The interior walls of the bathroom**

2. From the Draw toolbar, click and drag Block and choose Insert Block from the flyout.

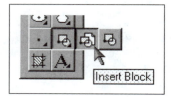

The Insert dialog box appears.

 **NOTE** The Insert dialog box lets you insert a block or an external file into your current drawing. You can also manually enter the insertion point and scale factor for blocks and external files.

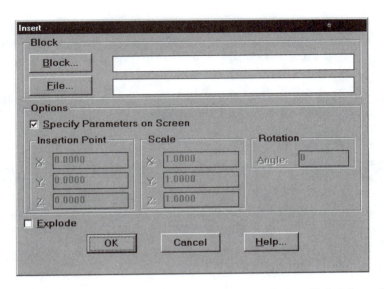

3. Click on the Block button at the top of the dialog box. The Defined Blocks dialog box appears, with a list of the available blocks in the current drawing.

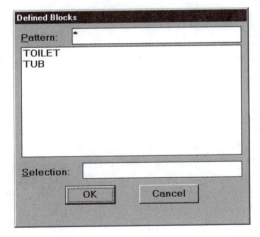

4. Double-click on the block name TUB. The Insert dialog box returns with TUB in the input box next to the Block button.

5. Click on OK, and AutoCAD LT prompts you for more information.

**6.** At the Insertion point: prompt, move the cursor across the screen slowly. Notice that a preview image of the tub now appears and follows the cursor. The upper-left corner you picked for the tub's base point is now on the cursor intersection.

**7.** Pick the upper-left intersection of the room as your insertion point. Notice that as you move your cursor, the preview image of the tub appears distorted.

> **NOTE** The X scale factor **and** Y scale factor **prompts let you stretch the block in one direction or another. You can even specify a negative value to mirror the block. The default value on these prompts is always 1. A scale factor of 1 will insert the block or file at the size it was created.**

**8.** At the X scale factor <1> / Corner / XYZ: prompt, press ↵ to accept the default, 1.

**9.** At the Y scale factor (default=X): prompt, press ↵ to accept (default=X). This means you are accepting that the X scale equals the Y scale, which in turn equals 1.

**10.** At the Rotation angle <0>: prompt, press ↵ to accept the default of 0. You should have a drawing that looks like panel 1 of Figure 4.2.

**11.** Repeat steps 2 through 10, but this time, in steps 3 and 4 click on the Block input box and enter **toilet**. Place the toilet along the top of the rectangle representing the room, just to the right of the tub at coordinate 5′-8″, 6′-10″, as shown in panel 2 of Figure 4.2.

You might have noticed that as you moved the cursor in step 7, the tub became distorted. This demonstrates how the X and Y scale factors can affect the item being inserted. Also, in step 10, you can see the tub rotate as you move the cursor. You can pick a point to fix the block in place, or you can enter a rotation value. The default 0° angle inserts the block or file with the orientation at which it was created.

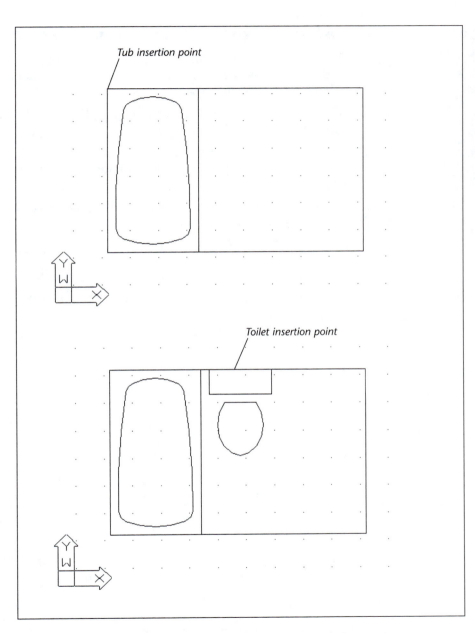

*Figure 4.2:*  **The bathroom, first with the tub and then with the toilet inserted**

## Using an Existing Drawing as a Symbol

Now you need a door into the bathroom. Since you have already drawn a door and saved it as a file, you can bring the door into this drawing file and use it as a block.

1. From the Draw toolbar, click and drag Block and choose Insert Block from the flyout.

2. In the Insert dialog box, click on the File button just below the Block button. The Select Drawing File dialog box appears.

> **TIP**   You can also browse your hard disk by looking at thumbnail views of the drawing files in a directory. See "Locating Files on Your Hard Disk" later in this chapter.

3. Double-click on the Door file name in the file list.

4. As you move the cursor around, you will notice the door appear above and to the right of the cursor intersection, as in Figure 4.3.

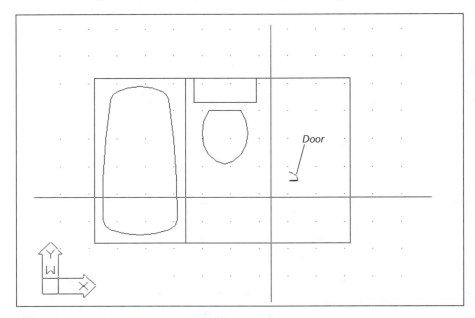

*Figure 4.3:*   **The door drawing being inserted in the Bath file**

5. At this point, the door looks too small for this bathroom. This is because you drew it 3 units long, which translates to 3″. Pick a point near coordinate 7′-2″, 2′-4″, so that the door is placed in the lower-right corner of the room.

6. If you take the default setting for the X scale of the inserted block, the door will remain 3″ long. However, as mentioned earlier, you can specify a smaller or larger size for an inserted object. In this case, you want a 3′ door. To get that from a 3″ door, you need an X scale factor of 12. (You may want to look again at Table 3.4 in *Chapter 3* to see how this is determined.) Enter **12** ↵ now, at the X scale factor prompt.

7. Press ↵ twice to accept the default y = x and the rotation angle of 0°.

Now the command prompt appears, but nothing seems to happen to the drawing. This is because, when you enlarged the door, you also enlarged the distance between the base point and the object. This brings up another issue to be aware of when you're considering drawings as symbols. All drawings have base points. The default base point is the absolute coordinate 0,0, otherwise known as the *origin,* which is located in the lower-left corner of any new drawing. When you drew the door in Chapter 2, you didn't specify the base point. So, when you try to bring the door into this drawing, AutoCAD LT uses the origin of the door drawing as its base point (see Figure 4.4).

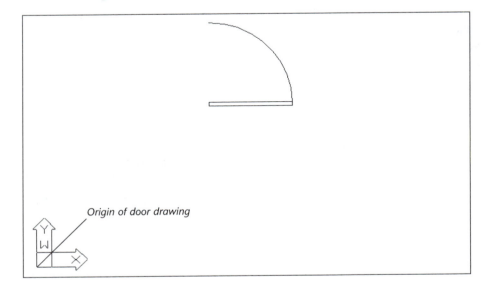

*Figure 4.4:* **The origin of the door drawing**

Since the door appears outside the bathroom, you must first click the Zoom All button on the Standard toolbar to display all of the drawing. Then use the Move command on the Modify toolbar to move the door to the right side wall of the bathroom. Let's do this now.

1. Click on Zoom All on the Standard toolbar. The view of the room shrinks away and the door is revealed. Notice that it is now the proper size for your drawing (see Figure 4.5).

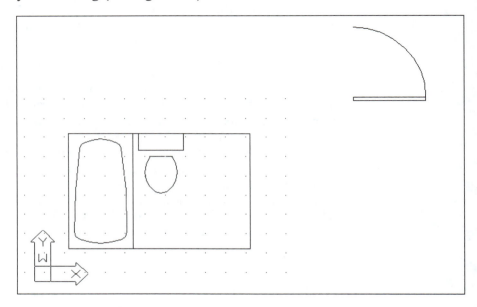

Figure 4.5:   *The enlarged door*

2. Choose Move from the Modify toolbar.

3. To pick the door you just inserted, at the Select objects: prompt, click on a point anywhere on the door and press ↵. Notice that now the entire door highlights. This is because a block is treated like a single object, even though it may be made up of several lines, arcs, etc.

4. At the Base point: prompt, pick the lower-left corner of the door.

5. At the Second point: prompt, use the Nearest Osnap override, and position the door so your drawing looks like Figure 4.6.

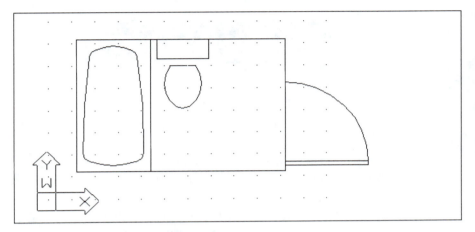

*Figure 4.6:*   **The door on the right side wall of the bathroom**

Because the door is an object you will use often, it should be a common size, so you don't have to specify an odd value every time you insert it. It would also be helpful if the door's insertion base point were in a more convenient location. Next, you will modify the Door block to better suit your needs.

## Unblocking and Modifying a Block

To modify a block, you break it down into its components, edit them, and then turn them back into a block. This is called *redefining* a block. If you redefine a block that has been inserted in a drawing, each occurrence of that block will change to reflect the new block definition. You can use this block redefinition feature to make rapid changes to a design.

To separate a block into its components, you use the Explode command. As of Release 3 of AutoCAD LT, you can explode blocks that are inserted with differing X, Y, and Z Scale values. You can also explode mirrored blocks.

1. Choose Explode from the Modify toolbar. You can also type **Explode** ↵ to start the Explode command.

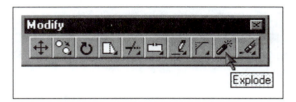

2. Click on the door and press ↵ to confirm your selection.

 **TIP** You can simultaneously insert and explode a block by clicking on the Explode check box in the lower-left corner of the Insert dialog box.

Now you can edit the individual objects that make up the door, if you so desire. In this case, you only want to change the door's insertion point, because you have already made it a more convenient size. So now you'll turn the door back into a block, this time using the door's lower-left corner for its insertion base point.

3. On the Draw toolbar, click on the Make Block button on the Block fly-out, or type **Bmake** ↵.

4. In the Block Definition dialog box, enter **Door** in the Block Name input box.

5. Click on the Select Objects button. You will exit the dialog box temporarily, and go back to the drawing editor.

6. Select the exploded door. You will return to the Make Block dialog box.

7. Click on the Select Point < button. You will exit again to the drawing editor. Use the Endpoint Snap to select the lower-left corner of the door as the Insertion base point.

8. When you return to the dialog box this time, click on OK. The following warning appears:

        A block with this name already exists in the drawing.
        Do you want to redefine it? <N>

AutoCAD LT provides this prompt so you won't inadvertently change a block you want to leave alone.

9. Click on the Redefine button.

10. Now insert the door again, using the Block button in the Insert dialog box. This time, however, use the Nearest Osnap override and pick a point on the right side wall of the bathroom, near coordinate 9′-4″, 2′-1″.

11. After you complete this, use the Grips feature to mirror the door, using the wall as the mirror axis so that the door is inside the room. Your drawing will look like Figure 4.7.

> **TIP** To mirror an object using Grips, first be sure Grips is on. Select the objects to mirror, click on a grip, and then press the right mouse button until you see the ** MIRROR ** message in the prompt.

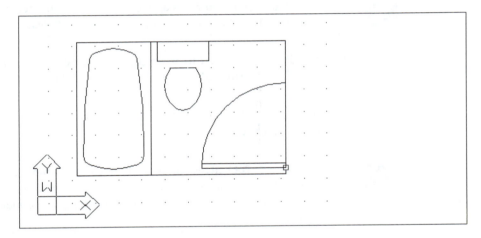

*Figure 4.7:* **The bathroom floor plan thus far**

## Saving a Block as a Drawing File

You've seen that, with very little effort, you can create a symbol that can be placed anywhere in a file. Suppose you want to use this symbol in other files. When you create a block using the Block command, the block exists within the current file only until you save it as a drawing file on disk. Likewise, if an existing drawing has been brought in and modified, such as the door, the drawing file on disk associated with that door is not automatically updated. To reflect the changes you made to the door block, you must update the door file. You do this using the Export option on the File menu. Let's see how this works.

In the next exercise, you'll get a chance to see how this works, and to try some new options in the File dialog box. Start by turning the tub and toilet blocks into individual files on disk.

1. Click on File ➤ Export. The Export Data dialog box opens. This dialog box is a simple file dialog box.

2. Open the List Files of Type drop-down list and select Drawing (\*.DWG).

3. Double-click on the File Name input box and enter **Tub**. The dialog box closes.

> **TIP** If you prefer, you can skip step 2, and then in step 3 enter the full file-name, including the .DWG extension, as in Tub.DWG.

4. At the Block name prompt, enter the name of the block you wish to save on disk as the tub file—in this case, also Tub. The tub block is now saved as a file.

5. Repeat steps 1 through 3 for the toilet block. Give the file the same name as the block.

> **NOTE** AutoCAD LT gives you the option to save a block's file under the same name as the original block or with a different name. Usually you will want to use the same name, which you can do by entering an equals sign (=) after the prompt.

### Replacing Existing Files with Blocks

The Wblock command does the same thing as File ➤ Export, but output is limited to AutoCAD LT .DWG files. (Experienced AutoCAD LT users will want to note that Wblock is now incorporated into the File ➤ Export command.) Let's try using the Wblock command this time, to save the door block you modified.

1. Issue the Wblock command by typing **Wblock** ↵.

2.  At the Create Drawing File dialog box, enter the file name **Door**. A warning message appears:

3.  In this case, you want to update the door you drew in *Chapter 2*, so click on Yes.

4.  At the command line prompt Block Name:, type **Door** or **=** (equals sign) followed by ↵. The new door will replace the old one.

5.  Save the current drawing.

    In this exercise, you typed the Wblock command at the command prompt instead of using File ➤ Export. The results are the same, regardless of which method you use.

## Other Uses for Blocks

So far, you have used the Block commands to create symbols, and the Export and Wblock commands to save those symbols to disk. As you can see, symbols can be created and saved at any time while you are drawing. You have made the tub and toilet symbols into drawing files that you can see when you check the contents of your current directory.

However, creating symbols is not the only use for Insert Block, Make Block, Export, and Wblock. You can use them in any situation that requires grouping objects. Export and Wblock also allow you to save a part of a drawing to disk. You will see instances of these other uses of Block, Export, and Wblock throughout *Chapters 5–8* and in *Chapter 12*.

Block, Export, and Wblock are extremely versatile and, if used judiciously, can boost your productivity and simplify your work. If you are not careful, however, you can also get carried away and create more blocks than you can keep track of. Planning your drawings helps you determine which elements will work best as blocks, and to recognize situations where other methods of organization will be more suitable.

## AN ALTERNATIVE TO BLOCKS

Another way to create symbols is by creating shapes. Shapes are special objects made up of lines, arcs, and circles. They can regenerate faster than blocks, and they take up less file space. Unfortunately, shapes are considerably more difficult to create and less flexible to use than blocks. Shapes can also be embedded into linetype definitions to create complex linetypes.

You create shapes by using a coding system developed by Autodesk. The codes define the sizes and orientations of lines, arcs, and circles. You first sketch your shape, then convert it into the code, and then copy that code into an ASCII shape file. However, you cannot copy, or *compile*, a shape file within AutoCAD LT. You must compile it using AutoCAD Release 3. You may then use the shape file in AutoCAD LT.

One way to get around the difficulty of creating shapes is to purchase one of the third-party software products available for this purpose. These are add-on programs capable of converting AutoCAD LT drawings into shape libraries. They usually require that you draw your shape within a predefined area in a special drawing file supplied with the software. If you intend to do drawings that will be composed mostly of very simple symbols, you may want to look into this alternative. Since AutoCAD LT fonts are created in the same way shapes are, these programs also make it possible to create your own fonts.

Another way of using symbols is to use AutoCAD LT's external reference capabilities. External referenced files are those inserted into a drawing in a way similar to blocks—the difference is that external referenced files do not actually become part of the drawing's database. Instead, they are loaded along with the current file at start-up time. It is as if AutoCAD LT opens several drawings at once: the main file you specify when you start AutoCAD LT, and any external referenced files associated with the main file.

By keeping external referenced files independent from the current file, you make sure that any changes made to the external referenced file will automatically appear in the current file. You don't have to update the external referenced file as you must for blocks. For example, if you used the Attach option on the External Reference toolbar (to be discussed in *Chapter 12*) to insert the Tub drawing, and you later made changes to the tub, the next time you opened the Bath file, you would see the new version of the tub.

External referenced files are especially useful in workgroup environments, where several people are working on the same project. One person might be updating several files that have been inserted into a variety of other files. Before external referencing was available, everyone in the workgroup would have had to be notified of the changes and update all the affected blocks in all the drawings that contained them. With external references, the updating is automatic. There are many other features unique to these files, discussed in more detail in *Chapters 6* and *12*.

## *Organizing Information with Layers*

Another AutoCAD LT tool for organization is the *layer*. Layers are like overlays on which you keep various types of information (see Figure 4.8). In a floor plan of a building, for example, you want to keep the walls, ceiling, plumbing fixtures, wiring, and furniture separate, so you can display or plot them individually or combine them in different ways. It's also a good idea to keep notes and reference symbols about each element of the drawing, as well as the drawing's dimensions, on their own layers. As your drawing becomes more complex, the various layers can be turned on and off to allow easier display and modification.

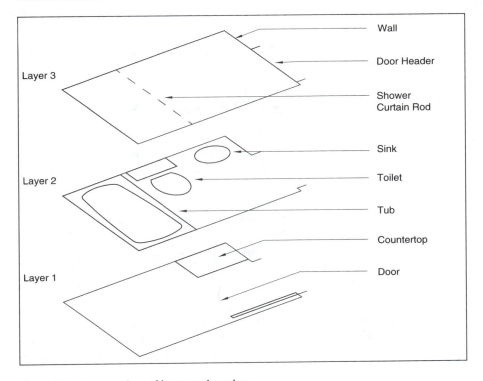

*Figure 4.8:* **A comparison of layers and overlays**

For example, one of your consultants may need a plot of just the dimensions and walls, without all the other information; another consultant may need only a furniture layout. Using manual drafting, you would have to redraw your plan for each consultant. With AutoCAD LT, you can turn off the layers you don't need and plot a drawing containing only the required information. A carefully planned layering scheme helps you produce a document that combines the different types of information needed in each case.

Using layers also enables you to modify your drawings more easily. For example, suppose you have an architectural drawing with separate layers for the walls, the ceiling plan, and the floor plan. If any change occurs in the wall locations, you can turn on the ceiling plan layer to see where the new wall locations will affect the ceiling, and then make the proper adjustments.

AutoCAD LT allows an unlimited number of layers, and you can name each layer anything you want.

### Creating and Assigning Layers

To continue with your bathroom, you will create some new layers.

1. Open the Bath file. To display the Layer Control dialog box, click on the Layers button on the Object Properties toolbar, or select Format ► Layers.

**NOTE** The Layer Control dialog box shows you at a glance the status of your layers. Right now, you have only one layer, but as your work expands, so will the number of layers. You will then find this dialog box indispensable.

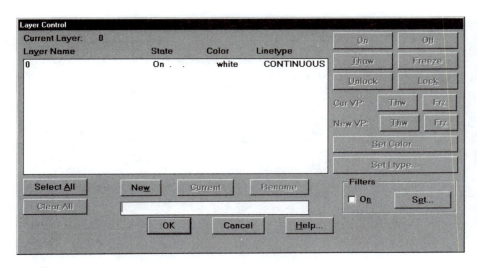

2. Type **Wall**; as you type, your entry appears in the input box at the bottom of the dialog box (just above the OK button).

3. When you are done typing, click on the New button just above the input box. The new layer appears in the large list box in the center of the dialog box.

4. Click on the Wall layer now shown in the list. The item is highlighted, and some of the buttons to the right become available (no longer grayed out).

5. Click on the Set Color button to display the Select Color dialog box, showing you the selection of colors available.

**NOTE** Though it isn't readily apparent, all the layer colors are designated by numbers. The first seven colors can be referred to either by name or color number and in this dialog box the color name is used. When you select a color after the seventh color, the color's number rather than its name appears in the Color input box at the bottom of the dialog box.

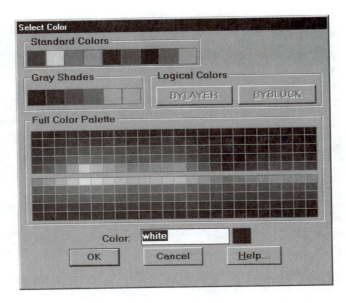

6. In the top row of Standard Colors, click on the green square and then on OK.

7. When the Layer Control dialog box returns, click on OK to close it.

### Controlling Layers through the Layer Command

You have seen how the Layer Control dialog box makes it easy to view and edit layer information, and how layer colors can be easily selected from an on-screen toolbar. But layers can also be controlled through the command window.

1. First press Esc to make sure any current command is canceled.

2. At the command prompt, enter **Layer** ↵. (You can type **La** ↵ for short.) The following prompt appears:

   ```
   ?/Make/Set/New/ON/OFF/Color/Ltype/Freeze/Thaw/Lock/
   Unlock:
   ```

   You'll learn about many of the options in this prompt as you work through this chapter.

3. Enter **N** ↵ to select the New option.

4.  At the New layer name(s) prompt, enter **Wall2** ↵. The ?/Make/Set/
    New... prompt appears again.

5.  Enter **C** ↵.

6.  At the Color prompt, enter **Yellow** ↵. Or you can enter **2** ↵, the
    numeric equivalent to the color yellow in AutoCAD LT.

7.  At the Layer Names for color 2 (yellow) <0>: prompt, enter **Wall2**
    ↵. The ?/Make/Set/New... prompt appears again.

8.  Press ↵ to exit the Layer command.

    Each method of controlling layers has its own advantages: The Layer
    Control dialog box offers more information about your layers at a
    glance. On the other hand, the Layer command offers a quick way to
    control and create layers if you're in a hurry. Also, if you intend to write
    custom macros, you will want to know how to use the Layer command
    as opposed to the dialog box, because dialog boxes cannot be con-
    trolled through scripts.

### Assigning Layers to Objects

When you create an object, that object is assigned to the current layer.
Until now, only one layer has existed, layer 0—which contains all the
objects you've drawn so far. Now that you've created some new layers,
you can reassign objects to them using the Properties button on the
Object Properties toolbar.

1.  Choose Properties from the Object Properties toolbar.

2.  At the Select objects prompt, click on the four lines representing the
    bathroom walls. If you have problems singling out the wall to the left,
    use a window to select the wall line.

3.  Press ↵ to confirm your selection. The Change Properties dialog box appears.

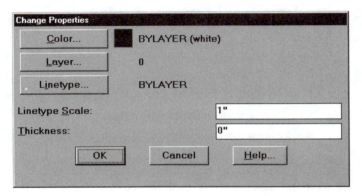

This dialog box allows you to change the layer assignment, color, linetype, and thickness of an object. You'll learn about linetypes and object thickness in later chapters.

4.  Click on the Layer button. Next you see the Select Layer dialog box, listing all the existing layers, including the ones you just created.

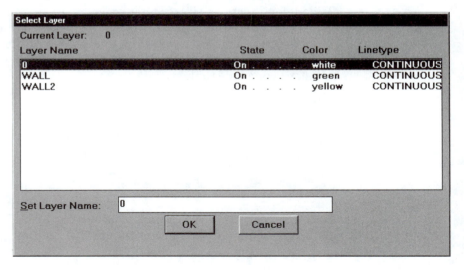

5. Double-click on the Wall layer. You return to the Change Properties dialog box.

6. Click on OK to close the dialog box.

The bathroom walls are now on the new layer, Wall, and the walls are changed to green. Layers are more easily distinguished from one another when colors are used to set them apart.

Next, you will practice the commands you learned in this section by creating some new layers and changing the layer assignments of the rest of the objects in your bathroom.

1. Bring up the Layer Control dialog box (use Format ➤ Layers, or click on the Layers button in the Object Properties toolbar). Create a new layer called **Fixture** and give it the color blue.

2. Use the Change Properties dialog box (click the Properties button on the Object Properties toolbar) to change the tub and toilet to the Fixture layer.

NOTE After a block is inserted you can change the color and linetype of the block using layer control. But only the objects within the block that are on layer 0 and assigned logical color *bylayer* and logical linetype *bylayer* may be changed. See the sidebar, "Controlling Colors and Linetypes of Blocked Objects."

3. Now create a new layer for the door, name the layer **Door,** and make it red.

4. Change the door to the Door layer.

5. Create three more layers for the ceiling, door jambs, and floor. Assign magenta to Ceiling, green to Jamb, and cyan to Floor.

NOTE The Properties button on the Object Properties toolbar issues one of two commands, based on how many objects you selected. Ddchprop is the command that opens the Change Properties dialog box; Ddmodify opens the Modify Properties dialog box.

In step 4, you used a dialog box that offered several options for modifying the block. When you click the Properties button on the Object Properties toolbar, the dialog box displayed will depend on whether you have selected one object or several. With only one object selected, AutoCAD LT presents all of the options that apply to that object. With several objects selected, you'll see a more limited set of options, because AutoCAD LT can change only the properties that are common to all the objects selected.

## CONTROLLING COLORS AND LINETYPES OF BLOCKED OBJECTS

Layer 0 has special importance to blocks. When objects assigned to layer 0 are used as parts of a block, those objects can take on the characteristics of the layer on which the block is inserted. As long as these objects are assigned logical color BYLAYER and logical linetype BYLAYER the contents of the block will display the color and linetype assigned to the insertion layer of the block. On the other hand, if those objects are on a layer other than 0, they will maintain their original layer characteristics even if you insert or change that block to another layer. For example, suppose the tub is drawn on the Door layer, instead of on layer 0. If you turn the tub into a block and insert it on the Fixture layer, the tub will display the color assigned to the Door layer, although the Tub block is assigned to the Fixture layer.

The source objects for a block can also be defined using BYBLOCK as the color and linetype. This allows each block insertion to have individual colors and linetype properties assigned directly to the block. The same block definition can be assigned any color and linetype directly, even BYLAYER.

## Working on Layers

So far you have created layers and then assigned objects to those layers. However, the current layer is still 0, and every new object you draw will be on layer 0. Here's how to change the current layer.

**NOTE** You can also use the Layer command to reset the current layer. To do this here, enter **Layer** at the command prompt, and at the ?/Make... prompt, enter **S** for set. At the New current layer prompt, enter **Jamb** and then press ↵ twice to exit the Layer command.

1. Click on the arrow button next to the layer graphic on the Object Properties toolbar. A drop-down list opens, showing you all the layers available in the drawing.

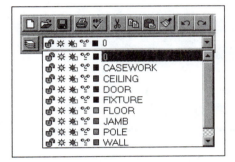

Notice the icons that appear next to the layer names; these control the status of the layer. You'll learn how to work with these icons later in this chapter. Also notice the box directly to the left of each layer name. This shows you the color of the layer.

2. Click on the Jamb layer name. The drop-down list closes, and "Jamb" appears in the toolbar's layer name box. Jamb is now the current layer.

3. Zoom in to the door, and draw a 5″ line; start at the lower-right corner of the door and draw toward the right.

4. Draw a similar line from the top-right end of the arc. Your drawing should look like Figure 4.9.

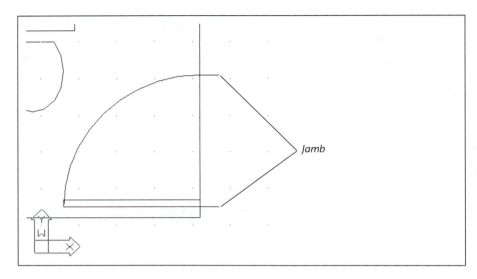

*Figure 4.9:*    **Door at wall with door jamb added**

Because you assigned the color green to the Jamb layer, the two lines you just drew to represent the door jambs are green. This gives you immediate feedback about what layer you are on as you draw.

Now you will use the part of the wall between the jambs as a line representing the door header (the part of the wall above the door). To do this, you will have to cut the line into three line segments, and then change the layer assignment of the segment between the jambs.

> **NOTE** You can also start the Break command by typing **Break** ↵ at the command prompt. Once you select an object, you enter **F** ↵ for the First point option, allowing you to select two points defining the location of the break. You then pick the break point and type **@** ↵.

1. From the Modify toolbar, click and drag the Break flyout and select Break 1 Point Select.

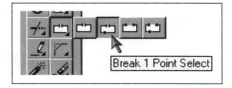

2. At the `Select objects` prompt, click on the wall between the two jambs.

3. At the `Enter first point` prompt, use the Intersection Osnap override to pick the intersection of the door's arc where it touches the wall.

 **NOTE** In step 4, notice that you don't have to reopen the flyout to get the 1 Point Select option; it is now the default option on the Modify Toolbar.

4. Click on Break 1 Point Select on the Break flyout on the Modify toolbar, and then repeat steps 2 and 3, this time using the jamb near the door hinge location to locate the break point.

5. Now change the line between the two jambs to the Ceiling layer using the Change button on the Object Properties toolbar. When you complete this change, the line turns to magenta, telling you it is now on the Ceiling layer.

6. Click on Zoom Previous on the Zoom flyout on the Standard toolbar to return to the previous view.

All of the buttons on the Break flyout issue the Break command. When you choose any of these options, you'll see `Break` appear at the command prompt, followed by another prompt. This command allows you to cut an object at a single point. You can also use Break to create a gap in an object.

Now you'll finish the bathroom by adding a sink to a layer named Casework.

1. Using the Layer Control dialog box, create a layer called **Casework**.

2. When the Casework layer name appears in the layer list, highlight it and click on the Current check box.

3. Click on the Set Color button. Using the Set Color dialog box, choose blue and click OK. When you exit the Layer Control dialog box, the status line indicates that the current layer is Casework.

Now you'll add the sink. Notice that as you draw, the objects will appear in blue, the color of the Casework layer.

4. Click on the Zoom All button on the Zoom flyout.

5. Click on Rectangle on the Polygon flyout of the Draw toolbar, and draw a rectangle 28″×18″ representing a sink countertop. Orient the countertop so that it fits into the upper-right corner of the room, as shown in Figure 4.10. Use coordinate 7′-0″, 5′-4″ for the lower-left corner of the countertop.

6. Use the Ellipse tool from the Draw toolbar and draw an ellipse 17″×14″ in the center of the countertop.

7. Use the Change Properties dialog box to change the ellipse to the Fixture layer. Your drawing will look like Figure 4.10.

## Controlling Layer Visibility

We mentioned earlier that at times you'll want to be selective about what layers you are working with on a drawing. In this bathroom, there is a door header that would normally appear only in a reflected ceiling plan. To turn off a layer so that it becomes invisible, use the Off button in the Layer Control dialog box.

1. Open the Layer Control dialog box.

2. Click on the Ceiling layer in the layer list.

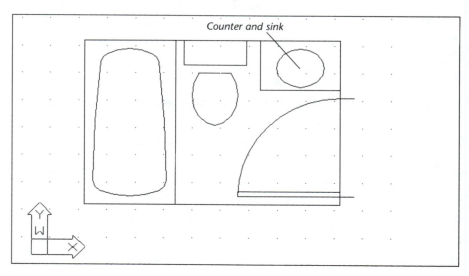

Figure 4.10: *Bathroom with sink and countertop added*

**3.** Click on the Off button to the right of the list.

**4.** Click on the OK button to exit the dialog box. When you return to the drawing, the header disappears because you have made it invisible by turning off its layer (see Figure 4.11).

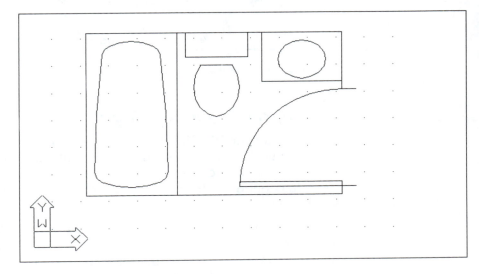

*Figure 4.11:*   **Bathroom with Ceiling layer turned off**

You can also control layer visibility using the layer drop-down list on the Object Properties toolbar.

**1.** On the Object Properties toolbar, click on the arrow button to open the layer name drop-down list.

**2.** Find the Ceiling layer, and notice the icon that looks like a face with its eyes closed. This tells you that the layer is off and not visible.

**3.** Click on the face icon; the eyes open.

**4.** Now click on the drawing area to close the layers list, and the door header reappears.

Figure 4.12 explains the role of the other icons in the layers drop-down list.

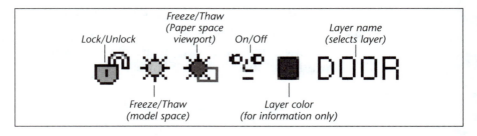

*Figure 4.12:*   **The drop-down layer list icons**

## Finding the Layers You Want

With only a handful of layers, it's fairly easy to find the layer you want to turn off. This becomes much more difficult, however, when the number of layers exceeds 20 or 30. The Layer Control dialog box offers the Filters option to help you search through your layer names to find specific ones.

To use filters, you click on the Set button of the Filters group at the lower-right of the Layer Control dialog box. In the Set Layer Filters dialog box, you can specify the layers you want to show in the layer list by indicating the layers' characteristics.

Now suppose you have several layers whose names begin with C-, such as C-lights, C-header, and C-pattern, and you want to display only those layers in the Layer Control dialog box. To do this, you enter **C★** in the Layer Names input box and then click on OK. Now only the layers whose names begin with C- will appear in the list of layers. You can then easily turn all these layers off, and change their color assignment or other settings quickly, without involving other layers you don't want to touch.

> **TIP** The asterisk in C-* is called a *wildcard character.* Wildcards can be used to help locate names in AutoCAD LT.

The other two input boxes, Colors and Ltypes, let you control what layers appear in the list by virtue of their color or linetype assignments. In the five drop-down lists at the top of the dialog box, you can designate the layers to include in the layer list by virtue of the status: On/Off, Freeze/Thawed, Locked/Unlocked, and so forth. See the sidebar, "Other Layer Options."

As the number of layers in a drawing grows, you will find layer filters to be an indispensable tool. Also, keep in mind the wildcard feature as you name layers: You can use it to group layers and later quickly select those groups to turn on and off.

> **NOTE** To delete all the objects on a layer, you can set the current layer to the one you want to edit, and then freeze or lock all the others. Click on Erase in the Modify toolbar. Then click and drag Select Window in the Standard toolbar and choose Select All from the flyout.

Now try changing the layer settings again, turning off all the layers except Wall and Ceiling and leaving just a simple rectangle. In the exercise, you'll get a chance to experiment with the On/Off options of the Layer Control dialog box.

1. Click on the Layers button in the Object Properties toolbar, or on Format ➤ Layers in the pull-down menus.

2. Click on the Select All button in the bottom-left corner of the dialog box to highlight the entire list of layers.

3. Click on the Wall and Ceiling layers to deselect them and thus exempt them from your next action.

4. Click on the Off button in the upper-right corner of the dialog box. The list changes to show that the selected layers have been turned off.

5. Click on the OK button. A message appears, warning you that the current layer will be turned off. Click on OK. The drawing now appears with only the Wall and Ceiling layers displayed (see Figure 4.13).

6. Open the Layer Control dialog box again, click on the Select All button, and then click on the On button to turn on all the layers at once.

7. Click on OK to return to the drawing.

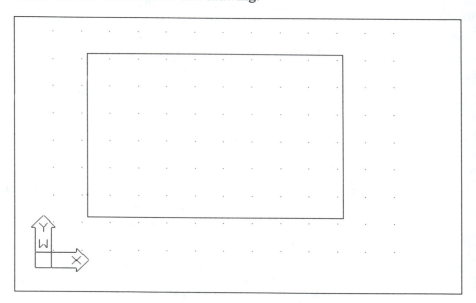

Figure 4.13:　**Bathroom with all layers except Wall and Ceiling turned off**

## OTHER LAYER OPTIONS

You may have noticed the Freeze and Thaw buttons in the Layer Control dialog box. These options are similar to the On and Off buttons—however, Freeze not only makes layers invisible, it also tells AutoCAD LT to ignore the contents of those layers when you use the All response to the Select object: prompt. Freezing layers can also save time when you issue a command that regenerates a complex drawing. This is because AutoCAD LT ignores objects on frozen layers during a regen. You will get firsthand experience with Freeze and Thaw in *Chapter 6*.

Another pair of Layer Control options, Lock and Unlock, offer a function similar to Freeze and Thaw. If you lock a layer, you will be able to view and snap to objects on that layer, but you won't be able to edit those objects. This feature is useful when you are working on a crowded drawing and you don't want to accidentally edit portions of it. You can lock all the layers except those you intend to edit, and then proceed to work without fear of making accidental changes.

### *Assigning Linetypes to Layers*

You will often want to use different linetypes to show hidden lines, center lines, fence lines, or other noncontinuous lines. You can set a layer to have not only a color assignment but also a linetype assignment. AutoCAD LT comes with several linetypes, as shown in Figure 4.14. You can also create your own linetypes (see *Chapter 17*).

AutoCAD LT stores linetype descriptions in an external file named ACLT.LIN. You can edit this file in a word processor to create new linetypes or to modify existing ones. You will see how this is done in *Chapter 17*.

To see how linetypes work, add a dash-dot line in the bathroom plan to indicate a shower-curtain rod.

**TIP**  If you are in a hurry, you can simultaneously load a linetype and assign it to a layer by using the Layer command. In this exercise, you would enter **Layer** ↵ at the command prompt, then enter **L** ↵, **dashdot** ↵, **pole** ↵, and then ↵ to exit the Layer command.

1. Click on the Layers button on the Object Properties toolbar or choose Format ➤ Layers.

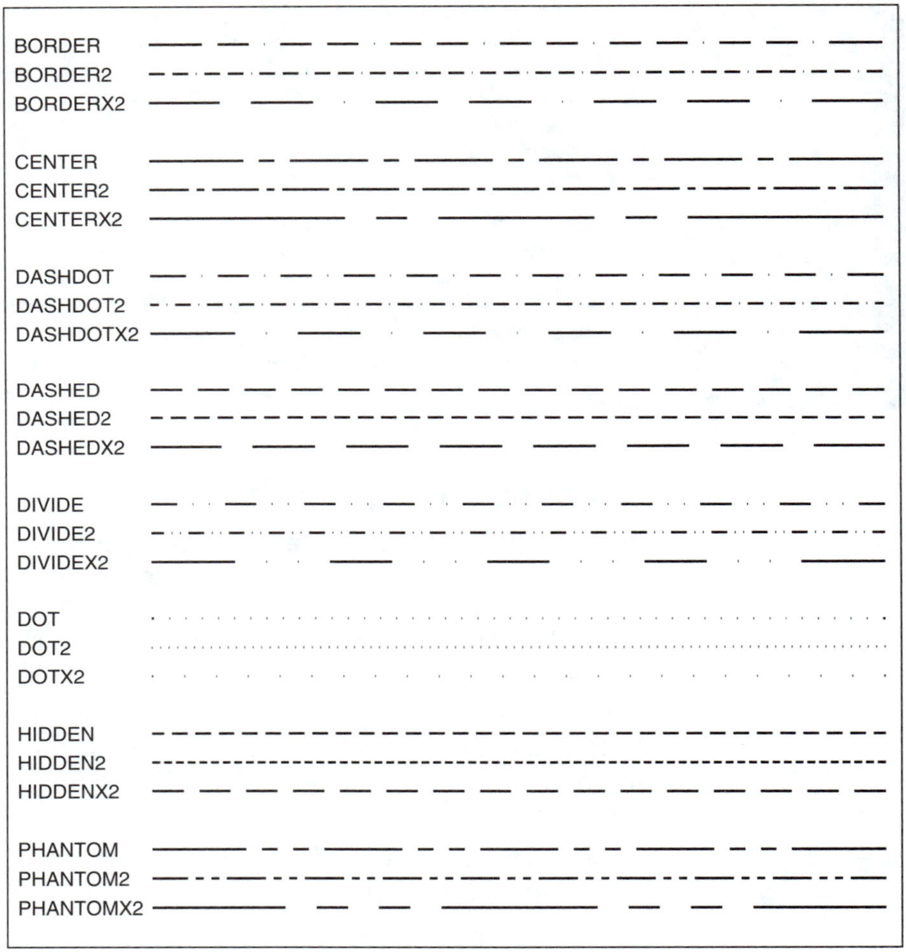

| | |
|---|---|
| BORDER | |
| BORDER2 | |
| BORDERX2 | |
| | |
| CENTER | |
| CENTER2 | |
| CENTERX2 | |
| | |
| DASHDOT | |
| DASHDOT2 | |
| DASHDOTX2 | |
| | |
| DASHED | |
| DASHED2 | |
| DASHEDX2 | |
| | |
| DIVIDE | |
| DIVIDE2 | |
| DIVIDEX2 | |
| | |
| DOT | |
| DOT2 | |
| DOTX2 | |
| | |
| HIDDEN | |
| HIDDEN2 | |
| HIDDENX2 | |
| | |
| PHANTOM | |
| PHANTOM2 | |
| PHANTOMX2 | |

*Figure 4.14:*    **Standard AutoCAD LT linetypes**

2. Enter **Pole** in the input box and click on New. Click on the Pole layer to highlight it in the layer list.

**3.** Click on the Set Ltype button to display the Select Linetype dialog box, showing the linetypes that have already been loaded into the drawing.

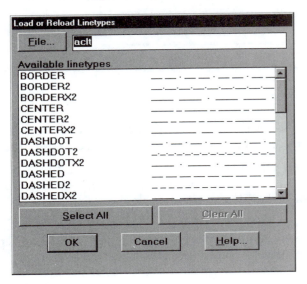

**4.** Click on the Load button at the bottom of the dialog box. The Load or Reload Linetype dialog box appears:

5. In the Available Linetypes list, click to highlight the sample view of the DASHDOT linetype, and then click on OK.

6. Notice that the DASHDOT linetype is now added to the linetypes available in the Select Linetype dialog box. Click to highlight this linetype, and then click on OK to exit the Select Linetype dialog box.

7. In the Layer Control dialog box, make sure the Pole layer is the current default layer by clicking on the Current button. DASHDOT is now listed as the linetype for the Pole layer.

8. Click on OK to exit the dialog box.

9. Draw a line across the opening of the tub area, from coordinate 4′-4″, 1′-10″ to coordinate 4′-4″, 6′-10″.

Although you have designated that this line is to be a DASHDOT line, it appears to be solid. Zoom in to a small part of the line, and you'll see that the line is indeed as you specified.

Since you are working at a scale of 1″=1′, you must adjust the scale of your linetypes accordingly. This, too, is accomplished in the Layer Control dialog box.

1. Click on the Linetype button on the Object Properties toolbar, or choose Format ➤ Linetype on the pull-down menus. The Select Linetype dialog box appears.

2. Double-click on the Linetype Scale input box, and type **12** ↵. This is the scale conversion factor for a 1″=1′ scale (see Table 3.3).

3. Click on OK. The drawing regenerates, and the shower-curtain rod is displayed in the linetype and at the scale you designated. Your drawing will look like Figure 4.15.

---

 **TIP**   You can also use the Ltscale system variable to set the linetype scale. Type **Ltscale** ↵, and at the `LTSCALE New scale factor <1.0000>` prompt, enter **12** ↵.

---

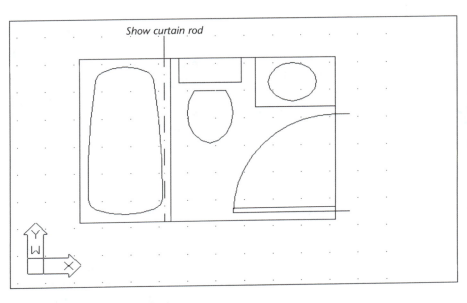

Show curtain rod

*Figure 4.15:* **The completed bathroom**

> **TIP** If you change the linetype of a layer or object but the object remains a continuous line, check the Ltscale system variable. It should be set to your drawing scale factor. If this doesn't work, set the Viewres system variable to a higher value (see *Chapter 6*).

Remember that if you assign a linetype to a layer, everything you draw on that layer will be of that linetype. This includes arcs, polylines, circles, and traces. As explained in the "Setting Individual Colors, Linetypes, and Linetype Scales" sidebar, you can also assign different colors and linetypes to individual objects, rather than relying on their layer assignment to define color and linetype. However, you may want to avoid assigning colors and linetypes directly to objects until you have some experience with AutoCAD LT and a good grasp of your drawing's organization.

The ability to assign linetype scales to individual objects is new in Release 3. You can now set the default linetype scale for all new objects with the Linetype button on the Object Properties toolbar. Change the value in the Linetype Scale input box as desired. You can also change the linetype scale of an *existing* object, using the Change Properties button on the Object Properties toolbar.

**NOTE** Prior to Release 3, linetype scale for the entire drawing (*global* line-type scale) was controlled by the system variable Ltscale. For the first time, with Release 3, you can set linetype scaling on a per object basis. *Object* line-type scale is controlled by a new system variable called Celtscale (Ce stands for "Current entity"). The object linetype scale setting is a *relative* setting. If the *global* linetype scale for the drawing is subsequently changed, then the scaling of the *object* will be automatically adjusted proportionally.

When individual objects are assigned a linetype scale, they are still affected by the global linetype scale set by the Ltscale system variable. For example, say you assign a linetype scale of 2 to the curtain rod in the previous example. This scale would then be multiplied by the global linetype scale (Lltscale) of 12, for a final linetype scale of 24. You can list any object to check the final linetype scale.

Linetype display can also be controlled using the system variable Psltscale, which controls linetypes viewed through a paper space view-port. Psltscale is a toggle, and is set equal to 0 or 1 where 1 is on and 0 is off. When it is turned on, the same linetype scale is applied to all objects in the viewport, even if external references are included in the viewport.

If the objects you draw appear in a different linetype from that of the layer they are on, you can change this in the following way.

1. Select the line object, and then click on the Properties button on the Object Properties toolbar. The Modify Line dialog box will appear.

2. Click on the Linetype... button. The Select Linetype list box will open.

3. Click on Bylayer. The appropriate linetype is applied to the selected object.

   Also, check the linetype scale of the object itself, using the Properties button. A different linetype scale can make a line appear to have an assigned linetype that may not be what you expect. See the sidebar, "Setting Individual Colors, Linetypes, and Linetype Scales."

   If you are working through the tutorial, your last task here is to set up an insertion point for the current drawing to facilitate its insertion into other drawings in the future.

1. Type **Base** ↵.
2. At the Base point <0´-0˝,0´-0˝>: prompt, pick the upper-left corner of the bathroom. The bathroom drawing is now complete.

## SETTING INDIVIDUAL COLORS, LINETYPES, AND LINETYPE SCALES

If you prefer, you can set up AutoCAD LT to assign specific colors and linetypes to objects instead of having objects take on the color and linetype settings of the layer on which they reside. Normally, objects are given a default color and linetype called Bylayer, which means each object takes on the color or linetype of its assigned layer. (You've probably noticed the word Bylayer in the Object Properties toolbar.)

Use the Properties button on the Object Properties toolbar to change the color or linetype of existing objects. This button opens a dialog box that lets you set the properties of individual objects. For new objects, use the Color button on the Object Properties toolbar to set the current default color to red (for example), instead of Bylayer. The Color button opens the Select Color dialog box, where you select your color from a toolbar. Then everything you draw will be red, regardless of the current layer color.

For linetypes, you can use the Linetype drop-down list in the Object Properties toolbar to select a default linetype for all new objects. The list only shows linetypes that have already been loaded into the drawing, so you must have first loaded a linetype before you can select it.

Another possible color and linetype assignment is Byblock, which is also set with the Properties button. Byblock makes everything you draw white, until you turn your drawing into a block and then insert the block on a layer with an assigned color. The objects then take on the color of that layer. This behavior is similar to that of objects drawn on layer 0. The Byblock linetype works similarly to the Byblock color.

Finally, if you want to set the linetype scale for each individual object, instead of relying on the global linetype scale (the Ltscale system variable), you can use the Properties button to modify the linetype scale of individual objects. Or you can use the Current Properties dialog box (via the Current Properties button in the Object Properties toolbar) to set the linetype scale to be applied to new objects. In place of using the Change Properties button to change the linetype scale, you can set the Celtscale system variable in the command window.

## Keeping Track of Blocks and Layers

The Properties button on the Object Properties toolbar can be used to examine, as well as to change, the properties of any AutoCAD LT object. The List button on the Object Properties toolbar gives similar information about objects in the text window.

1. Choose List from the Object Properties toolbar.

2. At the object-selection prompt, click on the tub and then press ↵. The AutoCAD LT Text Window appears.

**NOTE** The Space property you see listed for the Tub block designates whether the object resides in Model Space or Paper Space. You'll learn more about these spaces in *Chapters 6* and *12*.

3. In the Text Window, you will see not only the layer that the tub is on, but its space, insertion point, name, color, linetype, rotation angle, and scale.

**TIP** If you just want to quickly check what layer an object is on, click on the object in question, and then click on the Properties button in the Standard toolbar. You will get a dialog box showing you the basic properties of the object, including its layer setting.

You may wish to keep information from the text window, either as a text file or as hard copy. Click on Edit at the top of the Text Window, and select Copy History. This option allows you to select the contents of the text window and copy it to the Windows clipboard. Here's a way to get a permanent record of the layers and blocks within a drawing using the Copy History option.

1. Type **LAYER** ↵ at the command window, then **?** ↵ ↵. The Auto-CAD LT Text Window appears, and a listing of all the layers scrolls into view.

2. On the Text Window menu select Copy History from the Edit menu. This will transfer the contents of the Text Window to the Windows clipboard. A right-click in the Text Window will give the same menu choices on a cursor menu.

3.  Open the Windows Wordpad or any other word processor and click the paste icon, or type <Ctrl> and V, or select paste from the Edit menu.

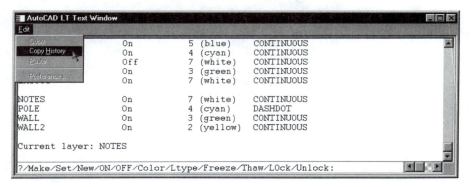

# Finding Files on Your Hard Disk

As your library of symbols and files grows, you may begin to have difficulty keeping track of them. Fortunately, AutoCAD LT offers a utility that lets you quickly locate a file anywhere in your computer. The Find File utility searches your hard disk for specific files. You can have it search one drive or several, or you can limit the search to one directory. You can limit the search to specific filenames or use wildcards to search for files with similar names.

The following exercise steps you through a sample Find File task:

>   **TIP**   Find File can also be accessed using the Find File button in any Auto-CAD LT file dialog box.

1.  Click on the Open icon on the Standard toolbar, or choose File ➤ Open. In the Select File dialog box, click on Find File to display the Browse/Search dialog box.

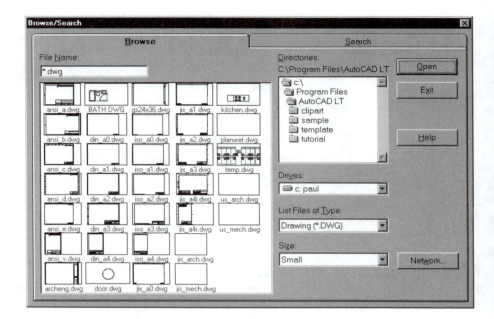

 **NOTE A drawing from an earlier version of AutoCAD LT will be represented as a box with an X through it.**

The Browse/Search dialog box has two tabs, Browse and Search. In the Browse page are all the drawings in the current directory, displayed as thumbnail views so you can easily identify them. You can open a file by double-clicking on its thumbnail view, or by entering its name in the File Name input box at the top.

The Size drop-down list in the Browse page of the Browse/Search dialog box lets you choose the size of the thumbnail views shown in the list box—small, medium, and large. You can scroll through the views using the scroll bars at the top and side of the list box.

2.  Click on the Search tab to open the page of Search functions. Use the
    Search Pattern input box to enter the name of the file for which you
    wish to search. The default is *.DWG, which will cause Find File to
    search for all AutoCAD LT drawing files. Several other input boxes
    help you set a variety of other search criteria, such as the date of the
    drawing, the type of drawing, and the drive and path to be searched.
    For now, leave these settings as is.

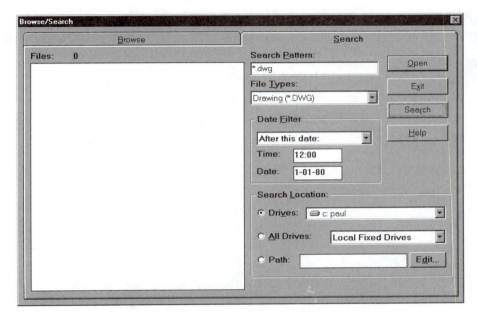

3.  Click on the Search button. In a few seconds, a listing of files that meet
    the criteria specified in the input boxes appears in the Files list on the
    left, along with thumbnail views of each file. You can click on a filename
    in the list, and then click on the Open button to open the file in the
    drawing editor.

4.  When you're ready, click on Exit to exit the Browse/Search dialog box,
    and then click on Cancel to exit the Open File dialog box.

In this exercise you performed a search using the default settings. These settings caused AutoCAD LT to search for files with the .DWG filename extension, created after 12:00 midnight on January 1, 1980.

Here are descriptions of the items in the Browse/Search dialog box:

**Search Pattern** lets you give specific filename search criteria using wildcard characters.

**File Types** lets you select from a set of standard file types.

**Time and Date** let you specify a cutoff time and date. Files created before the specified time and date are ignored.

**Drives** lets you specify the drives to search.

**All Drives** lets you search all the drives on your computer.

**Path** lets you specify a path to search.

The **Search** button begins the search process.

The **Open** button opens the file highlighted in the file list, after a search is performed.

The **Help** button provides information on the use of Browse/Search.

The **Edit** button next to the Path box opens another dialog box, displaying a directory tree from which you can select a search path.

### Inserting Symbols with Drag and Drop

If you prefer to manage your symbols library using the Windows Explorer, or to use another third-party file manager for locating and managing your symbols, you'll appreciate AutoCAD LT's support for Drag and Drop. With this feature, you can click and drag a file from the Explorer into the AutoCAD LT window. You may also use the Windows 95 Find button on the Start menu, then drag files from the search window into the AutoCAD LT drawing window. AutoCAD LT will automatically start the Insert command to insert a drawing file. Drag and Drop also works with a variety of other AutoCAD LT support files. Table 4.1 shows a list of files with which you can use Drag and Drop, and the functions associated with them. In addition to the file formats listed in Table 4.1 below, any Windows file formats that your system supports can be dragged into AutoCAD LT using the OLE feature.

Part
1

The Basics

*Table 4.1:*   **AutoCAD LT Support for Drag and Drop**

| File Type | Command Issued | Function Performed When File Is Dropped |
|---|---|---|
| .DXF | Dxfin | Imports .DXF files |
| .DWG | Insert, Plot | Imports or plots drawing files |
| .TXT | Dtext | Imports texts via Dtext |
| .LIN | Linetype | Loads line types |
| .MNU, .MNX | Menu | Loads menus |
| .SHX | Style | Loads fonts |
| .SCR | Script | Runs script |

## If You Want to Experiment...

If your application is not architecture, you may want to experiment with creating some other types of symbols. You might also start thinking about a layering system that suits your particular needs.

**TIP**   Use the Osnap modes you learned about in Chapter 2 to select the insertion points.

Open a new file called Mytemp. In it, create layers named 1 through 8 and assign each layer the color that corresponds to its number. For example, give layer 1 the color 1 (red), layer 2 the color 2 (yellow) and so on. Draw each part shown in Figure 4.16, and turn each part into a file on disk using the Wblock command. When Wblock prompts you for a filename, use the name indicated for each part in the figure. For the insertion point, also use the points indicated in the figure. Use the Osnap modes (*Chapter 2*) to select the insertion points.

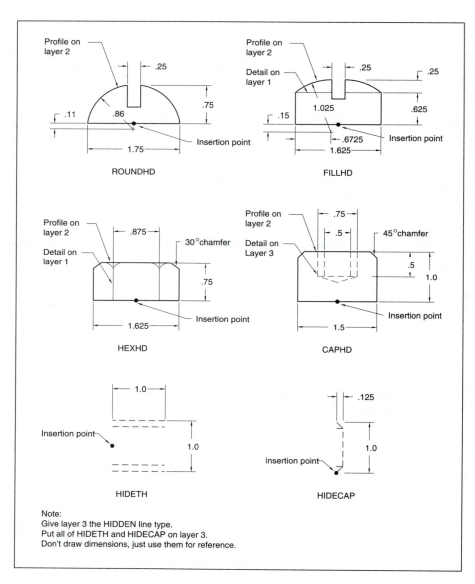

Figure 4.16:    *A typical set of symbols*

When you are done creating the parts, exit the file using File ➤ Exit, and then open a new file. Set up the drawing as an engineering drawing with a scale of ¼″=1″ on an 11″×17″ sheet. Create the drawing in Figure 4.17 using the Insert Block command to place your newly created parts.

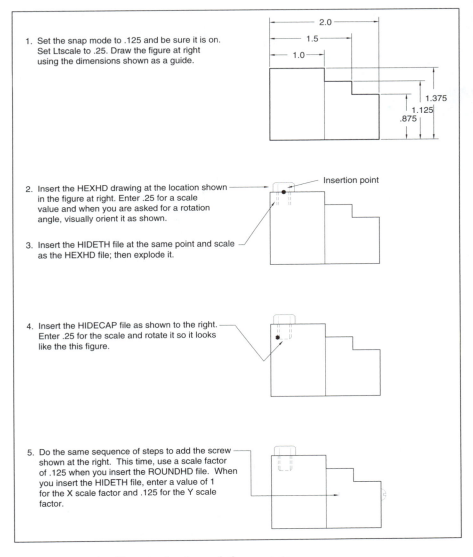

1. Set the snap mode to .125 and be sure it is on. Set Ltscale to .25. Draw the figure at right using the dimensions shown as a guide.

2. Insert the HEXHD drawing at the location shown in the figure at right. Enter .25 for a scale value and when you are asked for a rotation angle, visually orient it as shown.

3. Insert the HIDETH file at the same point and scale as the HEXHD file; then explode it.

4. Insert the HIDECAP file as shown to the right. Enter .25 for the scale and rotate it so it looks like the this figure.

5. Do the same sequence of steps to add the screw shown at the right. This time, use a scale factor of .125 when you insert the ROUNDHD file. When you insert the HIDETH file, enter a value of 1 for the X scale factor and .125 for the Y scale factor.

*Figure 4.17:* **Draw this part using the symbols you create.**

# Building on the Basics

Once you have the basics down, you will begin to explore AutoCAD LT in more detail. *Chapter 5: Editing for Productivity* tells you how to reuse drawing setup information and parts of an existing drawing. In *Chapter 6: Enhancing Your Drawing Skills*, you will learn how to assemble and edit a large drawing file. *Chapter 7: Printing and Plotting* shows you how to get your drawing onto hard copy. *Chapter 8: Adding Text to Drawings* tells you how to annotate your drawing and edit your notes. *Chapter 9: Using Dimensions* gives you practice in using automatic dimensioning, another unique CAD capability.

# Chapter 5

# Editing for Productivity

## *FAST TRACKS*

**T**HERE are at least five commands devoted to duplicating objects, ten if you include the Grips options. Why so many? If you're an experienced drafter, you know that technical drawing is often tedious. So AutoCAD LT offers a variety of ways to reuse existing geometry, thereby automating much of the repetitive work usually associated with manual drafting.

In this chapter, as you finish drawing the studio apartment unit, you will explore some of the ways to exploit existing files and objects while constructing your drawing. For example, you will use existing files as templates for new files, eliminating the need to set up layers, scales, and sheet sizes for similar drawings. With AutoCAD LT you can also duplicate objects in multiple arrays. You have already seen how to use the Osnap overrides on objects to locate points for drawing complex forms. We will look at other ways of using lines to aid your drawing.

And, because you will begin to use Zoom more in the exercises of this chapter, we will review this command as we go along. We'll also introduce you to the Pan command—another tool to help you get around in your drawing.

You're already familiar with many of the commands you will use to draw the apartment unit. So, rather than going through every step of the drawing process, we will sometimes ask you to copy the drawing from a figure, using notes and dimensions as guides and putting objects on the indicated layers. If you have trouble remembering a command you've already learned, just go back and review the appropriate section of the book.

# Using an Existing Drawing as a Template

AutoCAD LT allows you to use an existing drawing as the starting point, or *template,* for a new drawing. A template is a file that contains the necessary settings or objects for making a drawing.

You may have noticed the option Use a Template in the Create New Drawing dialog box. AutoCAD LT comes with a full set of *drawing templates,* called .DWT files, which you may wish to utilize. You can use them to start a drawing quickly without going through all the steps required to set it up.

Even if you choose the option Start from Scratch when you start a new drawing, AutoCAD LT will use one of its default templates: ACLT.DWT if you are using English meaurements; ACLTISO.DWT if you are using metric measurements.

You can also use your own files as templates. For example, you may want to create a second drawing with the same scale and sheet size as an existing drawing. You may even want to use some of the objects, layers, and blocks in it. By using the existing file to begin your new one, you can save a lot of time.

## Saving an Existing Drawing as a Template

In earlier exercises where you created new files, you typically selected Start from Scratch in the Create New File dialog box. This meant that you were working with the standard AutoCAD LT default settings.

You will probably want to create some standard templates which contain the settings you frequently use. In this case, you can create several empty drawing templates, each with its own default settings. One may have layers already set up; another may have predefined blocks ready to use. When you want to use one of these files as a template, you proceed as if you were opening a new file, and at the Create New File dialog box, you click on Use a Template. Then select the name of the template you want to use from the Select a Template list box.

The following exercise guides you through creating and using a template drawing for your studio's kitchenette. Because the kitchenette will use the same layers, settings, scale, and sheet size as the bathroom drawing, you can use the Bath file as a template. But first you will have to open the Bath drawing and save it as a template drawing.

1. Start AutoCAD LT in the usual way, and open your Bath drawing, or use BATH.DWG from the companion CD.

2. Click on File ➤ Save As. The Save Drawing As dialog box appears.

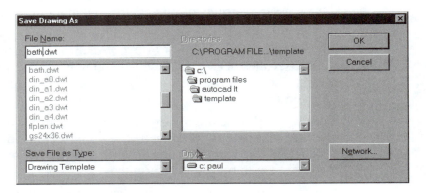

3. Click on the Save File as Type: drop-down list box and select Drawing Template.

4. Click on the File Name: input box, and type **Bath.dwt** as the name of the template file and press ↵. When the Template Description dialog box appears, enter an appropriate description that will assist you in remembering what the template is for. Type **Studio Floor Plan**, for example. Then click on the OK button.

5. Click on the New icon on the Standard toolbar to start a new drawing. The Create New Drawing dialog box appears.

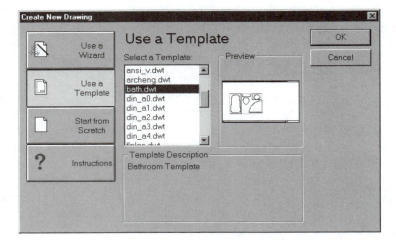

6. This time click on Use a Template. The Select a Template: list box replaces the Select Default Setting: list box. Select the Bath template you created (bath.dwt). A Preview of the drawing will appear in the Preview window, and the description you entered in step 4 will appear in the Template Description box. Click OK, and the bathroom drawing appears on the screen.

7. Click on File ➤ Save As, and save the unnamed drawing as **Kitchen**.

Although the drawing now in the drawing editor looks like the Bath drawing, this does not mean that you have opened the Bath file. Because the Kitchen file is using the Bath file as a template, the Kitchen drawing contains everything that's in the Bath drawing, including its objects. You don't need these objects, however, so erase them. Your new kitchenette file still contains the layers and settings used in the Bath file, and is already set up for a 1″=1′ drawing on an 8½″×11″ drawing area.

## OPENING A FILE AS READ-ONLY

When you open an existing file, you might have noticed the Read Only Mode check box in the Open Drawing dialog box. If you open a file with this option checked, AutoCAD LT will not let you save the file under its original name. You can still edit the drawing any way you please, but if you attempt to use File ➤ Save, you will get the message "Drawing file is write-protected." You can, however, save your changed file under another name.

The read-only mode provides a way to protect important files from accidental corruption. It also offers another method for reusing settings and objects from existing files by letting you open a file as a prototype, then saving the file under another name.

## Copying an Object Multiple Times

Now let's explore the tools that let you quickly duplicate objects. First you will draw the gas range top. In the process you will learn how to use the ARRAY command to create *arrays* (or multiple copies) of an object, and to control the number and orientation of the copies.

NOTE An array can be in either a circular pattern called a *polar array,* or a matrix of columns and rows called a *rectangular array.*

## Making Circular Copies

Before you start the range top, you have to first decide which layer you want to draw the range top on, and set this layer as the current layer. Then you will draw a circle representing the edge of one burner.

1.  Set the current layer to Fixture, and toggle the snap mode on.

2.  Click on Circle Center Radius from the Draw toolbar.

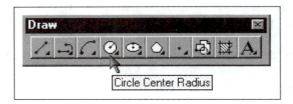

3.  At the 3P/TTR/<Center point>: prompt, enter **4´,4´**.

4.  At the Diameter/<Radius>: prompt, enter **3** ↵. The circle appears.

    Now you're ready to use the Array command to draw the burner grill. You will first draw one line representing part of the grill, and then use Array to create the copies.

---

**TIP**   You can also enter **C** ↵ at the command prompt to start the Circle command. The Center, Radius options are the defaults for Circle.

---

1.  Draw a line 4″ long starting from the coordinate 4´-1″, 4´-0″ and ending to the right of that point.

2.  Zoom into the circle and line to get a better view. Your drawing should look like Figure 5.1.

3.  Click and drag Duplicate Object from the Modify toolbar then select Polar Array.

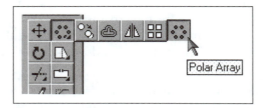

TIP   You can also type **Array** ↵ to start the Array command. Then, after confirming your selection of objects in step 5, type **P** ↵.

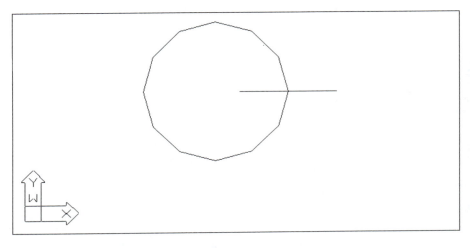

*Figure 5.1:   A close-up of the circle and line*

4. At the Select object: prompt, enter **L** ↵. This highlights the line you just drew.

5. Press ↵ to confirm your selection.

6. At the Center point of array prompt, pick the center of the circle using the Center Osnap override. Be sure you click on the circle's circumference.

7. At the Number of items prompt, enter **8** ↵. This tells AutoCAD LT you want seven copies plus the original.

8. At the Angle to fill (+=ccw,-=cw) <360>: prompt, press ↵ to accept the default. The default value of 360 tells AutoCAD LT to copy the objects so that they are spaced evenly over a 360° arc. (If you had instead entered 180°, the lines would be evenly spaced over a 180° arc, filling only half the circle.)

NOTE If you want to copy in a clockwise (CW) direction, you must enter a minus sign (–) before the number of degrees.

9. At the Rotate objects as they are copied? <Y>: prompt, press ↵ again to accept the default. The line copies around the center of the circle, rotating as it copies. Your drawing will look like Figure 5.2.

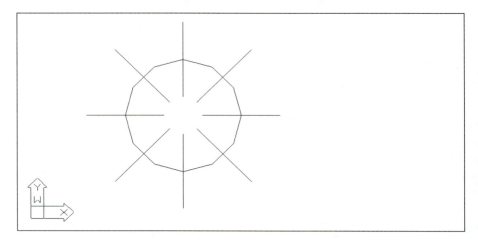

*Figure 5.2:* **The completed gas burner**

**NOTE** In step 9, you could have the line maintain its horizontal orientation as it is copied around, by entering **N** ↵. But since you want it to rotate about the array center, accept the default, **Y**.

## Making Row and Column Copies

Now you will draw the other three burners of the gas range by creating a rectangular array from the burner you just drew. You will first zoom back a bit to get a view of a larger area. Then you will proceed with the Array command.

1. Click on the ZoomOut button on the Standard toolbar. The view will zoom out **.5x**, and your drawing will look like Figure 5.3.

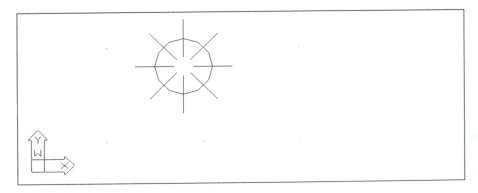

*Figure 5.3:* **A 0.5x magnification of the preceding view**

**TIP** If you're not too fussy about the amount you want to zoom out, you can choose Real-Time Zoom on the Zoom flyout to quickly zoom in and out by simply gliding the cursor up and down the screen until you get to the view you require. The Real-time Zoom icon looks like a magnifying glass with a small plus and minus beside it.

You may also specify the view magnification using View ➤ Zoom ➤ Scale and entering a value at the command line. If you specify a Scale value greater than 1 (5, for example), you will magnify your current view. If you leave off the *x*, your new view will be in relation to the drawing limits rather than the current view.

Now you will finish the range top. Here you will get a chance to use the Rectangular Array option to create three additional burners.

**2.** Click and drag Polar Array from the Modify toolbar, and then select Rectangular Array.

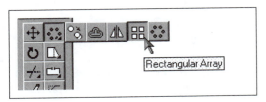

3. At the `Select objects:` prompt, use the Window selection option to window the entire burner. Then press ↵ to confirm your selection.

4. As mentioned earlier, a rectangular array is a matrix of columns and rows. At the `Number of rows ( – – – – ) <1>` prompt, enter **2** ↵. This tells AutoCAD LT the number of copies you want vertically.

5. At the `Number of columns ( ¦ ¦ ¦ ¦ ) <1>` prompt, enter **2** ↵ again. This tells AutoCAD LT the number of copies you want horizontally.

6. At the `Unit cell or distance between rows ( – – – – )` prompt, enter **14** ↵. This tells AutoCAD LT that the vertical distance between the rows of burners is 14″.

7. At the `Distance between columns ( ¦ ¦ ¦ ¦ )` prompt, enter **16** ↵ to tell AutoCAD LT you want the horizontal distance between the columns of burners to be 16″. Your screen will look like Figure 5.4.

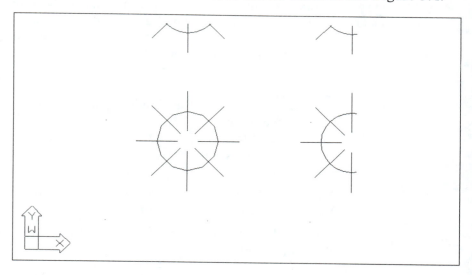

*Figure 5.4:    **The burners arrayed***

 **TIP** You can also type **Array** ↵ to start the Array command. Then, after confirming your selection of objects in step 4, type **R** ↵.

AutoCAD LT usually draws a rectangular array from bottom to top, and from left to right. You can reverse the direction of the array by giving negative values for the distance between columns and rows.

**TIP**   At times you may want to do a rectangular array at an angle. To accomplish this you must first set the Snap angle setting in the Drawing Aids dialog box (Options ➤ Drawing Aids) to the desired angle. Then proceed with the Array command.

You can also use the cursor to graphically indicate an *array cell* (see Figure 5.5). An array cell is a rectangle defining the distance between rows and columns. You may want to use this option when an object is available to use as a reference from which to determine column and row distances. For example, you may have drawn a crosshatch pattern, as on a calendar, within which you want to array an object. You would use the intersections of the hatch lines as references to define the array cell, which would be one square in the hatch pattern.

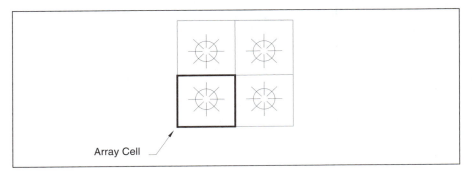

Array Cell

*Figure 5.5:*   **An array cell**

## Using Pan

Notice that most of the burners do not appear on the display shown in Figure 5.4. To move the view over so you can see all the burners, you can use the Pan command. Pan is similar to Zoom in that it changes your view of the drawing; however, Pan does not alter the magnification of the view the way Zoom does. Rather, Pan maintains the current magnification while moving your view across the drawing, just as you would pan a camera across a landscape.

> **NOTE** Pan is especially helpful when you have magnified an area to do some editing, and you need to get to part of the drawing that is near your current view. To start a Real-Time pan, enter **rtpan** ↵, or click on Real-Time Pan on the Pan flyout on the Standard toolbar.

1. Click and drag the Pan Point button on the Pan flyout on the Standard toolbar, or enter **p** ↵ at the command line to start the Pan command.

2. At the ´PAN Displacement: prompt, pick a point near coordinate 3´-7˝, 3´-7˝.

3. At the Second point: prompt, turn the ortho mode off if it is still on, and then move the cursor to the lower-left corner of the screen, as shown in Figure 5.6. The rubber-banding line you see indicates the pan displacement. Pick this point. Your drawing will be panned to the view shown in Figure 5.7.

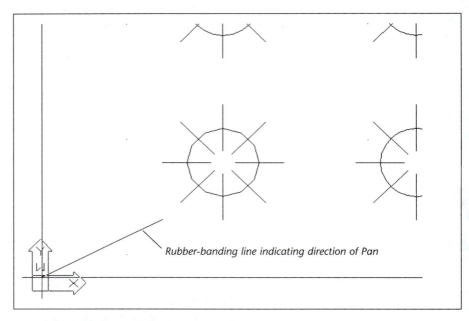

*Figure 5.6:* **A rubber-banding line indicating pan displacement**

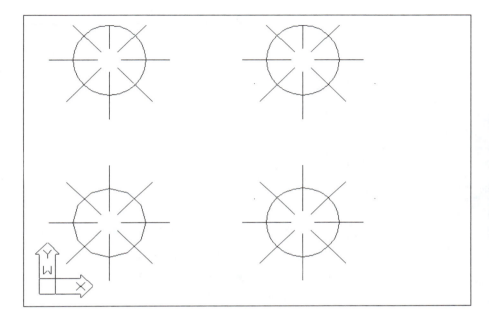

*Figure 5.7:* **The panned view of the gas range**

You may have noticed the other option on the Pan flyout: Real-time Pan. Real-Time Pan provides an easy way to pan your view in either direction. Real-time Pan provides continuous visual feedback as you move across your drawing. Use this option if you want to quickly pan across your view and you don't need to be exact about the distance or direction. The Pan options are also duplicated on the View menu.

The burners are still not entirely visible in your panned view, because the current zoom magnification is too great for you to see the entire range.

1. Type **Z** ↵.

2. At the All/Center... prompt, enter **e** ↵. This has the effect of zooming back out to include an area equivalent to the extents of your drawing.

3. Now complete the kitchenette as indicated in Figure 5.8.

   You will be using this drawing as a symbol, inserting it into the overall plan of the studio unit. To facilitate accurate placement of the kitchenette, you will want to change the location of the base point of this drawing to the upper-left corner of the kitchenette. This will then be the "handle" of the drawing.

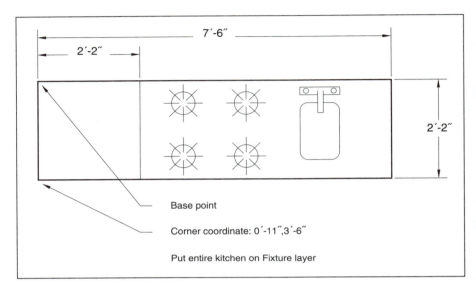

7'-6"

2'-2"

2'-2"

Base point

Corner coordinate: 0'-11",3'-6"

Put entire kitchen on Fixture layer

*Figure 5.8:    **Drawing the kitchenette***

1. At the command line, type **Base** ↵.

2. At the `Base point <1'-10",6'-10",0'-0">` prompt, pick the upper-left corner of the kitchenette as indicated in Figure 5.8. The kitchenette drawing is complete.

3. Click on the Save button on the Standard toolbar.

## MAKING MULTIPLE COPIES

The Array command is useful when you want to make multiple copies in a regular pattern. But what if you need to make copies at irregular intervals? You have two alternatives for accomplishing this: the Copy command's Multiple option, and the Grips feature's Move mode.

To use the Copy command to make random multiple copies:

1. Click on the Duplicate Objects button on the Modify toolbar to start the Copy command.

2. At the `Select object` prompt, select the objects you want to copy and press ↵ to confirm your selections.

3. At the `<Base point or displacement>/Multiple:` prompt, enter **M** ↵ to select the Multiple option.

## MAKING MULTIPLE COPIES (continued...)

4. At the Base point prompt, select a base point as usual.

5. At the Second point prompt, select a point for the copy. You will be prompted again for a second point, allowing you to make yet another copy of your object.

6. Continue to select points for more copies as desired.

7. Press ↵ to exit the Copy command when you are done.

When you use the Grips feature to make multiple random copies, you get an added level of functionality, since you can also rotate, mirror, and stretch copies by pressing the right mouse button. Of course, you must have the Grips feature turned on; it is usually on by default but you may find yourself on a system that has it turned off for some reason.

1. Press the Escape key twice to make sure you are not in the middle of a command, then select the objects you want to copy.

2. Click on a grip point as your base point. The ** STRETCH ** prompt appears, telling you that you are in the stretch mode.

3. Press the right mouse button once to change to the move mode. You'll see ** MOVE ** in the prompt area.

4. Move the cursor to the location for your copy and, while holding down the Shift key, click on the new location. Or you can enter **C** ↵ to issue the Copy option before you click on the new location.

5. If desired, click on other locations for more copies, without holding down the Shift key.

## *Developing Your Drawing*

As mentioned briefly in *Chapter 3*, when using AutoCAD LT, you first create the most basic forms of your drawing; then you refine them. In this section you will create two drawings—the studio apartment unit and the lobby—that demonstrate this process in more detail.

First you will construct a typical studio apartment unit using the drawings you have created thus far. In the process, you will explore the use of lines as reference objects.

You will also further examine how to use existing files as blocks. In *Chapter 4*, you inserted a file into another file. There is no limit to the size or number of files you can insert. As you may already have guessed, you can also *nest* files and blocks, that is, insert blocks or files within other blocks or files. Nesting can help reduce your drawing time by allowing you to build one block out of smaller blocks. For example, you can insert your door drawing into the bathroom plan. The bathroom plan can in turn be inserted into the studio unit plan, which also contains doors. Finally, the unit plan can be inserted into the overall floor plan for the studio apartment building.

## Importing Settings

In this exercise, you will insert the Bath *drawing* file into the studio unit plan. However, you must make a few changes to it first. Once the changes are made, you will import the bathroom and thereby import the layers and blocks contained in the bathroom file.

As you go through this exercise, observe how the drawings begin to evolve from simple forms to complex, assembled forms.

1. First, open your Bath file again, or use BATH.DWG from the companion CD.

2. Use the BASE command and select the upper-left corner of the bathroom as the new base point for this drawing, so you can position the Bath file more accurately.

3. Save the Bath file.

4. Create a new file called **Unit** by clicking on the New icon on the Standard toolbar; when the Create New Drawing dialog box opens, click on Use a Wizard and select Quick Set Up.

5. Next, use the Quick Set Up Step 1: Units to set the unit style to Architectural.

> **NOTE** If you need help setting up a drawing, turn to the instructions at the beginning of *Chapter 3*. Table 3.2 contains the information you need to specify the limits of your drawing area.

6. Use Quick Set Up Step 2: Area to set up a ¼″=1′-0″ scale, drawing on an 8½″×11″ sheet. This means your limits should include an area 528″ wide by 408″ long.

7. Click on the Done button to complete Quick Set Up.

8. Save your file as **Unit.dwg**.

9. Turn the snap mode on and set the grid aspect to 12″.

10. Begin the unit by drawing two rectangles, one 14′ wide by 24′ long, and the other 14′ wide by 4′ long. Place them as shown in Figure 5.9.

 **NOTE** The large rectangle represents the interior of the apartment unit, and the small rectangle represents the balcony.

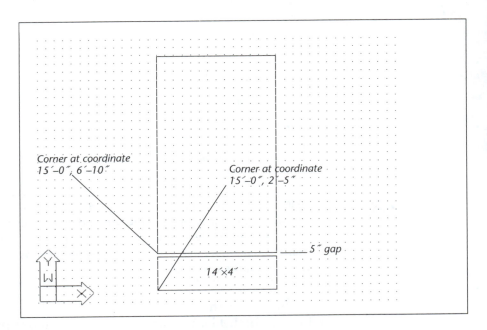

Figure 5.9: *The apartment unit interior and balcony*

11. Use Insert Block on the Draw toolbar to insert the bathroom drawing. When the Insert dialog box opens, click on the File button and select Bath.DWG. Use the upper-left corner of the unit's interior as the insertion point (see Figure 5.10). You can use the Endpoint Osnap override to accurately place the bathroom. Use a scale factor of 1.0 and a rotation angle of 0°.

12. Use the Properties button on the Object Properties toolbar to change all the lines you drew to the Wall layer.

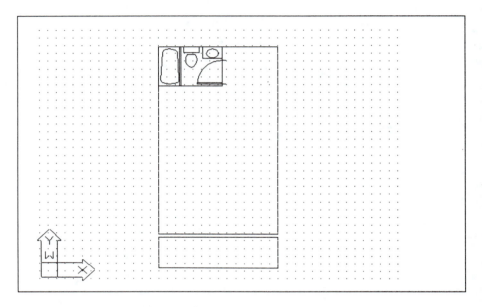

*Figure 5.10:*    **The unit after the bathroom is inserted**

**WARNING** If two drawings contain the same layers and blocks, and one of these drawings is imported into the other, the layer settings and block definitions of the *current* file will take priority over those of the *imported* file. This is a point to remember in cases where the layer settings and block definitions are different in the two files.

By inserting the bathroom, you imported the layers and blocks contained in the Bath file. You were then able to move previously drawn objects to the imported layers. As a quick way of setting up layers, you could set up several drawings containing different layering schemes and then insert them into new drawings. This method is similar to using an existing drawing as a template, but it allows you to start work on a drawing before deciding which template to use.

## Using and Editing Lines

You will draw lines in the majority of your work, so it is important to know how to manipulate lines to your best advantage. In this section, you will look at some of the more common ways to use and edit these fundamental drawing objects. The following exercises show you the process of drawing lines, rather than just how individual commands and options work.

### Roughing In the Line Work

The bathroom you inserted in the last section has only one side of its interior walls drawn (walls are usually shown by double lines). In this next exercise, you will draw the other side. Rather than trying to draw the wall in perfectly the first time, you will "sketch" in the line work and then work through a clean-up process, in a way similar to manual drafting.

1. Zoom into the bathroom so that the entire bathroom and part of the area around it are displayed on the screen, as in Figure 5.11.

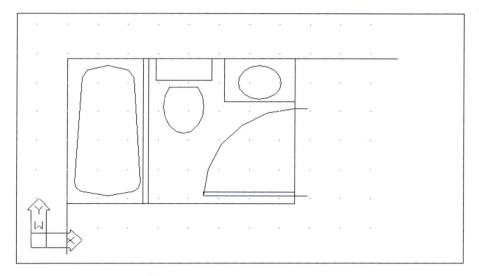

*Figure 5.11:* **The enlarged view of the bathroom**

2. Use the Layers drop-down list box to make Wall the current layer.

3. Start the Line command. Click on From on the Cursor menu (Shift-Right mouse-click). The From option lets you select a point relative to another point.

4. At the From prompt, click on the lower-right corner of the bathroom. Nothing appears in the drawing area yet.

5. Type **@5<–90** ↵. Now a line starts 5″ below the lower-right corner of the bathroom. Make sure that Ortho is highlighted on the status bar.

6. Continue the line horizontally to the left, to slightly cross the left wall of the apartment unit, as illustrated in the top panel of Figure 5.12.

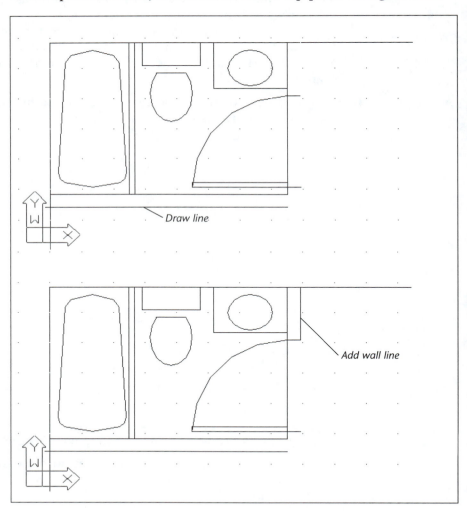

*Figure 5.12:*    ***The first wall line and the wall line by the door***

In the foregoing exercise, the From Osnap override allows you to spec-ify a point in space relative to the corner of the bathroom. In step 5, you used a polar coordinate to indicate the distance from the corner at which you wanted the line to start. You can also use relative or absolute Cartesian coordinates. Now let's continue with the line work.

**TIP** The Perpendicular Osnap override can also be used to draw a line per-pendicular to a nonorthogonal line—one at a 45° angle, for instance.

**Part 2**

**Building on the Basics**

1. Draw another line upward from the endpoint of the top door jamb at coordinate 22'-11", 29'-2" to meet the top wall of the unit. Use the Ortho mode and the Perpendicular Osnap override to pick the top wall of the unit. This causes the line to end precisely on the wall line in per-pendicular position, as in the bottom panel of Figure 5.12.

2. Draw a line connecting the two door jambs. Then change that line to the Ceiling layer.

3. Draw a line 6" downward from the endpoint of the jamb nearest the corner at coordinate 22'-11", 26'-0", as shown in the top panel of Fig-ure 5.13.

### Cleaning Up the Line Work

You've drawn some of the wall lines, approximating their endpoint locations. Next you will use the Fillet command to join lines exactly end to end.

**NOTE** The Chamfer command operates similarly to Fillet. Chamfer can be set to join two lines at a corner in exactly the same manner as Fillet. Unlike Fillet, however, Chamfer allows you to join two lines with an intermediate beveled line rather than an arc.

1. Click on the Feature flyout on the Modify toolbar, and then select Fillet.

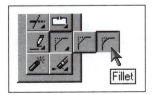

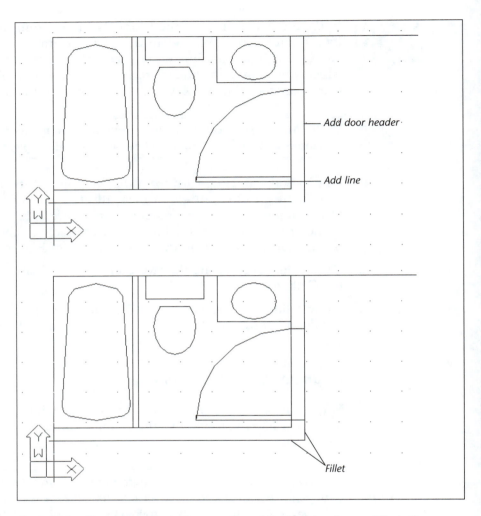

*Figure 5.13:* **The corner of the bathroom wall, and the filleted wall around the bathroom**

2. Type **R** ↵ **0** ↵ to set the fillet radius to 0, then press ↵ to repeat the Fillet command.

3. Fillet the two lines by picking the vertical line at coordinate 22′-11″, 25′-7″ and the horizontal line at coordinate 22′-0″, 25′-5″. Notice that these points lie on the portion of the line you want to keep. Your drawing will look like the bottom panel of Figure 5.13.

4. Fillet the bottom wall of the bathroom with the left wall of the unit. Make sure the points you pick on the wall lines are on the side of the line you want to keep, not the side you want trimmed.

5. Fillet the top wall of the unit with the right side wall of the bathroom.

6. Click on the Redraw View icon on the Standard toolbar to refresh the drawing. Your drawing should now look like Figure 5.14.

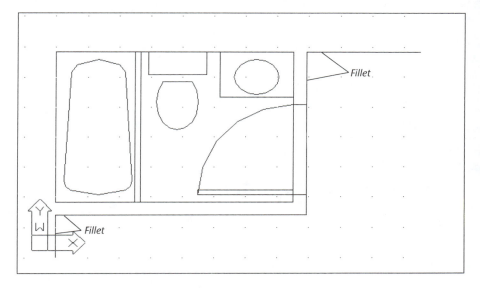

*Figure 5.14:    **The wall intersections, all cleaned up***

Fillet joins two nonparallel lines exactly end to end. Remember: Where you select the lines will affect how the lines are joined. As you select objects for Fillet, the side of the line you click on is the side that remains when the lines are joined. Figure 5.15 illustrates how Fillet works and shows what the fillet options do.

**NOTE** The Fillet command fillets *lines* only. If you created the rectangles in the unit drawing using the Rectang command rather than the Line command, you will have to explode the rectangles before you can fillet the segments. The rectangles are closed polylines, and you cannot fillet a polyline with a line.

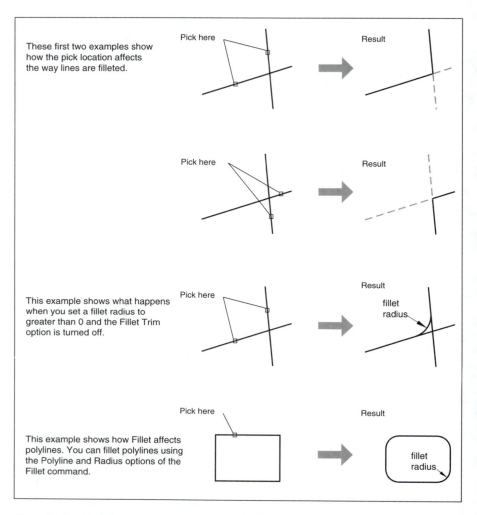

These first two examples show how the pick location affects the way lines are filleted.

This example shows what happens when you set a fillet radius to greater than 0 and the Fillet Trim option is turned off.

This example shows how Fillet affects polylines. You can fillet polylines using the Polyline and Radius options of the Fillet command.

*Figure 5.15:    The place where you click on the object to select it determines what part of an object gets filleted.*

Now let's finish this end of the Unit plan.

**TIP**  If you didn't complete the kitchen earlier in this chapter, you can insert the Kitchen file from the companion CD.

1. Use Insert Block from the Draw toolbar to place the kitchen drawing at the wall intersection at coordinate 15′-0″, 25′-5″. (You can also insert the kitchen at approximately the place where you want it, and then move it into a more exact position.)

2. Press ↵ three times to accept the default X and Y Scale factors of 1.0, and a Rotation Angle of 0°.

3. Pan your view so that the upper-right corner of the bathroom is in the center of the drawing area, as illustrated in the top panel of Figure 5.16.

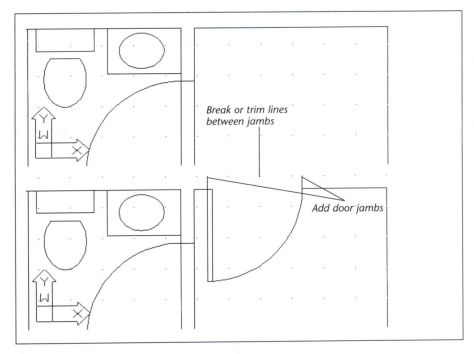

*Figure 5.16:*    ***The view after using Pan, with the door inserted and the jambs added***

4. Insert a door on the unit wall at coordinate 23′-4″, 30′-10″ and then press ↵ twice to accept the default Scale factors.

5. At the Rotation angle prompt, enter **270** ↵. Or use the cursor (make sure the Ortho mode is on) to orient the door so that it is swinging *into* the unit.

6. Make sure the door is on the Door layer.

**7.** Add 5″ door jambs, and use Modify ➤ Break ➤ 2 Points Select to break the header over the door (see the bottom panel of Figure 5.16). Be sure the door jambs are on the Jamb layer.

 NOTE If you need some help with the Break command, see "Modifying an Object" in *Chapter 3*, and the sidebar, "The Break Options," here in *Chapter 5*.

**8.** Draw the door header on the Ceiling layer.

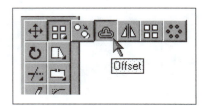

**9.** Click on the Duplicate flyout on the Modify toolbar and select Offset.

Offset the top wall lines of the unit and the door header up 5″, so they connect with the top end of the door jamb, as shown in Figure 5.17. Don't forget to include the short wall line from the door to the bathroom wall.

**10.** Save your file.

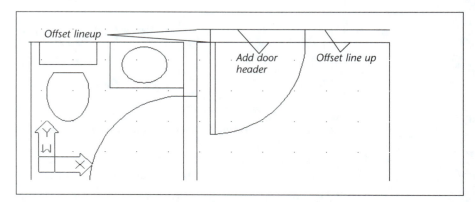

Figure 5.17:   *The other side of the wall*

## THE BREAK OPTIONS

In the exercise for finishing the Unit plan, you used a new option—2 Points Select—on the Break flyout on the Modify toolbar. Here are descriptions of all the options available on the Break flyout.

**1 Point Select** breaks an object at a single point, so the object becomes two contiguous objects. You are prompted to first select an object and then the point where the break is to occur.

**1 Point** performs the same function as 1 Point, but you are only prompted to select an object. The break is placed at the point of selection.

**2 Points Select** breaks an object so that there is a gap in the object. You are prompted to first select the object and then to pick two points defining the location of the gap.

**2 Points** also produces a gap in an object, but instead of prompting you to select the object and two points, 2 Point uses the point of selection as the first point in the gap. You are then prompted for the other end of the break or gap.

### Using Construction Lines as Tools

Now you need to extend the upper wall line 5″ beyond the right-side interior wall of the unit. To accomplish this, you will draw some line objects specifically designed to help with layout. Start by drawing a Ray line.

1. Click and drag Line from the Draw menu, and then select Ray.

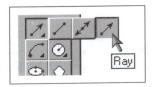

2. At the Start point prompt, start the Ray line from the upper-right corner of the unit at coordinate 29′-0″, 30′-10″ (see the upper panel of Figure 5.18).

3. At the Through point prompt, type **@1<45**. The Ray line appears. Press ↵ to exit the Ray command.

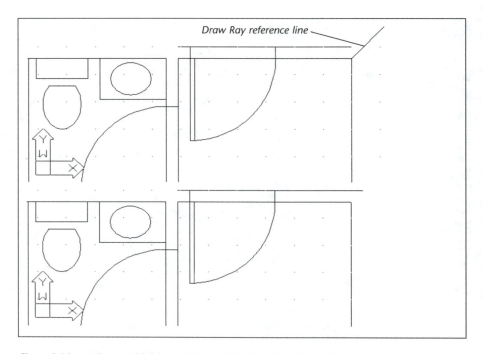

*Figure 5.18:    A Ray used to extend the wall line; and the line, extended*

> **NOTE** A Ray is a line of infinite length that starts from a point you select. For this reason, it didn't matter what length value you entered in step 3. As you continue this exercise, you will use the ray to help you locate the outer edge of a wall.

**4.** Fillet this Ray with the wall line you wish to extend, and then erase the Ray when you are done. Your drawing should look like the bottom panel of Figure 5.18.

**5.** Click on the Zoom Previous button on the Zoom flyout to view the left side of the unit.

**6.** Draw another Ray at 135°. Then use Fillet to join this line with the wall line (see Figure 5.19).

**7.** Erase the last Ray you drew.

**8.** Click on the Zoom All button on the Zoom flyout to view the entire drawing. It will look like Figure 5.20.

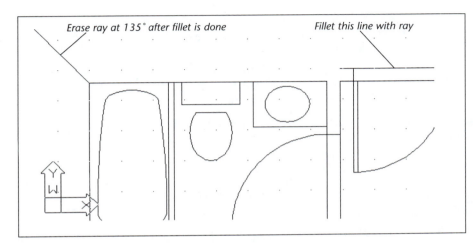

*Figure 5.19:* **The left-side wall line, extended**

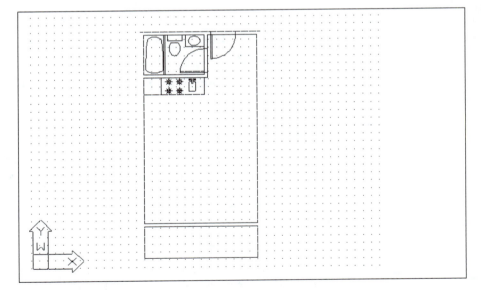

*Figure 5.20:* **The unit plan thus far**

In this exercise, you used Rays to help accurately position two other lines used for the exterior walls of the studio unit. This shows that you can freely use objects to help construct your drawing.

Now you will finish the balcony by adding a sliding glass door and a rail. Again, you will use lines for construction as well as for parts of the drawing. First, you'll add the door jamb by drawing an Xline. An Xline is a line that has an infinite length, but unlike the Ray, it extends in both directions. After drawing the Xline, you'll use it to quickly position the door jambs.

1. Zoom into the balcony area.

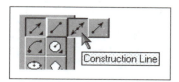

2. Click and drag Ray from the Draw toolbar, and then select Construction Line from the Line flyout. This starts the Xline command, and you'll see this prompt:

        Hor/Ver/Ang/Bisect/Offset/<From point>:

3. Type **O** ⏎ to select the Offset option of the Xline command.

4. At the `Offset distance` prompt, type **4** ⏎.

5. At the `Select object` prompt, click on the wall line at the right of the unit.

6. At the `Side to offset` prompt, click on a point to the left of the wall. The Xline appears (see the top panel of Figure 5.21).

7. At the `Select line object` prompt, click on the left wall line, and then click to the right of the wall to create another Xline.

8. Press ⏎ to exit the command.

   Next, you'll adjust the Xlines to form the jambs.

9. Click on Trim on the Modify toolbar.

10. At the `Select cutting edges:` prompt, select the Xlines and the two horizontal lines representing the wall between the unit and the balcony, and press ⏎.

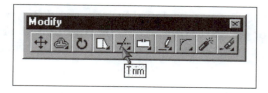

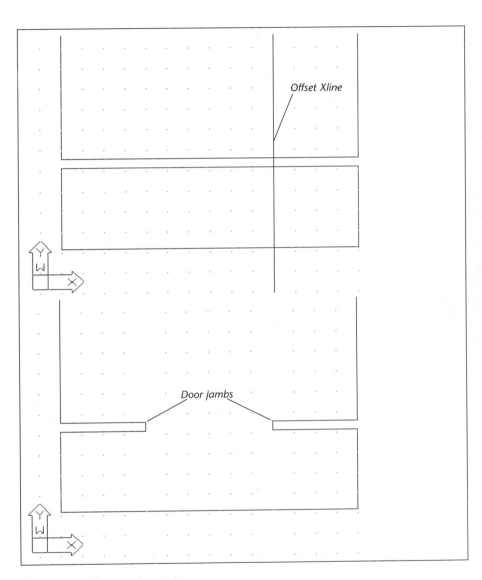

*Figure 5.21:* **The door opening**

11. At the Select object to trim: prompt, click on the horizontal lines at any point between the Xlines. Then click on the Xlines above and below the horizontal lines to trim them. Your drawing will look like the bottom panel of Figure 5.21.

**12.** Add lines on the Ceiling layer to represent the door header.

**13.** Now draw lines between the two jambs (on the Door layer) to indicate a sliding glass door (see Figure 5.22).

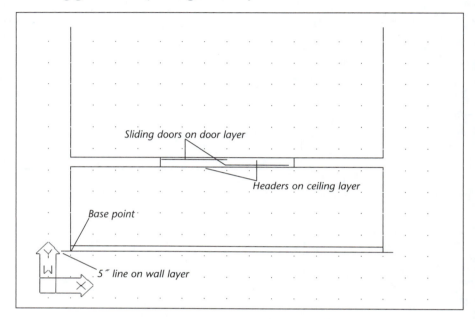

Figure 5.22:    **The sliding glass door**

### The Xline Options

There is more to the Xline command than you have seen in the exercises of this chapter. Here is a list of the other Xline options:

**Hor**    draws horizontal Xlines as you click on points.

**Ver**    draws vertical Xlines as you click on points.

**Angle**    draws Xlines at a specified angle as you pick points.

**Bisect**    draws Xlines bisecting an angle or a location between two points.

The wall facing the balcony is now complete. To finish off the unit, you need to show a hand rail and the corners of the balcony wall.

**1.** Offset the bottom line of the balcony 3″ toward the top of the drawing.

2. Create a new layer called **F-rail**, and assign this offset line to it.

3. Add a 5″ horizontal line to the lower corners of the balcony, as shown in Figure 5.22.

4. Now type **Base** ↵ to set the base point at the lower-left corner of the balcony, at the coordinates 15′, 2′-5″.

5. Change the lines indicating walls to the Wall layer, and put the sliding glass door on the Door layer (see Figure 5.22).

6. Zoom back to the previous view. Your drawing should now look like Figure 5.23.

7. Click on the Save button to save the drawing.

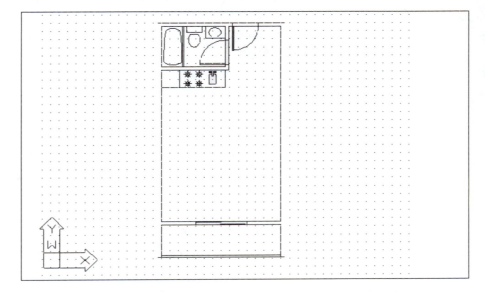

*Figure 5.23:* **The completed studio apartment unit**

Your studio apartment unit plan is now complete. The exercises you've just completed show you a typical set of operations you'll perform while building your drawings. In fact, nearly 80 percent of what you will do in AutoCAD LT is represented here.

Now, to review the drawing process, and to create a drawing you'll use later, draw the apartment house's lobby. As you follow the steps, refer to Figure 5.24.

> **NOTE** As is usual in floor plans, the elevator is indicated by the box with the large X through it, and the stair shaft is indicated by the box with the row of vertical lines through it.

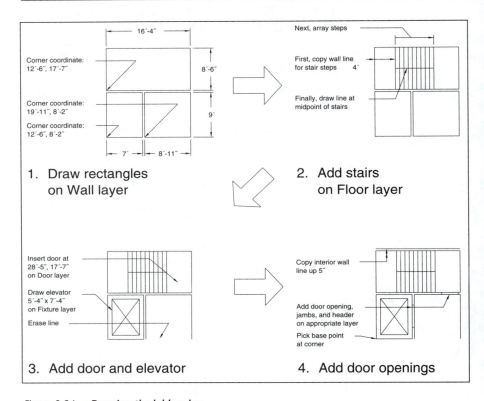

*Figure 5.24:* **Drawing the lobby plan**

1. Save the Unit file as a new file called **Lobby**. This enables you to utilize all of the settings that you created in the Unit drawing.

2. You do not need the unit line work, so erase the entire unit.

3. Begin by drawing the three main rectangles representing the outlines of the stair shaft, the elevator shaft, and the lobby.

4. To draw the stairs, offset the stair shaft's left wall to the right a distance of 4′. This creates the first line representing the steps.

5. Array this line in one row of ten columns, using a column spacing of 11 inches.

6. Draw the center line dividing the two flights of stairs.

7. Draw the elevator and insert the door. Practice using Xlines here.

8. Draw in the door jambs, and edit the door openings to add the door headers. Your plan should resemble the one in Figure 5.24, panel 4.

9. Now type **Basepoint** ↵, and select the lower-left corner of the elevator using the Endpoint Osnap.

10. Once you are finished, save the Lobby file.

## Finding Distances along Arcs

You've seen how you can use lines to help locate objects and geometry in your drawing. But if you need to find distances along a curved object such as an arc, lines don't always help. The following exercise shows a way of finding exact distances on arcs. Try this exercise when you're not working through the main tutorial.

### Finding an Exact Distance along an Arc

To find an exact distance along an arc (nonlinear), do the following:

**TIP** You can also set the point style by setting the Pdmode system variable to 3.

1. Type **Ddptype** ↵ or choose Format ➤ Point Style to open the Point Style dialog box.

2. At the Point Style dialog box, click on the icon that looks like an *X*, in the top row. Also be sure the Set Size Relative to Screen radio button is selected. Then click on OK.

3. Click and drag Point from the Draw toolbar then select Measure.

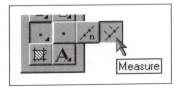

4. At the `Select object to measure` prompt, click on the arc near the end you want to measure from.

---

**TIP** The Block option of the Measure command allows you to specify a block to be inserted at the specified segment length, in place of the *X*s on the arc. You have the option of aligning the block with the arc as it is inserted. (This is similar to the polar array's Rotate Objects As They Are Copied option.)

---

5. At the `<Segment length>/Block` prompt, enter the distance you are interested in. A series of *X*s appears on the arc, marking off the specified distance along the arc. You can select the exact location of the *X*s using the Node Osnap override (Figure 5.25).

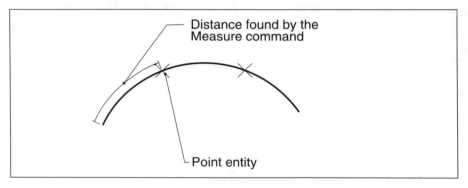

Distance found by the Measure command

Point entity

*Figure 5.25:* **Finding an exact distance along an arc using points and the Measure command**

The Measure command also works on Bezier curves. You'll get a more detailed look at the Measure command in *Chapter 13*.

As you work with AutoCAD LT, you'll find that creating temporary geometry such as the circle and points in the two foregoing examples will help you solve problems in new ways. Don't hesitate to experiment! Remember, you've always got the Save and U commands to help you recover from mistakes.

## Changing the Length of Objects

Suppose, after finding the length of an arc, you realize you need to lengthen the arc by a specific amount. The Lengthen command on the Resize flyout on the Modify toolbar lets you lengthen or shorten arcs, lines, splines, and elliptical arcs. Here's how to lengthen an arc:

1. Click and drag Stretch on the Modify toolbar, and then select Lengthen from the Resize flyout.

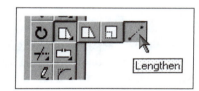

2. At the `DElta/Percent/Total/DYnamic/<Select object>:` prompt, type **T** ⤶.

3. At the `Angle/<Enter total length (1.0000)>:` prompt, enter the length you want for the arc.

4. At the `<Select object to change>/Undo:` prompt, click on the arc you wish to change. Be sure to click at a point nearest the end you want to lengthen. The arc increases in length to the size you specified.

Modify ➤ Lengthen will also shorten an object if it is currently longer than the value you enter.

In this short example, we have demonstrated how to change an object to a specific length. You can use other criteria to change an object's length, using these options available in the Lengthen command:

**DElta**  lets you lengthen or shorten an object by a specific length. To specify an angle rather than a length, use the Angle sub-option.

**Percent**  is for increasing or decreasing the length of an object by a percentage of its current length.

**Total**  lets you specify the total length or angle of an object.

**DYnamic**  lets you graphically change the length of an object using your cursor.

## Creating a New Drawing Using Parts from Another Drawing

In this section you will use the Wblock command (which you learned in *Chapter 4*) to create a separate stair drawing using the stair you've already drawn for the lobby. Later, in *Chapter 6*, you will use this new stair drawing for a fire escape. Although you haven't turned the existing stair into a block, you can still use Wblock to turn parts of a drawing into a file.

1. Click on File ➤ Export....

2. When the Export Data File dialog box appears, enter **Stair.dwg** in the filename input box and click on OK. You must include the .DWG filename extension to let AutoCAD LT know that you want to export to a drawing file and not some other format such as a .DXF or .WMF format file.

3. At the Block name prompt, press ↵. This tells AutoCAD LT that you want to create a file from part of the drawing, rather than a block.

4. At the Insertion base point: prompt, pick the lower-right corner of the stair shaft, at coordinate 28′-10″, 17′-7″. This tells AutoCAD LT the base point for the new drawing.

5. At the Select objects prompt, use a window to select the stair shaft, as shown in Figure 5.26.

6. When the stair shaft, including the door, is highlighted, press ↵ to confirm your selection. The stair disappears.

7. Since you want the stair to remain in the lobby drawing, use the Oops command to bring it back.

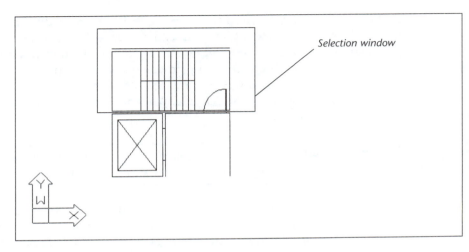

*Figure 5.26:* **A selection window enclosing the stair shaft**

## Eliminating Unused Objects from a Drawing

A template—or any drawing—may contain blocks, layers, linetypes, shapes, text styles, and dimension styles that you don't need in your new file. For example, the lobby you just completed contains the bathroom block because you used the Unit file as a basis. Even though you erased this block, it remains in the drawing file's database. It is considered "unused" because it doesn't appear as part of the drawing. Such extra blocks can slow you down by increasing the amount of time needed to open the file. They will also increase the size of your file unnecessarily. There are two commands for eliminating unused elements from a drawing: Purge and Wblock.

### Selectively Removing Unused Objects

The Purge command (Format ➤ Purge) is used to remove unused individual blocks, layers, linetypes, shapes, text styles, and dimension styles from a drawing file. You will want to purge your drawing of unused blocks, to help keep the file size down and to make layer maintenance easier.

As you will see in the Format ➤ Purge cascading menu and the Purge command window, you can purge other unused drawing elements, such as linetypes and layers, as well. Bear in mind, however, that Purge will not delete certain primary drawing elements—namely, layer 0, the Continuous linetype, and the standard text style. Unlike in previous versions of AutoCAD LT, you can now Purge at any time during your edit session.

NOTE External reference files do not have to be purged because they never actually become part of the drawing's database.

1.  Click on the Open icon and open the Lobby file. (Remember, you saved this file to disk, so now you are simultaneously closing the file and reopening the saved version.) If you did not create the Lobby file, use the drawing on the companion CD.

2.  Click on Format ➤ Purge ➤ Blocks.

3.  At the Purge block BATH? <N> prompt, enter **Y** ↵. The Purge block prompt will repeat for each unused block in the file. Continue to enter **Y** ↵ to all the prompts until the Purge command is completed.

4.  Use Save to save the file to disk.

    The Lobby file is now purged of most, but not all, of the unused blocks. Purge does not remove nested blocks on its first pass. For example, although you purged the Bath block from the Lobby file, it still contains the Tub and Toilet blocks that were nested in the Bath block. To remove them using Purge, you must start the command again and remove the nested blocks. For this reason, Purge can be a time-consuming way to delete large numbers of elements.

## If You Want to Experiment...

Try using the techniques you learned in this chapter to create new files. Use the files you created in *Chapter 4* as templates to create the symbols shown in Figure 5.27.

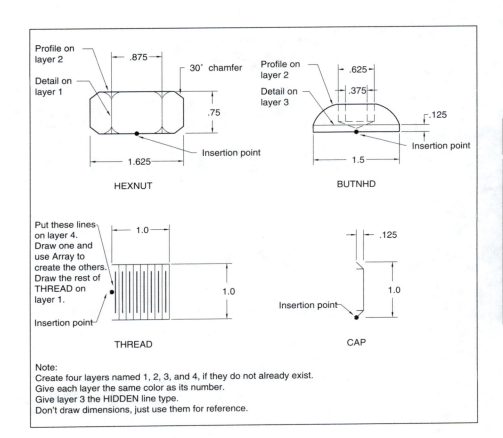

Figure 5.27: **Mechanical symbols**

# Chapter 6

# Enhancing Your Drawing Skills

## *FAST TRACKS*

**N**OW that you have created drawings of a typical apartment unit, and the apartment house's lobby and stairs, you can assemble them to complete the first floor of the apartment house. In this chapter, you will take full advantage of AutoCAD LT's features to enhance your drawing skills, as well as to reduce the time it takes for you to create accurate drawings.

As your drawing becomes larger, you will find that you need to use the Zoom and Pan commands more often. Larger drawings also require some special editing techniques. You will learn how to assemble drawings in ways that will save time and effort as your design progresses. Along the way, you'll see how you can enhance the appearance of your drawings by adding hatch patterns.

## Assembling the Parts

Start by creating a new file for the first floor, and inserting and copying the unit file.

1. Open a new file, which you will save as **Plan**, to contain the drawing of the apartment house's first floor. This is the file that you will use to assemble the unit plans into an apartment building.

2. Set up the drawing with Architectural units, using a ⅛″=1′-0″ scale on an 18″×24″ drawing area. Refer to Table 3.2 to determine the limits of your drawing area.

3. Create a layer called **Plan1** and make it the current layer.

4. Set the grid display to 5′.

5.  Insert the Unit.DWG drawing at coordinate 31´-5˝, 43´-8˝. Type **31´5˝, 43´8˝**. Accept the default values at all the prompts, since you want to insert this drawing just as you drew it.

6.  Click on the Zoom Extents button on the Zoom flyout to bring the apartment unit plan into view.

7.  Draw a line from the upper-right corner of the unit's interior, from coordinate 45´-5˝, 72´-1˝, to a point 2.5˝ to the right.

8.  Use the endpoint of the new 2.5˝ line to mirror the unit plan to the right. You will thus get a 5˝ wall thickness between studio units. Keep the original unit plan in place. Your drawing should look like Figure 6.1.

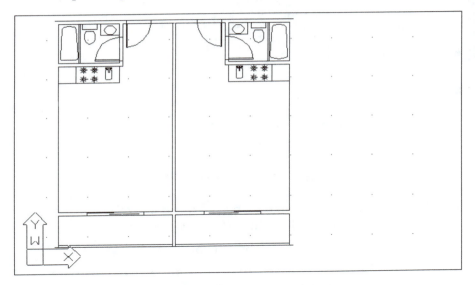

*Figure 6.1:* **The unit plan mirrored**

9.  Now erase the short line you used as a mirror reference, and draw another line vertically upwards from the same corner a distance of 24˝.

10. Use the endpoint of the 24˝ line to mirror the two unit plans on a horizontal axis.

NOTE The Extents option forces the entire drawing to fill the screen at the leftmost side of the display area.

11. Click on Zoom Extents again to get a view of the four plans. Your drawing will look like Figure 6.2.

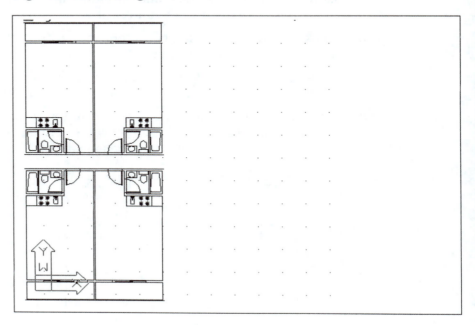

Figure 6.2:   *The unit plan, duplicated four times*

12. Erase the reference line, and copy the four units horizontally a distance of 28′-11″, the width of two units.

13. Insert the lobby at coordinate 89′-1″, 76′-1″.

14. Copy, or Mirror, all the unit plans to the right 74′-5″, the width of four units plus the width of the lobby.

15. Click on the Zoom All button on the Zoom toolbar ("Zoom All") to view the entire drawing, which will look like Figure 6.3.

 **NOTE** From this point on, we will use the name "Zoom All" to refer to this toolbar option.

16. Now use the Save option to save this file to disk.

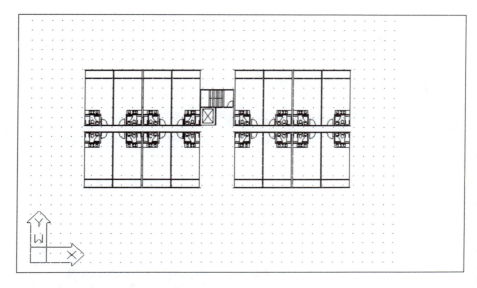

*Figure 6.3:* **The Plan drawing**

# Navigating Your Drawing Area

In the previous chapters we have used the Pan and Zoom options for moving around drawings. Now lets take a look at a tool that lets you navigate the drawing area. It's called the Aerial View.

## Using the Aerial View

1. Click on Aerial View on the Standard Toolbar. The Aerial View window appears, as shown in Figure 6.4.

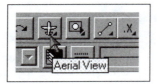

2. Move your cursor over to the Aerial View window. Notice that you have a dotted cross hair cursor in the window. This is the Aerial View zoom cursor.

> **TIP** The View ➤ Zoom ➤ Dynamic option performs a similar function to the Aerial View Window, but instead of opening a separate window, Dynamic temporarily displays the overall view in the drawing area.

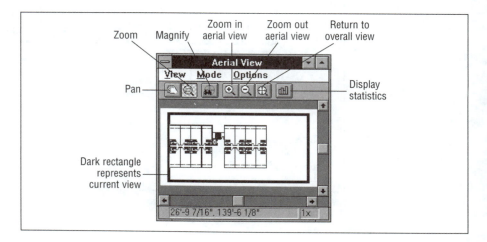

*Figure 6.4:* **The Aerial View window and its components**

**3.** Click on a point below and to the left of the apartment plan. A view window appears.

**4.** Click on a point above and to the right of the first unit in the lower left corner so the view window encloses the unit. Your view in the Drawing area enlarges to display the area you just selected. You also see a bold rectangle in the Aerial View window showing the location of your drawing area view.

The Aerial View doesn't zoom in. It continues to display the overall view of your drawing. The bold rectangle shows you exactly where you are in the overall drawing at any given time. This feature is especially useful when you need to zoom in close to a part of a drawing.

Now let's look at the Pan feature on the Aerial View toolbar. The Pan feature can be helpful if you are moving or copying objects from one part of a drawing to another.

**1.** Click on the Pan button on the Aerial View toolbar, or select Mode ➤ Pan from the Aerial View menu bar. Now as you move your cursor over the Aerial View window, you see a dotted rectangle. This lets you pan to any location in the view.

2. Move the dotted rectangle so it encloses the set of units above the ones currently being displayed in the drawing area. Click the mouse button. Your view immediately pans to that area.

Once again, the view in the Aerial View window doesn't change during the pan allowing you to visualize where you are in the overall drawing.

Now let's look at the magnified view feature: Locator Magnification. This feature lets you search for detail in your drawing, much as you would using a magnifying lens on a map.

 **NOTE** When the Locator Magnification feature is activated, the view in the Aerial View window shows an enlarged view of the area in that rectangle. As you move the rectangle in the drawing area, the Aerial View windows changes dynamically, like a magnifying glass passing over the drawing area.

1. Click and drag the Locate button that looks like a pair of binoculars, then drag your mouse into the drawing area. Notice that you now have a gray rectangle that follows the motion of your mouse.

2. Place the rectangle over a bathroom in one of the units, and then let go of the mouse button. Your drawing zooms into the bathroom area.

The Aerial View window is a great tool when you are working on a drawing that requires a lot magnification in your zoomed-in views. You may not find it very helpful on drawings that don't require lots of magnification, like the bathroom drawing you worked on in *Chapters 3* and *4*.

You were able to use the major features of the Aerial view in this exercise. Here are a few more features you can try on your own:

**Zoom In button**    zooms in on the view in the Aerial View window.

**Zoom Out button**    zooms out on the view in the Aerial View window.

**Global button**    displays an overall view of your drawing in the Aerial View window. Global is like a View ➤ Zoom ➤ Extents option for the Aerial View.

**Options ➤ Auto Viewport**    controls whether a selected viewport is automatically displayed in the Aerial View window. When checked, this option will cause the Aerial View window to automatically display the contents of a viewport when it becomes active. (See *Chapter 12* for more on viewports.)

**Options ➤ Dynamic Update**   controls how often changes in your drawing are updated in the Aerial View. When this option is checked, the Aerial View window is updated as you work. You may want to turn this feature off in very complex drawing as it can slow down redraw times.

**Options ➤ Locator Magnification...**   brings up a dialog box that lets you control the magnification of the Spyglass feature. A higher number increases magnification.

**Options ➤ Display Statistics... button**   displays WHIP display driver statistics.

## Saving Views

Now let's look at another way of navigating the drawing area, via saved views. A few walls in the Plan drawing are not complete. You'll need to zoom in to the areas that need work to add the lines, but these areas are spread out over the drawing. You could use the Aerial View window to view each area. There is, however, another way to edit widely separated areas: First, save views of the areas you want to work on, and then jump from saved view to saved view. This technique is especially helpful when you know you will often want to return to a specific area of your drawing.

**TIP**  A Saved View stores the location and scale of a viewport. This can be very useful when setting up a window for plotting.

1. First close the Aerial View window by clicking on the Close button in the upper-left corner of the window.

2. Click on Zoom All to get an overall view of the plan.

### OPENING A FILE TO A PARTICULAR VIEW

The Open Drawing dialog box contains a Select Initial View check box. If you open an existing drawing with this option checked, you are greeted with a Select Initial View dialog box just before the opened file appears on the screen. This dialog box lists any views saved in the file. You can then go directly to a view by double-clicking on the view name. If you have saved views and you know the name of the view you want, using Select Initial View saves time when you're opening very large files.

3. Click on Named Views... on the View flyout on the Standard toolbar. The View Control dialog box appears.

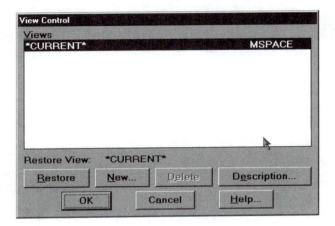

 **NOTE** From this dialog box, you can call up an existing view (Restore), create a new view (New...) or get detailed information about a view (Description...).

4. Click on the New... button. The Define New View dialog box appears.

5. Click on the Define Window radio button. Notice that the grayed options become available.

6. Click on Window <. The dialog boxes momentarily disappear.

7. At the First corner prompt, enter the coordinate **26´-3, 40´-1**.

8. At the Other corner prompt, enter the coordinate **91´-2, 82´-8**. The dialog boxes reappear.

9. In the New Name input box, type **First** for the name of the view you just defined.

10. Click on the Save View button. The Define New View dialog box closes, and you see FIRST listed in the View Control list.

11. Repeat steps 3 through 9 to define five more views, named SECOND, THIRD, etc. Use Figure 6.5 as a guide for where to define the windows. Click on OK when you are done.

Now let's see how you recall these views that you've saved.

1. With the View Control dialog box open, click on FIRST in the list of views.

2. Click the Restore button and then click OK. Your screen displays the first view you selected.

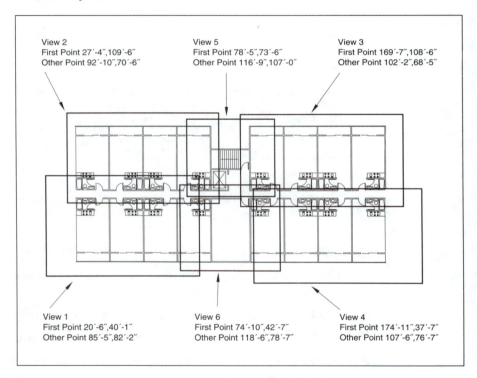

View 2
First Point 27'-4",109'-6"
Other Point 92'-10",70'-6"

View 5
First Point 78'-5",73'-6"
Other Point 116'-9",107'-0"

View 3
First Point 169'-7",108'-6"
Other Point 102'-2",68'-5"

View 1
First Point 20'-6",40'-1"
Other Point 85'-5",82'-2"

View 6
First Point 74'-10",42'-7"
Other Point 118'-6",78'-7"

View 4
First Point 174'-11",37'-7"
Other Point 107'-6",76'-7"

*Figure 6.5:* **Save view windows in these locations for the Plan drawing.**

3. Set the current layer to Wall, and proceed to add the stairs and exterior walls of the building, as shown in Figure 6.6.

4. Use the View Control dialog box again to restore the view named SECOND. Then add the exterior wall indicated in Figure 6.7.

5. Continue to the other views and add the rest of the exterior walls, as you have done with FIRST and SECOND. Use the three panels of Figure 6.8 as a guide to completing the views.

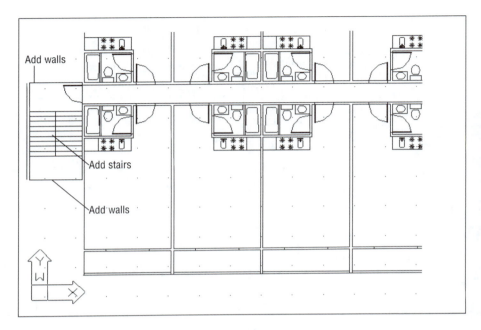

*Figure 6.6:* **The stairs and exterior walls added to the restored FIRST view**

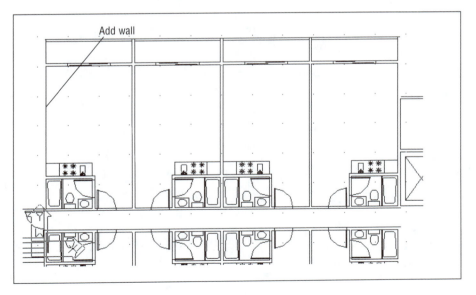

*Figure 6.7:* **An exterior wall added to the restored SECOND view**

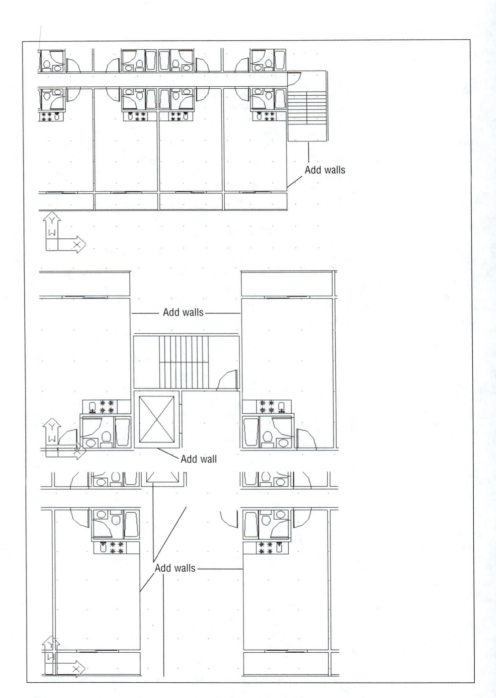

*Figure 6.8:* **The rest of the exterior walls added to the other views**

If you prefer, you can use the keyboard to invoke the View command and thus avoid all the dialog boxes.

1. Click on Zoom All.

2. Enter **View** ↵ at the command prompt.

3. At the View name to save prompt, enter **Overall** ↵.

4. Now save the Plan file to disk.

   As you can see, this is a quick way to save a view. With the name OVERALL assigned to this view, you can easily recall the overall view at any time.

Part
2

## ZOOMING AND PANNING DURING OTHER COMMANDS

At times you may want to perform a task that requires you to pan beyond the current view while you're in the middle of another command. For example, suppose you have the view named FIRST on screen and you want to draw a line from the lower-left corner of the building to the upper-right corner. You can start Draw ➤ Line, pick the starting point of the line, and then click on View ➤ Pan ➤ Point, and pan your view so that the upper-right corner of the building appears on the screen. Once the view appears, the Line command automatically continues and you can pick the other corner. Likewise, you can use the Aerial View window to zoom or pan over your drawing while in the middle of another command.

Commands that can be used in the middle of other commands are called *transparent commands*. A handful of standard AutoCAD LT commands, as well as all the system variables, are accessible as transparent commands. To use a command *transparently*, type an apostrophe immediately before the command. For example, at the command line type **'Grid** ↵, to turn on the grid in the middle of another command.

## Freezing Layers to Control Regeneration Time

As mentioned earlier, you may turn certain layers off altogether to plot a drawing containing only selected layers. But even when layers are turned off, AutoCAD LT still takes the time to redraw and regenerate them. The Layer command's Freeze option acts like the Off option, except that Freeze causes AutoCAD LT to ignore frozen layers when redrawing and regenerating a drawing. By freezing layers that are not needed for reference or editing, you can speed up redrawing time. But Freeze also affects blocks in a way that Off does not. Try this:

1. Using the Layer Control drop-down list box, set the current layer to 0. Press the down arrow to open the list box and then click on layer 0 to set it as the current layer.

2. Turn off the Plan1 layer. Nothing happens, because none of the objects were drawn on that layer.

3. Open the Layer Control list box again. Then choose the Plan1 layer from the list and click on Freeze. (Note that you cannot freeze the current layer.)

4. Click on OK. Every block you inserted disappears.

Even though none of the objects within the inserted blocks were drawn on layer Plan1, when Plan1 is frozen, so are the blocks assigned to that layer.

 **TIP** You can freeze and thaw individual layers by clicking on the Sun icon in the layer pop-up list in the Properties toolbar.

With respect to the Freeze option, External Reference files inserted using the Xref command also act like blocks. For example, you can Xref several drawings to different layers. Then, when you want to view a particular Xref drawing, you can freeze all the layers except the one containing that drawing.

 **NOTE** For more on External References vs. inserting, see "External Reference Drawings" later in this chapter.

Another technique is to use individual layers to store parts of a drawing that you may want to plot separately. For example, three floors in your apartment house plan may contain the same information, with some specific variation on each floor. You can have one layer contain blocks of the objects common to all the floors. Another layer might contain the blocks and objects specific to the first floor, and additional layers contain information specific to the second and third floors. When you want to view or plot one floor, you can freeze the layers associated with the others. You will practice this technique in *Chapter 12*.

Using layers and blocks in these ways requires careful planning and record keeping. If used successfully, however, layer-freezing techniques can save substantial time when you're working with drawings that use repetitive objects or that require similar information that can be overlaid.

Now "thaw" layer Plan1 that you froze earlier, turn off the Ceiling layer, and use File ➤ Exit to exit the Plan file.

# Understanding Model Space and Paper Space

So far, you've looked at ways to help you get around in your drawing by using saved views. You also have the capability to set up multiple views of your drawing, called *viewports*. Viewports are accessed by using two modes of display: *Paper Space* and *Model Space*.

To get a clear understanding of these two modes, imagine that your drawing is actually a full-size replica or model of the object you are drawing. Your computer screen is your window into a "room" where this model is being constructed, and the keyboard and mouse are your means of access to this room. You can control your window's position in relation to the object through the use of the Pan and Zoom commands. You can also construct or modify the model by using drawing and editing commands. This room is your *Model Space*.

So far, you have been working on your drawings by looking through a single "window." Now suppose you have the ability to step back and add windows with different views looking into your Model Space. The effect is as if you have several video cameras in your Model Space "room," each connected to a different monitor: You can view all your windows at once on your computer screen, or enlarge a single window to fill the entire screen. Additionally, you can control the shape of your windows and easily switch from one window to another. This is what *Paper Space* is like.

Paper Space lets you set up several views into your drawing Model Space. Each view acts like an individual screen. One window can have an overall view of your drawing, while another can be a close-up. Layer visibility can also be controlled individually for each window, allowing you to display different versions of the same area of your drawing. You can move, copy, and stretch viewports, and even overlap them, just as you do objects.

If you draw something in Paper Space, it doesn't become part of Model Space, but it can be plotted. This is significant because, as you will see in *Chapter 12*, Paper Space lets you plot several views of the same drawing on one sheet of paper. You can even include drawing borders and notes that appear only in Paper Space. In this function, you might think of Paper Space as a kind of page-layout area where you can "paste up" different views of your drawing. Figure 6.9 shows the Plan drawing set up in Paper Space mode to display several views.

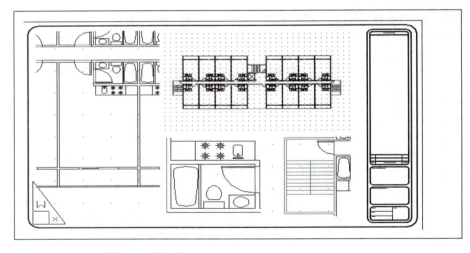

*Figure 6.9:    Different views of the same drawing in Paper Space*

We will discuss using Paper Space in more detail in *Chapter 12*. For now, let's continue with our look at working with large drawings.

**NOTE** In Model Space, you can use Vports to split your screen into several viewports, which can neither be plotted nor shaped and controlled individually the way Paper Space viewports can. See *Chapter 16* for details. The Vports command (View ➤ Tiled Viewports) only works in Model Space.

# Adding Hatch Patterns to Your Drawings

To help communicate your ideas to others, you will want to add special graphic elements that represent different types of materials, specific regions, or textures. AutoCAD LT provides *hatch patterns* for quickly placing a texture over an area of your drawing. In this section, you will add a hatch pattern to the floor of the studio apartment unit, thereby instantly enhancing the appearance of one drawing. Then later in the chapter you'll learn how you can quickly update all the units in the overall floor plan to reflect the changes in the unit.

### Setting Up for the Hatch

The first step is to provide a layer for the hatch pattern.

1. Open the Unit file and zoom into the bathroom and kitchenette area.

2. Create a new layer called **Flr-pat**.

3. Make Flr-pat the current layer.

### Defining the Hatch

1. Click on the Hatch button on the Draw Toolbar or type **Bhatch** ↵.

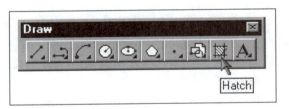

The Boundary Hatch dialog box appears.

**NOTE** The Boundary Hatch dialog box lets you set the hatch pattern (Pattern Type and Pattern Properties), pick a point that is bounded by the area to be hatched (Pick Points), select objects to define the hatch area (Select Objects), and use advanced boundary selection options for complex hatch patterns (Advanced...). Other options let you preview the hatch pattern in place (Preview Hatch), or view the hatch boundaries (View Selections).

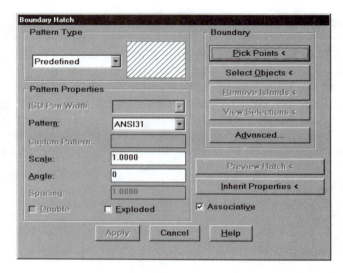

2. Under Pattern Type, open the pop-up list and select User-Defined. The User-Defined option lets you define a simple crosshatch pattern by specifying the line spacing of the hatch and whether it is a single- or double-hatch pattern. The Angle and Spacing input boxes become available in the Pattern Properties group, so you can enter values.

3. Double-click on the Spacing input box and enter **6**. This tells AutoCAD LT you want the hatch's line spacing to be 6″. Leave the Angle value at 0, since we want the pattern to be aligned with the bathroom walls.

4. Click on the Double check box (at the bottom of the Pattern Properties group). This tells AutoCAD LT you want the hatch pattern to run both vertically and horizontally.

5. Click on the Pick Points button. The dialog box momentarily disappears, allowing you to pick a point inside the area you want hatched.

6. Click on a point anywhere inside the bathroom floor area, away from the toilet. Notice that a highlighted outline appears in the bathroom. This is the boundary AutoCAD LT has selected to enclose the hatch pattern. It outlines everything including the door swing arc. Press ↵.

7. Click on the Preview Hatch button. The hatch pattern appears everywhere on the floor except where the door swing occurs. When the Boundary Hatch dialog box pops up, press the Continue button.

8. Click on Pick Points again, pick a point inside the door swing, and press ↵.

9. Click on Preview Hatch again. The hatch pattern now covers the entire floor area. When the Boundary Hatch dialog box pops up, press the Continue button.

10. Click on the Apply button to place the hatch pattern in the drawing.

Hatch lets you first define the boundary within which you want to place a hatch pattern. You do this by simply clicking on a location inside the boundary area, as in step 6. AutoCAD LT finds the actual boundary for you.

> **TIP**  Say you want to add a hatch pattern you have previously inserted. You may think that you have to guess at its scale and rotation angle. But with the Inherit Properties option in the Boundary Hatch dialog box, you can select a previously inserted hatch pattern as a prototype for the current hatch pattern. This feature does not work with Exploded hatch patterns however.

## Using the Advanced Hatch Options

You might have noticed that the toilet was automatically included as part of the boundary set for the hatch pattern. Think of the toilet as a "nested" boundary area to be excluded from hatching. You can control how AutoCAD LT treats these nested boundaries by selecting options available with the Advanced… button in the Boundary Hatch dialog box. This button displays the Advanced Options dialog:

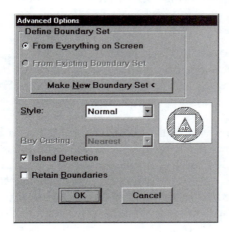

In addition to controlling the nesting of hatch patterns, the Advanced Options let you fine-tune other aspects of hatch pattern creation.

*Style*    The Style pop-up list in the middle of the dialog box controls how nested boundaries affect the hatch pattern. When you select a Style option, the graphic to the right of the pop-up list shows an example of the effect of the selected option. The Style options include the following:

**Normal**    causes the hatch pattern to alternate between nested boundaries. The outer boundary is hatched; then, if there is a closed object within the boundary, it is not hatched. If there is yet another closed object inside the *first* closed object, *that* object is hatched. This is the default setting.

**Outer**    applies the hatch pattern to an area defined by the outermost boundary and any boundaries nested within the outermost boundary. Any boundaries nested within the nested boundaries are ignored.

**Ignore**    applies the hatch pattern to the entire area within the outermost boundary, ignoring any nested boundaries.

NOTE Hatch patterns are like blocks, in that they act like single objects. You can explode a hatch pattern to edit its individual lines. You can also automatically explode the hatch after it is placed in the drawing, by selecting the Exploded check box in the Pattern Properties group of the Boundary Hatch dialog box.

**Make New Boundary Set button**    lets you select the objects from which you want AutoCAD LT to determine the hatch boundary. The screen clears and lets you select objects. This option discards previous boundary sets.

*Ray Casting*    This is a pull-down list that lets you control how Auto-CAD LT searches for a boundary when Island Detection (described next) is not used. The options are Nearest (the default), –X, +X, –Y, and +Y. With Nearest selected, AutoCAD LT searches for a boundary by starting with the object nearest to the point you pick when you use the Pick Points button in the Boundary Hatch dialog box. The –X and –Y options cause AutoCAD LT to search in negative X or negative Y direction for the first object in the boundary. The +X and +Y options cause AutoCAD LT to search in a positive X or positive Y direction.

*Island Detection*    This check box controls the Island Detection feature, a new method of finding boundaries used by AutoCAD LT Release 3. It is capable of finding nested areas and islands more easily than the older Ray Casting method.

*Retain Boundaries*    The Boundary Hatch command works by creating temporary polyline outlines of the hatch area. These polyline boundaries are automatically removed after the hatch pattern is inserted. If you want to retain the polyline boundaries in the drawing, make sure the Retain Boundaries check box is turned on. Retaining the boundaries can be useful if you want to know the hatched area's dimensions in square inches or feet. This option is available only if a boundary is already defined.

## Things to Watch Out For While Using Boundary Hatch

Here are a few tips on using the Boundary Hatch feature:

▶ Watch out for boundary areas that are part of a very large block. AutoCAD LT will examine the entire block when defining boundaries. This can take time if the block is quite large.

▶ The Boundary Hatch feature is view dependent; that is, it locates boundaries based on what is visible in the current view. To ensure that AutoCAD LT finds every detail, zoom in to the area to be hatched.

▶ If the area to be hatched will cover a very large area yet will require fine detail, first outline the hatch area using a polyline (see *Chapter 13* for more on Polylines). Then use the Select Object option in the Boundary Hatch dialog box to select the polyline boundary manually, instead of depending on Boundary Hatch to find the boundary for you.

▶ Consider turning off layers that might interfere with AutoCAD LT's ability to find a boundary. For example, in the previous exercise, you could have turned off the Door layer, and then used Pick Points to locate the boundary of the hatch pattern.

▶ Boundary Hatch works on nested blocks as long as the nested blocks are parallel to the current UCS.

## *Positioning Hatch Patterns Accurately*

In the last exercise, the hatch pattern was placed in the bathroom without regard for the location of the lines that make up the pattern. In most cases, however, you will want to control where the lines of the pattern are placed.

Hatch patterns use the same origin as the snap origin. By default, this origin is the same as the drawing origin, 0,0. You can change the snap origin (and thus the hatch pattern origin) by using the Snapbase system variable. The following exercise guides you through the process of placing a hatch pattern accurately, using the example of adding floor tile to the kitchenette.

1. Pan your view so that you can see the area below the kitchenette, and draw the 3'-0"×8'-0" rectangular outline of the floor tile area, as shown in Figure 6.10.

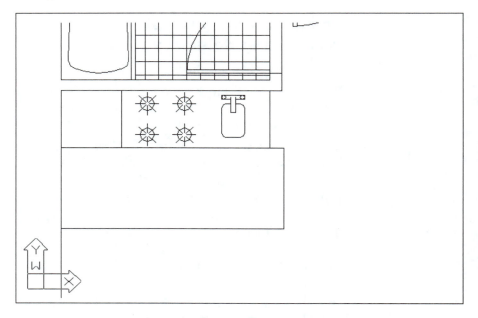

*Figure 6.10:* **The area below the kitchenette showing the outline of the floor tile area**

2. At the command line, type **Snapbase** ↵.

3. At the New value for SNAPBASE <0′-0″,0′-0″>: prompt, use the Endpoint Osnap override and click on the lower-left corner of the area you just defined (see Figure 6.10).

4. Click on the Hatch button on the Draw toolbar.

5. At the Boundary Hatch dialog box, make sure Predefined is selected in the Pattern Type pull-down list.

6. In the Pattern Properties group, open the Pattern pull-down list and select AR-PARQ1. The graphic to the right of the Pattern Type list box changes to show what AR-PARQ1 looks like.

---

**TIP**   You can also click on Hatch Pattern graphic icon in the Pattern Type list to "page" through each of the predefined hatch patterns.

---

7. Click on the Pick Points button.

8. Click on the interior of the area to be tiled, and press ↵. This will return you to the dialog box.

9. Make sure that the Associative check box is checked, and then click on Apply. A parquet-style tile pattern appears in the defined area.

Notice that each tile is shown whole; none of the tiles is cut off as in the bathroom example. This is because you first used the Snapbase system variable to set the origin for the hatch pattern. You can now move the Snapbase setting back to the 0,0 setting and not affect the hatch pattern.

In the foregoing exercise, you got a chance to use a predefined hatch pattern. Figure 6.11 shows you all the patterns available. You can also create your own custom patterns, as described in *Chapter 17*.

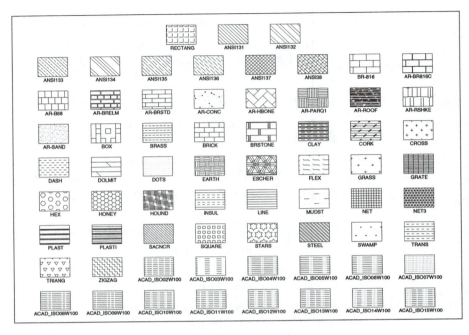

*Figure 6.11:　Predefined hatch patterns available in AutoCAD LT*

### Changing the Hatch Area

Suppose you want to enlarge the tiled area of the kitchenette by one tile. Here's how it's done.

1. Click on the outline border of the hatch pattern you just created. Notice the grips that appear around the hatch pattern area.

2. Shift-click on the grip in the lower-left corner of the hatch area.

3. With the lower-left grip highlighted, Shift-click on the lower-right grip.

4. Now click on the lower-left grip again, but don't Shift-click this time. Move the mouse and notice how the hatch boundary moves with it.

5. At the <Stretch to point>/Basepoint/Copy/Undo/eXit prompt, enter **@12<–90** to widen the hatch pattern by 1 foot. The hatch pattern adjusts to the new size of the hatch boundary.

## Modifying a Hatch Pattern

Like everything else, you or someone involved in your project will eventually want to change a hatch pattern in some way. In previous versions of AutoCAD LT, changing hatch patterns was a tedious process. Release 3 makes it a lot easier, as demonstrated in the following exercise.

1. Click and drag on the Special Edit flyout on the Modify toolbar, then select Edit Hatch, or type **Hatchedit** ↵ at the command prompt.

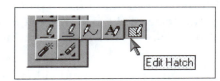

2. At the Select hatch object: prompt, click on the hatch pattern area. The Boundary Hatch dialog box appears again. You can now select any option that is available (not grayed out) to modify the hatch pattern.

3. Choose Predefined from the Pattern Type list box; then click on the graphic beside the Pattern Type list box. Notice how it changes and how, as it changes, the name of the pattern in the Pattern Properties group changes with it, to identify the pattern.

4. Choose AR-BRSTD from the Pattern pop-up list in the Pattern Properties group. Click the Apply button to change the hatch pattern area to the new pattern.

5. We want to keep the old pattern in our drawing, so click on the Undo button on the Standard toolbar or type **U** ↵ to return to the previous hatch pattern.

As you saw in the last exercise, not all the Boundary Hatch options are available to you. Still, you can change the pattern to a predefined or custom pattern, or to one that exists in the drawing. You can also change the angle and scale of a pattern, as well as the origin. Remember, in order to change the hatch origin, you must set the snap origin before you use the Hatchedit command.

## A Review of Other Boundary Hatch Options

Before exiting this section, you might want to look over the descriptions of options in the Boundary Hatch dialog box that weren't discussed in the exercises.

**ISO Pen Width**   lets you select a pen width to associate with the ISO standard hatch patterns supplied with AutoCAD LT. The pen-width option is available only when an ISO hatch pattern has been selected from the Pattern list box. These pen widths are meaningful only when used with the ISO standard hatch patterns. When you set the ISO pen width, the scale of the pattern is adjusted accordingly. However, you must manually set the width of the actual plotter pen at plot time.

**Exploded**   draws the hatch pattern as individual objects, instead of an associative hatch pattern.

**Associative**   draws a hatch pattern that will automatically update whenever the boundary of the hatch pattern changes.

**Remove Islands**   allows you to remove nested or island boundaries that have been included when you pick a point to define a boundary. This is useful when you want to force a hatch pattern to fall inside an island that occurs in a boundary.

**View Selections**   lets you review the boundaries that have been selected at any given time during the Boundary Hatch process.

**Inherit Properties**   lets you designate a hatch pattern, scale, and angle by selecting an existing hatch pattern in your drawing. When you choose this option, the dialog box momentarily disappears so that you can select a pattern from your drawing. The properties of the selected pattern become the settings for the current boundary hatch session.

## Updating Blocks

As you progress through a design project, you make countless revisions. With traditional drafting methods, revising a drawing like our studio apartment floor plan takes a good deal of time. If the bathroom layout is changed, for example, you have to erase every occurrence of the bathroom and redraw it 16 times. With AutoCAD LT, on the other hand, revising this drawing can be a very quick operation. The studio unit you just modified can be updated throughout the overall plan drawing by replacing the current Unit block with the updated Unit file. AutoCAD LT automatically updates all occurrences of the block. In the following exercise, we show you how this is accomplished.

1. Start by opening the Plan file.

> **NOTE** You need not wait for a drawing to regenerate in order to edit it, so canceling this regeneration can save some time when you update blocks.

2. When the drawing begins to appear, press the Escape key to cancel the initial regeneration.

3. Click on Insert Block from the Draw Toolbar.

4. Click on the File button, and from the Select Drawing File dialog box, double-click on the Unit filename.

5. Click on OK. A warning message tells you that a block already exists with the same name as the file. You have the option to cancel the operation or redefine the block in the current drawing.

6. Click on Redefine.

7. At the `Insertion point` prompt, press Esc. You do this because you really don't want to insert a Unit plan into your drawing, but rather are just using the Insert feature to update an existing block.

8. Now zoom in to one of the units. You will see that the floor tile appears in the unit as you drew it in the Unit file (see Figure 6.12).

Part
2

Building on the Basics

WARNING   This method does not update exploded blocks. If you plan to use this method to update parts of a drawing, do not explode the blocks you plan to update. See "Updating and Modifying a Block" in *Chapter 4*.

Nested blocks must be updated independent of the parent block. For example, if you had modified the Toilet block while editing the Unit file, and then updated the Unit drawing in the Plan file, the old Toilet block would not have been updated. Even though the toilet is part of the Unit file, it is still a unique, independent block in the Plan file, and AutoCAD LT will not modify it unless specifically instructed to do so. In this situation, you must edit the original Toilet file, and then update it in both the Plan and Unit files.

## SUBSTITUTING BLOCKS

In the example under the section "Updating Blocks," you update a block in your Plan file using the File option in the Insert dialog box. In that exercise, the block name and the filename were the same. You can also *replace* a block with another block or file of a different name. Here's how to do this:

1. Type **Insert** ↵ at the command prompt.

2. At the Block name (or ?) <>: prompt, enter **unit=alternate** ↵ where **alternate** is the name of the replacing block or filename. You will get the message Block unit redefined, and if REGENAUTO is turned off, your drawing will regenerate.

3. At the Insertion point: prompt, press the Esc.

You can use this method of replacing blocks if you would like to see how changing one element of your project can change your design. You might, for example, draw three different apartment unit plans, each with a unique name. You could then generate and plot three apartment house designs in a fraction of the time it would take you to do it by hand.

Block substitution can also reduce a drawing's complexity and accelerate regenerations. To do this, you temporarily replace large, complex blocks with schematic versions of those blocks. For example, you might replace the Unit block in the Plan drawing with another drawing that contains just a single-line representation of the walls and bathroom fixtures. You would still have the wall lines for reference when inserting other symbols or adding mechanical or electrical information, but the drawing would regenerate much faster. When doing the final plot, you would reinsert the original Unit block showing every detail.

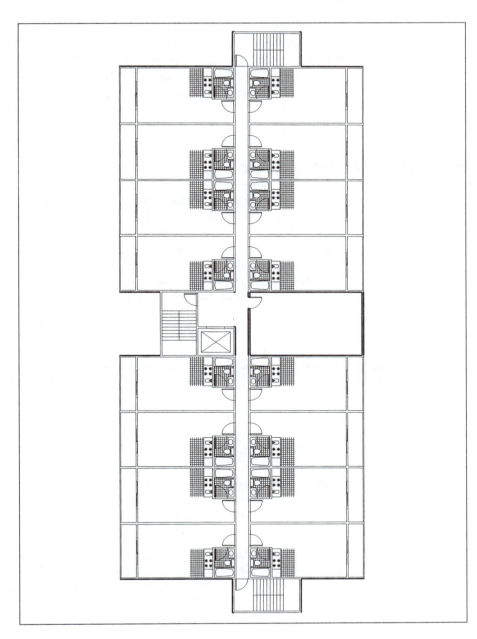

*Figure 6.12:* **The Plan drawing thus far**

Also, block references and layer settings of the current file take priority over those of the imported file. For example, if a file to be imported has layers of the same name as the current file, but those layers have color and line-type assignments that are different from the current file's, the current file's layer color and line-type assignments will determine those of the imported file. This does not mean, however, that the actual imported file on disk is changed; only the inserted drawing is affected.

## External Reference Drawings

In this chapter's discussion about freezing layers, we mentioned that you can use external reference (Xref) drawing files in a way similar to using blocks. To accomplish this, you use the Edit ➤ External Reference (Xref) command. The difference between these Xref files and files inserted with the Insert Block command is that Xref files do not actually become part of the drawing's database. Instead, they are "loaded" along with the current file at start-up time. It is as if AutoCAD LT were opening several drawings at once: the currently active file you specify when you start AutoCAD LT, and any file inserted with Xref.

> **NOTE** External Reference (Xref) files, like blocks, cannot be edited. You can, however, use Osnap overrides to snap to location in an Xref file, or freeze the Xref file's layer to make it invisible.

If you keep Xref files independent from the current file, any changes you make to the external reference will automatically appear in the current file. You don't have to manually update the Xref file as you do blocks. For example, if you used Xref to insert the Unit file into the Plan file, and you later made changes to the Unit file, the next time you opened the Plan file you would see the new version of the Unit file in place of the old.

Another advantage to external reference files is that since they do not actually become part of a drawing's database, drawing size is kept to a minimum. This translates to more efficient use of your hard disk space.

## Opening the External Reference Toolbar

The next exercise shows how you can use an external reference in place of an inserted block to construct the studio apartment building. You'll start by creating a new unit file by copying the old one. Then you bring a new toolbar, the External Reference toolbar, to the screen.

1. Open the the Unit file again and save a copy as **Unitxref.DWG**.

2. Open a new file called **Planxref**, and set up the drawing limits for a ⅛"=1′-0″ scale on an 11″×17″ drawing area.

3. Click on View ➤ Toolbars, click on the External Reference check box, and then press OK. This will load the External Reference toolbar. You can also click and drag the Aerial View icon on the standard toolbar then select External Reference. The new toolbar appears in the drawing area.

With the External Reference toolbar on the screen, you can access any of the External Reference functions with a single click.

## Attaching a Drawing as an External Reference

Now you're ready to do the actual attaching of a drawing.

NOTE Another way to attach a drawing is to enter **Xref** ↵ at the command prompt. The prompt response that you see contains the same options as those found on the External Reference toolbar. Since Attach is the default, option press ↵ to attach a file.

1. Click on Attach from the External Reference toolbar.

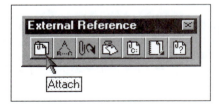

2. At the Select File to Attach dialog box, click on the file named Unitxref. You see the message Unitxref loaded in the prompt area.

3. At the `Insertion point:` prompt, insert the drawing at coordinate 31´-5″,43´-8″. The rest of the Xref command acts just like the Insert command. Press ↵ at all the prompts to accept the defaults.

4. Once the Unitxref file appears, make several copies of it in the same way you made copies of the Unit plan in the first part of this chapter.

5. Save the Planxref file. Then open Unitxref.

6. Erase the hatch pattern for the floors, and save the file.

7. Open Planxref again, and notice what happens to the Unitxref file you inserted using the External Reference command.

Here you saw how an external reference doesn't have to be updated the way blocks do. Also, you avoid the task of having to update nested blocks, since AutoCAD LT updates nested Xrefs, as well as Xrefs that are not nested.

### *Other Differences between Using External References and Inserting Files*

Here are a few other differences between xrefs and inserted files that you will want to keep in mind:

▶ Any new layers, text styles, or linetypes brought in with cross-referenced files do not become part of the current file. You must use the options on the Bind All flyout on the External Reference toolbar to import these items.

▶ If you make changes to the layers of an external reference file, those changes will not be retained when the file is saved, unless you set the Visretain system variable to 1. Visretain will then instruct AutoCAD LT to remember any layer color or visibility settings from one editing session to the next.

▶ To segregate layers on an external reference file from the ones in the current drawing, the Xref file's layers are prefixed with their file's name. A vertical bar separates the filename prefix and the layer name, as in Unitxref|wall.

**TIP**　You can convert a single Xref file into a block by typing Xref ↵ B ↵, then enter the name of the cross reference file to be converted.

▶ External Reference files cannot be exploded. You can, however, convert an Xref file into a block, and then explode it. To do this, you must use the Bind All option on the External Reference toolbar. This option converts all Xref files into blocks.

▶ If an External Reference file is renamed or moved to another location on your hard disk, AutoCAD LT won't be able to find that file when it opens other files to which the Xref is attached. If this happens, you must use the Path option on the External Reference toolbar to tell AutoCAD LT where to find the reference file.

External References are especially useful in workgroup environments where several people are working on the same project. For example, one person might be updating several files that are inserted into a variety of other files. Using blocks, everyone in the workgroup would have to be notified of the changes and would have to update all the affected blocks in all the drawings that contained them. With Xrefs, however, the updating is automatic, so you avoid confusion about which files need to have their blocks updated.

### *The External Reference Toolbar Options*

There are many other features unique to Xref files. Let's briefly look at some of the options under the External Reference toolbar we haven't yet discussed.

**Overlay**   attaches a file as an Xref without including any files that might be attached to the external reference. This avoids multiple attachments of other files and eliminates the possibility of circular references (referencing the current file into itself through another file).

**Reload**   lets you update an Xref file that has been modified since you opened your current file. This is useful when you are working in a network environment and you know that someone is concurrently editing an Xref file that you need.

**List**   displays a list of all the files attached to the current open file.

To aid in housekeeping, AutoCAD LT can maintain a log file that keeps a record of all your External Reference file activity. The log file is maintained only if the XREFCTL system variable is set to 1. The system default for this variable is 0. The name of the log file is the same as the drawing file it is associated with, except that the .XLG extension is used. This file stores a record of External Reference files and their associated blocks. AutoCAD LT creates this file automatically if it does not already exist. If it does exist, AutoCAD LT will append further records of Xref activity.

**TIP** External Reference log files can become quite large. If you find you are running out of disk storage space, you may want to delete any .XLG files you may accumulate as you work.

## If You Want to Experiment...

If you'd like to see firsthand how block substitution works, try doing the exercise in Figure 6.13. It shows how quickly you can change the configuration of a drawing by careful use of block substitution. As you work through the exercise, keep in mind that some planning is required to use blocks in this way. If you know that you will have to try various configurations in a drawing, you can plan to set up files to accommodate them.

You might also want to try the exercise using the External Reference toolbars Attach option in place of inserting files as blocks. Once you've attached the External Reference, try detaching it by using External Reference toolbar's Detach option. When you get the prompt <Xref(s) to Detach>, enter the name of the Xref.

By now, you may be anxious to see how your drawings look on paper. In the next chapter you will explore the use of AutoCAD LT's printing and plotting commands.

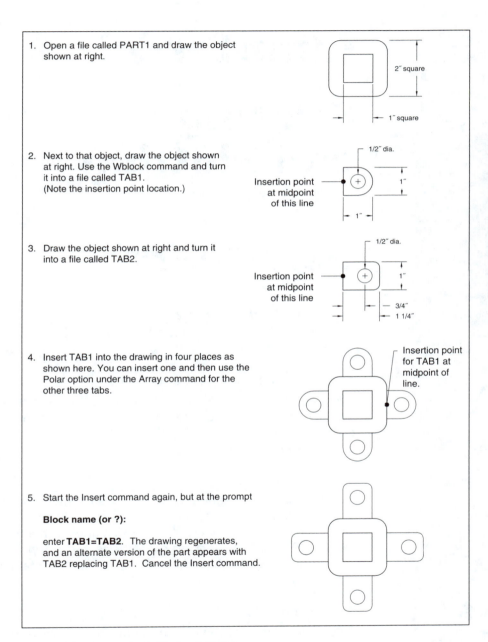

1. Open a file called PART1 and draw the object shown at right.

   2″ square

   1″ square

2. Next to that object, draw the object shown at right. Use the Wblock command and turn it into a file called TAB1. (Note the insertion point location.)

   1/2″ dia.

   Insertion point at midpoint of this line

   1″

   1″

3. Draw the object shown at right and turn it into a file called TAB2.

   1/2″ dia.

   Insertion point at midpoint of this line

   1″

   3/4″

   1 1/4″

4. Insert TAB1 into the drawing in four places as shown here. You can insert one and then use the Polar option under the Array command for the other three tabs.

   Insertion point for TAB1 at midpoint of line.

5. Start the Insert command again, but at the prompt

   **Block name (or ?):**

   enter **TAB1=TAB2**. The drawing regenerates, and an alternate version of the part appears with TAB2 replacing TAB1. Cancel the Insert command.

*Figure 6.13:* ***An exercise in block substitution***

# Chapter 7

# Printing and Plotting

## *Fast Tracks*

GETTING hard copy output from AutoCAD LT is something of an art. You'll need to be very familiar with both your output device and the settings available in AutoCAD LT. You will probably spend a good deal of time experimenting with AutoCAD LT's plotter settings and your printer or plotter to get your equipment set up just the way you want.

 **NOTE** For more information on choosing between printers and plotters, see *Appendix A.*

With the huge array of output options available, this chapter can only provide a general discussion of plotting. It is up to you to work out the details and fine-tune the way you and AutoCAD LT work together with your plotter. Here we'll take a look at the features available in AutoCAD LT and discuss some general rules and guidelines to follow when setting up your plots. We'll also discuss alternatives to using a plotter, such as plotter service bureaus and common dot-matrix printers. There won't be much in the way of a tutorial, so consider this chapter more of a reference.

## Plotting the Plan

To see firsthand how the Plot command works, try plotting the Plan drawing.

1. First, be sure your printer or plotter is connected to your computer and is turned on.

2. Start AutoCAD LT and open the Plan file.

3. Click on the Zoom All button on the Zoom flyout on the Standard toolbar to display the entire drawing.

4. Click on the Print button (Printer icon) on the Standard toolbar, or type **Plot** ↵ on the command line. The Plot Configuration dialog box appears.

**Plot Configuration**

Setup and Default Information
System Printer
[ Print/Plot Setup and Default Selection... ]

Pen Parameters
[ Pen Assignments... ]  [ Optimization... ]

Additional Parameters
- ⦿ Display      ☐ Hide Lines
- ○ Extents      ☐ Adjust Area Fill
- ○ Limits       ☐ Dithering
- ○ View         ☐ Use Previous Printer
- ○ Window       ☐ Plot To File

[ View... ]  [ Window... ]  [ File Name... ]

Paper Size and Orientation
- ⦿ Inches       [ Size... ]
- ○ MM

Plot Area 8.07 by 10.59.

Scale, Rotation, and Origin
[ Rotation and Origin... ]

Plotted Inches  =  Drawing Units
[ 8.07 ]  =  [ 18 ]
☑ Scaled to Fit

Plot Preview
[ Preview... ]   ⦿ Partial   ○ Full

[ OK ]   [ Cancel ]   [ Help... ]

5. Click on OK. The dialog box closes and you see the following message:

```
Command: PLOT Effective plotting area: 10.50 wide by
7.59 high
```

The width and height values shown in this message will depend on your system setup.

6. Your plotter or printer will print out the plan to no particular scale. You may see various messages while AutoCAD LT is plotting. When the plot is done, you see the message

```
Regeneration done 100% Plot complete.
```

You've just done your first printout. Now let's take a look at the wealth of settings available when you plot, starting with the selection of an output device.

## Selecting an Output Device

Many of you have more than one device for output. You may have a laser printer in addition to a plotter. You may also require PostScript file output for presentations. AutoCAD LT offers you the flexibility to use several types of devices quickly and easily.

When you install AutoCAD LT, any system printers which you have installed under Windows 95 will automatically become available to AutoCAD LT as output devices. The Windows 95 default system printer will also be the default for AutoCAD LT. You may, however, change the default for AutoCAD LT without changing the Windows 95 settings using the Print/Plot Setup and Default Selection button. The current default device is shown just above this button.

When you click this button, you will see the Print/Plot Setup and Default Selection dialog box with System Printer highlighted in the Select Device list box. You do not make your choice among the different System Printer options in this list box. Instead, click on the Print/Plot Setup... button in the lower-right corner of the dialog box. When the Print Setup dialog box opens, select the specific printer you require from the Printer Name drop-down list box. You may also change printing/plotting variables such as sheet size and orientation in this dialog box. Once you have set up your printer to match your current requirements, click on OK to return to the Print/Plot Setup and Default Selection dialog box.

AutoCAD LT will return to the default printer settings the next time you plot. If you want to continue to use the same (nondefault) printer settings the next time you plot, you may click on the Use Previous Printer option in the Additional Parameters group in this dialog box.

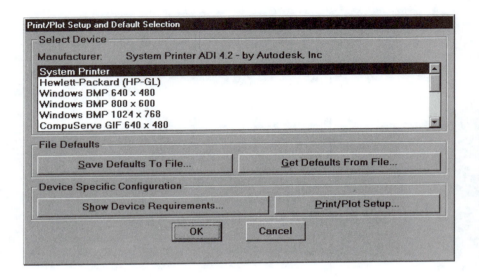

## Understanding Your Plotter's Limits

If you're familiar with a word processor or desktop publishing program, you know that you can set the margins of a page, thereby telling the program exactly how far from each edge of the paper you want the text to appear. With AutoCAD LT, you don't have that luxury. To accurately place a plot on your paper, you must know the plotter's *hard clip limits*. The hard clip limits are like built-in margins, beyond which the plotter will not plot. These limits vary from plotter to plotter (see Figure 7.1).

It is crucial that you know your printer/plotter's hard clip limits, in order to accurately place your drawings on the sheet. Take some time to study your plotter manual and find out exactly what these limits are. Then make a record of them and store it somewhere, in case you or someone else needs to format a sheet in a special way.

Hard clip limits for printers are often dependent on the software that drives them. You may need to consult your printer manual, or use the trial-and-error method of plotting several samples to see how they come out.

Once you've established the limits of your plotter or printer, you can begin to lay out your drawings to fit within those limits (see "Setting the Output's Origin and Rotation" later in this chapter). You can then establish some standard drawing limits based on your plotter's limits.

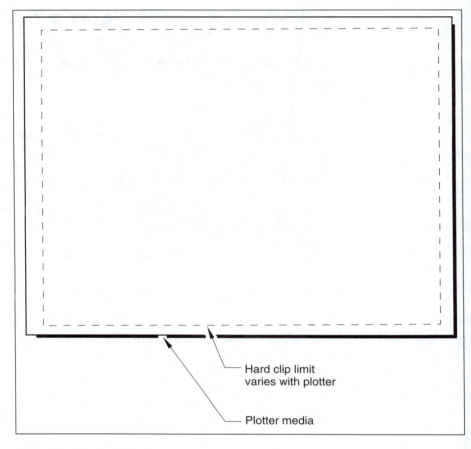

*Figure 7.1: **The hard clip limits of a plotter***

## Knowing Your Plotter's Origins

Another important consideration is the location of the origin on your plotter. For example, the Hewlett-Packard 7470 and 7475 use the lower-left corner of the plot area as the origin. Larger-format Hewlett-Packard plotters use the center of the plot area as the origin. When you plot a drawing that is too large to fit the sheet on a 7475 plotter, the image is pushed toward the top and to the right of the sheet (see Figure 7.2). When you plot a drawing that is too large to fit on an HP 7580 plotter, the image is pushed outward in all directions from the center of the sheet.

**NOTE** These origin placements also apply to plotter-emulation software that allows you to plot to a raster printer using, for example, the HPGL format.

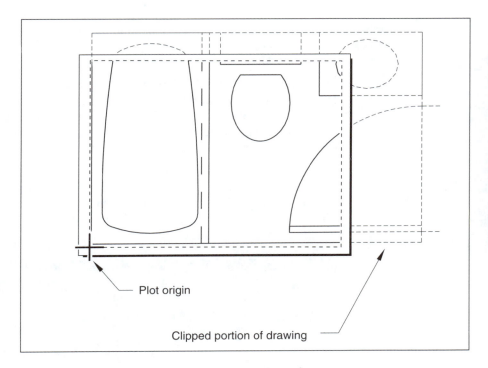

Plot origin

Clipped portion of drawing

*Figure 7.2:*   ***Plotting an oversized image on an HP 7475 plotter***

In each situation, the origin determines a point of reference from which you can relate your drawing in the computer to the physical output. Once you understand this, you are better equipped to accurately place your electronic drawing on the physical medium.

## Selecting a Paper Size and Orientation

Next let's look at the Paper Size and Orientation button group in the Plot Configuration dialog box. This is where you determine the size of your output sheet and the standard unit of measure you will use. The Inches and MM radio buttons let you determine the unit of measure you want to work with in this dialog box. This is the unit of measure you will use when specifying sheet sizes and view locations on the sheet. If you choose MM, sheet sizes are shown in millimeters, and you must specify distances and scales in millimeters for other options.

> **TIP**  If you need to convert from inches to millimeters, the scale factor is 1″ = 25.4 mm.

Near the Inches and MM radio buttons, you can see the Size button. If you are using the system printer, this button is grayed out. When you use the System Printer, the default paper size is set in the Windows 95 Control Panel. As we saw earlier in this chapter, you can modify paper size and orientation on the fly in the Print Setup dialog box.

In addition to the Windows 95 printer drivers, AutoCAD LT has its own printer drivers. If you are using one of these printers, or if you are printing to a file (described below), you may select the Paper Size here. Click on the Size... button to select an output sheet size. This brings up the Paper Size dialog box.

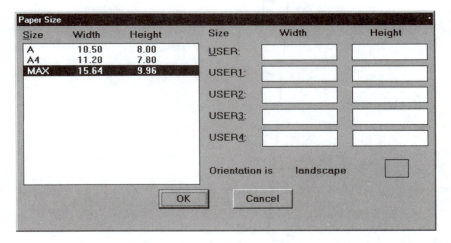

The range of sheet sizes will vary, depending on which plotter, or type of output file, you have selected in the Print/Plot Setup and Default selection option. To select a sheet size, you simply highlight it in the list box on the left and click on OK. Optionally, you can enter a non-standard sheet size in the input boxes to the right. As you can see, you can store up to five custom sheet sizes.

# Controlling the Appearance of Output

On the left side of the Plot Configuration dialog box is the Additional Parameters button group. These options give you the most control over the appearance of your plot. From here, you can control what gets plotted and how.

## Designating Hidden Lines, Fills, and Output Destination

Let's start by looking at the first three check boxes down the right side of this group. Using these check boxes, you can specify whether to plot a 3D drawing with hidden lines removed, whether your plotter is to compensate for pen widths when drawing solid fills, and whether your printer is to simulate more colors.

### Hide Lines

The Hide Lines check box is generally only used for 3D images. When this option is on, AutoCAD LT will remove hidden lines from a 3D drawing as it is plotted. This operation will add a minute or two to your plotting time.

Hide Lines is not required for Paper Space viewports that have been set to hide lines using the Hideplot option of the Mview command (View ➤ Floating Viewports ➤ Hideplot).

### Adjust Area Fill

Turning on Adjust Area Fill tells AutoCAD LT to compensate for pen width around the edges of a solid filled area in order to maintain dimensional accuracy of the plot. To understand this feature, you need to understand how most plotters draw solid areas.

**NOTE** Generally, compensation for pen width is critical only when you are producing drawings as a basis for photo etchings or similar artwork, where close tolerances must be adhered to.

Plotters draw solid fills by first outlining the fill area and then cross-hatching the area with a series of lines, much as you would do by hand. For example, if a solid filled area is drawn at a width of 0.090″, the plotter will outline the area using the edge of the outline as the centerline for the pen, and then proceed to fill the area with a cross-hatch motion. Unfortunately, by using the outline as the centerline for the pen, the solid fill's actual width is 0.090″ *plus* the width of the pen.

When you check the Adjust Area Fill box, AutoCAD LT pulls in the outline of the solid area by half the pen width. To determine the amount of offset to use, AutoCAD LT uses the pen width setting you enter under the Pen Assignments dialog box (described later in this chapter). Figure 7.3 illustrates the operation of Adjust Area Fill.

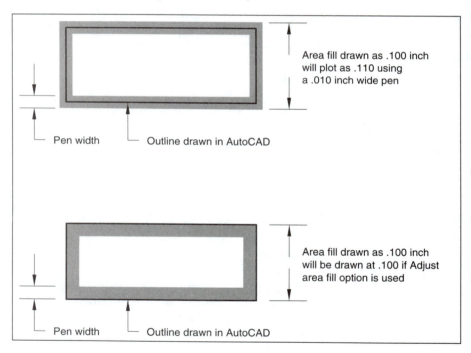

Figure 7.3:   *A solid area without pen-width compensation and with pen-width compensation*

## Dithering

When you click on the Dithering check box this sets the Dither system variable ON or OFF. This variable controls whether drawings that you print on your Windows 95 system printer are dithered. If dithering is ON, the printer will simulate more colors than it can actually print by combining colors and white space.

### Plot To File

We reviewed the Use Previous Printer option above. Now look at the Plot to File option. Using this option, you can tell AutoCAD LT to store the plot in a file on disk instead of sending the plot data to a plotter or printer for immediate output.

Turn this option on when you want to divert your printout to a file on disk and print it later. This can be useful if you are in an office in which a plotter is shared among several CAD stations. When the plotter is busy, plot to a file. Later you can download the plot file when your plotter is available, or send it out to an outside plotting service bureau.

To use this option, do the following:

1. Click the Plot To File check box.

2. Click on the File Name button (just below the check box). You'll see the Create Plot File dialog box, which is the same as the one used for most other file creation operations.

3. Enter the name for your plot file, or just accept the default filename, which is usually the same as the current file. The .PLT filename extension is the default.

4. Click on OK to accept the filename.

Use the above procedure to create a standard plot file. If you wish, you may create a raster format image from your drawing for use in other applications:

1. In the Print Configuration dialog box, click on Print/Plot Setup and Default Selection.

2. Select the file type extension you require from the Select Device list box: available raster image options are .BMP, .GIF, .PCX and .TIF. Then click on the Print/Plot Setup button.

3. In Print/Plot Setup dialog box, select the color output options and the background color, and press OK.

## Determining What to Print

The radio buttons on the left side of the Additional Parameters button group let you specify which part of your drawing you wish to plot.

### Display

This is the default option; it tells AutoCAD LT to plot what is currently displayed on the screen (see panel 1 of Figure 7.4). If you let AutoCAD LT fit the drawing onto the sheet—that is, you check the Scaled to Fit check box—the plot will be exactly the same as what you see on your screen (panel 2 of Figure 7.4).

### Extents

The Extents option draws all of the objects in the drawing, eliminating any space that may border the drawing (see Figure 7.5). If you let AutoCAD LT fit the drawing onto the sheet—that is, you check the Scaled to Fit check box—the plot will display exactly the same thing that you would see on the screen had you clicked on the Zoom Extents button.

> **WARNING** Using the Extents option can yield unexpected results. If you want reliable plotter output, avoid using Extents if possible. Instead, use the View ➤ Named Views... to save views for plotting.

At times when using the Extents plot option, you may find that you don't get exactly the same plot as your drawing extents. When a drawing changes in size, AutoCAD LT will often have to recalculate its size twice by performing two drawing regenerations to display the drawing extents. When plotting, AutoCAD LT doesn't do the second regeneration, so you end up with the wrong display. To avoid this problem, you may want to use the View command (View ➤ Named Views...) to set up a view of the area you want to plot, and then select the View... radio button. This will ensure that you will always get the plot you want, regardless of your drawing extents.

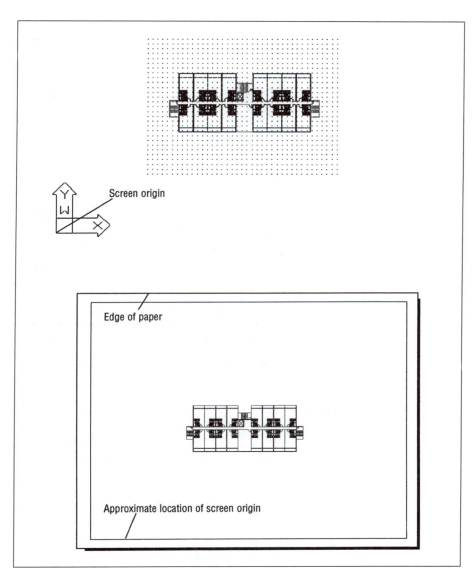

Screen origin

Edge of paper

Approximate location of screen origin

*Figure 7.4:* **The screen display and the printed output when Display is chosen and no Scale is used (the drawing is scaled to fit the sheet)**

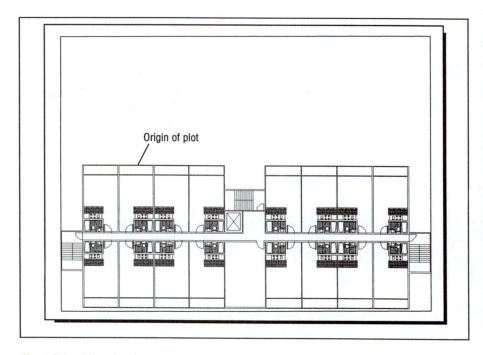

Figure 7.5:    *The printed output when Extents is chosen*

## Limits

The Limits printing option uses the limits of the drawing to determine what to print (see Figure 7.6). If, by selecting Scaled to Fit, you let AutoCAD LT fit the drawing onto the sheet, the plot will display exactly the same thing that you would see on the screen had you clicked on the Zoom All button.

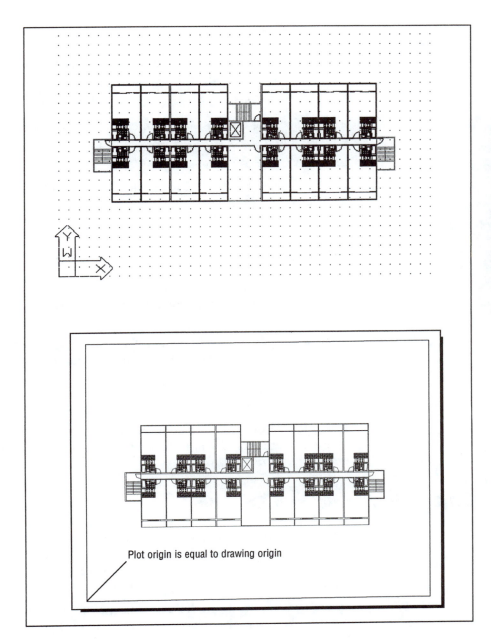

*Figure 7.6:* **The screen display and the printed output when Limits is chosen**

## View

The View printing option uses a previously saved view to determine what to print (see Figure 7.7).

1. Click on the View radio button in the Plot Configuration dialog box.

2. Then select the desired View name from the dialog box list that appears.

The view shown in Figure 7.7 corresponds to View 4, which you saved in the exercise in *Chapter 6*.

If, by selecting Scaled to Fit, you let AutoCAD LT fit the drawing onto the sheet, the plot will display exactly the same thing that you would see on the screen if you recalled the view you are plotting.

## Window

Finally, the Window option allows you to use a window to indicate the area you wish to plot (see Figure 7.8). Nothing outside the window will print.

To use this option, click on the Window... button. Then enter the coordinates of the window in the appropriate input boxes. Or you can click on the Pick button to indicate a window in the drawing editor. The dialog box will temporarily close to allow you to select points. When you're done, click on OK.

If you let AutoCAD LT fit the drawing onto the sheet using the Scaled to Fit check box, the plot will display exactly the same thing that you enclose within the window.

# Controlling Scale and Location

The Scale, Rotation, and Origin button group is where you tell Auto-CAD LT the scale of your drawing, as well as how the image is to be rotated on the sheet, and the location of the drawing origin on the paper.

In the previous section, the descriptions of several options indicate that the Scaled to Fit check box must be checked. Bear in mind that when you apply a scale factor to your plot, it changes the results of the Additional Parameters settings, and some subtle problems can arise. This is usually where most new users have difficulty.

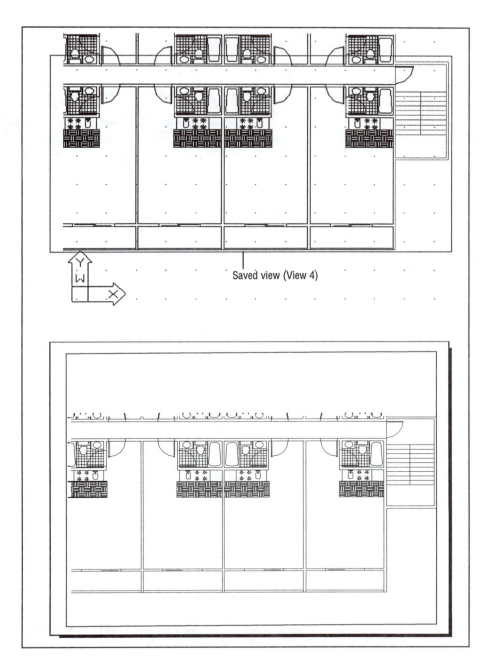

Saved view (View 4)

*Figure 7.7:* **A comparison of the saved view and the printed output**

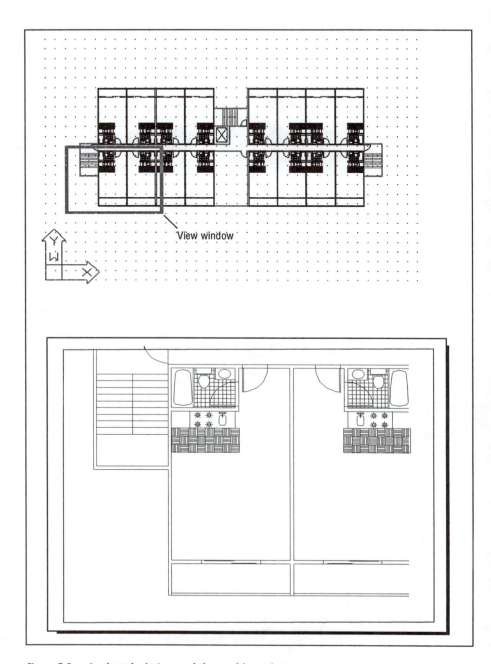

*Figure 7.8:* **A selected window and the resulting printout**

For example, the apartment plan drawing fits nicely on the paper when you use Scaled to Fit. But if you tried to plot the drawing at a scale of 1″=1′, you would probably get a blank piece of paper, because at that scale, hardly any of the drawing would fit on your paper. AutoCAD LT would tell you that it was plotting and then that the plot was finished. You wouldn't have a clue as to why your sheet was blank.

If an image is too large to fit on a sheet of paper because of improper scaling, the plot image will be clipped differently depending on whether the plotter uses the center of the image or the lower-left corner for its origin (see Figure 7.1). Keep this in mind as you specify Scale factors in this area of the dialog box.

**Part 2**

**Building on the Basics**

### Specifying Drawing Scale

To indicate scale, two input boxes are provided in the Scale, Rotation, and Origin button group: Plotted Inches (or Plotted MM if you use metric units) and Drawing Units. For example, if your drawing needs to plot at a scale of ⅛″ = 1′, then the scale factor is 96 (see Table 3.4), and you should do the following:

1.  Double-click on the Plotted Inches (or Plotted MM) input box, and enter **1** ↵.

2.  Double-click on the Drawing Units input box, and enter **96**.

    For a drawing set up using Architectural units, you can enter a scale as a fraction of 1″ = 1′. For example, for a ⅛″ scale drawing:

1.  Double-click on the Plotted Inches (or Plotted MM) input box, and enter **⅛″**.

2.  Double-click on the Drawing Units input box, and enter **1′**.

    You can specify a different scale from the one you chose while setting up your drawing, and AutoCAD LT will plot your drawing to that scale. You are not restricted in any way as to scale, but entering the correct scale is important: If it is too large, AutoCAD LT will think your drawing is too large to fit on the sheet, though it will attempt to plot your drawing anyway.

    The Scaled to Fit check box, as already described, allows you to avoid giving a scale altogether and forces the drawing to fit on the sheet. This works well if you are doing illustrations that are not to scale.

**NOTE** See *Chapter 3* for a discussion on drawing units and scale factors.

### Setting the Output's Origin and Rotation

To adjust the position of your drawing on the sheet, you enter the location of the view origin in relation to the plotter origin in x and y coordinates (see Figure 7.9).

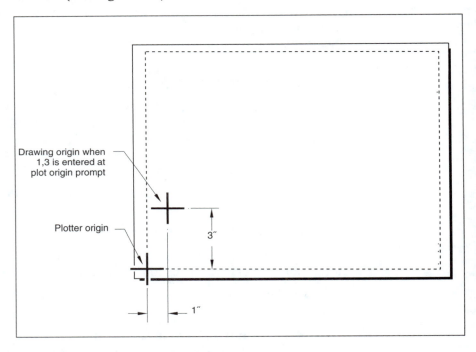

Drawing origin when
1,3 is entered at
plot origin prompt

Plotter origin

3″

1″

*Figure 7.9:  Adjusting the image location on a sheet*

For example, suppose you plot a drawing, then realize that it needs to be moved 1″ to the right and 3″ up on the sheet. You would replot the drawing by making the following changes:

1.  In the Plot Configuration dialog box, click the Rotation and Origin… button in the Scale, Rotation, and Origin button group. The Plot Rotation and Origin dialog box appears.

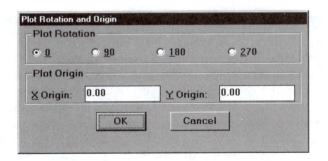

2. Double-click on the X Origin input box and type **1**.

3. Double-click on the Y Origin input box and type **3**.

4. Click on OK.

Now proceed with the rest of the plot configuration. With the above settings, when the plot is done, the image will be shifted on the paper exactly 1″ to the right and 3″ up.

**WARNING** If you encounter problems with rotating plots, try setting up a UCS that is rotated 90° from the world coordinate system. Then use the Plan command (View ➤ 3D Viewpoint ➤ Plan View) to view your drawing in the new rotated orientation. Next, save the view using the View command (View ➤ Named Views...). Once you do this, you can use the View button in the Additional Parameters group to plot the rotated view. See *Chapter 16* for more on UCS.

The four radio buttons labeled 0, 90, 180, and 270 allow you to rotate the plot on the sheet. Each value indicates the number of degrees of rotation for the plot. The default is 0, but if you need to rotate the image to a different angle, click on the appropriate radio button.

## *Adjusting Pen Parameters and Plotter Optimization*

The Pen Parameters group of the Plot Configuration dialog box contains two buttons: Pen Assignments..., which helps you control line weight and color, and Optimization..., which lets you control pen motion in pen plotters.

## Working with Pen Assignments and Line Weights

In most graphics programs, you control line weights by adjusting the actual width of lines in the drawing. In AutoCAD LT, you generally take a different approach to line weights. Instead of specifying a line weight in the drawing editor, you match plotter pen widths to colors in your drawing. For example, you might designate the color red to correspond to a fine line weight or the color blue to a very heavy line weight. To make these correlations between colors and line weights, you tell AutoCAD LT to plot with a particular pen or a particular line width for each color in the drawing. You can also control line weights through the use of polylines. See *Chapter 13* for details.

The Pen Assignments... button in the Plot Configuration dialog box is the entry point to setting the drawing colors for the pens or line widths on your plotter. When you click on this button, the Pen Assignment dialog box appears.

 **NOTE** This dialog box shows a listing for a Hewlett-Packard 7580 plotter.

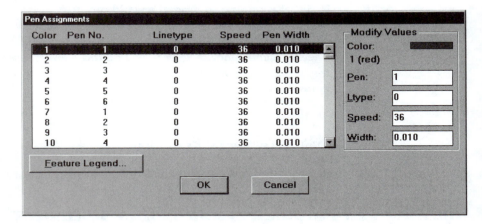

The predominant feature of this dialog box is the list of pen assignments. Color numbers in the first column of the list correspond to the colors in your drawing. The other columns show you what pen number, linetype, pen speed, and pen width are assigned to those colors.

To change these settings, you click on the item in the list you want to change. The values for that selected item appear in the appropriate input boxes under Modify Values at the right. You can then change the values in the input boxes. You can highlight more than one color at a time to change the pen assignments of several colors at once.

## ISO PEN WIDTHS

You may have noticed a setting called ISO Pen Widths in the Select Linetype dialog box discussed in *Chapter 4* (Format ➤ Linetype…) It will be grayed out unless an ISO linetype is loaded.

This setting is in the form of a drop-down list. When you select a pen width from that list, the linetype scale is updated to conform to the ISO standard for that width. This setting has no effect on the actual plotter output, however. If you are using ISO standard widths, it is up to you to match the color of the lines to their corresponding widths in the Plot Configuration dialog box. Use the Pen Assignments dialog box to set the line colors to pen widths.

### Pen No.

You assign line weights to colors by entering a pen number in the Pen input box. The default for the color red, for example, is pen 1. If you have a pen plotter, you can then place a pen with a fine tip in the slot designated for pen 1 in your plotter. Then everything that is red in your AutoCAD LT drawing will be plotted with the fine pen. If you have an ink jet plotter, you can set the width of pens through the plotter's control panel.

 **NOTE** If you have a Hewlett Packard ink jet plotter, you can also control pen settings through the HPCONFIG program.

### Ltype

Some plotters offer linetypes independent of AutoCAD LT's linetypes. Using the Ltype input box, you can force a pen assignment to one of these hardware linetypes. If your plotter supports hardware linetypes, you can click on the Feature Legend button to see what linetypes are available and their designations. Usually linetypes are given numeric designations, so a row of dots might be designated as linetype 2, or a dash-dot might be linetype 3.

If your plotter can generate its own linetypes, you can also assign line-types to colors. But this method is very seldom used, because it is simpler to assign linetypes to layers directly in the drawing.

## Speed

The pen Speed setting lets you adjust the pen speed in inches per second. This is important because various pens have their own speed requirements. Refillable technical pens that use India ink generally require the slowest settings; roller pens are capable of very high speeds. Pen speeds will also be affected by the medium you are using.

Selecting pens and media for your plotter can be a trial-and-error proposition. If you would like to learn more about the details of plotter pens and media, see *Appendix A*.

## Width

AutoCAD LT uses the Width setting in conjunction with the Adjust Area Fill option under the Additional Parameters button group. When creating solid fills, it draws a series of lines close together—much as you would do by hand (see Figure 7.10). To do this efficiently, the program must know the pen width. If the Width setting is too low, it will take longer than necessary to draw a solid fill; if it is too high, solid fills will appear as cross-hatches instead of solids.

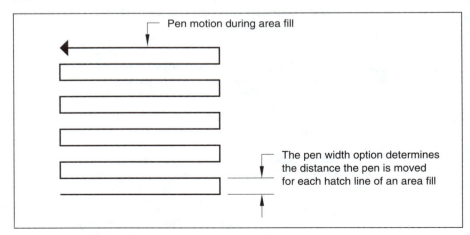

*Figure 7.10:* **How solid fill areas are drawn by a plotter**

## Optimizing Plotter Speed

AutoCAD LT does a lot of preparation before sending your drawing to the plotter. One of the things it does is optimize the way it sends vectors to your plotter, so your plotter doesn't waste time making frequent pen changes and moving from one end of the plot to another just to draw a single line.

The Optimization... button in the Pen Parameters group opens a dialog box that lets you control the level of pen optimization AutoCAD LT is to perform on your plots.

NOTE None of these options, except the No optimization and the Adds endpoint swap options, have any effect on dot-matrix and laser printers, or on ink-jet plotters.

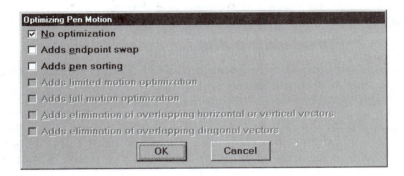

Here are brief descriptions of each setting:

**No optimization**   causes AutoCAD LT to plot the drawing just as it is regenerated on the screen.

**Adds endpoint swap**   forces the plotter to draw (as best it can) parallel lines in a back-and-forth motion, so that the pen moves the minimum distance between the end of one line and the beginning of another.

**Adds pen sorting**   sorts pens so that all of one color is plotted at once. This is fine if your plotter has a self-capping penholder, or if it is a single-pen plotter. You should disable this option if you have a multipen plotter that does not cap the pens.

**Adds limited motion optimization** and **Adds full motion optimization**    further minimize pen travel over a plot.

**Adds elimination of overlapping horizontal or vertical vectors** does just what it says: It eliminates overlapping lines. With pen plotters, overlapping lines can cause the weight of the line to increase noticeably. This setting helps reduce line weight build-up when a drawing contains numerous line overlaps. This setting does not affect raster plotters or printers.

**Adds elimination of overlapping diagonal vectors**    performs a similar function as the previous option, but on diagonal lines.

# Other Plot Controls

Here are a couple of other handy, timesaving features available to you in the Plot Configuration dialog box.

## Previewing a Plot

If you are an experienced CAD drafter, you're probably all too familiar with the following scenario:

You're rushing to meet a deadline. You've got one hour to plot a drawing that you know takes 45 minutes to plot. You set up AutoCAD LT and start the plot, then run off to finish some paperwork. When you come back 45 minutes later, the plot image is half the size it is supposed to be.

You can avoid facing predicaments like this one with the Plot Preview feature. Once you've made all the settings you think you need for plotting your drawing, turn on the Full radio button in the Plot Preview group, and then click on Preview…. AutoCAD LT will show you what your drawing will look like according to the settings you've chosen. Preview also lists any warning messages that would appear during the actual plotting process.

TIP  You can press the Esc key to speed up the preview. Once the preview plot is done, you are immediately returned to the Plot Configuration dialog box. You can also press Esc to terminate the preview generation when you've seen enough.

While in the Full Preview, you can zoom in on an area and pan around, but be aware that each zoom and pan requires the Preview function to "replot" the image.

The Full Preview can take some time, though not as long as an actual plot. If you're just interested in seeing how the drawing fits on the sheet, you can choose Partial instead of Full before clicking on Preview. The Partial option shows only the sheet edge, image orientation triangle, and the image boundary. The image itself is not shown. Using a small triangle in the corner of the drawing to indicate the lower-left corner of the drawing, AutoCAD LT shows you how your image is oriented on the sheet.

## Saving Your Settings

At times, drawings will require special plotter settings, or you may find that you frequently use one particular setting configuration. Instead of trying to remember the settings every time you plot, you can store settings as files that you can recall at any time. Here's how to do this:

1. Set up the plotter settings exactly as you want them.

2. Click the Print/Plot Setup and Default Selection... button.

3. In the Print/Plot Setup and Default Selection dialog box, click on the Save Defaults To File... button. The Save to File dialog box appears.

4. Enter a name for the group of settings. The default name is the same as the current drawing name, with the .PCP filename extension.

5. Click on OK to create your .PCP file of settings.

   To recall a settings file:

1. Click on File ➤ Print (or type **Plot** ↵ at the command line).

2. Click on the Print/Plot Setup and Default Selection... button.

3. In the Print/Plot Setup and Default Selection dialog box, click on the Get Defaults From File... button. The Obtain From File dialog box appears.

4. Click on the name of the desired plotter settings file.

5. Click on OK, and the settings will be loaded. You can then proceed with your plot.

The ability to store plotter settings in .PCP files gives you greater control over your output quality. It helps you to reproduce similar plots more easily when you need them later. You can store several different plotter configurations for one file, each for a different output device.

You can also open a .PCP file with a text editor. You can even create your own .PCP file by copying an existing one and editing it.

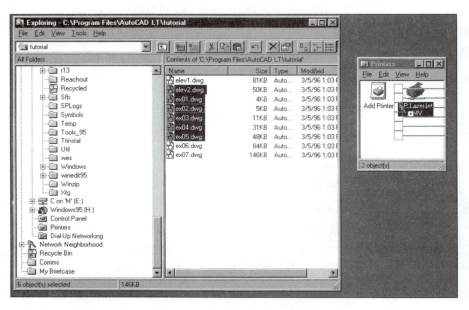

## Plotting Multiple Files from the Windows 95 Explorer

In Windows 95, you can use the drag-and-drop feature to plot a number of files sequentially.

1. Open the Windows Explorer and the Printers folder. (Choose Settings ➤ Printers on the Windows 95 Start menu to open the Printers folder.)

2. In the Explorer, open the folder in which your drawings are stored and highlight the files that you wish to print. You can select nonadjacent filenames by using the Ctrl-mouse click function.

3. Drag the selected files onto the system printer icon in the Printers folder, and release them. You will receive the following message:

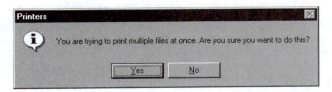

4. Click on Yes. Windows 95 will start AutoCAD LT (if it is not already active), open the drawing, and then open the Print Configuration dialog box.

5. At this point you can specify your preferred printer setup. Once your Printer is configured appropriately, click on OK.

This sequence is repeated in turn for each of the drawings you have selected. As each of the plots is processed, the drawing enters the print queue.

## Sending Your Drawings to a Service Bureau

Using a plotting service can be a good alternative to purchasing your own plotter. Or you might consider using a low-cost plotter for check plots, and then send the files to a service for your final product. Many reprographic services such as blueprinters offer plotting in conjunction with their other services. Quite often these services include a high-speed modem that allows you to send files over phone lines, eliminating the need for using courier services or regular mail.

Service bureaus will often use an *electrostatic plotter*—it's like a very large laser printer, and is often capable of producing color plots. These plotters are costly, and you probably won't want to purchase one yourself. However, they are excellent for situations requiring high volume and fast turnaround. The electrostatic plotter produces high-quality plots, often better than a laser printer, and it is fast: A 30″×42″ plot can take as little as two minutes.

Another device used by service bureaus is the *laser photo plotter*. This device uses a laser to plot a drawing on a piece of film. The film negative is later enlarged to the finished drawing size by means of standard reprographic techniques. Laser photo plotters yield the highest-quality output of any device, and they offer the flexibility of reproducing drawings at any size.

Finally, many service bureaus can produce full E-size plots of PostScript files. With AutoCAD LT's full PostScript support, you can get presentation-quality plots from any AutoCAD LT drawing.

## If You Want to Experiment...

At this point, since you aren't rushing to meet a deadline, you may want to experiment with some of the plotter and printer variables and see firsthand what each one does. Figure 7.11 contains an exercise you can do to try printing a view and scale different from those used in the exercises.

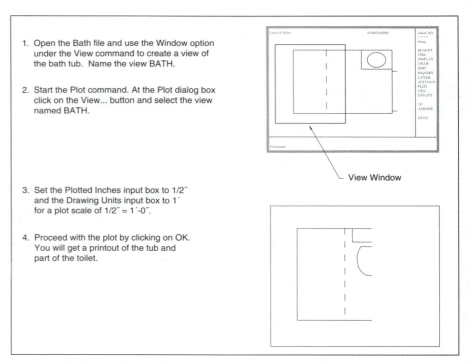

1. Open the Bath file and use the Window option under the View command to create a view of the bath tub.  Name the view BATH.

2. Start the Plot command. At the Plot dialog box click on the View... button and select the view named BATH.

View Window

3. Set the Plotted Inches input box to 1/2″ and the Drawing Units input box to 1′ for a plot scale of 1/2″ = 1′-0″.

4. Proceed with the plot by clicking on OK. You will get a printout of the tub and part of the toilet.

*Figure 7.11:*    **Printing the tub at ½″=1′-0″ scale**

# Chapter 8

# Adding Text to Drawings

## *FAST TRACKS*

### To continue text where you left off 288

*Start the Line Text command (Dtext) from the Draw toolbar. The last line of text you entered will be highlighted. Press ↵ at all the prompts until you see the* Text *prompt. A text cursor will appear just below the last text line.*

### To use TrueType or PostScript fonts in your drawing 298

*Choose Format ➤ Text Style, or type **ddstyle** on the command line. At the Text Style dialog box, create a new text style, if required. Then locate (via the Browse option) and double-click on the PostScript .PFB file, or TrueType .TTF file you want. Use Effects items at the bottom of the dialog box to specify height, width, or any other text effects you wish to apply.*

### To change the style of existing text 304

*Click on Properties on the Object Properties toolbar, and then click on the text whose style you want to change. In the Modify Text dialog box, click on the desired text style in the Style drop-down list.*

### To edit text 307

*Click on the Edit Text button on the Special Edit flyout on the Modify toolbar, or type **Ddedit** ↵ and click on the text you wish to edit. If the text is Line text (Dtext) the Edit dialog box appears with the text; if it is Paragraph text (MText), the Edit MText dialog box will open. In either case, you can use the standard input-box editing methods. When you are finished editing, click on OK. You may now click on a new text object to edit; or press ↵ when you are done.*

### To keep text from mirroring when included in a Mirror selection 308

*Type ´**Mirrtext** ↵ and then enter **0** ↵. From then on, the Mirror command and the \*\* MIRROR \*\* Grips option will not reverse text so it is unreadable, but rather will make copies of text mirroring their insertion points.*

**O**NE of the more tedious drafting tasks is applying notes to your drawing. Anyone who has had to draft a large drawing containing lots of notes knows the true meaning of writer's cramp. AutoCAD LT not only makes this job go faster by allowing you to type your notes, it also helps you to create more professional-looking notes by using a variety of fonts, type sizes, and type styles. And with Release 3, you have some new features to further improve text handling—such as a spelling checker and word wrap for large blocks of text.

In this chapter you will add notes to your apartment house plan. In the process, you will explore some of AutoCAD LT's text creation and editing features. You will learn how to control the size, slant, type style, and orientation of text, and how to import text files.

## Labeling a Drawing

In this first section, you will add some simple labels to your Unit drawing to identify the general design elements: the bathroom, kitchenette, and living room.

1. Start AutoCAD LT and open the Unit file. You may use 08-UNIT.DWG on the companion CD.

2. Turn off the Flr-pat layer. Otherwise, the floor pattern you added previously will obscure the text you will enter in this chapter.

**TIP** It's a good idea to keep your notes on a separate layer, so you can plot drawings containing only the graphics information, or freeze the notes layer to save redraw/regeneration time.

3. Create a layer called **Notes** and make it the current layer. Notes is the layer on which you will keep all your text information.

4. Click and drag the Text icon from the Draw toolbar and then select Line Text, or enter **Dtext** ↵ at the command prompt.

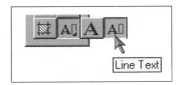

5. At the DTEXT Justify/Style/<Start point>: prompt, pick the starting point for the text you are about to enter, just below the kitchenette at coordinate 16′-2″, 21′-8″. By picking a point, you are accepting <Start point>, which is the default.

**NOTE** Why make the text so high? Remember that you are drawing at full scale, and anything you draw will be reduced in the plotted drawing. We will discuss text height in more detail later in this chapter.

6. At the Height <0′-0 3/16″>: prompt, enter **6** ↵ to indicate the text height.

7. At the Rotation angle <0>: prompt, press ↵ to accept the default, 0°. You can specify any angle other than horizontal if you want (for example, if you want your text to be aligned with a rotated object). You'll see a small square appear at the point you picked in step 5. This is your *text cursor*.

8. At the Text: prompt, enter the word **Kitchenette**. As you type, the word appears in the drawing.

**TIP** If you make a typing error, back up to the error with the Backspace key and then retype the rest of the word. If you need to, you can backspace over several lines.

9. Press ↵ to move the cursor down to start a new line.

10. This time you want to label the bathroom. Pick a point to the right of the door swing at coordinate 19′-11″, 26′-5″. The text cursor moves to that point.

11. Type **Bath** ↵. Figure 8.1 shows how your drawing should look now. (At this point, the text is in the default font, Txt; we'll discuss fonts later in this chapter.)

12. Press ↵ again to exit the Line Text command.

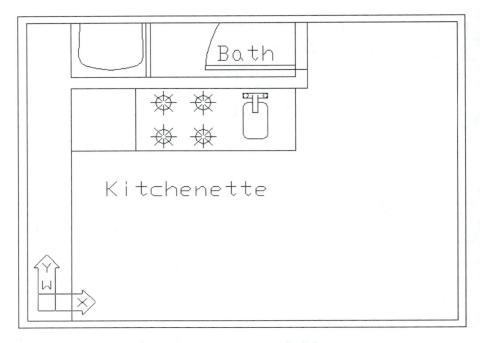

*Figure 8.1:*    **The Unit drawing with labels added for the kitchenette and bath**

As you have seen in the foregoing exercise, the Line Text command (Dtext) lets you enter a column of text by pressing ↵ at the end of each line. You can also click on a location for the next line, as you did in step 10.

## Justifying Text

When you pick a point at the Line Text's Justify/Style/<Start point>: prompt, your text is automatically justified to the left of the selected point, and the text uses that point as its *baseline* location. The *baseline* of text is an imaginary line on which the lowercase letters of the text sit. You can change the justification setting so that the text you enter will be justified either to the center or to the right. You can also specify whether the text baseline is on, above, or below the Start point prompt.

Here's how to change the justification setting:

 **NOTE** If you are working through the tutorial, you can skip this exercise. It's here for reference only.

1. Click on Line Text from the Draw toolbar or enter **Dtext** ↵, just as you would to start entering text.

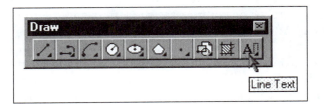

2. At the DTEXT Justify/Style/<Start point>: prompt, enter **J** ↵.

3. When you see this prompt:

   Align/Fit/Center/Middle/Right:

   select the justification style you want by typing the first letter of the style (**a**, **f**, **c**, **m**, or **r**) at the prompt.

4. Once you select a justification option, you are prompted for a point to locate your text. You can then start to enter your text.

   When you start to enter text, it will first appear as though no change has been made to the justification. The text will come in using the default, left-justification. Don't be alarmed—the text will move into position after you've exited the Line Text command.

## Justification Options

Here are descriptions of each justification option (we've left Align and Fit until last).

**Center**    causes the text to be centered on the start point, with the baseline on the start point.

**Middle**    causes the text to be centered on the start point, with the baseline slightly below the start point.

**Right**    causes the text to be justified to the right of the start point, with the baseline on the start point.

### Align and Fit Options

With the Fit and Align justification options, you must specify a dimension within which the text is to fit. For example, suppose you want the word *Refrigerator* to fit within the 26″-wide box representing the refrigerator. You can use either the Fit or the Align option to accomplish this. With Fit, AutoCAD LT prompts you to select start and end points, and then stretches or compresses the letters to fit within the two points you specify. You use this option when the text must be a consistent height throughout the drawing and you don't care about distorting the font. Align works like Fit, but instead of maintaining the current text style height, Align adjusts the text height to keep it proportional to the text width, without distorting the font. Use this option when it is important to maintain the font's shape and proportion. Figure 8.2 demonstrates how Fit and Align work.

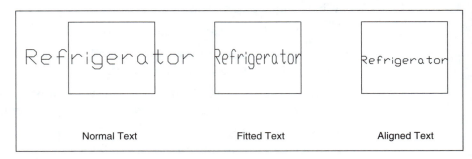

Normal Text          Fitted Text          Aligned Text

*Figure 8.2:*    **The word Refrigerator** *as it appears normally, and with the Fit and Align options selected*

## Understanding Text and Scale

Text scale conversion is a concept many people have difficulty grasping. As you discovered in previous chapters, AutoCAD LT allows you to draw at full scale—that is, to represent distances as values equivalent to the actual size of the object. When you plot the drawing later, you tell AutoCAD LT at what scale you wish to plot and the program reduces the drawing accordingly. This allows you the freedom to input measurements at full scale and not worry about converting them to various scales every time you enter a distance. Unfortunately, this feature can also create problems when you enter text and dimensions. Just as you had to convert the plotted sheet size to an enlarged size equivalent at full scale in the drawing editor, you must convert your text size to its equivalent at full scale.

To illustrate this point, imagine you are drawing the unit plan at full size on a very large sheet of paper. When you are done with this drawing, it will be reduced to a scale that will allow it to fit on an 8½″×11″ sheet of paper. So you have to make your text quite large to keep it legible once it is reduced. This means that if you want text to appear ⅛″ high when the drawing is plotted, you must convert it to a considerably larger size when you draw it. To do this, you multiply the desired height of the final plotted text by a scale conversion factor.

If your drawing is at ⅛″=1′ scale, you multiply the desired text height, ⅛″, by the scale conversion factor of 96 (found in Table 3.4) to get a height of 12″. This is the height you must make your text to get ⅛″-high text in the final plot. Table 8.1 shows you some other examples of text height to scale.

*Table 8.1:    Text ⅛″-High Converted to Size for Various Drawing Scales*

| Drawing Scale | Scale Factor | AutoCAD LT Drawing Height for ⅛″-High Text |
|---|---|---|
| ¹⁄₁₆″ = 1′-0″ | 192 | 24.0″ |
| ⅛″ = 1′-0″ | 96 | 12.0″ |
| ¼″ = 1′-0″ | 48 | 6.0″ |
| ½″ = 1′-0″ | 24 | 3.0″ |
| ¾″ = 1′-0″ | 16 | 2.0″ |
| 1″ = 1′-0″ | 12 | 1.5″ |
| 1½″ = 1′-0″ | 8 | 1.0″ |
| 3″ = 1′-0″ | 4 | 0.5″ |

# Entering a Column of Text

You will often want to enter a note or description of an object that requires more than one line of text. You've already had a glimpse of how to do this. The next exercise will let you try it out.

## Continuing Text from Where You Left Off

One feature of AutoCAD LT's Line Text function is that it lets you stop to do something else and then return to add text in a column below the last line you entered. This exercise shows you the process.

1. Click on Line Text from the Draw toolbar or enter **Dtext** ↵.

2. Click on a point at coordinate 24′-0″, 26′-5″ to locate the beginning of your text.

3. Enter **6** ↵ for the height and press ↵ at the Rotation Angle prompt.

4. Type **Entry** ↵, and then press ↵ again to exit the Line Text command.

   Now move to another part of the drawing to make changes. At this point, you've exited the Line Text command, and will return now to pick up where you left off.

5. Zoom in to the area where you just added the text.

6. Start Line Text again.

7. At the Justify/Style/<Start point>: prompt, press ↵. The Text prompt appears (skipping the prompts for height and insertion angle) and you see the Line Text cursor in the drawing area just below the word Entry.

8. Enter the entry dimensions **6′-0″ × 7′-0″** ↵. The cursor moves down a line.

9. Type the words **to the kitchenette** ↵. You should now have something that looks like Figure 8.3.

10. Press ↵ to exit the Line Text command.

## Working with the Text Command

Another way of entering text is to use the Text command. Although the Text command is somewhat less flexible than Line Text (Dtext), the Text command can be incorporated into menus, scripts (see *Chapter 17*), and

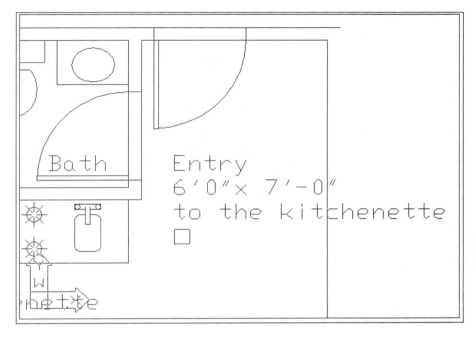

*Figure 8.3:*     **The column of text you entered from where you left off**

macros, where the Dtext command cannot. The Text command is best suited in menus and macros.

Text and Dtext work almost identically, except for the following:

▶ Text does not show your text in the drawing as you type.

▶ Text requires you to press ↵ twice between lines in a column of text.

▶ Text does not let you position text "on the fly" as Dtext does.

To get a feel for how Text works, try the following exercise:

1. Zoom back to your previous view.

2. At the command prompt, enter **Text** ↵. You get the same prompt for a starting point as when you use Line Text.

3. Pick a point on the balcony at coordinate 19′-8″, 4′-4″. Press ↵ twice to accept the default height and angle.

4. Type the word **Balcony**. As you type, the letters appear only in the prompt area. They do not appear in the drawing yet.

5.  Press ↵. The word "Balcony" appears in the drawing (see Figure 8.4), and the command prompt reappears.

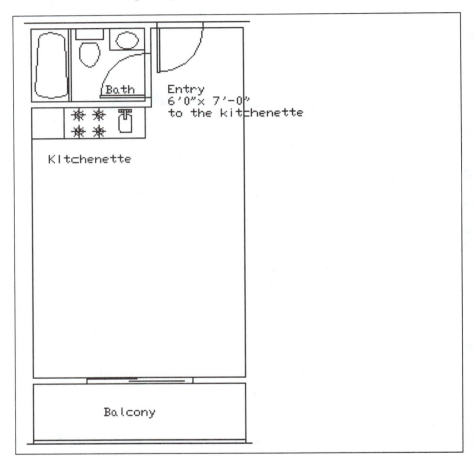

*Figure 8.4:*    **The word "Balcony," added with the Text command**

# Choosing Fonts and Special Characters

AutoCAD LT offers a choice of standard fonts that can be displayed in a number of different ways. The fonts include several specialized fonts, such as Greek and Cyrillic; symbols for astronomy, mapping, math, meteorology, and music are also provided. You can compress or expand these fonts and symbols, or you can modify them to create different type styles. Figure 8.5 (A/B) shows you the fonts and symbols available with AutoCAD LT.

 **NOTE** AutoCAD LT's own standard fonts are contained in files with the .SHX extension in your AutoCAD LT directory. The AutoCAD LT package also supplies a set of PostScript Type 1 fonts and a set of TrueType fonts for use in your drawings. To see samples of the TrueType fonts, open the truetype.dwg in the \sample directory.

**Part 2**

**Building on the Basics**

| | |
|---|---|
| This is Txt | |
| This is Monotxt | |
| This is Simplex | (Old version of Roman Simplex) |
| This is Complex | (Old version of Roman Complex) |
| *This is Italic* | (Old version of Italic Complex) |
| This is Romans | (Roman Simplex) |
| This is Romand | (Roman double stroke) |
| This is Romanc | (Roman Complex) |
| This is Romant | (Roman triple stroke) |
| *This is Scripts* | (Script Simplex) |
| *This is Scriptc* | (Script Complex) |
| *This is Italicc* | (Italic Complex) |
| *This is Italict* | (Italic triple stroke) |
| Τηισ ισ Γρεεκσ | (This is Greeks - Greek Simplex) |
| Τηισ ισ Γρεεκχ | (This is Greekc - Greek Complex) |
| Узит ит Вшсиллив | (This is Cyrillic - Alphabetical) |
| Тхис ис Чйрилтлч | (This is Cyriltlc - Transliteration) |
| 𝕿𝖍𝖎𝖘 𝖎𝖘 𝕲𝖔𝖙𝖍𝖎𝖈𝖊 | (Gothic English) |
| 𝕿𝖍𝖎𝖋 𝖎𝖋 𝕲𝖔𝖙𝖍𝖎𝖈𝖌 | (Gothic German) |
| 𝕺𝖍𝖎𝖘 𝖎𝖘 𝕲𝖔𝖙𝖍𝖎𝖈𝖎 | (Gothic Italian) |

*Figure 8.5A:*   ***The AutoCAD LT text fonts***

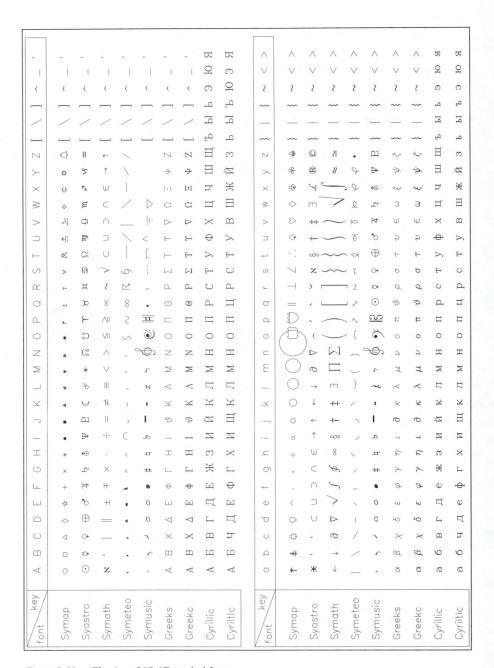

Figure 8.5B:    The AutoCAD LT symbol fonts

In addition, AutoCAD LT supplies a set of PostScript and TrueType fonts for applications in which you might want to use higher-quality display fonts. See "Using PostScript and TrueType Fonts" later in this chapter.

Bear in mind that the more complex the font, the longer it takes AutoCAD LT to regenerate your drawing. Before you choose a font for a particular job, consider how much text the drawing will contain. Use the Txt font if you like its look; it regenerates the fastest. Monotxt is a fixed-width font (like a typewriter font) that is useful for aligned columns of numbers or notes (see Figure 8.6). If you want something less boxy-looking, you can use the Romans font. Use the Romanc, Italicc, and other more complex fonts with discretion, as they will slow down the drawing regeneration considerably. Use the more complex fonts where you want a fancier type style, such as when drawing titles or labels in an exploded parts diagram (see Figure 8.7). You could use the Greeks font in conjunction with the Symath symbols for mathematical text.

| Room # | Door # | Thick | Rate | Matrl | Const |
|--------|--------|-------|------|-------|-------|
| 116 | 116 | 1 3/4" | 20 MIN | WOOD | SOLID CORE |
| 114 | 114 | 1 3/4" | 20 MIN | WOOD | SOLID CORE |
| 112 | 112 | 1 3/4" | 20 MIN | WOOD | SOLID CORE |
| 110 | --- | 1 3/4" | 45 MIN | METAL | MINERAL CORE |
| 108 | 108 | 1 3/4" | 20 MIN | WOOD | SOLID CORE |
| 106 | 106 | 1 1/2" | NO RATE | WOOD | HOLLOW |
| 102 | 102 | 1 1/2" | NO RATE | WOOD | HOLLOW |
| 104 | 104 | 1 3/4" | 20 MIN | WOOD | SOLID CORE |
| 107 | 107 | 1 3/4" | 45 MIN | METAL | MINERAL CORE |
| 105 | 105 | 1 3/4" | 20 MIN | WOOD | SOLID CORE |
| 101 | 101 | 1 3/4" | 20 MIN | WOOD | SOLID CORE |

| Room # | Door # | Thick | Rate | Matrl | Const |
|--------|--------|-------|------|-------|-------|
| 116 | 116 | 1 3/4" | 20 MIN | WOOD | SOLID CORE |
| 114 | 114 | 1 3/4" | 20 MIN | WOOD | SOLID CORE |
| 112 | 112 | 1 3/4" | 20 MIN | WOOD | SOLID CORE |
| 110 | --- | 1 3/4" | 45 MIN | METAL | MINERAL CORE |
| 108 | 108 | 1 3/4" | 20 MIN | WOOD | SOLID CORE |
| 106 | 106 | 1 1/2" | NO RATE | WOOD | HOLLOW |
| 102 | 102 | 1 1/2" | NO RATE | WOOD | HOLLOW |
| 104 | 104 | 1 3/4" | 20 MIN | WOOD | SOLID CORE |
| 107 | 107 | 1 3/4" | 45 MIN | METAL | MINERAL CORE |
| 105 | 105 | 1 3/4" | 20 MIN | WOOD | SOLID CORE |
| 101 | 101 | 1 3/4" | 20 MIN | WOOD | SOLID CORE |

*Figure 8.6:　Columns in the Txt and Monotxt fonts*

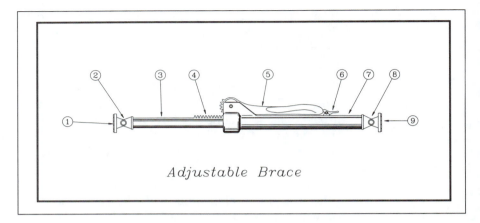

*Figure 8.7:    Italicc (Italic Complex) is used as the title of this parts diagram.*

## Creating a Type Style Using Fonts

Your drawings would look pretty boring if you used the same text style over and over. AutoCAD LT gives you the ability to create any number of text styles based on a set of predefined fonts. To create a style, you use Format ➤ Text Style… and then select from the fonts available from AutoCAD LT, or you can use the PostScript and TrueType fonts provided. This next exercise will show you how to create a text style quickly from the predefined set of AutoCAD LT fonts.

> **TIP**   Style is a command that can be used transparently (while another command is active). To use a command (or a system variable) transparently, put an apostrophe before it, as in ´ddstyle when entering it through the keyboard.

1. Click on Format ➤ Text Style or type **Ddstyle** ↵. The Text Style Dialog box appears.

2. In the Styles input box in the upper-left corner of the dialog box, you will see the name STANDARD. This is currently the default text style for any new drawing. To change the style, highlight STANDARD in the input box, type **Romans**, and then click the New button. The name ROMANS will appear in the list below the input box telling you that you've created a new text style.

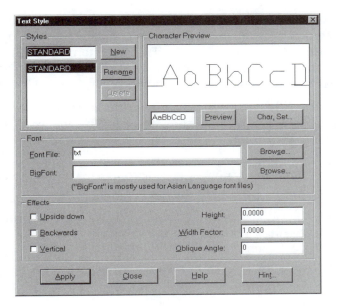

  **TIP** If you need to use several different text heights using the same text font in a drawing, you may want to keep the text height at 0. However, if you are using only two or three heights, you'll be better off creating two or three different type styles with specific heights.

3.  To select a font for your new style, first make sure that the Romans style name is highlighted in the list box. Click on the Browse button to the right of the Font file input box. This opens the Select Font File dialog box.

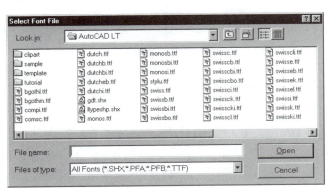

4. Locate and then double-click on the Romans .SHX font file. In this dialog box, you can select from the standard AutoCAD LT fonts, (.SHX), PostScript fonts (.PFB), or TrueType fonts (.TTF). Once you select a font you will be returned to the Text Style dialog box. The Character Preview window shows you what your text style looks like.

5. In the Effects option group near the bottom of this dialog box, locate the Height input box, then enter **6**. This will give the Romans style a fixed, 6″ text height.

   ▶ If you enter a value other than 0 at this prompt, it becomes the default height for this style. Then, when you use this style, you will not be prompted for a text height.

   ▶ If you accept the 0 value here, you will be prompted for a height setting whenever you use this style with the Line Text and the Text command.

6. Locate the Width factor input box and enter **.8** for this option. Here, you can compress or expand the font. Width factor values less than 1 will *compress* the font; values greater than 1 will *expand* the font. (You may find that you need a compressed font to fit into tight spaces. Or you may want to expand a font because of some graphic design consideration. See Figure 8.8.)

7. Click on the Preview button below the Character Preview window to review the effects of these settings on your new style.

8. Click on Apply. You now have a new text style called Romans that uses the Romans.SHX font and has a text height of 6 inches and a width factor of .8.

```
This is the Simplex font expanded by 1.4
This is the simplex font using a width factor of 1
This is the simplex font compressed by .6
```

*Figure 8.8:* **Examples of compressed and expanded fonts**

## Turning Text Upside Down and Backwards

In step 7 you got a preview of how the Width factor option in the Effects group affects the text style. The other Effects options—Oblique angle, Upside down, Backwards, and Vertical—offer further modifications to the style. The Oblique angle option lets you slant the text to create an italic look (see Figure 8.9).

> *This is the simplex font*
> *using a 12-degree oblique angle*

Figure 8.9: **The Simplex font with a 12-degree oblique angle**

The other check boxes do the following:

| | |
|---|---|
| Backwards? <N> | Makes the text appear backwards, as if in a mirror |
| Upside-down? <N> | Sets the style to appear upside-down, so you don't have to enter the text and rotate it |
| Vertical? <N> | Arranges lines of text vertically |

### Renaming a Type Style

In the last exercise, you named the new text style Romans—the same name as the font you selected. Giving the text style the same name as the font can help you remember what font you are using. But suppose you want to use another name for your newly created style. For example, you might want to create two styles of differing height using the same Romans font. Here's how you can change the style name:

1. Click on Format ➤ Rename... or enter **Ddrename** ↵ at the command prompt. The Rename dialog box appears.

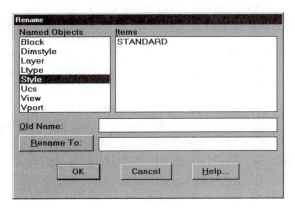

> **NOTE** The Ddrename command allows you to rename blocks, dimension styles, layers, line types, user coordinate systems, viewports, and views, as well as text styles.

2. In the Named Objects list box, click on Style.

3. Click on the name ROMANS that appears in the Items list to the right; this makes ROMANS appear in the Old Name input box below the list.

4. In the input box next to the Rename To: button, enter the name **NOTE2**.

5. Then click on the Rename To: button, and then on OK. (If you simply click on OK the object is not renamed.)

> **NOTE** You can also rename a text style via Format ➤ Text Style. When the Text Style dialog box opens, highlight the style name you want to change in the Styles input box. Type in the desired name and click on the Rename button. Click on the Close button to exit the dialog box.

Now that you have renamed Romans to Note2, Note2 is your current style. You'll get a chance to see how this style will look in your drawing, but first, let's look at another way of creating a text style.

## Using PostScript and TrueType Fonts

*Display fonts* are fonts used in situations where appearances are important. In a typical architectural project, for example, display fonts are frequently used for presentation drawings of floor plans and building elevations. With PostScript and TrueType support, you can add display fonts (see Figure 8.10) directly to your CAD drawings, thereby saving time and gaining the ability to make multiple copies of your artwork. Here's how it's done.

1. Select Format ➤ Text Style or enter **Ddstyle** ↵ at the command prompt. The Text Style dialog box appears, with **Note2** (the current default) highlighted in the Styles input box.

2. Type **Note** in place of Note2, and click on the New button.

**3.**  Click on the Browse button next to the Font File edit box. The Select Font File dialog box appears.

> **TIP**  You can use the PSout command (or the File ➤ Export option) to export your drawings as fully PostScript-compatible files. Then download the file to a PostScript device for more accurate text reproduction.

This is CIBT_____.pfb
*This is COBT_____.pfb*
This is EUR_____.pfb
*This is EURO____.pfb*
This is PAR.pfb
This is ROM_____.pfb
**This is ROMB____.pfb**
*This is ROMI___.pfb*
This is SAS_____.pfb
**This is SASB____.pfb**
***This is SASBO___.pfb***
*This is SASO_____.pfb*
This is SUE.pfb
THIS IS TE_____.PFB
THIS IS TEB_____.PFB
THIS IS TEL_____.PFB
Τηισ ισ ΘΜΑΤΗ·ττφ
*This is SWISSLI.ttf*
**This is VINET.ttf**
This is SWISSL.ttf
**This is SWISSEK.ttf**
This is SWISSKO.ttf
**This is SWISSEB.ttf**
This is SWISSE.ttf
***This is SWISSKI.ttf***
**This is SWISSK.ttf**
*This is SWISSI.ttf*

*This is SWISSCLI.ttf*
This is SWISSEL.ttf
This is SWISSCL.ttf
**THIS IS BGOTHL.TTF**
**THIS IS BGOTHM.TTF**
. % %® %® '_'_÷★⑩⑩™  **(compl.ttf)**
*This is COMPC.ttf*
This is DUTCH.ttf
**This is DUTCHB.ttf**
***This is DUTCHBI.ttf***
**This is DUTCHEB.ttf**
*This is DUTCHI.ttf*
This is MONOS.ttf
**This is MONOSB.ttf**
***This is MONOSBI.ttf***
*This is MONOSI.ttf*
This is STYLU.ttf
This is SWISS.ttf
**This is SWISSB.ttf**
***This is SWISSBI.ttf***
This is SWISSBO.ttf
This is SWISSC.ttf
**This is SWISSCB.ttf**
***This is SWISSCBI.ttf***
This is SWISSCBO.ttf
*This is SWISSCI.ttf*
**This is SWISSCK.ttf**
***This is SWISSCKI.ttf***

*Figure 8.10:  **PostScript and TrueType fonts supplied with AutoCAD LT***

4. Locate the PostScript font file TE_____.PFB, and double-click on it. (To quickly locate this file, use the Files of Type drop-down list at the bottom of the dialog box to select PostScript Font (\*.PFA, \*.PFB). This will cause the list box to display only the files with the .PFA or .PFB filename extensions.) Select TE_____.PFB, and click on the Open button.

5. In the Height input box, enter **6**.

6. Complete the rest of the input boxes just as you did in the previous exercise.

### The Textfill System Variable

Unlike the standard stick-like AutoCAD LT fonts, PostScript and True-Type fonts have filled areas. These filled areas take more time to generate, so if you have a lot of text in these fonts, your redraw and regen times will increase dramatically. To help reduce these, AutoCAD LT normally displays and plots these fonts as outline fonts, even though they are filled in their true appearance.

If you want, however, you can display and plot these fonts as solid filled fonts by adjusting the Textfill system variable. To change its setting, type **Textfill** ↵ and then type **1** ↵. This turns on text fill for PostScript and TrueType fonts. You can then plot your file with the text appearing as solid, filled text instead of outlined. When you are editing your file, you will want to turn Textfill off.

## Using a Type Style

Now let's see how to use the text styles you created. In the next exercise, you'll also get a chance to use center justification for your text.

1. Click on Line Text on the Draw toolbar.

2. At the DTEXT Justify/Style/<Start point>: prompt, enter **C** ↵.

3. Pick a point near the center of the living room at coordinate 21'-11", 15'-2".

4. At the Rotation angle prompt, press ↵ to accept the default 0 angle.

5. At the Text prompt, enter **Living room** ↵. (Your text will not be centered yet.)

6. Press ↵ again. This ends the Line Text command and executes the centering of your text on the selected point.

You might have noticed that in step 4 you got the Rotation angle prompt, skipping over the Height prompt. Remember that when you use a style with a height other than 0, AutoCAD LT doesn't bother to ask you what height you want. In this example, the text style has a preset height of 6″, so you are not prompted for a value.

> **NOTE** When you use the Style command, your default style becomes the one you most recently edited or created.

In the last exercise, you entered text using the current default style. If you want to use a style other than the current one, you can use the Current Properties dialog box to change the current style.

1. Choose Format ➤ Current Properties or click on the Current Properties button on the Object Properties toolbar. The Current Properties dialog box appears. Alternatively, you may type **Ddemodes** ↵ at the command line.

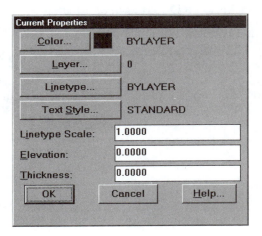

2. To change the current text style, click on Text Style…. The Text Style dialog box appears.

From here, you can choose from the list of styles available. The list only shows styles you've already created. You can also view the style's properties and see a sample.

**3.** Click on the STANDARD text style, and then on Close.

**4.** In the Current Properties dialog box, click on OK.

**5.** Click on Line Text from the Draw toolbar or enter **Dtext** ↵.

---

**TIP** If you remember all the justification options, you can enter them directly at the `Justify/Style/<Start point>` prompt and skip the `Justify` prompt.

---

**6.** Type **C** ↵.

**7.** Pick the point at coordinate 21′-11″, 14′-4″. This time the `Height` prompt appears, because you are now using a font whose height is set to 0. Notice how the default height is still at the last size you entered.

**8.** Press ↵ to accept the default height, and again to accept the default angle.

9. Enter **14′-0″ by 16′–5″** ↵.

10. Press ↵ again to exit Line Text.

11. Zoom in to this group of text. Now you can see the Note and Standard styles, as shown in Figure 8.11. The words "Living room" use the Technic font (TE_____.PFB) from the Note style, a smooth letterform. The dimensions 14′-0″ by 1′-5″ use the AutoCAD TXT font from the Standard text style.

12. Start Line Text again.

13. At the Starting point prompt, press ↵, and enter **230 square feet** ↵.

14. Press ↵ again to exit Line Text.

15. Now zoom to your previous view.

    Notice how the text you just entered is centered below the previously entered text (see Figure 8.12). AutoCAD LT remembers not only the location of the last text you entered, but the starting point you selected for it. If you had moved the last line of text, the new text would still appear below it.

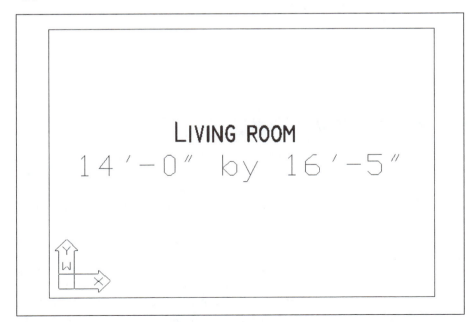

*Figure 8.11:* **A close-up showing the Note and Standard styles**

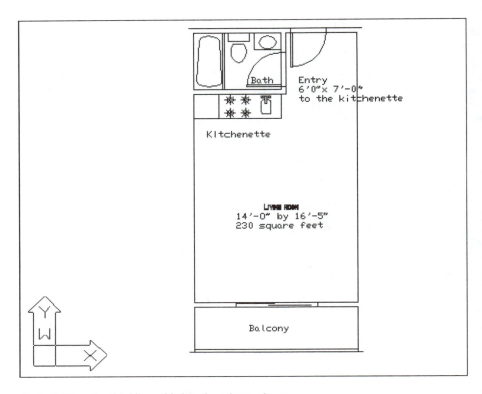

*Figure 8.12:*    **The third line added to the column of text**

# Modifying Existing Text

AutoCAD LT offers a variety of ways to modify text. Nearly every property associated with text can be edited. Of course, you can also edit the contents of the text. In this section, you will learn the various ways that text can be controlled to do exactly what you want it to do.

## Changing the Properties of Text

Perhaps the simplest way to modify text is to use the Properties button in the Object Properties toolbar. This option gives you access to virtually all of the properties that control the appearance of text. Let's see how it works. Before you start, save your existing drawing.

## ADDING SPECIAL CHARACTERS

You can add special characters to your text in AutoCAD LT. For example, you can place the degree symbol (°) after a number, or you can underscore (underline) text. To accomplish this, you use double percent (%%) signs in conjunction with a special code. For example, to underscore text, you enclose that text with the %% signs and follow it with the underscore code. So, to get this text:

This is <u>underscored</u> text.

you would enter this at the prompt:

**This is %%underscored%%u text.**

Overscoring (putting a line above the text) operates in the same manner.

To insert codes for symbols, you just place the codes in the correct positions for the symbols they represent. For example, to enter 100.5°, you type **100.5%%d**.

Here is a list of the codes you can use:

| Code | Special Characters |
| --- | --- |
| %%o | Toggles overscore on and off |
| %%u | Toggles underscore on and off |
| %%d | Places a degree sign (°) where the code occurs |
| %%p | Places a plus-minus sign where the code occurs |
| %%% | Forces a single percent sign; useful where you want a double percent sign to appear, or when you want a percent sign in conjunction with another code |
| %%*nnn* | Allows the use of extended ASCII characters when these characters are used in a text-definition file; *nnn* is the three-digit value representing the character |

1.  Zoom in to the entry area in the upper-right corner of the floor plan again.

2.  Click on the Properties button on the Object Properties toolbar.

**3.** At the `Select objects` prompt, click on the bottom line of the currently displayed text and then press ↵. The Modify Text dialog box appears; take a moment now to review the options.

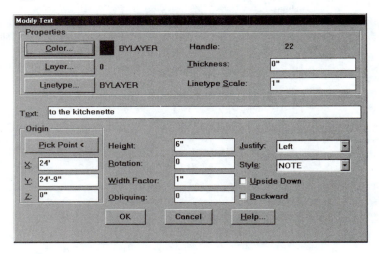

**4.** In the Modify Text dialog box, click on the arrow beside the Style pull-down list, which will then display all three text styles available in this file.

**5.** Click on NOTE, and the pull-down list closes.

**6.** Click on OK. The dialog box closes, and the text you selected changes to the new style (see Figure 8.13).

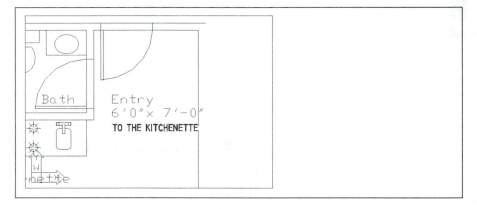

*Figure 8.13:*   ***After changing the style to NOTE***

The Modify Text dialog box lets you change everything—from the text's justification style to its contents.

## Text Editing Simplified

When you want to change the contents of several lines of text, you may find the Modify Text dialog box a bit unwieldy. With the Ddedit command, you can quickly edit several lines of text.

1. Click and drag the Edit Polyline flyout on the Modify toolbar and then select Edit Text, or enter **Ddedit** ↵.

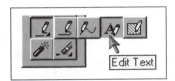

2. At the `<Select an Annotation object>/Undo:` prompt, click on the second-to-last line of text displayed on the screen. A dialog box appears displaying that text.

3. Click on the space between the *x* and the *7*.

4. Press the Backspace key to delete the letter *x*, and then enter **by**.

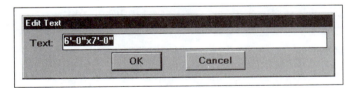

5. Click on OK, and the text in the drawing reflects your modifications.

6. At the `Select an Annotation object` prompt, click on the next line down. The Edit Text dialog box appears again, allowing you to make more changes.

7. Click on OK.

8. Now click on Undo from the Standard toolbar or enter **U** ↵. The text you just edited changes back to its previous form, and the `Select an Annotation object` prompt remains.

9. Press ↵ to exit Ddedit.

You can edit text in the Ddedit dialog box just as you would in any other input box. Just double-click on the input box and proceed to enter an entirely new line of text. Or, as you have just seen, you can easily edit one or two letters within the current line of text.

### Keeping Text from Mirroring

At times you will want to mirror a group of objects that contain some text. This operation will cause the mirrored text to appear backward. You can change a setting in AutoCAD LT to make the text read normally, even when it is mirrored.

**1.** Enter **Mirrtext** ↵.

**2.** At the New value for MIRRTEXT <1>: prompt, enter **0** ↵.

Now, any mirrored text that is not in a block will read normally. The text's *position*, however, will still be mirrored, as shown in Figure 8.14.

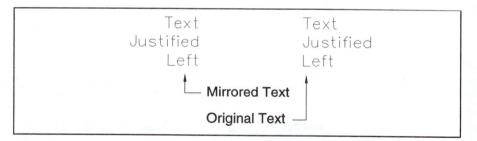

Figure 8.14: *Mirrored text, with MIRRTEXT set to 0*

## Entering Large Blocks of Text

If you have a substantial amount of text in a drawing, or a sheet of general notes for a set of drawings, you can use the Paragraph Text, or Multiline Text (MText), command to enter text. MText lets you enter and format entire paragraphs or lists. It offers features such as word wrapping to help you fit text in a specific area. Using specific command line codes, you can create variable text height, stacked fractions, and multiple styles. Here's how it works.

**1.** Click and drag the Text flyout from the Draw menu and select Paragraph Text, or type **MText** ↵.

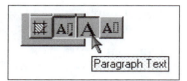

2. At the `Justify/Style/Height/ <Insertion point>` prompt, click on a point defining the upper-left corner of the area in which you want to place your word-wrapped text.

3. At the `Other corner` prompt, a window appears. Size the window to indicate the area within which you want to place your text. This text area is called the text boundary.

4. Once you've selected a text boundary, AutoCAD LT opens the Edit MText dialog box (see Figure 8.15).

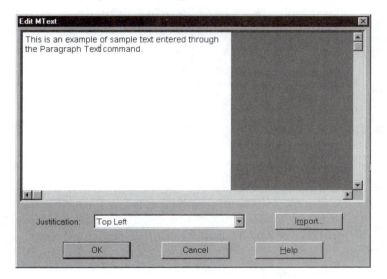

*Figure 8.15:* **The Edit MText dialog box**

5. Start typing your notes. As you type, the text appears in the window at the top of the dialog box just as it will appear in the drawing. Notice that the text appears in the white area of the window. This white area represents the width of the area you selected in step 2 and 3 when you defined the area within which you want to place your text. This width will vary depending on the width of the area you select and the size of the text style you are currently using.

6. When you are done entering your note, click on OK. The note appears in your drawing at the location you selected in step 2.

At any time while you are typing in step 5, you can make corrections to the text by moving the vertical bar text cursor to the location of your correction and making the appropriate changes. Just as with any text editor, you can highlight and replace whole blocks of text using your cursor.

As you can see from the prompt in step 2, you can set the rotation, style, height, and direction of the text before you enter it. You can also attach text to an existing text object. If you don't designate values for these other settings, AutoCAD LT will use the current default text settings.

## Editing and Formatting Paragraph Text

Paragraph, or Multiline text, offers many options for editing and formatting. In this section you'll take a closer look at that Edit MText dialog box and explore some of its other options.

The Edit MText dialog box doesn't appear only when you create new text. It also appears when you attempt to edit existing Multiline text. The following exercise demonstrates this.

1. Click on the Edit Text button on the Special Edit flyout on the Modify toolbar.

2. At the `Select an annotation object` prompt, click on the Multiline text.

3. The Edit MText dialog box appears with the selected text in its edit window. At this point, you can make changes to your text, and then click on OK to exit the dialog box. The changes appear in your drawing.

### Importing Text Files

With Multiline text objects, AutoCAD LT allows you to import standard ASCII text. Here's how you go about importing text files.

1. From the Edit MText dialog box, click on Import....

2. At the Import Text File dialog box, locate a valid text file. It must be a file in a raw text (ASCII) format such as a Notepad .TXT file.

3. Once you've highlighted the file you want, double-click on it or click on the Open button. The text appears in the Edit MText window.

4.  You can then click on OK and the text will appear in your drawing.

    In addition, you can use the Windows clipboard and Cut and Paste feature to add text to a drawing. To do this, take the following steps:

1.  Use the Cut or Copy option in any other Windows 95 program to place text into the Windows 95 clipboard.

2.  Go to AutoCAD LT, then choose Edit ➤ Paste. The text appears in the upper-left corner of the AutoCAD LT drawing window.

    Since AutoCAD LT is an OLE client, you can also attach other types of documents to an AutoCAD LT drawing file. See *Chapter 14* for more on AutoCAD LT's OLE support.

---

## EMBEDDING FORMAT CODES IN MULTIPLE-LINE TEXT

The formatting of Paragraph text is accomplished through the use of special codes at the command line. Here are the codes and their uses:

| | |
|---|---|
| \O | Start overline |
| \o | Stop overline |
| \U | Start underline |
| \u | Stop underline |
| \~ | Nonbreaking space (keeps words together on a line) |
| \\ | Literal backslash |
| \{ | Literal opening brace |
| \} | Literal closing brace |
| \C*<number>*; | Change to color *<number>* |
| \F*<filename>*; | Change to font *<filename>* |
| \H*<size>*; | Change to text height *<size>*; to indicate a size relative to the main body of text, you can use an x (as in .75x) |
| \S*<string>*; | Stack two strings, as in fractions |

To use these codes on blocks of text, you must enclose the coded text within braces. For example, to display this statement:

Include all new electrical equipment

with the words *all new* in red, you would type the following:

```
Include {\C1;all new} electrical equipment
```

Here C1 refers to the color number 1 (red); and the curly braces indicate the extent of text that is to be changed to red.

These codes are not available in the MText dialog box.

## *Checking Spelling*

Although AutoCAD LT is primarily a drawing program, you will find that some of your drawings contain more text than graphics. At long last, Autodesk has recognized this and has included a spelling checker in AutoCAD LT Release 3. If you've ever used the spelling checker in a typical Windows word processor, such as Microsoft Word for Windows, the AutoCAD LT spelling checker's operation will be familiar to you. Here's how it works:

1. Choose Tools ➤ Spelling…, or type **Spell** ↵ at the command prompt.

2. At the `Select object` prompt, select any text object(s) created with the Text, Line Text (Dtext), or Multiline Text (MText) commands, or enter **all**. When the spelling checker finds a word it does not recognize, the Check Spelling dialog box appears.

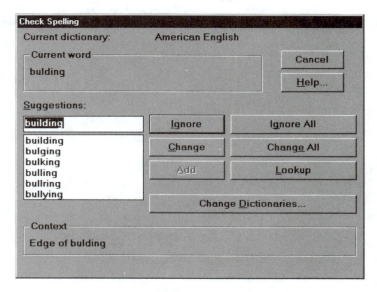

In the Check Spelling dialog box you'll see the word in question, along with the spelling checker's suggested alternate word, in the Suggestions input box. If the spelling checker finds more than one suggestion, a list of suggested replacement words appears below the input box. You can then highlight the desired replacement and click on the Change button to change the misspelled word, or click on Change All to change all occurrences of the word in the selected text. If the suggested word is inappropriate, choose another word from the replacement list (if any), or enter your own spelling. Then choose Change or Change All.

Here are the other options available to you in the Check Spelling dialog box:

**Ignore**   skips the word.

**Ignore All**   skips all the occurrences of the word in the selected text.

**Add**   adds the word in question to the current dictionary.

**Lookup**   checks the spelling of the word in the Suggestions box. This option is for the times when you decide to try another word that doesn't appear in the Suggestions input box.

**Change Dictionaries**   lets you use a different dictionary to check spelling. This option opens the Change Dictionaries dialog box, described in the upcoming section.

**Context**   displays the phrase in which the word in question was found.

### Choosing a Dictionary

The Change Dictionaries option opens the Change Dictionaries dialog box, where you can select a particular main dictionary for foreign languages, or create or choose a custom dictionary. Main dictionary files have the .DCT extension. The Main dictionary for the U.S. version of AutoCAD LT is ENU.DCT.

In this dialog box, you can also add or delete words from a custom dictionary. Custom dictionary files are ASCII files with the .CUS extension. Because they are ASCII files, they can be edited outside of AutoCAD LT. The Browse button lets you view a list of existing custom dictionaries.

If you prefer, you can also select a main or custom dictionary using the Dctcust and Dctmain system variables. See *Appendix D* for more on these system variables.

## Accelerating Zooms and Regens with Qtext

If you need to edit a drawing that contains lots of text, but you don't need to edit the text, you can use the Qtext command to help accelerate redraws and regenerations when you are working on the drawing. Qtext turns lines of text into rectangular boxes, saving AutoCAD LT from having to form every letter. This allows you to see the note locations so you don't accidentally draw over them.

To turn on Qtext:

1. Select Options ➤ Drawing Aids... and turn on the Quick Text check box, or enter **Qtext** ↵ at the command prompt.

2. At the ON/OFF <OFF>: prompt, enter **ON** ↵.

3. To display the results of Qtext, issue the Regen command from the prompt.

When Qtext is off, text is generated normally. When Qtext is on, rectangles show the approximate size and length of text, as shown in Figure 8.16.

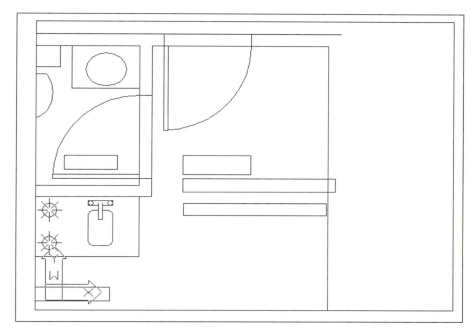

*Figure 8.16:*  **Text with Qtext off and on**

## If You Want to Experiment...

At this point, you may want to try adding some notes to drawings you have created in other "If You Want to Experiment..." sections of this book. Try the exercise shown in Figure 8.17. You might also try cutting and pasting a finish or door schedule from a word processor in the Monotxt font, to see how that works. If your application is mechanical, you might try importing a parts list.

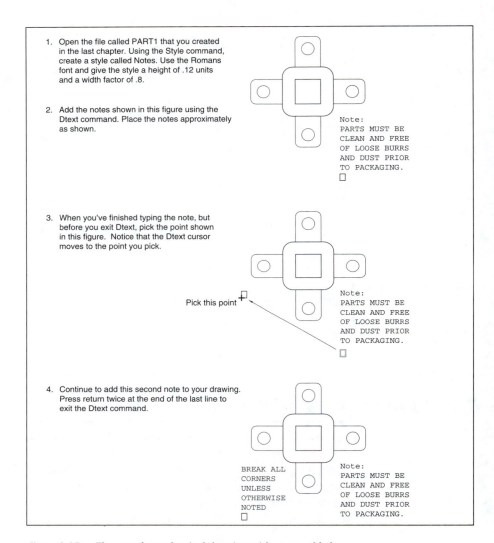

1. Open the file called PART1 that you created in the last chapter. Using the Style command, create a style called Notes. Use the Romans font and give the style a height of .12 units and a width factor of .8.

2. Add the notes shown in this figure using the Dtext command. Place the notes approximately as shown.

3. When you've finished typing the note, but before you exit Dtext, pick the point shown in this figure. Notice that the Dtext cursor moves to the point you pick.

Pick this point

4. Continue to add this second note to your drawing. Press return twice at the end of the last line to exit the Dtext command.

Note:
PARTS MUST BE
CLEAN AND FREE
OF LOOSE BURRS
AND DUST PRIOR
TO PACKAGING.

BREAK ALL
CORNERS
UNLESS
OTHERWISE
NOTED

*Figure 8.17:*     ***The sample mechanical drawing with notes added***

# Chapter 9
# Using Dimensions

## *FAST TRACKS*

**B**EFORE you determine the dimensions of a project, your design is in flux and many questions may be unanswered. Once you begin dimensioning, you begin to see if things fit or work together. Dimensioning can be crucial to how well a design works and how quickly it develops. Communicating even tentative dimensions to others can accelerate design development.

With AutoCAD LT, you can easily add tentative or final dimensions to any drawing. AutoCAD LT gives you an accurate dimension without your having to take measurements. You simply pick the two points to be dimensioned and the dimension line location, and AutoCAD LT does the rest. AutoCAD LT's *associative dimensioning* capability automatically updates dimensions whenever the size or shape of the dimensioned object is changed. These dimensioning features can save you valuable time and reduce the number of dimensional errors in your drawings.

AutoCAD LT's dimensioning feature has a substantial number of settings. Though they give you enormous flexibility in formatting your dimensions, all these settings can be somewhat intimidating to the new user. We'll ease you into dimensioning by first showing you how to create a *dimension style*.

# Creating a Dimension Style

Dimension styles are similar to text styles. They determine the look of your dimensions as well as the size of dimensioning features, such as the dimension text and arrows. You might set up a dimension style to have special types of arrows, for instance, or to position the dimension text above or in line with the dimension line.

AutoCAD LT gives you a default dimension style called Standard, which is set up for mechanical drafting. You will doubtless add many other styles to suit the style of drawings you are creating. You can also create variations of a general style for those situations that call for only minor changes in the dimension's appearance.

In this first section you'll see how to set up a dimension style that is more appropriate for architectural drawings (see Figure 9.1).

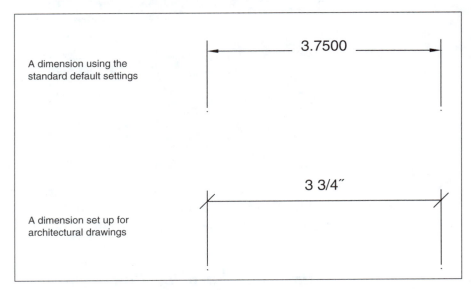

A dimension using the standard default settings

3.7500

A dimension set up for architectural drawings

3 3/4˝

*Figure 9.1:   AutoCAD LT's standard dimension style compared with an architectural-style dimension*

1.   Open the Unit file. Use the Unit file you created, or open 09-Unit.DWG from the companion CD. The drawing appears just as you left it in the last session.

2. You should create a new layer called DIM, and put your dimension information on this layer. This way, you will be able to turn dimension information on and off as required.

3. Click on Format ➤ Dimension Style..., or type **Ddim** ↵ at the command prompt. The Dimension Styles dialog box appears.

4. Double-click on the Name input box to highlight STANDARD, and then type in **architect**.

5. Click on Save.

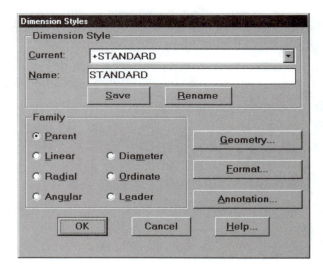

You've just created a dimension style called Architect, but at this point, it is identical to the Standard style on which it is based. Nothing has happened to the Standard style, of course; it is still available if you need to use it.

## Setting the Dimension Unit Style

Now you need to modify the new Architect dimension style so that it conforms to the architectural style of dimensioning. Let's start by changing the unit style for the dimension text. Just as you changed the overall unit style of AutoCAD LT to a foot-and-inches style for your toilet and tub drawing in *Chapter 3*, you must do the same with dimension styles.

1.  In the Dimension Styles dialog box, click on the Annotation... button. The Annotation dialog box appears.

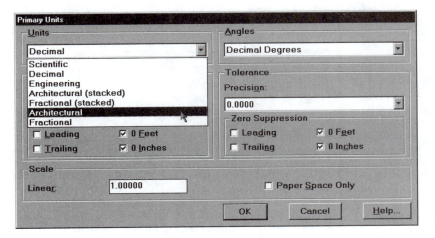

2.  In the Primary Units group, click on the Units... button. The Primary Units dialog box appears.

3.  Open the Units drop-down list and choose Architectural. Notice that this drop-down list contains the same unit styles as the main Units dialog box (Format ➤ Units...) plus "Stacked Architectural" and "Stacked Fractional."

4. In the Zero Suppression button group just below the Units list, click on 0 Inches to turn off this check box. If you leave it turned on, indications of 0 inches will be omitted from the dimension text. (In architectural drawings, 0 inches are shown as in this dimension: 12′-0″.)

5. Click on OK here and then again at the Annotation dialog box.

You have set up Architecture's dimension unit style to show dimensions in feet and inches, rather than inches and decimal inches.

**NOTE** Every dimension style setting has an equivalent system variable. See *Appendix D* for more on system variables that are directly associated with dimensions.

### Setting the Location of Dimension Text

AutoCAD LT's default setting for the placement of dimension text puts the text in line with the dimension line, as shown in the example at the top of Figure 9.1. However, we want the new Architectural style to put the text above the dimension line, as is done at the bottom of Figure 9.1. To do that, you will use the dimension style Format options.

1. In the Dimension Style dialog box, click on the Format... button. The Format dialog box appears.

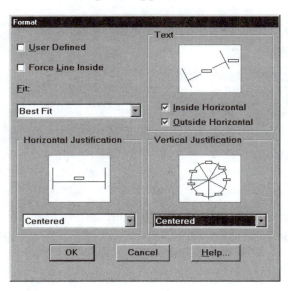

2. In the Vertical Justification box that occupies the lower-right corner of the dialog box, open the pull-down list and choose Above. The icon graphic changes to show you what this format will look like in your dimensions.

 **NOTE** You may click directly on any of the graphics in the Dimension Styles dialog boxes to cycle through all of the dimensioning options presented.

3. In the Text box (upper-right corner of the dialog box), click on the Inside Horizontal and Outside Horizontal check boxes to turn them both off. The graphic shows you the effect of these settings on your dimensions.

4. Now click OK to return to the Dimension Style dialog box.

## Choosing an Arrow Style and Setting the Dimension Scale

Next, you will want to specify a different type of arrow for your new dimension style. For linear dimension in architectural drawings, a diagonal line or "tick" mark is typically used, rather than an arrow.

In addition, you will want to set the scale for the graphical components of the dimension, such as the arrows and text. Recall from *Chapter 8* that text must be scaled up in size in order to appear at the proper size in the final output of the drawing. Dimensions, too, must be scaled so they look right when the drawing is plotted. For both the arrow and scale settings, you will use the Geometry settings.

1. In the Dimension Styles dialog box, click on the Geometry... button. The Geometry dialog box appears.

 **NOTE** You can create your own arrowheads. See *Appendix D* for details.

2. In the Arrowheads group, open the first pull-down list and choose Oblique. The graphic shows you what the arrow looks like. You can also cycle through all the arrow options by clicking on the graphic in the Arrowhead group.

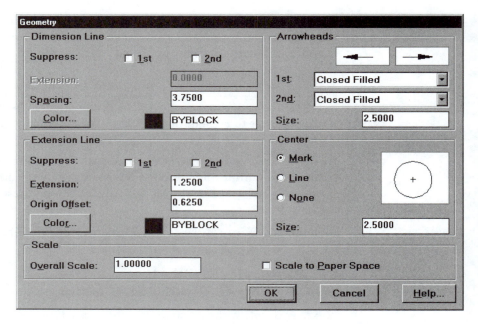

3. Locate the Overall Scale input box at the lower-left of the dialog box, and change this value to 48, the scale factor for a ¼″ scale drawing.

4. Click on OK here and then again at the Dimension Style dialog box. Now you're ready to add architectural dimensions.

TIP   Here's a simple way to figure out scale factors: Divide 12 by the decimal equivalent of the inch scale. So for ¼″ equals one foot, divide 12 by 0.25 to get 48. For ⅛″, divide 12 by 0.125 to get 96. For 1½″, divide 12 by 1.5 to get 8, and so on.

In this section, we've introduced you to the various dialog boxes that let you set the appearance of a dimension style. We haven't been able to discuss every option, of course, so if you want to learn more about the other dimension style options, consult *Appendix D*. There you'll find descriptions of all the items in the Dimension Styles dialog box, plus reference material covering the system variables associated with each option.

# Drawing Linear Dimensions

The most common type of dimension you'll be using is the linear dimension, which is an orthogonal dimension measuring the width and length of an object. AutoCAD LT offers three dimensioning tools for this purpose: Linear (Dimlinear), Continue (Dimcont), and Baseline (Dimbase). These options are readily accessible from the Dimensioning toolbar.

## Finding the Dimensioning Toolbar

Before you can apply any dimension, you'll want to open the Dimensioning toolbar. This toolbar contains nearly all of the commands necessary to draw and edit your dimensions.

Choose View ➤ Toolbars ➤ Dimensioning, or click on Dimensioning from the Tool Windows flyout on the Standard toolbar. The dimensioning toolbar appears.

Now you're ready to begin dimensioning.

## Placing Horizontal and Vertical Dimensions

Let's start by looking at the basic dimensioning tool, Linear. In Release 3, the Linear Dimension button (the Dimlinear command) on the Dimensioning toolbar accommodates both the horizontal and vertical dimensions.

In this exercise, you'll add a vertical dimension to the right side of the Unit plan. Dimension text can run either horizontally (always parallel to the bottom of the drawing) or parallel to the dimension line itself. This setting is controlled by the Dimension variable Dimtih. When Dimtih is ON, dimension text is drawn horizontally; when it is OFF, text is drawn parallel to the dimension line.

1. Set the Dimtih variable to OFF. Type **dimtih** ↵, and then type **OFF** ↵.

2. To start either a vertical or horizontal dimension, click on the Linear Dimension button on the Dimensioning toolbar, or enter **Dimlinear** ⏎ at the command prompt.

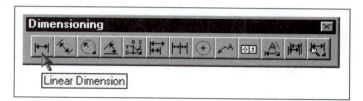

 **NOTE** Notice that the prompt in step 3 gives you the option of pressing ⏎ to select an object. If you do this, you are prompted to pick the object you wish to dimension, rather than the actual distance to be dimensioned. We'll look at this method later.

3. The prompt, `First extension line origin or RETURN to select:`, is asking you for the first point of the distance to be dimensioned. An extension line is the line that connects the object being dimensioned to the dimension line. Use the Endpoint Osnap override and pick the upper-right corner of the entry, at the coordinate 29′-0″, 30′-10″.

4. At the `Second extension line origin:` prompt, pick the lower-right corner of the living room, at coordinate 29′-0″, 6′-10″.

5. In the next prompt,

   ```
   Dimension line location (Text/Angle/Horizontal/Vertical/
   Rotated):
   ```

   the dimension line is the line indicating the direction of the dimension and containing the arrows or tick marks. As you move your cursor from left to right, you will see a temporary dimension appear. This allows you to visually select a dimension line location.

 **NOTE** You have the option to append information to the dimension's text or change the dimension text altogether. You'll see how later in this chapter.

6. Enter **@4′<0** ⏎ to tell AutoCAD LT you want the dimension line to be 4 feet to the right of the last point you selected. (You could pick a point using your cursor, but this doesn't let you place the dimension line as

accurately.) After you've done this, the dimension is placed in the drawing as shown in Figure 9.2.

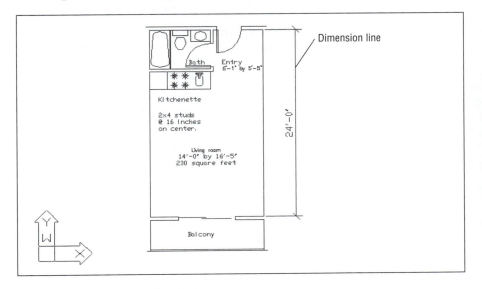

*Figure 9.2:* **The dimension line added to the unit drawing**

## Continuing a Dimension

You will often want to input a group of dimensions strung together in a line. For example, you may want to continue dimensioning the balcony and have the continued dimension aligned with the dimension you just entered. To do this, you use the Dimensioning menu's Continue option.

**1.** Click on the Continue Dimension button on the Dimensioning toolbar, or enter **Dimcont** ↵.

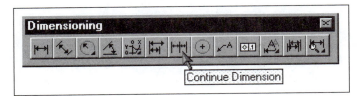

2.  At the Second extension line origin or RETURN to Select: prompt, pick the upper-right corner of the balcony at coordinate 29´-0″, 6´-5″. See the top panel of Figure 9.3 for the results.

3.  Pick the right end of the rail on the balcony, at coordinate 29´-0″, 2´-8″. See the bottom panel of Figure 9.3 for the results.

4.  Press ↵ twice to exit the Dimcont command.

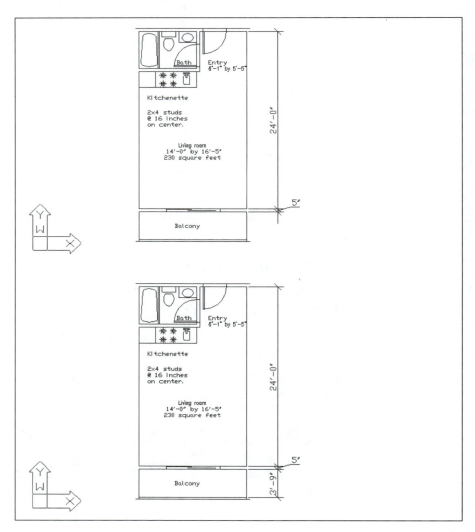

*Figure 9.3:    The dimension string continued*

The Continue option adds a dimension from where you left off. The last drawn extension line is used as the first extension line for the continued dimension. AutoCAD LT will keep adding dimensions as you continue to pick points, until you press ↵.

### Continuing a Dimension from an Older Previous Dimension

If you need to continue a string of dimensions from an older linear dimension, instead of the most recently added one, press ↵ at the Second extension line origin or RETURN to Select prompt you saw in step 2 of the previous exercise. Then, at the Select continued dimension prompt, click on the extension line from which you wish to continue.

## Drawing Dimensions from a Common Base Extension Line

Another method for dimensioning objects is to have several dimensions originate from the same extension line. To accommodate this, Auto-CAD LT provides the Baseline option on the Dimensioning menu. To see how this works, you will start another dimension—this time a horizontal one—across the top of the plan.

1. Click on the Linear button on the Dimensioning toolbar. Or, just as you did for the vertical dimension, you can type **Dimlinear** ↵ to start the horizontal dimension.

2. At the First extension line… prompt, pick the upper-left corner of the bathroom, near coordinate 15′-0″, 30′-10″.

3. At the Second extension line… prompt, pick the upper-right corner of the bathroom, near coordinate 22′-6″, 30′-10″.

4. At the Dimension line… prompt, pick a point near coordinate 22′-5″, 33′-5″ (see Figure 9.4).

    Now you're all set to draw another dimension continuing from the first extension line of the dimension you just drew.

5. Click on the Baseline Dimension button on the Dimensioning toolbar. Or you can type **Dimbase** ↵ at the command prompt to start a baseline dimension.

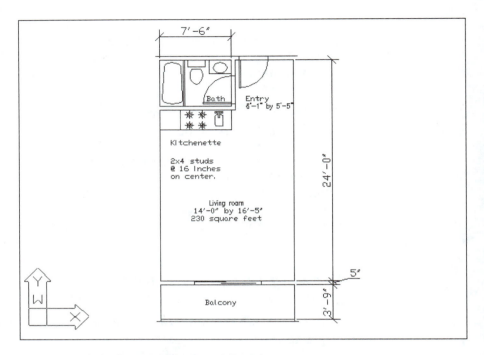

*Figure 9.4:    **The bathroom with horizontal dimension***

**6.** At the `Second extension line…` prompt, click on the upper-right corner of the entry as shown in Figure 9.5.

**7.** Click on the Zoom Out button until you see the entire drawing with the continued dimension, as shown in Figure 9.5.

**8.** Save the Unit drawing at this point. You will be using this version of the Unit drawing later, at the end of this tutorial.

In this example, you can see that the Baseline option is similar to the Continue option, except that Baseline allows you to use the first extension line of the previous dimension as the base for a second dimension.

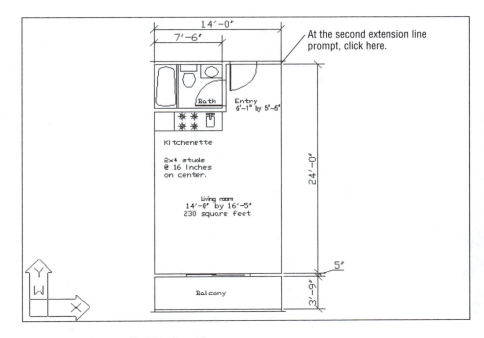

*Figure 9.5:* **The overall width dimension**

### Using an Older Previous Dimension

Just as with Continue Dimension (Dimcont command), you can draw baseline dimension from an older dimension by pressing ↵ at the Second extension line origin or RETURN to select prompt, and then selecting the dimension from which you want to draw the new baseline dimension.

## Editing Dimensions

As you begin to add more dimensions to your drawings, you will find that AutoCAD LT will occasionally place a dimension text or line in an inappropriate location, or you may need to make a modification to the dimension text. You cannot edit the individual elements of a dimension with the standard set of editing tools. In this section, you'll take an in-depth look at how dimensions can be modified to suit those special circumstances that always crop up.

## *Appending Data to Dimension Text*

So far in this chapter, you've been accepting the default dimension text. You know that if you need to, you can append information to the default dimension value as you select the dimension for annotation. When the Dimension line location prompt appears:

```
Dimension line location (Text/Angle/Horizontal/Vertical/
Rotated:)
```

type **T** ↵. On the Edit MText screen, add any required dimension information, either before or after the <> prompt. You may also change an existing dimension's text in much the same way.

### EDITING MULTIPLE DIMENSION TEXT USING DIMEDIT

The Dimedit command offers a quick way to edit existing dimensions. It adds the ability to edit more than one dimension's text at one time. The following example shows an alternative to the Properties option for appending text to a dimension.

1. Type **Dimedit** ↵.

2. At this prompt:

   ```
   Dimension Edit (Home/New/Rotate/Oblique)<Home>:
   ```

   type **N** ↵ to use the New option. When the Edit Mtext dialog box opens, type **to face of stud** ↵ after the <> prompt.

3. At the Select objects: prompt, pick the first dimension you wish to add the new text to. The Select objects: prompt remains, allowing you to select several dimensions.

4. Press ↵ to finish your selection. The dimensions change to include "to face of stud."

Dimedit is useful in editing dimension text, but you can also use this command to make graphical changes to the text. Here is a listing of the other Dimedit options:

**Home**   moves the dimension text to its standard default position and angle.

**Rotate**   allows you to rotate the dimension text to a new angle.

**Oblique**   skews the dimension extension lines to a new angle. See "Skewing Dimension Lines" later in this chapter.

**NOTE** You can also click on the Properties button on the toolbar, select a single dimension, and then, at the Modify Dimensions dialog box, click on Edit....

 **TIP** With Dimedit you can append text to several dimensions at once.

1. Click and drag Edit Polyline from the Modify toolbar, then select Edit Text.

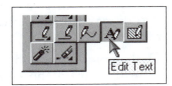

2. Next, click on the last horizontal dimension you added to the drawing at the top of the screen. The Edit MText dialog box appears. This is the same dialog box you saw in *Chapter 8* used for editing Multiline text. Notice the greater than and less than symbols (<>) in the window.

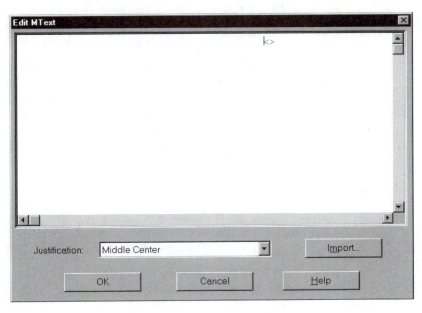

3. Move the cursor after the <> sign, then type "**to face of stud**".

4. Click on OK. The dimension changes to read "14′-0″ to face of stud". The text you entered is appended to the dimension text.

5. Because you don't really need the new appended text for the tutorial, click on the Undo button in the Standard toolbar to remove the appended text.

Using the Edit Text command, you were able to combine the dimension text "14′-0″" with the text "to face of stud".

In this exercise, you were only able to edit a single dimension. To append text to several dimensions at once, you need to use the Dimedit command. See the sidebar entitled "Editing Multiple Dimension Text Using Dimedit" for more on this command.

You can also have AutoCAD LT automatically add a dimension suffix or prefix to all dimensions, instead of just a chosen few, by using the Annotation option in the Dimension Styles dialog box. See *Appendix D* for more on this feature.

## Locating the Definition Points

AutoCAD LT provides the associative dimensioning capability to automatically update dimension text when a drawing is edited. Objects called *definition points* are used to determine how edited dimensions are updated.

The definition points are located at the same points you pick when you determine the dimension location. For example, the definition points for linear dimensions are the extension line origin and the intersection of the extension line/dimension line. The definition points for a circle diameter are the points used to pick the circle and the opposite side of the circle. For a radius, they are the points used to pick the circle, plus the center of the circle.

Definition points are actually point objects. They are very difficult to see because they are usually covered by the feature they define. You can, however, see them indirectly using grips. The definition points of a dimension are the same as the dimension's grip points. You can see them simply by clicking on a dimension. Try the following:

1. Make sure the Grips feature is turned on (see *Chapter 2* to refresh your memory on the Grips feature).

**2.** Click on the longest of the three vertical dimensions you drew in the earlier exercise. You will see the grips of the dimension, as shown in Figure 9.6.

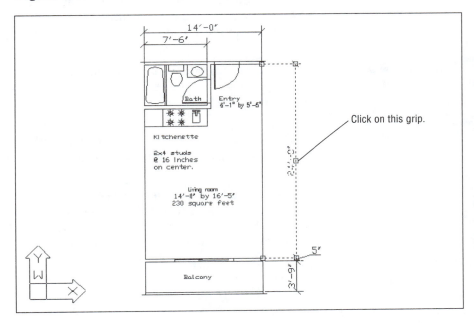

*Figure 9.6:* **The grip points are the same as the definition points on a dimension.**

## Making Minor Adjustments to Dimensions Using Grips

The definition points, whose location you can see through their grips, are located on their own unique layer called Defpoints. Definition points are displayed regardless of whether the Defpoints layer is on or off. To give you an idea of how these definition points work, try the following exercises, which show you how to directly manipulate the definition points.

**TIP** Since the Defpoints layer has the unique feature of being visible even when turned off, you can use it as a layer for laying out your drawing. While Defpoints is turned off, you can still see objects assigned to it, but the objects won't plot.

1. With the grips visible, click on the grip near the dimension text.

2. Move the cursor around. Notice that when you move the cursor verti-cally, the text moves along the dimension line. When you move the cur-sor horizontally, the dimension line and text move together, keeping their parallel orientation to the dimensioned floor plan.

**NOTE** Here the entire dimension line moves, including the text. In a later exercise, you'll see how you can move the dimension text independently of the dimension line.

3. Enter **@9′<0** ↵. The dimension line, text, and the dimension exten-sions move to the new location to the right of the text (see Figure 9.7).

**TIP** If you need to move several dimension lines at once, select them all at the command prompt; then Shift-click on one set of dimension-line grips from each dimension. Once you've selected the grips, click on one of the hot grips again. You can then move all the dimension lines at once.

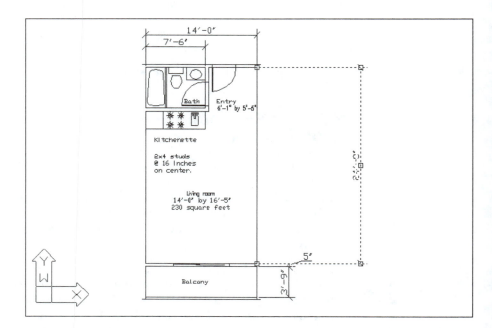

*Figure 9.7:*  **Moving the dimension line using its grip**

In step 3 of the last exercise you saw that you can specify an exact distance for the dimension line's new location by entering a relative polar coordinate. Cartesian coordinates work just as well. You can even use object snaps to relocate dimension lines. Next, try moving the dimension line back using the Perpendicular Osnap override.

1. Click on the grip at the bottom of the dimension line.

2. Shift-click the right mouse button to pop up the Osnap overrides menu, and choose Perpendicular.

3. Click on the vertical dimension line that dimensions the balcony. The selected dimension line moves to align with the other vertical dimension, back to its original location.

As you have seen in this section, the Grips feature is especially well suited to editing dimensions. With grips, you can stretch, move, copy, rotate, mirror, and scale dimensions.

## Editing Dimensions and Other Objects Together

Certainly it's helpful to be able to edit a dimension directly using its grips. But the key feature of AutoCAD LT's dimensions is their ability to *automatically* adjust themselves to changes in the drawing. As long as you include the dimension's definition points when you select objects to edit, the dimensions themselves will automatically update to reflect the change in your drawing.

To see how this works, try moving the living room closer to the bathroom wall. You can move a group of lines and vertices using the Stretch command and the Crossing option.

1. You won't need to save the changes you are about to make, so click on the Save button before you do anything else.

2. Click on Stretch on the Modify toolbar, or type **Stretch** ↵ and then **C** ↵. You will see the following prompt:

```
At the Select objects to stretch by crossing-window or
-polygon...

Select objects: C

First corner:
```

**TIP** To be more selective about the vertices you move, use a standard window instead of a crossing window to select the vertices. Then pick the individual objects whose vertices you wish to move.

3.  Pick a crossing window, as illustrated in Figure 9.8. Then press ↵ to confirm your selection.

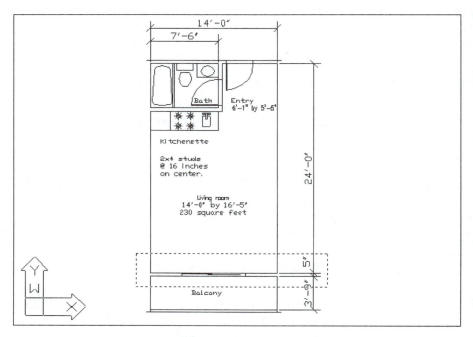

*Figure 9.8:* ***The Stretch crossing window***

4.  At the Base point prompt, pick any point on the screen.

5.  At the New point prompt, enter **@2′<90** to move the wall 2′ in a 90° direction. The wall moves, and the dimension text changes to reflect the new dimension, as shown in Figure 9.9.

6.  When you are done reviewing the results of this exercise, exit the file without saving it.

When you selected the crossing window corners, you included the definition points of both vertical dimensions. This allowed you to move the dimension extension lines along with the wall, thereby updating the dimensions automatically.

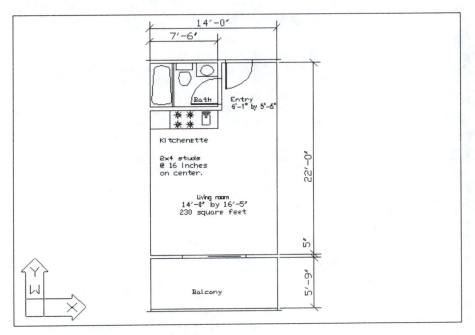

*Figure 9.9:* **The moved wall, with the updated dimensions**

You can also use the Mirror, Rotate, and Stretch commands with dimensions. The polar arrays will also work, and Extend and Trim can be used with linear dimensions.

When editing dimensioned objects, be sure you select the dimension associated with the object being edited. When you select objects, using the Crossing or Cpolygon selection options will help you include the dimensions. See the sidebar in *Chapter 2*, "Other Options in the Object Selection Settings Dialog Box," for more on these selection options.

## UNDERSTANDING THE STRETCH COMMAND

The tool you used for moving the wall and the dimension line extensions is the Stretch command. This is one of the most useful, yet least understood commands offered by AutoCAD LT. Think of Stretch as a vertex mover: Its sole purpose is to move the vertices (or endpoints) of objects.

Stretch actually requires you to do two things: select the objects you want to edit, and then select the vertices you wish to move. The crossing window and the Cpolygon window are convenient ways of killing two birds with one stone, because they select objects and vertices in one operation. But when you want to be more selective, you can click on objects and window vertices instead. For example, consider the exercise in this chapter where you moved a wall with the Stretch command. If you want to move the walls but not the dimension-line extensions, you could do that as follows:

1. Enter **Stretch** ↵ at the command prompt. (You enter Stretch via the prompt because the Stretch command in the Modify pull-down menu automatically uses the Crossing selection option.)

2. At the Select object: prompt, enter **W** ↵ (Window) or **WP** ↵ (Window Polygon).

3. Window the vertices you wish to move. Since the Window and Window Polygon selection options select objects completely enclosed within the window, most of the items you want to stretch will already be selected.

4. Click on the vertical walls to include them in the set of objects to be edited.

5. Press ↵ to finish your selection.

6. Indicate the base point and second point for the stretch.

You could also use the Remove selection option and click on the dimensions to deselect them in the previous exercise. Then, when you enter the base and second points, the walls would move but the dimensions would stay in place.

Stretch will stretch only the vertices included in the last window, crossing window, crossing polygon, or window polygon (see *Chapter 2* for more on these selection options). Thus, if you had attempted to window another part of your drawing in the wall-moving exercise, nothing would have moved. Before Stretch will do anything, objects need to be highlighted (selected) and their endpoints windowed.

The Stretch command is especially well suited to editing dimensioned objects, and when you use it with the crossing polygon (CP) or window polygon (WP) selection options, you have substantial control over what gets edited.

## Using Osnap While Dimensioning

> **WARNING**   There is a drawback to setting a constant Osnap mode: When your drawing gets crowded, you may end up picking the wrong point by accident.

You may find that when you pick intersections and endpoints frequently, as during dimensioning, it is a bit inconvenient to use the Osnap overrides menu. In situations where your drawing is not too crowded and you want to set an Osnap override as a default, you can do so in the following way:

▶ Either press F3, or click on the Running Object Snap button (the magnet icon) on the Snaps flyout on the Standard toolbar. In the Running Object Snap dialog box, select the desired default mode. You can even pick more than one mode, for instance Intersection, Endpoint, and Midpoint, so that whichever geometry you happen to be nearest will be the point selected.

**Running Object Snap**

Select Settings

☐ Endpoint      ☐ Intersection
☐ Midpoint      ☐ Insertion
☐ Center        ☐ Perpendicular
☐ Node          ☐ Tangent
☐ Quadrant      ☐ Nearest

Clear All

Aperture Size

Min    Max

◄ ▬▬▬▬▬▬ ►

OK      Cancel      Help...

▶ You may also open the Running Object Snap dialog box by typing **Ddosnap** ↵.

Once you've set your defaults, the next time you are prompted to select a point, the selected Osnap modes will be automatically activated. You can still override the default settings using the Osnap Cursor menu (Shift-click the right mouse button).

Part 2

Building on the Basics

# Dimensioning Nonorthogonal Objects

So far, you've been reading about how to work with linear dimensions. You can also dimension nonorthogonal objects, such as circles, arcs, triangles, and trapezoids. In this section you will practice dimensioning nonorthogonal objects by drawing an elevation of a window in the set of plans for your studio apartment building. You'll start by drawing the window itself.

1. Open a new file called **Window**.

2. Set the file up as an architectural drawing at a scale of 3″=1′-0″ on an 8½″×11″ sheet.

3. Click on Polygon on the Polygon flyout on the Draw menu or enter **Polygon** ↵.

4. At the Number of sides... prompt, enter **6** ↵.

5. At the Edge/<center of polygon> prompt, pick the center of the polygon at coordinate 1′-10″, 1′-6″. If you started the command with the keyboard, enter **C** ↵ at the Inscribe in circle/circumscribe... prompt.

6. At the Radius of circle: prompt, you will see the hexagon drag along with the cursor. You could pick a point with your mouse to determine its size.

7. Enter **8** ↵ to get an exact size for the hexagon.

8. Draw a circle with a radius of 7″ using coordinate 1′-10″, 1′-6″ as its center. Your drawing will look like Figure 9.10.

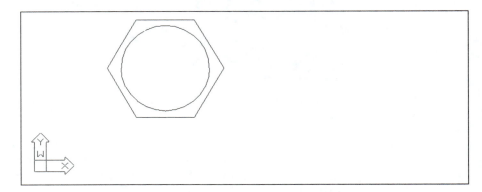

*Figure 9.10:*    ***The window frame***

## Dimensioning Nonorthogonal Linear Distances

Now you will dimension the window. The unusual shape of the window prevents you from using the horizontal or vertical dimensions you've used already. However, the Aligned option will allow you to dimension at an angle.

1. Start by setting the dimension scale to 4. A quick way to do this is by typing **Dimscale** ⏎ 4 ⏎.

2. Click on the Aligned Dimension button on the Dimensioning toolbar. You can also enter **Dimaligned** ⏎ to start the aligned dimension.

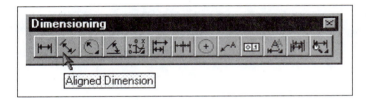

3. At the First extension line origin or RETURN to select: prompt, press ⏎. You could have picked extension line origins as you did in earlier examples, but using the ⏎ will show you firsthand how this option works.

4. At the Select object to dimension: prompt, pick the upper-right face of the hexagon near coordinate 2'-5", 1'-10". As the prompt indicates, you can also pick an arc or circle for this type of dimension.

 **TIP** Just as with linear dimensions, you can enter **T** ⏎ at step 5 to enter specific text.

5. At the Dimension line location (Text/Angle): prompt, pick a point near coordinate 2'-10", 2'-2". The dimension appears in the drawing as shown in Figure 9.11.

 **TIP** Remember that you can change the dimension text position using the Dimtih dimension variable. In Figure 9.11, the dimension text is aligned horizontally. This means Dimtih is ON. If the dimension text is aligned parallel to the dimension, this means Dimtih is set to OFF. Adjust the setting to match your drafting requirements.

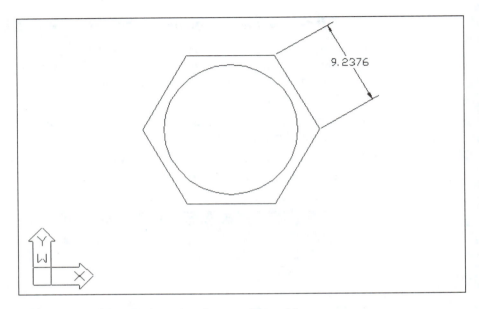

*Figure 9.11:* **The aligned dimension of a nonorthogonal line**

Next, you will dimension a face of the hexagon. Instead of its actual length, however, you will dimension a distance at a specified angle—the distance from the center of the face.

1. Click on the Linear Dimension button on the Dimensioning toolbar.

2. At the `First extension line origin or RETURN to select:` prompt, press ↵.

3. At the `Select object to dimension` prompt, pick the lower-right face of the hexagon near coordinate 2′-6″, 1′-4″.

4. At the `Dimension line location (Text/Angle/Horizontal/Vertical/Rotated):` prompt, type **R** ↵ to select the rotated option.

5. At the `Dimension line angle <0>` prompt, enter **30** ↵.

6. At the Dimension line location prompt, pick a point near coordinate 2′-11″, 0′-8″. Your drawing will look like Figure 9.12.

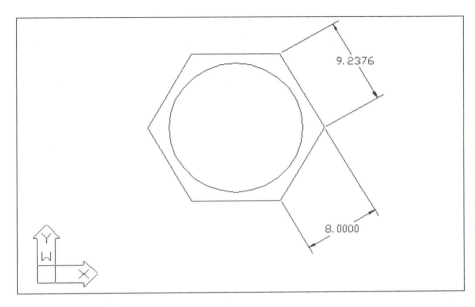

*Figure 9.12:* **A linear dimension using the rotated option**

## Dimensioning Radii, Diameters, and Arcs

To dimension circular objects, you use another set of options from the Dimensioning toolbar or the Dimension menu.

1. Click on the Angular Dimension button on the Dimensioning toolbar. Or you can enter **Dimangular** ⏎ to start the angular dimension.

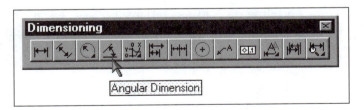

2. At the Select arc, circle, line, or RETURN: prompt, pick the upper-left face of the hexagon near coordinate 1′-3″, 1′-10″.

3. At the Second line: prompt, pick the top face at coordinate 1′-9″, 2′-2″.

4. At the Dimension line arc location (Text/Angle): prompt, notice how the dimension changes as you move the cursor. AutoCAD LT adjusts the dimension to fit the location.

5. Pick a point near coordinate 1′-8″, 1′-11″. The dimension is fixed in the drawing (see Figure 9.13).

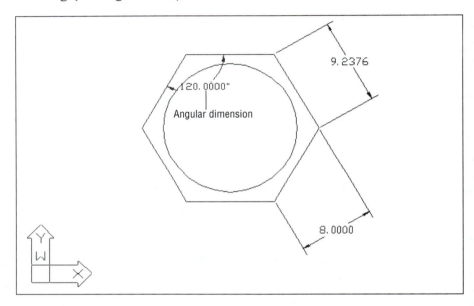

Figure 9.13:    *The angular dimension added to the window frame*

Now try the Diameter option, which shows the diameter of a circle.

1. Click and drag on Radius Dimension, then select Diameter Dimension. Or you can enter **Dimdiameter** ⏎ to start the diameter dimension.

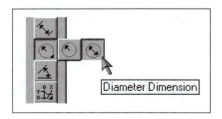

2.  At the `Select arc or circle:` prompt, pick the circle near coordinate 2'-5", 1'-6".

> **NOTE** If the dimension text can't fit within the circle, AutoCAD LT gives you the option to place dimension text outside the circle as you drag the temporary dimension to a horizontal position.

3.  At the `Dimension line location (Text/Angle):` prompt, you will see the diameter dimension drag with the cursor.

4.  Adjust your cursor so that the dimension looks like Figure 9.14, and then click the mouse/pick button.

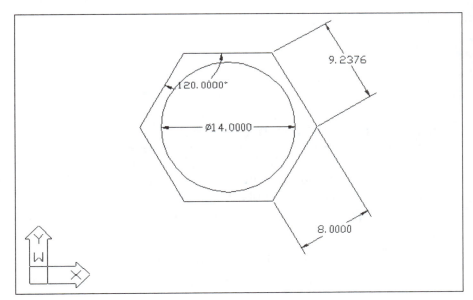

*Figure 9.14:* **Dimension showing the diameter of a circle**

The Radius Dimension option on the Dimensioning toolbar gives you a radius dimension (see Figure 9.15) just as Diameter provides a circle's diameter. The Center Mark option on the Dimensioning toolbar just places a cross mark in the center of the selected arc or circle.

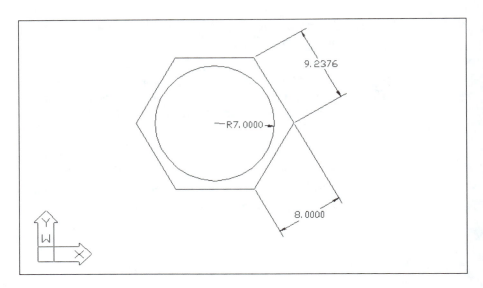

*Figure 9.15:*    **A radius dimension**

## Adding a Note with an Arrow

Finally, there is the Leader option on the toolbar or the Dimension menu, which allows you to add a note with an arrow pointing to the object the note describes.

1.  Click on the Leader button on the Dimensioning toolbar, or enter **Leader** ↵.

2.  At the From point: prompt, pick a point near coordinate 1′-4″, 2′-0″.

3.  At the To point: prompt, enter **@6<110** ↵. The leader appears.

4.  At the To point (Format/Annotation/Undo)<Annotation>: prompt, you can continue to pick points just as you would draw lines. For this exercise, however, press ↵ to finish drawing leader lines.

5.  Next, at the Annotation (or RETURN for options): prompt, type **Window frame** ↵ ↵ as the label for this leader. Your drawing will look like Figure 9.16.

**TIP**  You can also add Multiline text at the leader. See the upcoming section.

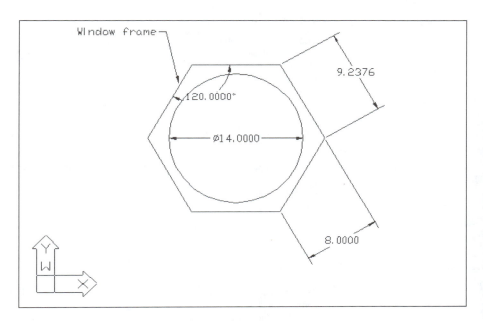

*Figure 9.16:* **The leader with a note added**

In this exercise, you used the default Annotation option in step 4 to add the text for the note. The Format option in this prompt lets you control the graphic elements of the leader. When you select the Format option by typing **F** ↵, you get the following prompt:

```
Spline/STraight/Arrow/None/<Exit>:
```

Choose Spline to change the leader from a series of line segments to a spline curve (see Figure 9.17). Often a curved leader shows up better than straight lines do. The STraight option changes the leader line to straight lines. None suppresses the arrowhead altogether, and Arrow restores it.

## Using Multiline Text with Leaders

You also have the option to add Multiline text at the leader. Take another look at step 5 in the previous exercise. To add Multiline text, you would press ↵ at the `Annotation (or RETURN for options):` prompt in this step. The next prompt to appear is:

```
Tolerance/Copy/Block/None/<Mtext>:
```

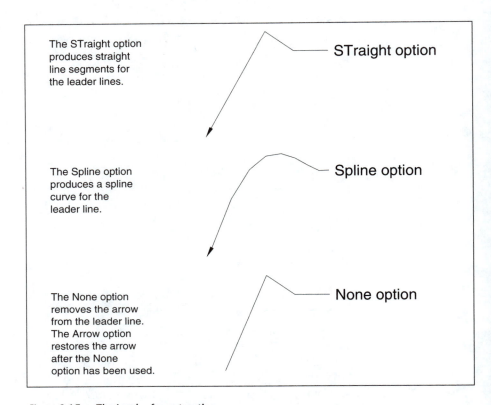

The STraight option produces straight line segments for the leader lines.

STraight option

The Spline option produces a spline curve for the leader line.

Spline option

The None option removes the arrow from the leader line. The Arrow option restores the arrow after the None option has been used.

None option

*Figure 9.17:* **The Leader format options**

Press ↵ again, and you will see the standard MText Editor (see *Chapter 8* for more on MText).

The other options in the Annotation prompt are as follows:

**Tolerance**   lets you insert a tolerance symbol. A dialog box opens, where you specify the desired type of tolerance annotation (see *Appendix D* for more on the Tolerance feature).

**Copy**   lets you copy text from another part of the drawing. You are prompted to select a text object to copy to the leader text location.

**Block**   lets you insert a block. You are asked for a block name, and then the command proceeds to insert the block—just like the Insert command (see *Chapter 3*).

Choose None if you don't want to do anything beyond drawing the leader arrow and line.

## Skewing Dimension Lines

At times, you may find it necessary to force the extension lines to take on an angle other than 90° to the dimension line. This is a common requirement of isometric drawings, where most lines are at 30° or 60° angles instead of 90°. To facilitate nonorthogonal dimensions like these, AutoCAD LT offers the Oblique option.

1.  Click and drag on the Dimension Styles button on the Dimensioning toolbar, then select Oblique Dimensions or type **Dimedit** ↵ **O** ↵.

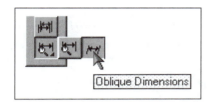

2.  At the `Select objects:` prompt, pick the aligned dimension at the upper-right of the drawing and press ↵ to confirm your selection.

3.  At the `Enter obliquing angle (RETURN for none):` prompt, enter **60** for 60°. The dimension will skew so that the extension lines are at 60°, as shown in Figure 9.18.

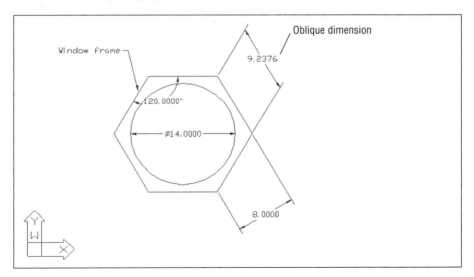

*Figure 9.18:* **A dimension using the Oblique option**

## Applying Ordinate Dimensions

In mechanical drafting, *ordinate dimensions* are used to maintain the accuracy of machined parts by establishing an origin on the part. All major dimensions are described as x or y coordinates of that origin. The origin is usually an easily locatable feature of the part, such as a machined bore or two machined surfaces. Figure 9.19 shows a typical application of ordinate dimensions.

To utilize AutoCAD LT's Ordinate dimensioning command, follow these steps:

1. Click on View ➤ Set UCS ➤ Origin or type **UCS** ↵ **Or** ↵.

2. At the Origin point <0,0,0>: prompt, click on the exact location of the origin of your part.

3. Toggle ORTHO mode on.

4. Click on the Ordinate Dimension button on the Dimensioning toolbar. You can also enter **Dimordinate** ↵ to start the ordinate dimension.

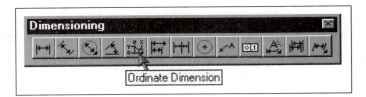

5. At the Select feature: prompt, use an Osnap to identify the specific point on an object that you want to dimension.

**NOTE** The direction of the leader will determine whether the dimension will be of the X datum or the Y datum.

6. At the Leader endpoint (Xdatum/tdatum/Text): prompt, indicate the length and direction of the leader. Drag the rubber-banding leader horizontally to get the Ydatum, and vertically to get the Xdatum (or

coordinate) of the feature. Then click on a point to define the endpoint of the leader.

In steps 1 and 2, you used the UCS feature to establish a second origin in the drawing. The Ordinate option then uses that origin to determine the ordinate dimensions. You will get a chance to work with the UCS feature in *Chapter 16*.

The other two options in the Ordinate flyout, Xdatum and Ydatum, force the dimension to be of the x coordinate or y coordinate no matter what direction the leader takes. The Ordinate option (see step 4) will make the best guess at which direction you want dimensioned, based on the orientation of the leader.

With ORTHO mode off, the dimension leader will be drawn with a jog, but will maintain orthogonal lines (see Figure 9.19).

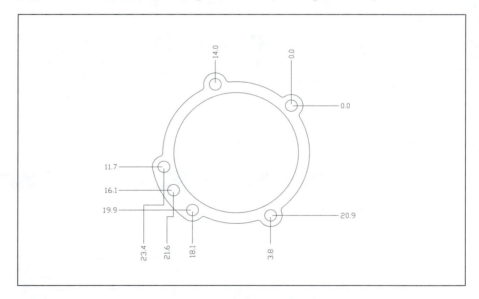

Figure 9.19:   **A drawing using ordinate dimensions. In the lower-left, note the two dimensions whose leaders are jogged. Also note the origin location in the upper-right.**

## Adding Tolerance Notation

In mechanical drafting, tolerances are a key part of a drawing's notation. To help facilitate tolerance notation, Release 3 of AutoCAD LT
provides the Tolerance command, which offers common ISO tolerance symbols together with a quick way to build a standard *feature
control* symbol. Feature control symbols are industry standard symbols used to specify tolerances. If you are a mechanical engineer or
drafter, AutoCAD LT's tolerance notation options will be a valuable
tool. A full discussion of tolerances, however, requires a basic understanding of mechanical design and drafting and is beyond the scope
of this book.

To use the Tolerance command, choose the Tolerance button from the
Dimensioning toolbar, or type **Tolerance** ↵ at the command prompt.

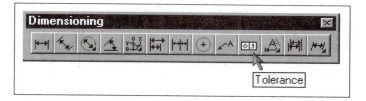

The Symbol dialog box appears.

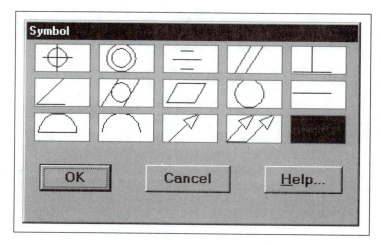

Figure 9.20 shows what each symbol represents.

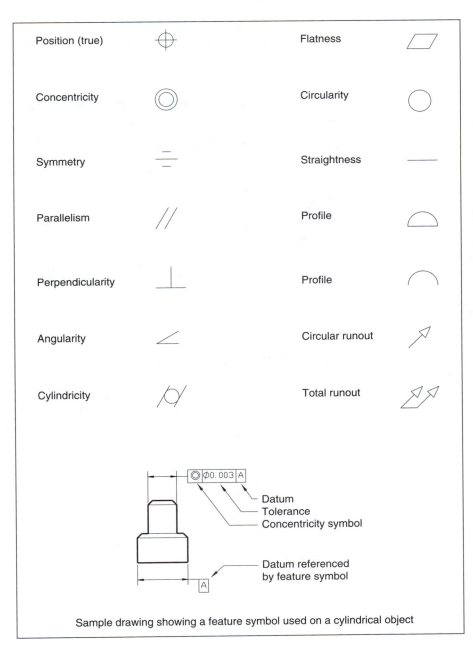

| | | | |
|---|---|---|---|
| Position (true) | ⊕ | Flatness | ▱ |
| Concentricity | ◎ | Circularity | ○ |
| Symmetry | ≡ | Straightness | — |
| Parallelism | // | Profile | ⌓ |
| Perpendicularity | ⊥ | Profile | ⌒ |
| Angularity | ∠ | Circular runout | ↗ |
| Cylindricity | ⌭ | Total runout | ⤴ |

⌽Ø0.003 A

— Datum
— Tolerance
— Concentricity symbol

— Datum referenced
by feature symbol

A

Sample drawing showing a feature symbol used on a cylindrical object

*Figure 9.20:* **The tolerance symbols**

Once you select a symbol, you then see the Geometric Tolerance dialog box. This is where you enter tolerance and datum values for the feature control symbol. You can enter two tolerance values and three datum values. In addition, you can stack values in a two-tiered fashion.

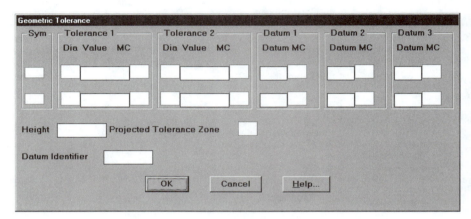

Now exit AutoCAD LT. You are done with the tutorials in this chapter.

## Update Dimension Settings Using Dimension Variables

Earlier in this chapter, when you created the current Dimension Style, you selected dimension settings via the Dimension Styles dialog boxes. Dimension settings are controlled by an extensive range of *dimension variables*. When you make selections in the dialog boxes, these system variables are modified to become the current default.

The dimensioning system variables control the following aspects of dimensioning: dimension scale; dimension offsets; tolerances; rounding values; dimension arrow styles; dimension text; dimension and extension line settings; and dimension color; as well as general dimension settings, such as dynamic updating of dimensions. All of these variables are listed and described in *Appendix D* of this book (see Table D.2, in particular).

You can use these dimension variables at the command line to change the Dimension Styles settings, or to change the settings of a specific dimension on-the-fly. Any changes which you make to the dimension variable will remain the current default until you change it again. So if you want to make a change to one dimension *only*, change the dimension variable, update the dimension following the procedure outlined below, and then change the dimension setting *back* to its original setting.

Using the Unit drawing that you worked on earlier in this chapter, let's now make some changes to the Dimension Style settings that you created. We are going to make changes to the position of the dimension text (using the Dimtih variable); to the display of zero values within dimension text (using the Dimzin variable); and to the dimension arrow setting (using Dimtsz). Once a setting has been changed, you will use the Update Dimension button on the Dimensioning toolbar to update each dimension as required.

1.   Open the Unit drawing that you saved earlier in this chapter.

2.   At the command line, type **Dimtih** ↵, then **On** ↵. This variable controls whether dimension text is aligned with the dimension line or positioned horizontally. An On value causes the text to be positioned horizontally.

3.   Click on the Update Dimension button on the Dimensioning toolbar. At the `Select Objects:` prompt click on the 24′0″ dimension on the right-side wall of the Unit. The dimension is immediately updated, with the text now positioned horizontally within the dimension line.

4.   At the command line, type **Dimzin** ↵, then **0** ↵. When this variable is set to 0, zero feet or zero inches values will not be displayed.

5. Click on the Update Dimension button on the Dimensioning toolbar. At the `Select Objects:` prompt click on the 24′0″ dimension again. The dimension is immediately updated, with the text now reading 24′ (without the zero inches).

6. At the command line, type **Dimtsz** ↵, then **0** ↵. When this variable is set to 0, the arrow style reverts to the default value—a standard arrowhead rather than the ticks that you selected when you created the Dimension Style.

7. Click on the Update Dimension button on the Dimensioning toolbar. At the `Select Objects:` prompt click on the 24′ dimension again. The dimension is immediately updated, with the standard arrow in place of the ticks displayed before.

So far, you have only modified the 24′ dimension. Now you should update all of the other dimensions in the Unit drawing so that they match this dimension.

8. Click on the Update Dimension button on the Dimensioning toolbar. At the `Select Objects:` prompt, select all of the remaining dimensions, and then press ↵.

You have now finished working with the dimensioning system variables. Before you save this drawing, let's make one final change to the dimensions of the Unit drawing. This final step demonstrates again dimensions being dynamically updated as you make changes to a drawing.

9. Select the 5″ dimension (between the unit and the balcony) and then click on the Erase button on the Modify toolbar. This dimension disappears.

10. Using the grips, click on the top extension line of the 3′9″ dimension, and drag it up to the bottom of the 24′ dimension. The dimension text changes to 4′2″.

11. Your drawing should now look like Figure 9.21. Save this drawing for use in future chapters.

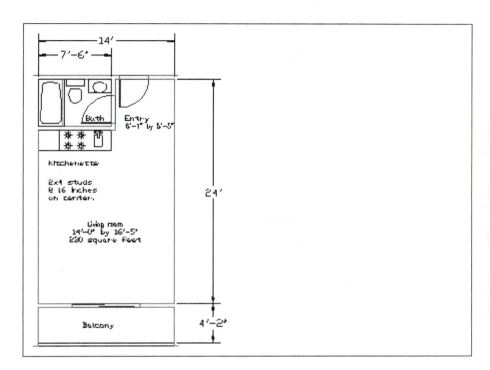

*Figure 9.21:*    **The finished Unit drawing with dimensions updated**

## If You Want to Experiment...

At this point, you might want to experiment with the settings described in this chapter to identify the ones that are most useful for your work. You can then establish these settings as defaults in a template drawing, or a series of different templates.

It's a good idea to experiment even with the settings you don't think you will need often—chances are you will have to alter them from time to time.

As an added exercise, try the steps shown in Figure 9.22. It will give you a chance to see how you can update dimensions on a drawing that has been scaled down.

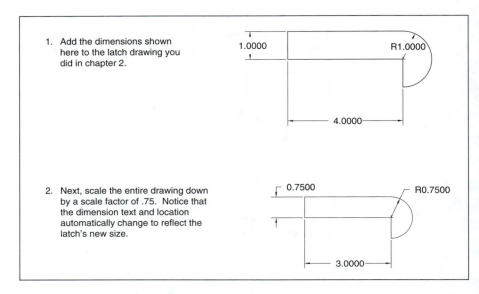

1. Add the dimensions shown here to the latch drawing you did in chapter 2.

2. Next, scale the entire drawing down by a scale factor of .75. Notice that the dimension text and location automatically change to reflect the latch's new size.

*Figure 9.22:* **A sample mechanical drawing with dimensions**

# Becoming an Expert

This part polishes your skills and gives you a few new ones.

*Chapter 10: Attributes—Storing Data with Graphics* tells you

how to attach information to drawing objects. In *Chapter 11:*

*Copying Pre-existing Drawings into AutoCAD LT*, you will learn

how to transfer paper drawings to AutoCAD LT. In *Chapter 12:*

*Power Editing*, you will gain some tips on working in groups.

*Chapter 13: Drawing Curves and Solid Fills* gives you an in-

depth look at some special drawing objects. *Chapter 14:*

*Getting and Exchanging Data from Drawings* will give you prac-

tice with getting information about a drawing, and you will

learn how AutoCAD LT can interact with other applications.

# Chapter 10

# Attributes—Storing Data with Graphics

## *FAST TRACKS*

**A**TTRIBUTES are unique to computer-aided design and drafting; nothing quite like them exists in traditional drafting. Because of this, they are often poorly understood. Attributes enable you to store information as text that you can later extract to use in database managers, spreadsheet programs, and word processors. By using attributes, you can keep track of virtually any object in a drawing.

**NOTE** For some of the exercises in this chapter, you will need to know how to create and edit ASCII files.

Keeping track of objects is just one way of using attributes. You can also use them in place of text objects in situations where you must enter the same text, with minor modifications, in many places in your drawing. For example, if you are drawing a schedule that contains several columns of information, you can use attributes to help simplify your data entry.

**TIP** You can even set up a default value for the attribute, such as *hollow core*, or *hc*. That way you only have to enter a value when it deviates from the default.

Attributes can also be used where you anticipate global editing of text. For example, suppose a note that refers to a part number occurs in several places. If you think you will want to change that part number in every note, you can make the part a block with an attribute. Later, when you know the new part number, you can use the global editing capability of the Attribute feature to change the old part number for all occurrences in one step.

In this chapter you will use attributes for one of their more common functions: maintaining lists of parts. In this case, the parts are doors. We will also describe how to import these attributes into a database program. As you go through these exercises, think about the ways attributes can help you in your particular application.

## Creating Attributes

Attributes depend on blocks. You might think of an attribute as a tag attached to a block, with the tag containing information about the block. For example, you could have included an attribute definition with the door drawing you created in *Chapter 2*. If you had, then every time you subsequently inserted the door you would have been prompted for a value associated with that door. The value could be a number, a height or width value, a name, or any type of text information you want. When you insert the block, you get the usual prompts, followed by a prompt for an attribute value. Once you enter a value, it is stored as part of the block within the drawing database. This value can be displayed as text attached to the door, or it can be made invisible. You can even specify what the prompts say in asking you for the attribute value.

But suppose you don't have the attribute information when you design the door. As an alternative, you can add the attribute to a *symbol* that is later placed by the door when you know enough about the design to specify what type of door goes where. The standard door type symbol suits this purpose nicely because it is an object that can be set up and used as a block independent of the actual door block.

NOTE A door type symbol is a graphic code used to indicate special characteristics of the associated door. The code refers to a note in another drawing or in a set of written specifications.

In the following exercises, you will create a door type symbol with attributes for the different values normally assigned to doors: size, thickness, fire rating, material, and construction.

## Finding the Attribute Toolbar

Before you start, you will need to load the Attribute toolbar. This toolbar contains many of the commands you will use to add, redefine, and edit attributes. To load the Attribute toolbar, choose View ➤ Toolbars ➤ Attribute, or click on the Attribute icon on the Tool Windows flyout on the Standard toolbar. The Attribute toolbar appears on the screen.

## Adding Attributes to Blocks

In this exercise, you will create a door type symbol, which is commonly used to describe the size, thickness, and other characteristics of any given door in an architectural drawing. The symbol is usually a circle, hexagon, or diamond, with a number in it. The number can be cross-referenced to a schedule that lists all the door types and their characteristics.

In this exercise, you will be creating a new file containing attribute definitions, but you can also include such definitions in blocks you create using the Block command or in files you create using the Wblock command. Just create the attribute definitions, and then include them with the Block or Wblock selections.

1. Open a new file and save it as **S-door** (for symbol-door). Since the symbol will fit in the default limits of the drawing, you don't have to change the limits setting.

2. Draw a circle with the center at 0,0, and a radius of 0.125 units. Next, zoom into the circle.

**TIP** Since this is a new drawing, the circle is automatically placed on layer 0. Remember that objects in a block that is on layer 0 will take on the color and linetype assignment of the layer on which the block is inserted. It is also a good idea when building blocks to use the default base point (0,0). For example, the center of a circle should optimally be at 0,0.

3. Click on the Define Attribute button on the Attribute toolbar, or type **Ddattdef** ↵.

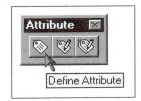

The Attribute Definition dialog box appears.

| Attribute Definition | |
|---|---|
| **Mode** | **Attribute** |
| ☐ Invisible | Tag: |
| ☐ Constant | Prompt: |
| ☐ Verify | Value: |
| ☐ Preset | |
| **Insertion Point** | **Text Options** |
| Pick Point < | Justification: Left |
| X: 0.0000 | Text Style: STANDARD |
| Y: 0.0000 | Height < 0.2000 |
| Z: 0.0000 | Rotation < 0 |
| ☐ Align below previous attribute | |
| OK   Cancel   Help... | |
| Null Tag not allowed. | |

4. Click on the input box labeled Tag in the Attribute group. Enter **d-type**.

**NOTE** The Attribute Tag is equivalent to the field name in a database; it can be up to 31 characters long but it cannot contain spaces. If you plan to use the attribute data in a database program, check that program's manuals for other restrictions on field names.

5.  Click on the input box labeled Prompt, and enter **Door type**. Here you enter the text for the prompt that will appear when you insert the block containing this attribute. Often the prompt is the same as the tag, but it can be anything you like. Unlike the tag, the prompt can include spaces.

**TIP** Use a prompt that gives explicit instructions so the user will know exactly what is expected. Consider including an example within the prompt. (Enclose the example in brackets to imitate the way AutoCAD LT prompts often display defaults.)

6.  Click on the input box labeled Value. This is where you enter a default value for the door type prompt. Enter a hyphen.

**TIP** If an attribute is to contain a number that will later be used for making sorts in a database, use a default such as 000 to indicate the number of digits required. The zeros may also serve to remind the user that values less than 100 must be preceded by a leading zero, as in 099.

7.  Click on the arrow on the Justification pull-down list, then highlight Middle. This will allow you to center the attribute on the circle's center. You might notice several other options in the Text Options group. Since attributes appear as text, you can apply the same settings to them as you would to ordinary text.

8.  Double-click on the input box next to the button labeled Height <, then enter **0.125**. This will make the attribute text 0.125 inches high.

9.  Check the box labeled Verify in the Mode group. This option instructs AutoCAD LT to verify any answers you give to the attribute prompts at insertion time. (You'll see later in this chapter how Verify works.)

10. Click on OK. You will see the attribute definition at the center of the circle (see Figure 10.1).

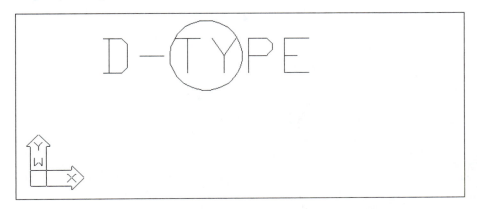

Figure 10.1:    *The attribute inserted in the circle and the second attribute added*

You have just created your first attribute definition. The attribute definition displays its tag in all uppercase to help you identify it. When you later insert this file into another drawing, you will see that the tag turns into the value you assign to it when it is inserted. If you want only one attribute, you can stop here and save the file. The next section shows you how you can quickly add several more attributes to your drawing.

## Changing Attribute Specifications

Next, you will add a few more attribute definitions, but instead of using the Attribute Definition dialog box, you will make an arrayed copy of the first attribute, then edit the attribute definition copies. This method can save you time when you want to create several attribute definitions that have similar characteristics. By making copies and editing them, you'll also get a chance to see firsthand how to make changes to an attribute definition.

Part
3

Becoming an Expert

1. Click on the Rectangular Array button on the Duplicate Objects flyout on the Modify toolbar. You can also type **Array** ↵ **R** ↵ to start the Array command.

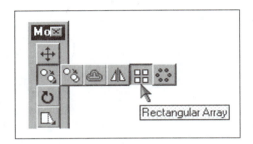

2. At the `Select objects` prompt, click on the attribute definition you just created, then press ↵.

3. At the `Number of rows` prompt, enter 7 ↵.

4. At the `Number of columns` prompt, press ↵.

5. At the `Distance between rows` prompt, enter **–.18** ↵. This is about 1.5 times the height of the attribute definition. Be sure to include the minus sign. This will cause the array to be drawn downward.

   Now you are ready to modify the copies of the attribute definitions.

> **TIP** You can type **Ddmodify** ↵ and then continue from step 2. The Ddedit command also lets you edit the tag, prompt, and default value of an attribute definition. It doesn't let you change an attribute definition's *mode,* however.

1. Click on the Properties button on the Object Properties toolbar.

2. At the `Select object to modify:` prompt, click on the attribute definition just below the original. The Modify Attribute Definition dialog box appears.

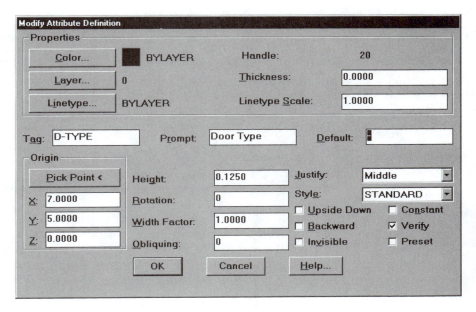

3. Click on the Invisible check box in the lower-right corner of the dialog box. This will cause this attribute to be invisible when the file is later inserted.

4. Double-click on the input box labeled Tag, then enter **d-size**.

5. Press Tab to move to the Prompt input box, then type **Door size**. The Default input box already contains a hyphen. Do not change this value.

6. Click on OK. You will see the attribute definition change to reflect the new tag.

7. Continue to edit the rest of the attribute definitions using the attributes settings listed in Table 10.1. Also make sure all but the original attributes have the Invisible option turned on.

8. Now you have finished creating your door type symbol with attributes. Save the S-door file. You will be inserting this block into the Plan drawing in the next exercise.

*Table 10.1:*    **Attributes for the Door Type Symbol**

| Tag | Prompt |
|-----|--------|
| D-number | Door number |
| D-thick | Door thickness |
| D-rate | Fire rating |
| D-matrl | Door material |
| D-const | Door construction |

When you later insert a file or block containing attributes, the attribute prompts will appear in the order that their associated definitions were created. If the order of the prompts at insertion time is important, you can control it by editing the attribute definitions so their creation order corresponds to the desired prompt order.

## UNDERSTANDING ATTRIBUTE DEFINITION MODES

In the Attribute Definition dialog box, you saw several check boxes in the Mode group. I've briefly described what two of these modes do. You won't be asked to use any of the other modes in this tutorial, so the following set of descriptions is provided in case they might be useful for your work.

**Invisible**    controls whether the attribute is shown as part of the drawing.

**Constant**    creates an attribute that does not prompt you to enter a value. Instead the attribute simply has a constant, or fixed, value you give it during creation. *Constant* is used in situations where you know you will assign a fixed value to an object. Once they are set in a block, constant values cannot be changed using the standard set of attribute editing commands.

**Verify**    causes AutoCAD LT to review the attribute values you enter at insertion time and asks you if they are correct.

**Preset**    causes AutoCAD LT to automatically assign a default value to an attribute when its block is inserted. This saves time, since a preset attribute will not prompt you for a value. Unlike the Constant option, you can edit an attribute that has the Preset option turned on.

You can have all four modes on, all four off, or any combination of modes. With the exception of the Invisible mode, none of these modes can be altered once the attribute becomes part of a block. Later in this chapter we will discuss how to make an invisible attribute visible.

## Inserting Blocks Containing Attributes

In the last section, you created a door type symbol at the desired size for the actual plotted symbol. This means that whenever you insert that symbol, you have to specify an X and Y scale factor appropriate to the scale of your drawing. This allows you to use the same symbol in any drawing, regardless of its scale. (You could have several door type symbols, one for each scale you anticipate using, but this would be inefficient.)

1. Open the Plan file. You may use the one you created, or open 10-PLAN.DWG on the companion CD. (If you have installed the tutorial drawings per the instructions in *Appendix C,* 10-PLAN.DWG will be in the Sample directory.)

2. Use the View command to restore view 1.

3. Be sure the Ceiling and Flr-Pat layers are off. Normally in a floor plan the door headers are not visible, and they will interfere with the placement of the door symbol.

4. Click on the Insert Block button on the Block flyout on the Draw toolbar, or type **Ddinsert** ↵.

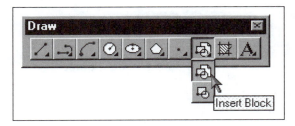

5. At the Insert dialog box, click on the File button.

6. Locate the S-door file in the file list and double-click on it.

7. Click on OK.

8. Insert the symbol at coordinate 41′-3″, 72′-4″.

9. At the X scale factor prompt, enter **96**.

10. Press ↵ at the Y scale factor prompt, and again at the Rotation angle prompt.

11. At the Door type <->: prompt, enter **A** ↵. Note that this prompt is the prompt you created. Note also that the default value is the hyphen you specified.

**12.** At the Door size <->: prompt, enter **7′-0″** ↵. This is also a prompt you created.

**13.** At the Door number <->: prompt, enter **116** ↵. Continue to enter the values for each prompt as shown in Table 10.2.

**14.** When you have finished entering the values, the prompts repeat themselves to verify your entry (because you selected Verify from the Modes group of the Attribute Definition dialog box). You can now either change an entry or just press ↵ to accept the original entry.

**15.** When you've finished and the symbol appears, the only attribute you can see is the one you selected to be visible: the door type.

**16.** Add the rest of the door type symbols for the apartment entry doors by copying or arraying the door symbol you just inserted. Use the previously saved views to help you get around the drawing quickly. Don't worry that the attribute values won't be appropriate for each unit. I'll show you how to edit the attributes in a later section of this chapter.

*Table 10.2:*　**Attribute Values for the Typical Studio Entry Door**

| Prompt | Value |
|---|---|
| Door type | A |
| Door number | Same as room number |
| Door thickness | 1 3/4″ |
| Fire rating | 20 min. |
| Door material | Wood |
| Door construction | Solid core |

As a review exercise, you'll now create another file for the apartment number symbol (shown in Figure 10.2). This will be a rectangular box with the room number that you will place in each studio apartment.

**1.** Save the Plan file, then open a new file called **S-apart** (for symbol-apartment).

2. Draw a rectangle per the dimensions shown in Figure 10.2, with the base point (the lower-left corner) at 0,0.

3. Give the apartment number symbol attribute the tag name **A-number**, the prompt **Enter apartment number**, a default value of **000**, and a text height of **0.125** inches.

4. Click on the button labeled Pick Point < in the Insertion Point group. The dialog box closes momentarily to let you pick a location for the attribute.

5. Click to pick the center of the rectangle. The center is at 0.2813, 0.125.

6. Save S-apart.

7. Open the Plan file again and insert the apartment number symbol (using an X scale factor of **96**) into the lower-left unit. Give this attribute the value of **116**.

8. Copy or array this room number symbol so that there is one symbol in each of the units. You'll learn how to modify the attributes to reflect their proper values in the following section, "Editing Attributes."

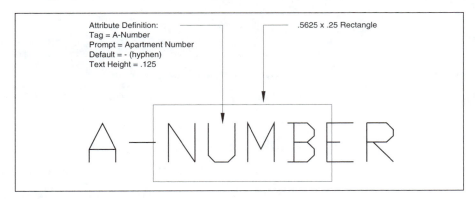

Attribute Definition:
Tag = A-Number
Prompt = Apartment Number
Default = - (hyphen)
Text Height = .125

.5625 x .25 Rectangle

*Figure 10.2:* **The apartment number symbol**

## Using a Dialog Box to Answer Attribute Prompts

You can set up AutoCAD LT to display an Enter Attributes dialog box (instead of command line prompts) for entering the attribute values at insertion time. Since this dialog box allows you to change your mind about a value before confirming your entry, the dialog box allows greater flexibility than individual prompts when entering attributes. You can also see all the attributes associated with a block at once, making it easier to understand what information is required for the block.

```
Edit Attributes
  Block Name:   S-DOOR

  DOOR TYPE              [A]
  DOOR SIZE             7'-0"
  DOOR NUMBER          116
  DOOR THICKNESS       1 3/4"
  FIRE RATING          20 MIN
  DOOR MATERIAL        WOOD
  DOOR CONSTRUCTION    SOLID CORE

        OK      Cancel    Previous    Next    Help...
```

To turn this feature on, do the following.

1. Enter **Attdia** ↵ at the command prompt.

2. At the New value for ATTDIA <0>: prompt, enter **1** ↵.

Attributes set with the Preset mode on will also appear in the dialog box and are treated no differently from other nonconstant attributes.

# *Editing Attributes*

Because drawings are usually in flux even after actual construction or manufacturing begins, you will eventually have to edit previously entered attributes. In the example of the apartment building, many things can change before the final set of drawings is completed.

Attributes can be edited individually (one at a time) or they can be edited globally (meaning you can edit several occurrences of a particular attribute tag all at one time). In this section you will make changes to the attributes you have entered so far, using both individual and global editing techniques, and you will practice editing invisible attributes.

## *Editing Attributes One at a Time*

AutoCAD LT offers an easy way to edit attributes one at a time through a dialog box. The following exercise demonstrates this feature.

1.  Click on the Named View button on the View flyout to restore view 1.

2.  Click on Edit Attribute on the Attribute toolbar, or enter **Ddatte** ↵ at the command prompt.

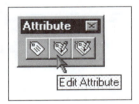

3.  At the `Select block` prompt, click on the apartment number attribute in the unit just to the right of the first unit in the lower-left corner. A dialog box appears, with the attribute value shown in an input box.

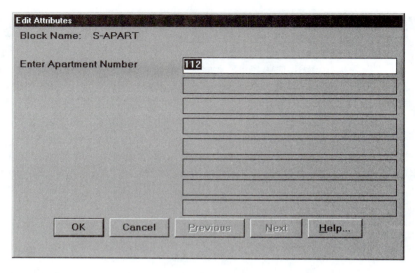

4.  Highlight the attribute value in the input box and enter **112**, and then click on OK to make the change.

5.  Do this for each room number, using Figure 10.3 to assign room numbers.

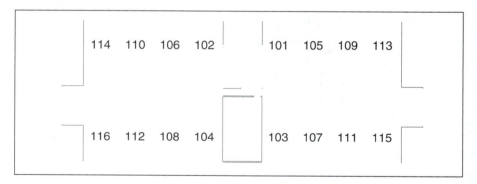

Figure 10.3:    *Apartment numbers for one floor of the studio apartment building*

## Editing Several Attributes in Succession

The Edit Attribute option is useful for reviewing attributes as well as editing them, because both visible and invisible attributes are displayed in the dialog box. This option is the same as the Ddatte command.

1. Click on Edit Attribute on the Attribute toolbar, or enter **Ddatte** ↵.

2. Click on a block containing attributes. The Edit Attributes dialog box appears as before.

3. Click on OK. To review and edit other attributes, repeat steps 1–3.

## Making Minor Changes to an Attribute's Appearance

Eventually, there will be situations where you will want to make a change to an attribute that doesn't involve its value, like moving the attribute's location relative to the block it's associated with, or changing its color, its angle, or even its text style. To make these types of changes, you must use the Attedit command. Here's how to do it.

1. Click on the Edit Attribute Globally button on the Attribute toolbar, or type **Attedit** ↵ at the command prompt.

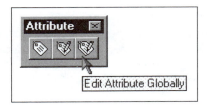

2. At the Edit attributes one at a time? <Y> prompt, press ↵ to accept the default Y.

3. At the Block name specification <*> prompt, press ↵. Optionally, you can enter a block name to narrow the selection to specific blocks.

4. At the Attribute tag specification <*> prompt, press ↵. Optionally, you can enter an attribute tag name to narrow your selection to specific tags.

5. At the Attribute value specification <*> prompt, press ↵. Optionally, you can narrow your selection to attributes containing specific values.

6.  At the Select Attributes prompt, you can pick the set of blocks that contain the attributes you wish to edit. Once you press ↵ to confirm your selection, one of the selected attributes becomes highlighted, and an × appears at its base point (see Figure 10.4).

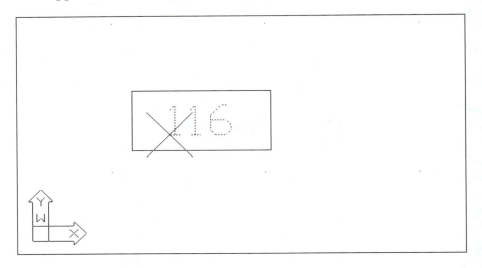

Figure 10.4:    *Close-up of attribute with* ×

7.  At the Value/Position/Height/Angle/Style/Layer/Color/Next <N>: prompt, you can enter the option that best describes the attribute characteristic you wish to change. After you make the change, the prompt returns, allowing you to make another change to the attribute. If you press ↵ to accept the default, *N*, another attribute highlights with an × at its base.

8.  The Value/Position/Height prompt appears again, allowing you to make changes to the next attribute.

9.  This process repeats until all the attributes have been edited or until you press Escape.

 **TIP**  **If you just want to change the location of individual attributes in a block, you can move attributes using grips.**

## Making Global Changes to Attributes

There will be times when you'll want to change the value of several attributes in a file to be the same value. You can use the Edit Attribute Globally option to make any global changes to attribute values.

Suppose you decide you want to change all the entry doors to a type designated as B, rather than A. Perhaps door type A was an input error, or type B happens to be better suited for an entry door.

1. Use the View command to restore view 4.

2. Click on Edit Attribute Globally on the Attribute toolbar, or type **Attedit** ↵.

3. At the Edit attributes one at a time? <Y> prompt, enter **N** ↵ for *No*. You will see the message Global edit of attribute values. This tells you that you are in the global edit mode.

4. At the Edit only attributes visible on screen? <Y> prompt, press ↵. As you can see from this prompt, you have the option to edit all attributes, including those out of the view area. You'll get a chance to work with this option later in the chapter.

5. At the Block name specification <*> prompt, press ↵. Optionally, you can enter a block name to narrow the selection to specific blocks.

6. At the Attribute tag specification <*> prompt, press ↵. Optionally, you can enter an attribute tag name to narrow your selection to specific tags.

7. At the Attribute value specification <*> prompt, press ↵. Optionally, you can narrow your selection to attributes containing specific values.

8. At the Select Attributes prompt, select the door type symbols for units 103 to 115.

9. At the String to change prompt, enter **A** ↵.

10. At the New string prompt, enter **B** ↵. The door type symbols all change to the new value.

The end results of the last four exercises in editing attributes are shown in Figure 10.5. This figure shows only the changes as they appear in View 4 of your drawing. You may check the other saved views also.

**Part 3**

**Becoming an Expert**

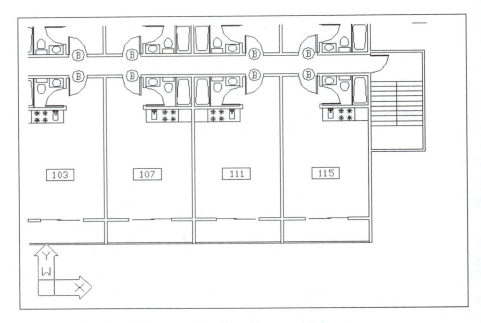

*Figure 10.5:* **View 4 with door symbols and apartment numbers added**

In step 8, you are asked to select the attributes to be edited. AutoCAD LT limits the changes to those attributes you select. If you know you need to change every single attribute in your drawing, you can do so by answering the series of prompts in a slightly different way, as in the following exercise.

1. Try the same procedure again, but this time enter **N** at the Edit only attributes visible on screen: prompt (step 4 in the previous exercise). The display will flip to text mode.

2. Once again, you are prompted for the block name, the tag, and the value (steps 5, 6, and 7 in the previous exercise). Respond to these prompts as you did before. Once you have done that, you get the message 16 attributes selected. This tells you the number of attributes that fit the specifications you just entered.

3. At the String to change: prompt, enter **A** ↵ to indicate you want to change the rest of the A attribute values.

4. At the New string: prompt, enter **B** ↵. A series of B's appear, indicating the number of strings that were replaced.

You may have noticed that the Select Attribute prompt is skipped and you go directly to the String to change prompt. AutoCAD LT assumes that you want it to edit every attribute in the drawing, so it doesn't bother asking you to select specific attributes.

## Making Invisible Attributes Visible

If an attribute has its invisible mode turned on, you cannot edit it using the global editing features described in the previous section. You can, however, make invisible attributes visible and *then* apply global edits to them. Here's how it's done.

1. Enter **Attdisp** ↵.

2. At the Normal/ON/OFF <Normal>: prompt, enter **ON** ↵. Your drawing will look like Figure 10.6. At this point you could edit the invisible attributes individually, as in the first attribute-editing exercise. For now, set the attribute display back to normal.

**NOTE** You'll get a chance to see the results of the ON and Normal options. The OFF option will make all attributes invisible, regardless of the mode used when they were created.

3. Enter **Attdisp** ↵ again; then at the Normal/ON/OFF prompt, enter **N** ↵ for normal. (Or you may click on the Undo button on the Standard toolbar.)

**TIP** You may also use the Options menu to change the display characteristics of attributes. Choose Options ➤ Display ➤ Attribute Display, then click on the desired option on the cascading menu.

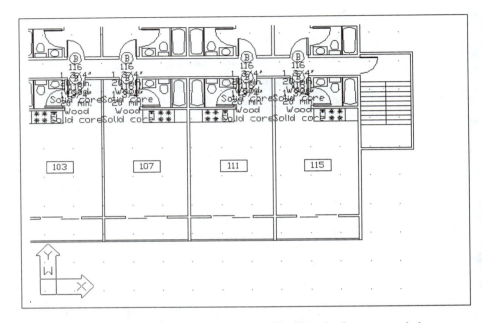

*Figure 10.6:*    **The drawing with all the attributes visible. Since the door type symbols are so close together, the attributes overlap.**

# Extracting and Exporting Attribute Information

Once you have entered the attributes into your drawing, you can extract the information contained in them and use it in other programs. You may, for example, want to keep track of the door information in a database manager. This is especially useful if you have a project that contains thousands of doors, such as a large hotel.

The first step in extracting attribute information is to create a "template" file using a text editor like the Windows 95 Notepad. The attribute template file is an ASCII text file containing a list of the attributes you wish to extract and their characteristics. You can also extract information about the block an attribute is associated with. The block's name, X and Y coordinates, layer, orientation, and scale are all available for extraction.

> **NOTE** Don't confuse this attribute template file with a drawing template, which you use to set up various default settings.

## Determining What to Extract

In the template file, for every attribute you wish to extract, you must give the attribute's tag name followed by a code that determines whether the attribute value is numeric or text, how many spaces to allow for the value, and, if it is a numeric value, how many decimal places to give the number. If you are familiar with database programs, you'll know these are typical variables you determine when you set up a database.

> **WARNING** You cannot have a blank line anywhere in the template file, or AutoCAD LT will reject it. Also, the last line in the file must end with a ↵, or your data will not extract. Equally, do not add an extra ↵, or the data will not extract.

For example, to get a list of rooms containing the B door type, you would create a text file with the following contents.

```
D-ROOM N005000

D-TYPE C001000
```

The first item on each line (D-ROOM and D-TYPE in this example) is the tag of the attribute you want to list. This is followed by at least one space, then a code that describes the attribute. This code may look a little cryptic at first glance. The following list describes how the code is broken down from left to right:

▶ The first character of the code is always a *C* or an *N* to denote a character (C) or numeric (N) value.

▶ The next three digits are where you enter the number of spaces the value will take up. You can enter any number from 001 to 999, but you must enter zeros for null values. The D-ROOM example shows the value of *005* for five spaces. The two leading zeros are needed because AutoCAD LT expects to see three digits in this part of the code.

▶ The last three digits are for the number of decimal places to allow if the value is numeric. For character values, these must always be zeros. Once again, AutoCAD LT expects to see three digits in this part of the code, so even if there are no decimal digits for the value, you must include *000*.

Now you will use the Windows Notepad application to create a template file. If you like, you can use any Windows word processor that is capable of saving files in the ASCII format.

1. Locate and start up the Notepad application from the Accessories program group on the Windows 95 Start Menu.

2. Enter the following text as it is shown. Press ↵ at the end of *each* line, including the last. Do not include an extra ↵ at the end, however.

    ```
    D-NUMBER C005000

    D-THICK  C007000

    D-RATE   C010000

    D-MATRL  C015000

    D-CONST  C015000
    ```

3. When you have finished entering these lines of text, click on File ➤ Save, then enter **Door.txt** for the filename. For ease of access, you should save this file to your current directory, the \AutoCAD LT directory.

4. Close the Notepad, and return to AutoCAD LT.

    You've just completed the setup for attribute extraction. Now that you have an attribute template file, you can extract the attribute data.

    ***Text Editor Line Endings***    It is very important that the last line of your file end with a single ↵. AutoCAD LT will return an error message if you either leave the ↵ off or have an extra ↵ at the end of the file.

### Performing the Extraction

AutoCAD LT allows you to extract attribute information from your drawing as a list in one of three different formats:

▶ CDF (comma-delimited format)

▶ SDF (space-delimited format)

▶ DXF (data exchange format)

## Using the CDF Format

The CDF format can be read by many popular database programs, as well as programs written in BASIC. This is the format you will use in this exercise.

1. Type **Ddattext** ↵. The Attribute Extraction dialog box appears.

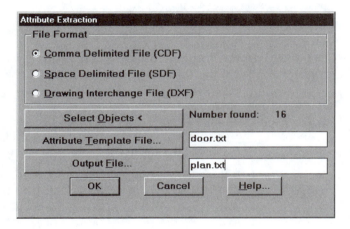

2. Click on the radio button labeled CDF.

3. Click on the Select Objects < button, and select all sixteen door symbols from the Plan drawing. Then press ↵ to end the selection set and return to the dialog box.

> **TIP**  You can select filenames of existing template and output files by clicking on the Template File or Output File buttons. The File dialog box appears, allowing you to select files from a list.

4. Double-click on the Attribute Template File button and select the Door.txt.

5. Press the Tab key to move from field to field to the Output File input box, then enter **Plan.txt**.

6. Click on OK. The computer will pause for several seconds, and when it is done, the message 16 records in extract file appears.

   If you get the error message Invalid character in filename, check your output filename and its path for spaces. This particular dialog box

**Part 3**

**Becoming an Expert**

field does not accept spaces in the path or filename. You must change the filename or path structure to complete this process. If the problem is in the path, tab to this input field, and type in just the filename.

---

 **NOTE** You may have noticed the Select Objects < button in the Attribute Extraction dialog box. When you click on this button, the dialog box temporarily closes to let you single out attributes to extract by picking their associated blocks from the display.

---

AutoCAD LT has created a file called Plan.txt that contains the extracted list. Let's take a look at its contents.

1. Open the Notepad again from the Accessories Program group.

2. Choose File ➤ Open to open Plan.txt from the current directory. (In this exercise, the output file is located in the \AUTOCAD LT directory.) You will get the following list:

```
'116','1 3/4"','20 MIN','WOOD','SOLID CORE'
'114','1 3/4"','20 MIN','WOOD','SOLID CORE'
'112','1 3/4"','20 MIN','WOOD','SOLID CORE'
'110','1 3/4"','20 MIN','WOOD','SOLID CORE'
'108','1 3/4"','20 MIN','WOOD','SOLID CORE'
'106','1 3/4"','20 MIN','WOOD','SOLID CORE'
'102','1 3/4"','20 MIN','WOOD','SOLID CORE'
'104','1 3/4"','20 MIN','WOOD','SOLID CORE'
'107','1 3/4"','20 MIN','WOOD','SOLID CORE'
'105','1 3/4"','20 MIN','WOOD','SOLID CORE'
'101','1 3/4"','20 MIN','WOOD','SOLID CORE'
'103','1 3/4"','20 MIN','WOOD','SOLID CORE'
'111','1 3/4"','20 MIN','WOOD','SOLID CORE'
'109','1 3/4"','20 MIN','WOOD','SOLID CORE'
'113','1 3/4"','20 MIN','WOOD','SOLID CORE'
'115','1 3/4"','20 MIN','WOOD','SOLID CORE'
```

Since you picked the comma-delimited format (CDF), AutoCAD LT placed commas between each extracted attribute value (or *field*, in database terminology).

The commas are used by some database management programs to indicate the separation of fields in ASCII files. This example shows everything in uppercase letters because that's the way they were entered when I inserted the attribute blocks in my own working sample. The extracted file maintains the case of whatever you enter for the attribute values.

**Part 3**

**Becoming an Expert**

***Using Other Delimiters with CDF*** Some database managers require the use of other symbols, such as double quotes and slashes, to indicate character values and field separation. AutoCAD LT allows you to use a different symbol in place of the single quote or comma. For example, if the database manager you use requires double-quote delimiters for text in the file to be imported, you can add the statement

```
c:quote  ″
```

to the template file to replace the single quote with a double quote. A line from an extract file using *c:quote ″* in the template file would look like this:

```
″115″, ″1 3/4 ″ ″,″20 MIN″,″WOOD″,″SOLID CORE″
```

Notice that the single quote (′) is replaced by a double quote (″).

You can also add the statement

```
c:delim  /
```

to replace the comma delimiter with the slash symbol. A line from an extract file using both *c:quote ″* and *c:delim /* in the template file would look like this:

```
″115″/″1 3/4 ″ ″/″20 MIN″/″WOOD″/″SOLID CORE″
```

Here the comma is replaced by a forward slash. You can add either of these statements to the beginning or end of your template file.

### Using the SDF Format

Like the CDF format, the space-delimited format (SDF) can be read by most database management programs. This format is the best one to use if you intend to enter information into a word-processed document, because it leaves out the commas and quotes. You can even import it into an AutoCAD LT drawing using the method described in *Chapter 8*. Now let's try using the SDF option to extract the same list we extracted a moment ago using CDF.

> **NOTE**  As an alternate, you can choose File ➤ Export, then at the Export Data dialog box, choose DXX Extract (*.DXX) from the List File of Type drop-down list. Enter a name for the extracted data file in the File name input box, then click on OK. Finally, in the drawing editor, select the attributes you want to extract.

1. Type **Ddattext** ↵ at the command prompt.

2. At the Attribute Extraction dialog box, use the same template filename, but for the attribute extract filename, use **Plan-sdf.txt** to distinguish this file from the last one you created.

3. Click on the SDF radio button, then click on OK.

4. After AutoCAD LT has extracted the list, use the Windows 95 Notepad to view the contents of the file. You will get a list similar to this one:

```
116 1 3/4" 20 MIN WOOD SOLID CORE
114 1 3/4" 20 MIN WOOD SOLID CORE
112 1 3/4" 20 MIN WOOD SOLID CORE
110 1 3/4" 20 MIN WOOD SOLID CORE
108 1 3/4" 20 MIN WOOD SOLID CORE
106 1 3/4" 20 MIN WOOD SOLID CORE
102 1 3/4" 20 MIN WOOD SOLID CORE
104 1 3/4" 20 MIN WOOD SOLID CORE
107 1 3/4" 20 MIN WOOD SOLID CORE
105 1 3/4" 20 MIN WOOD SOLID CORE
101 1 3/4" 20 MIN WOOD SOLID CORE
103 1 3/4" 20 MIN WOOD SOLID CORE
111 1 3/4" 20 MIN WOOD SOLID CORE
109 1 3/4" 20 MIN WOOD SOLID CORE
113 1 3/4" 20 MIN WOOD SOLID CORE
115 1 3/4" 20 MIN WOOD SOLID CORE
```

This format shows text without any special delimiting characters.

### Using the DXF Format

The third file format is the data exchange format (DXF). There are actually two methods for DXF extraction. The Attribute Extraction dialog box you saw earlier offers the DXF option. This option extracts only the data from blocks containing attributes. Choose the File ➤ Export option, then select .DXF from the List Files of Type: drop-down box to convert an entire drawing file into a special format for data exchange between AutoCAD LT and other programs (for example, other PC CAD programs). We will take a look at the DXF format in more detail in *Chapter 14*.

## Using Extracted Attribute Data with Other Programs

You can import any of these lists into any word-processing program that accepts ASCII files. They will appear as shown in our examples.

As we mentioned earlier, the extracted file can also be made to conform to other data formats.

*dBASE IV*   Suppose you want to import the list you just created in the exercises above into dBASE IV by using the CDF option. First, you create a database file with the same field characteristics you entered for the template file (i.e., length of fields and character or number). Then enter:

```
Append from \AutoCAD LT directory\Plan.txt Delimited
```

where *AutoCAD LT directory* is the directory where the Plan.txt file can be found.

To use the file created by the SDF option, replace **Delimited** in the line above with **SDF** and use **Plan-sdf.txt** instead of **Plan.txt**.

If you are using a database manager other than dBASE IV, find out what its format requirements are for imported files and use the quote and delim options described earlier to make adjustments. You may also have to rename the file in order to import it into the database manager. Requirements for two of the more popular database managers are described here.

*Lotus 1-2-3*    You can also use the SDF format for importing files into Lotus 1-2-3. However, you must change the SDF file extension from .txt to .prn. Once you have done this, you can use Lotus' File Import command to create a spreadsheet from this file. Use the Numbers option on the Lotus Import submenu to ensure that the numeric values are entered as discrete spreadsheet cells. Any items containing text are grouped together in one cell. For example, the last three items in the Plan-sdf.txt file are combined into one cell because each item contains text.

*Excel*    If you want to export data to Excel, you will have to use the CDF format. There are no other special requirements for Excel, but importing into Excel is made somewhat easier if you give your export file an extension that begins with XL, as in **Plan.xla**.

## Extracting Block Information Using Attributes

I mentioned that you can extract information regarding blocks, as well as attributes. To do this you must use the following format.

```
BL:LEVEL
  N002000

BL:NAME
  C031000

BL:X
  N009004

BL:Y
  N009004

BL:Z
  N009004

BL:NUMBER
  N009000

BL:HANDLE
  C009000

BL:LAYER
  C031000

BL:ORIENT
  N009004
```

```
BL:XSCALE
   N009004

BL:YSCALE
   N009004

BL:ZSCALE
   N009004

BL:XEXTRUDE
   N009004

BL:YEXTRUDE
   N009004

BL:ZEXTRUDE
   N009004
```

**WARNING** A template file containing these codes must also contain at least one attribute tag, because AutoCAD LT must know which attribute it is extracting before it can tell what block the attribute is associated with. The code information for blocks works the same as for attributes.

I have included some typical values for the attribute codes in this example. The following describes what each line in the above example is used for.

BL:LEVEL    returns the nesting level.

BL:NAME    returns the block name.

BL:X    returns the X coordinate of the insertion point.

BL:Y    returns the Y coordinate of the insertion point.

BL:Z    returns the Z coordinate of the insertion point.

BL:NUMBER    returns the order number of the block.

BL:HANDLE    returns the block's handle.

BL:LAYER    returns the layer the block is inserted on.

BL:ORIENT    returns the insertion angle.

BL:XSCALE    returns the X scale.

BL:YSCALE    returns the Y scale.

Part 3

Becoming an Expert

BL:ZSCALE    returns the Z scale.

BL:XEXTRUDE    returns the block's X extrusion direction.

BL:YEXTRUDE    returns the block's Y extrusion direction.

BL:ZEXTRUDE    returns the block's Z extrusion direction.

## *If You Want to Experiment...*

You can experiment with extracting information about the blocks in your drawing in the same way as you extracted attributes in the tutorial in this chapter. The block's name, X and Y coordinates, layer, orientation, and scale are all available for extraction. You can easily generate a text file listing all of these variables for any blocks that you select.

As you become more practiced with AutoCAD LT, you may want to develop a procedure to automate your checking procedures—for example, you might want to check that each block is on the correct layer, and at the correct scale.

First create a template called **Block.txt** using a text editor such as the Windows 95 Notepad. Remember, a template file is an ASCII file that contains a list of the attributes, or block information, that you wish to extract. For this exercise, include BL:NAME, BL:LAYER and BL:XSCALE in the template file. Refer to the "Extracting Block Information Using Attributes" section in this chapter for typical values for these variables.

Once you have created the template, follow the procedure described in the "Performing the Extraction" in this chapter. Use Plan.Dwg as before. After you click on the Select Objects < button in step 3 of the procedure, select all of the Toilet blocks in the drawing; select the Block.txt template file and save the information to an output file called **Toilet.txt**. Open and review your output file.

# Chapter 11

# Copying Pre-existing Drawings into AutoCAD LT

## *FAST TRACKS*

**To straighten sets of lines**

Turn on the Ortho mode. Type **Change** ↵. Select the lines you want to straighten, and then click on a point indicating, roughly, their endpoint location.

**To scale a drawing that contains curves without using a digitizer**

Draw a grid in AutoCAD LT that conforms to the area of the drawing you intend to scale. Plot the grid; then overlay the grid onto the paper drawing. Locate key points on the grid, and transfer those points back into the grid drawing in AutoCAD LT.

**A**T times you will want to turn a hand-drafted drawing into an AutoCAD LT drawing file. It may be that you are modifying a design you created before you started using AutoCAD LT, or that you are converting your entire library of drawings for future AutoCAD LT use. This chapter discusses three ways to enter a hand-drafted drawing: tracing, scaling, and scanning. Each of these methods of drawing input has its advantages and disadvantages.

**TIP** Even if you don't plan to trace drawings into AutoCAD LT, be sure to read the tracing information anyway, because some of it will help you with your editing. For example, because traced lines often are not accurately placed, you will learn how to fix such lines in the course of cleaning up a traced drawing.

Tracing with a digitizing tablet is the easiest method, but a traced drawing usually requires some cleaning up and reorganization. If dimensional accuracy is not too important, tracing is the best method for entering existing drawings into AutoCAD LT. It is especially useful for drawings that contain irregular curves, such as the contour lines of a topographical map.

Scaling a drawing is the most flexible method, since you don't need a tablet to do it and generally you are faced with less clean-up afterwards. Scaling also affords the most accurate input of orthogonal lines, because you can read dimensions directly from the drawing and enter those same dimensions into AutoCAD LT. The main drawback with scaling is that if the drawing does not contain complete dimensional information, you must constantly look at the hand-drafted drawing and measure distances with a scale. Also, irregular curves are difficult to scale accurately.

Of all the input methods, scanning produces a file that requires the most clean-up. In fact, you often spend more time cleaning up a scanned drawing than you would have spent tracing or scaling it. Even though some scanners can read straight text files, it is difficult to scan text in a drawing. Unfortunately, there is no easy way to transfer text from a hand-drafted drawing to an AutoCAD LT file. Scanning is best used for drawings that are difficult to trace or scale, such as complex topographical maps containing more contours than are practical to trace, or nontechnical line art.

## Tracing a Drawing

The most common and direct method for entering a hand-drafted drawing into AutoCAD LT is tracing. If you are working with a large drawing and you have a small tablet, you may have to cut the drawing into pieces that your tablet can manage, trace each piece, and then assemble the completed pieces into the large drawing. The best solution is to have a large tablet to begin with, but many of us do not have the budget for these large-format tablets.

NOTE If you don't have a digitizing tablet, you can use scaling to enter the utility room drawing used in this section's tracing exercise. (You will insert the utility room into your apartment house plan in *Chapter 12*.)

The following exercises are designed for an 11″×11″ or larger tablet. The sample drawings are small enough to fit completely on this size of tablet. You can use either a stylus or a puck to trace them, but the stylus will offer the most natural feel because it is shaped like a pen. A puck has crosshairs that you have to center on the line you want to trace, and this requires a bit more dexterity.

## Reconfiguring the Tablet for Tracing

When you first installed AutoCAD LT, you probably configured the tablet to use most of its active drawing area for AutoCAD LT's menu template. Since you will need the tablet's entire drawing area to trace this drawing, you now need to reconfigure the tablet to eliminate the menu. Otherwise, you won't be able to pick points on the drawing outside the 4″×3″ screen pointing area AutoCAD LT normally uses (see Figure 11.1).

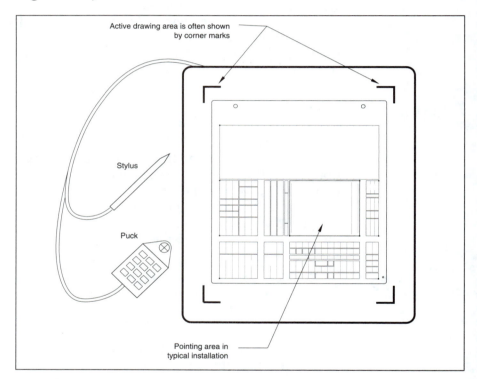

*Figure 11.1:* **The tablet's active drawing area**

1. Start AutoCAD LT and open a new file called Utility.

2. Set up the file as a ¼″=1′–scale architectural drawing on an 8½″×11″ sheet.

3. Choose Options ➤ Tablet ➤ Configure, or type **Tablet** ↵.

4. At the Option (ON/OFF/CAL/CFG): prompt, enter **CFG** ↵.

5. At the Enter number of tablet menus desired (0–4): prompt, enter **0** ↵.

6. At the Do you want to respecify the Fixed Screen Pointing Area? prompt, enter **Y** ↵.

> **NOTE** On some tablets, a light appears to show you the active area; other tablets use a permanent mark, such as a corner mark. AutoCAD LT won't do anything until you have picked a point, so you don't have to worry about picking a point outside this area.

7. At the Digitize lower left corner of screen pointing area: prompt, pick the lower-left corner of the tablet's active drawing area.

8. At the Digitize upper right corner of screen pointing area: prompt, pick the upper-right corner.

> **NOTE** When selecting points on the tablet, take care not to accidentally press the Pick button twice, as this will give you erroneous results. Many tablets have sensitive Pick buttons that can cause problems when you are selecting points.

Now as you move your stylus or puck you will notice a difference in the relationship between your hand movement and the screen cursor. The cursor moves more slowly and it is active over more of the tablet surface.

## *Calibrating the Tablet for Your Drawing*

Now make a photocopy of Figure 11.2, which represents a hand-drafted drawing of a utility room for your apartment building. Place the photocopied drawing on your tablet so that it is aligned with the tablet and completely within the tablet's active drawing area (see Figure 11.3).

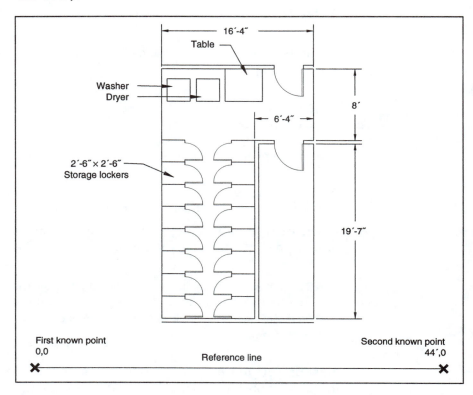

*Figure 11.2:    **The utility room drawing***

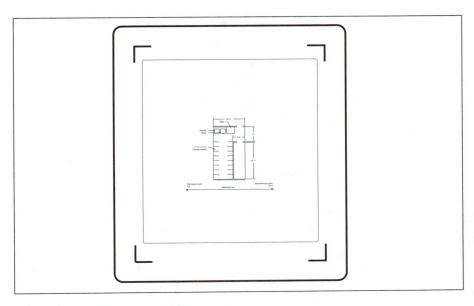

*Figure 11.3:*    **The drawing placed on the tablet**

 **NOTE** When you calibrate a tablet, you are setting ratios for AutoCAD LT; for example, that 2 inches on your tablet equals 16 feet in the drawing editor.

Before you can trace anything into your computer, you must calibrate your tablet. This means you must give some points of reference so AutoCAD LT can know how distances on the tablet relate to distances in the drawing editor. For example, you may want to trace a drawing that was drawn at a scale of ⅛"=1′–0". You will have to show AutoCAD LT two specific points on this drawing, as well as where those two points should appear in the drawing editor. This is accomplished by using the Tablet command's Cal option.

In Figure 11.2, we have already determined the coordinates for two points on a reference line.

1. Choose Options ➤ Tablet ➤ Calibrate, or enter **Tablet** ↵.

2. At the Option (ON/OFF/CAL/CFG): prompt, enter **Cal** ↵ at the command prompt.

3. The message "Calibrate tablet for use…Digitize first known point" appears, asking you to pick the first point for which you know the absolute coordinates. Pick the X on the left end of the reference line.

4. At the Enter coordinates for first point: prompt, enter **0,0** ↵. This tells AutoCAD LT that the point you just picked is equivalent to the coordinate 0,0 in your drawing editor.

5. Next, the Digitize second known point: prompt asks you to pick another point for which you know the coordinates. Pick the X on the right end of the reference line.

6. At the Enter coordinates for second point: prompt, enter the value **44′,0** ↵.

7. At the Digitize third known point (or RETURN to end): prompt, press ↵. The tablet is now calibrated.

The word Tablet appears on the status line to tell you that you are in tablet mode. If your digitizer does not have Wintab Support (see *Appendix A*) while in tablet mode, you can trace the drawing but you cannot access the Windows 95 menus. (Check your digitizer manual for further information.) If you want to pick a menu item, you must toggle the tablet mode off by using the F10 function key. Or you can enter commands through the keyboard.

### Calibrating More Than Two Points

In step 7 of the previous exercise, you bypassed the prompt that offered you the chance to calibrate a third point. In fact, you can calibrate as many as 31 points. Why would anyone want to calibrate so many points? Often the drawing or photograph you are trying to trace will be distorted in one direction or another. For example, blue-line prints are usually stretched in one direction because of the way prints are rolled through a print machine.

**NOTE** This section is not crucial to the tutorial and can be skipped for now. You may want to just skim through it and read it more carefully later on.

You can compensate for distortions by specifying several known points during your calibration. For example, we could have included a vertical distance on the utility room drawing to indicate a distance in the y-axis. You could have then picked that distance and calibrated its point. AutoCAD LT would then have a point of reference for the Y distance as well as the X distance. If you calibrate only two points, as you did in the exercise, AutoCAD LT will scale X and Y distances equally. Calibrating three points causes AutoCAD LT to scale X and Y distances separately, making adjustments for each axis based on their respective calibration points.

Now suppose you want to trace a perspective view of a building, but you want to "flatten" the perspective so that all the lines are parallel. You can calibrate the four corners of the building's facade to stretch out the narrow end of the perspective view to be parallel with the wide end. This is a limited form of what cartographers call "rubber-sheeting," where various areas of the tablet are stretched by specific scale factors.

When you select more than two points for calibration, you will get a message similar to that shown in Figure 11.4. Let's take a look at the parts of this message.

```
3 calibration points

Transformation type:           Orthogonal        Affine        Projective
--------------------------------------------------------------------------
Outcome of fit:                Success           Exact         Impossible
RMS Error:                     0.0202
Standard deviation:            0.0042
Largest residual:              0.0247
At point:                           2
Second-largest residual:       0.0247
At point:                           3

Select transformation type...
Orthogonal/Affine/<Repeat table>:
```

*Figure 11.4:  AutoCAD LT's assessment of the calibration*

Across the top, you see the labels "Orthogonal," "Affine," and "Projective." These are the three major types of calibrations or Transformation types. The orthogonal transformation scales the x- and y-axes using the same values. Affine scales the x- and y-axes separately and requires at least three points. The projective transformation stretches the tablet coordinates differently, depending on where you are on the tablet. It requires at least four calibration points.

Just below each of these labels you will see either "Success," "Exact," or "Impossible." This tells you whether any of these transformation types are available to you. Since this example shows what you see when you pick three points, you get Impossible for the projective transformation.

The far-left column tells you what is shown in each of the other three columns.

Finally, the prompt at the bottom of the screen lets you select which transformation type to use. If you calibrate four or more points, the projective transformation is added to the prompt. The Repeat Table option simply refreshes the table.

Take care when you calibrate points on your tablet. Here are a few things to watch out for when calibrating your tablet:

▶ Use only known calibration points.

▶ Try to locate calibration points that cover a large area of your image.

▶ Don't get carried away—try to limit calibration points to only those necessary to get the job done.

## Tracing Lines from a Drawing

Now you are ready to trace the utility room. If you don't have a digitizer, you can skip this exercise. We've included a traced file on the companion CD that you can use for later exercises.

**TIP** Once a tablet has been calibrated, you can trace your drawing from the tablet, even if the area you are tracing is not displayed in the drawing editor.

1.  Click on the Line button on the Draw toolbar, or type **Line** ↵.

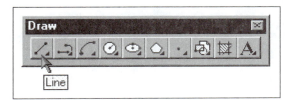

Part
3

Becoming an Expert

2.  Trace the outline of all the walls except the storage lockers.

3.  Add the doors by inserting the Door file at the appropriate points and then mirroring them. The doors may not fit exactly, but you'll get a chance to make adjustments later.

4.  Trace the washer and, since the washer and dryer are the same size, copy the washer over to the position of the dryer.

 **NOTE** The raggedness of the door arc is the result of the way AutoCAD LT displays arcs when you use the Zoom command; see *Chapter 6* for details.

At this point, your drawing should look something like panel 1 of Figure 11.5—a close facsimile of the original drawing, but not as exact as you might like. Zoom in to one of the doors. Now you can see the inaccuracies of tracing. Some of the lines are crooked, and others don't meet at the right points. These inaccuracies are caused by the limited resolution of your tablet, coupled with the lack of steadiness in the human hand. The best digitizing tablets have an accuracy of 0.001 inch, which is actually not very good when you are dealing with tablet distances of ⅛″ and smaller. In the following section, you will clean up your drawing.

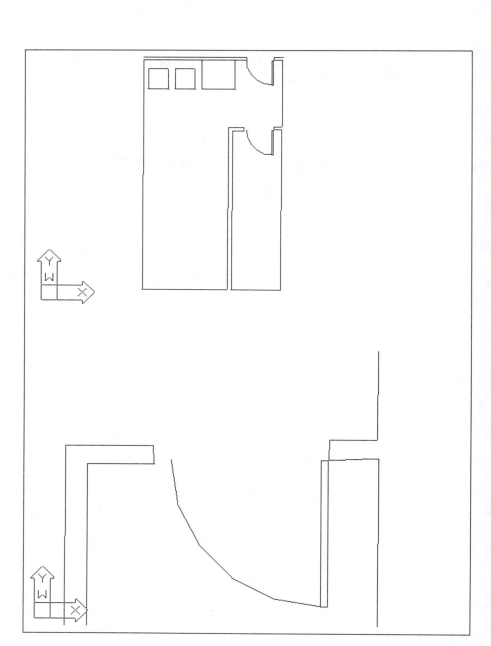

*Figure 11.5:* ***The traced drawing, with the door jamb in close-up in the bottom panel***

## Cleaning Up a Traced Drawing

In this section, you'll reposition a door jamb, straighten some lines, adjust a dimension, and add the storage lockers to the utility room.

In Figure 11.5, one of the door jambs is not in the right position (panel 2 gives you the best look). In this next exercise, you will fix this by repositioning a group of objects while keeping their vertices intact, using the Grips feature.

> **NOTE** If you skipped the last exercise, open the 11trace.DWG file from the companion CD to do the next exercise.

1. With the Verb/Noun selection setting and the Grips feature both turned on, pick a crossing window enclosing the door jamb to be moved (see panel 1 of Figure 11.6).

2. Shift-click on each of the grips at the end of the wall, in turn. You should have two hot grips at the door jamb.

3. Click on the lower of the two hot grips, without the Shift key this time, and drag the corner away to see what happens (see panel 2 of Figure 11.6).

4. Use the Endpoint Osnap override to pick the endpoint of the arc. The jamb repositions itself, and all the lines follow (see Figure 11.7).

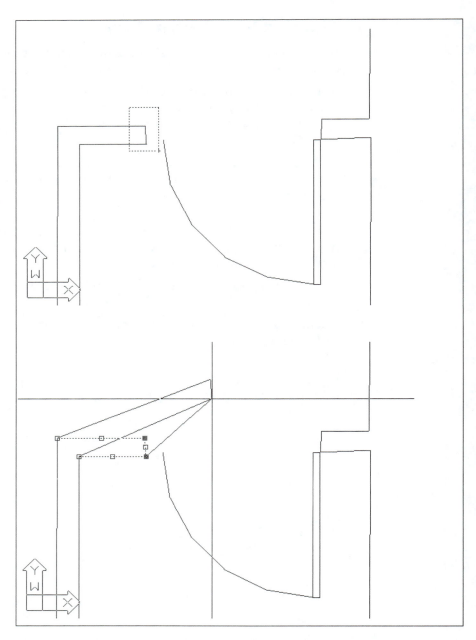

*Figure 11.6:* *A window crossing the door jamb, and the door jamb being stretched (bottom panel)*

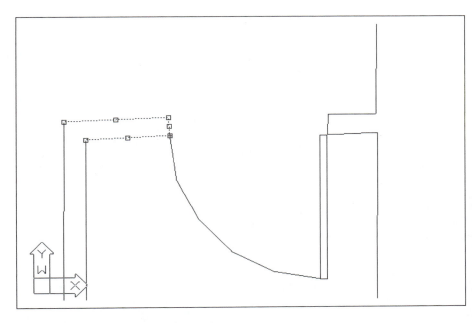

Figure 11.7: *The repositioned door jamb*

Another problem in this drawing is that some of the lines are not orthogonal. To straighten them, you use the Change command, together with the Ortho mode.

1. Toggle the Ortho mode on.

2. Type **Change** ↵ at the command prompt to start this operation.

3. At the `Select Objects` prompt, pick the two lines representing the wall just left of the door, and press ↵ to confirm your selection.

**WARNING** The Change command changes the location of the endpoint closest to the new point location. This can cause erroneous results when you are trying to modify groups of lines.

4. At the `Properties/<Change point>` prompt, use the Perpendicular Osnap override and pick the wall to the left of the lines you just selected. The two lines straighten out, and their endpoints align with the wall to the left of the two lines (see Figure 11.8).

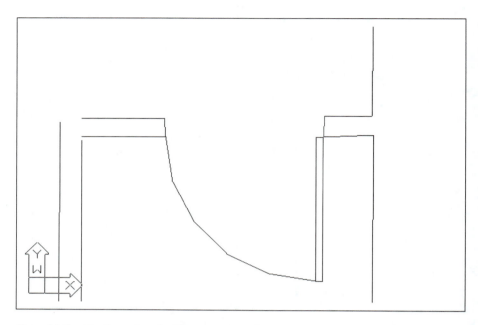

*Figure 11.8:    **The lines after the Change command is used***

As you have just seen, you can use the Change command not only to straighten lines, but to make them meet another line at a perpendicular angle. This only works with the Ortho mode on, however. To extend several lines to be perpendicular to a nonorthogonal line, you have to rotate the cursor to that line's angle (see panels 1 and 2 of Figure 11.9), using the Snapang system variable. (You can also use the Snap Angle input box in the Options ➤ Drawing Aids dialog box to rotate the cursor.) Then you use the process just described to extend or shorten the other lines (see panel 3 of Figure 11.9).

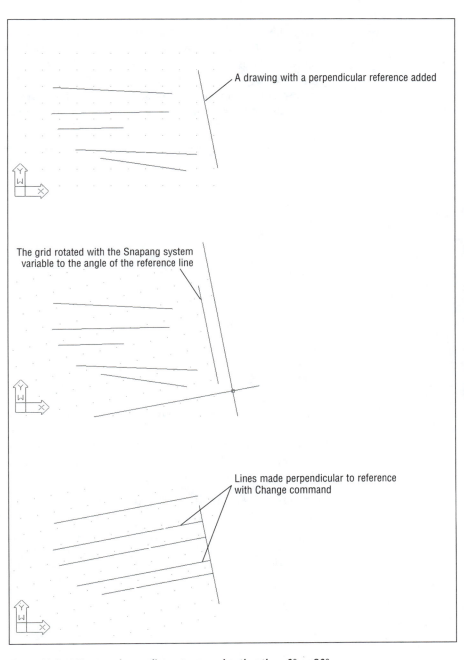

A drawing with a perpendicular reference added

The grid rotated with the Snapang system variable to the angle of the reference line

Lines made perpendicular to reference with Change command

*Figure 11.9:* **How to change lines at an angle other than 0° or 90°**

> **WARNING**  When changing several lines to be perpendicular to another line, you must be careful not to select too many lines. If the overall width of the group of lines is greater than the distance between the ends of the lines and the line to which they will be perpendicular, some of the lines will not change properly (see Figure 11.10). Once the lines have been straightened out, you can use the Fillet command to make the corners meet.

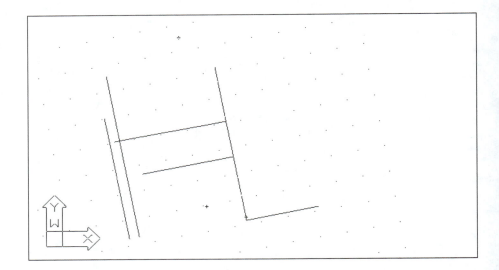

*Figure 11.10:* **Lines accidentally made perpendicular to the wrong point**

The overall interior dimension of the original utility room drawing is 16′–4″×28′–0″. Chances are the dimensions of the drawing you traced will vary somewhat from these.

1. Click and drag the Inquiry button on the Object Properties toolbar, then select Distance from the flyout to find your drawing's dimensions.

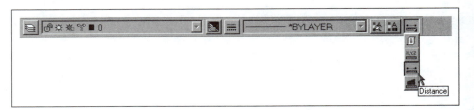

2. To adjust the walls to their proper positions (see Figure 11.11), either use the Grips feature, or click and drag the Resize button on the Modify toolbar, then select Stretch on the flyout.

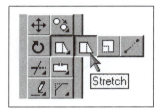

3. Use the Base ↵ command to make the base point the upper-left inside corner of the utility room, near coordinate 13′,30′.

4. To add the storage lockers, begin by drawing one locker accurately, using the dimensions provided on the traced drawing.

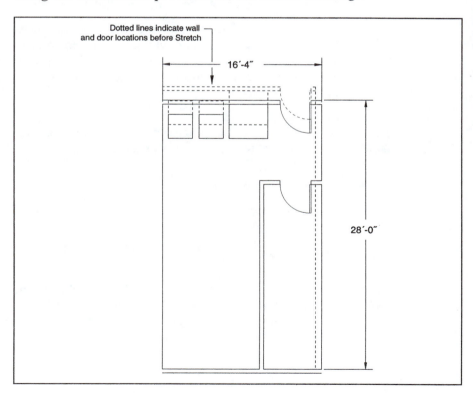

*Figure 11.11:*   ***The walls stretched to the proper dimensions***

5. Use the Mirror and Array commands to create the other lockers. Both of these commands are available on the Modify toolbar. (For entering objects repeatedly, this is actually a faster and more accurate method than tracing. If you traced each locker, you would also have to clean up each one.)

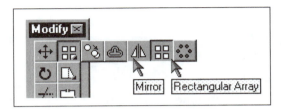

Finally, you may want to add the dimensions and labels shown earlier in Figure 11.2.

1. Create a layer called Notes to contain the dimensions and labels.

2. Set the Dimscale dimension setting to 48 before you start dimensioning. This can be done by clicking on Dimension Style from the Dimensioning toolbar, opening the Geometry dialog box, and then entering 48 in the Overall Scale input box (see *Chapter 9* for details on this process).

**NOTE** You can also set the Dimscale dimension setting by typing **Dimscale** ↵, and then entering the desired scale of 48.

3. Set the text height to 6″.

4. When you are done, save the file and exit AutoCAD LT.

## Working Smarter with Digitizers

**TIP** If you have only a small 12×12 format digitizer, but you need to digitize large drawings, consider hiring a finish carpenter to cut a hole in your table to accommodate the digitizer. You can then recess your digitizer into the table, so you can lay drawings flat over the digitizer.

In the first exercise of this chapter, you traced the entire drawing; however, you could have just traced the major lines with the ORTHO mode on, and then used the Offset command to draw the wall thickness. To do this, you would click and drag on the Copy objects button on the Modify toolbar, and then select Offset. Fillet and Trim (see *Chapter 5*) could then be used to "clean up" the drawing where lines cross or where they don't meet.

If you are a civil engineer, you would take a different approach. In laying out a road, for instance, you might first trace in the center lines, then use the Offset option on the Modify toolbar to place the curb and gutter. You could trace curved features using arcs (just to see what the radius of the curve is), and then redraw the arc accurately, joining straight line segments. The digitizer can be a great tool if it is used with care and a touch of creativity.

## Scaling a Drawing

When a hand-drafted drawing is to scale, you can read the drawing's own dimensions or measure distances using an architect's or engineer's scale, and then enter the drawing into AutoCAD LT as you would a new drawing using these dimensions. Entering distances through the keyboard is slower than tracing, but you don't have to do as much clean-up because you are entering the drawing accurately.

When a drawing contains lots of curves, you'll have to resort to a different scaling method that is actually an old drafting technique for enlarging or reducing a drawing. First, draw a grid in AutoCAD LT to the same proportions as your hand-drafted drawing. Plot this grid on translucent media and place it over the drawing. Then place points in the AutoCAD LT grid file relating to points on the grid overlay that intersect with the hand-drafted drawing (see Figure 11.12). Once you have positioned these points in your AutoCAD LT file, you can connect them to form the drawing by using polylines. This method is somewhat time-consuming and not very accurate, so if you plan to enter many drawings containing curves, it's best to purchase a tablet and trace them, or consider scanning or using a scanning service.

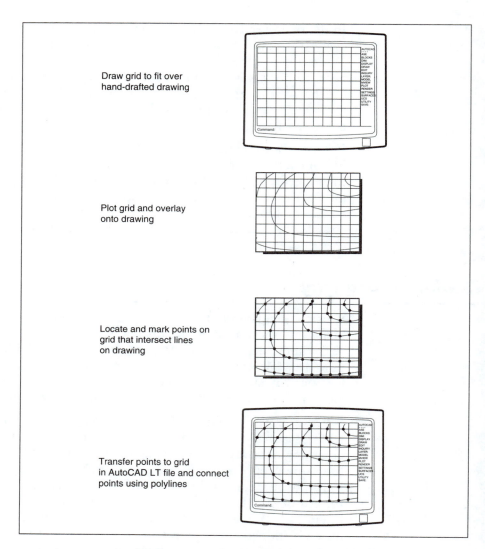

*Figure 11.12:* **Using a grid to transfer a hand-drafted drawing that contains curves**

## Scanning a Drawing

No discussion of drawing input can be complete without mentioning scanners. Imagine how easy it would be to convert an existing library of drawings into AutoCAD LT drawing files by simply running them through a scanning device. Unfortunately, scanning drawings is not quite that simple.

In scanning, the drawing size can be a problem. Desktop scanners are generally limited to an 8½″×14″ sheet size. Many low-cost hand-held scanners will scan a 22″×14″ area. Larger-format scanners are available but more expensive.

Once the drawing is scanned and saved as a file, it must be converted into a file AutoCAD LT can use. This conversion process can be time consuming and requires special translation software. Finally, the drawing usually requires some clean-up, which can take even longer than cleaning up a traced drawing. The poorer the condition of the original drawing, the more clean-up you'll have to do.

Whether a scanner can help you depends on your application. If you have drawings that would be very difficult to trace—large, complex topographical maps, for example—a scanner may well be worth a look. You don't necessarily have to buy one; some scanning services offer excellent value. And if you can accept the quality of a scanned drawing before it is cleaned up, you can save a lot of time. On the other hand, a drawing composed mostly of orthogonal lines and notes may be more easily traced by hand with a large tablet or entered directly by using the drawing's dimensions.

Despite the drawbacks of scanning, it can be an excellent document management tool for your existing paper drawings. You might consider scanning your existing paper drawings for archiving purposes. You can then use portions or all of your scanned drawings later, without committing to a full-scale, paper-to-AutoCAD LT scan conversion.

**Part 3**

**Becoming an Expert**

## HYBRID SCANNING SYSTEMS

A few software products use scanner technology to let you place a scanned image behind your drawing. With one such product, *CADRaster* from Man and Machine, Inc. (M+M), you can view a scanned image as a background while in AutoCAD LT. A drawing is first scanned using any one of several popular scanners. Using CADRaster, this file can be imported into AutoCAD LT as a background that you can trace over for your final drawing. The background image always remains in place in relation to your AutoCAD LT drawing, even when you perform a pan or zoom.

The conversion from scanned image to background is considerably faster than from scanned image to an AutoCAD LT file, and you can then build an intelligent drawing using the standard AutoCAD LT drawing objects. Products such as CADRaster offer a fast conversion method for many types of drawings. Or, if you need to, you can combine scanned images with AutoCAD LT drawings for output—for example, in civil applications where aerial photos are combined with roadway, site development, or parcel drawings.

## Importing Scanned Images

If you have a scanner and you would like to use it to import drawings into AutoCAD LT, you may do so using the Windows 95 cut and paste or drag-and-drop features. These features are discussed further in Chapter 14.

In the following section you will find step-by-step instructions on cutting and pasting a scanned image into AutoCAD LT for tracing or other purposes, using a .PCX file as an example.

Here are a few points you should consider if you plan to make use of scanned images:

▶ Scan in your drawing using a grayscale scanner, or convert your black-and-white scanned image to grayscale using your scanner software.

▶ Use a paint program or your scanner software to clean up unwanted gray or spotted areas in the file before cutting and pasting it into AutoCAD LT.

▶ If your scanner software or paint program has a de-speckle or de-spot routine, use it. It can help clean up your image and ultimately reduce AutoCAD LT file size.

▶ Scan at a reasonable resolution. Remember that the human hand is usually not more accurate than a few thousandths of an inch, so scanning at 150 to 200 dpi may be more than adequate.

▶ If you plan to make heavy use of scanned images, upgrade your computer to the fastest processor you can afford and don't spare the memory.

Scanned drawings can be used for applications other than tracing; you can cut and paste paper maps or plans into AutoCAD LT for presentations. We know of one architectural firm that produces some very impressive presentations with very little effort by combining 2D scanned images with 3D massing models for urban design studies. If you have the memory capacity, you can include raster images on 3D surfaces to simulate storefronts, people, or other surface features.

## If You Want to Experiment...

If you want to see firsthand how a scanned image can be brought in to AutoCAD LT, and you have a .PCX file, try the following exercise. Or better yet, if you have a scanner (a hand-scanner will do) scan Figure 11.2 and try importing it.

1. Open the scanned image in either your scanning software, or in a Paint program.

2. Select the scanned image and copy it to the Windows 95 clipboard (Ctrl-C).

3. Switch to AutoCAD LT and open the target drawing for your scanned image. (This will be a new drawing if you plan to use your image as a basis for tracing.)

4. Paste the scanned image from the clipboard into your AutoCAD LT drawing (Ctrl-V).

The image is inserted at the upper-left corner of the drawing area. You can click on it and drag it into position and/or re-size it using the object "handles."

Once the image is in, you can use it as a background to trace over, and then discard the image when you are done. The tracing capabilities of AutoCAD LT are limited. You cannot zoom or pan across the drawing while tracing, or your tracing will disappear behind the background. If you plan to scan a lot of drawings, you might consider some additional scanning software, such as the package described in the sidebar in this chapter.

Or you may use the image as a part of your drawing in its own right.

# Chapter 12
# Power Editing

## *Fast Tracks*

**To insert an Xref drawing** 454

*Click on Attach from the External Reference toolbar. At the dialog box, locate the file you wish to reference and double-click on it. Answer the prompts for insertion point, scale, and angle.*

**To import a named object (layer or block) from an Xref** 460

*Click and drag on Bind All on the External Reference toolbar to open the Bind flyout, then click on the button for the type of object you want to import. Enter the name of the object, including the filename prefix.*

**To enter Paper Space or return to Model Space** 463

*Double-click on the Tile button on the status bar, or type **Tilemode** ↵ **0** ↵.*

**To create a Paper Space viewport** 467

*While in Paper Space, click on View ➤ Floating Viewports; then select the type or number of desired viewports. You can also type **Mview** ↵ while in Paper Space and then answer the prompts.*

**To accurately scale a view in a Paper Space viewport** 469

*While in Paper Space, enter **MS** ↵, click on the viewport to be set, type **Zoom** ↵, and then type the inverse of the desired scale factor of the view, followed by **XP**. For example, for a 1/4″=1′ scale view, you would enter **1/48XP**.*

**To freeze a layer in a particular viewport** 472

*While in Paper Space, enter **MS** ↵, click on the viewport to be set, and then click on the Layers button on the Object Properties toolbar. Click on the layer you wish to freeze. Then click on the Frz button across from the Cur VP: label.*

**To match the properties of another object in a drawing** 474

*Click on the Property Painter icon on the Standard toolbar (the paintbrush icon), or type **Painter** ↵. Select a Source Object to copy from. In the Property Painter dialog box, select the properties you wish to match. Select one or more objects to copy these properties to, and then click on Apply.*

**B**ECAUSE you may not know all of a project's requirements when it begins, you usually base the first draft of a design on projected needs. As the plan goes forward, you make adjustments for new requirements as they arise. As more people enter the project, additional design restrictions come into play and the design is further modified. This process continues throughout the project, from first draft to end product.

In this chapter you will review much of what you've already learned. In the process, you will look at some techniques for setting up drawings to help manage the continual changes a project undergoes. You will also discover some steps you can take to minimize duplication of work. AutoCAD LT can be a very powerful timesaving tool. In this chapter, we'll examine methods of harnessing that power.

## Editing More Efficiently

The apartment building plan you've been working on is currently incomplete. For example, you need to add the utility room you created in *Chapter 11*. In the real world, this building plan would also undergo innumerable changes as it was developed. Wall and door locations would change, and more notes and dimensions would be added. In the space of this book's tutorials, we can't develop these drawings to completion. However, we can give you a sample of what is in store while using AutoCAD LT on such a project.

In this section, you will add a closet to the Unit plan. (You will update the Plan file later in this chapter.) In the editing you've already done, you've probably found that you use certain commands frequently: Move, Offset, Fillet, Trim, Grips, and the Osnap overrides. Now you will learn some ways to shorten your editing time by using them more efficiently.

## QUICK ACCESS TO YOUR FAVORITE COMMANDS

As you continue to work with AutoCAD LT, you'll find that you use a handful of commands 90 percent of the time. You can collect your favorite commands into a single toolbar using AutoCAD LT's toolbar customization feature. This way, you can have ready access to your most frequently used commands.

In addition, if you find yourself using one particular flyout menu over and over, you can easily turn it into a stand-alone floating toolbar for quick access. *Chapter 17* gives you all the information you need to customize your own toolbars.

**Part 3**

**Becoming an Expert**

### Editing an Existing Drawing

First, let's look at how you can add a closet to the unit plan. You'll begin by copying existing objects to provide the basis for the closet. You should use the Unit drawing that you worked on in *Chapter 9*. If you did create a Unit drawing, use the 12-UNIT.DWG on the companion CD.

1. Open the Unit plan, and freeze the Notes, Dimension (Dim), and Flr-pat layers. This will keep your drawing clear of objects you won't be editing.

2. If they are not already on, turn on Noun/Verb Selection and the Grips feature by selecting Options ➤ Selection and Options ➤ Grips.

3. Click on the right side wall, and then click on its midpoint grip.

4. Enter **C** ↵ to start the Copy mode; next enter **@2´<180** and then press ↵ twice to exit the command (see Figure 12.1).

5. Use the Zoom Window option on the Zoom flyout to zoom in to the entry area.

6. Issue the Offset command (click on the Offset button on the Duplicate Objects flyout on the Standard toolbar). At the Offset distance or through prompt, use the Nearest Osnap override and pick the outside wall of the bathroom near the door, as shown in Figure 12.2.

7. At the Second point: prompt, use the Perpendicular Osnap override and pick the other side of that wall (see Figure 12.2).

**8.** Click on the copy of the wall line you just created, and then on a point to the left of it.

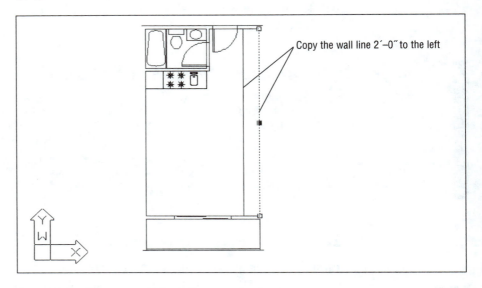

*Figure 12.1:* **Where to copy the wall to start the closet**

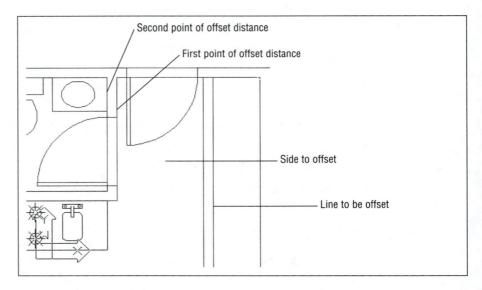

*Figure 12.2:* **How to use an existing wall as a distance reference for copying**

In steps 7 and 8, you determined the offset distance by selecting existing geometry. If you know you want to duplicate a distance, but don't know what that distance is, you can often use existing objects as references.

Next, use the same idea to copy a few more lines for the other side of the closet.

1. Zoom back so you can see the kitchenette in your screen view.

2. Click to highlight the two lines that make up the wall at the top of your view.

3. Shift-click on the midpoint grips of these lines (see Figure 12.3).

4. Click again on one of the midpoint grips, and then enter **C** ↵ to select the Copy option.

5. Enter **B** ↵ to select a base point option.

6. Use the upper-right corner of the bathroom for the base point, and the lower-right corner of the kitchenette as the second point.

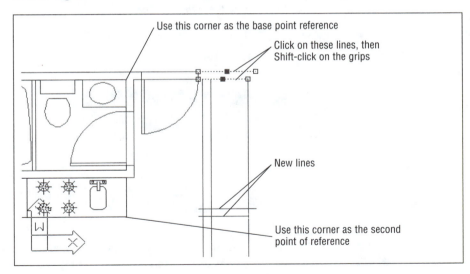

*Figure 12.3:* **Adding the second closet wall**

Now you've got the general layout of the closet. The next step is to clean up the corners. First, you'll have to do a bit of prep work and break the wall lines near the wall intersections, as shown in Figure 12.4.

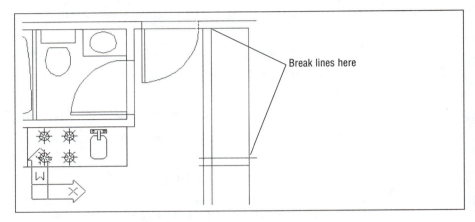

*Figure 12.4:* **Where to break the wall lines**

1. Click on Break 1 Point on the Modify toolbar. This tool breaks a line at a point on the object.

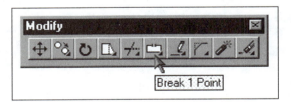

2. Click on the vertical wall to the far right at a point near the location of the new wall (see Figure 12.4).

NOTE When you click on an object in steps 2 and 3, nothing seems to happen. Since the lines are broken at a point, no gap appears, so you really can't see any change—but the lines are, in fact, broken into two line segments. The 1 Point Select option on the 1 Point flyout performs the same function as the 1 Point option but also allows you to select the break point with more accuracy.

3. Click on Break 1 Point again; then click on the horizontal line just below the topmost line on the screen (see Figure 12.4).

4. Click on the Fillet button on the Feature flyout, or type **Fillet** ↵ to join the wall lines that don't meet (see Figure 12.5).

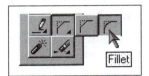

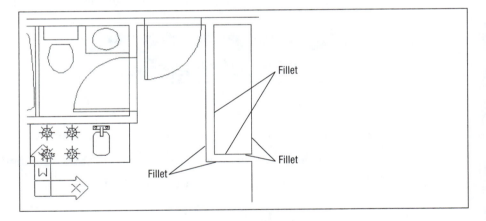

*Figure 12.5:* **Where to fillet the corners**

 **NOTE** Check that the Fillet radius is equal to zero if you want the filleted lines to be joined with a corner. (It is shown at the first Fillet command line prompt.) If the fillet radius is other than zero, the filleted lines will be joined with an arc.

Part
3

Becoming an Expert

In steps 2 and 3, you didn't have to be too exact about where to pick the break points, because Fillet takes care of joining the wall lines exactly. Now you are ready to add the finishing touches.

1. At the closet door location, draw a line from the midpoint of the interior of the closet wall to the exterior of the closet wall (see Figure 12.6). Make sure this line is on the Jamb layer.

2. Offset the new line 3′ in both directions. These new lines are the closet door jambs.

3. Click on Trim on the Modify toolbar, then click on the two jambs, and then press ↵. (The jambs are the "cutting edge" for the Trim function.)

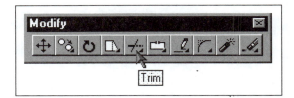

4. Click on the two vertical lines between the jambs.

5. Add door headers and sliding doors as shown in **Figure 12.6**.

6. Click on the Save button to save the file.

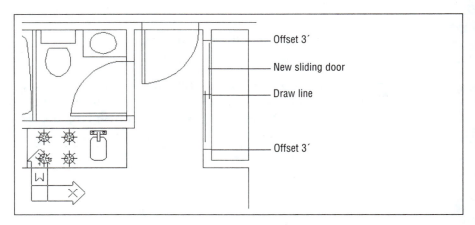

*Figure 12.6:*    ***Constructing the closet door jambs***

Sometimes it's easier to trim lines back and then draw them in again, as in the previous steps 4 and 5. At first this may seem counterproductive, but trimming the lines and then drawing in headers actually takes fewer steps and is a less tedious operation than some other routes. And the end result is a door that is exactly centered on the closet space. Figure 12.7 shows the finished closet fully-dimensioned, for your reference.

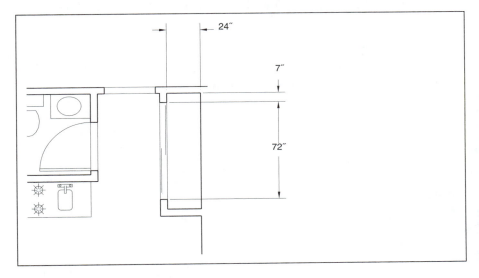

Figure 12.7:   **The finished closet with dimensions shown**

## Building on Previously Drawn Objects

Suppose your client decides your apartment building design needs a few one-bedroom units. In this exercise, you will use the studio unit drawing as a basis for the one-bedroom unit. To do so, you will double the studio's size, add a bedroom, move the kitchenette, rearrange and add closets, and move the entry doors. In the process of editing this new drawing, you will see how you can build on previously drawn objects.

Start by setting up the new file. As you work through this exercise, you'll be using commands that you've seen in previous exercises, so we won't bother describing every detail. But do pay attention to the process taking place, as shown in Figures 12.8 through 12.12.

1. Save the Unit.DWG file as a new file called **Unit2**.

2. Turn on the Notes, Flr-pat, and Dimension layers.

3. Later you will move the kitchenette, so erase its floor pattern.

4. Move the dimension string at the right of the unit, 14′–5″ to the right, and copy the unit the same distance to the right. Your drawing should look like Figure 12.8.

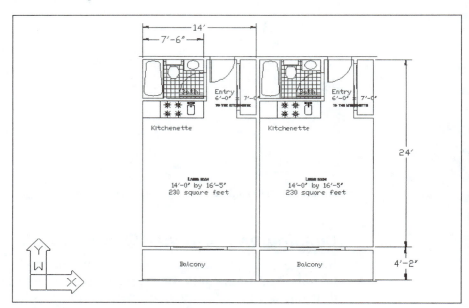

*Figure 12.8:* **The copied unit**

5. Now erase the bathroom, kitchenette, door, closet, and wall lines, as shown in Figure 12.9. You should do this in two steps. First, use a window to select and erase the bathroom, kitchen, and closet objects. The topmost line of the bathroom wall extends outside the window, and so it will remain. You should click on it and erase it.

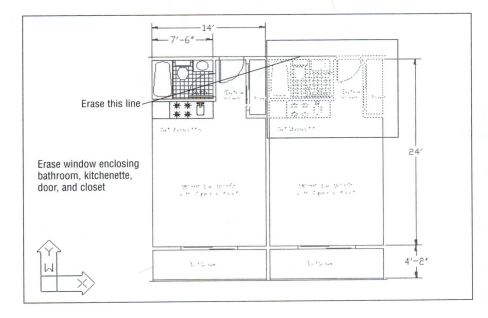

Figure 12.9: **Objects to be erased**

6. Copy the short interior wall of the closet to the right about 4′, to replace that side of the wall (see Figure 12.10).

7. Use Fillet on the Modify toolbar to join and extend walls where they have been broken (see Figure 12.10).

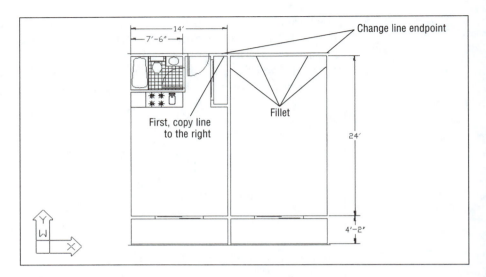

*Figure 12.10:* **Replacing erased walls**

8. Extend the topmost line so its endpoint is 5″ beyond the right interior wall line. (You've already done this once before in *Chapter 5.*)

9. Move the kitchenette to the opposite corner of the unit, as shown in Figure 12.11.

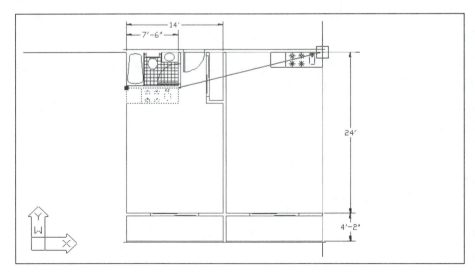

*Figure 12.11:* **Where to move the kitchenette**

10. Move the remaining closet down 5′–5″, as shown in Figure 12.12. You can use the corners of the bathroom as reference points.

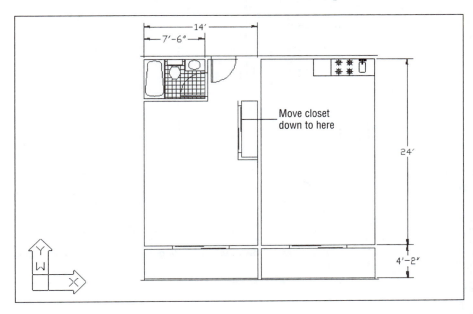

*Figure 12.12:* **The closet's new location**

Next, you'll work on finishing the new bedroom door and entry.

1. Zoom in to the area that includes the closet and the two doors.

2. Copy the existing entry door downward, including header and jambs (see Figure 12.13).

3. Clean up the walls by adding new lines and filleting others, as shown in Figure 12.14.

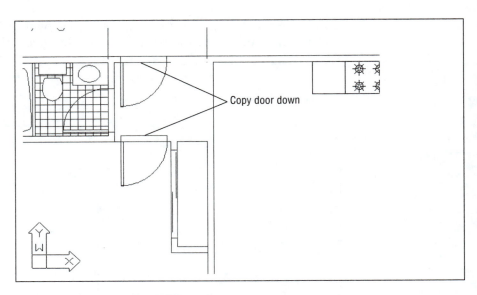

*Figure 12.13:* **How to use an existing door to create a door opening**

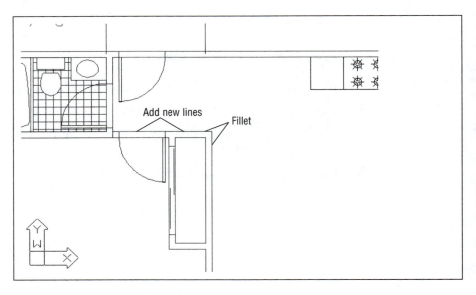

*Figure 12.14:* **Cleaning up the walls**

4. Mirror the door you just copied so it swings in the opposite direction.

 **TIP** Use the midpoint of the door header as the first axis endpoint.

5. Use the Stretch command (click on Stretch on the Modify toolbar) to move the entry door from its current location to near the kitchenette, as shown in Figure 12.15.

6. Once you've moved the entry door, mirror it in the same way you mirrored the other door.

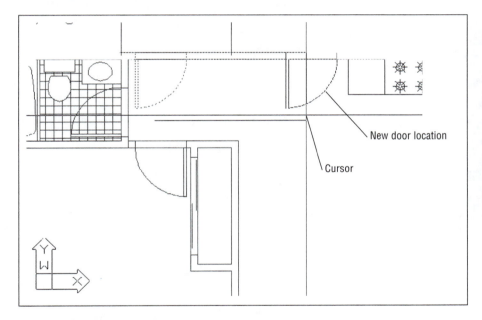

New door location

Cursor

*Figure 12.15:* ***Where to move the door***

In the previous exercise, you once again used parts of the drawing instead of creating new parts. In only a few instances are you adding new objects. In the exercise that follows, you will again use existing geometry to create new features. You will *extend* the walls of the existing closet to add a new closet. Just as with the Trim command, the

Extend command requires that you first select a set of objects to define the boundary of the extension, and then select the objects you wish to extend.

1. Now set the view of your drawing so it looks similar to Figure 12.16.

2. Click on the Extend button on the Feature flyout on the Modify toolbar, or type **Extend** ↵ at the command line. (You can use the command shortcut **Ex** ↵ rather than typing the whole word.)

3. At the Select boundary edge(s)… Select object: prompt, pick the wall at the bottom of the screen, as shown in Figure 12.16, and press ↵.

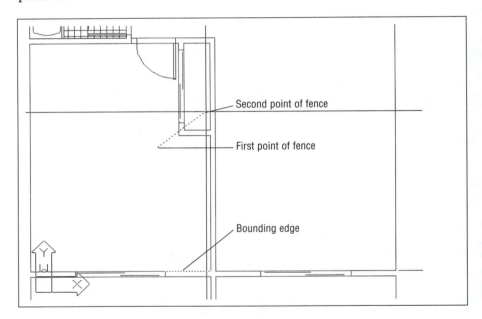

Figure 12.16: *Where to extend the lines*

4. At the Select object to extend: prompt, you need to pick the two lines just below the closet door. To do this, first enter **F** ↵ to use the Fence selection option.

5. At the `First Fence point` prompt, pick a point just to the left of the lines you want to extend.

6. At the `Undo/<Endpoint of line>` prompt, pick a point to the right of the two lines, so the fence crosses over them (see Figure 12.6).

7. Press ↵. The two lines extend to the wall.

8. Use a combination of Trim and Fillet to clean up the places where the walls meet.

9. Add another closet door on the right side of the new closet space you just created. Your drawing should look like Figure 12.17.

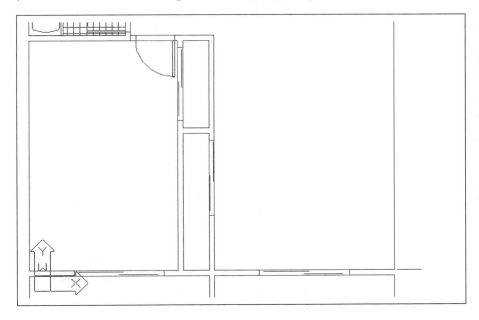

*Figure 12.17:* **The second closet added**

## Using Grips to Simplify Editing

Now suppose you want to change the location and orientation of the kitchenette. You will use the Grips feature to do just that.

1. Set up a view similar to the one in Figure 12.18.

2. Click on the kitchenette.

3. Click on the grip in the upper-left corner to make it a hot grip. The grip changes from hollow to solid.

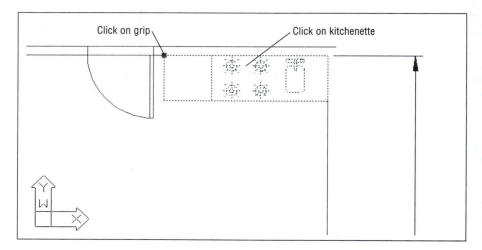

Click on grip    Click on kitchenette

*Figure 12.18:*    ***The rotation base point***

4. Press the ↵ key two times until you see the *** ROTATE *** message at the prompt.

5. Enter **–90**.

6. Click on the kitchenette's grip again; then, using the Endpoint Osnap override, click on the upper-right corner of the room. Your drawing should look like Figure 12.19.

**TIP** Remember that the Spacebar acts the same as the ↵ key for most commands, including the Grips modes.

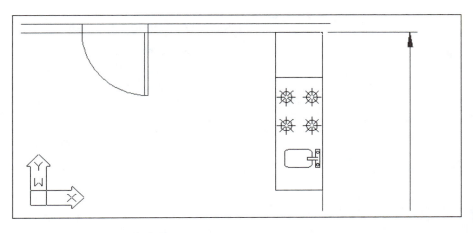

*Figure 12.19:* **The revised kitchenette**

Part
3

Becoming an Expert

 **NOTE** Typically the grip point of a block is the same as its insertion point—as long as the Enable Grips Within Blocks option is not activated. If you wish to enable grips *within* a block, choose Options ➤ Grips, or type **ddgrips** ↵, and then click on the second check box in the Grips dialog box.

Since the kitchenette is a block, its grip point is the same as its insertion point. This makes the kitchenette block—as it does all blocks—a great candidate for grip editing. Remember that the door, too, is a block.

Now suppose you want to widen the entrance door from 36″ to 42″. Try the following exercise involving a door and its surrounding wall.

1. Use a crossing window to select the door jamb.

2. Shift-click on both of the door jamb's grips.

3. Click on one of the grips again. It is now a hot grip.

4. At the ** Stretch ** prompt, enter **@6<180**. The door should now look like Figure 12.20.

 **NOTE** The Stretch hot-grip command will ignore a block as long as you do not include its insertion point in the stretch window.

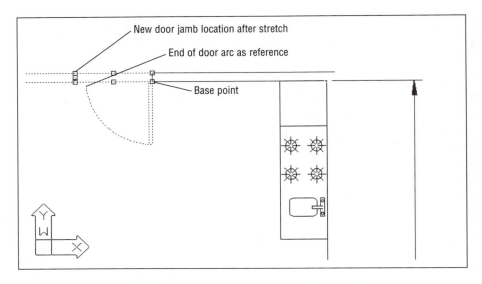

*Figure 12.20:*    **The widened door opening**

Notice that in step 4 you don't have to specify a base point to stretch the grips. AutoCAD LT assumes the base to be the original location of the selected hot grip.

Now you can enlarge the door using the Grips command's Scale mode. Scale allows you to change the size of an object or a group of objects. You can change the size visually by entering a scale value or by using an object for reference. In this exercise, you will use the current door width as a reference.

1.  Press the Escape key to clear your selection set.

2.  Click on the door, and then on the door's grip point.

3.  Press ↵ three times to get to the Scale mode.

4. At the `<Scale factor>/Base point/Copy/Undo/Reference/eXit:` prompt, enter **R** ↵ to select the Reference option.

5. At the `Reference length <0´−1″>:` prompt, click on the door's grip point.

6. At the `Second point:` prompt, click on the endpoint of the door's arc at the wall line. As you move the cursor, the door changes in size relative to the distance between the grip and the end of the arc.

7. At the `<New length>/Base point/Copy/Undo/Reference/eXit:` prompt, use the Endpoint Osnap override and click on the door jamb directly to the left of the arc endpoint. The door enlarges to fit the new door opening (see Figure 12.21).

8. Save the file.

Part
3

Becoming an Expert

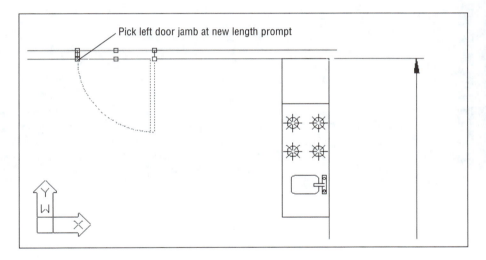

*Figure 12.21:* **The enlarged door**

You could have used the Scale option on the Resize flyout on the Modify toolbar to accomplish the operation performed in the above exercise with the Scale hot-grip command. The advantage to using grips is that you don't need to use the Osnap overrides to select exact grip locations, thereby reducing the number of steps you must take to accomplish this task.

In the next section, you will update the Plan file to include the revised studio apartment and the one bedroom unit you have just created (see Figure 12.22). You will be making changes such as these throughout the later stages of your design project. As you have seen, AutoCAD LT's ability to make changes easily and quickly can ease your work and help you test your design ideas more accurately.

## SELECTION CYCLING

In the exercises in this chapter, you may encounter situations where you need to select an object that is overlapping or very close to another object. Prior to Release 3 of AutoCAD LT, this was a difficult task; you had no control over what would be selected when you clicked on two overlapping objects.

Release 3 comes with a feature that eliminates the hassle of selecting overlapping objects. *Selection cycling* lets you cycle through objects that overlap until you select the one you want. To use this feature, simply hold down the Ctrl key while clicking on an object. If the first object highlighted is not the one you want, click again. When several objects are overlapping, just keep clicking until the right object is highlighted and selected.

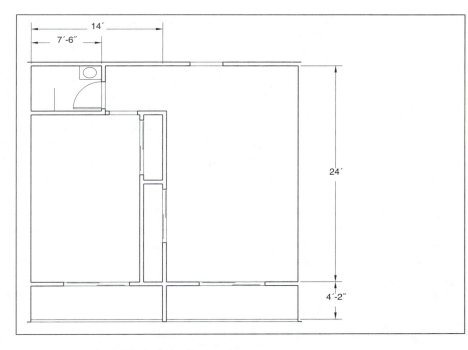

*Figure 12.22:*     **The finished one-bedroom unit**

# Using External References (Xrefs)

We mentioned in *Chapter 6* that careful use of blocks, external references, and layers can help you improve your productivity. In this section you will see firsthand how to use these elements to help reduce design errors and speed up delivery of an accurate set of drawings. You do this by controlling layers in conjunction with blocks and externally referenced files (Xrefs) to create a common drawing database for several drawings.

## *Preparing Existing Drawings for Cross-Referencing*

In *Chapter 6* we discussed using the Layers ➤ Freeze option to control layers. You can set up layers to represent the z-coordinate locations in your drawing. For example, you can create a layer for each of the three floors of your apartment building and then insert the Unit blocks on the appropriate layers. A fourth layer can contain the blocks common to all the floors, such as the lobby, stairs, utility room, and some of the units (see Figure 12.23). To display or plot a particular floor, you freeze all of the layers except that floor and the layer containing the common information. The following exercise shows you how to do all of this.

**NOTE** If you prefer, you can skip this exercise. For the later exercises that call for the elements created here you can use the Plan, Col-gr, Floor1, Floor2, and Common files (supplied on the companion CD).

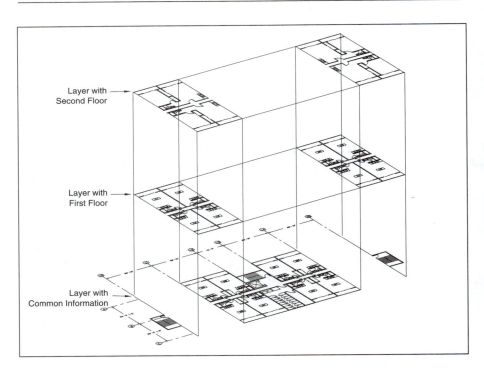

Layer with
Second Floor

Layer with
First Floor

Layer with
Common Information

*Figure 12.23:    A 3D representation of layers*

1. Open the Plan file. If you do not have a finished Plan drawing, use 12-PLAN.DWG on the companion CD.

2. Create a layer called **Gridline**, and add the grid and dimension information shown in Figure 12.24.

NOTE Gridline and related dimensions are used in architectural drawings as a system to establish references from which accurate dimensions can be taken. They are usually based on key structural elements, such as columns and foundation wall locations.

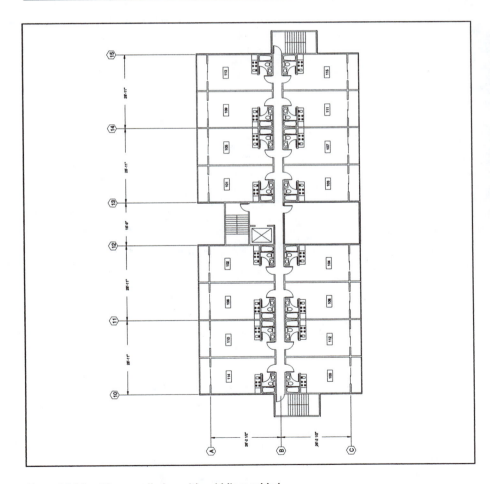

*Figure 12.24: The overall plan with grid lines added*

3.  Use Properties on the Object Properties toolbar and assign a Center linetype to the gridlines. This is a typical center-line composed of a long line, then a short dash, then another long line, usually used to denote the center of an object—in this case, a wall. Be sure Ltscale is set to 96 (click on Options ➤ Linetypes ➤ Global Linetype Scale, and specify 96).

4.  Use the Wblock command (or use File ➤ Export) to write the gridlines and other grid information to a file named **Col-gr.DWG**. Use the drawing origin, 0,0, for the insertion base point.

5.  Use the Wblock command again, and write the eight units in the corners of your plan to a file called **Floor1.DWG** (see Figure 12.25). When you select objects for the Wblock, be sure to include the door symbols for those units. Use 0,0 again for the Wblock insertion base point.

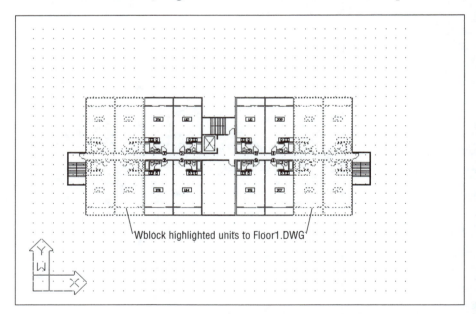

*Figure 12.25:*    ***Units to be exported to the Floor1 file***

6. Using Figure 12.26 as a guide, insert Unit2 into the corners where the other eight units were previously. Notice that when you insert the upper left-side unit, you must specify a minus y value (–1) in order to "mirror" the unit.

7. Once you've accurately placed the corner units, use the Wblock command to write these corner units to a file called **Floor2.DWG**. Again, use the 0,0 coordinate as the insertion base point for the Wblock.

8. Now use the Wblock command to turn the remaining set of unit plans into a file called **Common.DWG**. Remember that you can select everything in the drawing by entering **ALL** ↵ at the Select objects prompt.

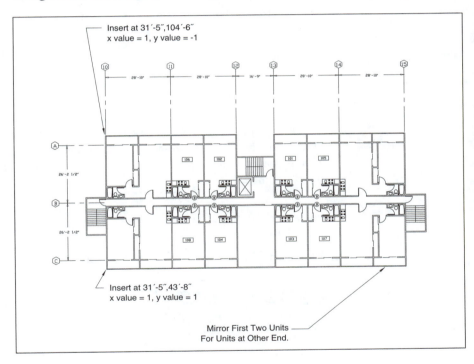

*Figure 12.26:* **Insertion information for Unit2**

You've just created four files: Col-gr, Floor1, Floor2, and Common. Each of these files contains unique information about the building. Next, you'll use the Xref command to recombine these files for the different floor plans in your building.

## Assembling External References to Build a Drawing

Next, you will create composite files for each floor, using cross-references of only the files needed for the individual floors. You will use the Attach option of the Xref command to insert all the files you exported from the Plan file.

1. Close the Plan file (don't save the changes) and open a new file and save it as **Xref-1**.

2. Set up this file as an architectural drawing 18″×24″ with a scale of ⅛″=1′.

3. Set Ltscale to 96.

 **TIP** Although it is not necessary in these exercises, it is generally a good practice to create a separate layer for each external reference file you attach. This increases your flexibility, as you can turn ON and OFF, or FREEZE/THAW the different Xrefs.

4. Open the External Reference toolbar by choosing View ➤ Toolbars ➤ External Reference.

5. Click on the Attach button on the External Reference toolbar.

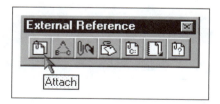

The Select File to Attach dialog box appears.

6. Double-click on the Common filename.

7. At the Insertion point prompt, enter **0,0** ↵.

8. Press ↵ at the X and Y Scale factor prompts and the rotation angle prompt.

9. Repeat the Attach option to insert the Floor1 file and the Col-gr file. You now have the plan for the first floor.

10. Save this file.

> **NOTE** Because the insertion points of all the files are the same, they will fit together perfectly when they are inserted into the new files.

11. Create a new file called **Xref-2**. Repeat steps 2 through 9 (you won't have to repeat step 4), but in step 9, insert the Floor2 file instead. This new file represents the plan for the second floor.

12. Save this file.

> **WARNING**  AutoCAD LT will not be able to find an external reference that has been moved to another disk or directory, and will issue an error message. If this happens, you must use the Path option on the External Reference toolbar to tell AutoCAD LT the new location of the external reference.

Now when you need to make changes to Xref-1 or Xref-2, you can edit the individual external reference files that make them up. Then, the next time you open either Xref-1 or Xref-2, the updated Xrefs will automatically appear in their most recent forms.

External references need not be permanent. You can attach and detach them easily at any time. This means that if you need to get information from another file—to see how well an elevator core aligns, for example—you can temporarily cross-reference the other file to quickly check alignments, and then detach it when you are done.

Think of these composite files as final plot files that are only used for plotting and reviewing. Editing can then be performed on the smaller, more manageable Xrefs. Figure 12.27 diagrams the relationship of these files.

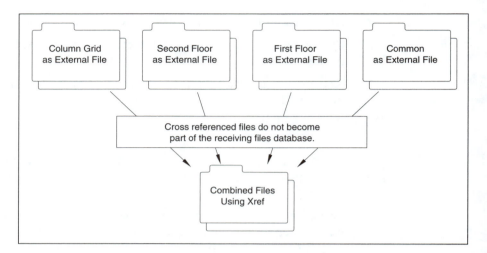

*Figure 12.27:*    ***Diagram of external reference file relationships***

The combinations of Xrefs are limited only by your imagination, but avoid multiple references of the same file.

## Updating Blocks in External References

There are several advantages to using external references. Since the Xrefs don't become part of the drawing file's database, these composite files remain quite small. Also, because Xrefs files are easily updated, work can be split up among several people in a workgroup environment or on a network. One person can be editing the Common file while another works on Floor1, and so on. The next time the composite file is opened, it will automatically reflect any new changes made in the external references. Now let's see how to set this up.

1. Open the Common file.

2.  Now you need to update the Unit plan you edited earlier in this chapter. Click on the Insert Block button on the Block flyout on the Draw toolbar.

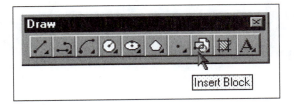

3.  At the Insert dialog box, click on the File button and click on the Unit filename. Then click on OK here, and again in the Insert dialog box.

4.  At the warning message, click on OK.

5.  At the Insertion point: prompt, press Esc.

6.  Enter **Regen** ⏎ to regenerate the drawing. You will see the new Unit plan in place of the old one (see Figure 12.28). You will also see all the dimensions and notes for each unit.

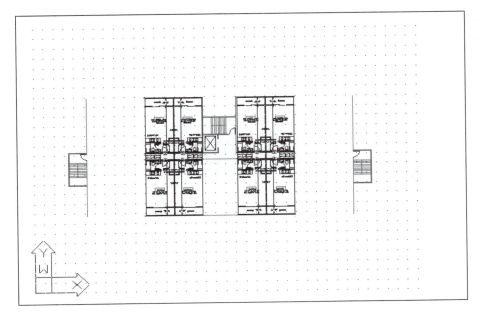

*Figure 12.28:  **The Common file with the revised Unit plan***

7. Open the Layer Control drop-down list on the Object Properties tool-bar and locate the Notes and Dimensions layers. Click on the Freeze/Thaw icon (it looks like a sun) to freeze this layer and keep the notes from interfering with the drawing. The Sun icon turns into a snowflake icon showing you that the layer is now frozen.

8. Click in the drawing area to close the list. Your drawing should now look like Figure 12.29.

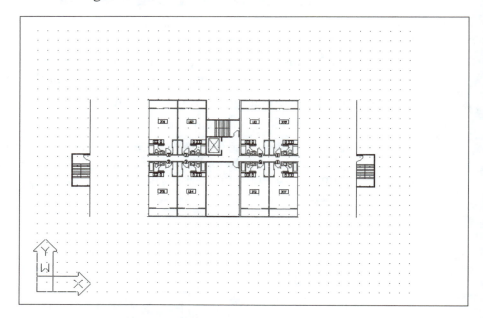

Figure 12.29:   *The Common file with the Notes layer frozen*

 Using Insert Block on the Draw toolbar again, replace the empty room across the hall from the lobby with the utility room you created in *Chapter 11* (see Figure 12.30). If you didn't create the utility room drawing, use the UTIL.DWG file on the companion CD.

NOTE When you created the Utility room file in *Chapter 11*, you were not asked to create specific layers for objects in the drawing, except for the Notes layer for text objects. So the layering is not consistent with other parts of the current drawing. The Utility drawing on the companion CD has the required layers added to the drawing. Use this drawing if you prefer not to revise your Utility drawing at this point. You can use the new Property Painter feature to match the drawing layers. See "Matching Object Properties" later in this chapter for a description of the Property Painter.

9. Save the Common file.

10. Now open the Xref-1 file. You will see the utility room and the typical units in their new form. Your drawing should look like Figure 12.31.

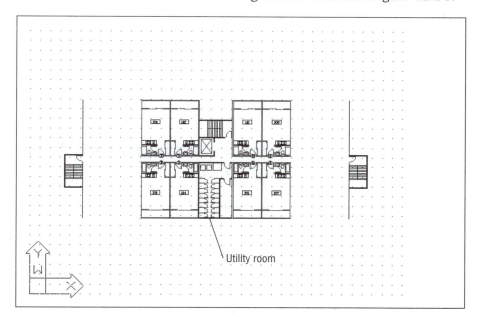

Figure 12.30:    *The utility room installed*

Part
3

Becoming an Expert

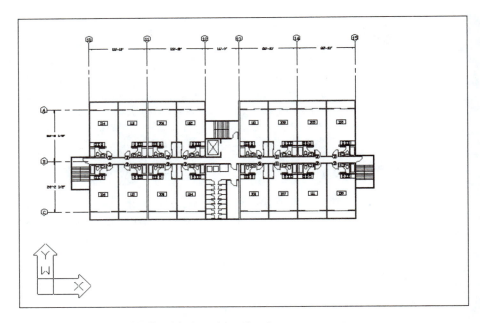

*Figure 12.31:* **The Xref-1 file with the units updated**

## Importing Named Objects from External References

In *Chapter 5*, we discussed how layers, blocks, linetypes, and text styles—called *named elements*—are imported along with a file that is inserted into another. Xref files, on the other hand, do not import named elements. You can, however, review their names and use a special command to import the ones you want to use in the current file.

AutoCAD LT renames named elements from Xref files by giving them the prefix of the filename from which they come. For example, the Wall layer in the Floor1 file will be called Floor1|wall in the Xref-1 file; the Toilet block will be called Floor1|toilet. You cannot draw on the layer Floor|wall, nor can you insert Floor1|toilet; but you can view the Xref's layers in the Layer Control dialog box, and you can view blocks in the Xref file using the Insert dialog box.

**TIP** You can set the Visretain system variable to 1 to force AutoCAD LT to retain layer settings of external reference files (see *Appendix D* for details).

Next you'll look at how AutoCAD LT identifies layers and blocks in external references, and you'll get a chance to import a layer from an Xref.

1. While in the Xref-1 file, click on the Layers button on the Object Properties toolbar. Notice that the names of the layers from the external reference files are all prefixed with the filename and the | vertical bar character. Exit the Layer dialog box.

> **NOTE** You can also open the Layer Control drop-down list to view the layer names.

2. Click and drag on the Bind All button on the External Reference toolbar to open the Bind flyout, and then select Bind Layer, or enter **Xbind ↵ LA ↵**.

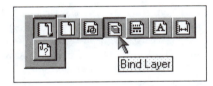

3. At the Dependent Layer Name(s): prompt, enter **Floor1|Wall ↵**. You then see the next message, Scanning... 1 Layer(s) bound. You have now imported the Wall layer from the Floor1 file. However, AutoCAD LT maintains the imported layer's uniqueness by giving it another name.

4. Click on the Layers button, and open the Layer Control dialog box again.

5. Scroll down the list of layer names until you get to the ones that start with the Floor1 prefix. Notice that Floor1|wall no longer exists. In its place is a layer called Floor1$0$wall.

> **TIP** You can now use **Ddrename** to rename the $0$ layer names to more intuitive ones if you choose.

As you can see, when you use the Bind option (Xbind) to import a named item, such as the Floor1|wall layer, the vertical bar (|) is replaced by two dollar signs surrounding a number, which is usually zero. (If for some reason the imported layer name Floor1$0$wall already exists, then the zero in that name is changed to 1, as in *Floor1$1$wall*.) Other named items are also renamed in the same way, using the $0$ replacement for the vertical bar.

## NESTING EXTERNAL REFERENCES AND USING OVERLAYS

External references can be nested. For example, the COMMON.DWG file created in this chapter might use the UNIT.DWG file as an external reference rather than an inserted block, and you would get the same result in the XREF-1.DWG file. That is, you would see the entire floor plan, including the unit plans, when you open XREF-1.DWG. In this situation, UNIT.DWG is nested in the COMMON.DWG file, which is in turn referenced in the XREF-1.DWG file.

Nested Xrefs can be useful: typically, in new construction, the column grid is referenced into the floor plans, and the floor plans are referenced into, for example, the furniture plans. However, nested external references can lead to problems in environments where multiple users share drawings. Unless external references are very carefully managed, circularity in Xrefs can easily occur, where Drawing X references Drawing Y, while at the same time Drawing Y references Drawing X.

To avoid this problem, you can use the Overlay option of the Xref command, which is new with Release 3. An overlaid external reference cannot be nested. For example, if you *attached* the COMMON.DWG file, as an xref into Floor1 and Floor2 in the conventional way, the COMMON.DWG would become a part of the XREF1.DWG. However, if you *overlaid* the COMMON.DWG file into the FLOOR1.DWG and FLOOR2.DWG files, then the COMMON.DWG file would not be displayed when you opened the XREF-1.DWG file. Overlays provide a useful way of sharing drawings for comparison purposes.

## Switching to Paper Space

Your set of drawings for this studio apartment building would probably include a larger-scale, more detailed drawing of the typical unit plan. You already have the beginnings of this drawing in the form of the Unit file.

As you have seen, the notes and dimensions you entered into the Unit file can be frozen in the Plan file so they don't interfere with the graphics of the drawing. The Unit file can be part of another drawing file that contains more detailed information on the typical unit plan on a larger scale. To this new drawing you can add other notes, symbols, and dimensions. Whenever the Unit file is altered, you update its occurrence in the large-scale drawing of the typical unit as well as in the Plan file. The units are thus quickly updated, and good correspondence is ensured among all the drawings for your project.

Now suppose that you want to combine drawings having different scales in the same drawing file—for example, the overall plan of one floor plus an enlarged view of one typical unit. This can be accomplished by using the Paper Space mode first discussed in *Chapter 6*. First, let's see how to get into Paper Space.

Your gateway to Paper Space is the setting of the Tilemode system variable. When Tilemode is set to 1 (On), the default setting, you cannot enter Paper Space; when it is set to 0 (Off), you can freely move from Paper Space to Model Space.

1. If it isn't already open, open the Xref-1 file, making sure your display shows all of the drawing.

2. Double-click on the Tile button on the status bar, choose View ➤ Paper Space, or enter **Tilemode** ↵ **0** ↵. Your screen goes blank and your UCS icon changes to a triangular shape. Also note the Model/Paper Space button on the status bar; it shows "PAPER," which tells you at a glance that you are in Paper Space.

The new UCS icon tells you that you are in Paper Space. But where did your drawing go? Before you can view it, you must create the windows, or *viewports*, that let you see into Model Space. But before you do that, let's explore Paper Space.

1. Click on Format ➤ Drawing Limits or enter **Limits** ↵ at the command prompt. Then note the default value for the lower-left corner of the Paper Space limits. It is 0′–0″, 0′–0″.

2. Press ↵ and note the current default value for the upper-right corner of the limits. It is 1′–0″, 9″, which is the standard default for a new drawing. This tells us that the new Paper Space area is 12″ wide by 9″ high—an area quite different from the one you set up originally in this drawing.

3. Click on Format ➤ Drawing Limits again.

4. At the ON/OFF: prompt, press ↵.

5. At the upper-right corner: prompt, enter **42,30** ↵ to designate an area that is 42″×30″.

6. Click on Zoom All.

Now you have your Paper Space set up. The next step is to create viewports so you can begin to paste up your views.

7. Click on View ➤ Floating Viewports ➤ 3 Viewports.

8. At the Horizontal/Vertical/Above/Below/Left/<Right>: prompt, enter **A** ↵ for Above. This option creates one large viewport along the top half of the screen, with two smaller viewports along the bottom.

9. At the Fit/<first point>: prompt, enter **F** ↵ for the Fit option. Three rectangles appear in the formation shown in Figure 12.32. Each of these is a viewport to your Model Space. The viewport at the top fills the whole width of the drawing area; the bottom half of the screen is divided into two viewports.

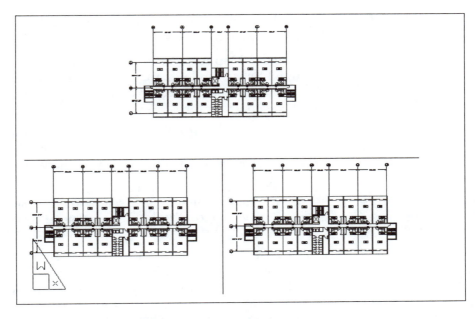

*Figure 12.32:    **The newly created viewports***

Now you need to get access to the viewports in order to display and edit your drawing.

**10.**  Double-click on the Paper button on the status bar; it changes to "MODEL." This gives you control over Model Space. (Or you can click on View ➤ Floating Model Space. You can also enter **Mspace** or **MS** ↵ to enter Model Space mode.)

**11.**  Be sure the top viewport is the current one (if not, click on it); then click on the Zoom Extents button on the Standard toolbar Zoom fly-out. The view enlarges to fill in the current active viewport.

**12.**  Click on the lower-left viewport to activate it.

**13.**  Click on the Zoom Window button and window the elevator area.

---

 **TIP**  If your drawing disappears from a viewport, you can generally retrieve it by using the Zoom Extents option (**Zoom** ↵ **E** ↵).

---

**14.** Click on the lower-right viewport and use the Zoom Window button to enlarge your view of a typical unit.

When you use **Mspace** ↵ or View ➤ Model Space (Floating), to move into Model Space mode, the UCS icon again changes shape—instead of one triangular-shaped icon, you have three arrow-shaped ones, one for each viewport on the screen.

Also, as you move your cursor into the currently active viewport, the cursor changes from an arrow into the usual crosshair. Another way to tell which viewport is the active one is by its double border.

**WARNING**  **You cannot move between viewports while in the middle of the Snap, Zoom, Vpoint, Grid, Pan, Dview, or Vplayer commands.**

You can move from viewport to viewport even while you are in the middle of most commands. For example, you can issue the Line command, then pick the start point in one viewport, then go to a different viewport to pick the next point, and so on. To activate a different viewport, you simply click on it (see Figure 12.33).

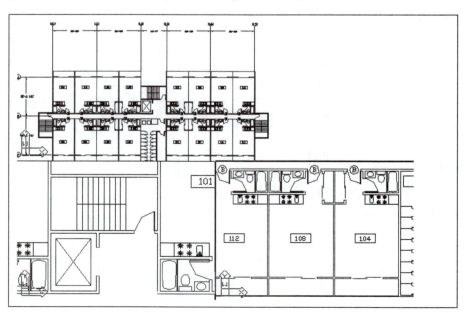

*Figure 12.33:*    **The three viewports with the plan in view**

## Getting Back to Model Space

Once you've created viewports, you can then reenter Model Space through the viewport using View ➤ Floating Model Space. But what if you want to quickly get back into the old full-screen Model Space you were in before you entered Paper Space? The following exercise demonstrates how this is done.

1.  Double-click on the Tile button on the status bar, or enter **Tilemode** ↵ 1 ↵. Your drawing returns to the original full-screen view—everything is back to normal.

2.  Double-click on Tile again, or enter **Tilemode** ↵ 0 ↵. You are back in Paper Space. Notice that all the viewports are still there when you return to Paper Space. Once you've set up Paper Space, it remains part of the drawing until you delete all of the viewports.

You should do most of your drawing in Model Space and use Paper Space for setting up views for plotting and for inserting your title blocks. Since viewports are retained, you won't lose anything when you go back to Model Space to edit your drawing.

## Working with Paper Space Viewports

Paper Space is intended as a page-layout or composition tool. You can manipulate viewports' sizes, scale their views independently of one another, and even set layering and linetype scale independently. Let's try manipulating the shape and location of viewports, using the Modify command options.

1.  Click on Stretch on the Modify toolbar and stretch the two viewport corners. Use a crossing window, as shown in Figure 12.34. Notice how the view within each viewport changes.

2.  Click on Modify ➤ Erase; then click on the frame of the lower-right viewport.

3.  Use the Move command to move the lower-left viewport to a new position, as shown in Figure 12.34.

 **NOTE** You can also click on the viewport frames and then stretch their corners using their grips. A viewport remains rectangular even when you try to stretch only one corner of it.

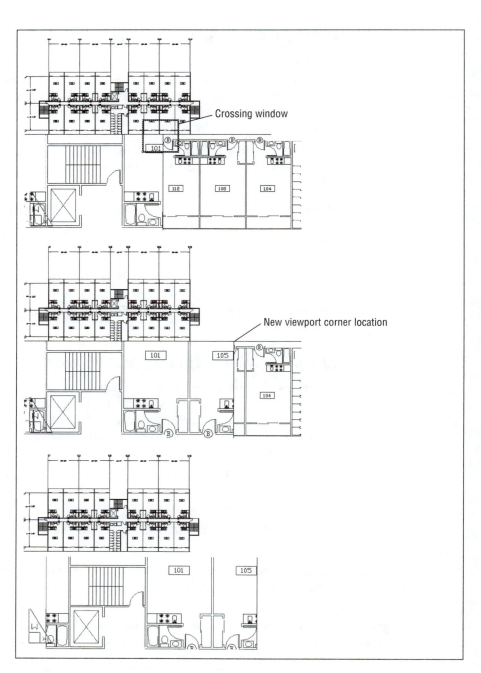

*Figure 12.34:* **Stretching, erasing, and moving viewports**

Viewports are actually objects, so they can be manipulated by all the editing commands just like any other object. In the foregoing exercise you moved, stretched, and erased viewports. Next, you'll see how layers affect viewports.

1.  Create a new layer called **Vport**.

2.  Use the Properties button on the Object Properties toolbar to change the viewport borders to the Vport layer.

3.  Finally, turn off the Vport layer. The viewport borders will disappear.

A viewport's border can be assigned a layer, color, or linetype. If you put the viewport's border on a layer that has been turned off, that border will become invisible, just like any other object on such a layer. Making the borders invisible is helpful when you want to compose a final sheet for plotting. Even when turned off, the active viewport will show a heavy border around it to simplify editing, and all the viewports will still display their views.

## Scaling Views in Paper Space

Paper Space has its own unit of measure. You have already seen how you can set the limits of Paper Space independently of Model Space. When you first enter Paper Space, regardless of the area your drawing occupies in Model Space, you are given limits that are 12 units wide by 9 units high. This may seem incongruous at first, but if you keep in mind that Paper Space is like a paste-up area, then this difference of scale becomes easier to comprehend. Just as you might paste up photographs and maps representing several square miles onto an 11″×17″ board, so can you use Paper Space to paste up views of scale drawings representing city blocks or houses.

NOTE While in Paper Space, you cannot edit objects in Model Space, and vice versa. You must use View ➤ Floating Model Space and View ➤ Paper Space to move from one mode to the other. Paper Space and Model Space each have separate scales, just as they have separate objects.

You must carefully consider scale factors when composing your Paper Space paste-up. Let's see how to put together a sheet in Paper Space and still maintain accuracy of scale.

1. Double-click on the Paper/Model Space button on the status bar, click on View ➤ Model Space (Floating), or enter **MS** ↵ to return to Model Space.

2. Click on the top view to activate it.

3. Pan the view so that the plan is centered in the viewport (see Figure 12.35).

4. Click on the Zoom Scale button, or enter **Zoom** ↵ (or **Z** ↵).

5. At the All/Center/Dynamic/Extents… prompt, enter **1/96xp** ↵. The **xp** suffix appended to the **1/96** tells AutoCAD LT that the current view should be scaled to ¹⁄₉₆ of the Paper Space scale. You get the **1/96** simply by taking the inverse of the drawing's scale factor, 96.

6. Click on the lower viewport.

7. Pan the view so that two of the typical units are centered in the viewport (see Figure 12.35).

8. Choose the Zoom Scale button again, and enter **1/24xp** ↵ at the All/Center/Dynamic prompt. Your view of the unit will be scaled to ¼″=1′ in relation to Paper Space.

It's easy to adjust the width, height, and location of the viewports so that they display only the parts of the unit you want to see; just go back to the Paper Space mode and use the Stretch, Move, or Scale commands. The view within the viewport itself will remain at the same scale and location, while the viewport changes in size. You can use these commands on a viewport with no effect on the size and location of the objects within the view.

You can also overlap viewports. Use the Osnap overrides to select geometry within each viewport, even while in Paper Space. This allows you to align one viewport on top of another at exact locations.

You can also add a title block at a 1:1 scale to frame your viewports, and then plot this drawing while still in Paper Space at a scale of 1:1. Your plot will appear just as it does in Paper Space.

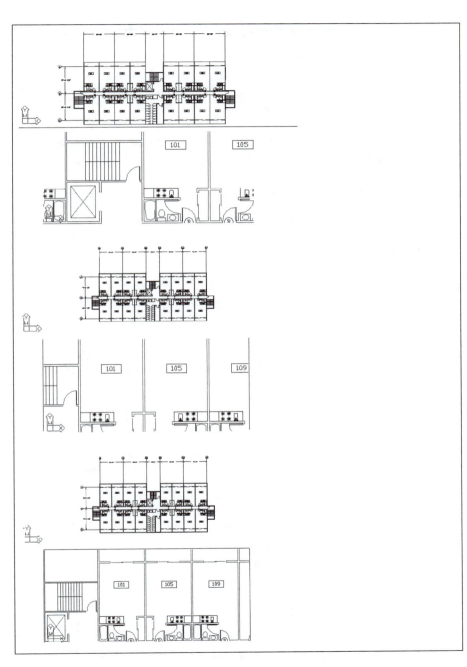

*Figure 12.35:* **Setting viewport views to scale**

## *Setting Layers in Individual Viewports*

Another unique feature of Paper Space viewports is their ability to freeze layers independently. You could, for example, display the usual plan information in the overall view of a floor but show only the walls in the enlarged view of one unit.

> **WARNING**  The Cur VP and New VP options in the Layer Control dialog box cannot be used if Tilemode is set to 1 (On).

1.  Activate the lower viewport.

2.  Click on the Format the Layers button to open the Layer Control dialog box.

3.  Click on COMMON|FIXTURE in the list of layers to highlight it.

4.  Click on the Frz button next to the Cur VP: label.

5.  Click on OK. The active viewport will regenerate, with the Fixture layer in the COMMON Xref invisible in the current viewport. The Fixture layer contains the kitchenette and the bathroom fixtures. Notice that the fixtures still remain visible in the upper viewport, and also in Unit 109, which is not a part of the Common Xref (see Figure 12.36).

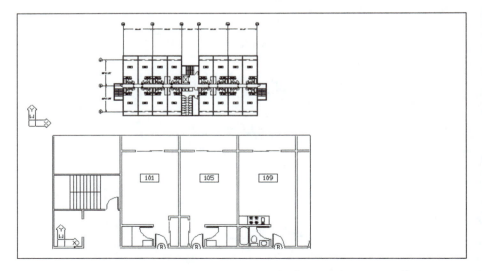

*Figure 12.36:*  ***The drawing editor with the Fixture layer turned off in the active viewport (Common Xref only)***

You might have noticed the other two similar buttons next to the label New VP. These two buttons control layer visibility in any new viewports you might create next, rather than controlling existing viewports.

If you prefer, you can also use the Layer Control drop-down list in the toolbar to freeze layers in individual viewports. Select the layer from the list, then click on the Sun icon with the small rectangle below it. This is equivalent to the Frz and Thw buttons in the Layer Control dialog box.

Now save and exit the Xref-1 file.

This section concludes the apartment building tutorial. Although you haven't drawn the complete building, you've already learned all the commands and techniques you need to do so. Figure 12.37 shows you a completed plan of the first floor; to complete your floor plans and get some practice using AutoCAD LT, you may want to add the symbols shown in this figure to your Plan file.

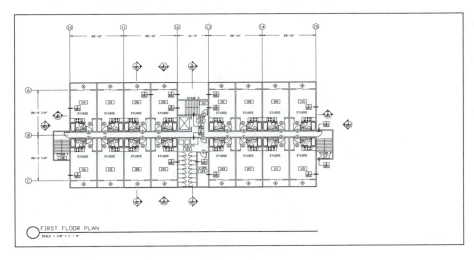

*Figure 12.37:* **A completed floor of the apartment building**

Since buildings like this one often have the same plans for several floors, the plan for the second floor can also represent the third floor. Combined with the first floor, this will give you a three-level apartment building. This project might also have a ground-level garage, which would be a separate file. The Gridline file you created earlier can be used in the garage file as a reference for dimensions. The other symbols can be blocks stored as files that can be retrieved in other files.

## *Matching Object Properties*

In the exercises in this chapter, you have assembled drawings from component parts of other drawings. This occurs frequently in real-life design situations. Often the component drawings have been created by different CAD operators, and they may not adhere to the same standards with respect to layers, linetypes, or object color, for example.

When you integrate different drawings, you need to match the properties of the objects within the drawing. Prior to Release 3, in order to match properties, first you would use List to identify the properties of the source object, and then use the Change Properties command to match these properties in the target object. The latest version of AutoCAD LT contains a new feature, called Property Painter, which allows you to copy all or a specified subset of properties from a source object to one or more objects.

1. To activate the Property Painter, click on the Property Painter button on the standard toolbar.

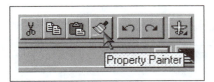

2. At the Select a Source Object: prompt, click on the object you wish to match. The Property Painter dialog box opens. By default, all of the Property options are checked, and the Source Object properties are displayed.

3. Clear all of the properties that you do not want to copy.

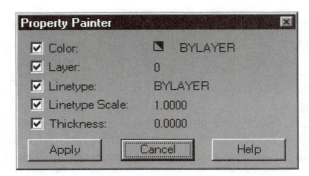

4.  At the `Select a Destination Object(s):` prompt, click on all of the objects that you want to match to the Source object.

5.  Click on the Apply button in the Property Painter dialog box.

## *If You Want to Experiment...*

You may want to experiment further with Paper Space in order to become more familiar with it. Try the following exercise. In it you will add two more viewports using the View ➤ Floating Viewports options (Mview) and Copy commands.

1.  Open the Xref1 file you used for the earlier Paper Space exercise.

2.  Choose View ➤ Paper Space or type **Pspace** ↵ to go to Paper Space.

3.  Turn on the Vport layer, and Stretch the lower viewport so that it occupies the lower-right third of the screen (see panel 1 of Figure 12.38).

4.  Choose View ➤ Floating Viewports ➤ 1 Viewport or type **Mview** ↵ to create a new viewport.

5.  At the `OFF/ON/Hideplot` prompt, pick the lower-left corner of the screen.

6.  At the `Other corner` prompt, size the viewport so that it is similar to the viewport on the right, as shown in panel 1 of Figure 12.38.

7.  Press Esc to stop the drawing regeneration.

8.  Use the Copy command to copy the lower-right viewport to the left. This time, let the drawing regeneration occur. Notice that the view in the copied viewport is identical to that in the original.

9.  At the command prompt, type **Mspace** ↵ to switch over to Model Space.

10. Pick the lower-left viewport.

11. Type **Regen** ↵. Notice that only the current viewport regenerates.

12. Issue the Zoom command and use the Dynamic option to move your view to the elevator area. You get a miniature version of the Dynamic Zoom view.

13. Arrange the views in the other viewport to look like panel 2 of Figure 12.38.

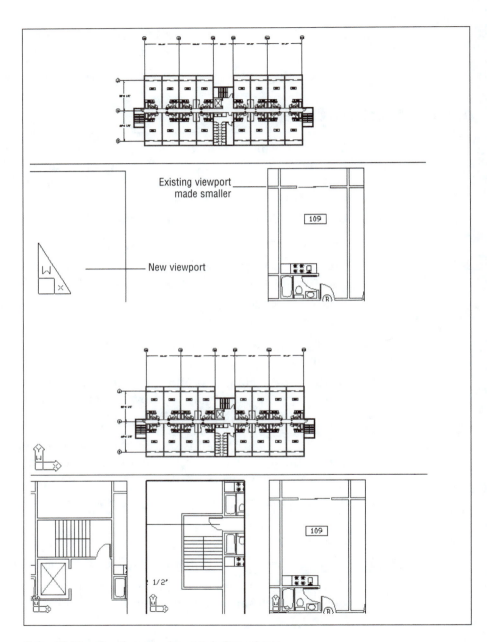

*Figure 12.38:    Creating new viewports in Paper Space*

# Chapter 13

# Drawing Curves and Solid Fills

## *FAST TRACKS*

**S**o far in this book, you've been using basic lines, arcs, and circles to create your drawings. In this chapter, it's time to add polylines and spline curves to your repertoire. Polylines offer many options for creating forms, including solid fills. Spline curves are perfect for drawing smooth, nonlinear objects. The splines are true NURBS curves. NURBS stands for Non-Uniform Rational B-Splines—but all you really need to know about the meaning of NURBS is that their curve information is mathematically accurate. Previous versions of AutoCAD LT provided only *polyline splines*, which created approximations of curves through short line segments.

## Introducing Polylines

Polylines are typically composed of one or more connected line segments or arcs. A polyline may look like a series of line segments, but it acts like a single object. This characteristic makes polylines useful for a variety of applications, as you'll see in the upcoming exercises.

### Drawing a Polyline

First, to introduce you to the polyline, you will begin a drawing of the top view of the joint in Figure 13.1.

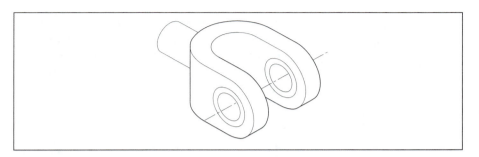

*Figure 13.1:*   **A sketch of a metal joint**

Part
3

1.  Open a new file and save it as **Joint2d**. Don't bother to make special setting changes, as you will do this drawing with the default settings.

2.  Click the Polyline button on the Polyline flyout on the Draw toolbar. You may also type **Pline** ↵ at the command line.

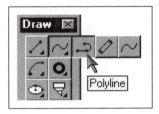

3.  At the From point prompt, enter a point at coordinate 3,3 to start your polyline.

NOTE **You can draw polylines just as you would with the Line command. Or you can use the other Pline options to enter a polyline arc or specify polyline thickness.**

4.  At the prompt:

    Arc/Close/Halfwidth/Length/Undo/Width/<Endpoint of line>:

    enter **@3<0** ↵ to draw a horizontal line of the joint.

5.  At the Arc/Close/Halfwidth... prompt, enter **A** ↵ to continue your polyline with an arc.

Becoming an Expert

NOTE The Arc option allows you to draw an arc that starts from the last point you selected. As you move your cursor, an arc follows it in a tangent direction from the first line segment you drew. You may click on a point to specify the Endpoint, or optionally enter **S** ↵ to add a Second point prior to the Endpoint.

6.   At the prompt:

```
Angle\CEnter\CLose\Direction\Halfwidth\Line\Radius\
Second pt\Undo\Width\<Endpoint of arc>:
```

enter **@4<90** ↵ to draw a 180° arc from the last point you entered. Your basic drawing should now look like Figure 13.2, although the position of the rubber banding line will depend upon the location of your cursor.

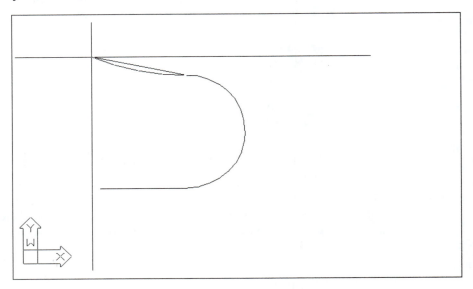

*Figure 13.2:   A polyline line and arc*

7.   Continue the polyline with another line segment. To do this, enter **L** ↵.

8.   At the Arc\Close\Halfwidth... prompt, enter **@3<180** ↵. Another line segment continues from the end of the arc.

9.   Press ↵ to exit Pline.

You now have a sideways, U-shaped polyline that you will use in the next exercise to complete the top view of your joint.

## Polyline Options

Let's pause from the tutorial to look at some of the Polyline options you didn't use.

**Close** draws a line segment or arc from the last endpoint of a sequence of lines to the first point picked in that sequence.

**Length** enables you to specify the length of a line that will be drawn at the same angle as the last line entered.

**Halfwidth** creates a line segment or arc by specifying half its beginning and ending widths (see Figure 13.3).

**Width** creates a tapered line segment or arc by specifying the full width of the segment's beginning and ending points.

**Undo** deletes the last line segment drawn.

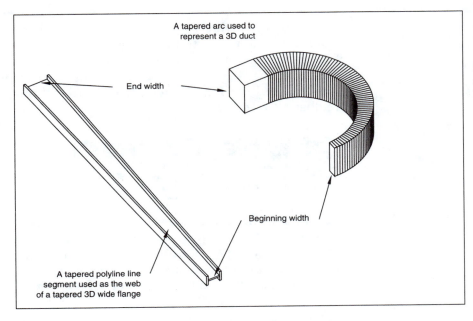

*Figure 13.3:* **Tapered line segment and arc created with Halfwidth**

If you want to break down a polyline into simple lines and arcs, you can use the Explode option on the Modify toolbar, just as you would with blocks. Once a polyline is exploded, it becomes a set of individual line segments or arcs. Since they are not polylines, the new objects will no longer have polyline properties, such as thickness.

**NOTE** The Fillet option on the Modify toolbar can be used to fillet all the vertices of a polyline composed of straight line segments. To do this, click the Fillet button on the Feature flyout on the Modify toolbar. Set your fillet radius, start Fillet again, then select the Polyline option under the Fillet command, and pick the polyline you want to fillet.

To turn off the filling of solid polylines, click on Options ➤ Display and turn off the Solid Fill option. (The Display options are explained in detail later in this chapter, in the section on solid fills.)

## Editing Polylines

You can edit polylines with many of the standard editing commands. To change the properties of a single polyline, click on the Properties button on the Object Properties toolbar (Ddmodify). The Stretch command on the Modify toolbar can be used to displace vertices of a polyline, and the Trim, Extend, and Break commands on the Modify toolbar also work with polylines.

In addition, there are many editing capabilities offered for polylines only. For instance, later you will see how you can smooth out a polyline using the Fit option under the Edit Polyline (Pedit) command. Let's take a closer look at some of the other Edit Polyline options by continuing the work on our top view of the joint.

In the following exercise, you'll use the Offset command on the Modify toolbar to add the inside portion of the joint.

 **TIP** A very complex polyline containing hundreds of vertices may not offset properly. If this happens, you can break the polyline up into smaller segments using the Break 1 Point option on the Modify toolbar, and then try the Offset command on these segments.

1. Click the Offset button on the Duplicate Objects flyout on the Modify toolbar, or type **Offset** ↵.
2. At the Offset distance prompt, enter **1**.
3. At the Select object prompt, pick the U-shaped polyline you just drew.
4. At the Side to offset prompt, pick a point toward the inside of the U. A concentric copy of the polyline appears (see Figure 13.4).

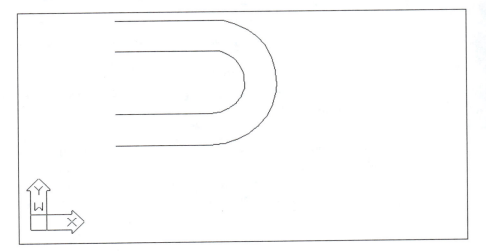

*Figure 13.4:* **The offset polyline**

The concentric copy of a polyline can be very useful when you need to draw complex parallel curves like the ones in Figure 13.5.

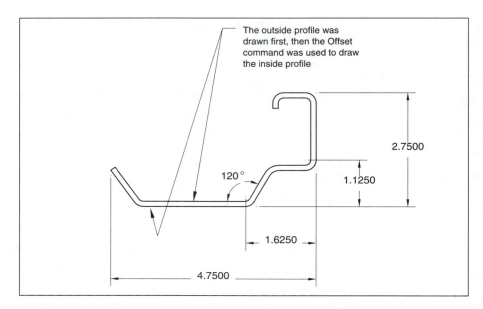

*Figure 13.5:* **Sample complex curves drawn by using offset polylines**

Next, complete the top view of the joint.

**1.** Connect the ends of the polylines with two short line segments (see Figure 13.6).

> **WARNING** The objects to be joined must touch the existing polyline exactly endpoint to endpoint, or else they will not join. To ensure that you place the endpoints of the lines exactly on the endpoints of the polylines, use the Endpoint Osnap override to select each polyline endpoint.

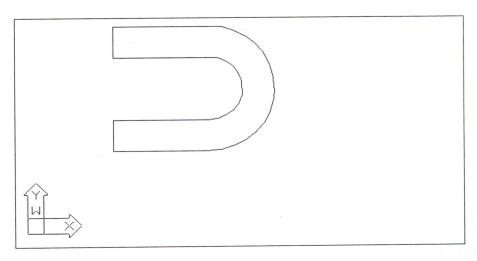

*Figure 13.6:*    ***The joined polyline***

**2.** Click on the Edit Polyline button on the Modify toolbar, or type **Pedit** ⏎.

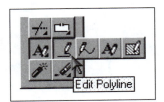

**3.** At the `Select polyline` prompt, pick the outermost polyline.

**4.** At the `Close/Join/Width…` prompt, enter **J** ⏎ for the Join option.

**5.** At the `Select objects` prompt, pick all the objects you have drawn so far.

**6.** Once all the objects are selected, press ⏎ to join them all into one polyline, and then ⏎ to exit the command.

By using the Width option under Edit Polyline, you can change the thickness of a polyline. Let's change the width of your polyline, to give some thickness to the outline of the joint.

1. Click on the Edit Polyline button on the Modify toolbar and select the polyline again.

2. At the `Open/Join/Width…` prompt, enter **W** ↵ for the Width option.

3. At the `Enter new width for all segments:` prompt, enter **.03** ↵ for the new width of the polyline. The line changes to the new width (see Figure 13.7), and you now have a top view of your joint.

4. Press ↵ to exit the Pedit command.

5. Save this file.

---

**TIP**  You can add thickness to regular lines and arcs by using the Edit Polyline (Pedit) command to change them into polylines, and then using the Width option to give them a width.

---

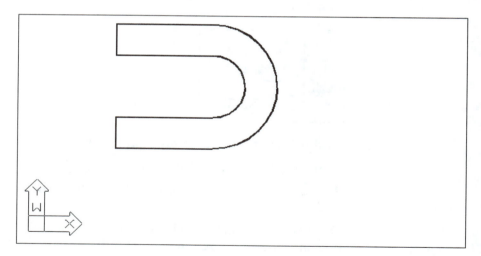

*Figure 13.7:*  **The polyline with a new thickness**

Now here's a brief look at a few of the Edit Polyline (Pedit) options you didn't try firsthand.

**Close**    connects the two endpoints of a polyline with a line segment or arc. If an arc was the last object drawn, Close will use an arc to complete the polygon. If the polyline you selected to be edited is already closed, this option changes to Open.

**Open**    removes the last segment added to a closed polyline.

**Spline**    smooths a polyline into a Bézier curve (discussed in detail later in this chapter).

**Decurve**    changes a smoothed polyline into one made up of straight line segments.

**Edit Vertex**    lets you edit each vertex of a polyline individually (discussed in detail in the next section).

**Fit**    turns polyline segments into a series of arcs.

**Ltype Gen**    controls the way noncontinuous linetypes are generated. When Ltype Gen is ON, the linetype is generated in a continuous pattern through the vertices of the polyline; when it is OFF, the pattern is restarted at each vertex. If you have a fitted or spline curve with a noncontinuous linetype, you will want to turn this option ON.

## Smoothing Polylines

There are many ways to create a curve in AutoCAD LT. If you don't need the representation of a curve to be exactly accurate, you can use a polyline curve. In the following exercise, you will draw a polyline curve to represent a contour on a topographical map.

1.  Open the TOPO.DWG drawing that is included on the CD that comes with this book. You will see the drawing of survey data shown in the top panel of Figure 13.8. Some of the contours have already been drawn in between the data points.

2.  Zoom in to the upper-right corner of the drawing, so your screen looks like panel 2 of Figure 13.8.

Part
3

Becoming an Expert

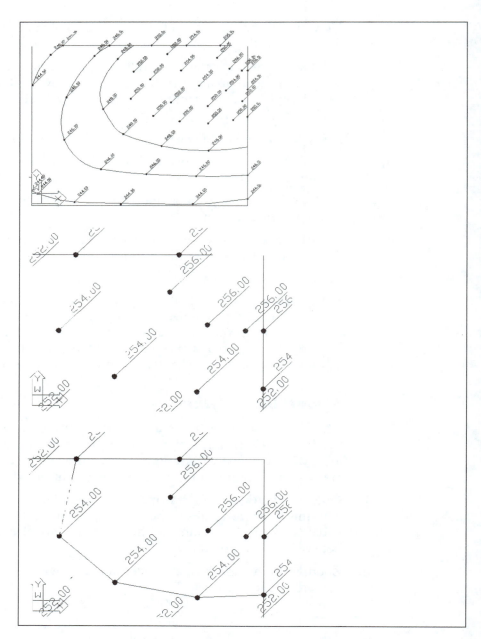

*Figure 13.8:    The TOPO.DWG drawing shows survey data portrayed in an AutoCAD LT draw-ing. Notice the dots indicating where elevations were taken. The actual elevation value is shown with a diagonal line from the point.*

3.  Click on the Polyline button on the Draw toolbar. Using the Center Osnap mode, draw a polyline that connects the points labeled "254.00" in the upper-right corner of the drawing. Your drawing should look like panel 3 of Figure 13.8.

4.  When you have drawn the polyline, press ↵.

Next you will convert the polyline you just drew into a smooth contour line.

1.  Click the Edit Polyline button on the Modify toolbar or type **Pedit** ↵.

2.  At the PEDIT Select objects: prompt, pick the contour line you just drew.

3.  At the prompt

    ```
    Close/Join/Width/Edit vertex/Fit/Spline/Decurve/Ltype
    gen/Undo/eXit:
    ```

    press **F** ↵ to select the Fit option. This causes the polyline to smooth out into a series of connected arcs that pass through the data points.

4.  At the prompt

    ```
    Close/Join/Width/Edit vertex/Fit/Spline/Decurve/Ltype
    gen/Undo/eXit:
    ```

    press ↵ to end the command.

Your contour is now complete. The Fit curve option on the Edit Polyline (Pedit) command causes AutoCAD LT to convert the straight-line segments of the polyline into arcs. The endpoints of the arcs pass through the endpoints of the line segments, and the curve of each arc depends on the direction of the adjacent arc. This gives the effect of a smooth curve. Next, you'll use this polyline curve to experiment with some of the editing options unique to the Edit Polyline command.

## TURNING OBJECTS INTO POLYLINES AND POLYLINES INTO SPLINES

There may be times when you will want to convert regular lines, arcs, or even circles into polylines. You may want to change the width of lines, or join lines together to form a single object such as a boundary. Here are the steps to take to convert lines, arcs, and circles into polylines.

1. Click on the Edit Polyline button on the Special Edit flyout on the Modify toolbar. You can also type **Pedit** ↵ at the command prompt.

2. At the Select polyline prompt, pick the object you wish to convert. If you want to convert a circle to a polyline, you must first break the circle (Break option on the Modify toolbar).

3. At the prompt

       Object selected is not a polyline. Do you want to turn it
       into one? <Y>

   press ↵. The object is converted into a polyline.

4. If your original object was a circle, you should now use the Close option on the Edit Polyline (Pedit) command to close the object again.

   If you have a polyline you would like to turn into a true spline curve, do the following:

1. Click and drag the Edit Polyline button on the Modify toolbar, or type **Pedit** ↵. Select the polyline you want to convert.

2. Type **S** ↵ to turn it into a polyline spline; then type ↵ to exit the Edit Polyline (Pedit) command.

3. Click on the Spline button on the Polyline flyout on the Draw toolbar. Or you may type **Spline** ↵.

4. At the Object/<Enter first point>: prompt, type **O** ↵ for the Object option.

5. At the Select object prompt, click on the polyline. Though it may not be immediately apparent, the polyline has been converted into a spline object.

## Editing Vertices

One of the Pedit options we haven't yet discussed, Edit Vertex, is almost like a command within a command. Edit Vertex has numerous suboptions that allow you to fine-tune your polyline by giving you control over its individual vertices. We'll discuss this command in depth in this section.

1. First, turn off the Data and Border layers to hide the data points and border, and set layer zero as the current layer.

2. Click on the Edit Polyline button on the Modify toolbar. Then select the polyline you just drew.

3. Type **E** ↵ to enter the Edit Vertex mode. An X appears at the beginning end of the polyline, indicating the vertex that will be affected by the Edit Vertex options.

### Edit Vertex Suboptions

When you select Edit Vertex, you get the prompt

```
Next/Previous/Break/Insert/Move/Regen/Straighten/Tangent/
Width/eXit <N>:
```

***Next and Previous*** The Next and Previous options enable you to select a vertex for editing. When you started the Edit Vertex option, an X appeared on the selected polyline to designate its beginning. As you select Next or Previous, the X moves from vertex to vertex to show which one is being edited. Let's try this out.

1. Press ↵ a couple of times to move the X along the polyline. (Since Next is the default option, you need only press ↵ to move the X.)

2. Type **P** ↵ for Previous. The X moves in the opposite direction. Notice that now the default option becomes P.

> **TIP** To determine the direction of a polyline, note the direction the X moves in when you use the Next option. Knowing the direction of a polyline is important for some of the other Edit Vertex options.

***Break*** The Break option breaks the polyline between two vertices.

1. Position the X on one end of the segment you want to break (see Figure 13.9).

2. Enter **B** ↵ at the command line.

3. At the `Next/Previous/Go/eXit <N>:` prompt, use Next or Previous to move the X to the other end of the segment to be broken.

4. When the X is in the right position (see Figure 13.9, again), pick Go from the Edit Vertex menu or enter **G** ↵, and the polyline will be broken.

**NOTE** You can also use the Break and Trim options on the Modify toolbar to break a polyline anywhere, as you did when you drew the toilet seat in *Chapter 3*.

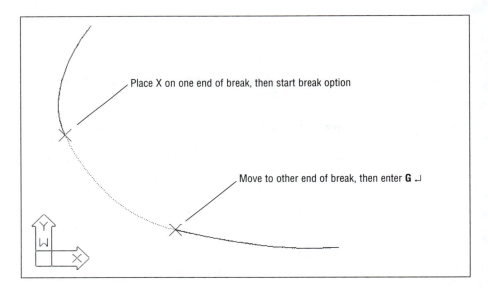

*Figure 13.9:*    ***How the Break option works***

*Insert*    Next, try the Insert option, which inserts a new vertex:

1. Type **X** ↵ to temporarily exit the Edit Vertex option. Then type **U** ↵ to undo the break.

2. Type **E** ↵ to return to the Edit Vertex option, and position the X before the point at which you want to insert a new vertex (see Figure 13.10).

3. Enter **I** ↵ to select the Insert option.

**4.** When the prompt Enter location of new vertex: appears, along with a rubber-banding line originating from the current X position (see Figure 13.10), pick a point indicating the new vertex location. The polyline is redrawn with the new vertex.

**TIP**  If a curve is not smooth enough or does not conform to a particular shape, you can use the Edit Vertex/Insert option to add vertices to a polyline, thereby giving you more control over its shape.

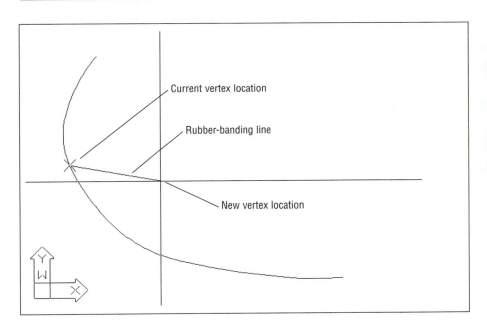

*Figure 13.10:*    **The new vertex location**

Notice that the inserted vertex appears between the currently marked vertex and the *next* vertex because the Insert option is sensitive to the direction of the polyline. If the polyline is curved, the new vertex will not immediately be shown as curved (see panel 1 of Figure 13.11). You must smooth it out by exiting the Edit Vertex option and then using the Fit option (see panel 2 of Figure 13.11).

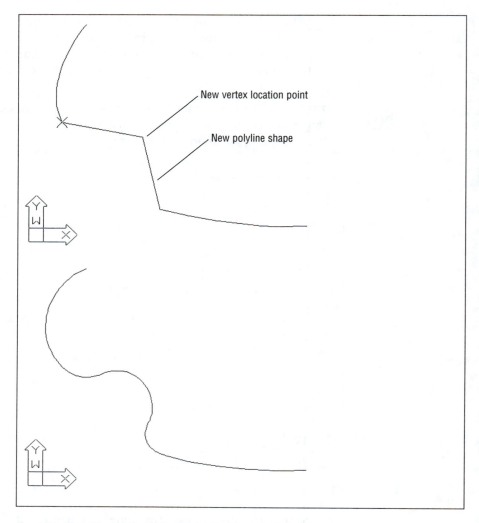

*Figure 13.11:* **The polyline before and after the curve is fitted**

*Move*   In this brief exercise, you'll use the Move option to move a vertex.

1.  Undo the inserted vertex by exiting the Edit Vertex option (**X** ↵) and typing **U** ↵.

2.  Restart the Edit Vertex option, and use the Next or Previous option to place the X on the vertex you wish to move (see panel 1 of Figure 13.12).

3.  Enter **M** ↵ for the Move option.

4.  When the Enter new location: prompt appears, along with a rubber-band line originating from the X (see panel 1 of Figure 13.12), pick the new vertex. The polyline is redrawn (see panel 2 of Figure 13.12). Again, if the line is curved, the new vertex appears as a sharp angle until you use the Fit option (see panel 3 of Figure 13.12).

---

TIP   The quickest way to move a polyline vertex is by using its grip. Click on the polyline to highlight its grips. Click on the vertex you want to move. It becomes a "hot grip," which you can then drag to a new location. You can also use the Stretch option to move a polyline vertex.

---

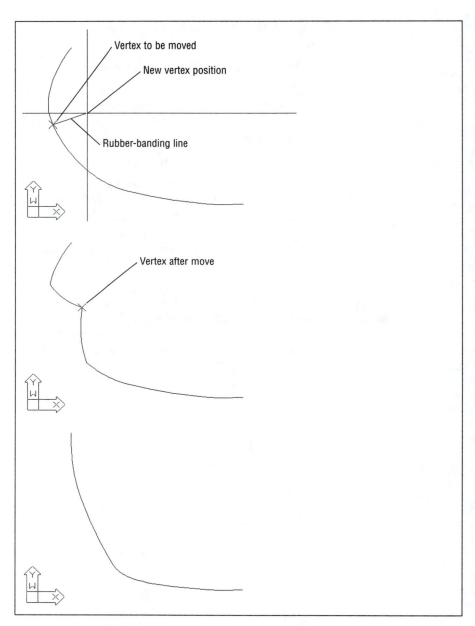

*Figure 13.12:*    **Picking a new location for a vertex, with the polyline before and after the curve is fitted**

***Straighten*** The Straighten option straightens all the vertices between two selected vertices, as shown here:

1. Undo the moved vertex (from previous exercise).

2. Start the Edit Vertex option again, and select the starting vertex for the straight line (see Figure 13.13).

3. Enter **S** ↵ for the Straighten option.

4. At the `Next/Previous/Go/eXit:` prompt, move the X to the other end of the straight line.

5. Once the X is in the proper position, enter **G** ↵ for the Go option. The polyline straightens between the two selected vertices (see Figure 13.13).

**TIP** The Straighten option offers a quick way to delete vertices from a polyline.

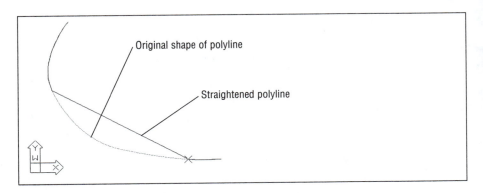

Original shape of polyline

Straightened polyline

*Figure 13.13:* **A polyline before and after straightening**

***Tangent*** Next is the Tangent option, which alters the direction of a curve on a curve-fitted polyline.

1. Undo the straightened segment from the previous exercise.

2. Restart the Edit Vertex option, and position the X on the vertex you wish to alter (see panel 1 of Figure 13.14).

3. Enter **T** ↵ for the Tangent option. A rubber-banding line appears.

**Part 3**

**Becoming an Expert**

4. Point the rubber-banding line in the direction for the new tangent, and click the mouse. An arrow appears, indicating the new tangent direction (see panel 2 of Figure 13.14).

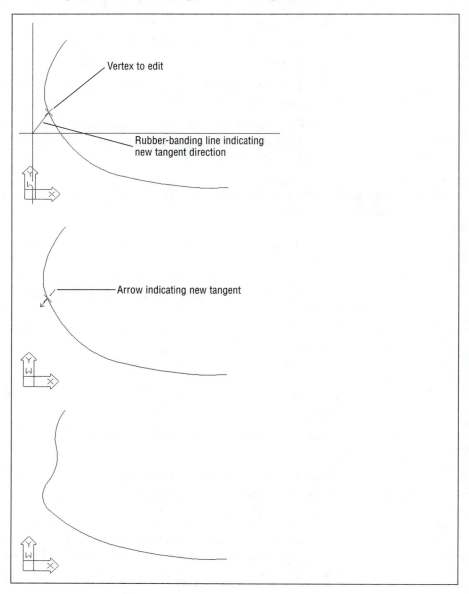

*Figure 13.14:* **Picking a new tangent direction**

Don't worry if the polyline shape does not change. You must use Fit (use X ↵, then F ↵) to see the effect of Tangent (see panel 3 of Figure 13.14).

*Width*   Finally, try out the Width option. Unlike the Pedit command's Width option, Edit Vertex/Width enables you to alter the width of the polyline at any vertex. Thus you can taper or otherwise vary polyline thickness.

1. Undo the tangent arc from the previous exercise.

2. Return to the Edit Vertex option, and place the X at the beginning vertex of a polyline segment.

3. Enter **W** ↵.

4. At the Enter starting width prompt, enter a value, 1′ for example, indicating the polyline width desired at this vertex.

5. At the Enter ending width prompt, enter the width, 3′ for example, for the next vertex.

Again (as with Straighten), don't be alarmed if nothing happens after you enter this Width value. To see the result, you must exit the Edit Vertex command (see Figure 13.15).

**NOTE** The Width option is useful when you want to create an irregular or curved area in your drawing that is to be filled in solid. This is another option that is sensitive to the polyline direction.

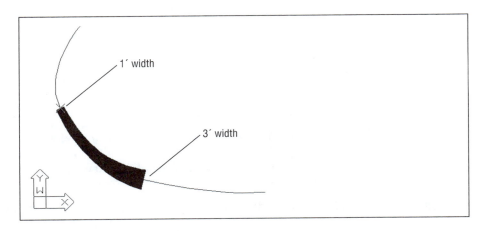

*Figure 13.15:   A polyline with the width of one segment increased*

**Part 3**

**Becoming an Expert**

As you have seen throughout these exercises, you can use the Undo option to reverse the last Edit Vertex option used. And you can use the eXit option to leave Edit Vertex at any time. Just enter **X** ⏎, and this brings you back to the Edit Polyline Close/Join/Width... prompt.

## Creating a Polyline Spline Curve

The Edit Polyline (Pedit) command's Spline option offers a way to draw smoother and more controllable curves than those produced by the Fit option. A polyline spline does not pass through the vertex points as a fitted curve does. Instead, the vertex points act as weights pulling the curve in their direction. The polyline spline only touches its beginning and end vertices. Figure 13.16 illustrates this concept.

NOTE A polyline spline curve does not represent a mathematically true curve. See "Using True Spline Curves" later in this chapter to learn how to draw a mathematically accurate spline curve.

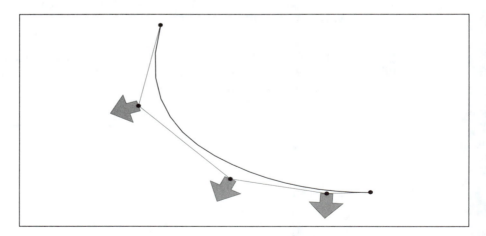

*Figure 13.16:* **The polyline spline curve pulled toward its vertices**

Let's see how using a polyline spline curve might influence the way you edit a curve.

1. Undo the width changes you made in the previous exercise.

2. To change the contour into a polyline spline curve, click on Edit Polyline on the Modify toolbar. Then pick the polyline you just edited.

3. At the `Close/Join/Width…` prompt, enter **S** ↵. Your curve will change to look like Figure 13.17.

4. Press ↵ to exit Edit Polyline.

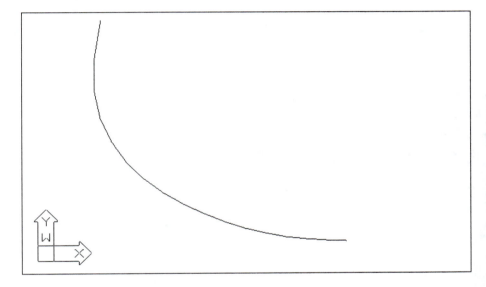

Figure 13.17:   *A spline curve*

The curve takes on a smoother, more graceful appearance. It no longer passes through the points you used to define it. To see where the points went and to find out how spline curves act, do the following:

1. Make sure the Noun/Verb Selection mode and the Grips feature are turned on (select Options ➤ Selection and Options ➤ Grips).

2. Click on the curve. You'll see the original vertices appear as grips.

3. Click on the grip that is second from the top of the curve, and move the grip around. Notice how the curve follows, giving you immediate feedback on how the curve will look.

Pick a point as shown in the bottom panel of Figure 13.18. The curve is fixed in its new position.

Use the Undo command to undo the change to this vertex.

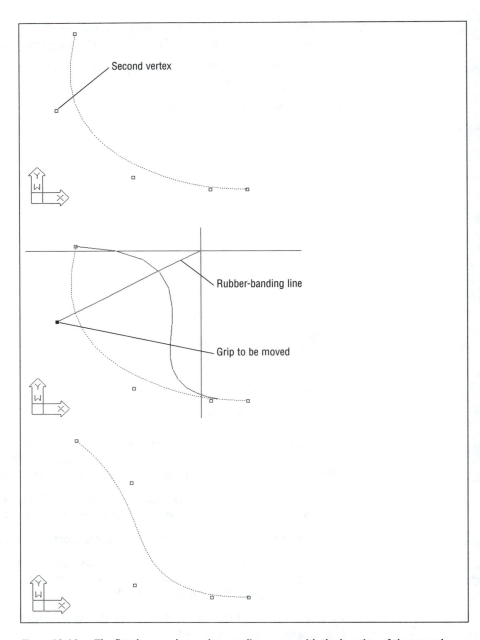

*Figure 13.18:* **The fitted curve changed to a spline curve, with the location of the second vertex and the new curve**

# Using True Spline Curves

So far, you've been working with polylines to generate spline curves. The advantage to using polylines for curves is that they can be enhanced in other ways—you can modify their width, for instance, or join several curves together. But at times you will need a more exact representation of a curve. The Spline object offers a more accurate model of spline curves, as well as more control over its shape.

### Drawing a Spline

The next exercise demonstrates the creation of a spline curve.

1. Turn the Data layer on so you can view the data points.

2. Adjust your view so you can see all the data points with the elevation of 250.00 (see Figure 13.19).

3. Click on the Spline button on the Polyline flyout on the Draw toolbar.

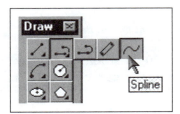

4. At the Object/<Enter first point>: prompt, use the Center Osnap override to start the curve on the first data point in the lower-right corner (see Figure 13.19). The prompt changes to Close/Fit Tolerance/<Enter point>:.

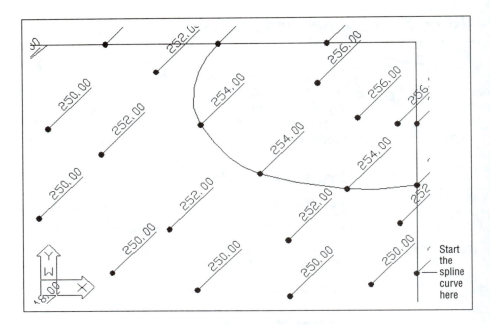

*Figure 13.19:* **Starting the spline curve at the first data point**

5. Continue to select the 250.00 data points until you reach the last one. Notice that as you pick points, a curve appears, and bends and flows as you move your cursor.

6. Once you've selected the last point, press ↵.

   Notice that the prompt changes to Enter start tangent:. Also, a rubber-banding line appears stretching from the first point of the curve to the cursor. As you move the cursor, the curve adjusts to the direction of the rubber-banding line. Here, you can set the tangency of the first point of the curve (see the top panel of Figure 13.20).

7. Press ↵. This causes AutoCAD LT to determine the first point's tangency based on the current shape of the curve. A rubber-banding line appears from the last point of the curve. As with the first point, you can indicate a tangent direction for the last point of the curve (see bottom panel of Figure 13.20).

8. Press ↵ to exit the Spline command without changing the endpoint tangent direction.

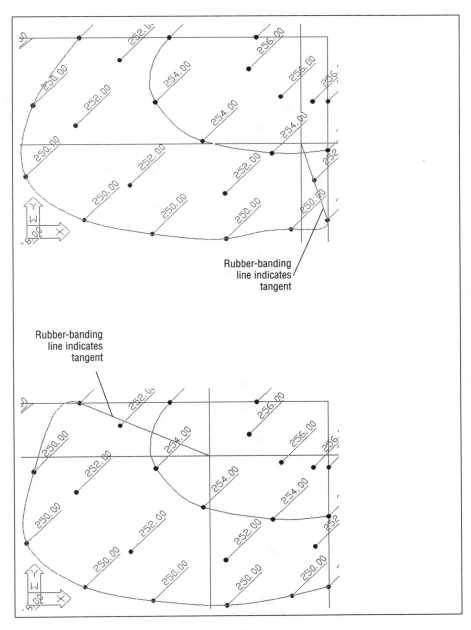

*Figure 13.20:* **The last two prompts of the Spline command let you determine the tangent direction of the spline.**

TIP    See *Chapter 2* for more detailed information on grip editing.

You now have a smooth curve that passes through the points you selected. These points are called the *control points*. If you click on the curve, you'll see the grips appear at the location of these control points, and you can adjust the curve simply by clicking on the grip points and moving them.

You may have noticed two other options—Fit Tolerance and Close—as you were selecting points for the spline in the last exercise. Here is a description of these options:

**Fit Tolerance**    lets you change the curve so that it doesn't actually pass through the points you pick. When you select this option, you get the prompt Enter Fit Tolerance <0.0000>:. Any value greater than 0 will cause the curve to pass close to, but not actually through the points. A value of 0 causes the curve to pass through the points. (You'll see how this works in a later exercise.)

**Close**    lets you close the curve into a loop. If you choose this option, you are prompted to indicate a tangent direction for the closing point.

## Fine-Tuning Spline Curves

Spline curves are different from other types of objects, and many of the standard editing commands won't work on splines. AutoCAD LT offers the Edit Spline option on the Special Edit flyout on the Modify toolbar (Splinedit command) for making changes to splines. The following exercise will give you some practice with this command. You'll start by focusing on Splinedit's Fit Data option, which lets you fine-tune the spline curve.

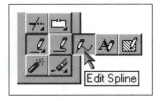

### Controlling the Fit Data of a Spline

The following exercise will demonstrate how the Fit Data option lets you control some of the general characteristics of the curve.

1. Click on the Edit Spline button on the Special Edit flyout on the Modify toolbar, or type **Splinedit** ↵ at the command line.

2. At the Select Spline prompt, select the spline you drew in the previous exercise.

3. At the prompt

   ```
   Fit Data/Close/Move Vertex/Refine/rEverse/Undo/eXit <X>:
   ```

   type **F** ↵ to select the Fit Data option.

4. At the next prompt,

   ```
   Add/Close/Delete/Move/Purge/Tangents/toLerance/eXit <X>
   ```

   type **T** to select the Tangents option. Move the cursor, and notice that the curve changes tangency through the first point, just as it did when you first created the spline (see Figure 13.20 above).

5. Press ↵. You can now edit the other endpoint tangency.

6. Press ↵ again. You return to the Add/Close/Delete... prompt.

7. Now add another control point to the spline curve. At the Add/Close/Delete... prompt, type **A** ↵ to access the Add option.

8. At the Select point prompt, click on the second point from the bottom end (see panel 1 of Figure 13.21). A rubber-banding line appears from the point you selected. That point and the next point are highlighted. The two highlighted points tell you that the next point you select will fall between these two points.

9. Click on a new point. The curve changes to include that point. In addition, the new point becomes the highlighted point, indicating that you can continue to add more points between it and the other highlighted point (see panel 2 of Figure 13.21).

10. Press ↵. The Select point prompt appears, allowing you to add another point if you so desire.

11. Press ↵ again to return to the Add/Close/Delete... prompt.

Part
3

Becoming an Expert

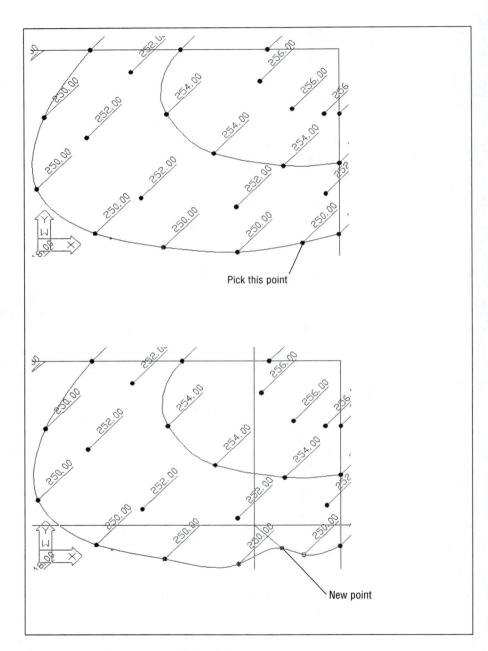

*Figure 13.21:* **Adding a new control point to a spline**

Before we end our examination of the Fit Data options, let's look at how toLerance works.

1.  At the Add/Close/Delete... prompt, type **L** ↵ to select the toLerance option. This option sets the tolerance between the control point and the curve.

2.  At the Enter fit tolerance <0.0000>: prompt, type **30** ↵. Notice how the curve no longer passes through the control points, except for the beginning and endpoints (see Figure 13.22). The fit tolerance value you enter determines the maximum distance away from any control point the spline can be.

3.  Type **X** ↵ to exit the Fit Data option.

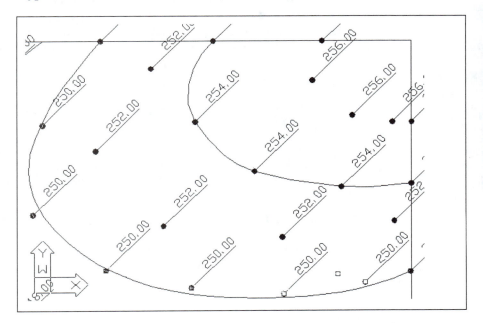

*Figure 13.22:*   **The spline after setting the control point tolerance to 30**

Part
3

Becoming an Expert

You've seen how you can control many of the shape properties of a spline through the Fit Data option. Here are descriptions of the other Fit Data options you didn't try in these exercises:

**Delete**   removes a control point in the spline.

**Close**   lets you close the spline into a loop.

**Move**   lets you move a control point.

**Purge**   deletes the fit data of the spline, thereby eliminating the Fit Data option for the purged spline. (See "When Can't You Use Fit Data?" just below.)

*When Can't You Use Fit Data?*   The Fit Data option of the Splinedit command offers many ways to edit a spline; however, this option is not available to all spline curves. When you use certain of the other Splinedit options, a spline curve will lose its fit data, thereby disabling the Fit Data option. These options are as follows:

►   Refining the spline (Splinedit/Refine)

►   Purging the spline of its fit data using the Purge option (Splinedit/ Fit Data/Purge)

Also, note that the Fit Data option is not available when you edit spline curves that have been created from polyline splines. See the sidebar, "Turning Objects into Polylines and Polylines into Splines."

## Adjusting the Control Points with the Refine Option

While you are still in the Splinedit command, let's look at another of its options—Refine—with which you can fine-tune the curve.

1. At the `Fit Data/Open/Move Vertex/Refine…` prompt, type **R** ↵. The Refine option lets you control the "pull" exerted on a spline by an individual control point. This isn't quite the same effect as the Fit Tolerance option you used in the previous exercise.

2. At the prompt

   ```
   Add Control Point/Elevate Order/Weight/eXit <X>:
   ```

   type **W** ↵. The first control point is highlighted.

3. At the next prompt,

   ```
   Next/Previous/Select Point/eXit/<Enter new weight>
     <1.0000> <N>:
   ```

   press ↵ to move the highlight to the next control point.

4. Type **25** ↵. The curve not only moves closer to the control point, it also bends around the control point in a tighter arc (see Figure 13.23).

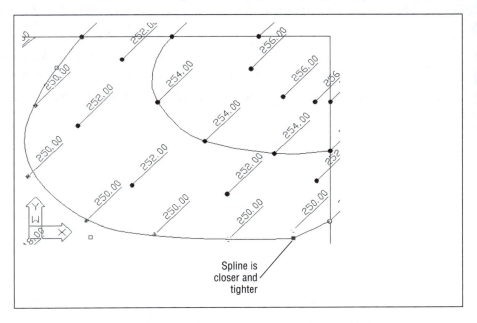

Spline is
closer and
tighter

*Figure 13.23:* **The spline after increasing the Weight value of a control point**

You can use the Weight value of Splinedit's Refine option to pull the spline in tighter. Think of it as a way to increase the "gravity" of the control point, causing the curve to be pulled closer and tighter to the control point.

Continue your look at the Splinedit command by adding more control points—without actually changing the shape of the curve. You do this using Refine's Add Control Point and Elevate Order options.

1.  Type **X** ↵ to exit the Refine/Weight option; then type **A** ↵ to select the Add Control Point option.

2.  At the Select a point on the spline: prompt, click on the second-to-last control point toward the top end of the spline (see panel 1 of Figure 13.24). The point you select disappears and is replaced by two control points roughly equidistant from the one you selected (see panel 2 of Figure 13.24). The curve remains unchanged. Two new control points now replace the one control point you selected. Press ↵ to end the selection, then ↵ again to exit the Add Control Point option.

3.  Now type **E** ↵ to select the Elevate Order option.

4.  At the Enter new order <4>: prompt, type **6** ↵. The number of control points increases, leaving the curve itself untouched.

5.  Type ↵ twice to exit the Refine option and then the Splinedit command.

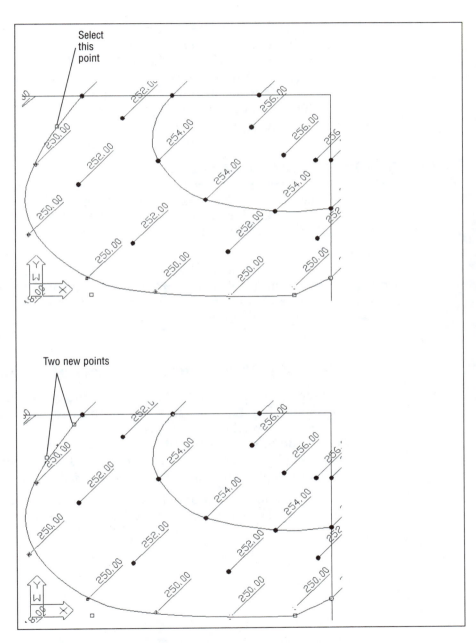

*Figure 13.24:* **Adding a single control point using the Refine option**

You would probably never edit contour lines of a topographical map in quite the way these exercises have shown. But by following this tutorial you have explored all the potential of the AutoCAD LT's spline object. Aside from its usefulness for drawing contours, it can be a great tool for drawing freeform illustrations. It is an excellent tool for mechanical applications, where precise, nonuniform curves are required, such as drawings of cams or sheet metal work.

## Marking Divisions on a Curve

Perhaps one of the most difficult things to do in manual drafting is to mark regular intervals on a curve. AutoCAD LT offers the Divide and Measure commands to help you perform this task with speed and accuracy.

**NOTE** The use of Divide and Measure are discussed here in conjunction with polylines, but you can use these commands on many other objects, such as lines, arcs, and splines.

### Dividing Objects into Segments of Equal Length

Divide can be used to divide an object into a specific number of equal segments. For example, suppose you needed to mark off the contour you've been working on in this chapter into nine equal segments. One way to do this is to first find the length of the contour by using the List command, and then sit down with a pencil and paper to figure out the exact distances between the marks. But there is another, easier way.

Divide will place a set of point objects on a line, arc, circle, or polyline, marking off exact divisions. This next exercise shows how it works.

1. Click and drag the Point button on the Draw toolbar, and select Divide on the flyout, or type **Divide** ↵ at the command line.

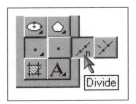

2. At the `Select objects to divide:` prompt, pick the contour line at elevation 254.

3. The `<Number of segments>/Block:` prompt that appears next is asking for the number of divisions you want on the selected object. Enter 9 ↵.

   The command prompt now returns, and it appears that nothing has happened. But AutoCAD LT has placed several points on the contour indicating the locations of the nine divisions you have requested. To see these points more clearly, do the following:

4. Click on Format ➤ Point Style, or type **Ddptype** ↵. The Point Style dialog box appears.

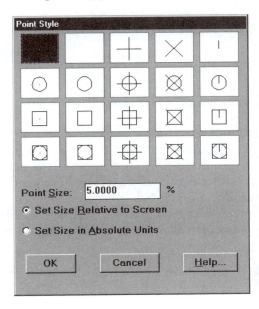

5. Click on the X point style on the top line of the dialog box, click on the Set Size Relative to Screen radio button, and then click on OK.

6. Enter **Regen** ↵. A set of Xs appears, showing the nine divisions (see Figure 13.25).

TIP You can also change the point style by changing the Pdmode system variable. When Pdmode is set to 3, the point appears as an X. See *Appendix D* for more on Pdmode.

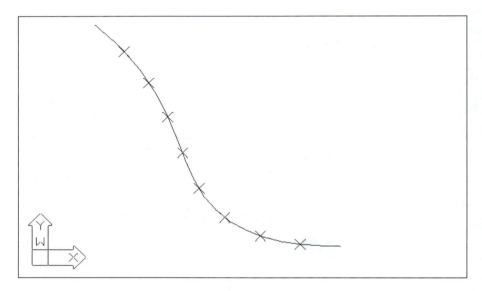

*Figure 13.25:* **Using the Divide command on a polyline**

The Divide command uses *Point* objects to indicate the division points. Point objects are created by using the Point command; they usually appear as dots. Unfortunately, such points are nearly invisible when placed on top of other objects. But, as you have seen, you can alter their shape using the Point Style dialog box. You can use these X points to place objects or as reference points to break the object being divided. (Divide does not actually cut the object into smaller divisions.)

TIP To snap to point objects, you can use the Nodes Osnap override.

## Dividing Objects into Specified Lengths

The Measure command acts just like Divide; however, instead of dividing an object into segments of equal length, Measure marks intervals of a specified distance along an object. For example, suppose you need to mark some segments exactly 5′ apart along the contour. Try the following exercise to see how Measure is used to accomplish this task.

> **NOTE** Measure is AutoCAD LT's equivalent of the divider tool in manual drafting. A divider is a V-shaped instrument, similar to a compass, used to mark off regular intervals along a curve or line.

Part 3

1. Use the Undo command until the points added by the Divide command disappear from the contour line.

2. Click and drag the Point button on the Draw toolbar, and select Measure on the flyout.

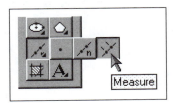

3. At the `Select object to measure:` prompt, pick the same contour as before at a point closest to its lower endpoint. We'll explain shortly why this is important.

4. At the `<Segment length>/Block:` prompt, enter 5′↵. The X points appear at the specified distance.

5. Now exit this file.

   Bear in mind that the point you pick on the object to be measured will determine where Measure begins measuring. In the last exercise, for example, you picked the contour near its bottom endpoint. If you had picked the top of the contour, the results would have been different, because the measurement would have started at the top, not the bottom.

Becoming an Expert

## MARKING OFF INTERVALS USING BLOCKS INSTEAD OF POINTS

You can also use the Block option under the Divide and Measure commands to place blocks at regular intervals along a line, polyline, or arc. Here's how to use blocks as markers:

1. First be sure the block you want to use is part of the current drawing file.

2. Start either the Divide or Measure command by dragging on the Point button on the Draw toolbar, and then selecting Divide or Measure from the flyout.

3. At the Number of segments: prompt, enter **B**.

4. At the Block name to insert: prompt, enter the name of a block.

5. At the Align block with object? <Y> prompt, press ⏎ if you wish the blocks to follow the alignment of the selected object. (Entering **N** ⏎ causes each block to be inserted at a 0° angle.)

6. At the Number of segments: prompt, enter the number of segments. The blocks appear at regular intervals on the selected object.

One example of using Divide's or Measure's Block option is to place a row of sinks equally spaced along a wall. Or you might use this technique to make multiple copies of an object along an irregular path defined by a polyline, like a railroad track, for example.

# Filling In Solid Areas

You have learned how to create a solid area by increasing the width of a polyline segment. But suppose you want to create a simple solid shape or a very thick line. AutoCAD LT provides the Solid and Donut commands to help you draw simple filled areas.

## Drawing Large Solid Areas

We've seen people use hatch patterns to fill in solid areas—and that's a great way to fill an irregular shape. However, hatches tend to increase the size of a file dramatically, thereby increasing loading and regeneration time. To keep file size down, use solids and polylines to do solid fills whenever possible.

*Solids* are three- or four-sided polygons that are filled solid. They also plot as solid fills. Following are the steps for drawing a solid.

1. Click and drag the 2D Solid button from the Polygon flyout on the Draw toolbar, or type **Solid** ↵ at the command prompt.

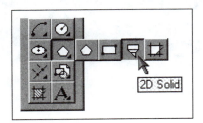

2. The Solid command draws a three- or four-sided solid area, so the first point you pick will be one of the area's corners. At the First point: prompt, pick a point indicating the first corner of the solid filled area.

3. At the Second point: prompt, pick the next corner of your solid area.

4. Selecting the third point is where things get a little tricky. In this exercise, you are drawing a square first, so your third point is the corner diagonal to the last corner you picked (see Figure 13.26). At the Third point: prompt, pick the point that is diagonal to the second point you picked for the rectangular area you are filling. (Imagine that you are drawing a Z pattern.)

5. At the Fourth point: prompt, pick the final corner of your fill. A solid area appears between the four points you selected.

6. When the Third point: prompt appears again, you have an opportunity to continue your fill pattern. You can select a sequence of points in a Z pattern again. Or you can press ↵ to complete the Solid command.

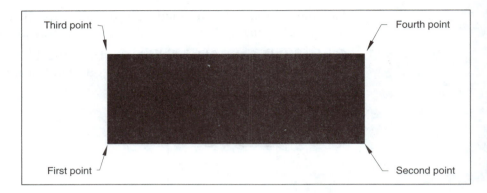

*Figure 13.26:    Points for a solid square*

**TIP**  If you need to fill in an irregular shape, you can use several short solids or even triangular shapes. To create a triangular solid, pick the first three points, and then press ↵ to complete the triangle. You can ignore the prompt for **Fourth Point**:.

If you were to pick points in a circular rather than a Z pattern, you would end up with a filled area shaped like a bow tie (see Figure 13.27). You can create solid filled areas with more than four sides by entering more points in a Z pattern (see Figure 13.28). There is no limit to the number of points you can select.

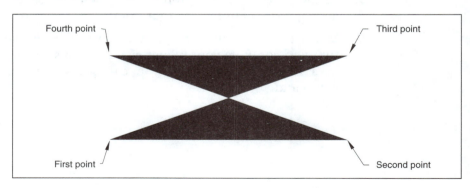

*Figure 13.27:    An area filled by picking points in a clockwise pattern*

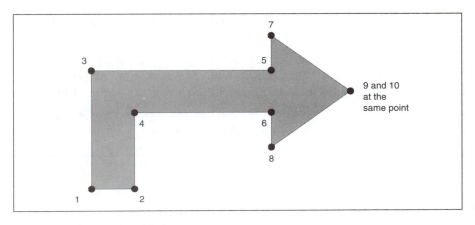

*Figure 13.28: How to use Solid to fill in an odd shape*

To end the Solid command, press ↵ without picking a point.

## Drawing Filled Circles

If you need to draw a thick circle like an inner tube, or a solid filled circle, take the following steps:

1. Click on the Donut button on the Circle flyout on the Draw toolbar, or enter **Donut** ↵ at the command line.

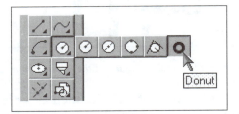

2. At the Inside diameter: prompt, enter the desired diameter of the donut "hole." This value determines the opening at the center of your circle.

Part
3

Becoming an Expert

3. At the Outside diameter: prompt, enter the overall diameter of the circle.

4. At the Center of doughnut: prompt, click on the desired location for the filled circle. You can continue to select points to place multiple donuts. Figure 13.29 shows a sample drawing that uses the Donut command.

5. Press ⏎ to exit this process.

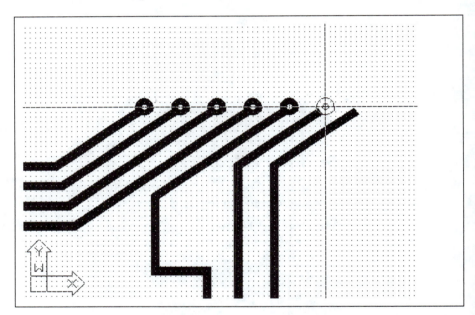

*Figure 13.29:*    **Circuit board layout showing use of the Donut command**

If you need to fill only a part of a circle, such as a pie slice, you can use the Donut command to draw a full circle, and then use the Trim or Break options on the Modify toolbar to cut out the portion of the donut you don't need.

## Toggling Solid Fills On and Off

Once you have drawn a solid area with the Pline, Solid, Trace, or Donut commands, you can control whether the solid area is actually displayed as filled in. When Options ➤ Display ➤ Solid Fill does not show a check mark, thick polylines, solids, and donuts appear as outlines of the solid areas (see Figure 13.30).

NOTE You can shorten regeneration and plotting time if solids are not filled in.

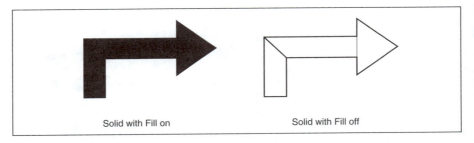

| Solid with Fill on | Solid with Fill off |

*Figure 13.30:* **A solid displayed with the Fill option turned on and turned off**

Turning the solid filled areas on and off is easy. Just select Options ➤ Display ➤ Solid Fill to toggle solid fills on and off. Or enter **Fill** ↵ at the command line; then, at the ON/OFF <ON>: prompt, enter your choice of on or off.

You can also control the visibility of solid fills by using the Solid Fill check box in the Drawing Aids dialog box (Options ➤ Drawing Aids...).

## Overlapping Solid Lines and Shaded Fills

If you use a raster plotter or laser printer that can convert solid areas into screened or gray-shaded areas, you may encounter the problem of shading areas overlapping lines and hiding them. This problem may not be apparent until you actually plot the drawing; it frequently occurs when a gray area is bounded by lines (see Figure 13.31).

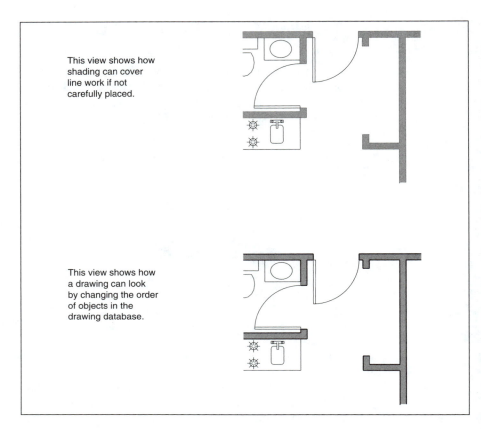

This view shows how
shading can cover
line work if not
carefully placed.

This view shows how
a drawing can look
by changing the order
of objects in the
drawing database.

*Figure 13.31:* **Problems that occur with overlapping lines and gray areas**

Most other graphics programs have specific tools to handle this difficulty. These tools are commonly named Move To Front or Move To
Back, indicating that you move an object in front of or behind another
object. Although AutoCAD LT does not have a specific command to
perform a "move to front," there is hope. The following list shows how
to bring one object in front of another.

1. Select the objects that you want to move in front of the gray surfaces.

2. Click on Duplicate Objects on the Modify toolbar, or type **Copy** ↵.

3. At the `Base point of displacement:` prompt, enter @.

4. At the `Second point of displacement:` prompt, enter @ again.

5. Click on the Erase button on the Modify toolbar.

6. At the `Select objects:` prompt, enter **P** ↵ to select the previously selected objects, and then press ↵ to complete the command.

7. Before you plot, click on Options ➤ Selection... and then click on the Object Sort Method... button.

8. Make sure the Plotting check box is checked. If you are sending your plots to a PostScript device, make sure the PostScript Output check box is checked.

## If You Want to Experiment...

There are many valuable uses for polylines beyond those covered in this chapter. We encourage you to become familiar with this unique object so you can take full advantage of AutoCAD LT.

To further explore the use of polylines, try the exercise illustrated in Figure 13.32. It will give you an opportunity to try out some of the options discussed in this chapter that weren't included in the exercises.

**Part 3**

**Becoming an Expert**

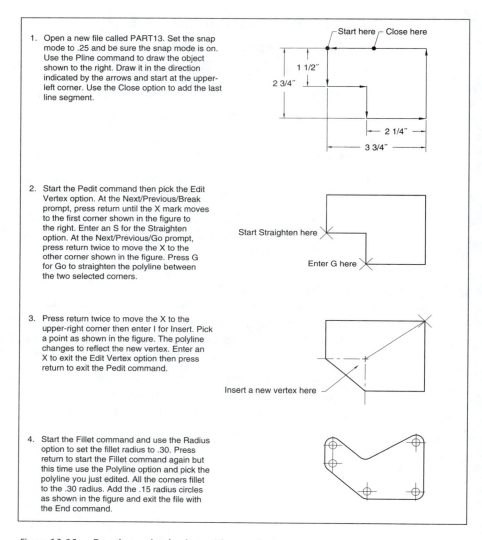

1.  Open a new file called PART13. Set the snap mode to .25 and be sure the snap mode is on. Use the Pline command to draw the object shown to the right. Draw it in the direction indicated by the arrows and start at the upper-left corner. Use the Close option to add the last line segment.

2.  Start the Pedit command then pick the Edit Vertex option. At the Next/Previous/Break prompt, press return until the X mark moves to the first corner shown in the figure to the right. Enter an S for the Straighten option. At the Next/Previous/Go prompt, press return twice to move the X to the other corner shown in the figure. Press G for Go to straighten the polyline between the two selected corners.

3.  Press return twice to move the X to the upper-right corner then enter I for Insert. Pick a point as shown in the figure. The polyline changes to reflect the new vertex. Enter an X to exit the Edit Vertex option then press return to exit the Pedit command.

4.  Start the Fillet command and use the Radius option to set the fillet radius to .30. Press return to start the Fillet command again but this time use the Polyline option and pick the polyline you just edited. All the corners fillet to the .30 radius. Add the .15 radius circles as shown in the figure and exit the file with the End command.

*Figure 13.32:  **Drawing a simple plate with curved edges***

# Chapter 14

# Getting and Exchanging Data from Drawings

## *FAST TRACKS*

**A**UTO**CAD LT** drawings contain a wealth of data. In them you can find graphic information such as distances and angles between objects, as well as precise areas and the properties of objects. But as you become more involved with AutoCAD LT, you will find that you also need data of a different nature. For example, as you begin to work in groups, the various settings in a drawing become important. Statistics on the amount of time you spend on a drawing are needed when you are billing computer time. As your projects become more complex, file maintenance requires a greater degree of attention. To take full advantage of AutoCAD LT, you will want to exchange much of this data with other people and other programs.

In this chapter, you will explore the ways in which all types of data can be extracted from AutoCAD LT and made available to you, your coworkers, and other programs. First, you will discover how to get specific data on your drawings. Then you will look at ways to exchange data with other programs—such as word processors, desktop publishing software, and even other CAD programs.

## Getting Information about a Drawing

AutoCAD LT can instantly give you precise information about your drawing, such as the area, perimeter, and location of an object; the base point, current mode settings, and space used in a drawing; and the time when a drawing was created and last edited. In this section you will practice extracting this type of information from your drawing using options on the Object Properties Inquiry flyout. The Inquiry flyout is located at the far right of the Object Properties toolbar.

> **TIP** To find exact coordinates in a drawing, use the ID command. Choose the Point Location button on the Inquiry flyout on the Object Properties toolbar, or type **ID** ↵. At the prompt ID Point, use the Osnap overrides to pick a point, and its x, y, and z coordinates will be displayed on the prompt line.

## Finding the Area or Location of an Object

Architects, engineers, and facilities planners often need to know the square-foot area of a room or a section of a building. A structural engineer might want to determine the cross-sectional area of a beam. In this section you will practice determining the areas of both regular and irregular objects. First you will find out the square-foot area of the living room and entry of your studio unit plan.

1. Start AutoCAD LT and open the Unit file you created earlier, or use the 14-UNIT.DWG file on the companion CD.

2. Turn off all unnecessary layers: doors, fixtures, dimensions, annotation, and floor pattern, if these are on.

3. Use the Zoom Window option on the Zoom toolbar to create a window which includes both the living room and entry area.

4. Click on the Area button on the Inquiry flyout on the Object Properties toolbar, or type **Area** ↵ on the command line.

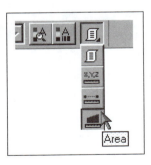

5. At the <First point>/Object/Add/Subtract: prompt, pick the lower-left corner of the living room near coordinate 15′–0″,6′–10″ (see Figure 14.1).

6. At the Next point: prompt, pick the upper-left corner of the living room near coordinate 15′–0″, 25′–5″.

7. Continue to pick the corners, as shown in Figure 14.1, outlining the living room and entry area until you have come full circle to the first point. You don't need to pick the first point a second time.

8. When you complete the circuit, press ↵. You get the message

    Area = 39570.00sq in (274.79171 sq ft), Perimeter = 76′–0″

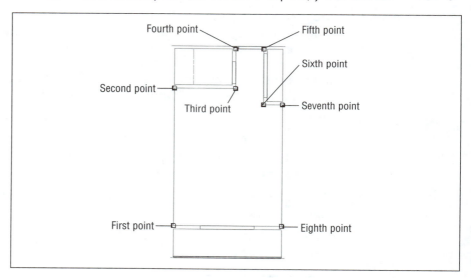

*Figure 14.1:* **Selecting the points to determine the area of the living room and entry**

There is no limit to the number of points you can pick to define an area. This means you can obtain the areas of very complex shapes.

## Using Boundary

Using the Object option of the Area command, you can also select circles and polylines for area calculations. Using this option in conjunction with another AutoCAD LT utility called Boundary, you can quickly get the area of a bounded space. You will recall from the discussion on hatch patterns in *Chapter 6* that a polyline is drawn when you use the Boundary Hatch (Bhatch) function. The Boundary command generates a polyline outline without adding the hatch. Here's how to use it.

> **WARNING**   There is one caveat to using Boundary: You must be sure the area you are trying to define has a continuous border. If there are any gaps at all, no matter how small, Boundary will give you an error message.

1. Check that the layers are set so the doors are turned off (Door layer) but the door headers are on (Ceiling layer).

2. Click on the Boundary button on the Polygon flyout on the Draw toolbar to open the Boundary Creation dialog box.

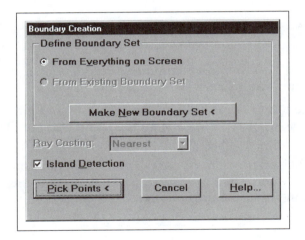

3. Click on the Pick Points < button. The dialog box closes.

4. At the `Select internal point` prompt, click on the interior of the unit plan. The outline of the interior is highlighted temporarily (see Figure 14.2).

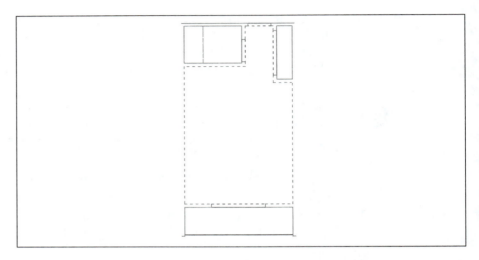

*Figure 14.2:*　　***Once you select a point on the interior of the plan using Boundary, an outline of the area is highlighted.***

5. Press ↵. The Boundary command has drawn an outline of the floor area using a polyline.

6. Click on the Area button on the Inquiry flyout on the Object Properties toolbar, or type **Area** ↵ on the command line. Then enter **O** ↵ to select the Object option.

7. Ctrl-click on the right-hand wall of the unit until the boundary is highlighted; when it is highlighted, press ↵. You get the same Area... message you got in the previous exercise.

---

**TIP**　If you need to recall the last area calculation value you received, you can enter ´**Setvar** ↵ **Area** ↵. The area will be displayed in the command window. Enter ´**Perimeter** ↵, and you get the last perimeter calculated.

---

The Boundary command creates a polyline that conforms to the boundary of an area. This feature, combined with the ability of the Area command to find the area of a polyline, makes short work of area calculations.

## Finding the Area of Complex Shapes

The Boundary command works well if the shape or the area you want to find is not complex. For complex objects, you must also enlist the aid of the other Area command options: Object, Add, and Subtract. Using Add and Subtract, you can maintain a running total of several separate areas being calculated. This gives you flexibility in finding areas of complex shapes.

The exercise in this section guides you through the use of these options. First, you'll look at how you can keep a running tally of areas. In preparation for the exercise, follow these steps:

1. Exit the Unit file, and open the file named **Flange** from the companion CD (see Figure 14.3). Don't bother to save changes in the Unit file. You do not want to keep the Boundary polygon as a part of your drawing.

2. Use the Edit Polyline (Pedit) option on the Modify toolbar (the Pedit command is described in *Chapter 13*) to turn the arcs which make up the perimeter of the flange into polyline arcs before you start the Area command.

3. Use the Edit Polyline command's Join option to join the polyline arcs into a single bounding polyline.

> **NOTE** Area does not calculate areas for arc objects, but it does for polylines. You must change all arc objects into polyline arcs before using Area.

### Finding the Gross Area

First use the Area command to find the gross area of the flange.

1. Click on Area on the Inquiry flyout on the Object Properties toolbar to start the Area command.

2. Type **A** ↵ for the Add option.

3. Type **O** ↵ for the Object option.

4. Click on the polyline which defines the perimeter of the flange:

```
Area = 27,7080, Perimeter = 30,8496
Total area = 27,7080
<First point /Object/Subtract:
```

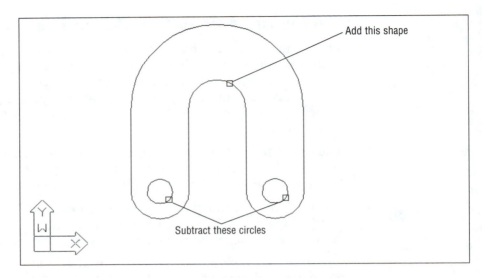

*Figure 14.3:* **The Flange drawing showing areas to add and to subtract**

## Subtracting Unwanted Areas from the Area Calculation

Now that you have the gross area, you must take the areas that you don't want to include as part of the area count and subtract them from the current running total area. (Some area geometries make it impossible to obtain the gross area first. In these situations, you can use the Subtract option first to find the negative areas, and then use Add to find the gross areas.)

1. At the `First point/Object/Subtract:` prompt, enter **S** ⏎.

2. At the `<First point>/Object/Add:` prompt, type **O** ⏎ to pick the Object option again. You are going to subtract the area defined by the circles. (Notice that when you are in Subtract mode, Add becomes the current area-selection option in the prompt.)

3. At the `<SUBTRACT mode> Select objects:` prompt, pick the two circles inside the flange, as shown in Figure 14.3. As you pick the objects, the running total is displayed again above the prompt.

4. Once you are done, you see the final total area above the prompt line:

```
Total area = 26.4940
<SUBTRACT mode> Select object:
```

5. To exit the Area command, press ↵ twice.

It is important to remember that whenever you press ↵ during an area calculation, AutoCAD LT automatically connects the first and last points and returns the area calculated. You can then continue to select more points or objects defining areas, but the additional areas will be calculated from the *next* point you pick.

In this example, you obtained the area of a mechanical object. However, the same process works for any type of area you want to calculate. It can be the area of a piece of property on a topographical map, or the area of a floor plan. For example, you can use the Object option to find an irregular area like the one shown in Figure 14.4, as long as it is a polyline. Remember: If the polyline is not closed, the Area command assumes the first and last points picked are connected, and calculates the area accordingly.

**Part 3**

**Becoming an Expert**

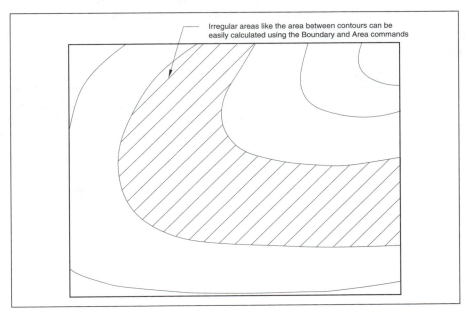

Irregular areas like the area between contours can be easily calculated using the Boundary and Area commands

*Figure 14.4:* **The site plan with an area to be calculated**

### Recording Area Data in a Drawing File

Once you find the area of an object, you'll often need to record it somewhere. You can write it down in a project log book, but this is easy to overlook. A more dependable way to store area information is to use *attributes*.

For example, in a building project, you can create a block that contains attributes for the room number, room area, and the date when the room area was last taken. You might make the area and date attributes invisible, so only the room number appears. This block could then be inserted into every room. Once you find the area, you can easily add it to your block attribute with the Ddatte command. In fact, such a block could be used with any drawing in which you wished to store area data.

## Keeping Track of Time

The Time command allows you to keep track of the time spent on a drawing for billing or analysis purposes. You can also use Time to check the current time and find out when the drawing was created and most recently edited. Because the AutoCAD LT timer uses your computer's time, be sure the time is set correctly in the Windows Control Panel.

**TIP** You can modify your system Time and Date without going through Settings ➤ Control Panel. Right-click on the Time/Date display on the right-hand side of the Windows 95 taskbar. When the Options menu appears, click on Adjust Date/Time. This opens the Date/time Properties dialog box where you can set the date and time as required.

To access the Time command, enter **Time** ↵ at the command prompt, or select Tools ➤ Time. You get a message like the one in Figure 14.5.

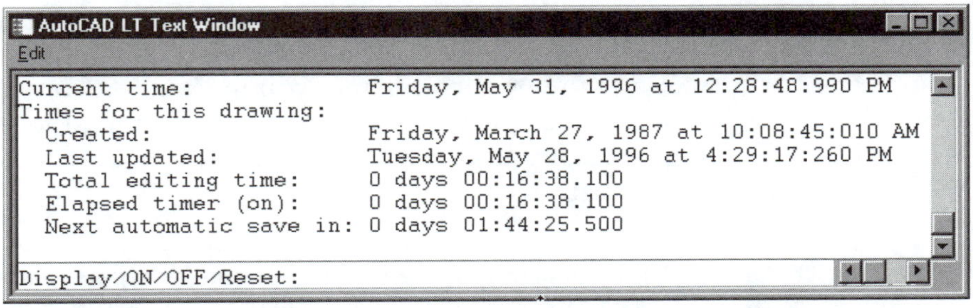

```
AutoCAD LT Text Window                                    _  □  ×
Edit
Current time:              Friday, May 31, 1996 at 12:28:48:990 PM  ▲
Times for this drawing:
  Created:                 Friday, March 27, 1987 at 10:08:45:010 AM
  Last updated:            Tuesday, May 28, 1996 at 4:29:17:260 PM
  Total editing time:      0 days 00:16:38.100
  Elapsed timer (on):      0 days 00:16:38.100
  Next automatic save in:  0 days 01:44:25.500                      ▼
Display/ON/OFF/Reset:                                   ◄  □  ►
```

*Figure 14.5:*    **The Time screen**

The first three lines tell you the current date and time, the date and time the drawing was created, and the last time the drawing was saved or ended.

The fourth line shows the total time spent on the drawing from the point of its creation. This elapsed timer lets you time a particular activity, such as changing the width of all the walls in a floor plan or redesigning a piece of machinery. You can turn the elapsed timer on or off or reset it by entering **on**, **off**, or **reset** at the prompt shown as the last line of the message. The timer will not show any time spent on a drawing between the last time it is saved and the time a Quit command is issued.

The last line tells you when the next automatic save will be.

## Getting Information from System Variables

If you've been working through this book's tutorial, you'll have noticed that sometimes a *system variable* is used in conjunction with a command. You can check the status or change the setting of any system variable while you are in the middle of another command. To do this, you simply type an apostrophe ('), followed by the name of the system variable at the command prompt.

For example, if you have started to draw a line, and you decide you need to rotate your cursor 45°, you can do the following:

1. At the To point prompt, enter '**snapang**.

2. At the New value for SNAPANG prompt, enter a new cursor angle. Once you have entered an angle value, you are returned to the Line command with the cursor in its new orientation.

**Part**
**3**

**Becoming an Expert**

You can also recall information such as the last area or distance calculated by AutoCAD LT. Since the Area system variable duplicates the name of the Area command, you must enter ´**Setvar** ↵ **Area** ↵ to read the last area calculation. The Setvar command lets you list all the system variables and their status, as well as access each system variable individually.

> **TIP**  If you can't quite recall the name of a particular variable, you can use SETVAR to list all of the system variables, or selected subsets using a wildcard character (*). For example, if you want to list all of the text-related variables, type **Setvar** ↵ **?** ↵. Then type **Text\*** ↵.

Many of the system variables give you direct access to detailed information about your drawing. They also let you fine-tune your drawing and editing activities. In *Appendix D* you'll find all the information you need to familiarize yourself with the system variables available. Don't feel that you have to memorize them all at once; just be aware that they are available.

## Storing System Data for Later Retrieval

If you are working in groups, it is often quite helpful to have a record of the editing time and system variables for particular files readily available to other group members. It is also convenient to keep records of block and layer information, so you can see if a specific block is included in a drawing or what layers are normally on or off.

The following exercise demonstrates how you can get a record of the information displayed by many of the AutoCAD LT commands:

1.  Click on Tools ➤ Preferences… to open the Preferences dialog box.

2.  In the Work Space tab, click on the check box labeled Log File in the Settings group, and then click on OK.

> **TIP**  As a shortcut, you can quickly turn the Log File feature on and off by typing **Logfileon** ↵ and **Logfileoff** ↵ at the command prompt in AutoCAD LT.

As long as the Log File option is turned on, the contents of the AutoCAD LT text window are continuously added to a file called ACLT.LOG in the AutoCAD LT program directory. The following steps allow you to check this.

3. Click on Tools ➤ Time. The drawing time will be recorded in the text window.

4. Return to the Preferences dialog box and click on the Log File check box again to remove the check mark from the check box. Click on OK to exit the dialog box.

5. Start the Windows Wordpad or any text editor.

6. With the text editor, open the file called ACLT.LOG. It should contain the time data on your current drawing.

The Log File stores all text data from the command window whenever the Log File option is turned on. You must turn off the Log File feature before you can actually view this file.

 **NOTE** You can also Cut and Paste directly from the Text Window, without going through the Log File. This procedure is covered later in this chapter.

Since the Log File is a standard text file, you can easily send it to other members of your workgroup, or print it out for a permanent record.

## EASY ACCESS TO THE AUTOCAD LT LOG FILE

If you want to have easy access to the ACLT.LOG file, you may place it on the desktop. Here's how it's done:

1. Open the Windows 95 Explorer, then locate and double-click on the ACLT.LOG file. The Open With dialog box will appear. This dialog box allows you to choose the program you wish to use to open the file.

2. In the scrolling list box, locate the text editor you want to use with the ACLT.LOG file. Typically, this would be the Windows 95 Wordpad. Click on the desired program and press OK. The ACLT.LOG file will open in the text editor of your choice.

3. Return to the Explorer and right-click on the ACLT.LOG file. When the Options menu appears, click on Create Shortcut. "Shortcut to aclt.log" appears highlighted in the Explorer.

4. Drag the Shortcut from the Explorer and drop it onto your Windows 95 desktop. You can edit the text below the icon by clicking on it once, and then pressing F2. You may change the text to "Open Logfile," for example.

Once this is done, you can open the ACLT.LOG file by double-clicking on the icon on your desktop.

# Managing Files in AutoCAD LT

As your projects become more complex and your library of drawings and symbols expands, you will find yourself devoting a good deal of effort to organizing your files. Backing up, deleting, renaming, and even merely searching for files begins to take more of your time. Fortunately, AutoCAD LT offers a variety of ways to let you keep up your file housekeeping with a minimum of hassle.

## Using the File Utilities

You can perform a series of simple file operations directly from Auto-CAD LT by selecting an option from the File ➤ Management cascading menu.

The function of each of these options is described here.

**Unlock Files**...   unlocks drawing and other AutoCAD LT files that have been locked (see Table 14.1).

**Audit**   checks the current file for any errors and displays the results in the text window.

**Recover**   attempts to recover damaged or corrupted AutoCAD LT files. The current file is closed in the process as Recover attempts to open the file to be recovered.

## Unlocking Files on a Network

On a network, there is always the potential for more than one person to access a file at the same time. For this reason, AutoCAD LT provides file-locking capability.

Whenever a file is opened for editing, AutoCAD LT creates a small lock file that exists only during the time the drawing file is being edited. Once the file is closed, the lock file is erased. If you try to edit this drawing at the same time someone else is editing it, AutoCAD LT will detect the lock file and return a message like the following:

```
Waiting for file: Plan1.DWG
Locked by John Doe at 11:55 am on 12/25/95
Press Esc to cancel
```

AutoCAD LT repeatedly attempts to access the file every five seconds until either the drawing file is closed by the other user or you cancel the operation by pressing the Esc key. If you cancel, you get the following message and must then wait your turn to access this file:

```
Access denied: Plan1.DWG
Press RETURN to continue:
```

Table 14.1:   *AutoCAD LT Filename Extensions and Their Lock File Counterparts*

| File Description | Standard Extension | Lock File Extension |
| --- | --- | --- |
| Audit files | .ADT | .ADK |
| Drawing backup | .BAK | .BKK |
| AutoCAD LT configuration (NT only) | .CFG | .CFK |
| Drawing | .DWG | .DWK |
| Binary data exchange | .DXB | .DBK |
| DXF drawing interchange | .DXF | .DFK |
| Attribute data in DXF format | .DXX | .DXK |
| Linetype definition | .LIN | .LIK |
| Compiled menu | .MNX | .MNK |
| Plot configuration parameters | .PCP | .PCK |
| Plot file | .PLT | .PLK |
| Slides | .SLD | .SDK |
| Attribute template | .TXT | .TXK |
| Xref log | .XLG | .XLK |

Part
3

Becoming an Expert

Sometimes, however, a lock file may exist even though its associated drawing file has been closed. This can occur when someone aborts an editing session by using the Ctrl-Alt-Del key combination. When such an orphaned lock file exists, you must manually unlock the file by using File ➤ Management ➤ Unlock Files.... (You can also delete the lock file in the Windows Explorer.)

Drawing files are not the only files that are locked. Nearly all types of AutoCAD LT files—from menu files to font files—are locked while they are being read from disk. They are unlocked, however, once file access has been completed and the file in question has been loaded. You can recognize a lock file by its filename extension. Table 14.1 lists lock file extensions and their AutoCAD LT file counterparts.

WARNING  If you are using AutoCAD LT on a network, be certain that the file you are trying to load is not currently being edited before you try to unlock it.

## Exchanging CAD Data with Other Programs

AutoCAD LT offers many ways to share data with other programs. Perhaps the most common type of data exchange is to simply share drawing data with other CAD programs. In this section, you'll look at how you can export and import CAD drawings using the DXF file format. You'll also look at how you can use bitmap graphics, both to and from AutoCAD LT, through the Windows clipboard.

We'll look at how you can include text, spreadsheet, and database files in a drawing, or include AutoCAD LT drawings in other program files using a Windows feature called Object Linking and Embedding (OLE).

# EXCHANGING FILES WITH EARLIER RELEASES OF AUTOCAD LT AND OTHER AUTOCAD VERSIONS

AutoCAD LT Release 3 has a file structure that is radically different from earlier versions of AutoCAD LT. Fortunately, you can still exchange files with previous versions of the program.

1. Choose File ➤ Save As…. The Save Drawing As dialog box appears.

2. Click on the Save File as Type: list box arrow to display the range of choices.

3. Select AutoCAD LT Release 2, or AutoCAD LT Release 1.

4. Enter a new drawing name, if required, and click on OK.

You don't get something for nothing, however; there are certain things you will lose when you save a file from AutoCAD LT Release 3 in the earlier format. Bear these considerations in mind when using this option. Here is a list of the features you will lose:

► Splines become polyline splines.

► Ellipses are converted to polylines. Linetypes with embedded shapes lose the embedded shape definitions.

► Dimension styles are not completely translated.

► Paragraph text is converted to multiple text objects. TrueType fonts are not supported in earlier versions and so are converted to txt.shx fonts.

► Rays and Xlines are converted to line objects and truncated at the drawing limits.

► OLE objects, External Reference Overlays, Previews, and new system variables are ignored.

When you save a file to an earlier format, you will receive a message telling you how the file has been modified to accommodate the earlier format. Press F2 to open the text window and read the often lengthy message. You may wish to copy this log via the clipboard to a word processor, or use the Logfileon command to store the conversion message for future reference.

In the Save Drawing As dialog box, the Save File as Type: list box also provides options to convert AutoCAD LT drawings to regular AutoCAD Release 11, 12, and 13 format. AutoCAD Release 11 and Release 12 have the same file format as earlier versions of AutoCAD LT. Conversion to this format is subject to the restrictions described above. These restrictions do not apply when you convert a drawing to AutoCAD Release 13 format.

Part
3

Becoming an Expert

## Using the .DXF File Format

A .DXF file is a DOS text file containing all the information needed to reconstruct a drawing. It is often used to exchange drawings created with other programs. Many micro-CAD programs, including some 3D perspective programs, can generate or read files in .DXF format. You may want to use a 3D program to view your drawing in a perspective view, or you may have a consultant who uses a different CAD program that accepts .DXF files. There are many 3D rendering programs that read .DXF files. Most 2D drafting programs also read and write .DXF files.

You should be aware that not all programs that read .DXF files will accept all the data stored therein. Many programs that claim to read .DXF files will "throw away" much of their information. Attributes are perhaps the most commonly ignored objects, followed by many of the 3D objects, such as meshes and 3Dfaces. But .DXF files, though not the most perfect medium for translating data, have become something of a standard.

### Exporting .DXF Files

To export your current drawing as a .DXF file, try the following:

1. Enter **DXFout** ↵. The Create .DXF File dialog box appears.

2. In the File Name: input box, enter the name you wish to give your .DXF file, and click OK.

3. At the next prompt,

   ```
   Enter decimal places of accuracy (0 to
   16)/Objects/Binary <6>:
   ```

   press ↵ to accept the default, or enter a value to increase or decrease the decimal accuracy of your .DXF file.

In step 3 above, you have two additional options:

▶ To specify that your .DXF file be written in a binary format, enter **B** ↵ for Binary. This helps make the file smaller, but some other CAD programs are unable to read the binary (.DXB) version of .DXF files.

▶ To select specific objects for export, enter **O** ↵. You are then prompted to select objects. Once you are done, you see the Enter decimal places of accuracy prompt again.

NOTE You can also click on File ➤ Export..., then select .DXF in the Save File As Type: list box, and enter the name of your export file. AutoCAD LT will skip the prompt in step 3 and proceed to create the .DXF file.

### Importing .DXF Files

To import .DXF files, follow these steps:

1. Click on File ➤ Import..., or enter **DXFin** ↵. The Import File dialog box appears.

2. Choose .DXF from the pop-up list at the bottom of the dialog box (you don't need to do this if you enter **DXFin** at the command prompt).

3. Locate and select the .DXF file you wish to import.

4. Double-click on the filename to begin importing it.

    If the import drawing is large, AutoCAD LT may take several minutes.

## Using AutoCAD LT in Desktop Publishing

As you probably know, AutoCAD LT is a natural for creating line art, and because of its popularity, most desktop publishing programs are designed to import AutoCAD LT drawings in one form or another. Those of you who employ desktop publishing software to generate user manuals or other technical documents will probably want to be able to use AutoCAD LT drawings in your work. In this section, we will examine ways to output AutoCAD LT drawings for use by the two most popular desktop publishing programs available for the IBM PC: PageMaker and Ventura.

## Exporting Drawings to Desktop Publishing Programs

There are two methods for transferring AutoCAD LT drawings to a desktop publishing program. Since most of these programs accept HPGL and PostScript files, you can either have AutoCAD LT plot to a file using an HPGL plotter configuration, or you can use the PostScript Out option found under File ➤ Export ➤ PostScript.

**TIP**  If you are a circuit board designer or drafter, you will want to use the PostScript Out option to output your layout to linotronic typesetting devices. This will save time and file size because this option converts AutoCAD LT entities into true PostScript descriptions.

### HPGL Output

First, let's look at how you export an HPGL file.

1. Configure your plotter setting for a Hewlett-Packard plotter (HPGL). Just about any of the Hewlett-Packard plotter options will work.

2. Click on File ➤ Print. Then use the Print/Plot Set Up and Default Selection dialog box to set the default plotter to Hewlett-Packard, and press OK.

3. In the Plot Configuration dialog box, click on the Plot to File check box.

4. Click on the Filename button and then type in a filename for your Plot file and press ↵; or just press ↵ to accept the .DWG filename as your Plot filename.

### PostScript Output

Another method for file transfer is to use the Encapsulated PostScript (.EPS) format. If you use PostScript fonts in your drawing, then the PostScript output file will contain the proper code to utilize the true PostScript fonts in your output device.

**TIP**  You can also choose File ➤ Export, then select Encapsulated PS (*.EPS) from the Save File as Type drop-down list in the Export Data dialog box. Enter a name for your file, then click on OK. AutoCAD LT will skip steps 2 through 7 and immediately start to write the drawing to an .EPS file.

1. At the command prompt, type **Psout** ↵.

2. Enter a name for your file and include the filename extension, then click OK.

3. At the `What to plot…` prompt, select an option.

4. At the `Include a screen preview image in the file? (None/EPSI/TIFF) <None>:` prompt, press ↵.

5. At the `Size units (Inches or Millimeters) <Inches>:` prompt, press ↵.

6. At the `Output Inches=Drawing Units or Fit or ? <Fit>:` prompt, press ↵. You then see the following list:

**Standard Values for Output Size**

| Size | Width | Height |
|------|-------|--------|
| A | 8.00 | 10.50 |
| B | 10.00 | 16.00 |
| C | 16.00 | 21.00 |
| D | 21.00 | 33.00 |
| E | 33.00 | 43.00 |
| F | 28.00 | 40.00 |
| G | 11.00 | 90.00 |
| H | 28.00 | 143.00 |
| J | 34.00 | 176.00 |
| K | 40.00 | 143.00 |
| A4 | 7.80 | 11.20 |
| A3 | 10.70 | 15.60 |
| A2 | 15.60 | 22.40 |
| A1 | 22.40 | 32.20 |
| A0 | 32.20 | 45.90 |
| USER | 7.50 | 10.50 |

 **TIP** You can increase the "resolution" and accuracy of your exported drawings by using the larger output sizes.

7. At the `Enter the Size or Width, Height (in Inches) <A>:` prompt, enter the appropriate sheet size. Chances are, if you are importing AutoCAD LT documents into PageMaker or Ventura, you'll want the A size, or you can enter a custom width and height at this prompt.

**Part 3**

**Becoming an Expert**

8. AutoCAD LT displays the message

   ```
   Effective plotting area:  X.XX wide by Y.YY high
   ```

   where *X.XX* and *Y.YY* are the width and height of the output image. AutoCAD LT will take a moment to generate the file and then return to the command prompt.

   If you chose to enter **EPSI** or **TIFF** when you were asked if you want a preview image (at step 4 above), you will get this prompt:

   ```
   Screen preview image size (128x128 is standard)?
   (128/256/512) <128>:
   ```

   In this case, you can enter a value for the image size in pixels. The preview image is somewhat crude but is provided only to allow easy identification of the art when it is pasted into a document. For this reason, you may not need to increase the size unless the image cannot be identified easily using the default value.

## Adding Sound, Motion, and Photos to Your Drawings

Perhaps the most exciting addition to AutoCAD LT in this release is its ability to include data from other Windows sources. These include scanned photographs in the form of bitmap files, sound files, and even live action video and animation. Imagine how you might be able to enhance your drawings with photographs, sound, and full motion video. You can include voice annotation, or, if the file is to go to a client, an animated video clip of your building or mechanical design. The potential for this feature is enormous.

You can also insert more typical types of data like spreadsheets and databases into your AutoCAD LT drawing. A spreadsheet inserted into an AutoCAD LT drawing can be set up to automatically reflect changes in the original spreadsheet document, in much the same way that Xref drawings are automatically updated.

This ability to import data from non-CAD sources is called Object Linking and Embedding, or OLE. Many programs now support OLE. If you are using the Microsoft Office Suite, for example, you will be able to use this feature with AutoCAD LT.

Here's a step-by-step description of how to import data from an Excel spreadsheet:

1. Open AutoCAD LT, then start Excel, and open the spreadsheet file that you want to import.

2. Highlight the cells you want to bring into your AutoCAD LT file, and then choose Edit ➤ Copy (Ctrl+C) from the Excel menu bar.

3. Return to AutoCAD LT, then choose Edit ➤ Paste Special. The Paste Special dialog box appears. You may use this dialog box to specify how the spreadsheet data should be imported.

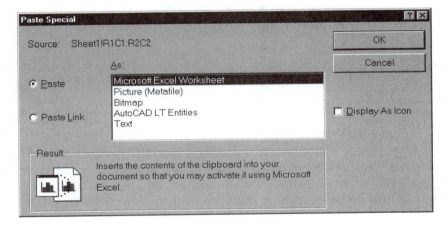

4. Click on the Paste Link radio button on the left side of the dialog box. This option causes the pasted spreadsheet to be linked to the source file. (The next section, "Choosing Between Linking and Embedding," describes the difference between a simple Paste and a Paste Link.)

5. Notice that the Results graphic and description change when you toggle the Paste Link button, and that the MicroSoft Excel Worksheet is selected. Click on OK. The spreadsheet will appear in the open Auto-CAD LT drawing.

Remember that you can paste data into AutoCAD LT only from applications that support OLE. You can also use the Windows 95 drag-and-drop feature to insert objects into AutoCAD LT. To do this, locate the file using the Windows Explorer or via the Drive options under the My Computer icon on your Desktop. Once you've located the file, drag it into the AutoCAD LT drawing editor. By using the Ctrl and Shift keys, you can control how the file is pasted into AutoCAD LT.

| Drag only | Result determined by target and source |
| Shift+drag | Move the file |
| Ctrl+drag | Copy the file |
| Shift+Ctrl-drag | Link the file |

If AutoCAD is minimized to a button, drag the file over the button, wait until AutoCAD LT opens, then drop the file into the AutoCAD LT drawing area. If the pasted object is an image file, such as a TIFF or Targa file, the image will appear. If it's a data file, like a spreadsheet or database, the data will appear as it does in the application it came from. A sound file will appear as an icon representing the application you have associated with the sound file. Video files display their first frame.

To edit or play back the pasted object, double-click on it. The application associated with the object will start up and the object will appear in the application. You can then make your changes and then select File ➤ Update to return to AutoCAD LT (Update replaces the usual Save option in the File menu of many object applications). Sound and video play back when you double-click on the sound icon or video image.

If you want to create or edit a new spreadsheet or image and paste it into AutoCAD LT, you can choose Edit Insert ➤ Object..., or type **Insertobj** ↵. The Insert Object dialog box appears.

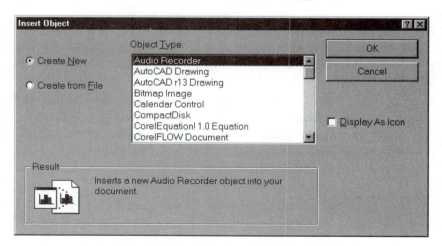

This dialog box shows a list of the programs/files currently on your system which support OLE. The contents of the Object Type: list box will depend on the applications you have installed on your system. Choose an item on the list to create a new object or edit an existing file. If you select MicroSoft Excel Worksheet, for example, Excel will open a blank worksheet to which you can add data. If you choose a bitmap image, the Windows Paint application will open, and a bitmap image will appear in the AutoCAD LT drawing area. As you begin to draw in the Paint program, the image is replicated in the AutoCAD LT pasted image.

### Choosing between Linking or Embedding

When you paste a data object into your AutoCAD LT file, you have the option to have it *linked* to the source file or to *embed* it. If you link it to the source file, then the pasted object can be updated whenever the source file is modified. This is similar to an AutoCAD LT external reference file (see *Chapter 12* for more on external references).

> **NOTE** When editing a linked object from within AutoCAD LT, the Save option in the File pull-down menu of that object's application changes to Update.

If a file is not linked to its source file, then it is considered an embedded object. You can still open the application associated with the object by double-clicking on the object, but the object is no longer associated with the source file. This is similar to a drawing inserted as a block, where changes in the source drawing file have no effect on the inserted block.

To control whether an object is linked or embedded, choose the Paste Link (linked) or Paste (embedded) radio button from the Paste Special dialog box.

### Editing Links

You can make changes to a linked object by right-clicking on it. You'll see a pop-up menu with the options Cut, Copy, Clear and Undo. (If it's an Excel Worksheet, you will also see Worksheet Object.) Cut, Copy, and Clear perform the standard Windows Clipboard functions. For example, if you want to delete a pasted object, right-click on it and choose Clear from the pop-up menu.

The Undo option will undo the last command or option chosen. Click on the WorkSheet Object; you will see Edit, Open, and Convert options. Both Edit and Open let you make changes to the source file. The Convert Option opens the Convert dialog box.

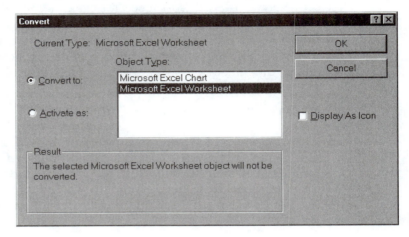

The list box offers conversion options. You may also change the pasted spreadsheet into an icon, if you prefer.

Other types of objects will offer different options at the bottom of the pop-up menu. Bitmap images will show *Bitmap Image Object*, for example. The subsidiary options of Edit, Open, and Convert remain the same.

### Controlling and Updating Links

Once you've pasted an object with links, you can control the link by selecting Edit ➤ Links... (Olelinks). You can set AutoCAD LT to update links when information in the source changes, either automatically or manually. If there are no linked objects in the drawing, this option does nothing; otherwise, it opens the Links dialog box:

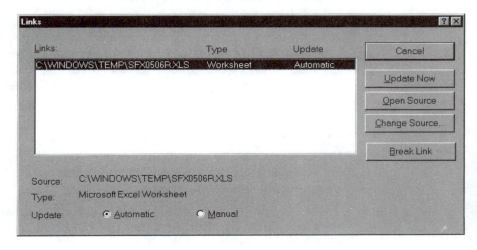

The following describes the options available in this dialog box:

**Automatic** and **Manual**   radio buttons control whether linked objects are updated automatically or manually.

**Update Now**   updates an objects link when the Manual option is selected.

**Break Link**   does just that. It cancels the link between a pasted object and its source file. Once this option is used, changes in the source file have no effect on the pasted object. This is similar to using the Bind option in the Xref command.

**Change Source...**   lets you change the object's link to a different file. When you select this option, AutoCAD LT opens the Change Source dialog box, which lets you select another file of the same type.

**Open Source**   opens the application associated with the object and lets you edit it.

## *Using the Clipboard to Export AutoCAD LT Drawings*

Just as you can cut and paste data into AutoCAD LT from applications that support OLE, you can also cut and paste AutoCAD LT images to other applications. This can be useful as a way of including AutoCAD LT images into word processed documents, spreadsheets, or desktop publishing documents. It can also be useful in creating background images for visualization programs like 3D Studio, or paint programs like Fractal Painter.

The receiving application need not support OLE, but if it does, then the drawing can be edited with AutoCAD LT and will maintain its accuracy as a CAD drawing. Otherwise, the AutoCAD LT image will be converted to a bitmap graphic.

To use the clipboard to export a specific view from your AutoCAD LT drawing, select the Edit ➤ Copy Link (Copylink) option. Here's an example of the steps to take.

1. While in AutoCAD LT, set up the view you want exported.

2. Choose Edit ➤ Copy Link or type **Copylink** ↵. AutoCAD LT will pause for a second, and then the command prompt will return.

3. Open the receiving application and file, then choose Paste Special… from the Edit pull-down menu to paste and link the AutoCAD LT image to the file.

The receiving file and application must support OLE in order to link or embed the AutoCAD LT image. Otherwise, the image will be pasted as a simple bitmap image with no links to AutoCAD LT.

If you want to be more selective about what you are copying to the clipboard, you can choose Edit ➤ Copy or Edit ➤ Cut from the AutoCAD LT menu bar in step 2. You are then prompted to select specific objects you want to copy to the clipboard.

## COPYING AND PASTING IN THE TEXT WINDOW

We've described how you can record the text from the AutoCAD LT text window using the Log File feature. You can also record the entire contents of the text window to the Windows clipboard. Here's how it's done:

1. Move the arrow cursor to the command prompt window at the bottom of the AutoCAD LT window.

2. Right-click on the mouse. A pop-up menu appears.

3. Click on Copy History. The entire contents of the text window is copied to the clipboard.

If you want to copy only a portion of the text window to the clipboard, do the following:

1. Press the F2 function key to open the text window.

2. Using the I-beam text cursor, highlight the text that you wish to copy to the clipboard.

3. Right-click on your mouse, then click on Copy from the pop-up menu. You can also click on Edit ➤ Copy from the text window's menu bar. The highlighted text is copied to the clipboard.

You may notice two other options on the pop-up menu: Paste and Preferences.... Paste will paste the first line of the contents of the clipboard into the command line. This can be useful for entering repetitive text or for storing and retrieving a frequently used command. Preferences... will open the Preferences dialog box, where you can control aspects of the screen, work space, and file system.

# If You Want to Experiment...

If you use Word for Windows (or another word processor which supports OLE) in your work, you may want to experiment with various ways of exporting AutoCAD LT files to that program and vice versa. Try using cut and paste and drag-and-drop.

1. Open the Unit plan.

2. Zoom out until you have the entire Unit Plan on the screen.

3. Choose Edit ➤ Copy Link, or type **Copylink** ↵.

4. Open your word processing program, and start a new file called **Unitfile**.

From the word processor menu bar, choose Edit ➤ Paste Special.

You can choose whether to paste the Unit plan as a .DWG file, a .PCX, or a .BMP file. Make your selection and click on OK.

The Unit Plan appears immediately above your cursor in the word processor.

To reposition or resize the file, drag it up or down the page. Or select it and copy it (Ctrl C) or cut it and paste it (Ctrl-X, Ctrl-V) to another part of the document, assuming you have some text in the document.

Now try adding a few notes to your drawing, and then print out the file.

In this chapter, you have seen how AutoCAD LT allows you to access information ranging from the areas of objects to information from other programs. You may never use some of these features, but knowing they are there may at some point help you to solve a production problem.

You've just completed Part 3 of our tutorial. If you've followed the tutorial from the beginning, this is where you get a diploma. You have reached Expert status in 2D drawing and have the tools to tackle any drawing project thrown at you. You need only to log in some time on a few real projects to round out your experience.

From now on, you won't need to follow the book's chapters in order. If you're interested in 3D, go ahead and continue to Part 4, where you'll get thorough instructions on 3D drawing with AutoCAD LT. Otherwise, you can skip to Part 5 to become a full-fledged AutoCAD LT power-user.

Also, don't miss the appendices—they are packed with information that will answer many of your specific questions or problems. Of course, the entire book is a ready reference to answer questions as they arise or to refresh your memory about specific commands.

Good luck!

# Working in Three Dimensions

While 2D drafting is AutoCAD LT's workhorse application, AutoCAD LT's 3D capabilities give you a chance to expand your ideas and look at them in a new light. *Chapter 15: Creating 3D Models* covers AutoCAD LT's basic features for creating three-dimensional drawings. *Chapter 16: Navigating in 3D Space* introduces you to two different methods for orienting and viewing your 3D models.

# Chapter 15
# Creating 3D Models

## *Fast Tracks*

**V**IEWING an object in three dimensions lets you have a sense of its true shape and form. It also helps you conceptualize the design, which results in better design decisions. Finally, using three-dimensional objects helps you communicate your ideas to those who may not be familiar with the plans, sections, and side views of your design.

A further advantage to drawing in three dimensions is that you can derive 2D drawings from your 3D model, which might otherwise take considerably more time with standard 2D drawing methods. For example, you could model a mechanical part in 3D and then quickly derive its top, front, and right-side views using the techniques discussed in this chapter.

AutoCAD LT allows you to turn any 2D drawing you create into a 3D model by changing the properties of the objects making up the drawing.

In this chapter, you will use AutoCAD LT's 3D capabilities to see what your studio apartment looks like from various angles.

## Creating a 3D Drawing

The way AutoCAD LT creates three-dimensional forms is by *extruding* two-dimensional objects. For example, to draw a cube using this process, you first draw a square, and then extrude the square by giving its lines a *thickness* (see Figure 15.1). This thickness is a value given as a z coordinate. Imagine that your screen's drawing area is the drawing surface. A z coordinate of 0 is on that surface. A z coordinate greater than 0 is a position closer to you and above that surface. Figure 15.2 illustrates this concept.

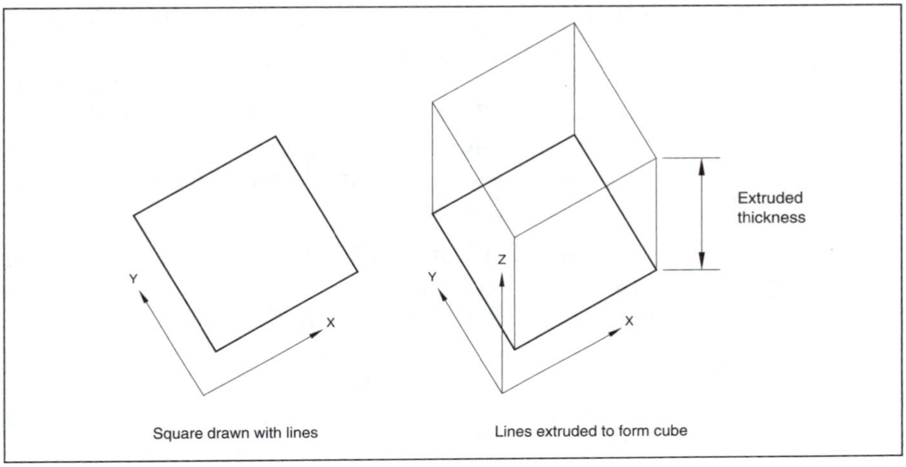

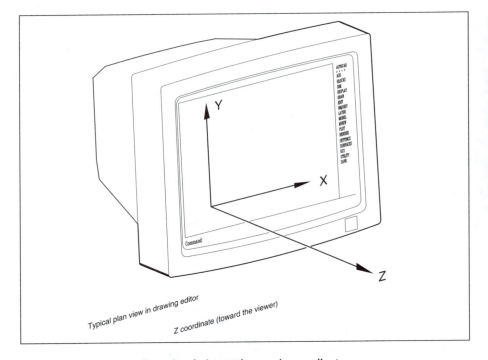

*Figure 15.1:*   **How to create a cube using extrusion**

*Figure 15.2:*   **The z coordinate in relation to the x and y coordinates**

Part
4

Working in
Three Dimensions

When you draw an object with thickness, you don't see the thickness until you view the drawing from a different angle. This is because normally your view is perpendicular to the imagined drawing surface. At that angle, you cannot see the thickness of an object because it projects toward you—just as a sheet of paper looks like a line when viewed from one end. Thus, to view an object's thickness, you must change the angle at which you view your drawing.

You can set AutoCAD LT so that everything you draw has an *elevation*. Normally, you draw on the imagined surface, but you can set the z coordinate for your drawing elevation so that whatever you draw is above that surface. An object with an elevation value other than 0 rests not *on* the imagined drawing surface but *above* it (or *below* it if the z coordinate is a negative value). Figure 15.3 illustrates this concept.

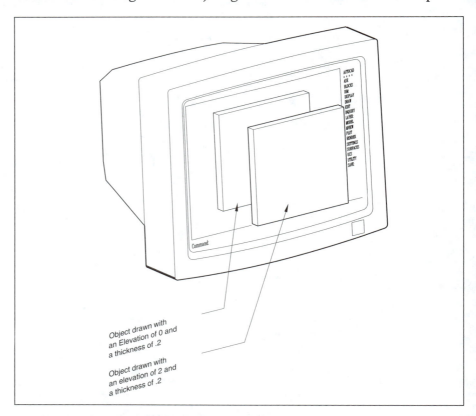

*Figure 15.3:* ***Two identical objects at different z coordinates***

## Changing a 2D Plan into a 3D Model

In this exercise, you will turn the 2D studio unit drawing into a 3D drawing by changing the properties of the wall lines. You will also learn how to view the 3D image.

1. Start AutoCAD LT and open the Unit file and Save it as **3Dunit. DWG**. Use the unit drawing you have been working on, or open 15-UNIT.DWG on the companion CD. (If you have installed the tutorial drawings per the instructions in *Appendix C*, 15-UNIT.DWG will be in the Sample directory.)

2. Set the current layer to Wall, and turn off all the other layers except Jamb.

3. Turn on the grid (if it isn't on already). Your screen should look like Figure 15.4.

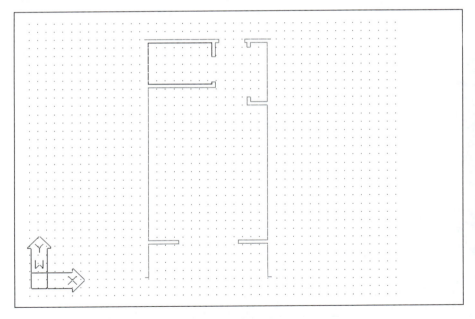

*Figure 15.4:*    **The plan view of the walls and door jambs**

4. Before you go any further, you will need to explode the Bath drawing. You cannot directly modify objects within a block. So you will not be able to apply elevation or thickness to the bathroom walls unless you explode the block. Click on the Explode button on the Modify toolbar (or type **Explode** ↵), and then select the Bath block and press ↵.

5. Click on View ➤ 3D Viewpoint ➤ Vector, or type **Vpoint** ↵ at the command prompt. This starts the Vpoint command that allows you to view the studio unit in 3D.

6. At the Rotate/<viewpoint><0′–0″,0′–0″,0′–1″>: prompt, enter **–1,–1,1** ↵. The default value is a list of the x, y, and z coordinates of your last viewing location relative to your object. Your view looks as if you are standing below and to the left of your drawing, rather than directly above it (see Figure 15.5). The grid shows you the angle of the drawing surface.

TIP To accomplish the same result, you can use View ➤ 3D Viewpoint ➤ SW Isometric, or click on the SW Isometric button on the View flyout on the Standard toolbar. The SW Isometric view is located at –1, –1, 1.

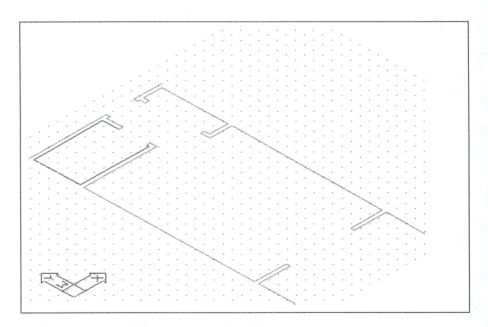

Figure 15.5: *A 3D view of the floor plan*

7. Click on the Properties button on the Object Properties toolbar, or type **Ddchprop** ↵.

8. At the object-selection prompt, use a crossing window to pick the entire drawing and press ↵.

9. At the Change Properties dialog box, double-click on the Thickness input box, enter **8′**, and click on OK. The walls and jambs now appear to be 8′ high.

10. Click on the Zoom Out button on the Standard toolbar to zoom the view out again.

   Figure 15.6 shows the extruded wall lines. You are able to see through the walls because this is a *wireframe view*. A wireframe view shows the volumes of a 3D object by showing the lines representing the intersections of surfaces. Later we will review how to make an object's surfaces opaque.

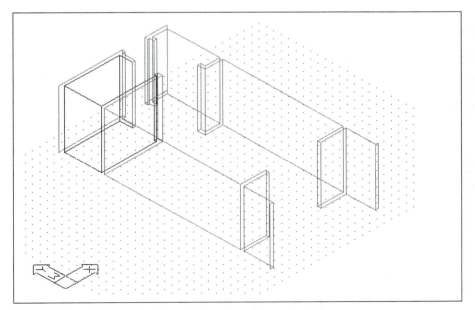

*Figure 15.6:* **The wall lines, extruded (wireframe view)**

Next you will change the elevation of the door headers by moving them in the z-axis using grips.

1. Turn on the Ceiling layer. The door headers appear as lines on the floor where the door openings are located.

2. Click on the two magenta lines representing the header at the balcony door.

3. Shift-click on the midpoint grips of these two lines.

4. Click again on one of the hot grips, without holding down the Shift key. This establishes the base point from which to move.

5. At the ** STRETCH ** prompt, enter **@0,0,7′** ⏎. The header lines move to a new position 7′ above the floor (see Figure 15.7).

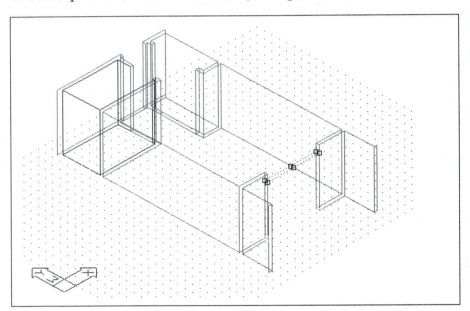

*Figure 15.7:* **The balcony header lines at the new elevation**

6. Click on the Properties button on the Object Properties toolbar and change the thickness of the header to 1′ using the Thickness input box. Click on OK.

7. Click on the lines representing the door headers for the bathroom, closet, and entry.

**8.** Repeat steps 3 through 6. Your drawing will look like Figure 15.8.

> **TIP** If you are having difficulty selecting the door headers, turn the wall layer off temporarily. This will make it easier to select the header lines. Turn the walls layer back on when you finish.

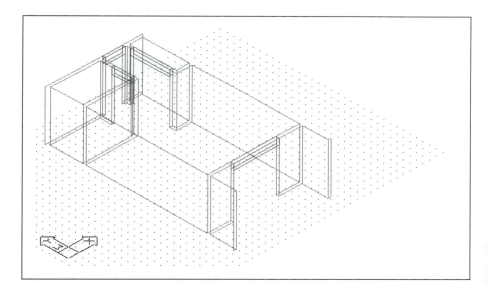

*Figure 15.8:* **The headers with the new thickness**

You could have used the Move command to move the lines to their new elevation, entering the same *@0,0,7'* at the Second point prompt for Move. Since you must select objects to edit them using grips, with Move you save a step by not having to select the lines a second time for the Ddchprop command (Properties button on the Object Properties toolbar).

## Creating a 3D Object

Though you may visualize a design in 3D, you will often start sketching it in 2D and later generate the 3D views. When you know from the start what the thickness and height of an object will be, you can set these values so that you don't have to extrude the object later. The following exercise shows you how to set elevation and thickness before you start drawing.

1.  Click on the Properties button on the Object Properties toolbar.

The Current Properties dialog box appears.

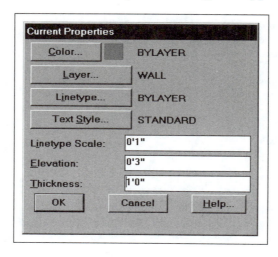

2.  Enter **3″** in the Elevations input box.

3.  Enter **12″** in the Thickness input box.

4.  Click on OK. The grid changes to the new elevation. Now as you draw objects, they will appear 12″ thick at an elevation of 3″.

5.  Draw a circle representing a planter at one side of the balcony (see Figure 15.9). Make it 18″ in diameter. The planter appears as a 3D object with the current thickness and elevation settings.

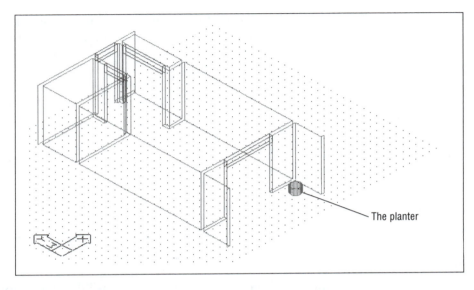

The planter

*Figure 15.9:* **The planter**

Extruding forms is a very simple process, as you have seen. You just have to keep track of thicknesses and elevations. With these two properties, you can create nearly any three-dimensional form you need. If you use the same thickness and elevation often, you can create a default thickness and elevation for new objects using the Elev command. You can also use the Elevation and Thickness *system variables* to set the default elevation and thickness for new objects.

Next you will discover how to control your view of your drawing.

## Viewing a 3D Drawing

Your first 3D view of a drawing is a wireframe view. It appears as an open model made of wire; none of the sides appear solid. This section describes how to manipulate this wireframe view so you can see your drawing from any angle. We will also describe how, once you have selected your view, you can view the 3D drawing as a solid object with the hidden lines removed. In addition, we will cover methods for saving views for later recall.

1. Click on View ➤ 3D Viewpoint ➤ Tripod, or enter **Vpoint** ↵ ↵ at the command prompt. You get a screen that helps you visually select your 3D view (see Figure 15.10). The three lines converging at one point compose the *coordinate tripod*.

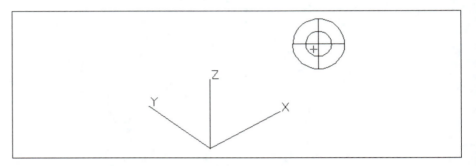

*Figure 15.10:* **The coordinate tripod and target**

2. Move your mouse around, and watch how the tripod rotates to show your orientation *in relation to the x-, y-, and z-axes of your drawing*. Each line is labeled to indicate which axis it represents. Above and to the right of the tripod is a target with a small cursor. As you move your mouse, the cursor follows, staying near or within the target.

3. Move the cursor around the center of the target. Note how the tripod appears to rotate, indicating your changing view (see Figure 15.11). This target shows you your viewpoint in relation to the drawing.

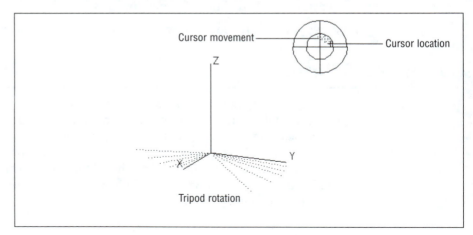

*Figure 15.11:* **The tripod rotates as you move the cursor around the target's center.**

4. If it isn't on already, toggle on the dynamic coordinate readout. As you move the cursor, the readout tells you *your x,y coordinates in relation to the target's center.*

5. Move the cursor closer to the center. The coordinate readout approaches 0,0, and the z-axis of the tripod begins to foreshorten until it is no longer visible (see Figure 15.12). This shows that you are almost directly above the drawing, as you would be in a 2D view.

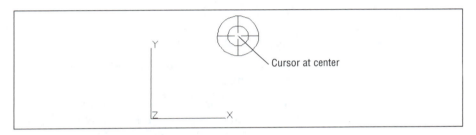

*Figure 15.12:* **The z-axis foreshortened**

6. Position the cursor as shown in Figure 15.12 and pick the point indicated. Or you may type **0,0,1** at the Vpoint Rotate… prompt on the command line. Your drawing will look something like Figure 15.13. Now you can see that your view does indeed look like a plan view. The closer to the target's center you move the cursor, the higher in elevation your view will be.

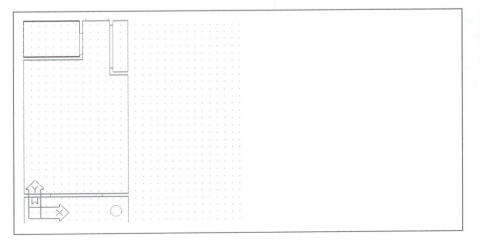

*Figure 15.13:* **A 3D view that looks like a 2D view**

## *Understanding Coordinate Values and the Viewpoint Prompt*

Let's take a moment to study the relationship between the coordinate values you enter at the Viewpoint prompt, and the coordinate tripod. In an earlier exercise, when you entered a coordinate value at the Viewpoint prompt, what you were specifying were the x, y, and z values for your position in relation to the origin of the coordinate tripod. The coordinate tripod graphically shows your orientation to the drawing. The coordinate values are not meaningful in themselves, but only in relation to each other.

The origin of the coordinate tripod, in this case, is your entire drawing—not the actual drawing origin (see Figure 15.14).

In addition, the coordinate readout offers some additional help when using the coordinate tripod. The following list describes how positive and negative coordinate values affect your view.

▶   The negative x value places your viewing position to the left (or west) of your drawing.

▶   The negative y places your position 270° (or south) in relation to your drawing.

▶   The positive 1 value for the z-axis lifts your view above the surface.

As you go through the following exercise in the next section, you will see more clearly the relationship between your view and these coordinates.

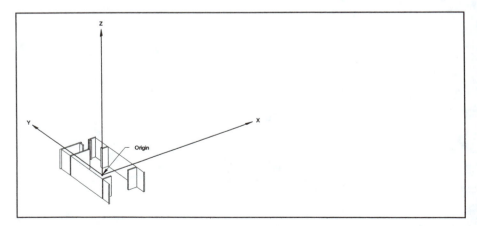

*Figure 15.14:    **The coordinate tripod, superimposed on the plan***

## Understanding the Viewpoint Axes Target

The cursor's position in relation to the target's center represents your viewpoint in relation to your drawing. You might think of the target as a schematic-plan view of your drawing, with the cursor being your position in relation to the plan (see Figure 15.15). For example, if you place the cursor just below and to the left of the center, your view will be from the lower-left corner of your overall drawing, like your view of the floor plan in the first exercise. If you place the cursor above and to the right of the center, you will view your drawing from the upper-right corner.

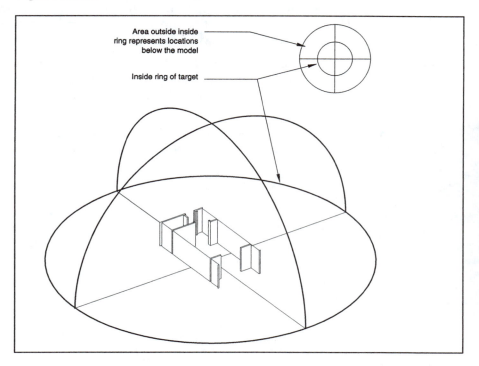

Area outside inside ring represents locations below the model

Inside ring of target

*Figure 15.15:*    **This diagram shows how the viewpoint axes target relates to your drawing.**

NOTE *Vpoint Defaults:* At first the x and y values are very low, while the z value is relatively high. This indicates that you are very close to the origin in the x- and y-axes, but far from it in the z-axis. For a typical plan view, the view coordinates would be 0,0,1.

In the following exercise, you'll see firsthand how the tripod cursor affects your 3D views.

1.  Click on View ➤ 3D Viewpoint ➤ Tripod. The tripod and target appear.

2.  Look at the target. As you move the cursor closer to its inner ring, the x and y lines begin to flatten until, as you touch the circle, they are parallel (see Figure 15.16). This first ring represents a directly horizontal position on your drawing surface.

3.  Position the cursor as shown in Figure 15.16 and click on this position. Your drawing will look as if you are viewing the drawing surface edge-on, and the walls from the side (see Figure 15.17).

 NOTE *Vpoint Defaults:* This time the x and y values are high, while the z value is 0 or close to it. This indicates the view is from an elevation of 0 (ground level).

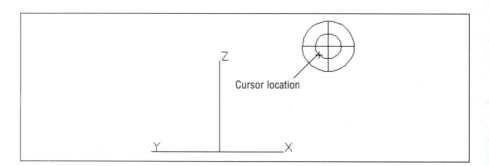

Figure 15.16:    *The parallel x- and y-axes*

 TIP   If you find it a little difficult to tell what is going on because you can see right through the walls, don't worry—as you work with 3D, you will become more accustomed to this type of view.

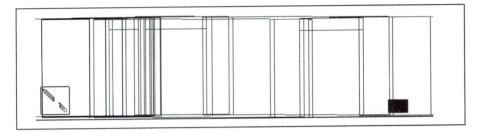

*Figure 15.17:* **View of walls from side**

4. Click on View ➤ 3D Viewpoint ➤ Tripod again.

5. Move the cursor to the outer ring of the target. The z-axis line foreshortens again. This ring represents a view located underneath your drawing, as if you are looking at the back of the screen.

6. Pick a point just inside this outer ring, as shown in Figure 15.18. You will get a view something like Figure 15.19.

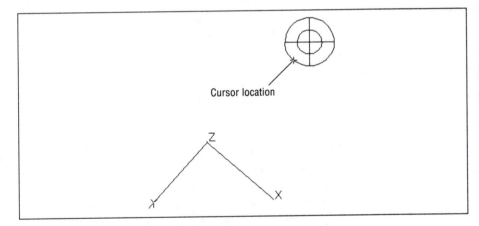

*Figure 15.18:* **The cursor location for an underside view**

Part
4

Working in
Three Dimensions

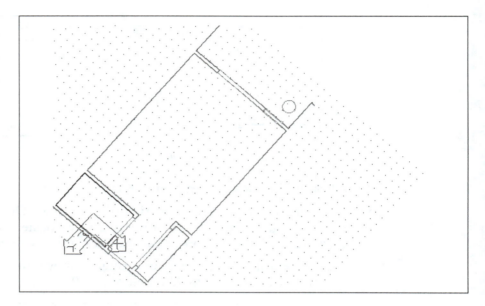

*Figure 15.19:* **The plan from below the drawing surface**

 **NOTE** If you want to get back to a plan view of your drawing, click on the Top View button on the View flyout on the Standard toolbar or type **Plan** ↵. You will notice that your 2D view looks just the way it did before you extruded the walls. This is because you are viewing the wall lines edge-on.

At first you might think that your view (as shown in Figure 15.19) is just another view from above the drawing. However, if you look carefully at the position of the bathroom in relation to the rest of the unit, you will notice that it appears to be mirrored, just like any drawing viewed from the back of the drawing sheet.

Now let's return to the view you used to edit the Unit drawing.

1.  Click on View ➤ 3D Viewpoint ➤ Vector, or type **Vpoint** ↵.

2.  Enter **–1,–1,1** ↵. You will see the drawing from a viewpoint similar to the one you started with.

3.  Using View ➤ Named Views…, save this view, and give it the name **3D**.

4.  Finally, turn on all the layers except Notes. You will see the rest of the drawing still in a 2D form.

## Using the Vpoint Rotate Option

A more direct way of obtaining a view from a 3D drawing is by using the Vpoint command's Rotate option.

1. Turn off all the layers except Wall and Ceiling.

2. Click on View ➤ 3D Viewpoint ➤ Vector, and then type **R** ↵.

3. Look at the Enter angle in X–Y plane in X axis <225>: prompt. The number in brackets tells you the rotational angle for the current view. If you imagine looking at a 2D view of the apartment, as in Figure 15.4, this value represents a position toward the lower-left of the view. Enter 45 ↵ now to get a view at the opposite side of the apartment.

4. Now look at the number in brackets in the Enter angle from X–Y plane <35>: prompt. It tells you the angle of the current view above the current floor elevation. If you imagine looking at the side of the apartment as in Figure 15.17, this value represents the direction of your point of view above the floor. Press ↵ to accept the default value. You get a new view of the apartment from the opposite side of your current view (see Figure 15.20).

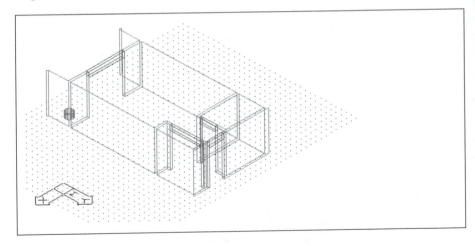

*Figure 15.20:* **The new view of the apartment**

Figure 15.21 illustrates what these view values represent.

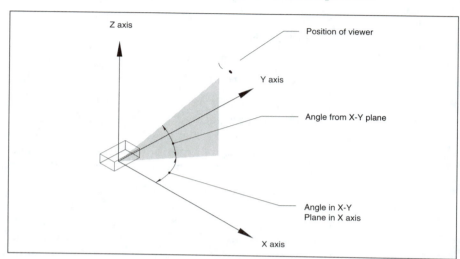

*Figure 15.21:*    **The view angles and what they represent**

If you like, you can visually choose the rotational angle of your view. To do this, follow these steps:

1.  Click and drag the Point Location button on the Inquiry flyout on the Object Properties toolbar. You can also type **ID** ↵ and pick a point at the center of the apartment. If you do not have a Snap on, this command will locate a 2D point at the current elevation. If you Snap to an object, it will locate the actual x, y, and z coordinates. Using the ID command lets you set up a new last point, which can be accessed by using the "@" during any point prompt.

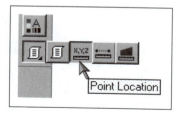

2.  Start the Vpoint command and select the Rotate option as you did in the previous exercise. A rubber-band line will appear, with one end at the point you selected and the other end on the cursor (see Figure 15.22).

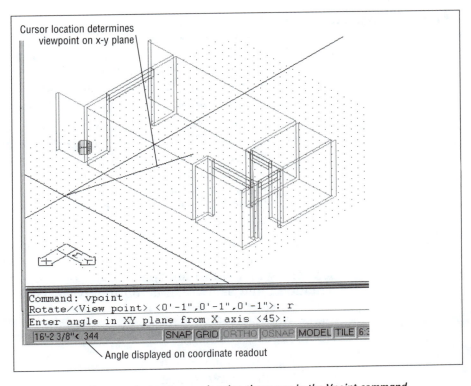

Figure 15.22: **How to select a view angle using the cursor in the Vpoint command**

 **NOTE** In the Vpoint command, you can use the position of the cursor to determine your view position. With the Osnap modes you can even use part of your apartment model as a reference.

3. At the Enter angle from XY plane from X Axis prompt, pick a point indicating the position from which you wish to view the model.

4. At the Enter angle from the x,y plane prompt, enter a value indicating the angle above the floor plane.

Your view will change to reflect your new view angle.

 **WARNING** You cannot use the rubber-band line to select the view height; you must enter a value.

# Visualizing Your Model

From time to time, you will want to get an idea of how your model looks with hidden lines removed. This is especially true of complex 3D models. Frequently, object intersections and shapes are not readily apparent until you can see what object lies in front of others.

AutoCAD LT provides two helpful viewing commands, both on the View menu, for this situation. First, the Hide command allows you to quickly view your drawing with hidden lines removed. You can then assess where surfaces are and get a better feel for the model. Hide is also an option at plot time, allowing you to create hard copy line drawings of a 3D model. You can then render the hard copy using manual techniques if you want.

The second command, Shade, lets you add a sense of solidity to the image by adding color to surfaces. Shade has a variety of settings for controlling how colors are applied. This option is better suited to presentations, and as a visualization tool when Hide proves inadequate. Unfortunately, you cannot plot a view generated by the Shade command. You can, however, store the view as a slide file for independent viewing.

Let's begin by looking at the Hide command; we'll discuss Slides in more detail later in the chapter.

## Removing Hidden Lines

You'll start by getting a quick hidden line view.

1. Restore the view you saved earlier with the name 3D.

2. Click on View ➤ Hide, or enter **Hide** ↵ at the commandline. AutoCAD LT will display this message:

```
HIDE Regenerating drawing
Hiding lines value% done
```

where *value%* change as the command calculates the hidden line removal. (On a fast computer you won't notice the value change.) When AutoCAD LT is done, the *value%* reads 100% and the image appears with hidden lines removed (see Figure 15.23). Hide does not hide text objects; Shade, however, does.

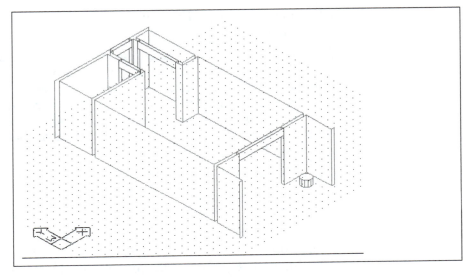

*Figure 15.23:*   **The apartment with hidden lines removed**

This hidden-line view will remain until your drawing is regenerated. Note that you cannot use the View command to save a hidden-line view. You can, however, save this view as a slide. You can also plot a view with hidden lines removed by checking the Hide Lines check box in the Plot Configuration dialog box before you start your plot. Using the Hide Lines option will generally add only a few minutes to your plot time.

## Shading Your 3D Model

If you're used to looking at wireframe 3D images, the Hide command is usually good enough to give you an idea of how your model looks. But when you want to get an even better visualization of the form your model is taking on, it's time for the Shade command. To see how it works, try the following exercise:

1. Click on View ➤ 3D Viewpoint ➤ Vector.

2. At the prompt, enter **–2,–4,3**. This changes the view so you have a different line of sight to each wall surface.

3.  Select View ➤ Shade. Four shading options are shown on the Shade submenu.

You can also start the Shade command by typing **Shade** ↵ at the command line. The type of shading generated in that case will be determined by the current Shadedge setting. To produce a different type of shading, change the setting of this system variable before using the Shade command. Each of the four menu options represents a different Shadedge value (0–3). Here are descriptions of each of the four shading settings:

| | |
|---|---|
| **256 Color** | Shades the surfaces with no edge highlighting (Shadedge = 0) |
| **256 Color Edge Highlight** | Shades the surfaces and highlights the edges (Shadedge = 1) |
| **16 Color Hidden Line** | The surfaces are not filled; the edges are drawn with the object color (Shadedge = 2) |
| **16 Color Filled** | Shades the surface with the object color and the edges with the background color (Shadedge = 3) |

4.  Click on 16 Color Filled. Just as with the Hide command, AutoCAD LT displays a message telling you that it is regenerating the drawing. In a short time, the shaded view appears.

5.  Click again on View ➤ Shade, and this time select 256 Color Edge Highlight. Notice that the shaded image now looks more realistic and less like a cartoon (see Figure 15.24).

6.  Click again on View ➤ Shade, and this time select 256 Color.

7.  The drawing is shaded for the third time. This time only the surfaces appear, with no edges showing.

8.  Save your drawing as 3Dunit.DWG, if you haven't already done so.

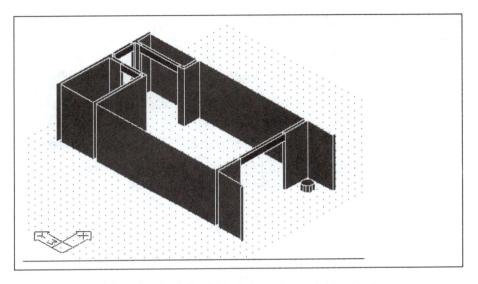

*Figure 15.24:* **The Unit plan shaded with Shadedge system variable set to 1**

In step 2, you changed your view slightly so your line of sight to the various walls was at a different angle. Had you not changed your view, the Shade command would have shaded all the walls with the same intensity in steps 5 and 7. This is because Shade renders a view as if a light source emanates from the same direction as the viewer. Thus, when all the walls are at the same angle to the view, they all receive and reflect the same amount of light. With the model slightly turned, however, light then reflects off each surface differently.

You probably noticed a fifth option on the Shade submenu: Diffuse. This option invokes another system variable, Shadedif, which controls the contrast of colors among different surfaces. A higher Shadedif number increases contrast; a lower number decreases contrast. The value can range from 0 to 100, with a default setting of 70. You may want to experiment with this setting on your own.

# Getting the 3D Results You Want

Working in 3D is tricky because you can't see exactly what you are drawing. You must alternately draw and then hide or shade your drawing from time to time to see exactly what is going on. Here are a few tips on how to keep control of your 3D drawings.

## Making Horizontal Surfaces Opaque

To make a horizontal surface appear opaque, you must draw it with a wide polyline or a solid. Consider a table, for example: You might represent the table top with a rectangle and give it the appropriate thickness, but the top would appear to be transparent when the lines were hidden. Only the sides of the table top would become opaque. To make the entire table top opaque, you can use the Solid command (or a wide polyline) to draw a filled rectangle and give it the appropriate thickness. When the lines are hidden, the table top appears to be opaque (see Figure 15.25). This technique works even with the Fill setting off.

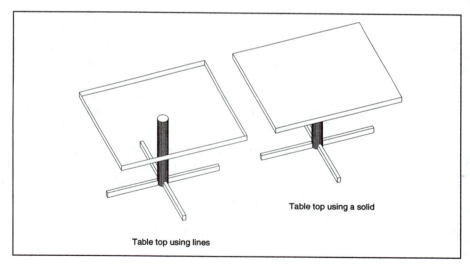

Table top using a solid

Table top using lines

*Figure 15.25:* **One table using lines for the top, and another using a solid**

When a circle is used as an extruded form, the top surface appears opaque when you use the Hide command. Where you want to show an opening at the top of a circular volume, as in a circular chimney, you can use two 180° arcs (see Figure 15.26).

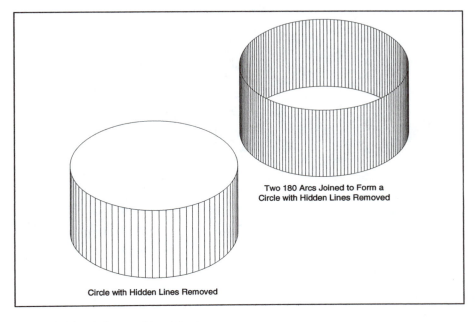

Two 180 Arcs Joined to Form a
Circle with Hidden Lines Removed

Circle with Hidden Lines Removed

*Figure 15.26:   A circle and two joined arcs*

To create complex horizontal surfaces, you can use a combination of wide polylines and solids. For example, a sidewalk on a street corner would use a donut for the rounder corner, then solids at either side for the straight portion of the sidewalk. It's okay to overlap surfaces to achieve the effect you want.

## Setting Layers Carefully

Bear in mind that the Hide command hides objects that are obscured by other objects on layers that are turned off. For example, if a couch in the corner of the studio unit is on a layer that is off when you use Hide, the lines behind the couch are hidden even though the couch does not appear in the view (see Figure 15.27). You can, however, freeze any layer containing objects that you do not want affected by the hidden-line removal process.

Part
4

Working in
Three Dimensions

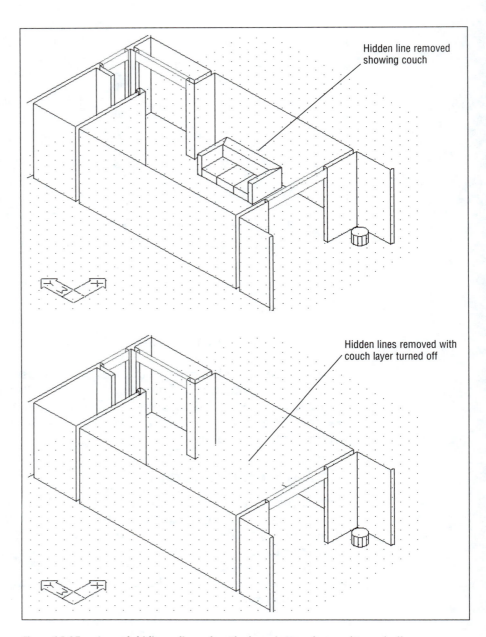

*Figure 15.27:    A couch hiding a line, when the layer is turned on and turned off*

## Using Filters

Specifying 3D coordinates is the same as specifying 2D coordinates, with the addition of a third dimension, the z-axis. AutoCAD LT offers a method for specifying 3D points, called *filtering*, that allows you to build a 3D coordinate relative to existing geometry by using *parts* of existing coordinates. For example, you could filter the x and y coordinates using an Osnap from an existing object. You would then enter the missing z dimension via the keyboard.

To use the Point Filters:

1. Click on the Point Filters flyout on the Standard toolbar. The available filters are .X, .Y, .Z, and .XY, .XZ, .YZ.

2. Click on the 3D filter you require.

3. Specify a point, or choose an Object Snap and select an existing object.

4. At the next To Point: prompt, specify the required value(s) to complete the coordinate. If you don't specify a z coordinate, the current elevation setting is assumed.

Filters can also be used in a 2D drawing to select an x or y component of an object with which to align a point.

---

### EDITING 3D OBJECTS

As you can see from this chapter, AutoCAD LT has limited 3D capabilities. You cannot create 3D faces, 3D meshes, or 3D solids in AutoCAD LT. Since AutoCAD Release 13 and AutoCAD LT Release 3 share a common drawing format, you can, however, open Release 13 drawings which contain 3D objects in AutoCAD LT. You can edit the 3D objects using standard editing commands, but you have to be careful when editing in 3D. Here are a few tips to keep in mind:

➤ The Scale command will scale an object's z coordinate value, as well as the standard x and y coordinates. (Click on the Scale button on the Resize flyout on the Modify toolbar.) Suppose you have an object with an elevation of two units. If you use the Scale command to enlarge that object by a factor of 4, the object will have a new elevation of 2 units times 4, or 8 units. If, on the other hand, that object has an elevation of 0, its elevation will not change, because 0 times 4 is still 0.

> **EDITING 3D OBJECTS (continued...)**
>
> ➤ Array, Mirror, and Rotate (on the Modify toolbar) can also be used on 3D lines, 3D faces, and 3D shapes, but these commands won't affect their z coordinate values. Z coordinates can be specified for base and insertion points, so take care when using these commands with 3D models.
>
> ➤ Using the Move, Stretch, and Duplicate Object commands (on the Modify toolbar) with object snaps can produce some unpredictable and unwanted results. Point filters are a useful tool when selecting 3D points with Osnap overrides. For example, to move an object from the endpoint of one object to the endpoint of another on the same z coordinate, invoke the .xy filter at the `Base point` and `Second point` prompts *before* issuing the endpoint override. Proceed to pick the endpoint of the object you want; then enter the z coordinate, or just pick any point to use the current default z coordinate.
>
> ➤ When you create a block, the block will use the UCS that is active at the time the block is created to determine its own local coordinate system. When that block is later inserted, it will orient its own coordinate system with the current UCS. (UCS is discussed in more detail in *Chapter 16*.)

## Creating and Using Slides

3D graphics are often handy for presentations, and 3D AutoCAD LT images are frequently used for that purpose, as well as for producing drafted 2D drawings. You may want to show off some of your 3D work directly from the computer screen. If your drawings are complicated, however, your audience may get impatient waiting for the hidden lines to be removed. Fortunately, AutoCAD LT provides two commands on the File ➤ Slide menu that let you save a view from your screen in a form that will display quickly.

**NOTE** Slides can be used with Autodesk Animator Pro to become part of animations or other presentation material. From Animator Pro, you can then export your slides to Autodesk 3D Studio for texture maps.

The Mslide and Vslide commands will save a view as a file on disk. Such a view is called a slide. You can display a slide any time you are in the AutoCAD LT drawing editor. Slides display at redraw speed, no matter how complex they may be. This means you can save a slide of a hidden-line view of your 3D drawing and recall that view quickly at any time.

Slides can also be used for reference during editing sessions, instead of panning, zooming, or viewing. A slide cannot be edited, however, nor will it be updated, when you edit the drawing.

## Creating Slides

In the following exercise, you will make a few slides of the the 3D version you have just created of the Unit file (3DUNIT.DWG).

1.  Open the 3D Unit file, if it is not already open. If you have not created this drawing, open 3DUNIT.DWG on the companion CD.

2.  Click on View ➤ Hide to get a hidden-line view of the unit.

3.  Choose File ➤ Slide ➤ Create…, or type **Mslide** ↵ on the command line.

4.  At the Create Slide File dialog box, click on OK to accept the default filename, 3Dunit.SLD. (The default slide name is the same name as the current drawing, with the extension .SLD.) The actual drawing file is not affected.

5.  Zoom in to the bathroom, and use File ➤ Slide (Mslide) to save another view called Unitbath, this time without the hidden lines removed.

6.  When the Create Slide File dialog box appears, highlight the File input box at the bottom of the dialog box, enter **Unitbath** ↵, and click on OK.

## Viewing Slides

Now that you've saved two views, let's see how to view them.

1.  Zoom back to the previous view and choose File ➤ Slide ➤ View…, or enter **Vslide** ↵.

2.  At the Select Slide File dialog box, highlight the **Unitbath** slide file and click on OK. The slide of the bathroom appears. You can move the cursor around the view and start commands in the normal way, but you cannot edit or obtain information from this slide.

3.  Start Vslide again.

4.  This time, click on OK at the dialog box to accept the default slide filename, 3DUnit. The 3D view of the unit appears with its hidden lines removed. Since slides display at redraw speed, you don't have to wait to view the unit without its hidden lines.

**Part 4**

**Working in Three Dimensions**

>  **NOTE** Any command that performs a redraw will also return you to the current drawing.

5. Click on the Redraw button on the Standard toolbar to return to the drawing being edited.

6. Open the Plan file. If you have not created this drawing, use 15-PLAN. DWG on the companion CD.

7. Use the Vslide command to view the Unitbath slide again. As you can see, you are able to call up the slide while working in any file, not just the one you were in when you created the slide.

8. Click on the Redraw button to bring the Plan drawing back onto the screen.

9. Now create a slide of the Plan file and call it **Plan1**.

Next, you'll get to see how you can automate a slide presentation using the slides you just created.

## Automating a Slide Presentation

AutoCAD LT has a Script facility, which will read a sequence of commands from a text file. Let's create a script file to automatically show the slides you made in the last exercise.

First you'll create a script file outside of AutoCAD LT, using a text editor (such as Windows Notepad) or a word processor which saves the file in ASCII format. You will later use the script file to run a slide show. You'll add the Delay command to the script. Delay's function is to pause a script for a specific length of time.

1. Open a new file called **Show**.

2. Use a text editor to create a file called **Show.SCR**, and insert the following lines into this file, pressing ↵ at the end of each line, including the last.

```
vslide 3DUnit
delay 3000
vslide Unitbath
delay 3000
vslide Plan1
```

These lines are a sequence of predetermined instructions to AutoCAD LT that can be played back later. When you play this script file, each line is entered at the AutoCAD LT command prompt, just as you would enter it through the keyboard. Notice that the Vslide command is executed before each slide, which is then followed by the line delay 3000, which tells AutoCAD LT to pause roughly 3,000 milliseconds after each Vslide command is issued (you can substitute another value if you like). If no delay is specified, the next slide will come up as soon as the previous slide is completed.

You can also have the slides repeat themselves continuously by adding the Rscript command at the very end of the Show.SCR file. You may want to do this in a presentation intended for casual viewing as an exhibit in a display area with people passing through. To stop a repeating script, press the Escape (or the Backspace) key.

Now try playing the script.

1. Return to AutoCAD LT, then click Tools ➤ Run Script... or enter **Script** ↵.

2. At the Select Script File dialog box, highlight and pick the file you just created (Show.SCR) from the file list, and then click OK.

The slides you saved will appear on the screen in the sequence in which you entered them in the Show.SCR file.

## If You Want to Experiment...

Part 4

Don't forget that 3D modeling can be fun as well as productive. You get to see your ideas take shape. 3D helps you visualize concepts more clearly, and in some cases can show you things that a traditional 3D chipboard model cannot.

The following exercise is really just for fun. It shows you how to do a limited form of animation, using View ➤ 3D Viewpoint, the Mslide command, and scripts.

1. Open the 3DUnit drawing.

2. Do a hidden-line removal; then use Mslide to create a slide called **V1**.

3. Click and drag the Inquiry button on the Object Properties toolbar, the select Locate Point on the flyout. Pick a point in the center of the floor plan. This marks the view center for the next step.

**Working in Three Dimensions**

4. Enter **Vpoint** ↵ **R** ↵ at the command prompt.

5. At the Enter angle at XY plane prompt, enter **235** ↵; at the next prompt, press ↵.

6. Do another hidden-line removal, and use Mslide again to create a slide called **V2**.

7. Repeat steps 4 through 6, but this time increase by 10 the angle value you entered at step 5 (to **245**). At step 6, increase the slide name by 1 (to **V3**).

8. Keep repeating steps 4 through 6, increasing the angle value by 10 each time and increasing the slide filename by 1. Repeat these steps at least five more times.

9. Use a text editor to create a script file called **Animate.SCR**, containing the following lines, pressing ↵ at the end of each line:

```
Vslide v1
Vslide v2
Vslide v3
Vslide v4
Vslide v5
Vslide v6
Vslide v7
Vslide v8
Rscript
```

10. Return to AutoCAD LT. At the command prompt, enter **Script** ↵ and select Animate.SCR in the Select Script File dialog box. Then click on OK and watch the show.

11. Press Esc or Backspace to end the show.

You might also want to try creating an animation that moves you completely around the unit plan.

Here's another suggestion for experimenting: To practice drawing in 3D, turn the kitchenette of your 3D unit drawing into a 3D object. Make the cooking top 30″ high and add some cabinet doors.

# Chapter 16

# Navigating in 3D Space

## *FAST TRACKS*

N the previous chapter you learned how to generate three-dimensional models in AutoCAD LT. This chapter focuses on the command options available to view and edit your models in 3D space.

## Mastering the User Coordinate System

The User Coordinate System (UCS) allows you to define a coordinate system in 3D space. All the same commands used in 2D drawings can be applied to 3D drawings.

By now you are familiar with the L-shaped icon in the lower-left corner of the AutoCAD LT screen, containing the letters *W*, *X*, and *Y*. The W indicates that you are currently in what AutoCAD LT calls the World Coordinate System (WCS); the X and Y indicate the positive directions of the x- and y-axes. WCS is a global system of reference from which you can define other user coordinate systems.

It may help to think of these AutoCAD LT user coordinate systems as different drawing surfaces, or two-dimensional planes. You can have several user coordinate systems at any given time. By setting up these different UCSs, you are able to draw as you would in the WCS in 2D, yet draw a 3D image. Let's say you want to draw a house in 3D with doors and windows on each of its sides. You can set up a UCS for each of the sides; then you can move from UCS to UCS to add your doors and windows (see Figure 16.1). Within each of these UCSs, you draw your doors and windows as you would in a typical 2D drawing. You can even insert elevation views of doors and windows that you have created in other drawings.

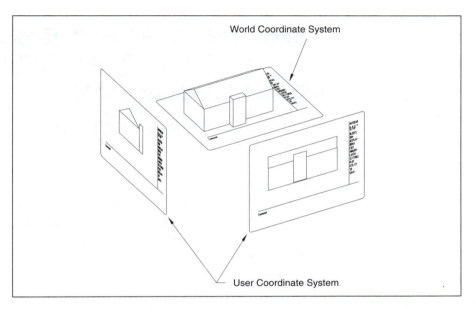

Figure 16.1: **Different user coordinate systems in a 3D drawing**

In this chapter you will be experimenting with a number of different views and UCSs. All of the commands you will use are available both at the command line and also via the AutoCAD LT menus. Additionally, a number of the View and UCS commands can be accessed from the UCS and View toolbars. The first thing to do is to open these toolbars to have access to their buttons.

## Loading the View and UCS Toolbars

To display the View and UCS toolbars, choose View ➤ Toolbars, check the View and UCS checkboxes in the Toolbars list box, and then click on OK. When the toolbars appear on your screen, you may drag them into a convenient location at the side of your screen. Both of these toolbars are also available as flyouts on the Standard toolbar.

**Part 4**

**Working in Three Dimensions**

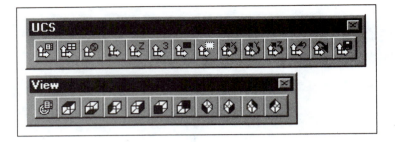

## Defining a UCS

In the first set of exercises, you will draw a chair that you can later add to your 3D Unit drawing. In drawing this chair, you will be exposed to the use of the UCS, as well as to some of the other 3D capabilities available in AutoCAD LT.

Begin the chair by drawing the seat and legs.

1.  Start AutoCAD LT, open a new file, and save it as **Barcelon**.

2.  Set up your drawing as an architectural drawing with a scale of 1″= 1′–0″ on an 8½″×11″ sheet. Then click the Zoom All button on the Zoom flyout on the Standard toolbar.

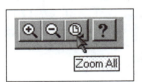

3.  To draw the seat of the chair, click Rectangle on the Draw toolbar. Draw a rectangle measuring 20″ in the x-axis and 30″ in the y-axis. Position the rectangle so the lower-left corner is at the coordinate 2′–0″,2′–0″ (see Figure 16.2). At the First Corner: prompt, type **24,24** ↵. At the Other corner: prompt, type **@20,30** ↵.

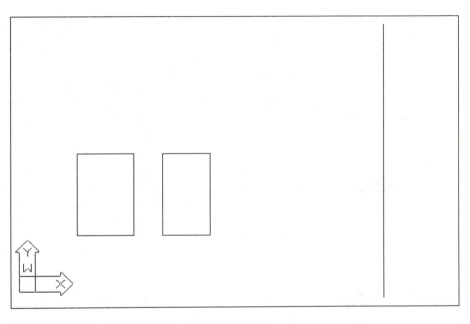

*Figure 16.2:* **The chair seat and back in plan view**

4. To draw the back of the chair, draw another rectangle 17″ in the x-axis and 30″ in the y-axis, just to the right of the previous rectangle (see Figure 16.2). At the First Corner: prompt, type **55,24** ↵. At the Other corner: prompt, type **@17,30** ↵.

5. Create a new layer called Chair, and make it the current layer. Click on the Layers button on the Object Properties toolbar, type **Chair** in the input box, and click on the New button. To make this exercise easier, you should assign a different color to this new layer. Highlight the Chair layer in the list box; click on the Set Color... button, and select Red from the Standard Colors selection bar at the top of the Select Color dialog box. Click on OK twice to return to the drawing editor.

**Part 4**

**Working in Three Dimensions**

6. You are now going to create two *solid* rectangles, using the 2D rectangles as a basis. (Once you have created the 3D solids, you will dispense with the 2D rectangles.) Type **Solid** ↵. As you are prompted for the first, second, third, and fourth points, click on each corner of the first rectangle, and then press ↵. Remember that you do not click in a clockwise or anti-clockwise fashion, but rather in a Z pattern. You can review this process in Chapter 13, if you need to. Once you have created the first solid rectangle, repeat the process for the second one.

TIP   To assist you in selecting the corners, you should turn on the Endpoint Running Osnap. Type **Ddosnap** ↵. Click on the checkbox beside Endpoint and press OK. When you have finished creating the rectangles, you should clear the Endpoint Osnap by opening the dialog box again, and deselecting the Endpoint Osnap.

7. Click on the Properties button on the Object Properties toolbar.

8. At the Select objects: prompt, select the two solids.

9. At the Change Properties dialog box, enter **3** in the Thickness input box and click on OK. This gives the seat and back a thickness of 3″.

10. Click on the SW Isometric button on the View flyout on the Standard toolbar. (See *Chapter 15* if you need to refresh your memory on this command.) This gives you a 3D view from the lower-left of the rectangles.

11. Click on the Zoom Out button on the Standard toolbar to zoom out a bit and give yourself some room to work.

   Notice that the UCS icon appears in the same plane as the current coordinate system. The icon will help you keep track of which coordinate system you are in. If the UCS icon is not showing on your screen, choose Options ➤ UCS Icon ➤ On, or type **Ucsicon** ↵, then **On** ↵ to turn it on.

   Now you can see the chair components as 3D objects. Next, you will define a UCS based on one side of the seat.

1.  Click on the 3 Point UCS button on the UCS toolbar. You may also choose View ➤ Set UCS ➤ 3 Point, or type **UCS** ⏎ **3** ⏎. This option allows you to define a UCS based on three points that you select.

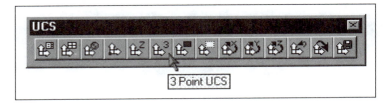

2.  At the Origin point <0,0,0>: prompt, use your cursor and the Endpoint Osnap override to pick the bottom of the lower-left corner of the rectangle representing the seat (see label 1 in Figure 16.3). This now becomes the origin point of your UCS.

3.  At the next prompt:

    ```
    Point on positive portion of the X axis <2′–1″,2′–0″,
    0′–0″>:
    ```

    use your cursor and the Endpoint Osnap override to pick the bottom of the lower-right corner of the rectangle (see label 2 in Figure 16.3). The default value for the prompt in this step, 2′–1″,2′–0″,0′–0″, indicates the positive direction of the x-axis of the current coordinate system.

    **NOTE** The prompts in steps 3 and 4 are asking you for the direction of the x-axis (step 3) and of the y-axis (step 4) in your new UCS.

4.  At the next prompt:

    ```
    Point on positive – Y portion of the UCS X–Y plane
    <2′–0″,2′–0″,2′–1″>:
    ```

    pick the top of the left-hand corner of the rectangle, just above the corner you picked for the origin of the UCS (see label 3 in Figure 16.3). Both the crosshair and the UCS icon align with your new UCS.

Part
4

Working in
Three Dimensions

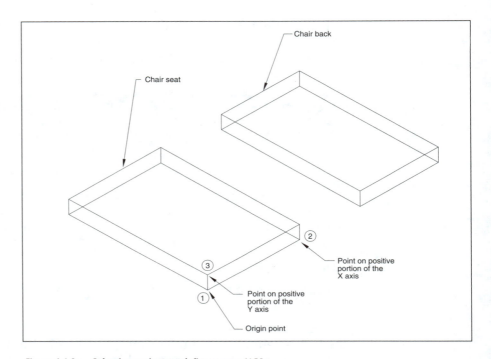

*Figure 16.3:    **Selection points to define a new UCS***

**5.** Now that you have defined a UCS, you may want to save it so that you can return to it in a later editing session. Click on Save UCS from the UCS toolbar or choose View ➤ Set UCS ➤ Save. You can also type **UCS ↵ S ↵**.

**6.** At the ?/Name of UCS: prompt, enter the name **Side**.

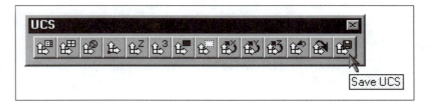

> **NOTE** An alternative way to save a UCS that you have created is as follows: Click on the Named UCS button on the UCS toolbar, or type **Dducs** ↵. In the UCS Control dialog box, highlight the \*No Name\* UCS. In the input box, enter the new name and click on the Rename To button. (You cannot do this with either \*WORLD\* or \*PREVIOUS\*, as these are names reserved for the world coordinate system and the UCS command's Previous option.)

Once you have saved the UCS, you can issue the Named UCS command and make this named UCS the current one whenever you want to return to this UCS. Click on Named UCS button on the UCS toolbar, or type **Dducs** ↵. In the dialog box, click on the name of the UCS you wish to recall. Click on the Current button and then on OK.

## Viewing a UCS in Plan

Next, you will want to arrange the seat and back and draw the legs of the chair. All of this will be easier to accomplish by viewing the chair from the side. To do this, you need to view your newly created UCS as if it were a 2D view. First, save the current 3D view so you can return to it easily later on.

1. Click on Named Views from the View toolbar, or use View ➤ Named Views.... You can also type **Ddview** ↵.

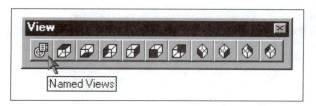

Part
4

Working in
Three Dimensions

The View Control dialog box appears.

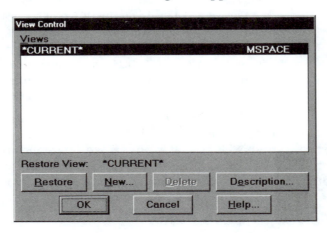

2. Click on the New button to save this view. The Define New View dialog box opens.

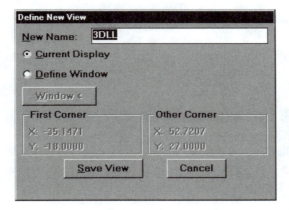

3. Give the new view the name **3DLL**, and then click on the Save View button.

4. Click on OK to return to the drawing.

5.  Click on View ➤ 3D Viewpoint ➤ Plan View ➤ Current. You can also type **Plan** ↵ ↵ to issue the Plan command. The view changes to show the two objects from their sides (see Figure 16.4).

6.  Click on the Zoom Out button on the Standard toolbar to view more of the drawing and to give yourself some room to work.

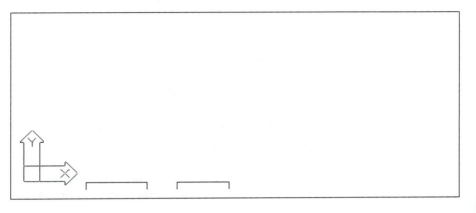

*Figure 16.4:*   **The newly defined UCS in plan view**

## Working in a UCS

You could have given these rectangles a different elevation to lift them off the WCS plane. Instead, you will change their elevation by using the standard Move command while viewing them edge-on. In this exercise you will see how you can use standard editing commands to draw in 3D.

1.  Click on the Move button on the Modify toolbar, or type **Move** (or **M** for short) ↵. Use a crossing window to select the chair seat and back.

2.  Move them vertically in the current UCS y-axis 8.5″, just as you would if you were moving any object in 2D. Your screen should look like Figure 16.5.

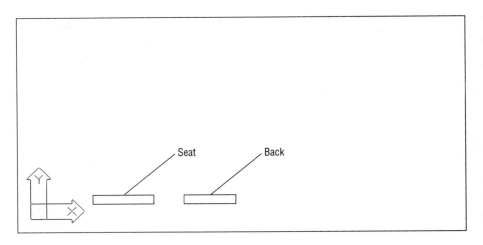

*Figure 16.5:    Elevating the chair seat and back*

Now you need to move the chair seat and back to their proper locations. Grips will make quick work of this operation.

**TIP   If this exercise doesn't seem to be working, check to see if Grips and Noun/Verb Selection are both turned on (see *Chapter 2* if you need help).**

3. Click on the solid rectangle that represents the seat back.

4. Click on the lower-left grip, and then press ↵ twice to get to the ✶✶ ROTATE ✶✶ mode.

5. At the Rotation angle prompt, enter **80** ↵ for a rotation angle of 80°. You can also select a rotation angle visually using your cursor.

6. Click on the same grip again, and this time press ↵ once to get to the ✶✶ MOVE ✶✶ mode.

7. Using the Endpoint Osnap override, click on the upper-right corner of the other solid rectangle to the left, as shown in Figure 16.6.

8. Select both solids; then click on the same grip point that you used previously at the intersection of the two solids.

9. Press ↵ twice to get to ** ROTATE ** mode, and then enter **–10** to rotate both solids –10°. Use Figure 16.6 as a guide.

10. To get a 3D view of the chair to see your progress, click on the Named Views button on the Views toolbar, or choose View ➤ Named Views… to restore the view you saved earlier as 3DLL. Your screen should look like Figure 16.7.

11. You may now remove the 2D rectangles (in layer zero) which were created for construction purposes only. Select both of the rectangles and click on the Erase button on the Standard toolbar.

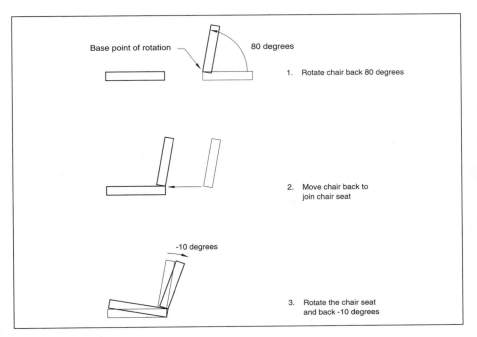

*Figure 16.6:* **Positioning the chair seat and back**

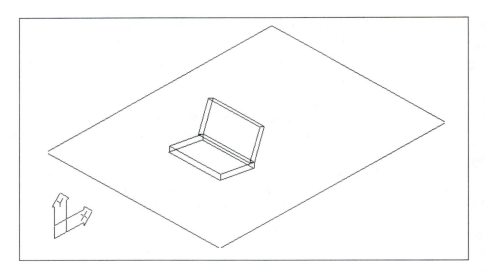

*Figure 16.7:    The 3D view of your drawing so far*

## Controlling the UCS Icon

So far, you have used only the UCS 3 Point option (View ➤ Set UCS ➤ 3 Point) to create an alternative coordinate system. There are several other options available to allow easy creation of and access to the UCS function. In the following section, "Using Viewports to Aid in 3D Drawing," you will want to set the UCS icon to show the current UCS *origin* as well as its *orientation*.

Make sure your view is similar to the one in Figure 16.7, then click on Options ➤ UCS Icon ➤ Origin, or type **Ucsicon** ↵ **OR** ↵. Do this now in your current drawing, and the UCS icon will move to a location below the chair.

Now, whenever a new UCS is defined, the UCS icon will shift its location to show you not only the orientation of the UCS but also its origin. This will be useful in later exercises.

Let's take a moment to look at the options offered by the Ucsicon command.

    **Origin**    (the option you used just above as Options ➤ UCS Icon ➤ Origin) forces the UCS icon to appear at the location of the current UCS's 0,0,0 origin point. If the UCS's origin is off the screen, the UCS icon appears in the screen's lower-left corner.

**On**    controls whether the UCS icon is displayed or not. When this option is checked the icon is displayed; when it is not checked the icon is turned off.

## Using Viewports to Aid in 3D Drawing

In *Chapter 12*, you were introduced to AutoCAD LT's viewports. In this next section, you will use viewports to see your 3D model from several sides at the same time. This is helpful in both creating and editing 3D drawings, since it allows you to refer to different portions of the drawing without having to change views. In *Chapter 12*, you created viewports from Paper Space. This time, you'll create viewports directly in Model Space.

1. Click on View ➤ Tiled Viewports ➤ 3 Viewports.

2. At the `Horizontal/Vertical/Above/Below/Left <Right>:` prompt, press ↵ to accept the default Right option. This causes the right viewport to occupy half the screen, while the left half is divided into two smaller viewports.

   Now you see three of the same images in each viewport. Each viewport can display a different view of your drawing. In step 2, the prompt gives you the option to divide the screen horizontally in three equal viewports (Horizontal) or vertically into three equal viewports (Vertical). Above, Below, and Left each divide the screen into unequally sized viewports, with the option name indicating where the larger of the three viewports is placed.

3. Click on the upper-left viewport to activate it. Then click on View ➤ 3D Viewpoint ➤ Plan View ➤ World, or type **Plan** ↵ **W** ↵. (The W is the World option of the Plan command—it sets your view up as a plan view of the WCS.) The view changes to a plan view of your chair.

4. Use the Zoom command to enlarge your view. Do this by entering **Z** ↵ **.7x** ↵.

5. Activate the lower-left viewport.

6. Click on View ➤ 3D Viewpoint ➤ Plan View ➤ Current to get a plan view of the current UCS. The side view of your chair will appear in this viewport.

7. Enter **Z** ↵ **.7x** ↵ again to allow some room in this view.

8. Pan this view up so you can draw the legs of the chair more easily. (You can use the Real-time Pan option on the Standard toolbar.)

9. Switch to the 3D view on the right and use the Zoom Window option to enlarge it to get a better look at the chair in 3D. You should have a screen similar to Figure 16.8.

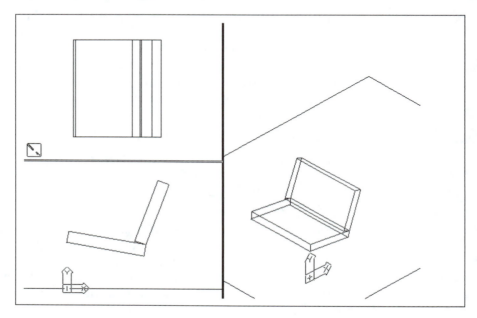

*Figure 16.8:*    **Three viewports, each displaying a different view**

## Adding the Legs

Now let's finish off the chair by adding legs.

**NOTE** Polylines are the best objects to use for 3D, because you can generate complex shapes easily by giving the polylines thickness and width. Using a Spline object will not work, since you cannot give a real Spline a thickness or width.

1. Go to the side view of the chair and draw two curved polylines, as shown in Figure 16.9. At this point, just approximate the curves with several straight polyline segments. You don't have to be absolutely perfect about placing or shaping these lines either.

2. Use the Edit Polyline command (Pedit) to spline-fit them. Click on the Edit Polyline button on the Special Edit flyout on the Modify toolbar, or type **Pedit** ↵. Select the polylines you created. Then type **S** ↵ ↵.

3. Use the control point grips of the spline-fit polylines to adjust their curve, if necessary (see Figure 16.9).

4. Use the Edit Polyline command again to give the polylines a width of 0.5″.

5. Use the Properties button on the Object Properties toolbar to open the Modify polyline dialog box and give the polylines a thickness of –2″. Notice that as you draw and edit a polyline, it appears in both the plan and 3D views.

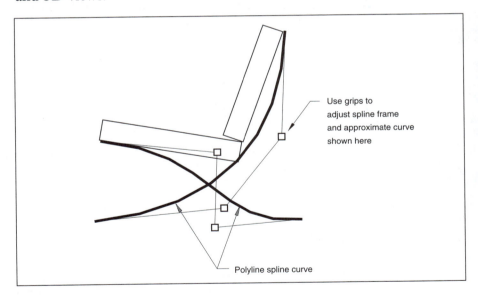

Use grips to adjust spline frame and approximate curve shown here

Polyline spline curve

*Figure 16.9:* **Drawing the legs of the chair**

6. Click on the upper-left viewport to move to the plan view.

**7.** Click on the Named UCS button on the UCS toolbar.

**8.** At the UCS Control dialog box, click on \*WORLD\*, then on the Current button, and finally on OK.

**9.** Toggle the Ortho mode on and Mirror the polylines representing the chair legs to the opposite side of the chair in roughly the same location. Your screen should look similar to Figure 16.10.

> **NOTE** Notice that the broken-pencil UCS icon has shifted to the viewport in the lower-left corner. This icon tells you that the current UCS is perpendicular to the plane of that view.

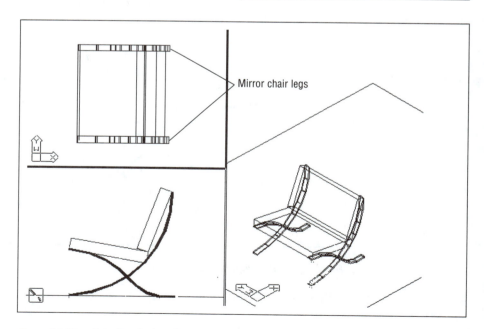

Mirror chair legs

*Figure 16.10:   Copying the legs from one side to another*

Your chair is now complete. Let's finish up by getting a better look at it.

1. Click on the viewport to the right.

2. Type **Hide** ↵ to see what the chair actually looks like when it is viewed as a solid (see Figure 16.11). You can also use View ➤ Hide.

3. Click on View ➤ Tiled Viewports, and choose 1 Viewport in the cascading menu.

4. Click on OK. The 3D view fills the screen in preparation for the next set of exercises.

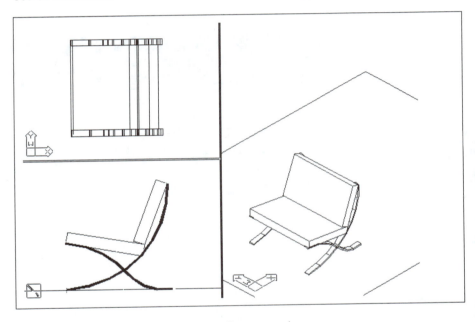

*Figure 16.11:* **The chair in 3D with hidden lines removed**

## Controlling the UCS

There are a number of other ways to define a UCS. In the following set of exercises, you will get some practice moving your UCS around. Learning how to move effortlessly between UCSs is crucial to your mastering the creation of 3D models, so you'll want to pay special attention to the command options shown in these procedures. You'll be using the options of the UCS command (**UCS** ↵). These options are

**Part 4**

**Working in Three Dimensions**

also accessible either via the View ➤ Set UCS cascading menu or the UCS toolbar.

### Orienting a UCS in the View Plan

Before you begin with the exercises, you'll need to define a UCS in the current view plane. To do this, click on the View UCS button on the UCS toolbar or choose View ➤ Set UCS ➤ View. You can also type **UCS** ↵ **V** ↵. The UCS icon changes to show that the UCS is aligned with the current view.

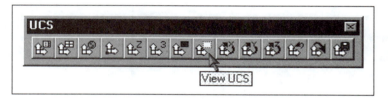

AutoCAD LT uses the current UCS origin point for the origin of the new UCS. By defining a view as a UCS, you can enter text to label your drawing, as you would in a technical illustration. Text entered in a plane created in this way will appear normal (see Figure 16.12).

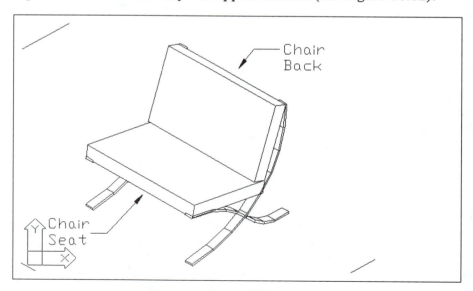

Figure 16.12:   *You can add text to a 3D view using the View option of the UCS command.*

## UCS Based on Object Orientation

You can also define a UCS based on the orientation of an object. This is helpful when you want to work on a predefined object to fill in detail on its surface plane.

1. Click on the Object UCS button on the UCS toolbar, or choose View ➤ Set UCS ➤ Object. You can also type **UCS** ↵ **OB** ↵.

2. At the `Select Objects:` prompt, click on the seat cushion to align the UCS. The UCS icon, indicating the UCS origin, will position itself at the lower-left corner of the seat cushion—the first point selected when creating the solid object.

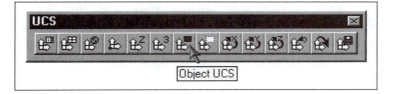

 **NOTE** The origin of the UCS varies with the type of object selected: for Text, Blocks, and Attributes, the insertion point establishes the UCS origin; for Solids, the first point of the solid becomes the UCS origin; for a Line object, the endpoint nearest the pick point becomes the origin; for Arc and Circle objects, the center becomes the origin; and for Dimensions, the midpoint of the dimension text establishes the origin of the UCS.

## UCS Based on an Offset Orientation

There may be times when you want to work in a UCS that has the same orientation as the current UCS but is offset. For example, you may be making a drawing of a building that has several parallel walls offset with a sawtooth effect (see Figure 16.13). You can easily hop from one UCS to another, parallel UCS by using the Origin option.

**Part 4**

**Working in Three Dimensions**

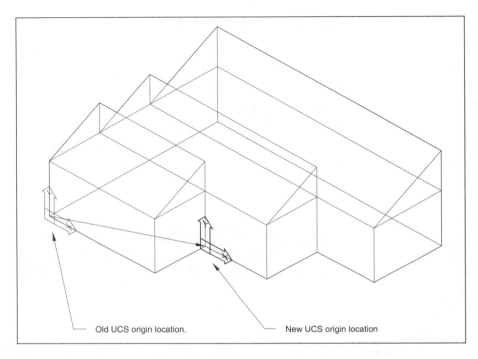

*Figure 16.13:* ***Moving the origin of the UCS***

1. Click on the UCS Origin button on the UCS toolbar, or choose View ➤ Set UCS ➤ Origin. You can also type **UCS** ↵ **O** ↵.

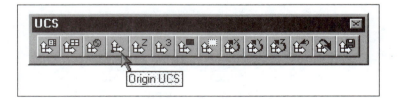

2. At the Origin point <0,0,0>: prompt, pick the bottom end of the chair leg, just below the current UCS origin. The UCS icon shifts to the end of the leg, with its origin at the point you picked (see Figure 16.14).

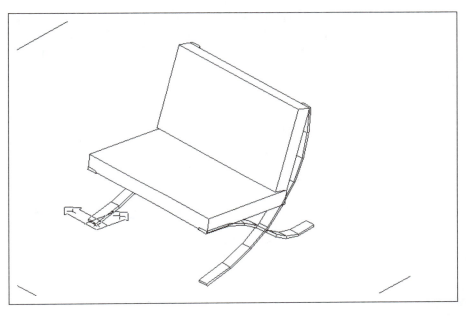

*Figure 16.14:* **Using the Origin option to shift the UCS**

### UCS Rotated Around an Axis

Now suppose you want to change the orientation of the x-, y-, or z-axis of the current UCS. You can accomplish this by using the X, Y, or Z options of the UCS command. Let's try rotating the UCS about the z-axis to see how this works.

1. Click on the Z Axis Rotate UCS button on the UCS toolbar or choose View ➤ Set UCS ➤ Z Axis Rotate. You can also type **UCS** ↵ **Z** ↵. This will allow you to rotate the current UCS about the z-axis.

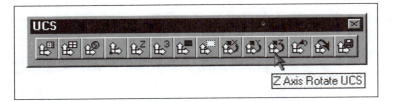

**Part 4**

**Working in Three Dimensions**

**2.** At the Rotation angle about Z axis <0>: prompt, enter **–90** to rotate the UCS 90° clockwise. The UCS icon rotates to reflect the new orientation of the current UCS (see Figure 16.15).

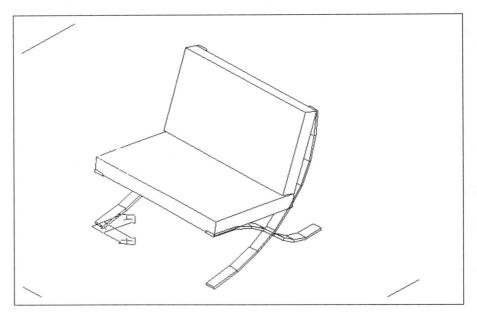

*Figure 16.15:* **Rotating the UCS about the z-axis**

Similarly, the X and Y options allow you to rotate the UCS about the current x- and y-axis, respectively, just as you did for the z-axis just above.

Finally, you can skew the UCS by using the Z Axis Vector option. This is useful when you need to define a UCS based on a z-axis determined by two objects.

**1.** Click on the Z Axis Vector UCS button on the UCS toolbar, or choose View ➤ Set UCS ➤ Z Axis Vector. You can also type **UCS ↵ ZA ↵**.

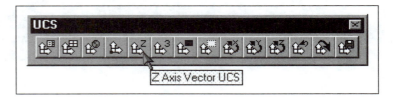

WARNING  Because your cursor location is in the plane of the current UCS, it is best to pick a point on an object using either the Osnap overrides or the coordinate filters.

2. At the Origin point <0,0,0>: prompt, press ⏎ to accept the default, which is the current UCS origin. You can shift the origin point at this prompt if you like.

3. At the next prompt:

   Point on positive portion of Z-axis <0'−0",0'−0",0'−1">:

   use the Endpoint Osnap override and pick the other chair leg end, as shown in Figure 16.16. The UCS twists to reflect the new z-axis of the UCS.

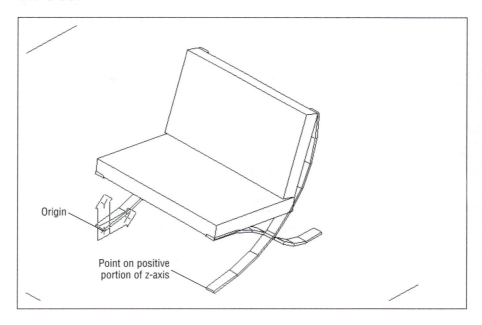

*Figure 16.16:*  **Picking points for the Z-Axis Vector option**

Now we've finished our tour of the UCS command. Set the UCS back to the world coordinate system and save this file.

# True Perspective Views

So far, your views of 3D drawings have been in *parallel projection*. This means parallel lines appear parallel on your screen. Though this type of view is helpful while constructing your drawing, you will want to view your drawing in true perspective from time to time to get a better feel for what your 3D model actually looks like. In the first part of this chapter, you will explore the use of the Dview command (View ➤ 3D Dynamic View), which allows you to see your drawing in *true perspective*.

Using Dynamic view, you can create both parallel projection and true perspective views. In a perspective view, an object is shown smaller or larger as the viewing distance increases or decreases. With dynamic viewing, you can also see the effects of changing your viewpoint on-the-fly, as you actually change the viewpoint. To simplify the view, you may want to remove hidden lines. You can use the Hide command that you learned in *Chapter 15*, or the Hide option on the Dview command.

## Setting Up Your Perspective View

Dview is a complex command, so this chapter's exercises are brief, presenting the use of each Dview option in turn. With this in mind, you may want to begin these exercises when you know you have an hour or so to complete them all at one sitting.

Now let's begin!

1.  The following exercises continue with the Barcelon file. If you did not complete the exercises in the earlier part of this chapter, use the copy of this file supplied on your companion CD. Be sure you are in the world coordinate system, and then issue the Plan command (**Plan ↵**) so you have a plan view of the chair.

2.  Click on Zoom All on the Zoom flyout on the Standard toolbar to get an overall view of the drawing.

3.  Click on View ➤ 3D Dynamic View, or enter **Dview** ↵ at the command prompt.

4.  At the object selection prompt, pick the chair seat and back. You will use these objects as references while using the Dview command.

5.  Next you will see the Dview prompt:

    ```
    CAmera/TArget/Distance/POints/PAn/Zoom/TWist/CLip/Hide/
    Off/Undo/<eXit>:
    ```

    AutoCAD LT uses the analogy of a camera to help determine your perspective view. As with a camera, your perspective view is determined by the distance from the object, camera position, view target, and camera lens type.

    Follow these steps to determine the camera and target positions:

1.  At the Dview prompt, enter **PO** ↵ for the Points option.

2.  At the Enter target point <current point>: prompt, pick the center of the chair seat. This will allow you to adjust the camera target point, which is the point at which the camera is aimed.

3.  At the Enter camera point <current point>: prompt, pick the lower-left corner of the screen. This places the camera location (the position from which you are looking) below and to the left of the chair, on the plane of the WCS (see Figure 16.17).

WARNING   When selecting views in this set of exercises using Dview and its options, be sure you click the Mouse/Pick button as indicated in the text. If you press the ↵ key (or click the ↵ button on the mouse), your view will return to the default orientation, which is usually the last view selected.

Part
4

Working in
Three Dimensions

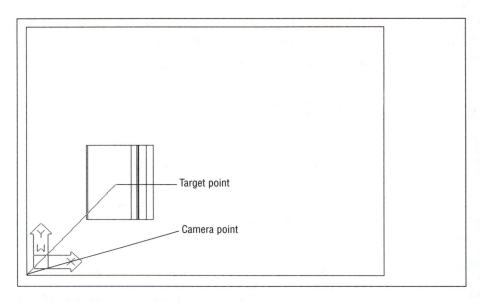

*Figure 16.17:* ***The target and camera points***

Your view now changes to reflect your target and camera locations, as shown in Figure 16.18. The Dview prompt returns, allowing you to further adjust your view.

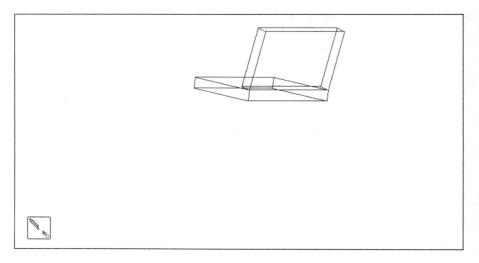

*Figure 16.18:* ***The view with the camera and target positioned***

If you like, you can press ↵ at the object-selection prompt without pick-ing any object, and you will get the default image, a house, to help you set up your view (see Figure 16.19).

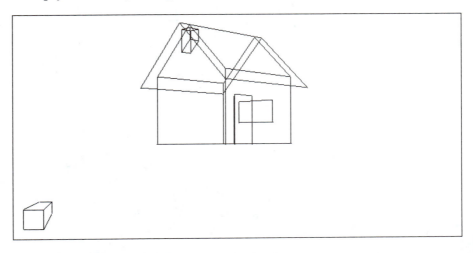

*Figure 16.19:* **The default sample image used with Dview**

## Adjusting Distances

Next, you will adjust the distance between the camera and target.

1. At the DVIEW prompt, enter **D** ↵ for the Distance option. A slide bar appears at the top of the screen.

2. At the New camera/target distance <current distance>: prompt, move your cursor from left to right. The chair appears to enlarge and reduce. You can also see that the position of the diamond in the slide bar moves. The slide bar gives you an idea of the distance between the camera and the target point in relation to the current distance.

3. As you move the diamond, you see lines from the diamond to the 1× value (1× being the current view distance). As you move the cursor toward the 4× mark on the slide bar, the chair appears to move away from you. Move the cursor toward 0×, and the chair appears to move closer.

4. Move the cursor further to the left. As you get to the extreme left, the chair appears to fly off the screen. This is because your camera location has moved so close to the chair that the chair disappears beyond the view of the camera—as if you were sliding the camera along the floor toward the target point. The closer to the chair you are, the larger and farther above you the chair appears to be (see Figure 16.20).

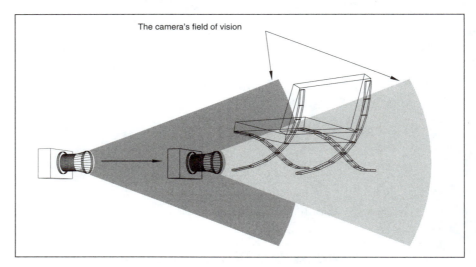

Figure 16.20:    *The camera's field of vision*

 **NOTE** The Distance option actually serves two functions: Aside from allowing you to adjust your camera to target distance, it also turns on the perspective view mode. The Off option of Dview changes the view back to a parallel projection.

5. Adjust your view so it looks like Figure 16.21. To do this, move the diamond to between 1× and 4× in the slide bar.

6. When you have the view you want, click the mouse/pick button. The slide bar disappears and your view is fixed in place. Notice that your UCS icon has changed to the perspective icon.

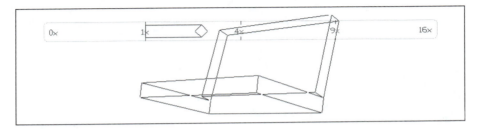

*Figure 16.21:* **The chair and diamond cursor while using the Distance option**

## Adjusting the Camera and Target Positions

Next, you will want to adjust your view so you can see the whole chair. You are still in the Dview command.

1. At the DVIEW prompt, enter **TA** ↵ for the Target option. The chair will temporarily disappear from view.

2. At the prompt

   ```
   Toggle angle in/Enter angle from X-Y plane <.00>:
   ```

   move your cursor very slowly in a side-to-side motion. Keep the cursor centered vertically, or you may not be able to find the chair. The chair moves in the direction of the cursor in an exaggerated manner. The sideways motion of the cursor simulates panning a camera from side to side across a scene (see Figure 16.22).

NOTE Using Dview's Target option is like standing in one location while moving the camera angle around.

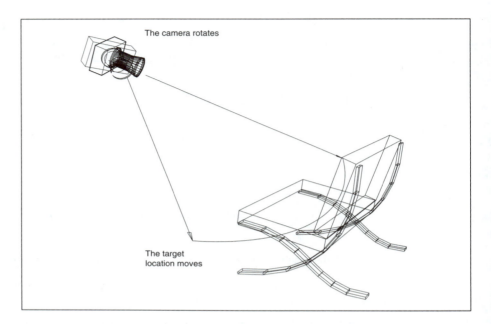

*Figure 16.22:    Adjusting the target option is like panning your camera across a scene.*

3.  Center the chair in your view, and then move the cursor slowly up and down. The chair moves in the opposite direction to the cursor. The up-and-down motion of the cursor simulates panning a camera up and down.

4.  Watch the coordinate readout as you move the cursor up and down. It displays the camera's vertical angle as you move the cursor. Moving the cursor down causes the readout to list increasing negative numbers; moving the cursor up causes the readout to list increasing positive numbers. This coincides with the prompt that asks for an angle from the X-Y plane. If you knew the exact camera angle you wanted from the X-Y plane, you could enter it now.

**TIP** If you lose your view of the chair but remember your camera angle, you can enter it at the `Enter angle in X-Y plane` **prompt to help relocate your view.**

5. When you're ready, enter **T** ↵ to select the Toggle angle option. The prompt changes to

    ```
    Toggle angle from/Enter angle in X-Y plane from X axis
    <current angle>:
    ```

6. Move your cursor from left to right; now the coordinate readout displays the angle of the camera relative to the x-axis of the horizontal (X-Y) plane. As you move the cursor from left to right, the coordinate readout shows the direction the camera is pointing relative to the x-axis. If you knew the exact camera angle you wanted from the x-axis of the X-Y plane, you could enter it now.

7. Position the view of the chair so it looks like Figure 16.23, and click the Mouse/Pick button. You've now fixed the target position.

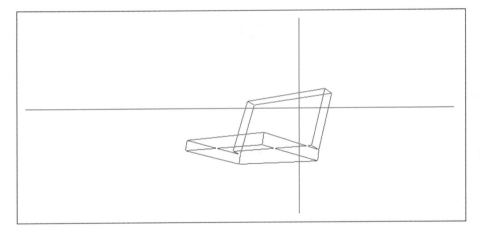

*Figure 16.23:* **While in the Dview Target option, set up your view so it looks like this figure.**

In steps 4 and 6 above, we mentioned that you could enter an angle value indicating either the vertical or horizontal angle to the target. Once you enter that value (or just press ↵), the angle becomes fixed in either the vertical or horizontal direction. Then, as you move your cursor, the view's motion will be restricted to the remaining unfixed direction.

## Changing Your Point of View

Next, you will want to adjust the camera location to one that is higher in elevation.

1.  At the DVIEW prompt, enter **CA** ↵ to select the Camera option.

2.  At the prompt

    ```
    Toggle angle in/Enter angle from XY plane <11>:
    ```

    move your cursor slowly up and down. As you move the cursor up, your view changes as if you were rising above the chair (see Figure 16.24). The coordinate readout displays the camera's angle from the horizontal X-Y plane as you move the cursor.

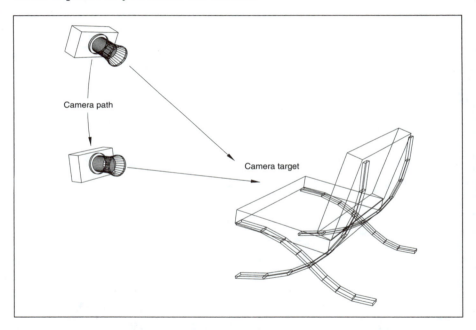

*Figure 16.24:*    *While in the Camera option, moving the cursor up and down is like moving your camera location up and down in an arc.*

3. Move the cursor down so you have a view that is roughly level with the chair, and then move the cursor from side to side. Your view changes as if you were walking around the chair, viewing it from different sides (see Figure 16.25).

**NOTE** Using Dview's Camera option is like changing your view elevation while constantly looking at the chair.

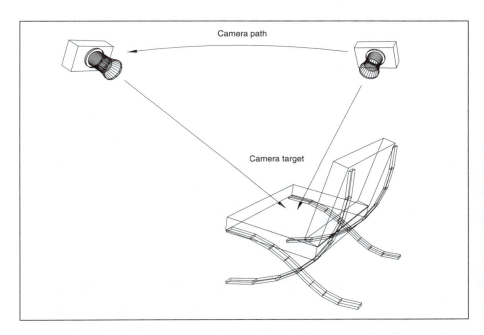

*Figure 16.25:* ***Moving the cursor from side to side is like walking around the target position.***

4. When you are ready, enter **T** ↵ to choose the `Toggle angle in/Enter angle from XY plane` option. This toggles the prompt to:

```
Toggle angle from/Enter angle in XY plane from x axis
<-144>:
```

5. Now when you move the cursor from side to side, the coordinate readout lists the camera's angle to the target point relative to the x-axis.

6.  Position your view of the chair so it is similar to the one in Figure 16.26, and click the mouse/pick button.

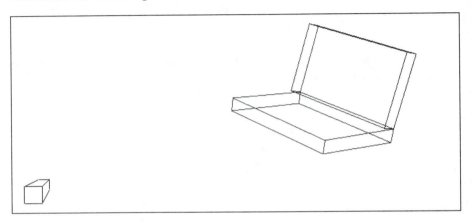

*Figure 16.26:    Set up your camera location so you have a view similar to this one.*

In steps 2 and 5, we mentioned that you could enter an angle value indicating either the vertical or horizontal angle to the camera. Once you indicate a value, either by entering a new one or by pressing ↵, the angle becomes fixed in either the vertical or horizontal direction. Then, as you move your cursor, the view's motion will be restricted to the remaining unfixed direction.

### Using the Zoom Option as a Telephoto Lens

The Zoom option of Dview allows you to adjust your view's cone of vision, much like a telephoto lens in a camera. You can expand your view to include more of your drawing, or narrow the field of vision to focus on a particular object.

1.  At the DVIEW prompt, enter **Z** ↵ for the Zoom option. Move your cursor from side to side, and notice that the chair appears to shrink or expand. You also see a slide bar at the top of the screen, which lets you see your view in relation to the last Zoom setting, indicated by a diamond. You can enter a value for a different focal length, or you can visually select a view using the slide bar.

2.  At the Adjust lenslength <50.000mm>: prompt, press ↵ to accept the 50.000mm default value.

**NOTE** If you don't have a perspective view (obtained by using the Distance option) and you use the Zoom option, you will get the prompt Adjust zoom scale factor <1>: instead of the Adjust lenslength prompt. The Adjust zoom... prompt acts just like the standard Zoom command.

## Twisting the Camera

The Twist option lets you adjust the angle of your view in the view frame—like twisting the camera to make your picture fit diagonally across the frame.

1. At the DVIEW prompt, enter **TW** ↵ for the Twist option. Move your cursor, and notice that a rubber-band line stretches out from the view center; the chair also appears to rotate, and the coordinate readout changes to reflect the twist angle.

2. At the New view twist <0>: prompt, press ↵ to keep the current 0° twist angle.

3. Press ↵ again to exit the Dview command, and the drawing regenerates, showing the chair in perspective (see Figure 16.27).

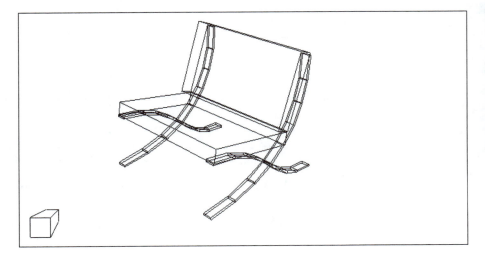

*Figure 16.27:* ***A perspective view of the chair***

In the next section, you will look at one special Dview option—Clip— that lets you control what is included in your 3D views.

## Using Clip Planes to Hide Parts of Your View

At times, you may want a view that would normally be obscured by objects in the foreground. For example, if you try to view the interior of your Unit drawing, the walls closest to the camera obscure your view. The Dview command's Clip option allows you to eliminate objects in either the foreground or the background, so you can control your views more easily. In the case of the apartment unit, you can set the Clip/Front option to delete any walls in the foreground that might obscure your view of its interior (see Figure 16.28).

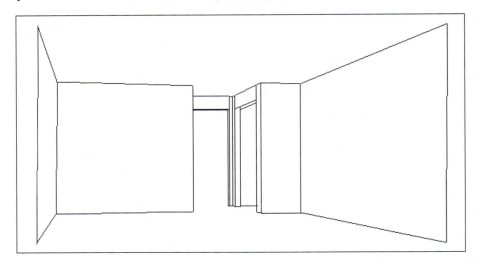

Figure 16.28:    *A view of an apartment unit interior using the Clip/Front plane*

1.  Open the Unit file that you turned into a 3D model (3DUNIT.DWG) in *Chapter 15*, and set up a perspective view using Figure 16.29 as a guide. You can also use the 3DUNIT.DWG file on the companion CD.

2.  Click on View ➤ 3D Dynamic View or enter **Dview** ↵ at the command prompt.

3.  At the Object-selection prompt, select the entire drawing.

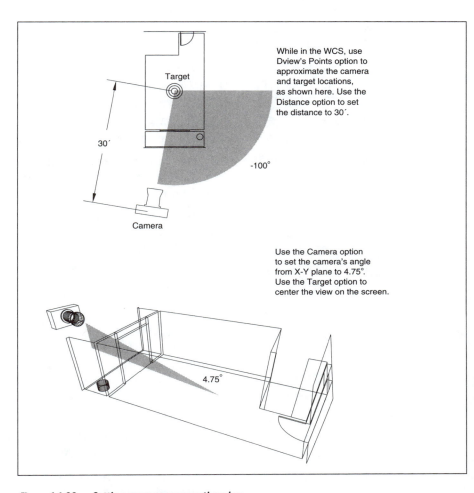

While in the WCS, use Dview's Points option to approximate the camera and target locations, as shown here. Use the Distance option to set the distance to 30´.

Target

30´

-100°

Camera

Use the Camera option to set the camera's angle from X-Y plane to 4.75°. Use the Target option to center the view on the screen.

4.75°

Part
4

Working in
Three Dimensions

*Figure 16.29:* **Setting up your perspective view**

**4.** Using the Points option (**PO** ↵), first place the target at the center of the living room, then place the camera location toward the bottom of the screen at a slight angle, as shown at the top of Figure 16.29. Use the dynamic coordinate readout to help you locate the camera in relation to the target point.

5. Use the Distance option (**D** ↵) and enter **30′** to set the target-to-camera distance accurately.

6. Use the Camera option (**CA** ↵) and enter **4.75** at the Toggle angle in/Enter angle from XY plane <0.0000>: prompt to place the camera angle at 4.75° from the floor.

7. When the Camera option's Toggle angle from/Enter angle in XY plane from X axis: prompt appears, press ↵ to accept the default.

8. Use the Target option (**TA** ↵) to center the room on the screen. Remember to move the cursor slowly to center the view in the screen. When your view looks roughly like Figure 16.28, press the left mouse button.

With this view, the walls between the interior of the unit and the balcony obscure the interior. Next you will learn how to make the wall invisible, using Dview's Clip option.

1. While still in the Dview command, enter **CL** ↵ for the Clip option.

2. At the Back/Front<off>: prompt, enter **F** ↵ for the Front option. A slide bar appears at the top of the screen.

3. As you move the diamond on the slide bar from left to right, the walls in the foreground begin to disappear, starting at the point closest to you. Moving the diamond from right to left brings the walls back into view. You can select a view either by using the slide bar or by entering a distance from the target to the Clip plane.

4. At the Eye/<distance from target>< current distance>: prompt, move the slide bar diamond until your view looks similar to Figure 16.29. Then click the mouse/pick button to fix the view.

5. To make sure the Clip plane is in the correct location, preview your perspective view with hidden lines removed. Enter **H** ↵ at the DVIEW prompt. The drawing regenerates, with hidden lines removed.

There are several other Dview Clip options that let you control the location of the Clip plane. These options are described as follows:

**Eye**   places the Clip plane at the position of the camera itself.

**Back**   operates in the same way as the **Front** option, but it clips the view behind the view target instead of in front (see Figure 16.30).

**Off**   turns off any Clip planes you may have set up.

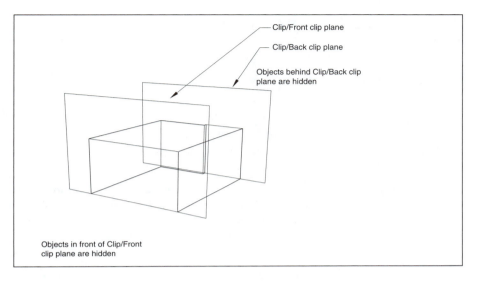

*Figure 16.30:* **Effects of the Clip planes**

You've now completed the Dview command exercises and should have a better understanding of how Dview can be used to get exactly the image you want.

> **TIP** The quickest and easiest way to establish a perspective view is to first use Vpoint (View ➤ 3D Viewpoint ➤ Vector) to set up your 3D view orientation, then start Dview, and use the Distance option right off the bat to set your camera-to-target distance. Once this is done, you can easily use the other Dview options as needed, or exit Dview to see your perspective view.

If you like, you can use View ➤ Named Views to save your perspective views. This is helpful when you want to construct several views of a drawing to play back later as part of a presentation. You can also use the Hide and Shade options on the Tools pull-down menu to help you visualize your model.

# *If You Want to Experiment...*

You've covered a lot of ground in this chapter, so it might be a good idea to play with the commands you've explored here to help you remember what you've learned.

To test what you've learned about Dview, try the following exercise:

1. Make a copy of the Unit plan. Insert several copies of the the Barcelon chair you created earlier in this chapter.

WARNING   When you are using the Insert command, the UCS of the inserted drawing will be made parallel to the current UCS of the current drawing. Also, insertions will use the current elevation setting. So check your current UCS and elevation *before* you use Insert.

2. Once you have inserted the chairs, use the Dview command to create an interior view. Repeat the Dview Clip exercise in "Using Clip Planes to Hide Parts of Your View."

3. Once you have completed the view on screen, save the file as 3DROOM.DWG, and then exit AutoCAD LT.

# Customizing AutoCAD LT

In this last part of the book, you will learn how you can take control of AutoCAD LT. *Chapter 17: Integrating AutoCAD LT into Your Projects and Organization* shows you how you can create toolbars and menus that adapt AutoCAD LT to your own work style.

# Chapter 17

# Integrating AutoCAD LT into Your Projects and Organization

## *FAST TRACKS*

### To create a custom toolbar button 649

*Right-click on any toolbar button to open the Customize Toolbars dialog box. Click on Modify..., then in the Modify Toolbars dialog box, click on Custom on the pull-down list. Click and drag a blank button from the Modify Toolbars dialog box to your toolbar, then right-click on the new blank button. In the Button Properties dialog box, add a name, help comment, and macro. Select an icon from the icon scroll box or click Edit to create a new icon.*

### To pause for input in a menu option 661

*Enter the backslash (\) where you want AutoCAD LT to pause in the command keystroke sequence of your menu item.*

### To create a cascading menu 662

*Start the bracketed label with –>, as in [–>line]. The following lines of the menu group will be part of the cascading menu until AutoCAD LT encounters <– in a menu label.*

### To place dividing lines in a pull-down menu 662

*Insert a label containing double hyphens, as in [––].*

### To create a custom linetype 669

*Enter Linetype ↵ at the command prompt, then C ↵, and then the name for your new linetype. Select the ACLT.LIN file at the dialog box, or enter a name for a new linetype file. Then enter a description for your new linetype. Finally, enter the length of each line segment of your new linetype, including blank lengths, separated by commas. For example, if you enter 1.5,–1.5, you will have a linetype pattern of a line for 1.5 units, and then 1.5 blank units before the next 1.5-unit line segment, and so on.*

**T**HIS latest release of AutoCAD LT offers a high degree of flexibility and customization, allowing you to tailor the software's look and feel to your requirements. In this final chapter, you will examine how AutoCAD LT can be made to fit into your work group and office environment.

The first part of the chapter shows how you can adapt AutoCAD LT to fit your particular needs. You will learn how to customize AutoCAD LT by modifying its toolbars and menus to incorporate commands that your work group uses frequently.

Then we'll examine some general issues surrounding the use of Auto-CAD LT in an office. You may find help with some problems you have encountered when using AutoCAD LT in a work group. We'll also discuss the management of AutoCAD LT projects.

## Customizing Toolbars

The most direct way to adapt AutoCAD LT to your way of working is to customize the toolbars. AutoCAD LT for Windows 95 offers all users an easy route to customization. You can create new toolbars, customize buttons, and even create new icons. In this section, you'll discover how easy it is to add features to AutoCAD LT.

## Turning a Flyout into a Toolbar

No two people will use AutoCAD LT in exactly the same way, so AutoCAD LT has a built-in feature that "remembers" the last button selected from a flyout menu. The theory is that you will use one particular button from a flyout repeatedly. This theory doesn't always work, however. You may in fact find that you frequently use several options from the same flyout. This situation can quickly become bothersome.

The solution is to simply open the flyout as a floating toolbar. In the following example, you'll see how to turn the Arc flyout of the Draw toolbar into a toolbar. Flyouts are actually toolbars that are incorporated into another toolbar. So you can use the same method you used in earlier chapters to load a toolbar.

1. Choose View ➤ Toolbars.... The Toolbars dialog box appears.

2. Place a check in the checkbox beside Arc. The Arc flyout opens as a floating toolbar in the drawing editor.

Now you have ready access to all the different methods for drawing arcs. To close the toolbar, click on the rectangle in the upper-right of the toolbar.

**TIP** For added convenience, you might want to make the Tool Windows toolbar appear as a standard part of the AutoCAD LT screen. The Tool Windows toolbar lets you open all the other main toolbars at a click of a button. To locate and open the Tool Windows toolbar, follow the instructions outlined below.

The only difficulty that you might encounter is in locating some of the flyouts by name. The majority of the toolbars are very clearly named: Arc, Line, Hatch, and so on. A few of the flyout/toolbar names are not quite so intuitive: Special Edit, Feature, and Inquiry, for example.

You can easily familiarize yourself with the few unusual toolbar names. *Special Edit* includes Edit Polyline, Edit Spline, Edit Text, and Edit Hatch. *Feature* includes the Fillet and Chamfer commands. *Inquiry* includes List, Point Location, Distance, and Area. Or you can turn a flyout directly into a floating toolbar—without knowing its name—using the following two-step procedure.

1. Right-click on the flyout button. For example, if you want to turn the Arc flyout into a toolbar, right-click on the Arc button which is currently displayed. The Customize Toolbars dialog box appears, with the parent toolbar name highlighted. For example, if you clicked on one of the Arc buttons, the *Draw* toolbar will be highlighted.

2. Left-click on the same flyout button this time. A copy of the desired flyout appears as a floating toolbar.

You may use either of the above methods (View ➤ Toolbars… or Right-click/Left-click) depending upon your preference or what is most convenient.

### Creating Your Own Toolbar

You may find that instead of using one toolbar or flyout, you are moving from flyout to flyout from a variety of different toolbars. If you keep track of the tools you use most frequently, you can create your own custom toolbar containing your favorite tools. Here's how it's done.

1. Choose Tools ➤ Customize Toolbars… from the menu bar to open the Customize Toolbars dialog box. (You can also right-click on any button in any toolbar to open this dialog box.)

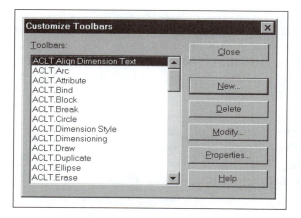

Before we continue, let's review the options in the Customize Toolbars dialog box.

**Close**    closes the dialog box.

**New**    lets you create a new toolbar.

**Delete**   deletes a toolbar from the list.

**Modify...**   opens the Modify Toolbar dialog box, from which you can click and drag predefined buttons.

**Properties...**   opens the Toolbar Properties dialog box. Use this dialog box to review or modify the toolbar name and help line.

**Help**   displays the Autocad LT Help screens for the Customize Toolbars dialog box.

You'll get to use most of these options in the following sections.

2.   Click on the New... button. The New Toolbar dialog box appears.

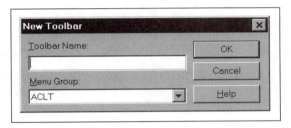

3.   Enter **My Toolbar** in the Toolbar Name input box and then click on OK. A blank toolbar appears in the AutoCAD LT window. The "toolbar" is only one button wide at this point. Drag it to a convenient location on the AutoCAD LT window.

Notice that ACLT.My Toolbar now appears in the Customize Toolbars dialog box list. You can now begin to add buttons to your toolbar.

4.   Click on Modify... from the Customize Toolbars dialog box. The Modify Toolbar dialog box appears.

**Part 5**

**Customizing AutoCAD LT**

5. Click on the arrow to open the Categories pull-down list. Notice that the list contains the main categories of commands.

6. Choose Draw from the list. The list box displays all the Icon buttons available for the Draw category. The buttons on the top line of the list are *flyouts* (indicated by the small triangle). From the second line of the list are the *individual buttons* that issue the single commands.

7. Click and drag the Circle *flyout* button on the top line from the Modify Toolbars dialog box, and drop it onto the new toolbar you created in step 3. The button now appears in your toolbar. If you click on it, the full set of circle options is displayed.

8. Click and drag the Line button on the second line onto your new toolbar. This time you have added only the Line command button, not the Line flyout. Now click on Close to exit the Modify Toolbar dialog box, and then again to close the Customize Toolbars dialog box.

You now have a custom toolbar with two buttons. You can add buttons from different categories if you like. You are not restricted to buttons from one category.

Typically, AutoCAD LT stores new toolbars and buttons in the ACLT.MNS file (see the sidebar entitled "The AutoCAD LT Menu Files"). AutoCAD LT will treat your custom toolbar just like any other toolbar. It will appear when you start AutoCAD LT and will remain on the screen until you close it. You can recall it at any time using View ➤ Toolbars....

NOTE As you are dragging and dropping buttons from the Modify Toolbars dialog box onto your custom toolbar, you may accidentally release one onto the drawing editor. A new toolbar will automatically be created, entitled "Toolbar 1." Simply closing this toolbar does not remove it. You should return to the Customize Toolbars dialog box and use the Delete button to remove ACLT.Toolbar 1.

## Customizing Buttons

Now let's move on to some more serious customization. Suppose you want to create an entirely new button with its own functions. For example, you may want to create a set of buttons that will insert your favorite symbols. Or you might want to create a special toolbar containing a set of buttons that opens some of the existing flyouts as toolbars.

### Creating a Custom Button

In the following set of exercises, you'll create a button that inserts a door symbol, and then add your custom button to the toolbar you just created.

1. Open the Customize Toolbars dialog box again, then click on Modify....

2. Select Custom from the Categories pull-down list. The list box now shows two blank buttons, one for a single command and another for flyouts (the one for flyouts has a small triangle in the lower-right corner).

3. Click and drag the single command blank button to your new toolbar.

4. Right-click on the blank button on your new toolbar. The Button Properties dialog box appears.

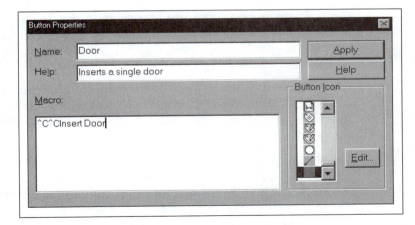

5. This dialog box lets you define the purpose of your custom button.

Let's pause for a moment to look at this dialog box. The Name input box lets you enter a name for your button. This name will appear as a tool tip. You must enter a name before AutoCAD LT will create the new button definition.

The Help input box just below the name lets you add a help message. This message will appear in the status bar in the lower-left corner of the AutoCAD LT window when you point to your button.

The Macro area is the focus of this dialog box. Here, you can enter the keystrokes you want to "play back" when you click on this button.

Finally, to the right, you see a scroll bar that lets you scroll through a set of icons. You can also see a button labeled Edit. When you highlight an icon in the scroll box, then click on Edit, an Icon editor tool appears allowing you to edit an existing icon, or create a new icon.

Now let's go ahead and add a macro and new icon to this button.

1. In the Name input box, enter **Door**. This will be your tool tip for this button.

2. In the Help input box, enter **Inserts a single door**. This will be the Help message for this button.

3. In the Macro input box, enter **^c^cinsert door**.

   Note that the two ^c's already appear in the Macro input box. These represent two Cancels being issued. This is the same as pressing the Escape key twice. It ensures that when the macro starts, it cancels any unfinished commands.

   You follow the two cancels with the Insert command as it is issued from the keyboard. If you need help finding the keyboard equivalent of a command, consult *Appendix E*, which contains a list of all the command names.

   After the Insert command, there is a space. A space, or a semi-colon, is used to indicate a ⏎. The name door follows the ⏎. This is the same sequence of keystrokes you would enter at the command line to insert the door drawing you created in *Chapters 2* and *3*. You could go on to include an insertion point, scale factor, and rotation angle in this macro, but these options are better left for the time when the door is actually inserted.

You can put any valid string of keystrokes in the Macro input box, including DIESEL (Direct Interpretively Evaluated String Expression Language) functions. See "Using DIESEL Macro Language in Custom Menus" later in this chapter for more information. You can also include pauses for user input using the backslash (\) character. See "Pausing for User Input" later in this chapter.

**WARNING** It is important that you enter the exact sequence of keystrokes that follow the command, otherwise your macro may get out of step with the command prompts. This will take a little practice and some going back and forth between testing your button and editing the macro.

### Creating a Custom Icon

You have all the essential parts of the button defined. Now you just need to add an icon to go with your door button. If you prefer, you can use any of the predefined icons in the scroll box. Just click on the icon you want to use, then click on Apply. To create your own custom icon, follow the procedure below.

1. In the Icon scroll box, scroll down the list until you see a blank icon.

2. Click on the blank icon, then click on the Edit button. The Button Editor appears.

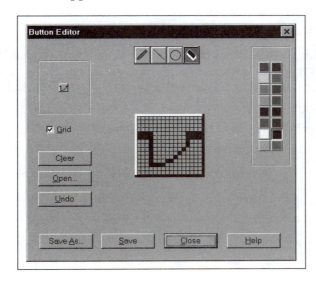

Part
5

Customizing
AutoCAD LT

The button editor is like a very simple paint program. Across the top are the tools to draw lines, circles, and points, as well as an eraser. Along the right side, you see a color toolbar from which you can choose colors for your icon button. In the upper-left, you see a preview of your button. The following describes the rest of the options.

**Grid** turns a grid on and off in the drawing area. This grid can be an aid in drawing your icon.

**Clear** erases the entire contents of the drawing area.

**Open** opens a .BMP file to import an icon. The .BMP file must be small enough to fit in the 16 by 16 pixel matrix provided for icons (24 by 24 for large format icons).

**Undo** lets you undo the previous step.

**Save As...** saves your icon as a .BMP file under a name you enter.

**Save** saves your icon. If you have not named your icon at this point, it will be saved as ICON.BMP.

**Close** exits the Button Editor.

**Help** displays helpful information about the features of the Button Editor.

Now let's continue by creating a new icon.

3. Draw the door icon shown here. Don't worry if its not perfect. You can always go back and fix it.

4. Click on Save, then Close the Button Editor.

5. In the Button Properties dialog box, click on Apply. You'll see the icon appear in the button in your toolbar. Click on the X in the upper-right of the dialog box to close the Button Properties dialog box.

6. Now click on the Close button on the Customize Toolbars dialog box.

7. Click on the Door button of your new toolbar. The door appears in your drawing ready to be placed.

For the button macro to work, the Door drawing must be in the Auto-CAD LT default directory, or in a specified support directory before the door button will be inserted. (To specify additional support directories, choose Tools ➤ Preferences... ➤ File System ➤ Support Dirs.)

You can continue to add more buttons to your toolbar to build a toolbar of symbols. Of course, you're not limited to a symbols library. You can also incorporate the macros you accumulate as you work with AutoCAD LT.

### Adjusting the Properties of Flyouts

Just as you added a custom button to your toolbar, you can also customize flyouts. Remember that a flyout is really just a toolbar that is attached to another toolbar. When you created your custom toolbar (My Toolbar), you added a copy of the Circle flyout to it. This next example shows how you can make adjustments to the properties of the flyout.

1.  Right-click twice on the Circle flyout button on your custom toolbar. First the Customize Toolbars then the Flyout Properties dialog box appears.

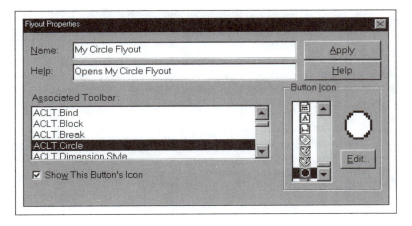

Notice how this dialog box resembles the Button Properties dialog box you used in the previous exercise. But instead of the Macro input box, you see a list of button toolbars, with ACLT.Circle highlighted.

2. Enter **My Circle Flyout** in the Name input box. Enter **Opens My Circle flyout** in the Help input box. The simple circle icon in the icon scroll box is highlighted.

3. Click on the check box labeled Show This Button's Icon so that a check mark appears in the box.

4. Click on Apply. The flyout button in the My Toolbar toolbar shows the icon you selected.

5. Close the Flyout Properties and the Customize Toolbars dialog boxes, then place the arrow cursor on the flyout to display its tool tip. Notice that your new tool tip and help message appear.

6. Click and drag the circle icon, then select Donut from the flyout and draw a Donut. Notice that even though you selected donut, the circle icon remains as the top icon for the flyout.

Step 6 demonstrates that you have disabled the feature that causes the last flyout to appear as the default on the toolbar. You disabled this feature in step 3 by checking the Show This Button's Icon check box.

TIP To delete a button from a toolbar, right-click on the button to open the Customize Toolbars dialog box, then click on Modify.... When the Modify Toolbars dialog box appears, click and drag the button you want to delete out of the toolbar and into the drawing area.

### Modifying Existing Button Properties

If you want to modify an existing button or flyout, you can go directly to either the Button Properties or the Flyout Properties dialog box by double right-clicking on the button you want to modify. Once one of these dialog boxes is open, you can make changes to any component of the button definition.

## THE AUTOCAD LT MENU FILES

As you create and modify icon buttons and toolbars, you may have noticed the message `Compiling menu file…` appearing briefly in the status line at the bottom of the AutoCAD LT window. The message is telling you that AutoCAD LT is updating the menu files. AutoCAD LT uses several menu files to maintain the button and menu definitions.

**ACLT.MNU** is the menu template file that contains the information required to build the original AutoCAD LT menu. Most users don't need to edit this file.

**ACLT.MNS** is the source menu file. It contains the information used to create the ACLT.MNC and ACLT.MNR files.

**ACLT.MNC** is the compiled menu file. AutoCAD LT translates or "compiles" the ACLT.MNS file so that it can read the menu faster.

**ACLT.MNR** is the menu resource file. It is a binary file that contains the bitmap images used for buttons and other graphics.

As you create or edit icon buttons and toolbars, AutoCAD LT first adds your custom items to the ACLT.MNS file. It then compiles this file into the ACLT.MNC and ACLT.MNR files for quicker access to the menus.

The new menu and toolbar information should not be added to the ACLT.MNU file. Custom *partial menus* should be created, which will operate alongside the *base menu*. If at any time you are dissatisfied with the results of your customization, and wish to return to the original AutoCAD LT menus, you can delete the .MNS, .MNC, and .MNR files. Exit from the program. AutoCAD LT will then automatically recreate these menu files from the original .MNU file when you reopen the program. Or you can unload and then reload the ACLT.MNU via the Menu Customization dialog box (Tools ➤ Customize Menus). Remember to insert all of the menus (starting with Help and ending with File) into the right-hand side of the Menu Bar tab after you reload.

## Adding Your Own Pull-down Menu

In addition to adding buttons and toolbars, AutoCAD LT lets you add pull-down menu options. This section looks at how you might add a custom pull-down menu. There is a fair amount of trial-and-error in getting menu options to work. You may wish to make backup copies of the .MNS, .MNC, and .MNR files before you start. You can restore these copies later, if your custom menu gets into trouble. Alternatively, you can restore the original .MNU file as a last resort (see the sidebar "The AutoCAD LT Menu Files").

## Creating Your First Pull-down Menu

The reason that you create new menus is to increase your productivity—you can combine the steps of a complex task into a single menu option. Let's start by trying the following exercise to create a simple pull-down menu file called My Menu:

1. Using a text editor, like the Windows 95 Notepad, create a file called **Mymenu.MNU**, containing the following lines:

```
***POP1
[My 1st Menu]
[Line]^c^c_line
[-]
[->More]
[Arc-3Pt]^c^c_arc \
[<-Rotate 90]Rotate single \@;90;
***POP2
[My 2nd Menu]
[door]^c^cInsert door
[Continue Line]^C^CLINE;;
```

 **WARNING** Pay special attention to the spaces between words and letters in the commands in this exercise and elsewhere in this chapter. A space in menu syntax is equivalent to a carriage return (↵). You need not worry much about whether to type upper- or lowercase letters.

2. Save this file, and be sure you place it in your AutoCAD LT directory.

Once you've stored the file, you've got your first custom pull-down menu. You may have noticed some familiar items among the lines you entered. The menu contains the Line and Arc commands.

Now let's see how My Menu works in AutoCAD LT.

## Loading a Menu

In the following exercise, you will load the menu you have just created and test it out. The procedure described here for loading menus is the same for all menus, regardless of their source.

1.  Click on Tools ➤ Customize Menus.... The Menu Customization dialog box appears.

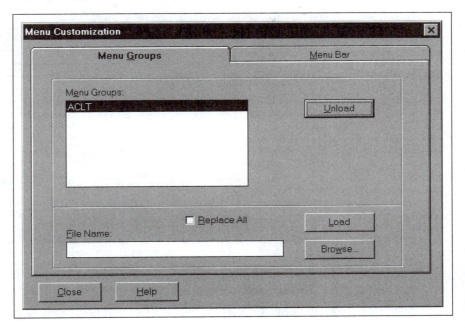

2.  Click on Browse at the bottom of the dialog box. The Select Menu file dialog box appears.

3.  Locate the Mymenu.MNU file, highlight it, then click on the Open button. The dialog box closes and you see the name of the file in the File Name input box of the Menu Customization dialog box.

4.  Click on Load. The Mymenu.MNU filename appears in the list box. You can ignore the warning message about overwriting existing customization, since this is the first time that you have loaded Mymenu.MNU. Also, it will not overwrite any customization within the ACLT menu files (see the sidebar entitled "The AutoCAD LT Menus").

5. Highlight Mymenu.MNU in the list box, then click on the tab at the top of the dialog box labeled Menu Bar. The dialog box switches to the Menu Bar tab, which displays two lists.

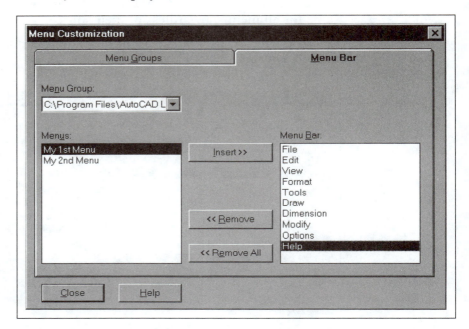

On the left is a list of the menus available in your Mymenu file. The list on the right shows the currently loaded pull-down menus.

6. Highlight Help in the right hand column. This tells AutoCAD LT you want to add your pull-down in front of the Help pull-down.

7. Highlight My 1st Menu from the list on the left, then click on the button labeled Insert >>. My 1st Menu moves into the right hand column and it appears in the AutoCAD LT menu bar between Options and Help (see Figure 17.1).

*Figure 17.1:* **The My 1st Menu menu**

8. Highlight Help on the right-hand list again, highlight My 2nd Menu from the list on the left, then click on Insert >> again. My 2nd Menu is copied to the right-hand column, and it too appears in the menu bar (see Figure 17.1).

9. Close the Menu Customization dialog box.

10. Draw some objects on the screen, then try the My 1st Menu ➤ More ➤ Rotate 90 option (see Figure 17.2).

*Figure 17.2:* **The My 1st Menu cascading menu**

## How the Pull-down Menu Works

With just an 11-line menu file, you created a menu that contains many of the tools used to build menus. Now let's take a more detailed look at the menu syntax, or how menu files work. In this next section, we will review each of the syntax options used in this exercise, and further develop our menus. Table 17.1 contains a list of the special characters used to build a menu.

### Menu Titles and Labels

Let's take a closer look at the Mymenu.MNU file. The first item in the file, ★★★POP1, identifies the beginning of a pull-down menu. The item just below this is the phrase "My 1st Menu" in square brackets. This is the *title* of the pull-down menu; it is what appears in the menu bar. Every pull-down menu must have this title element.

Following the title, each item on the list starts with a word enclosed in brackets; these words are the options, or *labels*, that actually appear when you open the pull-down menu. The text that follows the label tells AutoCAD LT what to do when the menu option is selected.

Finally, in the Mymenu sample, you see ★★★POP2. This is the beginning of a second pull-down menu. Again, you must follow this with a pull-down menu title in square brackets. Below the title, you can add other menu options.

Table 17.1: **Menu Syntax Reference: Special menu characters**

| Character | Description |
|---|---|
| ★★★ | Indicates section title |
| ★★ | Indicates submenu section label or alias |
| [...] | Encloses a label |
| ; | Issues a carriage return |
| SPACE | Issues a carriage return |
| \ | Pauses for user input |
| _ | Translates AutoCAD LT commands and keywords |
| + | Continues menu macro to the next line (if last character) |
| =★ | Displays the current image tile, pull-down, or cursor menu |
| ★^C^C | Indicates a prefix for a repeating item |
| $ | Indicates a special character code to load a menu section or introduce a conditional DIESEL macro expression ($M=) |
| ^B | Turns Snap mode on/off (CTRL+B) |
| ^D | Turns coordinates on/off (CTRL+D) |
| ^E | Sets the next isometric plane (CTRL+E) |
| ^G | Turns Grid mode on/off (CTRL+G) |
| ^H | Issues a backspace |
| ^O | Turns ORTHO mode on/off (CTRL+L) |
| ^P | Turns menu echoing on/off |
| ^V | Changes current viewport (CTRL+R) |
| ^Z | Indicates null character; suppresses the automatic addition of SPACEBAR at the end of a menu item |

## Calling Commands

Now look at the Line option in the Mymenu.MNU listing. The two Ctrl-C (^C) elements that follow the square brackets will cancel any command that is currently operative. The Line command follows, written just as it would be entered via the command line. Two Cancels are issued in case you are in a command that has two levels, such as the Edit Vertex option of the Pedit command (Modify ➤ Edit Polyline ➤ Edit Vertex).

The underline that precedes the Line command tells AutoCAD LT that you are using the English-language version of this command. This feature allows non-English versions of AutoCAD LT to use custom menus by translating the English-language command to the appropriate commands in their versions.

You may also notice that there is no space between the second ^C and the New command. A space in the line would be interpreted as a ↵. If there were a space between these two elements, a ↵ would be entered between the last Ctrl-C and the New command, causing the command sequence to misstep.

Another way to indicate a ↵ is by using the semicolon, as in the example that follows. When you have many ↵s in a menu macro, using semicolons instead of spaces can help make your macro more readable.

```
[Continue Line]^C^CLINE;;
```

In this sample menu option, the Line command is issued, and then an additional ↵ is added. The two semicolons (or carriage returns) following the word Line tell AutoCAD LT to continue the line from the endpoint of the last line entered. AutoCAD LT automatically inserts a single ↵ at the end of a menu line. If you want two ↵s, they should be entered as semicolons. It is less desirable to enter two *spaces* at the end of a menu line: spaces are not visible when you are checking your menu code, and some text editors do not allow trailing blanks.

## Pausing for User Input

Another symbol used in the menu file is the backslash (\\), used when a pause is required for user input. For example, when you selected the Arc-3Pt option in My Menu, it started the Arc command and then paused for your input.

**Part 5**

**Customizing AutoCAD LT**

```
[Arc-3Pt]^c^c_arc \
```

The space between ^c^c_arc and the backslash (\) represents the pressing of the ↵. The backslash indicates a pause to allow the AutoCAD LT user to select the three points for the arc.

### Creating a Cascading Menu

Look at the More option in the File pull-down menu group; it starts with these characters: −>. This is the way you indicate a menu item that opens a cascading menu. Everything that follows the [−>More] menu item will appear in the cascading menu. To indicate the end of the cascading menu, you use the characters <−, as in the [<−Rotate 90] menu item farther down. Anything beyond this <− item appears in the main part of the menu.

### Placing Division Lines in Pull-down Menus

Compare My 1st Menu and My 2nd Menu by clicking on the menu titles in turn. (Do not actually click on any of the options.) Both menus have two options, but on My 1st Menu the options are separated by a horizontal line.

Look at your menu code. The *double-hyphen* symbol (−−) on the fourth line of your menu is used to place dividing lines between options in pull-down menus. You may add a [−−] line between [Door] and [Continue Line] if you would prefer a dividing line in My 2nd Menu.

**NOTE** If you make any changes to a menu, you will have to unload and then reload the .MNU file for the changes to be implemented in the current drawing session.

### Creating a Menu Group

It is a good practice, especially if you are doing extensive customization, to create a menu group for your custom menus. If, for example, you develop different menus to match different project automation requirements, this will give you additional flexibilty in loading the custom menu set for a given project.

To give your pull-down menu file a menu group name, add the following line at the top of the file:

```
***MENUGROUP=MYMENU
```

where *MYMENU* is the name you want for your menu group name.

Having a named menu group has two additional advantages:

▶ You will be able to associate custom toolbars with your menu group. When you create a new toolbar, you have the option in the New Toolbar dialog box to select a menu group other than the ACLT menu group. Your new toolbar will be loaded whenever your custom menu is loaded.

▶ A separate menu group helps AutoCAD LT isolate your file and its help messages from other menus that might be loaded along with yours.

### Adding Help Messages to Pull-down Menu Items

Earlier in this chapter, you learned how to include a help message with an Icon button. The help message appears in the status bar of the AutoCAD LT window when you highlight an option. You can also include a help message with a pull-down menu item. Here's how.

You will have to add an ID name to each menu item that requires a help message. The following shows a sample of how this might be done for the My 1st Menu example you used earlier:

```
***MENUGROUP=MYMENU

***POP1

[My 1st Menu]

ID_1line    [Line]^c^c_line

[--]

[->More]

ID_1Arc-3Pt [Arc-3Pt]^c^c_arc \

ID_1Rot90   [<-Rotate 90]Rotate single \@;90;
```

The ID name starts with the characters ID followed by an underline, and then the name for the menu item. Several spaces are added so that the menu items align for clarity. Each menu item must have a unique ID name.

Finally, you add a section at the end of your file called ***HELP-STRINGS. For this example, it would look like this:

```
***HELPSTRINGS

ID_1line      [Draws a line]

ID_1Arc-3Pt   [Draws an arc with 3 Points]

ID_1Rot90     [Rotates an object 90 degrees]
```

The menu item ID names are duplicated exactly, followed by several spaces, and then the actual text you want to have appear in the status line enclosed in brackets. The spaces between the ID and the text are for clarity.

Once you've done this, and then loaded the menu file, you will see these same messages appear in the status bar when these menu options are highlighted. In fact, if you browse your ACLT.MNU file, you will see similar ID names. If you prefer, you can use numbers in place of names.

## Using DIESEL Macro Language in Custom Menus

So far, you have used only command keystroke sequences for your menu items. You can also include DIESEL string expressions in menu files to expand the repertoire of your menus. DIESEL (Direct Interpretively Evaluated String Expression Language) is a macro language. DIESEL macros can pass string values to AutoCAD LT commands that request information. They can also pass data values to the menu, and cause changes to the menu itself.

DIESEL is not a complete programming language, but it performs basic arithmetic functions and "if statements." A summary of the DIESEL string functions is presented in Table 17.2. For further information on any of these functions, consult the Catalog of DIESEL String Functions in the AutoCAD LT Online Help.

*Table 17.2:* **DIESEL Functions**

| Function | Description | Usage example |
| --- | --- | --- |
| + | addition | $(+, value1, value2) |
| - | subtraction | $(-, value1, value2) |
| * | multiplication | $(*, value1, value2) |
| / | division | $(/, value1, value2) |
| = | equal to | $(=, value1, value2) |
| < | less than | $(< , value1, value2) |
| > | greater than | $(>, value1, value2) |
| != | not equal to | $(!=, value1, value2) |
| <= | less than or equal to | $(<=, value1, value2) |
| >= | greater than or equal to | $(>=, value1, value2) |
| and | logical and | $(and, value1, value2) |
| angtos | convert angle to string | $(angtos, value, mode, precision) |
| edtime | date and time string | $(edtime, time, picture) |
| eq | test equal strings | $(eq, value1, value2) |
| eval | evaluate diesel string | $(eval, string) |
| fix | convert decimal to integer | $(fix, value) |
| getenv | get environment value | $(getenv, variable-name) |
| getvar | get system variable | $(getvar, system-variable) |
| if | conditional expression | $(if, expression, action-if-true, action-if-not) |
| index | value of nth element in string | $(index, number, comma-delimited-string) |
| linelen | length of status line | $(linelen) |
| nth | nth value in a series | $(nth, number, list-arguments) |
| or | logical or | $(or, value1, value2) |
| rtos | convert decimal to string | $(rtos, value, mode, precision) |
| strlen | length of string | $(strlen, string) |
| substr | extract part of string | $(substr, string, start-position, length) |
| upper | convert string to upper case | $(upper, string) |
| xor | logical xor | $(xor, value1, value2) |

**Part 5**

**Customizing AutoCAD LT**

When you include a DIESEL macro in a menu item, it must be preceded by $M=. A dollar sign ($) on its own instructs AutoCAD LT to load a menu section. The $M= command instructs a menu item to get information from a DIESEL macro. If you were to include the DIESEL getvar function in a menu item, for example, the function call plus string would be as follows:

```
$M=$(getvar, system-variable)
```

Let's use one of these DIESEL strings in your custom menu.

1. Open Mymenu.MNU using the Windows 95 Notepad.

2. At the bottom of My 2nd Menu add the following line:

```
[Current Layer]*^c^cchprop;single;\la;$M=$(getvar,
clayer);;
```

This menu item enables you to change selected objects (one at a time) to the current layer.

**\*** The asterisk allows the command to repeat indefinitely (see Table 14.1), so you can continue selecting objects and changing them to the current layer. Press Esc to terminate the command.

**^c^cchprop;** cancels any previous commands and then issues the Change Properties command, followed by ↵.

**single;** allows the user to select only one object to change.

**\la;$M=** pauses for input, selects **LA**yer to change, and then calls the DIESEL macro, which supplies the current layer value to the command.

You can easily add two further menu items based on the one you have just created.

1. Copy the above menu line twice more in your menu file, and edit it as shown below.

```
[Current Linetype]*^c^cchprop;single;\lt;$M=$(getvar,
celtype);;

[Current Color]*^c^cchprop;single;\c;$M=$(getvar,
cecolor);;
```

Now, in short measure, you have three menu items which enable you to change any object in your drawing to the current layer, linetype, or color.

2. If you want to add dividing lines between your menu items, add [−−} between each item in My 2nd Menu, then save your .MNU file.

3. Return to AutoCAD LT and unload and then reload Mymenu.MNU so that these changes will take effect.

# Creating Custom Linetypes and Hatch Patterns

As your drawing needs expand, you may find that the standard linetypes and hatch patterns are not adequate for your application. Fortunately, you can create your own. This section explains how to go about creating custom linetypes and hatch patterns.

## Viewing Available Linetypes

AutoCAD LT provides the standard linetypes most commonly used in drafting. These were reviewed in Chapter 4, Table 4.14. It also supplies a library of ISO linetypes and a few complex linetypes, which are reviewed below. You may find that the dashes and dots are not spaced the way you would like, or that you want an entirely new linetype.

You can create a custom linetype in either of two ways:

▶ You can edit (or copy then edit) an existing linetype file. This is the easier method.

▶ Or you can use the Linetype command and create a linetype and linetype file from scratch.

To understand how either of these methods works, let's take a look at a typical linetype file. AutoCAD LT stores the standard linetypes in a file called ACLT.LIN, in ASCII format. In this exercise, we will open and review the ACLT.LIN file.

1. Open the Windows 95 Explorer, and locate the ACLT.LIN file in your AutoCAD LT directory.

2. Double-click on the ACLT.LIN file. Windows 95 Notepad will load and open the file. You will see the listing shown in Figure 17.3.

A linetype definition is a two-line definition: the first line gives the name of the linetype, followed by a text description and/or a graphic representation; the second line contains the actual numerical definition, which describes the line segments, points, and blanks which make up the linetype.

```
Standard AutoCAD Line Types

*BORDER,__ __ . __ __ . __ __ . __ __ . __ __ .
A,.5,-.25,.5,-.25,0,-.25
*BORDER2,__ . __ . __ . __ . __ . __ . __ . __ .
A,.25,-.125,.25,-.125,0,-.125
*BORDERX2,____ . ____ ____ . ____ ____ .
A,1.0,-.5,1.0,-.5,0,-.5
*CENTER,____ _ ____ _ ____ _ ____ _ ____ _
A,1.25,-.25,.25,-.25
*CENTER2,___ _ ___ _ ___ _ ___ _ ___ _
A,.75,-.125,.125,-.125
*CENTERX2,_____ __ _____ __ _____ __
A,2.5,-.5,.5,-.5
*DASHDOT,__ . __ . __ . __ . __ . __ . __ .
A,.5,-.25,0,-.25
*DASHDOT2,_._._._._._._._._._._._._._._._._.
A,.25,-.125,0,-.125
*DASHDOTX2,____ . ____ . ____ . ____ . ____ .
A,1.0,-.5,0,-.5
*DASHED,__ __ __ __ __ __ __ __ __ __ __
A,.5,-.25
*DASHED2,_ _ _ _ _ _ _ _ _ _ _ _ _ _ _ _ _
A,.25,-.125
*DASHEDX2,____ ____ ____ ____ ____ ____
A,1.0,-.5
*DIVIDE,__ . . __ . . __ . . __ . . __ . .
A,.5,-.25,0,-.25,0,-.25
*DIVIDE2,_ . . _ . . _ . . _ . . _ . . _ . . _ .

A,.25,-.125,0,-.125,0,-.125
*DIVIDEX2,____ . . ____ . . ____ . .
A,1.0,-.5,0,-.5,0,-.5
*DOT,. . . . . . . . . . . . . . . . . . . . .
A,0,-.25
*DOT2,.......................................
A,0,-.125
*DOTX2,. . . . . . . . . . . . . . .
A,0,-.5
*HIDDEN,__ __ __ __ __ __ __ __ __ __ __ __
A,.25,-.125
*HIDDEN2,_ _ _ _ _ _ _ _ _ _ _ _ _ _ _ _ _
A,.125,-.0625
*HIDDENX2,____ ____ ____ ____ ____ ____
A,.5,-.25
*PHANTOM,_____ __ __ _____ __ __
A,1.25,-.25,.25,-.25,.25,-.25
*PHANTOM2,____ _ _ ____ _ _ ____ _ _ ____

A,.625,-.125,.125,-.125,.125,-.125
*PHANTOMX2,_____ ____ ____ _____
A,2.5,-.5,.5,-.5,.5,-.5


Iso Line Types

; dashed line
*ACAD_ISO02W100,__ __ __ __ __ __ __ __ __ __ __
A,12,-3
; dashed space line
*ACAD_ISO03W100,__   __   __   __   __   __   __
A,12,-18
; long dashed dotted line
*ACAD_ISO04W100,____ . ____ . ____ . ____ . ____ .
A,24,-3,.5,-3
; long dashed double dotted line
*ACAD_ISO05W100,____ .. ____ .. ____ .. ____ ..
A,24,-3,.5,-3,.5,-3
; long dashed triplicate dotted line
*ACAD_ISO06W100,____ ... ____ ... ____ ... ____
A,24,-3,.5,-3,.5,-3,.5,-3
; dotted line
*ACAD_ISO07W100,. . . . . . . . . . . . . . . . . .
A,.5,-3
; long dashed short dashed line
*ACAD_ISO08W100,____ __ ____ __ ____ __ ____ __
A,24,-3,6,-3
; long dashed double-short-dashed line
*ACAD_ISO09W100,____ __ __ ____ __ __ ____ __ __
A,24,-3,6,-3,6,-3
; dashed dotted line
*ACAD_ISO10W100,__ . __ . __ . __ . __ . __ . __ .
A,12,-3,.5,-3
; double-dashed dotted line
*ACAD_ISO11W100,__ __ . __ __ . __ __ . __ __ .
A,12,-3,12,-3,.5,-3
; dashed double-dotted line
*ACAD_ISO12W100,__ . . __ . . __ . . __ . . __ . .
A,12,-3,.5,-3,.5,-3
; double-dashed double-dotted line
*ACAD_ISO13W100,__ __ . . __ __ . . __ __ . . __ __
A,12,-3,12,-3,.5,-3,.5,-3
; dashed triplicate-dotted line
*ACAD_ISO14W100,__ . . . __ . . . __ . . . __ . . .
A,12,-3,.5,-3,.5,-3,.5,-3
; double-dashed triplicate-dotted line
*ACAD_ISO15W100,__ __ . . . __ __ . . . __ __ . . .
A,12,-3,12,-3,.5,-3,.5,-3,.5,-3
```

Figure 17.3:  *A listing of standard linetypes; the lines in the figure were generated with the underline key and the period, and are only rough representations of the actual lines.*

3. If you scroll down the ACLT.LIN file to the ISO Linetypes (see the lower panel of Figure 17.3), you will notice that a third descriptive line has been added to each entry. This is not a part of the actual definition, but a comment which has been added later.

4. Exit the Notepad, and return to AutoCAD LT.

**WARNING** If you accidentally leave the ACLT.LIN file open in the Notepad, and then return to AutoCAD LT and try to edit it, AutoCAD LT will create a lock file (ACLT.LIK) and deny you access to the .LIN file. If this happens, exit Notepad, open the Windows 95 Explorer, and delete the .LIK file in your AutoCAD LT directory. Or you can choose File ➤ Management ➤ Unlock Files... as described in *Chapter 14*.

### Creating a New Linetype

Next, try creating a new linetype.

1. Enter **Linetype** ↵ at the command line.

2. At the ?/Create/Load/Set: prompt, enter **C** ↵.

3. At the Name of linetype to create: prompt, enter **Custom** ↵ as the name of your new linetype.

   Notice that the file dialog box you see next is named Create or Append Linetype File. If you pick the default linetype file, ACLT.LIN, your new linetype will be added to that file. If you choose to create a new linetype file, AutoCAD LT will open a file containing the linetype you create and add .LIN to the filename you supply.

4. To start a new linetype file, enter **Newline** in the File Name input box, and click on OK.

**NOTE** If you had chosen the default linetype file, ACLT, the prompt in step 5 would read Wait, checking if linetype already defined.... This protects you from inadvertently overwriting an existing linetype you may want to keep.

5. At the `Creating new file… Descriptive text:` prompt, enter the name of your linetype, and a text description of it. You can use any keyboard character as part of your description, but the actual linetype can be composed only of a series of lines, points, and blank spaces. For this exercise, enter

   `Custom - My own center line` _____ _ _____ ↵

   using the underline key to simulate the appearance of your line.

6. At the `Enter pattern (on next line):` prompt, enter the following numbers (after the A that appears automatically):

   `1.0,-.125,.25,-.125` ↵

7. At the `New definition written to file. ?/Create/Load/Set:` prompt, press ↵ to exit the Linetype command.

   Remember, once you've created a linetype, you must load it in order to use it. Type **Linetype** ↵, **L** ↵ and enter the name of the linetype you require. This is discussed in more detail in the "Assigning Linetypes to Layers" section of *Chapter 4*.

## Setting the Current Linetype Default

The Set option of the Linetype command allows you to set the new linetype as the current default. This will override any layer settings.

▶ If the linetype is a standard AutoCAD LT linetype, and is stored in ACLT.LIN, you can use the Set option to simultaneously load and set the linetype as current. Type **Linetype** ↵, **S** ↵ and enter the name of the new linetype, followed by ↵. The new linetype will immediately appear in the Linetype Control window on the Object Properties toolbar.

▶ If the linetype is stored in a custom linetype file (as in the exercise above), then you must first load it, using the Linetype command. Type **Linetype** ↵, **L** ↵, and enter the name of the new linetype, followed by ↵. When the Select Linetype dialog box opens, select the .LIN file that contains the required linetype, (for example Newline.LIN), and press OK. You may now use the S option of the Linetype command (see above) to set the linetype. Or simply type ↵ to end the Linetype command, and set the linetype by clicking on its name in the Linetype Control list box on the Object Properties toolbar.

### The Linetype Code

In step 6 of the previous exercise, you entered a series of numbers separated by commas. This is the linetype code, representing the different lengths of the components that make up the linetype. The separate elements of the linetype code are explained as follows:

► The 1.0 following the *A* defines the length of the first part of the line: one unit. (The *A* that begins the linetype definition is a code that is applied to all linetypes.)

► The first –.125 is the short blank or broken part of the line. The minus sign tells AutoCAD LT that the line is *not* to be drawn for the specified length, which is 0.125 units in this example.

► Next comes the positive value of 0.25. This tells AutoCAD LT to draw a short line segment 0.25 units long after the blank part of the line.

► Finally, the last negative value, –.125, again tells AutoCAD LT to skip drawing the line for the distance of 0.125 units.

This short series of numbers represents a simple segment that is repeated to form the line (see Figure 17.4). You would need to define a much longer series to create a very complex linetype like the random broken line shown in Figure 17.5.

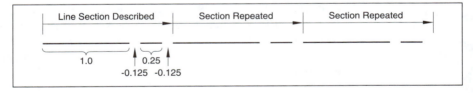

*Figure 17.4:* **Linetype description with plotted line**

*Figure 17.5:* **Random broken line**

**Part 5**

**Customizing AutoCAD LT**

You may be wondering what purpose the *A* serves at the beginning of the linetype code. A linetype is composed of a series of line segments and points. The *A*, which is supplied by AutoCAD LT automatically, is a code that forces the linetype to start and end on a line segment rather than a blank space in the series of lines. At times, AutoCAD LT stretches the last line segment to force this condition, as shown in Figure 17.6.

*Figure 17.6:* **AutoCAD LT stretches the beginning and end of the line as necessary**

As mentioned in the beginning of this section, you can also create linetypes outside AutoCAD LT by using a word processor or text editor such as Windows 95 Notepad. If you need a new linetype, open the ACLT.LIN file, choose a linetype close to the one you need, make a copy of it (you can copy it to the clipboard and then into another linetype file, if required), and then edit it as needed.

### Creating Complex Linetypes

A complex linetype is one that incorporates text or special graphics. AutoCAD LT comes with a sample set of complex linetypes. These are the top seven linetypes shown in Figure 17.7. A more extensive library of complex linetypes is provided on the companion CD. Installation and use of the library of linetypes is described in *Appendix C*.

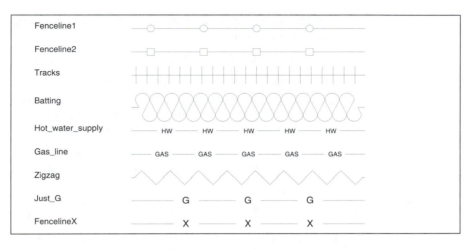

*Figure 17.7:* **Samples of complex linetypes**

In this section, we will create the extra two linetypes shown in Figure 17.7. You might prefer to show an underground gas line with an intermittent *G*, as shown in Figure 17.7, rather than with GAS spelled out. Fences are often shown with an intermittent *X*. Let's go ahead and build both of these lines.

For the graphics needed to compose complex linetypes, you can use any of the symbols found in the AutoCAD LT font files shown in *Chapter 8*. Just create a text style using these symbols fonts, and then specify the appropriate symbol by using its corresponding letter in the linetype description.

To create a linetype that includes text, follow the same syntax for creating a new linetype as shown in the previous section, and add the necessary font file information in brackets. You cannot add complex linetype coding at the command line. You must add it to an existing .LIN file. For example, say you want to create the linetype for the underground gas line mentioned above. You would add the following to your ACLT.LIN file:

```
*Gas line — G — G —
a,1.0,−0.25,["G", standard, S=.2, R=0, X=−.1, Y=−.1],−0.25
```

The information in the square brackets describes the characteristics of the text. The text that you want to appear in the line is surrounded by quotes. Next come the text style, scale, rotation angle, x displacement, and y displacement.

You can substitute the rotation angle (the R value) with an A, as in the following example:

```
a,1.0,-0.25,["G", standard, S=.2 A=0, X=.1, Y=.1],-0.25
```

This keeps the text at the same angle, regardless of the line's direction. Notice that in this sample, the X and Y values are a −.1; this will center the Gs on the line. The scale value of .2 will cause the text to be .2 units high, so the −.1 is half the height.

Now that you have created the linetype with "G," you can simply copy the linetype definition in the ACLT.LIN file, and edit it to look like this:

```
*Fence line — X — X —
a,1.0,-0.25,["X", standard, S=.2, R=0, X=-.1, Y=-.1],-0.25
```

In addition to fonts, you can also specify shapes for linetype definitions. Instead of letters, shapes display symbols. Shapes are stored not as drawings, but as definition files, similar to text-font files. In fact, shape files have the same .SHX extension as text and are defined similarly. In AutoCAD LT, although you cannot *create* shape files, you can use *existing shape files* to create complex linetypes. All of the shape files used in the sample linetypes shown in Figure 17.7 are supplied in a file called LTYPESHP.SHX in your AutoCAD LT directory. They are: CIRC1, BOX, TRACK, BAT, and ZIG.

To use a shape in a linetype code, you use the same format as shown previously for text; instead of using a letter and style name, however, you use the shape name and the shape filename, as in the following example:

```
*Boxline, ====
a,1.0,-0.25,[BOX,LTYPESHP.SHX,S=.2,R=0,X=-.1,Y=-.1],-0.25
```

This example uses the Box symbol from the LTYPESHP.SHX shape file. The symbol is scaled to .2 units with 0 rotation and an X and Y displacement of −1.

## Creating Hatch Patterns

AutoCAD LT provides several predefined hatch patterns you can choose from (see Figure 17.8), but you can also create your own. This section demonstrates the basic elements of pattern definition.

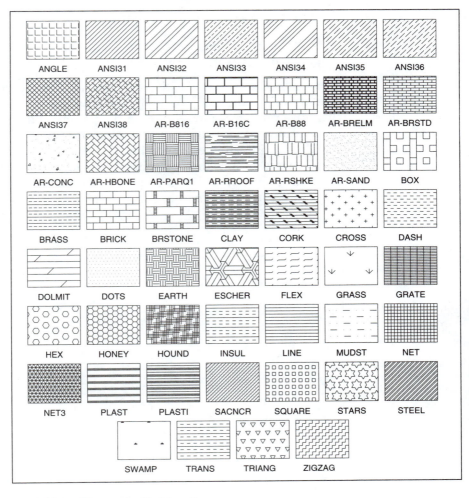

*Figure 17.8:* **The standard hatch patterns**

Unlike linetypes, hatch patterns cannot be created while you are in an AutoCAD LT file. The pattern definitions are contained in an external file named ACLT.PAT. This file can be opened and edited with a text editor that can handle ASCII files, like the Windows 95 Notepad. Here is one hatch pattern definition from that file:

```
*square,Small aligned squares
0, 0,0, 0,.125, .125,-.125
90, 0,0, 0,.125, .125,-.125
```

You can see some similarities between pattern descriptions and line-type descriptions. They both start with a line of descriptive text, and then give numeric values defining the pattern. The numbers in pattern descriptions have a different meaning, however. This example shows two lines of information. Each line represents a line in the pattern. The first line determines the horizontal line component and the second line represents the vertical component of the pattern. Figure 17.9 shows the hatch pattern defined in the example.

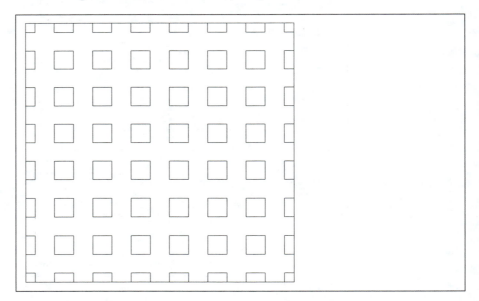

Figure 17.9: *Square pattern*

A pattern is made up of *line groups*. A line group is like a linetype that is arrayed a specified distance to fill the area to be hatched. A line group is defined by a line of code, much as a linetype is defined. In the square pattern, for instance, two lines—one horizontal and one vertical—are used. Each of these lines is duplicated in a fashion that makes the lines appear as boxes when they are combined. Figure 17.10 illustrates this point.

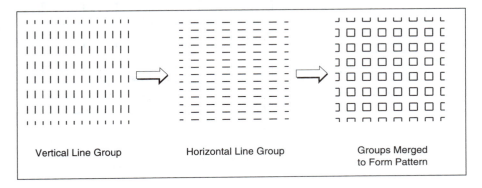

Vertical Line Group    Horizontal Line Group    Groups Merged to Form Pattern

*Figure 17.10:* **The individual and combined line groups**

Look at the first line in the definition:

    0, 0,0, 0,.125,  .125,-.125

This example shows a series of numbers separated by commas, and it represents one line group. It actually contains four sets of information, separated by blank spaces:

---

NOTE **If you have forgotten the numeric values for the various directions, refer back to Figure 2.4 in** *Chapter 2*, **which shows AutoCAD LT's system for specifying angles.**

---

▶ The first component is the 0 at the beginning. This value indicates the angle of the line group, as determined by the line's orientation. In this case it is 0 for a horizontal line that runs from left to right.

▶ The next component is the origin of the line group, 0,0. This does not mean that the line actually begins at the drawing origin (see Figure 17.11). It gives you a reference point to determine the location of other line groups involved in generating the pattern.

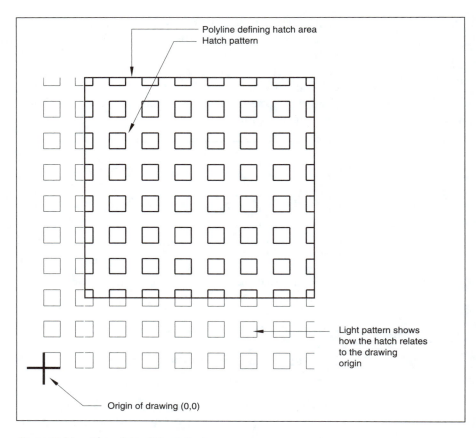

*Figure 17.11:*  **The origin of the patterns**

▶   The next component is 0,.125. This determines the distance for arraying the line and in what direction, as illustrated in Figure 17.12. This
value is like a relative coordinate indicating x and y distances for a rectangular array. It is not based on the drawing coordinates, but on a coordinate system relative to the orientation of the line. For a line oriented
at a 0° angle, the code 0,.125 indicates a precisely vertical direction. For
a line oriented at a 45° angle, the code 0,.125 represents a 135° direction. In this example, the duplication occurs 90° in relation to the line
group, because the x value is 0. Figure 17.13 illustrates this point.

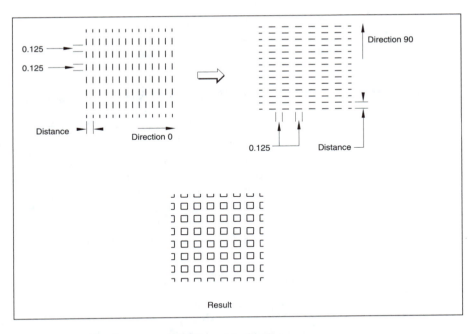

*Figure 17.12:* **The distance and direction of duplication**

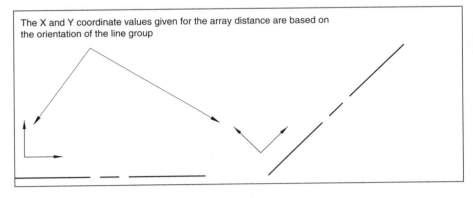

*Figure 17.13:* **How the direction of the line group copy is determined**

▶ The last component is the actual description of the line pattern. This value is equivalent to the value given when you create a linetype. Positive values are line segments, and negative values are blank segments. This part of the line group definition works exactly as in the linetype definitions you studied in the previous section.

This system of defining hatch patterns may seem somewhat limiting, but you can actually do a lot with it. Autodesk managed to come up with 53 patterns—and that was really only scratching the surface.

# Supporting Your System and Working in Groups

So far in this book you have worked with AutoCAD LT as an individual learning a program. However, you are usually not alone when you use AutoCAD LT on a project. Your success with AutoCAD LT may depend as much on the people you work with as on your knowledge of the program. In the last half of this chapter, we'll look at some of the issues you may face as a member of an interactive group: selecting a system and obtaining support for it, what happens once that system arrives in the office, and some ways you can manage your system.

## Getting Outside Support

It helps to have knowledgeable people to consult when questions arise. Most often, the vendor who sells the CAD system is also the source for technical support. Another source is the independent CAD consultant. And don't overlook colleagues who have had some solid experience with AutoCAD LT. Most likely, you will tap all three of these sources at one point or another as you start to implement an AutoCAD LT system in your work.

It can be difficult to find a vendor who understands your special needs. This is because the vendor must have specialized knowledge of computers as well as design or production. A good vendor should offer training and phone support, both of which are crucial to productive use of a program with as much complexity as AutoCAD LT. Some vendors even offer user groups as a means of maintaining active and open communication with their clients. Here are some further suggestions:

▶ Find an independent consultant who is familiar with AutoCAD LT. Although it may be harder to find a good CAD consultant than to find a good vendor, the consultant's view of your needs is unbiased by the motivation to make a sale. The consultant's main goal is to help you gain productivity from your CAD system, so he or she will be more helpful in these areas than your average vendor.

▶ Get references before you use anyone's services. Your own colleagues may be the best source of information on vendors, consultants, and even hardware. You can learn from their good fortune or mistakes.

▶ Don't rely on magazine reviews and product demonstrations at shows. These can often be misleading or offer incomplete information. If you see something you like, test it before you buy it. For some products this may be difficult, but because of the complex nature of computer-aided design and drafting, it is important to know exactly what you are getting.

## Choosing In-House Experts

Perhaps even more important than a good vendor is an individual within your office who knows your CAD system thoroughly. Ideally, everyone closely involved in your drafting and design projects should be a proficient AutoCAD LT user, but it is impractical to expect everyone to give time to system management. Usually one individual is chosen for this task. It can often be a thankless one, but when the going gets rough, an in-house expert is indispensable.

In a smaller office, the in-house authority may need to be an expert on design, production, and computers, all rolled into one. The point is that to really take advantage of AutoCAD LT or any CAD system, you should provide some in-house expertise. AutoCAD LT is a powerful tool, but that power is wasted if you don't take advantage of it.

If you find that a task can be automated, a knowledgeable in-house person can create custom macros and commands on the spot, saving your design or production staff hundreds of work hours—especially if several people are performing that task. Your in-house authority can also train new personnel and answer users' questions. You must be aware, however, that the role of the in-house expert will require significant time spent away from other tasks. Dealing with questions about the program's use can be disruptive to the expert's own work, and writing custom applications is often at least a part-time job in itself. Keep this under consideration when scheduling work or managing costs on a project. It also pays to keep the following in mind:

▶ The in-house expert should be a professional trained in your firm's field of specialization, rather than someone with a computer background. Every architect or engineer on your staff represents years of training. Learning AutoCAD LT can take a matter of weeks or months.

**Part 5**

**Customizing AutoCAD LT**

The expert-to-be, however, should be willing to develop some computer expertise.

▶ Running a CAD system is not a simple clerical task. It takes not only clear thinking and good organizational skills, but good communication skills as well. The in-house authority should have some interest in teaching, and the ability to be patient when dealing with interruptions and "stupid" questions. He or she may well be a manager and will need access to the same information as any key player on your design team.

▶ If you have several computers, you may also want to obtain some general technical support. Especially if your company is implementing its first computer environment, many questions will arise that are not directly related to AutoCAD LT. The technical support person will be able to answer highly technical questions for which a computer background is required more so than familiarity with your professional specialty.

▶ Consider contracting with an outside consultant to occasionally provide additional support. This will allow development of custom applications without waiting for your staff to develop the necessary skills. A consultant can also help train your staff and even fill in from time to time when production schedules become too tight.

## Acclimatizing the Staff

Once an AutoCAD LT system is installed and operational, the next step is to get the staff acquainted with that system. This can be the most difficult task of all. In nearly every office, there is at least one key person who resists the use of computers. This can be a tremendous obstacle, especially if that individual is at management level—though nearly anyone who is resisting the project goals can do damage. The human capacity to undermine the sincerest efforts is astounding, and when coupled with a complex computer system, the results can be disastrous. Unfortunately, there is no easy solution to this problem aside from fostering a positive attitude toward the CAD system's capabilities and its implementation.

AutoCAD LT has a way of adding force to everything you do, both good and bad. Because it is capable of reproducing work rapidly, it is very easy to unintentionally multiply errors until they are actually out of hand. This also holds true for project management. Poor management tends to be magnified when AutoCAD LT comes into the picture. You are managing yet another dimension of information—blocks, symbols, and layers. If the users cannot manage and communicate this information, problems are sure to arise.

On the other hand, a smoothly running, well-organized project is reflective of the way AutoCAD LT enhances your productivity. In fact, good management is essential for realizing productivity gains with AutoCAD LT. A project on AutoCAD LT is only as good as the information you provide and the manner in which the system is administered. Open communication and good record keeping are essential to the development and integrity of a design or a set of drawings. The better managed a project is, the fewer problems arise, and the less time is required to get results.

Discussing CAD management procedures in your project kickoff meetings will help get people accustomed to the idea of using the system. Exchanging information with your consultants concerning your CAD system standards is also an important step in keeping a job running smoothly from the start, especially if they are also using AutoCAD LT.

## *Learning the System*

Learning AutoCAD LT can be time consuming. If you are the one who is to operate the AutoCAD LT system, at first you won't be as productive as you were when you were doing everything manually, and don't expect to perform miracles overnight. Once you have a good working knowledge of the program, you still have to integrate it into your day-to-day work. It will take you a month or two, depending on how much time you spend studying AutoCAD LT, to get to a point where you are entering drawings with any proficiency. It also helps to have a real project you can work on while you are in training. Choose a job that doesn't have a tight schedule, so that if anything goes wrong you have enough time to make corrections.

Remember that it is important to communicate to others what they can expect from you. Otherwise, you may find yourself in an awkward position because you haven't produced the results that someone anticipated.

## Managing an AutoCAD LT Project

If you are managing a project that is to be put on AutoCAD LT, be sure you understand what it can and can't do. If your expectations are unreasonable, or if you don't communicate your requirements to the design or production team, friction and problems may occur. Open and clear communication is of the utmost importance, especially when using AutoCAD LT or any CAD program in a workgroup environment. Here are some further points to consider:

▶   If your office is just beginning to use AutoCAD LT, be sure you allow time for staff training. Generally, an individual can become independent on the program after 24 to 36 hours of training. ("Independent" means able to produce drawings without having to constantly refer to a manual or call in the trainer.) This book should provide enough guidance to accomplish this level of skill.

▶   Once at the point of independence, most individuals will take another month or so to reach a work rate comparable to hand drafting. After that, the individual's productivity will depend on his or her creativity and problem-solving ability. These are very rough estimates, but they should give you an idea of what to expect.

As you or your staff members are becoming familiar with AutoCAD LT, you will need to learn how to best utilize this new tool in the context of your office's operations. This may mean rethinking how you go about running a project. It may also mean training coworkers to operate differently.

For example, one of the most common production challenges is scheduling work so that check plots can be produced on a timely basis. Normally, project members are used to looking at drawings at convenient times as they progress, even when there are scheduled review dates. With AutoCAD LT, you won't have that luxury. You will have to consider plotting time when scheduling drawing review dates. This means the person doing the drawings must get accurate information in time to enter last-minute changes and to plot the drawings.

# Establishing Office Standards

Communication is especially important when you are one of many people working on the same project on separate computers. A well-developed set of standards and procedures helps to minimize problems that might be caused by miscommunication. In this section, you'll find some suggestions on how to set up these standards.

## Establishing Layering Conventions

You have seen how layers can be a useful tool. But they can easily get out of hand when you have free reign over their creation and naming. This can be especially troublesome when more than one person is working on the same set of drawings. The following scenario illustrates this point.

One day the drawing you are working on has twenty layers. Then the next day, you find that someone has added six more, with names that have no meaning to you whatsoever. You don't dare delete those layers or modify the objects on them, for fear of retaliation from the individual who put them there. You ask around, but no one seems to know anything about these new layers. Finally, after spending an hour or two tracking down the culprit, you discover that the layers are not important at all.

> **TIP** If you are an architect, engineer, or in the construction business, check out some of the CAD layering standards set forth by the American Institute of Architects (AIA) and the Construction Standards Institute (CSI).

With an appropriate layer-naming convention, you can minimize this type of problem (though you may not eliminate it entirely). A too-rigid naming convention can cause as many problems as no convention at all, so it is best to give general guidelines rather than force everyone to stay within narrow limits. As mentioned in *Chapter 6*, you can create layer names in a way that allows you to group them using wildcards. AutoCAD LT allows up to 31 characters in a layer name, so you can use descriptive names.

Line weights should be standardized in conjunction with colors. If you intend to use a service bureau for your plotting, check with them first; they may require that you conform to their color and line-weight standards.

## Establishing Drawing Name Conventions

As with layers, you will also need a system to keep track of your drawing files and blocks. Blocks on AutoCAD LT can have 31-character names, but because you will want to turn blocks into external files, you should limit block names to eight characters.

Design a filenaming system that allows you to identify your drawing files by job number, drawing type, and revision number. For instance, the job number can be three digits, the drawing type can be an alphabetic code, and the revision can be an alphanumeric code. With this system, a coded filename would look like this: *704B061A.DWG*. Here, the first three numbers are an abbreviation of job number 8704. The next two characters are a symbol for drawing type B on sheet number 6. Finally, the last two characters indicate revision number 1 and series designation A. You may even want to include a code number to designate symbols.

Unfortunately, this type of code is difficult to remember. Most people prefer easily recognizable names, such as *ELM02.DWG* for Elm Street project sheet number 2. Although this recognizable type of name can't convey as much information as a coded name, it is usually better to base your filenaming system on recognizable names—most designers and drafters have enough to think about without having to learn special codes. You may be able to devise a combination of names plus numbers that offers a word or phrase in conjunction with a code.

## Labeling Hard Copies

A problem you will run into once you start to generate files is keeping track of which AutoCAD LT file goes with which hardcopy drawing. It's a good idea to place an identifying tag on the drawing (that will plot with the drawing) in some inconspicuous place. As well as the filename, the tag should include such information as the date and time the drawing was last edited, who edited it, and what submission the plot was done for. All these bits of information can prove helpful in the progress of a design or production project (see Figure 17.14).

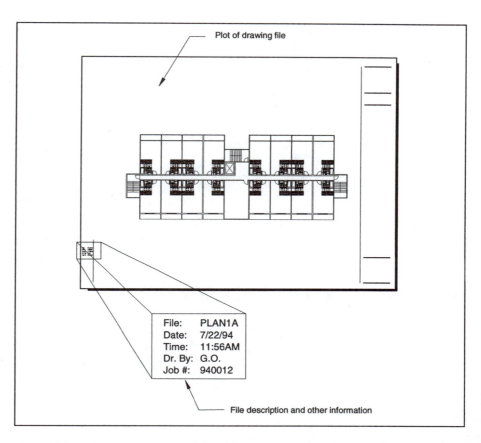

Plot of drawing file

File: PLAN1A
Date: 7/22/94
Time: 11:56AM
Dr. By: G.O.
Job #: 940012

File description and other information

*Figure 17.14:* **You can promote good drawing management by using a small note identifying the file used to generate the drawing.**

If you don't have time to develop your own custom drawing stamp, you can use the one supplied by AutoCAD LT. In Release 3, Autodesk has added the Revdate command, which allows you to insert and update the operator name, drawing name, and the revision date into the Title Block.

1. On the command line, type **Revdate** ↵. The first time that you use Revdate in a drawing, you will be prompted for insertion information.

2. At the REVDATE block insertion point <0,0>: prompt, select an insertion point for the block. AutoCAD LT presumes that you will place Revdate in your Title Block. It automatically creates a new layer TITLE_BLOCK, and places Revdate on it. (If this layer name does

not match your current layering conventions, use Ddrename to rename the layer.)

3. At the REVDATE block rotation (0 or 90 degrees <0>: prompt, press ↵ or enter **90** ↵. Revdate is typically positioned horizontally or vertically in the drawing border.

When you subsequently use the Revdate command, the attribute information in the block will be updated. The three Revdate attributes are as follows:

**Revdate**   The date and time.

**Fname**   The drawing name (not including the path or extension).

**User**   The name of the person revising the drawing. Revdate uses the logon name. If you wish to change this, choose Tools ➤ Preferences... ➤ User and change the user name as appropriate.

## Using Networks with AutoCAD LT

In an effort to simplify your file maintenance, you may want to consider installing a network to connect your computers electronically. Networks offer a way to share files and peripherals among computers in different locations. They come in a variety of styles—from very simple software and cable connectors to systems that use what are called *dedicated file servers*, whose special hardware and fiber optics communicate with the computers on the network.

In simplified terms, a *dedicated file server* is a storage device, often a computer with a large-capacity hard disk, that acts as a repository of data. A server will often have a tape-backup device to facilitate regular system backup.

Two basic types of networks can be used with AutoCAD LT: *server/client systems* and *peer-to-peer systems*. The file server offers you a way to maintain files on a single computer. The computers connected to the server are referred to as *clients* or *nodes*. You can store all of your common symbols, custom menus, and working files on the server, thus reducing the risk of having duplicate files. The client computers are simpler and less powerful. They use the server as their main storage device, accessing the programs and data stored on the server through the network. Networks with servers also have all the peripheral output devices connected to the server. This centralized type of system offers the user an easier way of managing files.

A peer-to-peer network does not use a server. Instead, each computer has equal status and can access files and peripherals on other computers on the network. Generally, this type of network is less expensive, since you don't need to dedicate a computer to the single task of server. Peripherals such as plotters and printers are shared among computers. Even hard disks are shared, though access to directories can be controlled at each computer.

Networks can be useful tools in managing your work, but they can also introduce new difficulties. For some network users, file-version control becomes a major concern. Speed of file access can be another problem. No matter what form of network you install, you will need a system manager whose duties include backing up files in the server and making sure the network's output devices are operating as they should. Used properly, a network can save time by easing the flow of information between computer users; it must, however, be managed carefully.

Here are some tips on using AutoCAD LT on a network:

▶ If you can afford it, use a star topology for your network, with an active hub and a dedicated server.

▶ Configure AutoCAD LT to store temporary and swap files on the client or node computer (see *Appendix A* for more on setting this up).

▶ Store the AutoCAD LT configuration settings locally on the client or node computer(s), so that the users can maintain their own customized menu and environment settings (see *Appendix B* for more information).

## Keeping Records

Computers are said to create "the paperless office." As you work more and more with them, however, you may find that quite the opposite is true. Although you can store more information on magnetic media, you will spend a good deal of time reviewing that information on hardcopy, because it is very difficult to spot errors on a computer monitor. When you use AutoCAD LT on large projects, another level of documentation must also exist: a way of keeping track of the many elements that go into the creation of drawings.

**Part 5**

**Customizing AutoCAD LT**

Because job requirements vary, you may want to provide a layer log to keep track of layers and their intended uses for specific jobs. Also, to manage blocks within files, a log of block names and their insertion values can help. Finally, plan to keep a log of symbols. You will probably have a library of symbols used in your workgroup, and this library will grow as your projects become more varied. Documenting these symbols will help to keep track of them.

Another activity that you may want to keep records for is plotting—especially if you bill your clients separately for computer time or for analyzing job costs. A plot log might contain such information as the time spent on plotting, the type of plot done, the purpose of the plot, and even a list of plotting errors and problems that arise with each drawing.

Although records may be the last thing on your mind when you are working to meet a deadline, in the long run they can save time and aggravation for you and the people you work with.

## Understanding What AutoCAD LT Can Do for You

Many of us have only a vague idea of what AutoCAD LT can contribute to our work. We think it will make our drafting tasks go faster, but we're not sure exactly how; or we believe it will make us produce better-quality drawings. Some people expect AutoCAD LT will make them better designers or allow them to produce professional-quality drawings without having much drawing talent. All these things are true to an extent, and AutoCAD LT can help you in some ways that are less tangible than speed and quality.

### Seeing the Hidden Advantages

We have discussed how AutoCAD LT can help you meet your drafting and design challenges, by allowing you to visualize your ideas more clearly and by reducing the time it takes to do repetitive tasks. AutoCAD LT also forces you to organize your drawing process more efficiently. It changes your perception of problems and, though it may introduce new ones, the additional accuracy and information AutoCAD LT provides will minimize errors.

AutoCAD LT also provides drawing consistency. A set of drawings done on AutoCAD LT is more legible and consistent, reducing the possibility of errors caused by illegible handwriting or poor drafting. In our litigious culture, this is a significant feature.

Finally, because AutoCAD LT systems are becoming more prevalent, it is easier to find people who can use it proficiently. As this group of experts grows, training will become less of a burden to your company.

## Taking a Project Off AutoCAD LT

As helpful as AutoCAD LT can be, there are times when making revisions on AutoCAD LT is simply not worth the effort. Last-minute changes that are minor but pervasive throughout a set of drawings are best made by hand on the most up-to-date hardcopy. That way, you don't waste time and drawing media in plotting drawings.

Also, it is a good idea to have a label on every hardcopy of a file so that users know which file to edit when the time comes to make changes.

Only your experience can help you determine the best time to stop using AutoCAD LT and start making changes by hand. Many factors will influence this decision—the size and complexity of the project, the people available to work on it, and the nature of the revisions, to name just a few.

 **TIP** Once your project is done, go back and enter the final changes in AutoCAD LT just to keep your files up-to-date.

As you have seen, AutoCAD LT is a powerful software tool, and like any powerful program, it is difficult to master. I hope this last chapter has given you the incentive to take advantage of AutoCAD LT's full potential. Remember—even after you've learned how to use AutoCAD LT, there are many other issues that you must confront while using AutoCAD LT in an office environment.

Unlike words, drawings have few restrictions. The process of writing requires adherence to the structures of our language. The process of drawing, on the other hand, has no fixed structure. There are a million ways to draw a face or a building, for example. For this reason, your use of AutoCAD LT is much less restricted, and there are certainly potential uses for it that are yet to be discovered. We encourage you to

Part
5

Customizing
AutoCAD LT

experiment with AutoCAD LT and explore the infinite possibilities it offers for solving your design problems and communicating your ideas.

We hope *Mastering AutoCAD LT for Windows 95 and Windows NT* has been of benefit to you and that you will continue to use it as a reference. If you have comments, criticisms, or ideas about how we can improve the next edition of this book, write or e-mail me at the addresses below. And thanks for choosing *Mastering AutoCAD LT for Windows 95 and Windows NT*.

George Omura
Omura Illustration
P.O. Box 357
Albany, CA 94706-0357
E-Mail: 76515.1250@compuserve.com

# Appendices

*Appendix A: Hardware and Software Tips* should give you a start on selecting hardware appropriate for AutoCAD LT. If AutoCAD LT is not already installed on your system, read *Appendix B: Installing and Setting Up AutoCAD LT*, which contains an installation and configuration tutorial that you should follow before starting *Chapter 1. Appendix C: Using the CD-ROM* describes the utilities available on the companion CD. *Appendix D: System and Dimension Variables* will illuminate the references to the system variables scattered throughout the book. Finally, *Appendix E: Standard AutoCAD LT Commands* provides a listing of all the AutoCAD LT commands.

# Appendix A

# Hardware and Software Tips

**B**ECAUSE some of the items that make up an AutoCAD LT system are not found on the typical desktop system, I have provided this appendix to help you understand some of the less common items you may need. This appendix also discusses ways you can improve AutoCAD LT's performance through software and hardware.

## The Graphics Display

There are two issues to consider concerning the graphics display: resolution and performance.

If you are running Windows 95 software, then you probably already have a high-resolution display card for your monitor. If you haven't set up your system yet, then a high-resolution display card and monitor is a must. SVGA display cards are inexpensive and offer high-quality display.

Graphics performance all comes down to speed. To enhance graphics performance you need to consider the following:

**Local bus** Contemporary motherboards use high-speed local bus architecture (VESA), which accelerates video throughput. Check that yours is local bus. If you are shopping for a graphics card, make sure that it is VESA—and preferably PCI (plug-and-play) for ease of installation.

**Video RAM** If you are shopping for a display system, you should also make sure that it has 2–4MB of *video RAM*. Standard video cards typically have only 1MB of video RAM. 2–4MB will give you noticeably better performance with AutoCAD LT.

In previous versions of AutoCAD LT, it was advisable to obtain *display list* software to improve graphics performance. With Release 3, this is no longer necessary—AutoCAD LT already comes equipped with it. The display list gives you nearly instantaneous pans and zooms, but it comes at the cost of consuming more of your memory.

# Pointing Devices

Our most basic means of communicating with computers is the keyboard and pointing device. Most likely, you will use a mouse, but if you are still in the market for a pointing device, choose an input device that generates smooth cursor movement. Some of the lesser-quality input devices cause erratic movement. When looking for an input device other than a mouse, choose one that provides positive feedback, such as a definitive button click when you pick an object on the screen. Many low-cost digitizers have a very poor button feel that can cause errors when you are selecting points or menu options.

In general, use a high-resolution mouse if you do not plan to do any tracing. If you must have the use of a tablet menu, or if you know you are going to trace drawings, then get a digitizer, but be sure it is of good quality.

## The Digitizing Tablet

If you need to trace drawings, you should consider a digitizing tablet. It is usually a rectangular object with a pen-like *stylus*, or a device called a *puck*, which resembles a mouse. It has a smooth surface on which to draw. The most popular size is 11″×11″, but digitizing tablets are available in sizes up to 60″×70″. The tablet gives a natural feel to drawing with the computer because the movement of the stylus or puck is directly translated into cursor movement. While many digitizers come with a stylus, you will want a multi-button puck to work with Auto-CAD LT.

A digitizing tablet's puck often has *function buttons*. These buttons can be programmed through the AutoCAD LT menu file system to start your most frequently used commands. This is much faster than searching through an on-screen menu. You can also select commands from the tablet's surface if you install the *menu template* supplied with Auto-CAD LT. A menu template is a paper or plastic overlay sheet with the

AutoCAD LT commands printed on it. You can select commands simply by pointing at them on the template. If you have a digitizing tablet, refer to *Appendix B*, which tells you how to install a template.

AutoCAD LT supports Wintab-compatible digitizers. If your digitizer has a Wintab driver, you can use your digitizer as both a *tracing device* (to trace drawings on a tablet), and also as a *pointing device* (to choose AutoCAD LT or Windows 95 menu items).

Your Wintab digitizer must first be installed and configured under Windows 95. Check that it is working in Windows 95 before enabling it in AutoCAD LT. Otherwise, you will not be able to use the digitizer as a pointing device (mouse). To enable the digitizer in AutoCAD LT, choose Tools ➤ Preferences… Work Space Tab. Then select the Tablet or Mouse option under Digitizer Input.

## Output Devices

Output options vary greatly in quality and price. Quality and paper size are the major considerations for both printers and plotters. Nearly all printers give accurate drawings, but some produce better line quality than others. Some plotters give merely acceptable results, while others are quite impressive in their speed and accuracy.

AutoCAD LT for Windows 95 can use the Windows 95 *system printer*, so any device that Windows 95 supports is also supported by Auto-CAD LT. AutoCAD LT also gives you the option of plotting directly to an output device. By plotting directly to the output device instead of going through Windows 95, AutoCAD LT can offer more control over the final output.

### Printers

Depending on your budget and the requirements of your office— whether you need high-quality final output or not, for example—there are a number of different options for you to consider.

**Laser Printers** produce high quality line work output. The standard office laser printer is usually limited to 8½″×11″ paper. However, 11″×17″ laser printers for graphics and CAD work are now becoming affordable, and are commonly used for proof plots. Resolution and speed are the major considerations if you are buying a laser printer.

300 DPI (dots per inch) output produces very acceptable plots, but 600 DPI is fast becoming the standard. You should also look for a laser printer with sufficient built-in memory to improve spooling and plotting speeds.

**Ink-jet or Bubble-jet Printers**    offer speed and quality output. Some ink-jet printers even accept 17″×22″ paper and offer Post-Script emulation at up to 720 DPI. Since ink-jet printers are competitively priced, they can offer the best solution for low-cost check plots. And the 17″×22″ paper size is quite acceptable for half-size plots, a format that more architects and engineers are using.

**PostScript Printers**    If you want to use a PostScript device to output your drawings, the best method is to either select File ➤ Export or use the Psout command. These options convert your drawing into a true PostScript file. You can then send your file to a PostScript printer or typesetting machine. This can be especially useful for PCB layout where you require photo negatives for output. If you are an architect who needs presentation-quality drawings, you may want to consider using the Encapsulated PS (*.EPS) option in the Export Data dialog box. Often service bureaus who offer a raster plotter service can produce E-size PostScript output from a Post-Script file. The uses of this option are really quite open-ended.

## *Plotters*

A plotter is a mechanical drafting device used to draw a computer image on sheets of paper, vellum, or polyester film. Some plotters use pens, though most offer ink-jet, laser, thermal, or electrostatic technology to get the image on paper.

If your drawing is fairly simple, a pen plotter can give you results in minutes. However, many applications require fairly complex drawings, which in turn take much longer to plot. A typical architectural drawing, for example, takes 45 minutes on a good-quality, large-format plotter using wet-ink pens on polyester film. By using pens capable of faster speeds, you can reduce the time it takes to plot a drawing by 40 percent and still get an accurate reproduction. When you want large plots, sharp clear lines, or reproduction quality, the pen plotter is the way to go.

**App.
A**

**Hardware and
Software Tips**

Raster plotters, especially ink-jet plotters, are perhaps the most flexible general-purpose output devices available. These plotters can produce large-format drawings in less than half the time taken by pen plotters. Many ink-jet plotters offer high speed and good quality at a competitive price. If speed and large-format drawings are top priorities, nothing can match these devices.

If you need large plots but feel you can't afford a large plotter, many service bureaus (or blueprint companies) offer plotting as a service. This can be a very good alternative to purchasing your own plotter. Check with your local service bureau.

## Memory and AutoCAD LT Performance

Next to your computer's CPU, memory has the greatest impact on AutoCAD LT's speed. How much you have, and how you use it, can make a big difference in whether you finish that rush job on schedule or work late nights trying. In this section, I hope to clarify some basic points about memory and how AutoCAD LT uses it.

AutoCAD LT Release 3 for Windows 95 and NT is a virtual memory system. This means that when your RAM memory resources reach their limit, part of the data stored in RAM is temporarily moved to your hard disk to make more room in RAM. This temporary storage of RAM to your hard disk is called memory *paging*. Through memory paging, AutoCAD LT will continue to run, even though your work might exceed the capacity of your RAM.

AutoCAD LT uses memory in two ways. First, it stores its program code in RAM. The more programs you have open under Windows, the more RAM will be used. Windows controls the use of memory for program code, so if you start to reach the RAM limit, Windows will take care of memory paging. The second way AutoCAD LT uses memory is for storing drawing data. AutoCAD LT always attempts to store as much of your drawing in RAM as possible. Again, when the amount of RAM required for a drawing exceeds the actual RAM available, AutoCAD LT will page parts of the drawing data to the hard disk. The paging of drawing data is controlled strictly by AutoCAD LT. Since RAM is shared with both program code and drawing data, your drawing size and the number of programs you have open under Windows will affect how much RAM you have available. For this reason, if you find that your AutoCAD LT editing session is slowing down, try closing other applications you might have open. This will free up more memory for AutoCAD LT and the drawing file.

### AutoCAD LT and Your Hard Disk

You will notice that AutoCAD LT will slow down when paging occurs. If this happens frequently, the best thing to do is add more RAM. But you can also improve the performance of AutoCAD LT under these conditions by ensuring that you have adequate hard disk space and that any free hard disk space has been *defragmented* or *optimized*. A defragmented disk will offer faster access, thereby improving paging speed.

With previous versions of AutoCAD LT, you were advised to set up a permanent swap file. With the Windows 95 version, this is not necessary. Windows 95 dynamically allocates swap-file space. However, you should make sure that there is enough free space on your hard disk to allow Windows 95 to set up the space. As a general rule, allow enough space for a swap file that is four times the size of your RAM capacity. If you have 16MB of RAM, you need to allow space for a 64MB swap file (at a minimum). This will give your system 64MB of virtual memory.

### What to Do for Out of RAM and Out of Page Space Errors

After you have used AutoCAD LT for awhile, you may find some odd-looking files with a .AC$ extension in the directory where your drawings are stored. These files are the temporary files for storing unused portions of a drawing. They often appear if AutoCAD LT has been terminated abnormally. You can usually erase these files without any adverse effect.

**WARNING** If you are in a network environment, check the time and date of any .AC$ files before you remove them. They may belong to another user's current editing session, in which case you should not erase them.

If you've discarded all the old swap files and your disk is still unusually full, there may be some lost file clusters filling up your hard disk. Lost clusters are pieces of files that are not actually assigned to a specific

App.
A

Hardware and
Software Tips

file. Often they crop up when a program has terminated abnormally. To eliminate them and free up the disk space they're using, exit Auto-CAD LT and run Scandisk.

Finally, if you are not in the habit of emptying your Recycle bin, you should do so now. Every file that you "delete" using the Windows 95 Explorer is actually passed to the Recycle bin. You need to clear this out regularly.

## AutoCAD LT on a Network

If you are using a network version of AutoCAD LT, each computer on the network that uses AutoCAD LT must have its own configuration file. This means you must set the /C command switch to a local drive and directory (this process is described in *Appendix B*). Once this is done, you must run the AutoCAD LT configuration for each client computer. This will ensure that each node will have its own network node name and default log-in name.

Another point to consider is the location of swap files. When drawing files get large, AutoCAD LT makes heavy use of your hard disk. Swap files are constantly being written and updated. If you are working with AutoCAD LT on a network, it is especially important to pay attention to where swap files are being written. If you are using a server-client network system, and the network client or node has its own hard disk, you can improve AutoCAD LT's performance by forcing the program to place drawing swap files on the local drive, instead of on the server. This reduces network traffic, thereby improving Auto-CAD LT's and the network's performance. The following steps show how this is done.

1.  Start AutoCAD LT from the node, then choose Tools ➤ Preferences…, and click on the File System tab.

2.  Select the Other Directory button in the Temporary Files section at the top left of the tab.

3.  Use the Browse button to locate a directory on your local drive, such as a TEMP directory you have created for this purpose. Double-click on the chosen directory name in the Edit Directory dialog box.

4.  When the directory name appears in the Path: input box, click first on the Change button and then on the Close button.

5. Click on OK to exit the Preferences dialog box.

All temporary files will now be placed in your chosen local directory.

# When Things Go Wrong

AutoCAD LT is a complex program, and occasionally you will run into problems. Here are a few tips on what to do when things don't work.

### Difficulty Starting Up or Opening a File

If you've recently installed AutoCAD LT but you cannot get it started, you may have a configuration problem. Before you panic, try reinstalling your system from scratch. If you are installing the CD version, this won't take long (see *Appendix B* for installation instructions).

Another common problem is having files locked and unavailable. This can happen to drawing files as well as support files, such as linetype, hatch pattern, menu, and shape files. If a file is reported as being locked by AutoCAD LT, and you know no one else is using the system, locate the file in question, and then remove its lock file. See *Chapter 14* for a complete listing of files and their lock file equivalents.

If you are on a single-user system, you may want to turn off the file-locking feature altogether. This can save you the frustration of having to unlock files that are accidentally locked as a result of system crashes.

### Restoring Corrupted Files

Hardware failures can result in data files becoming corrupted. When this happens, AutoCAD LT is unable to open the drawing file. Fortunately, there is hope for damaged files. In most cases, AutoCAD LT will run through a file-recovery routine automatically when it attempts to load a corrupted file. If you have a file you know is corrupted, you can start the file-recovery utility by clicking on File ➤ Management ➤ Recover. This opens the Recover File dialog box, allowing you to select the file you want to recover. Once you enter the name, AutoCAD LT goes to work. You get a series of messages, most of which have little meaning to the average user. Then the recovered file is opened. You may lose some data, but a partial file is better than no file at all, especially when the file represents several days of work.

Another possibility is to attempt to recover your drawing from the .BAK file—the last saved version before your drawing was corrupted. Rename the .BAK file to a .DWG file with a different name, and then open it up. The drawing will contain only what was in your drawing when it was previously saved.

There may be situations when a file is so badly corrupted it cannot be restored. By backing up frequently, the inconvenience of such an occurrence can be minimized. You may also want to consider the Microsoft Office Plus package, which allows you to schedule backups and scan and defragment your drives during off hours. Programs such as Scandisk can spot problem areas on your hard disk before they cause trouble.

## Troubleshooting

This section covers a few of the more common problems experienced while using AutoCAD LT.

### You can see but cannot select objects in a drawing someone else has worked on

This may be happening because you have a Paper Space view instead of a Model Space view. To make sure you're in Model Space, type **Tilemode** ⏎ and then type **1** ⏎. Or you can turn on the UCS icon by typing **Ucsicon** ⏎ **On** ⏎, and if you see the triangular UCS icon in the lower-left corner, then you are in Paper Space. You must go to Model Space before you can edit the drawing.

### Grips do not appear when objects are selected

Make sure the Grips feature is enabled (Options ➤ Grips). See *Appendix B* for details.

### When you select objects, it doesn't work the way it appears in this book

Check the Selection settings to make sure they are set the same way as the exercise specifies (Options ➤ Selection). See *Chapter 2* for details.

## Text appears in the wrong font style, or an error message says AutoCAD LT cannot find font files

When you are working on files from another company, it's not uncommon that you will encounter a file that uses special third-party fonts that you do not have. You can usually substitute standard AutoCAD LT fonts for any fonts you don't have without adverse effects. AutoCAD LT automatically presents a dialog box letting you select font files for the substitution. You can either choose a font file or press the Esc key to ignore the message (see *Chapter 8* for more on font files). If you choose to ignore the error message, you may not see some of the text that would normally appear in the drawing.

## DXF files do not import

Various problems can occur during the DXF import, the most common of which is that you are trying to import a DXF file into an existing drawing rather than a new drawing. Under some conditions, you can import a DXF file into an existing drawing, but AutoCAD LT may not import the entire file.

To ensure that your entire DXF file is safely imported, open a brand-new file using the standard AutoCAD LT defaults. Choose File ➤ New, and at the dialog box, make sure the No Prototype option is checked. Once the new file is opened, proceed with the DXFIN command or use File ➤ Import and select *.DXF from the File Type Pull-down list.

## A file cannot be saved to disk

Frequently, a hard drive will fill up quickly during an edit session. AutoCAD LT can generate temporary and swap files many times larger than the file you are editing. This can leave you with no room left to save your file. If this happens, you can empty the Recycle bin to clear some space on your hard drive, or delete old AutoCAD LT.BAK files you don't need. *Do not delete AutoCAD LT temporary files.*

### AutoCAD LT does not display all the Paper Space viewports

AutoCAD LT uses substantial memory to display Paper Space viewports. For this reason, it limits the number of viewports it will display at one time. Even though viewports don't display, they will still plot. Also, if you zoom in on a blank viewport while in Paper Space, you will be able to see its contents. The viewport regains visibility because you are reducing the number of viewports shown on the screen at one time.

You can increase the number of viewports AutoCAD LT will display at one time by resetting the *Maxactvp* system variable. (This is usually set to 16.) Be forewarned, however, that increasing the Maxactvp setting will cause AutoCAD LT to use more memory. If you have limited memory on your system, this will slow down AutoCAD LT considerably.

### AutoCAD LT becomes impossibly slow when adding more Paper Space viewports

As mentioned for the preceding problem, AutoCAD LT consumes memory quickly when adding viewports. If your system resources are limited, you can reduce the *Maxactvp* system variable setting so that AutoCAD LT displays fewer viewports at one time. This will let you work on a file that has numerous viewports without causing a decrease in your computer's performance. Try reducing Maxactvp to 8, and then reduce or increase the setting until you find the optimum value for your situation. Alternatively, you can use the Mview OFF option to turn off viewports when you are not working in them.

### AutoCAD LT won't open a large file, and displays a "Page file full" message

AutoCAD LT will open drawing files larger than can fit into your system's RAM. In order to do this, however, AutoCAD LT attempts to store part of the drawing in a temporary file on your hard drive. If there isn't room on the hard drive, AutoCAD LT will give up. To remedy this problem, clear off some space on your hard drive. It is not uncommon for AutoCAD LT to require as much as 10MB of hard disk space for every 1MB of a drawing file.

### The keyboard shortcuts for commands are not working

If you are working on an unfamiliar computer, chances are the keyboard shortcuts (or abbreviations) have been altered. These usually reside in the ACLT.PGP file. See *Appendix E* for information on adding or changing keyboard abbreviations.

### Plots come out blank

Check the scale factor you are using for your plot. Often, a blank plot means your scale factor is making the plot too large to fit on the sheet. Try plotting with the Scale to Fit option. If you get a plot, then you know your scale factor is incorrect. See *Chapter 7* for more on plotting options. Check your output before you plot by using the Full Preview option in the Plot Configuration dialog box.

### You cannot get your drawing to be properly oriented on the sheet

If you want to change the orientation of your drawing on a plotted sheet, and the Plot Configuration orientation options don't seem to work, try rotating the UCS to align with your desired plot view, and then type **Plan** ↵. Adjust the view to display what you want to have plotted, then use the View command (View ➤ Named Views…) to save this view. When you are ready to plot, use the View option in the Plot Configuration dialog box and plot the saved view, instead of rotating the plot.

# Appendix B

# Installing and Setting Up AutoCAD LT

## Before You Do Anything, Back Up the Disks

Whether you purchased the full disk set or the disk/CD-ROM version, you will want to back up the AutoCAD LT disks. To copy the disks, open the Windows 95 Explorer and go to My Computer. Click on the icon for your floppy drive, and then use the Copy Disk option (right-click on the drive icon or choose File ➤ Copy Disk).

> **WARNING** If you have a tablet, do not put disks on top of it, because the tablet uses a small electrical field to operate. This field can destroy data on a disk.

Be sure to label your copies the same way the originals are labeled, including the serial number from your Personalization Disk. Put your originals in a safe place, away from any magnetic sources.

Once you have completed installation, we suggest that you back up the contents of your hard disk so that, in the event you experience problems with the hard disk, you won't have to re-install AutoCAD LT and other programs and files that reside there.

You cannot back up the CD-ROM unless you have an optical drive.

## Before Installing AutoCAD LT

Before you begin the installation process, be sure you have a drive with at least 70MB of free disk space: 35MB to install all files; 32MB for use as virtual memory.

You will also want to have at least an additional 64MB of free disk space for AutoCAD LT *temporary files* and *swap files*, plus another 10MB for the tutorial files you will create. (Temporary and swap files are system files AutoCAD LT creates as it works. You don't have to deal with these files directly—Windows 95 manages the swap files for you, but you do have to allow room for them.

## Installing the AutoCAD LT Software

After you've checked that you've got enough disk space, proceed with the following steps to install AutoCAD LT.

1. Start Windows 95 and make sure no other applications are running.

2. Insert the AutoCAD LT Set-up disk in your floppy drive, or, if you have the CD-ROM version of AutoCAD LT, place the AutoCAD LT CD-ROM in your CD-ROM drive.

3. Open the Run... option on the Start menu.

4. Type the following into the Open input box:

    *d*: setup

   and press OK. The *d* in the above example should be replaced by the drive letter that contains the AutoCAD LT Set-up diskette or CD-ROM. For example, if your CD-ROM is drive F, you would type **f** in place of the *d* in the example.

5. When the AutoCAD LT Welcome screen appears, press the Next Button to begin program installation.

6. When prompted, insert the disk labeled Personalization Disk. Make sure it is not write-protected. Place the disk in drive A or B. If you are installing from a CD-ROM, be sure the AutoCAD LT CD is in your CD-ROM drive.

7. To personalize AutoCAD LT, you are asked for your name and company. This information will be displayed on the opening AutoCAD LT screen, so don't enter anything you'll regret later.

8. Next, you are prompted where to place your AutoCAD LT files. The Set-up program offers the default installation directory of c:\Program Files\AutoCAD LT. Unless you are an experienced computer user, press ↵ to accept these defaults when you see the prompts.

9. You will then be prompted to select the type of installation desired.

   **Typical**   installs all files: program files, support files, clipart files, sample drawings, templates, tutorial files, Help files, Dictionary files, and Font files.

   **Compact**   installs only the program files and support files—the minimum required to run AutoCAD LT.

   **Custom**   allows you to choose any set of the above files from a dialog box.

10. You will then be prompted to select the folder where the AutoCAD LT program icons will be placed. Make any changes required, or choose Next to accept the default presented.

11. Once you answer all these questions, AutoCAD LT will display all of the selections that you have made. If you need to change any of these, click on Back and change the setting(s). If you are satisfied with the settings, click on Next. The actual installation begins and you are prompted for each disk as it is needed. (If you are installing from a CD-ROM disk, you are asked to indicate the CD-ROM drive, and the installation continues uninterrupted.)

12. At the end of the installation, click on the Finish button. You see a new program group called AutoCAD LT. It includes on-line documentation (a Readme file) and the AutoCAD LT Help file, as well as the programs themselves. The Readme file provides the latest information about AutoCAD LT.

### The Program Files

In the \Program Files\AutoCAD LT directory, you will see a number of subdirectories. Here are brief descriptions of the contents of each subdirectory:

**Clipart**    contains a set of Windows metafiles (.WMF format.)

**Sample**    contains Sample drawings supplied with AutoCAD LT. If you install the tutorial drawings for this book, you should place them in this directory.

**Template**    contains a set of drawing template (.DWT) files. *Chapter 5* discusses using template files.

**Tutorial**    contains the drawings supplied by AutoCAD LT for its own tutorial. This is a different tutorial from the one supplied with this book. (The tutorial drawings for this book should be copied into the \Sample directory.)

## Setting Preferences

Once you've done the basic installation, you are ready to use AutoCAD LT. The tutorials in this book assume that you are using the default Preference settings. As you become more familiar with the workings of AutoCAD LT, you may want to make adjustments to the way AutoCAD LT works throughout the Preferences dialog box.

This dialog box can be accessed by clicking on Options ➤ Preferences…(or right-click in the command window, and click on the Preferences… in the options menu). The dialog box is further divided into sections shown as tabs across the top. The following describes the settings available in each of these sections according to button groups.

App.
B

Installing and Setting
Up AutoCAD LT

## Workspace

The Workspace tab options control AutoCAD LT's appearance and input options as well as the time interval for AutoCAD LT's automatic save feature.

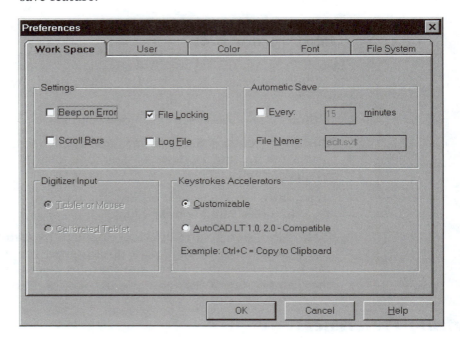

### Settings

Here is a list of the options available under the Workspace tab.

**Beep on Error**    toggles an audible warning when you make an error.

**Scroll Bars**    toggles the scroll bars of the drawing area on and off.

**File Locking**   prevents other users on a network from updating files that are in use.

**Log File**   allows you to record the data from the command line. When the Check box is checked, the AutoCAD LT text window is recorded in a log file.

## Automatic Save

This group lets you control the time interval between automatic saves. You can also use the Savetime system variable.

## Digitizer Input

If you are using a digitizer *and* a mouse, this pair of radio buttons let you control whether the mouse is recognized by AutoCAD LT.

**Tablet or Mouse**   let you switch between a digitizer and mouse, simply by moving from one pointing device to the other.

**Calibrated Tablet**   causes AutoCAD LT to accept input from the digitizer only.

## Keystroke Accelerators

Many of AutoCAD LT's drafting tools are controlled by keystroke combinations. These keystrokes can conflict with some of the Windows 95 accelerator keystrokes. This pair lets you control which set of conflicting keystrokes take precedence.

**AutoCAD LT 1.0, 2.0**   causes AutoCAD LT to accept the Ctrl key options that were standard in earlier versions of AutoCAD LT, such as Ctrl-C to cancel a command.

**App. B**

**Installing and Setting Up AutoCAD LT**

**Customizable**   forces the standard Windows 95 keyboard accelerators, such as Ctrl–C to Copy to the Clipboard and Esc to cancel a command, to take precedence.

### Font

The Font tab opens a dialog box that lets you select a font for program text display. This has no effect on the text in the AutoCAD LT drawings, only on text in the Text Window or command line.

### Color

The Color tab opens a dialog box that lets you select colors for the various components of the AutoCAD LT window. You can, for example, use this button to change the background color of the drawing area.

### File System

The settings under the File System tab tell AutoCAD LT where to look for files it needs during the course of its operation.

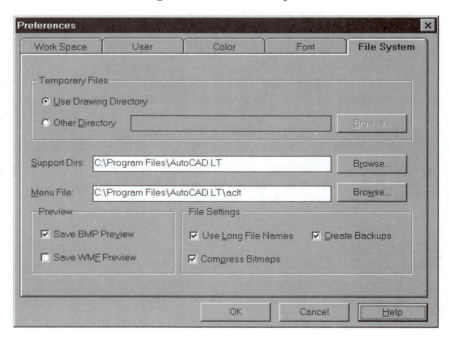

**Temporary Files** sets the location for temporary swap files. Set this to a drive that has a lot of free space for optimum AutoCAD LT performance. If you are working over a network, set up a temporary directory on your local drive to reduce traffic on the network.

**Support Dirs:** sets the location of support files such as fonts, menus, hatch patterns, linetypes, and drawing libraries. If you add a symbols library, you will want to include the library's path in this input box.

**Menu File** allows you to specify a different directory for your menu file.

**Browse** can be used with any of the input boxes to help locate a directory or file.

**Preview** allows you to select with radio buttons a bitmap format (.BMP) or a Windows metafile (.WMF) for the drawing preview.

**File Settings** enables or disables the use of long filenames, creation of backups, and compression of bitmaps created by AutoCAD LT.

## User

The settings under the User tab in the Preferences dialog box are as follows:

**User Name** shows the user name and company name entered when you installed AutoCAD LT. AutoCAD LT inserts this into your drawing title block when you use the Revdate command. You may change the user name if required.

**Spelling Dialects** shows the language and dialect that is in effect in the Spell Checker at the time.

**Measurement** shows whether the English (feet and inches) or metric measurement system is in effect.

## Understanding the ACLT.INI File

The settings that are maintained in the Preferences... dialog boxes are contained in the ACLT.INI file. If you are comfortable with editing Windows .INI files, you can view and edit the ACLT.INI files to set up AutoCAD LT to your liking. All of the Preferences options reviewed in the previous section are stored in the ACLT.INI file. Here is a listing of the main headings in the ACLT.INI file and their meaning.

**[General]**   controls many of the environment settings. For your reference, Table B.1 shows all of the environment settings that are contained in this category.

**[Command Line Windows]**   controls the appearance of the text window.

**[Application Window]**   controls the location and size of the Auto-CAD LT window.

**[Drawing Window]**   controls the appearance of the drawing window.

**[Toolbars]**   controls the appearance of toolbars.

**[Partial Menus]**   tracks the menu name, menu group name, and position of the drop-down menus, both AutoCAD LT-supplied and custom menus.

**[Aerial View]**   controls the default options for the Aerial View window.

**[Browse/Search]**   controls the options for the Browse/Search option under the Open File dialog box. The variables in this section should *not* be modified.

*Table B.1:*   **The AutoCAD LT General Environment Variables**

| Environment Variable | Purpose |
| --- | --- |
| Autosave | Turns automatic save on or off |
| AutoSaveFile | Sets the name and path of the automatic save file |
| AutoSaveInterval | Sets the number of minutes |
| BeepOnError | Turns audible beep on or off |
| BmpOutCompression | Turns BMP compression on or off |

*Table B.1:* **The AutoCAD LT General Environment Variables (continued)**

| Environment Variable | Purpose |
|---|---|
| CreateBackupFiles | Turns backup creation on or off |
| Customcolors | Sets the colors AutoCAD LT uses |
| Dither | Turns dither on or off |
| Fastersplash | Splash screen appears more quickly |
| FileLocking | Turns file locking on or off |
| Font | Sets font for text window |
| KeystrokeAccelerators | Use customizable (Windows-style) or AutoCAD LT-compatible |
| LastDwg | Tracks last selected drawing |
| LastTemplate | Tracks last selected template |
| LastWizard | Tracks last selected Wizard |
| LogFileOpen | Turns logfile creation on or off |
| MaxArray | Maximum number of objects to array, using Array command (100–10000000) |
| MaxHatch | Maximum number of points or lines in a hatch pattern (100–10000000) |
| NoStartUpDialog | Automatic display of Start Up dialog box or not |
| StartUpType | Last selected button in Start Up dialog box |
| Support | Sets the path to the support files directory |
| TempFilesDefault | Sets the path to temporary (swap) file directory |
| UseLongFiles | Turn long filename support on or off |
| UsePreviousPrinter | Use previously selected printer rather than Windows default |
| UserName | Name of user given at installation |
| Visible | Turns the text window on or off |
| WindowPosition | Sets the size and position of the text window |

**App.
B**

**Installing and Setting
Up AutoCAD LT**

### Changing Environment Settings at the Command Line

If you look closely at Table B.1, you will recognize about 75% of the variables listed there. You reviewed them in the Preferences... dialog box above. The remaining 25%, however, cannot be changed in Preferences.... A few can be accessed via other dialog boxes. The balance can only be set either directly in the .INI file, or by using the Getenv and Setenv commands.

If you want to check an environment setting variable, type **Getenv** ↵, followed by the variable's name. The value of this setting is displayed. To change an environment setting—for example, if you wish to turn off the dialog box that is always displayed when you open a drawing, do the following:

1. Enter **Setenv** ↵.

2. Type **nostartupdialog** ↵. (You don't have to worry about upper- and lowercase letters. AutoCAD LT will respond to either.)

3. Enter **1** ↵.

This will turn off the automatic display of the Start Up screen.

## Relocating Configuration Files on a Network

AutoCAD LT stores its configuration information in two files. These files are ACLT.INI for the Windows 95 version, and ACLTNT.CFG for the Windows NT version. When you first install and configure Auto-CAD LT, these two files are created and placed in the AutoCAD LT directory. If you install AutoCAD LT on a network, Auto CAD LT is installed on the server drive.

You may want to move the .INI and .CFG files from the network directory to your own personal directory. That way you can store your own personal menu and environment settings. To do this, you need to first create a local directory; then create a shortcut which will start and run AutoCAD LT from the network, if you don't already have one; and finally, you need to specify a new configuration directory by setting the /C command line switch.

1. First, create a subdirectory on your local drive for your custom versions of ACLT.INI and ACLT.CFG. Call this directory **Custom**.

2. Next, create a shortcut to start and run AutoCAD LT, if you don't already have one.

3. Right-click on the Windows 95 Desktop. An options menu appears.

4. Choose New ➤ Shortcut. The Create Shortcut dialog box opens.

5. Use the Browse button to locate the ACLT.EXE file on the network server. If it was installed in the default directory, it will be in \Program Files\AutoCAD LT on the network drive.

6. Click on the ACLT.EXE file. It appears in the Command Line of the Create shortcut dialog box. Then click on Next.

7. You are now prompted for a Title for your shortcut. Type **My Auto-CAD LT** in place of ACLT.EXE. Then click on the Finish button. The AutoCAD LT icon with the title My AutoCAD LT will appear on the Desktop. (You can edit the title on the Desktop at any time by highlighting it and pressing the F2 key.)

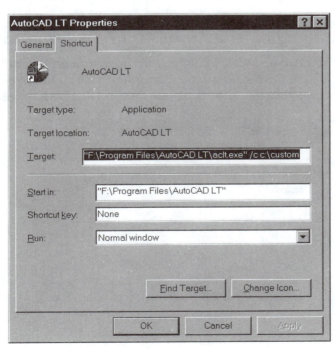

Now that you have created your shortcut, you need to relocate the .INI and/or the Windows NT configuration file to your local Custom directory.

8.  Right-click on the shortcut on your desktop and select Properties... from the option menu. When the AutoCAD LT Properties dialog box opens, click on the Shortcut tab.

9.  Edit the contents of the Target: input box so that it shows the following:

    ```
    F:\Program Files\AutoCAD LT /C C:\CUSTOM
    ```

10. When you are done, click on OK. Your new configuration is set up. The next time that you use this shortcut to open AutoCAD LT, the .INI and .CFG files will be copied to your Custom directory.

In step 8, the Target: input box tells Windows 95 where to find the AutoCAD LT program. The */C* in the example is called a command line switch. The switch appears first in the line, followed by a space, and then the file location. This example assumes that AutoCAD LT is installed on network drive F, and that your local drive is C. Be sure you specify the correct drive for your particular installation.

### Changing the AutoCAD LT Program Icon

You can optionally change the shortcut icon to a different one by clicking on the Change Icon button in the AutoCAD LT Properties dialog box after step 2. This brings up the Change Icon dialog box.

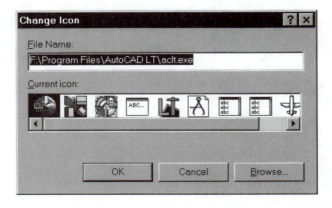

You can select from a set of pre-defined icons that are included with the ACLT.EXE file.

1. Click on the Change Icon button in the AutoCAD LT Properties dialog box. You are initially offered the Windows 95 default icon set.

2. Use the Browse button to locate ACLT.EXE. Double-click on ACLT.EXE. You will be presented with a set of AutoCAD LT icons to choose from.

3. Highlight the icon of your choice, and click on OK. Click on OK to exit the AutoCAD LT properties dialog box.

# Configuring Your Digitizing Tablet

If you are using a digitizer with AutoCAD LT for Windows, you will need to select some additional configuration options. These other options allow you to add flexibility to your digitizer, or to add a menu template. As an alternative, you may choose to configure your tablet as the Windows pointing device; in this case, the options in this section will not apply.

## Configuring the Tablet Menu Area

If you own a digitizing tablet, and you would like to use it with the AutoCAD LT tablet menu template, you must configure your tablet menu first.

1. The first step is to securely fasten your tablet menu template to the tablet. Be sure the area covered by the template is completely within the tablet's active drawing area.

2. Choose Options ➤ Tablet ➤ Configure. You will get the prompt

        Enter the number of tablet menus desired (0-4)<0>:

For the next series of prompts, you will be locating the four tablet menu areas, starting with menu area 1 (see Figure B.1).

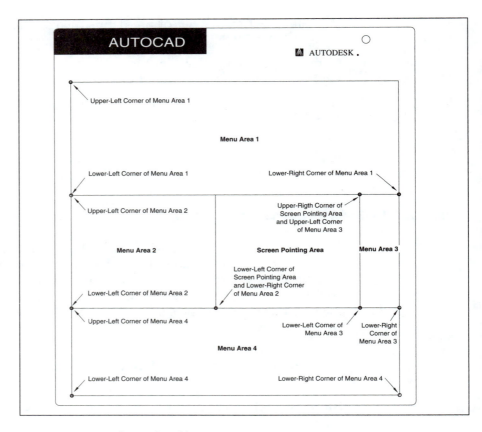

*Figure B.1:*    ***How to locate the tablet menu areas***

3.    At the prompts, pick the upper-left, lower-left, and lower-right corners of menu area 1. Use Figure B.1 for reference.

4.    When you are prompted as follows, press ↵ to accept the default:

    Enter the number of columns for menu area 1, 0 to 499 <25>:

    Enter the number of rows for menu area 1, 0 to 1839 <9>:

5.    At the prompts, pick the upper-left, lower-left, and lower-right corners of menu area 2. Use Figure B.1 for reference.

6. When you are prompted as follows, press ↵ to accept the default:

   ```
   Enter the number of columns for menu area 2, 0 to 2202
   <11>:

   Enter the number of rows for menu area 2, 0 to 1809 <9>:
   ```

7. At the prompts, pick the upper-left, lower-left, and lower-right corners of menu area 3. Use Figure B.1 for reference.

8. When you are prompted as follows, press ↵ to accept the default:

   ```
   Enter the number of columns for menu area 3, 0 to 539 <9>:

   Enter the number of rows for menu area 3, 0 to 1806 <13>:
   ```

9. At the prompts, pick the upper-left, lower-left, and lower-right corners of menu area 4. Use Figure B.1 for reference.

10. When you are prompted as follows, press ↵ to accept the default:

    ```
    Enter the number of columns for menu area 4, 0 to 5004
    <25>:

    Enter the number of rows for menu area 4, 0 to 1407 <7>:
    ```

11. When you are done selecting the menu areas, you will get the prompt

    ```
    Do you want to respecify the Fixed Screen Pointing Area:
    ```

    Type **Y** ↵.

12. When prompted, digitize the lower-left and upper-right of the fixed screen pointing area. Pick the positions indicated in Figure B.1.

    The three prompts that remain refer to the *floating screen pointing area.* This is an area on your tablet that allows you to select menu options and other areas on your screen outside the drawing area. This option is necessary because when you set up a digitizer for tracing, access to areas outside the drawing area is temporarily disabled. The floating screen pointing area lets you access pull-down menus and the status bar during tracing sessions (see *Chapter 11*).

    If you never intend to trace drawings with your tablet, then answer **N** to all three prompts. Otherwise do the following:

13. At the following prompt

    ```
    Do you want to specify the Floating Screen Pointing
    Area? <N>:
    ```

    type **Y** ↵.

**14.** At the prompt

```
Do you want the Floating Screen Pointing Area to be the
same size as the Fixed Screen Pointing Area? <Y>:
```

type **Y** ↵ if you want the Floating Screen Pointing Area to be the same as the Fixed Pointing Screen area. Type **N** ↵ if you want to use a separate area on your tablet for the Floating Screen Pointing Area.

**15.** The last prompt asks you if you want to use the F12 function key to toggle the Floating Screen Area on and off. (This is similar to the F10 key function of earlier releases of AutoCAD LT). Enter **Y** ↵ or **N** ↵, depending on whether you want to specify a different function key for the Floating Screen Area or not.

AutoCAD LT will remember this configuration until you change it again. Quit this file by clicking on File ➤ Exit.

## Turning on the Noun/Verb Option

If, for some reason, the Noun/Verb selection method is not available, here are instructions on how to turn it back on.

**1.** Choose Options ➤ Selection to display the Object Selection Settings dialog box.

2. In the Selection Modes button group, find the Noun/Verb Selection setting. Click on the check box to turn this option on.

3. Click on OK.

   If it wasn't there before, you should now see a small square at the intersection of the crosshair cursor. This square is actually a pickbox superimposed on the cursor. It tells you that you can select objects, even while the command prompt appears at the bottom of the screen and no command is currently active. As you have seen earlier, the square will momentarily disappear when you are in a command that asks you to select points.

   You can also turn on Noun/Verb selection by entering **´Pickfirst** ↵ at the command prompt. When you are asked for New value for Pickfirst <0>:, enter **1** ↵ (entering 0 turns the Pickfirst function off). The Pickfirst system variable is stored in the AutoCAD LT configuration file. See *Appendix D* for more on system variables.

### Other Selection Options

The Object Selection Settings dialog box lets you control the degree to which AutoCAD LT conforms to standard graphical user interface (GUI) methods of operation. It also lets you adjust the size of the object selection pickbox.

In *Chapter 2*, you practiced selecting objects using the Noun/Verb Selection setting—one of several AutoCAD LT settings that make the program work more like other GUI-environment programs. If you are used to working with other GUIs, you may want to turn on some of the other options in the Selection Settings dialog box. Here are descriptions of them; in brackets are the names of the system variables that control these features.

**Use Shift to Add [Pickadd]**   With this option checked, you can use the standard GUI method of holding down the Shift key to pick multiple objects. When the Shift key is not held down, only the single object picked or the group of objects windowed will be selected. Previously selected objects are deselected, unless the Shift key is held down during selection. To turn this feature on using system variables, set Pickadd to 0.

***Press and Drag [Pickdrag]***   With this option checked, you can use the standard GUI method for placing windows: You first click and hold down the pick button on the first corner of the window; then, while holding down the pick button, you drag the other corner of the window into position. When the other corner is in place, you let go of the pick button to finish the window. This setting applies to both Verb/Noun and Noun/Verb operations. In the system variables, set Pickdrag to 1 for this option.

***Implied Window [Pickauto]***   When this option is checked, a window or crossing window will automatically start if no object is picked at the `Select objects:` prompt. This setting has no effect on the Noun/Verb setting (preselection of objects). In the system variables, set Pickauto to 1 for this option.

## *Turning on the Grips Feature*

If for some reason the grips feature is not available, here are instructions for turning it back on.

**1.**   Choose Options ➤ Grips…. The Grips dialog box appears:

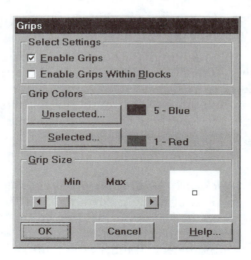

2. At the top of the dialog box are the Select Settings check boxes. Click on the Enable Grips check box.

3. Click OK, and you are ready to proceed.

The Grips dialog box also lets you determine whether grips appear on objects that compose a block (see *Chapter 4* for more on blocks), as well as set the grip color and size. These options can also be set using system variables described in *Appendix D*.

You can also turn the Grips feature on and off by entering ´**Grips** ↵. At the prompt New value for Grips <0>:, enter a **1** to turn Grips on, or **0** to turn Grips off. Grips is a system variable that is stored in the AutoCAD LT configuration file.

# Using Dialog Boxes

Now that you've seen AutoCAD LT's workspace layout, you'll want to familiarize yourself with *dialog boxes*. As with pull-down menus, dialog boxes offer an easy way to communicate with the program by offering you command options in an easy-to-understand visual format. If you've used Microsoft Windows or any other graphical user interface, you should feel right at home with AutoCAD LT Release 3's dialog boxes. If not, here is a brief primer.

## The Components

Figure B.2 shows two dialog boxes, each with a set of typical dialog box elements. There are three major components to dialog boxes: the title, the button groups, and the options. At the top of the dialog box is the title, which identifies the dialog box for you. Dialog boxes are divided into groups, enclosed by a rectangle and labeled at the top. We will refer to these groups as *button groups*, even though they don't always contain buttons. Scattered over the dialog boxes are the various buttons, boxes, and so forth (described in the following sections) that you use to specify your choices.

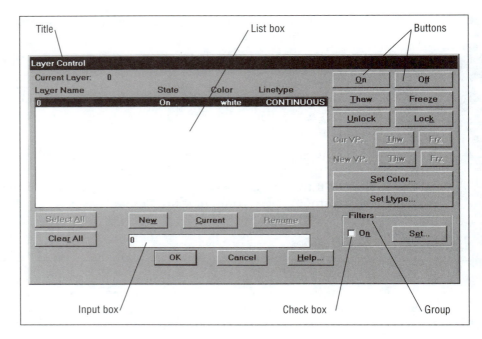

*Figure B.2:*     **The parts of a dialog box**

## Labeled Buttons

Whenever you see a rectangular button with a *label* on it, you know that clicking on it will immediately execute the action described in the label. Buttons whose labels are followed with an ellipsis (...) tell you that a dialog box will be opened when you click. Buttons with a < symbol following the label tell you that the screen will clear, allowing you to perform some activity, such as picking points. When you see a button that is heavily outlined, it means that button is the default choice and will be activated when you press ↵. Dimmed buttons are unavailable in the current use of the dialog box.

Here is a typical set of labeled buttons:

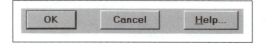

## Radio Buttons

When a set of mutually exclusive options are available, they are usually presented as *radio buttons*. These are small square buttons with labels to their right and usually found in groups. You activate a radio button option by clicking on the button itself to fill it in. Here is a set of radio buttons; the Decimal option is turned on:

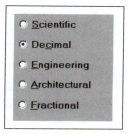

## Check Boxes

Toggled options are presented as *check boxes*. These are squares that are blank when the option is turned off, or have an *X* in them when the option is turned on. To turn on a check box, you click the square. Here is a set of check boxes; all options except Ortho and Quick Text are turned on:

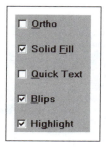

## List Boxes

You will often be presented with a list of items to choose from. These lists appear in *list boxes*, and you select items from the list by clicking on them. When the list is too long to fit in the list box, a scroll bar appears to the right of the box. You can search for specific items in a

App.
B

Installing and Setting
Up AutoCAD LT

list box by typing the first character of the item you are looking for. Edit boxes, explained just below, are often associated with list boxes.

Here is a sample list box; notice the scroll bar on the right:

| Layer Name | State | Color | Linetype |
|---|---|---|---|
| 0 | On . . . . | white | CONTINUOUS |
| ART | On . . . . | white | CONTINUOUS |
| ART1 | On . . . . | white | CONTINUOUS |
| DEFPOINTS | On . . . . | white | CONTINUOUS |
| DIM1 | On . . . . | red | CONTINUOUS |
| DIMS | On . . . . | red | CONTINUOUS |
| MESSAGES | On . . . . | magenta | CONTINUOUS |
| MESSAGES1 | . . . . . | magenta | CONTINUOUS |
| TEXT | On . . . . | blue | CONTINUOUS |

## Pull-down Lists

Sometimes, a *pull-down list* is used instead of a list box. This list first appears as a rectangle with a downward pointing arrow on the right side, and the default item in the rectangle. To pull down the list, you click the arrow, and then you click on the desired option. If the list is long, a scroll bar is provided.

Here is a sample pull-down list shown closed and opened with the scroll bar:

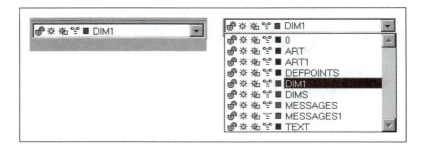

## Edit Boxes

If an option requires keyboard input from you, an *edit box* or *input box* is provided. When you click on the edit box, it displays a vertical bar cursor. You can then enter a name, number, or other value for the option next to the box, or you can correct any existing value in the box. Here is a typical group of edit boxes:

| | |
|---|---|
| X Spacing | 0.5000 |
| Y Spacing | 0.5000 |
| Snap Angle | 0 |
| X Base | 0.0000 |
| Y Base | 0.0000 |

If something already appears in an edit box, you can double-click on the box to highlight the entire text. Then begin to type, and your typing will completely replace the original entry. Clicking once in the text in the box moves the vertical bar cursor to that location, and you can edit or enter from that point. Just as in a word processor, you can toggle between Insert and Overtype modes by pressing the Ins key, and you can use the ← and → keys to move the vertical bar cursor. To highlight a group of characters in the input box, click and drag with the mouse.

## Keyboard Shortcuts

You may have noticed that the labels for the various buttons and boxes have underlined characters in them. Another way to select an option from a dialog box is by holding down the Alt key and pressing the underlined character in the option name. The option label is then highlighted. You can move to any other option in the dialog box by just pressing the underlined character (without Alt), or you can move sequentially from option to option by pressing the Tab key.

Once a button is highlighted, changing the option with the keyboard depends on the type of button it is. To activate radio buttons and check boxes, you use the Spacebar. To open pull-down lists, you press the ↓ key. You can then move up and down in the list using the ↑ and ↓, and use the Esc key to close it. To activate labeled buttons, press ↵ when they are highlighted.

You may want to try using the keyboard shortcuts for a while to see if you like them. They are not for everyone, but since you have one hand free while mousing around, you might as well put it to work.

App. B

Installing and Setting Up AutoCAD LT

# Appendix C
# Using the CD-ROM

**T**HIS appendix describes the software supplied on the companion CD-ROM that comes with this book. The CD contains a number of useful utilities and resources that you can load and run at any time. Before you use them, however, it's best to get familiar with AutoCAD LT. Many of these utilities work within AutoCAD LT from the command line or from options from pull-down menus, and they offer prompts in a way similar to most other AutoCAD LT commands.

## The Files on the CD

Look at the contents of the companion CD-ROM, and you'll see a bewildering variety of files and directories. Don't be alarmed. You won't have to deal with the majority of these files. Most of the files you see are program files for the AutoCAD LT Resource Guide. Let's look at what's available on the CD.

### The AutoCAD LT Resource Guide

The AutoCAD Resource Guide is an online encyclopedia of nearly all the third party add-on products available for Autodesk programs, including hardware and software. If you want to know if a particular add-on exists, use the Resource Guide to find it. Since it's set up as a Windows Help file, you won't have to learn anything new to use it.

The Resource Guide is divided into five main topics: Software Solutions, Hardware Solutions, Learning Resources (including Autodesk Training Centers, and AutoCAD User Groups), Consulting Partners, and New Products Showcase. The Resource Guide comes with a search feature called *Powersearch*. You can search for topics using keywords within each topic, or do a global search. You can also do searches with the product or company name, among other categories.

### Installing the AutoCAD LT Resource Guide

1. Click on Run... on the Windows 95 Start menu, and use the Browse button to locate the setup file: SETUP.EXE.

2. Select the SETUP.EXE, and click on the Open button.

3. When the filename appears in the Open: field in the Run dialog box, click on OK, then follow the instructions to install the Resource Guide.

   If you accept the default settings, the AutoCAD Resource Guide will be installed in the C:\ARG directory. The Setup program will create a program group and icon that will start the AutoCAD Resource Guide application. You can click and drag the Resource Guide icon to your AutoCAD LT program group for easier access.

   Note that to use the Resource Guide, you must have the companion CD in your computer.

### Using the AutoCAD LT Resource Guide

If you've ever used a Windows Help file, you should have no trouble using the AutoCAD Resource Guide. Once you've installed the guide, double click on its icon. At the opening screen of the Resource Guide simply click on the appropriate button to review the topic that you are interested in. You may wish to browse the Introductory and How to... information for the AutoCAD Resource Guide before reviewing the five major topic categories (Software, Hardware, Learning Resources, Consulting Partners, New Products). You can use the Powersearch feature or the Index to locate topics. Return to the opening screen at any time via the Go Back button.

The Resource Guide describes close to two thousand products which complement Autodesk software.

## The Mastering AutoCAD LT Bonus Software

To help you get the most from AutoCAD LT and this book, we've included a set of programs and files from the author. Locate the MASTERING AUTOCAD LT directory on the companion CD. Take a look at the contents of the \MASTERING AUTOCAD LT directory on the CD. It contains the following subdirectories:

**AEC**    contains a set of symbols and utilities described later in this appendix. These utilities will enhance your use of AutoCAD LT regardless of your profession.

**CUSTOM LINETYPES**    contains a library of Complex Linetypes for use in AutoCAD LT.

**SAMPLE DRAWINGS**    contains an archive of all of the tutorial drawings used in this book.

All of the programs and files in these subdirectories are offered to you free as a part of this book. The following sections describe how to install and use the bonus files found on the CD.

Since you will need the SAMPLE DRAWINGS to complete the tutorials in this book, let's take a look at installing these files first. Then we will review installation and use of the AEC and CUSTOM LINETYPES packages.

## Installing and Using the Sample Drawing Files

The sample drawing files for the exercises in this book are contained in the SAMPLE DRAWINGS subdirectory under the MASTERING AUTOCAD LT directory on the companion CD. These drawings are provided for you in the event that you decide to skip some of the book's tutorial material. With these files, you can open the book to any chapter and start working, without having to construct the drawings from earlier chapters. An icon in each exercise, like the one shown here in the margin, lets you know when a file is available in the exercise sequence.

Here's how to install the sample files:

1. Locate the \Sample subdirectory within AutoCAD LT on your own system. If you installed AutoCAD LT per the defaults, this will be

   ```
   C:\Program Files\Autocad LT\Sample
   ```

2. Copy all of the sample drawing files from the \MASTERING AUTO-CAD LT\SAMPLE DRAWINGS subdirectory on the CD into the \Sample directory on your system.

Once you've installed the sample files, you have free access to them during the exercises. To open the sample drawings, click on the Open button (File folder) on the Standard toolbar, locate the Sample sub-directory and double-click on the name of the drawing you require. Table C.1 contains a list of all of the Sample Drawings for each Chapter.

*Table C.1:* **Sample Drawings for the Mastering AutoCAD LT Tutorials**

| Chapter | Drawing Name | Description |
|---------|--------------|-------------|
| Chapter 1 | NOZZLE3D.DWG | Sample drawing for *Open an Existing File*. |
| Chapter 1 | DHOUSE.DWG | Sample drawing in *If You Want to Experiment*.... |
| Chapter 2 | DOOR.DWG | Door drawing created in this chapter. |
| Chapter 3 | 3-01.DWG | Bath Outline as per Figure 3.1. |
| Chapter 3 | 03-08.DWG | Bath layout per Figure 3.8. |
| Chapter 4 | 04-BATH.DWG | Bathroom drawing as completed in Chapter 3. |
| Chapter 4 | TOILET.DWG | Toilet block/drawing. |
| Chapter 4 | TUB.DWG | Tub block/drawing. |
| Chapter 4 | 04-03.DWG | Bathroom with tub and toilet inserted. |
| Chapter 4 | 04-07.DWG | Bathroom with door inserted. |
| Chapter 4 | BATH.DWG | Completed Bathroom drawing. |
| Chapter 5 | 05-01A.DWG | Gas burner per Figure 5.1. |
| Chapter 5 | 05-08.DWG | Kitchenette per Figure 5.8. |
| Chapter 5 | 05-09A.DWG | Unit outline per Figure 5.9. |
| Chapter 5 | 05-20.DWG | Unit plan per Figure 5.20 |

App.
C

Using the CD-ROM

*Table C.1:*    **Sample Drawings for the Mastering AutoCAD LT Tutorials (continued)**

| Chapter | Drawing Name | Description |
| --- | --- | --- |
| Chapter 5 | KITCHEN.DWG | As completed in Chapter 5. |
| Chapter 5 | LOBBY.DWG | As completed per Figure 5.24. |
| Chapter 5 | UNIT.DWG | Unit drawing as completed in Chapter 5. |
| Chapter 6 | 06-UNIT.DWG | Unit drawing as completed in Chapter 5. |
| Chapter 7 | 07-PLAN.DWG | Plan drawing as created in Chapter 6. |
| Chapter 8 | 08-UNIT.DWG | Unit drawing with Floor Patterns added in Chapter 6. |
| Chapter 9 | 09-UNIT.DWG | Unit drawing with text added in Chapter 8. |
| Chapter 10 | 10-PLAN.DWG | Plan drawing (unchanged since Chapter 6). |
| Chapter 10 | S-DOOR.DWG | Door type symbol. |
| Chapter 10 | S-APART.DWG | Apartment number symbol. |
| Chapter 10 | DOOR.TXT | Template file for attribute extraction. |
| Chapter 11 | 11-TRACE.DWG | Traced Utility room per Figure 11.5. |
| Chapter 11 | UTIL.DWG | Utility room with lockers added. |
| Chapter 12 | 12-PLAN.DWG | Plan drawing with door and apartment symbols added in Chapter 10. |
| Chapter 12 | 12-UNIT.DWG | Unit drawing with dimensioning added in Chapter 9. |

*Table C.1:* **Sample Drawings for the Mastering AutoCAD LT Tutorials (continued)**

| Chapter | Drawing Name | Description |
|---------|--------------|-------------|
| Chapter 12 | 12-UNIT2.DWG | One bedroom unit as per Figure 12.22. |
| Chapter 12 | COL-GR.DWG | Column grid as per Figure 12.24. |
| Chapter 12 | FLOOR1.DWG | Eight studio corner units per Figure 12.25. |
| Chapter 12 | FLOOR2.DWG | Eight one-bedroom corner units per Figure 12.26. |
| Chapter 12 | COMMON.DWG | Remaining units and common areas in Plan drawing. |
| Chapter 12 | UTIL.DWG | Utility room for insertion across from Lobby per Figure 12.30. |
| Chapter 12 | XREF-ALL.DWG | Drawing containing all of the Reference drawings. |
| Chapter 13 | TOPO.DWG | Contour drawing for Editing exercise. |
| Chapter 14 | 14-UNIT.DWG | Unit drawing (with layers turned off). |
| Chapter 14 | FLANGE.DWG | Sample drawing for complex area calculations. |
| Chapter 15 | 15-UNIT.DWG | Unit drawing (unchanged since Chapter 9). |
| Chapter 15 | 15-3DUNIT.DWG | Plan drawing for Slide Presentation (SW Isometric view). |
| Chapter 15 | 3DUNIT.DWG | 3D Unit in Plan view. |
| Chapter 16 | BARCELON.DWG | 3D Chair drawing created in this chapter. |

## On-Screen AEC

On-Screen AEC is a set of macros and architectural symbols, all integrated with a standard AutoCAD LT menu and toolbars. This package offers the basic tools you'll need to start drawing architectural drawings. In addition, it contains many time-saving tools to aid all users—not just architects—in editing your drawings.

### Installing On-Screen AEC

Here's how to install On-Screen AEC:

1. Create a subdirectory called **AEC** under \Program Files\AutoCAD LT.

2. Copy the contents of the AEC directory on the CD-ROM into the \Program Files\AutoCAD LT\AEC subdirectory.

3. Start AutoCAD LT and choose Tools ➤ Preferences....

4. Click on the File System tab at the top of the dialog box. The File system Options appear.

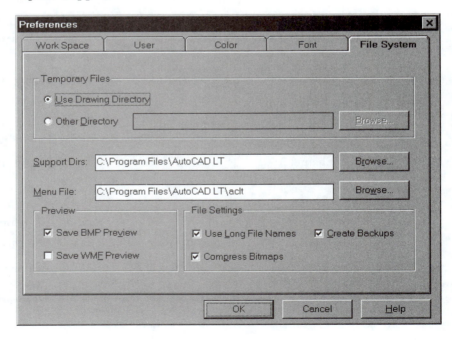

5. Next, in the Support Dirs: input box, add ***drive:\ Program Files\ AutoCAD LT\AEC*** to the end of the line shown there. The line should be similar to the following:

```
C:\Program Files\AutoCAD LT;C:\Program Files\
AutoCAD LT\AEC
```

This example shows a typical listing in the Support Dirs: input box, where AutoCAD LT is installed on drive C. Replace the C in this example with the drive letter where AutoCAD LT is installed in your system.

6. Click on OK, then close and restart AutoCAD LT.

On-Screen AEC is now installed and ready for use. The next section describes how to load the On-Screen AEC menus.

### Loading the On-Screen AEC Menu

Now you are ready to load the On-Screen AEC menus to give you access to the symbols and utilities offered there. Here's how it's done.

1. Once back in AutoCAD LT, choose Tools ➤ Customize Menu or type **Menuload** ↵. The Menu Customization dialog box appears.

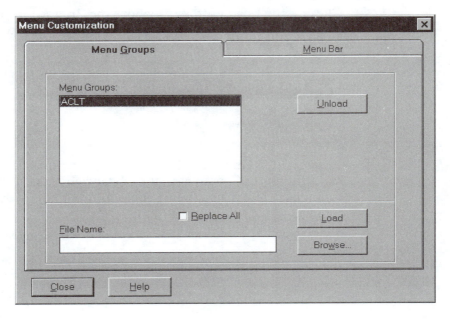

2.  Click on the Browse button at the bottom of the dialog box. The Select Menu File dialog box appears.

3.  Locate the filename OSAEC.MNU, then double-click on it. You return to the Menu Customization dialog box and the OSAEC.MNU filename appears in the File Name input box.

4.  Click on the Load button just above the Browse button. AutoCAD LT takes a moment to load the menu. The AEC Tools toolbar will appear on the screen.

5.  In the Menu Group list box in the upper portion of the dialog box, highlight OSAEC, then click the tab labeled Menu Bar at the top of the dialog box. The dialog box changes to reveal the Menu Bar options.

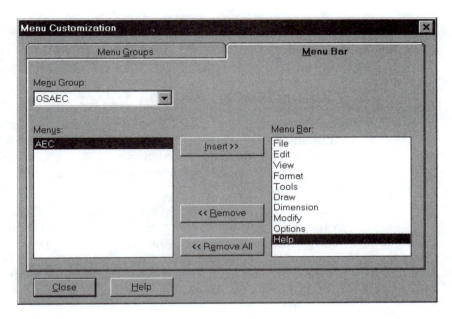

Notice that a menu called AEC appears in the Menus list box to the left. This is a pull-down menu that is contained in the OSAEC.MNU file.

6. In the Menu Bar list box to the right, click on Help to highlight it. This determines where the AEC pull-down menu will appear in the menu bar.

7. Click on the button labeled Insert >>. AEC will appear just above Help in the Menu Bar list box and you will see AEC appear in the AutoCAD LT menu bar at the top of the AutoCAD LT Window.

You are now ready to use On-Screen AEC. Follow the instructions presented in the following section.

## Using the AEC Utilities

On-Screen AEC is a basic architectural symbols library package. This package supplies utilities for creating doors, plumbing and electrical fixtures, wall patterns, and wall intersection clean-up. Even if your application doesn't involve architecture, you may want to install On-Screen AEC just to take advantage of these utilities.

> **WARNING** You should turn off any running object snaps before using these utilities, as the Osnaps will interfere with the accuracy of point selections.

## Getting Started with On-Screen AEC

Once you've installed the AEC software, you can begin to use On-Screen AEC. In the AEC directory, there is a Word file called AECLT.DOC that contains very detailed instructions on the use of this package. This appendix provides summary instructions on each of the options available in this package.

You may want to start by clicking on the Sheet Setup Drawing option in the AEC pull-down menu to bring up a dialog box you can use to set up your drawing. Once the setup is done, you will have a drawing area equivalent to your sheet size, with a grid representing 1″ intervals on the final plot area. Text size for the Standard text style and dimension styles will also be set up for you.

## Using AEC to Add Walls, Doors, Symbols, and Stairs

Let's begin by taking a look at some of the basic architectural features available with AEC.

### Adding Walls

On-Screen AEC LT makes use of the Dline command found in Auto-CAD LT. The Dline command draws two parallel lines (double lines) to create walls in a single step rather than drawing one side and then copying or offsetting to finish the wall. We've included a button on the On-Screen AEC LT toolbar for your convenience.

### Adding a Door

The door utility can be used only in the world coordinate system. If you are in another UCS, switch back to the WCS temporarily to insert a door using this utility. In order to place doors, you must have drawn walls using the Wall utility.

Adding a door is a two step process. First, you create an opening in a wall, then you place a door. First, lets look at how you create an opening.

1. Choose AEC ➤ Opening, then select an opening size from the cascading menu that appears. Alternately, you can choose an opening size from the 12″ Wall Opening flyout menu on the AEC Tools toolbar.

2. Click on one side of the wall, locating the center of the opening.

3. Click on the opposite side of the wall. After a moment, the opening will appear.

    To place a door, do the following:

1. Choose AEC ➤ Doors, then select a door type, or choose a door from the AEC Tools toolbar Door flyout.

2. Select the hinge corner of the opening.

3. Select the opposite side of the door opening. At this point, you see the door appear.

4. Select the hinge corner again.

5. Select the opposite side of the door opening again to set the rotation angle of the door.

### Adding a Wall Pattern

Here's how to select and pick points for a wall pattern:

1. Choose AEC ➤ Wall Pattern, then from the cascading menu, select the wall pattern you want, or click on Open Toolbar to open the Wall Pattern toolbar. Or select a wall pattern from the wall pattern flyout menu on the AEC Tools Toolbar.

2. Click on a point within the wall that is to receive the wall pattern. (If you select the Steel wall pattern, you need to select both sides of the wall.)

    The wall pattern appears between the first and last points you selected.

### Adding Symbols

Here are the steps to add symbols to a drawing. If you would like to modify the AEC-supplied symbols to fit your own work environment, you can find them in the AEC subdirectory.

1. Pull down the AEC menu, and choose one of the three categories of symbols. A cascading menu appears, with a list of symbols. For the Electrical and Reference symbols, you must also choose a scale.

2. Choose the name of the symbol you want to use.

3. Answer the Insertion point and rotation angle prompts on the command line. The symbol appears in the location you select.

   Alternatively, you may pick a symbol from the symbol toolbars. Figure C.1 shows a representative set of the AEC symbol toolbars. Electrical and Reference have ½″, ¼″, ⅛″, and ¹⁄₁₆″ scale toolbars, as well as a Custom scale option.

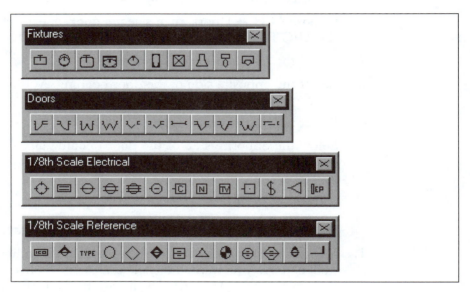

Figure C.1:    *The symbol toolbars available on the AEC menu*

## Using the Wall Cleanup Utilities

The cleanup utilities will join double lines into tee, corner, and cross formations. The lines joined must be simple lines, not polylines.

### Cleaning Up Tee Wall Intersections

To clean up tee wall intersections, do the following:

1. Click on AEC ➤ Wall Cleanup ➤ Tee, or select the Tee button on the AEC Tools toolbar.

2. Click on one corner of the tee.

3. Click on the other corner of the tee.

4. Click on the second corner of the tee again. The wall lines will join to form a tee.

### Cleaning Up Corner Wall Intersections

To clean up corner wall intersections, do the following:

1. Click on AEC ➤ Wall Cleanup ➤ Corner, or select Corner from the Tee flyout on the AEC Tools toolbar.

2. Click on the outer-most intersection of the wall corner.

3. Click on the inner corner of the wall intersection.

4. Click on the inner corner again. The corner will join.

### Cleaning Up Crossing Wall Intersections

This function only works if all the lines forming the walls are continuous through the intersection. If this is the case, do the following:

1. Click on AEC ➤ Wall Cleanup ➤ Intersect, and then click on the Intersection button of the Tee flyout on the AEC Tools toolbar.

2. Click on a corner of the intersection.

3. Click on the corner that is diagonal from the first corner you selected.

4. Click on the second corner again. The wall will be cleaned to form a wall intersection.

### 3D Objects Toolbar

AutoCAD LT for Windows 95 is 100% file-compatible with AutoCAD Release 13. This means that any Release 13 drawing can be opened and edited by AutoCAD LT. There are some objects, notably 3D solids, that can be created in AutoCAD Release 13 and imported into Auto-CAD LT. However, AutoCAD LT cannot by itself create these objects.

Now you can use 3D solids in your AutoCAD LT session by loading the 3D Objects toolbar.

1. Select menu item AEC ➤ Toolbars ➤ 3D Objects.

2. Click the required shape on the toolbar, and AEC will insert a block containing the desired object.

The block may then be exploded, and the object edited just like any other AutoCAD LT object.

### Installing and Using the Custom Linetypes

The CUSTOM LINETYPES subdirectory is located under the MASTERING AUTOCAD LT directory on the companion CD. It contains a library of Complex Linetypes for use in AutoCAD LT. The library contains source shape files, compiled shape files, and linetype definitions as well as two drawing files that display the standard AutoCAD LT linetypes and the bonus complex linetypes.

To install the complex linetype library:

1. Copy the Linetype files from the CUSTOM LINETYPES directory on the CD into your AutoCAD LT directory on your hard drive. Alternatively, you may drag the entire CUSTOM LINETYPES folder and copy it onto your system as a subdirectory of your AutoCAD LT program directory.

2. Use the Linetype command or Linetype button on the Object Properties toolbar to load the linetypes from file PWRLTYPE.LIN.

3. Open the drawing file LTYPES02.DWG to view and experiment with these linetypes.

NOTE Complex linetypes that have embedded text use the font file Romans.shx. You must have a text style which uses Romans defined in your drawing for these linetypes to work.

# Appendix D

# System and Dimension Variables

**T**HIS appendix discusses AutoCAD LT's system variables. It is divided into two sections: *system variables* and *dimension variables*. The general system variables let you fine-tune your AutoCAD LT environment. Dimension variables govern the specific dimensioning functions of AutoCAD LT.

System variables are accessible directly from the command prompt, and transparently (while in another command), by entering the variable name preceded by an apostrophe.

We've divided this appendix into two main sections: Setting System Variables and Setting Dimension Variables. This division is somewhat artificial, because as far as AutoCAD LT is concerned, there is no difference between system variables and dimension variables—you use both types of variables the same way. But because the set of dimension variables is quite extensive, they are separated here for clarity.

## Setting System Variables

Table D.1 lists the variables, and notes whether they are read-only or adjustable. Most of these variables have counterparts in other commands, as listed in the table. For example, Angdir and Angbase can be adjusted using the Ddunits command (Format ➤ Units). Others, such as Highlight and Expert, do not have equivalent commands. These must be adjusted at the command line.

Table D.1: **System Variables**

| Variable Name | Associated Command | Where Saved | Use |
|---|---|---|---|
| ACLTPREFIX | Preferences | *NA* | The ACAD environment setting. |
| ACLTVER | *NA* | *NA* | The AutoCAD LT version number. |
| AFLAGS | Units | With drawing | Controls attribute mode settings: 1 = invisible; 2 = constant; 3 = verify; 8 = preset. |
| ANGBASE | Units | With drawing | Controls direction of 0 angle, relative to the current UCS. |
| ANGDIR | Units | With drawing | Controls positive direction of angles: 0 = counterclockwise; 1 = clockwise. |
| APERTURE | Aperture | With configuration | Controls the Osnap cursor target height in pixels. |
| AREA (read-only) | Area | *NA* | Displays last area calculation; use with Getvar function. |
| ATTDIA | Insert/ Attribute | With drawing | Controls the Attribute dialog box: 0 = no dialog box; 1 = dialog box. |
| ATTMODE | Attdisp | With drawing | Controls attribute display mode: 0 = off; 1 = normal; 2 = on. |

App.
D

System and
Dimension Variables

*Table D.1:*   **System Variables (continued)**

| Variable Name | Associated Command | Where Saved | Use |
|---|---|---|---|
| ATTREQ | Insert | With drawing | Controls the prompt for attributes: 0 = no prompt or dialog box for attributes (attributes use default values); 1 = normal prompt or dialog box upon attribute insertion. |
| AUDITCTL | Config | With configuration | Controls whether an audit file is created: 0 = disable; 1 = enable creation of .ADT file. |
| AUNITS | Units | With drawing | Controls angular units: 0 = decimal degrees; 1 = degrees-minutes-seconds; 2 = grads; 3 = radians; 4 = surveyor's units. |
| AUPREC | Units | With drawing | Controls the precision of angular units determined by decimal place. |
| BACKZ (read-only) | Dview | With drawing | Displays distance from Dview target to back clipping plane. |
| BLIPMODE | *NA* | With drawing | Controls appearance of blips: 0 = off; 1 = on. |

*Table D.1:*  **System Variables (continued)**

| Variable Name | Associated Command | Where Saved | Use |
|---|---|---|---|
| CDATE (read-only) | Time | *NA* | Displays calendar date/time (YYYYMMDD.HHMMSSMSEC). |
| CECOLOR | Color | With drawing | Controls current default color assigned to new objects. |
| CELTSCALE | *NA* | With drawing | Controls current linetype scale for individual objects. |
| CELTYPE | Linetype | With drawing | Controls current default linetype assigned to new objects. |
| CHAMFERA | Chamfer | With drawing | Controls first chamfer distance. |
| CHAMFERB | Chamfer | With drawing | Controls second chamfer distance. |
| CHAMFERC | Chamfer | With drawing | Controls chamfer distance for Angle option. |
| CHAMFERD | Chamfer | With drawing | Controls chamfer angle for Angle option. |
| CHAMMODE | Chamfer | With drawing | Controls method of chamfer: 0 = use 2 distances; 1 = use distance and angle. |
| CIRCLERAD | Circle | *NA* | Controls the default circle radius: 0 = no default. |
| CLAYER | Layer | With drawing | Sets the current layer. |

**App. D**

*Table D.1:* **System Variables (continued)**

| Variable Name | Associated Command | Where Saved | Use |
|---|---|---|---|
| CMDACTIVE (read-only) | *NA* | *NA* | Displays whether a command, script, or dialog box is active: 1 = command active; 2 = transparent command active; 4 = script active; 8 = dialog box active (values are cumulative, so 3 = command and transparent command are active). |
| CMDDIA | *NA* | With configuration | Controls use of dialog boxes for some commands: 0 = use command line; 1 = use dialog box. |
| CMDNAMES (read-only) | *NA* | *NA* | Displays the English name of the currently active command. |
| COORDS | F6, Ctrl-D | With drawing | Controls coordinate readout: 0 = coordinates displayed only when points are picked; 1 = absolute coordinates dynamically displayed as cursor moves; 2 = distance and angle displayed during commands that accept relative distance input. |

*Table D.1:* **System Variables (continued)**

| Variable Name | Associated Command | Where Saved | Use |
|---|---|---|---|
| CVPORT (read-only) | Vports | With drawing | Displays ID number of current viewport. |
| DATE (read-only) | Time | *NA* | Displays date and time in Julian format. |
| DCTCUST | Spell | With configuration | Sets default custom spelling dictionary file name, including path. |
| DCTMAIN | Spell | With configuration | Sets default main spelling dictionary file name; requires specific keywords for each language. Use AutoCAD LT Help for complete list of keywords. |
| DELOBJ | *NA* | With drawing | Controls whether source objects used to create new objects are retained: 0 = delete objects; 1 = retain objects. |
| DISTANCE (read-only) | Dist | *NA* | Displays last distance calculated by Dist command. |
| DITHER | *NA* | ACLT.INI | Controls whether drawings are dithered (additional colors are simulated in drawing output). On Windows 95 system printers only: 0 = Off; 1 = On. |

**App. D**

**System and Dimension Variables**

Table D.1:    **System Variables (continued)**

| Variable Name | Associated Command | Where Saved | Use |
|---|---|---|---|
| DONUTID | Donut | *NA* | Controls default inside diameter of a donut. |
| DONUTOD | Donut | *NA* | Controls default outside diameter of a donut. |
| DWG-CODEPAGE (read-only) | *NA* | With drawing | Displays code page of drawing (see Syscodepage). |
| DWGNAME (read-only) | Open | *NA* | Displays drawing name and drive/ directory, if specified by user. |
| DWGPREFIX (read-only) | *NA* | *NA* | Displays drive and directory of current file. |
| DWGTITLED (read-only) | *NA* | *NA* | Displays whether a drawing has been named: 0 = untitled; 1 = named by user. |
| DWGWRITE (read-only) | *NA* | *NA* | Displays read/write status of current drawing: 0 = read-only; 1 = read/write. |
| EDGEMODE | Trim, Extend | With configuration | Controls how trim and extend boundaries are determined: 0 = boundaries defined by object only; 1 = boundaries defined by objects and their extension. |

*Table D.1:* **System Variables (continued)**

| Variable Name | Associated Command | Where Saved | Use |
|---|---|---|---|
| ELEVATION | Elev | With drawing | Controls current 3D elevation relative to current UCS. |
| EXEDIR (read-only) | *NA* | *NA* | Displays the directory path of the AutoCAD LT executable file. |
| EXPERT | *NA* | *NA* | Controls prompts, depending on level of user's expertise: 0 = normal prompts; 1 = suppresses About to regen and Really want to turn the current layer off prompts; 2 = suppresses Block already defined and A drawing with this name already exists prompt for Block command; 3 = suppresses An item with this name already exists prompt for the Linetype command; 4 = suppresses An item with this name already exists for the UCS and Vports Save options; 5 = suppresses An item with this name already exists for Dimstyle/Save and Dimoverride commands. |

Table D.1:    **System Variables (continued)**

| Variable Name | Associated Command | Where Saved | Use |
|---|---|---|---|
| EXTMAX (read-only) | Zoom | With drawing | Displays upper-right corner coordinate of extents. view. |
| EXTMIN (read-only) | Zoom | With drawing | Displays lower-left corner coordinate of extents view. |
| FFLIMIT | Style (fonts) | With configuration | Sets number of Post-Script and TrueType fonts that can be stored in memory, from 0 to 100; 0 = no limit. |
| FILEDIA | Dialog box | With configuration | Sets whether a file dialog box is used by default: 0 = don't use unless requested with a ~; 1 = use whenever possible. |
| FILLETRAD | Fillet | With drawing | Controls fillet radius. |
| FILLMODE | Fill | With drawing | Controls fill status: 0 = off; 1 = on. |
| FRONTZ (read-only) | Dview | With drawing | Controls front clipping plane for current viewport; use with Viewmode system variable. |
| GRIDMODE | Grid | With drawing | Controls grid: 0 = off; 1 = on. |

*Table D.1:* **System Variables (continued)**

| Variable Name | Associated Command | Where Saved | Use |
|---|---|---|---|
| GRIDUNIT | Grid | With drawing | Controls grid spacing. |
| GRIPBLOCK | Grips | With configuration | Controls display of grips in blocks: 0 = show insertion point grip only; 1 = show grips of all objects in block. |
| GRIPCOLOR | Grips | With configuration | Controls color of unselected grips. Choices are integers from 1 to 255; default is 5. |
| GRIPHOT | Grips | With configuration | Controls color of hot grips. Choices are integers from 1 to 255; default is 1. |
| GRIPS | Grips | With configuration | Controls use of grips: 0 = grips disabled; 1 = grips enabled (default). |
| GRIPSIZE | Grips | With configuration | Controls grip size (in pixels), from 1 to 255 (default is 3). |
| HANDLES (read-only) | *NA* | With drawing | Displays status of object handles: 0 = off; 1 = on. |

*Table D.1:*    **System Variables (continued)**

| Variable Name | Associated Command | Where Saved | Use |
|---|---|---|---|
| HIGHLIGHT | Select | *NA* | Controls whether objects are highlighted when selected: 0 = none; 1 = highlighting. |
| HPANG | HATCH | *NA* | Sets default hatch pattern angle. |
| HPDOUBLE | Hatch | *NA* | Sets default hatch doubling for user-defined hatch pattern: 0 = no doubling; 1 = doubling at 90˚. |
| HPNAME | Hatch | *NA* | Sets default hatch pattern name; use a period (.) to set to no default. |
| HPSCALE | Hatch | *NA* | Sets default hatch pattern scale factor. |
| HPSPACE | Hatch | *NA* | Sets default line spacing for user-defined hatch pattern; cannot be 0. |
| INSBASE | Base | With drawing | Controls insertion base point of current drawing. |
| INSNAME | Insert | *NA* | Sets default block or file name for Insert command; enter a period (.) to set to no default. |
| LASTANGLE (read-only) | Arc | *NA* | Displays ending angle for last arc drawn. |

*Table D.1:*     **System Variables (continued)**

| Variable Name | Associated Command | Where Saved | Use |
| --- | --- | --- | --- |
| LASTPOINT | *NA* | With drawing | Sets or displays coordinate normally referenced by the @. |
| LENS-LENGTH (read-only) | Dview | With drawing | Displays focal length of lens used for perspective display. |
| LIMCHECK | Limits | With drawing | Controls limit checking: 0 = no checking; 1 = checking. |
| LIMMAX | Limits | With drawing | Controls coordinate of drawing's upper-right limit. |
| LIMMIN | Limits | With drawing | Controls coordinate of drawing's lower-left limit. |
| LOCALE (read-only) | *NA* | *NA* | Displays ISO language code used by your version of AutoCAD LT. |
| LONG-FNAME (read-only) | *NA* | With configuration | Indicates whether long file name support is enabled or disabled: 0 = disabled; 1 = enabled. |
| LTSCALE | Ltscale | With drawing | Controls the global linetype scale factor. |

**App. D**

**System and Dimension Variables**

*Table D.1: System Variables (continued)*

| Variable Name | Associated Command | Where Saved | Use |
|---|---|---|---|
| LUNITS | Units | With drawing | Controls unit styles: 1 = scientific; 2 = decimal; 3 = engineering, 4 = architectural, 5 = fractional. |
| LUPREC | Units | With drawing | Controls unit accuracy by decimal place or size of denominator. |
| MACRO-TRACE | Diesel | *NA* | Controls debugging tool for DIESEL expressions: 0 = disabled; 1 = enabled. |
| MAXACTVP | Viewports/ Vports | *NA* | Controls maximum number of viewports to regenerate at one time. |
| MAXSORT | *NA* | With configuration | Controls maximum number of items to be sorted when a command displays a list. |
| MENUECHO | *NA* | *NA* | Controls messages and command prompt display from commands embedded in menu: 0 = display all messages; 1 = suppress menu item name; 2 = suppress command prompts; 4 = disable ^P toggle of menu echo; 8 = debugging aid for DIESEL expressions. |

*Table D.1:* **System Variables (continued)**

| Variable Name | Associated Command | Where Saved | Use |
| --- | --- | --- | --- |
| MIRRTEXT | Mirror | With drawing | Controls mirroring of text: 0 = disabled; 1 = enabled. |
| MODE-MACRO | *NA* | *NA* | Controls display of user-defined text in status line. |
| MTEXTED | Mtext | With configuration | Controls name of program used for editing MText objects. |
| OFFSET-DIST | Offset | With drawing | Controls default offset distance. |
| ORTHO-MODE | F8, Ctrl-O, ORTHO | With drawing | Controls ortho mode: 0 = off; 1 = on. |
| OSMODE | Osnap | With drawing | Sets current default Osnap mode: 0 = none; 1 = endpoint; 2 = midpoint; 4 = center; 8 = node; 16 = quadrant; 32 = intersection; 64 = insert; 128 = perpendicular; 256 = nearest; 512 = quick. If more than one mode is required, enter the sum of those modes. |
| PDMODE | Ddptype | With drawing | Controls type of symbol used as a point during Point command. |

*Table D.1:*    **System Variables (continued)**

| Variable Name | Associated Command | Where Saved | Use |
|---|---|---|---|
| PDSIZE | Point | With drawing | Controls size of symbol set by PDMODE. |
| PELLIPSE | Ellipse | With drawing | Controls type of object created with Ellipse command: 0 = true NURBS ellipse; 1 = polyline representation of ellipse. |
| PERIMETER (read-only) | Area, List | *NA* | Displays last perimeter value derived from Area and List commands. |
| PICKADD | Select | With configuration | Determines how items are added to a selection set: 0 = only most recently selected item(s) become selection set (to accumulate objects in a selection set, hold down Shift while selecting); 1 = selected objects accumulate in a selection set as you select them (hold down Shift while selecting items to remove those items from the selection set). |

*Table D.1:* **System Variables (continued)**

| Variable Name | Associated Command | Where Saved | Use |
|---|---|---|---|
| PICKAUTO | Select | With configuration | Controls automatic window at Select objects prompt: 0 = window is enabled; 1 = window is disabled. |
| PICKBOX | Select | With configuration | Controls size of object-selection pickbox (in pixels). |
| PICKDRAG | Select | With configuration | Controls how selection windows are used: 0 = click on each corner of the window; 1 = Shift-click and hold on first corner, then drag and release for the second corner. |
| PICKFIRST | Select | With configuration | Controls whether you can pick object(s) before you select a command: 0 = disabled; 1 = enabled. |
| PLATFORM (read-only) | *NA* | *NA* | Identifies the version of AutoCAD LT being used. |

**App. D**

**System and Dimension Variables**

*Table D.1:* **System Variables (continued)**

| Variable Name | Associated Command | Where Saved | Use |
|---|---|---|---|
| PLINEGEN | Pline/Pedit | With drawing | Controls how polylines generate line types around vertices: 0 = linetype pattern begins and ends at vertices; 1 = linetype patterns ignore vertices and begin and end at polyline beginning and ending. |
| PLINEWID | Pline | With drawing | Controls default polyline width. |
| PLOTID | Plot | With configuration | Sets default plotter based on its description. |
| PLOTROT-MODE | Plot | With drawing | Controls orientation of your plotter output. |
| PLOTTER | Plot | With configuration | Sets default plotter, based on its assigned integer ID. |
| POLYSIDES | Polygon | *NA* | Controls default number of sides for a polygon. |

*Table D.1:*   **System Variables (continued)**

| Variable Name | Associated Command | Where Saved | Use |
|---|---|---|---|
| PROJMODE | Trim, Extend | With drawing | Controls how Trim and Extend affect objects in 3D: 0 = true 3D mode (no projection); 1 = trims/extends based on a plane parallel to the current UCS; 2 = trims/extends based on a plane parallel to the current view plane. |
| PSLTSCALE | Pspace | With drawing | Controls Paper Space linetype scaling. |
| PSPROLOG | Psout | With configuration | Controls what portion of the ACLT.PSF file is used for the prologue section of a Psout output file. Set this to the name of the section you want to use. |
| QTEXT-MODE | Qtext | With drawing | Controls the quick text mode: 0 = off; 1 = on. |
| RASTER-PREVIEW | Save | With drawing | Controls whether raster preview images are saved with the drawing and sets the format type: 0 = BMP only; 1 = BMP and WMF; 2 = WMF only; 3 = No preview image created. |

**App. D**

**System and Dimension Variables**

*Table D.1:*   **System Variables (continued)**

| Variable Name | Associated Command | Where Saved | Use |
|---|---|---|---|
| SAVEFILE (read-only) | Autosave | With configuration | Displays filename that is autosaved. |
| SAVENAME (read-only) | Save | *NA* | Displays user file name under which file is saved. |
| SAVETIME | Autosave | With configuration | Controls time interval between automatic saves, in minutes: 0 = automatic save disabled. |
| SCREENSIZE (read-only) | *NA* | *NA* | Displays current viewport size in pixels. |
| SHADEDGE | Shade | With drawing | Controls how drawing is shaded: 0 = faces shaded, no edge highlighting; 1 = faces shaded, edge highlighting; 2 = faces not filled, edges in object color; 3 = faces drawn in object color, edges in background color. |
| SHADEDIF | Shade | With drawing | Sets difference between diffuse reflective and ambient light. Value represents percentage of diffuse reflective light. |

*Table D.1:* **System Variables (continued)**

| Variable Name | Associated Command | Where Saved | Use |
|---|---|---|---|
| SNAPANG | Snap | With drawing | Controls snap and grid angle. |
| SNAPBASE | Snap | With drawing | Controls snap, grid, and hatch pattern origin. |
| SNAPISO-PAIR | Snap | With drawing | Controls isometric plane: 0 = left; 1 = top; 2 = right. |
| SNAPMODE | F9, Snap | With drawing | Controls snap toggle: 0 = off; 1 = on. |
| SNAPSTYL | Snap | With drawing | Controls snap style: 0 = standard; 1 = isometric. |
| SNAPUNIT | Snap | With drawing | Controls snap spacing given in $x$ and $y$ values. |
| SORTENTS | *NA* | With configuration | Controls whether objects are sorted based on their order in database: 0 = disabled; 1 = sort for object selection; 2 = sort for object snap; 4 = sort for redraws; 8 = sort for Mslide; 16 = sort for regen; 32 = sort for plot; 64 = sort for Psout. |

**App. D**

**System and Dimension Variables**

*Table D.1:*    **System Variables (continued)**

| Variable Name | Associated Command | Where Saved | Use |
|---|---|---|---|
| SPLFRAME | Pline, Pedit | With drawing | Controls display of spline vertices, defining mesh of a surface-fit mesh, and display of "invisible" edges of 3Dfaces: 0 = no display of spline vertices, only fit surface of a smoothed 3Dmesh, and no display of "invisible" edges of 3Dface; 1 = spline vertices are displayed, only defining mesh of a smoothed 3Dmesh is displayed, "invisible" edges of 3Dface are displayed. |
| SPLINESEGS | Pline, Pedit | With drawing | Controls number of line segments used for each spline patch. |
| SPLINETYPE | Pline, Pedit | With drawing | Controls type of spline curve generated by Pedit spline: 5 = quadratic B-spline; 6 = cubic B-spline. |
| SYSCODE-PAGE (read-only) | *NA* | With drawing | Displays system code page specified in ACAD.XMF. |

*Table D.1:* **System Variables (continued)**

| Variable Name | Associated Command | Where Saved | Use |
|---|---|---|---|
| TABMODE | Tablet | *NA* | Controls Tablet mode: 0 = off; 1 = on. |
| TARGET (read-only) | Dview | With drawing | Displays coordinate of perspective target point. |
| TDCREATE (read-only) | Time | With drawing | Displays time and date of file creation in Julian format. |
| TDINDWG (read-only) | Time | With drawing | Displays total editing time in days and decimal days. |
| TDUPDATE (read-only) | Time | With drawing | Displays time and date of last file update in Julian format. |
| TDUSRTIMER (read-only) | Time | With drawing | Displays user-controlled elapsed time in days and decimal days. |
| TEXTFILL | Text | With drawing | Controls display of Bitstream, TrueType, and PostScript Type 1 fonts: 0 = outlines; 1 = filled. |

**App. D**

**System and Dimension Variables**

*Table D.1:* **System Variables (continued)**

| Variable Name | Associated Command | Where Saved | Use |
|---|---|---|---|
| TEXTQLTY | Text | With drawing | Controls resolution of Bitstream, True-Type, and PostScript Type 1 fonts: values from 1.0 to 100.0. The lower the value, the lower the output resolution. Higher resolutions improve font quality but decrease display and plot speeds. |
| TEXTSIZE | Text, Dtext | With drawing | Controls default text height. |
| TEXTSTYLE | Text, Dtext | With drawing | Controls default text style. |
| THICKNESS | Elev | With drawing | Controls default 3D thickness of object being drawn. |
| TILEMODE | Mspace/ Pspace | With drawing | Controls Paper Space and Viewport access: 0 = Paper Space and viewport objects enabled; 1 = strictly Model Space. |
| TOOLTIPS | Icon toolbars | With configuration | Controls display of ToolTips: 0 = off; 1 = on. |

*Table D.1:*    **System Variables (continued)**

| Variable Name | Associated Command | Where Saved | Use |
|---|---|---|---|
| TRIMMODE | Chamfer, Fillet | With configuration | Controls whether lines are trimmed during Chamfer and Fillet commands: 0 = no trim; 1 = trim |
| UCSFOLLOW | UCS | With drawing | Controls whether AutoCAD LT automatically changes to plan view of UCS while in Model Space: 0 = UCS change does not affect view; 1 = UCS change causes view to change with UCS. |
| UCSICON | Ucsicon | With drawing | Controls UCS icon: 1 = on; 2 = UCS icon appears at origin. |
| UCSNAME (read-only) | UCS | With drawing | Displays name of current UCS. |
| UCSORG (read-only) | UCS | With drawing | Displays origin coordinate for current UCS relative to world coordinate system. |
| UCSXDIR (read-only) | UCS | With drawing | Displays x direction of current UCS relative to world coordinate system. |

*Table D.1:* **System Variables (continued)**

| Variable Name | Associated Command | Where Saved | Use |
|---|---|---|---|
| UCSYDIR (read-only) | UCS | With drawing | Displays y direction of current UCS relative to world coordinate system. |
| UNITMODE | Units | With drawing | Controls how AutoCAD LT displays fractional, foot-and-inch, and surveyor's angles: 0 = industry standard; 1 = AutoCAD LT input format. |
| VIEWCTR (read-only) | *NA* | With drawing | Displays center of current view in coordinates. |
| VIEWDIR (read-only) | Dview | With drawing | Displays camera viewing direction in coordinates. |
| VIEWMODE (read-only) | Dview | With drawing | Displays view-related settings for current viewport: 0 = off; 1 = perspective on; 2 = front clipping on; 4 = back clipping on; 8 = UCS follow on; 16 = front clip not at a point directly in front of the viewer's eye. |

*Table D.1:* **System Variables (continued)**

| Variable Name | Associated Command | Where Saved | Use |
|---|---|---|---|
| VIEWSIZE (read-only) | *NA* | With drawing | Displays height of current view in drawing units. |
| VIEWTWIST (read-only) | Dview | With drawing | Displays twist angle for current viewport. |
| VISRETAIN | Layer | With drawing | Controls whether layer setting for Xrefs is retained: 0 = current layer color; line type and visibility settings retained when drawing is closed; 1 = layer settings of Xref drawing always renewed when file is opened. |
| VSMAX (read-only) | *NA* | *NA* | Stores coordinates for upper-right corner of the current viewport's virtual display. |
| VSMIN | *NA* | *NA* | Displays coordinates for lower-left corner of virtual display. |
| WORLDUCS (read-only) | UCS | *NA* | Displays status of WCS: 0 = current UCS is not WCS; 1 = current UCS is WCS. |

**App. D**

**System and Dimension Variables**

Table D.1: **System Variables (continued)**

| Variable Name | Associated Command | Where Saved | Use |
|---|---|---|---|
| WORLDVIEW | Dview, Vpoint | With drawing | Controls whether Dview and Vpoint operate relative to UCS or WCS: 0 = current UCS is used; 1 = WCS is used. |
| XREFCTL | Xref | With configuration | Controls whether Xref log files are written: 0 = no log files; 1 = log files written. |

# Setting Dimension Variables

In *Chapter 9*, nearly all of the system variables related to dimensioning are shown with their associated options in the Dimension Styles dialog box. Later in the appendix, you'll find a complete discussion of all elements of the Dimension Styles dialog box and how to use it.

This section provides further information about the dimension variables. For starters, Table D.2 lists the variables, their default status, and a brief description of what they do. You can get a similar listing by entering **Dimstyle** ↵ at the command prompt, then typing **ST** to select the Status option. Alternatively, you can use the AutoCAD LT Help system. This section also discusses a few system variables that do not show up in the Dimension Styles dialog box.

*Table D.2:*    **The Dimension Variables**

| General Dimension Controls | | |
| --- | --- | --- |
| **Dimension Variable** | **Default Setting** | **Description** |
| DIMASO | On | Turns associative dimensions on and off. |
| DIMSHO | On | Updates dimensions dynamically while dragging. |
| DIMSTYLE | STANDARD | Name of current dimension style. |
| DIMUPT | Off | Controls text positioning control during dimension input: 0 = no text positioning, uses settings; 1 = text positioning allowed during input. |

**Scale**

| Dimension Variable | Default Setting | Description |
|---|---|---|
| DIMSCALE | 1.0000 | Overall scale factor of dimensions. |
| DIMTXT | .18 (approx. ³⁄₁₆″) | Text height. |
| DIMASZ | .18 (approx. ³⁄₁₆″) | Arrow size. |
| DIMTSZ | 0″ | Tick size. |
| DIMCEN | .09 (approx. ³⁄₃₂″) | Center mark size. |
| DIMLFAC | 1.0000 | Linear unit scale factor. |

**Offsets**

| Dimension Variable | Default Setting | Description |
|---|---|---|
| DIMEXO | .0625 or ¹⁄₁₆″ | Extension line origin offset. |
| DIMEXE | .18 (approx. ³⁄₁₆″) | Amount extension line extends beyond dimension line. |
| DIMDLI | .38 (approx. ³⁄₈″) | Dimension line offset for continuation or base. |
| DIMDLE | 0″ | Amount dimension line extends beyond extension line. |

| Tolerances | | |
| --- | --- | --- |
| **Dimension Variable** | **Default Setting** | **Description** |
| DIMALTTZ | 0 | Controls zero suppression of tolerance values: 0 = no suppression; 1 = suppression. |
| DIMDEC | 4 | Sets decimal place for primary tolerance values. |
| DIMTDEC | 4 | Sets decimal place for tolerance values. |
| DIMTP | 0″ | Plus tolerance. |
| DIMTM | 0″ | Minus tolerance. |
| DIMTOL | Off | When on, shows dimension tolerances. |
| DIMTOLJ | 1 | Controls vertical location of tolerance values relative to nominal dimension: 0 = bottom; 1 = middle; 2 = top. |
| DIMTZIN | 0 | Controls supression of 0 dimensions in tolerance values: 0 = no supression; 1 = supression. |
| DIMLIM | Off | When on, shows dimension limits. |

| Rounding | | |
| --- | --- | --- |
| **Dimension Variable** | **Default Setting** | **Description** |
| DIMRND | 0″ | Rounding value. |
| DIMZIN | 0 | Controls display of 0 dimensions: 0 = leaves out zero feet and inches; 1 = includes zero feet and inches; 2 = includes zero feet; 3 = includes zero inches. |

**Dimension Arrow and Text Control**

| Dimension Variable | Default Setting | Description |
| --- | --- | --- |
| DIMAUNIT | 0 | Controls angle format for angular dimensions; settings are the same as for Aunits system variable. |
| DIMBLK | "" | arrow block name. |
| DIMBLK1 | "" | User-defined arrow block name used with Dimsah. |
| DIMBLK2 | "" | User-defined arrow block name used with Dimsah. |
| DIMFIT | 3 | Controls location of text and arrows for extension lines: 0 = both arrows and text placed outside extensions if space isn't available; 1 = text has priority, so if only enough space for text, arrows are placed outside extension lines; 2 = AutoCAD LT chooses between text and arrows, based on best fit; 3 = a leader is drawn from dimension line to dimension text when space for text not available (see Dimjust). |
| DIMGAP | 0.09 (approx. ³⁄₃₂″) | Controls distance between dimension text and dimension line. |
| DIMJUST | 0 | Controls horizontal dimension text position: 0 = centered between extension lines; 1 = next to first extension line; 2 = next to second extension line; 3 = above and centered on first extension line; 4 = above and centered on second extension line. |

| Dimension Arrow and Text Control (continued) | | |
|---|---|---|
| **Dimension Variable** | **Default Setting** | **Description** |
| DIMSAH | Off | Allows use of two different arrowheads on a dimension line. See Dimblk1 and Dimblk2. |
| DIMTFAC | 1.0″ | Controls scale factor for dimension tolerance text. |
| DIMTIH | On | When on, text inside extensions is horizontal. |
| DIMTOH | On | When on, text outside extensions is horizontal. |
| DIMTAD | 0 | When on, places text above the dimension line. |
| DIMTIX | Off | Forces text between extensions. |
| DIMTVP | 0 | Controls text's vertical position based on numeric value. |
| DIMTXSTY | STANDARD | Controls text style for dimension text. |
| DIMUNIT | 2 | Controls unit style for all dimension style groups except angular. Settings are same as for Lunit system variable. |

**System and Dimension Variables**

**Dimension and Extension Line Control**

| Dimension Variable | Default Setting | Description |
|---|---|---|
| DIMSD1 | Off | Suppresses the first dimension line. |
| DIMSD2 | Off | Suppresses the second dimension line. |
| DIMSE1 | Off | When on, suppresses the first extension line. |
| DIMSE2 | Off | When on, suppresses the second extension line. |
| DIMTOFL | Off | Forces a dimension line between extension lines. |
| DIMSOXD | Off | Suppresses dimension lines outside extension lines. |

**Alternate Dimension Options**

| Dimension Variable | Default Setting | Description |
|---|---|---|
| DIMALT | Off | When on, alternate units selected are shown. |
| DIMALTF | 25.4000 | Alternate unit scale factor. |
| DIMALTD | 2 | Alternate unit decimal places. |
| DIMALTTD | 2 | Alternate unit tolerance decimal places. |
| DIMALTU | 2 | Alternate unit style. See Lunits system variable for values. |
| DIMALTZ | 0 | Suppresses zeroes for alternate dimension values: 0 = no supression; 1 = supression. |
| DIMPOST | "" | Adds suffix to dimension text. |
| DIMAPOST | "" | Adds suffix to alternate dimension text. |

| Colors | | |
| --- | --- | --- |
| **Dimension Variable** | **Default Setting** | **Description** |
| DIMCLRD | 0 | Controls color of dimension lines and arrows. |
| DIMCLRE | 0 | Controls color of dimension extension lines. |
| DIMCLRT | 0 | Controls color of dimension text. |

Finally, for those of you who might want to write macros, or scripts, to control dimension styles, we'll talk about using two options of the Dimstyle command to set and recall dimension styles from the command line: Dimstyle ↵ S ↵ and Dimstyle ↵ R ↵. If you are familiar with the command sequences required to save and restore dimension styles, you will also be able to assign a macro to a menu or a toolbar button to load specific dimension styles within your drawing.

If you want to change a setting through the command line instead of through the Dimension Styles dialog box, you can enter the system variable name at the command prompt, or, again, assign a macro to a menu or a button.

## Controlling Associative Dimensioning

As discussed in *Chapter 9*, you can turn off AutoCAD LT's *associative dimensioning* by changing the Dimaso setting. The default for Dimaso is *On*.

The Dimsho setting controls whether the dimension value is dynamically updated while a dimension line is being dragged. The default for this setting is *On*.

## Storing Dimension Styles through the Command Line

Once you have set the dimension variables as you like, you can save the settings by using the Dimstyle command. The Dimstyle/Save command records all of the current dimension variable settings (except Dimaso and Dimsho) with a name you specify.

1. At the command prompt, enter **Dimstyle** ↵.

2. At the Save/Restore/STatus/Apply/?: prompt, type **S** ↵.

3. When the ?/Name for new dimension style: prompt appears, you can enter a question mark (**?**) to get a listing of any dimension styles currently saved, or you can enter a name under which you want the current settings saved.

For example, suppose you change some of your dimension settings through dimension variables instead of through the Dimension Styles dialog box, as shown in the following list:

| | |
|---|---|
| Dimtsz | 0.044 |
| Dimtad | On |
| Dimtih | Off |
| Dimtoh | Off |

These settings are typical for an architectural style of dimensioning; you might save them under the name Architect, as you did in an exercise in *Chapter 9*. Then suppose you change other dimension settings for dimensions in another format—surveyor's dimensions on a site plan, for example. You might save them with the name Survey, again using the Save option of the Dimstyle command. When you want to return to the settings you used for your architectural drawing, you use the Restore option of the Dimstyle command, described in the next section.

## Restoring a Dimension Style from the Command Line

To restore a dimension style you've saved using the Dimstyle Save option:

1. At the command prompt, enter **Dimstyle** ↵.

2. At the Save/Restore/STatus/Apply/?: prompt, type **R** ⏎. The following prompt appears:

```
?/Enter dimension style name or RETURN to select
dimension:
```

Here you have three options: Enter a question mark (**?**) to get a listing of saved dimension styles; or enter the name of a style, such as Arch, if you know the name of the style you want; or you can use the cursor to select a dimension on the screen whose style you want to match.

## Notes on Metric Dimensioning

This book assumes you are using feet and inches as units of measure. The AutoCAD LT user community is worldwide, however, and many of you may be using the metric system in your work. As long as you are not mixing U.S. (feet and inches) and metric measurements, using the English version of AutoCAD LT is fairly easy. With the Units command, set your measurement system to decimal, then draw distances in millimeters or centimeters. At plot time, select the MM radio button (millimeters) under Paper Size and Orientation in the Plot Configuration dialog box. Also, be sure you specify a scale that compensates for differences between millimeters (which are the AutoCAD LT base unit when you are using the metric system) and centimeters.

If your drawings are to be in both foot-and-inch and metric measurements, you will be concerned with several settings, as follows:

**Dimlfac**   sets the scale factor for dimension values. The dimension value will be the measured distance in AutoCAD LT units times this scale factor. Set Dimlfac to 25.4 if you have drawn in inches but want to dimension in millimeters. The default is 1.00.

**Dimalt**   turns the display of alternate dimensions on or off. Alternate dimensions are dimension text added to your drawing in addition to the standard dimension text.

**Dimaltf**   sets the scale factor for alternate dimensions (i.e., metric). The default is 25.4, which is the millimeter equivalent of 1″.

**Dimaltd**   sets the number of decimal places displayed in the alternate dimensions.

**Dimapost**   adds a suffix to alternate dimensions, as in 4.5mm.

If you prefer, you can have AutoCAD LT use a template drawing called ACLTISO.DWT. This drawing is set up for metric/ISO standard drawings. See *Chapter 5* for more on using drawing templates.

# A Closer Look at the Dimension Styles Dialog Box

As you saw in *Chapter 9*, you can control the appearance and format of dimensions through dimension styles. To get the Dimension Styles dialog box, click on the Dimension Styles button on the Dimensioning Toolbar, or enter **Ddim** ↲ at the command line.

The three buttons in the Dimension Styles dialog box—Geometry, Format, and Annotation—open related dialog boxes that control the variables associated with these three aspects of AutoCAD LT's dimensioning system. You'll get a closer look at these dialog boxes in the next section.

Within the Dimension Styles dialog box, dimensions are divided into "families" as a way of classifying the different types of dimensions available in AutoCAD LT. The dimension families are angular, diameter, linear, leader, ordinate, and radial. The Parent family affects all the dimension families globally. You can fine-tune your dimension styles by making settings to each family independently. If you don't set any of the families, their settings default to the Parent settings. To change the settings of a family, click on the family name's radio button before making changes in the Geometry, Format, or Annotation dialog boxes.

The following paragraphs describe the options in the Geometry, Format, and Annotation subdialog boxes. Each description specifies the dimension variables (in parentheses) that are related to the dialog box option. As you work through this appendix, you may want to refer back to *Chapter 9*'s figures that illustrate these subdialog boxes.

## The Geometry Dialog Box

This dialog box lets you control the placement and appearance of dimension lines, arrowheads, extension lines, and center marks. You can also set a scale factor for these dimension components.

### The Dimension Line Group

Refer to Figure D.1 for examples of the effects of these options.

**Suppress (Dimsd1, Dimsd2)**  suppresses the dimension line to the left or right of the dimension text.

**Extension (Dimdle)**  sets the distance that dimension lines are drawn beyond extension lines when using the standard AutoCAD LT dimension tick for arrows. This option is unavailable (grayed out) when the filled arrow is selected in the Arrowheads group.

**Spacing (Dimdli)**  determines the distance between dimension lines from a common extension line generated by the Baseline Dimension or Continue Dimension options on the Dimensioning toolbar.

**Color (Dimclrd)**  sets the color of dimension lines. The standard AutoCAD LT Color dialog box appears, allowing you to visually select a color.

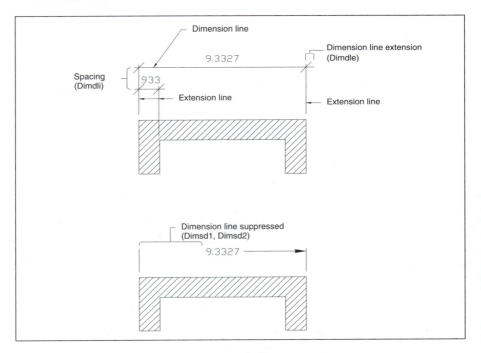

*Figure D.1:*  **Examples of how the Dimension Line options affect dimensions**

## The Extension Line Group

Refer to Figure D.2 for examples of the effects of these options.

**Suppress (Dimse1, Dimse2)**    suppresses the first or the second dimension extension line.

**Extension (Dimexe)**    sets the distance that extension lines extend beyond the dimension line.

**Origin Offset (Dimexo)**    sets the distance the extension line is offset from its point of origin on the object being dimensioned.

**Color (Dimclre)**    sets the color of extension lines. The standard AutoCAD LT Color dialog box appears, allowing you to visually select a color.

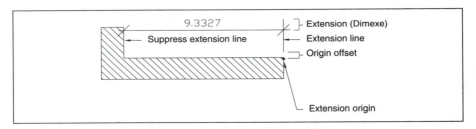

*Figure D.2:*    *Examples of how the Extension Line options affect extension lines*

## The Arrowheads Group

These options let you control the type of arrowhead AutoCAD LT applies to dimensions.

**1st**    shows you a pull-down list of choices to set the arrowheads at both ends of the dimension line. When you select an arrowhead, the graphic above the group shows you how the arrow will look. You can also click on the graphic to cycle through the selections.

**2nd**    shows you a pull-down list of choices to set different arrowheads for each side of a dimension. This option works like the first option, but only sets one arrowhead.

**Size (Dimasz)**    sets the size of the arrowhead.

In the first and second pull-down lists is a choice called User; this lets you use a block in place of the standard arrows. A dialog box opens, in which you enter the name of the block you wish to use for the arrow. The block must already exist in the drawing before you can add it, and it must follow the guidelines described in the "Using Alternate Dimension Arrows" section of this appendix.

### The Center Group

These options let you determine what center mark is drawn when using the Dimcenter command. Center marks are also drawn when dimension lines are placed outside a circle or arc using the Diameter or Dimradius commands. All these settings are controlled by the Dimcen system variable.

**Mark**   adds a center mark.

**Line**   creates a center mark and lines.

**None**   suppresses the creation of center marks and lines.

**Size**   controls the size of the center marks.

### The Scale Group

These options let you control the overall scaling of dimensions.

**Overall Scale (Dimscale)**   sets the scale factor for the size of dimension components, text and arrow size, and text location. This setting has no effect on actual dimension text or the distances being dimensioned.

**Scale to Paper Space**   is meaningful only if you dimension objects in a Model Space viewport while you're in Paper Space. When this option is enabled, AutoCAD LT adjusts the scaling of dimension components to Paper Space.

## The Format Dialog Box

This subdialog box contains the following general settings:

**User Defined (Dimupt)**    overrides the dimension text location settings and lets you place the text manually when the dimensions are drawn.

**Force Line Inside (Dimtofl)**    forces a dimension line to be drawn between extension lines under all conditions.

**Fit (Dimfit)**    lets you determine how dimension text and arrows are placed between extension lines. In the pull-down list, Text and Arrows causes both arrows and text to be placed outside extensions if space isn't available. Text Only gives text priority, so that if space is available for text only, arrows will be placed outside extension lines. With the Best Fit option, AutoCAD LT determines whether text or arrows fit better, and draws the dimension accordingly. Leader draws a leader line from the dimension line to the dimension text when space for text is not available.

The settings in the Format subdialog box control the location of dimension text. The **Text, Horizontal Justification**, and **Vertical Justification** groups include a graphic that demonstrates the effect of your selected option on the dimension text. You can also click on the graphic to scroll through the options.

### The Text Group

These options let you control the text location.

**Inside Horizontal (Dimtih)**    orients text horizontally between extension lines, regardless of the dimension lines' orientations. If this option is not selected, text is aligned with the extension line.

**Outside Horizontal (Dimtoh)**    orients text horizontally when it occurs outside the extension lines, regardless of the dimension lines' orientations. If this option is not selected, text is aligned with the extension line.

### The Horizontal Justification Group

These settings can also be controlled using the Dimjust system variable.

**Centered**    centers the dimension text between the extension lines.

**1st Extension Line**    places the text next to the first extension line.

**2nd Extension Line**    places the text by the second extension line.

**Over 1st Extension**    places the text over the first extension line, aligned with the extension line.

**Over 2nd Extension**    places the text over the second extension line, aligned with the extension line.

### Vertical Justification

These options can also be set using the Dimtad system variable.

**Centered**    centers the dimension within the dimension lines.

**Above**    places the text above the dimension line, as is typical for architectural dimensioning. The distance from the text to the dimension line can be set with the Gap option in the Annotation subdialog box.

**Outside**    places the text outside the dimension line at a point farthest away from the origin point of the first extension line. This effect is similar to the Above option, but is more apparent in circular dimensions.

**JIS**    places text in conformance with the Japanese Industrial Standards.

## *The Annotation Dialog Box*

This dialog box controls the dimension text. You can determine the style, color, and size of text, as well as the unit style, tolerance, and alternate dimensions.

### *Primary Units and Alternate Units*

These two groups offer the same options. The Primary Units options affect only the main dimension text, and the Alternate Units options control alternate units when they are enabled. Alternate units are dimension values that are shown in brackets next to the standard dimension value, and are helpful when two unit systems, such as U.S. (feet and inches) and metric, are used in the same drawing. The Enable Units check box turns on the alternate units (see Figure D.3).

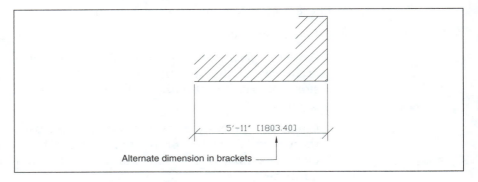

*Figure D.3:*    ***An example of alternate units***

**Prefix** lets you include a prefix in dimension text, and **Suffix** lets you include a suffix in dimension text. For the primary dimension text, Prefix and Suffix are controlled by the same Dimpost system variable. For alternate dimension text, Prefix and Suffix share the Dimapost system variable. See Table D.2 for details on Dimpost and Dimapost.

Both the Primary Units and Alternate Units groups have a Units button, which you click to bring up the Primary Units and Alternate Units dialog boxes. These dialog boxes contain the same options; when enabled, the Primary Units options affect only the main dimension text, and the Alternate Units options affect only alternate dimension text. Here are descriptions of these options:

**Units** and **Angles**   let you select the unit and angle styles (which are the same styles as for the Units command described in *Chapter 3*). For Primary Units, the Units option is controlled by the Dimunit system variable, and the Angles option is controlled by the Dimaunit system variable. For Alternate Units, the Units option is controlled by the Dimaltu.

**Dimension Precision** and **Tolerance Precision (Dimdec, Dimtdec, Dimaltd, Dimalttd)**   set the number of decimal places you want to use for these values. Dimension precision can also be set using the Dimdec system variable, and tolerance precision using Dimtdec. For Alternate Units, dimension precision can be set using Dimaltd, and tolerance precision using Dimalttd.

**Dimension Zero Suppression (Dimzin, Dimaltz)**   controls how AutoCAD LT handles zeroes in dimensions. The Leading option suppresses leading zeroes in a decimal dimension (for example, 0.3000 becomes .3000). The Trailing option suppresses trailing zeroes (so that 8.8000 becomes 8.8, or 45.0000 becomes 45). The 0 Feet option suppresses zero feet values in an architectural dimension so that 0′–4″ becomes 4″.

**0 Inches**   suppresses zero inch values in an architectural dimension, so that 12′–0″ becomes 12′. The Dimzin system variable controls this option for Primary Units; the Dimaltz system variable controls this option for Alternate Units.

**Tolerance Zero Suppression (Dimtzin, Dimalttz)**   controls how AutoCAD LT handles zeroes in tolerance dimensions. (See the description for Dimension Zero Suppression, just above.) The Dimtzin system variable controls this option for Primary Units; Dimalttz controls this option for Alternate Units.

**Scale**    lets you specify a scale factor to linear dimensions. This setting affects the dimension text value. For example, say you have drawn an object to one-half its actual size. To have your dimensions reflect the true size of the object, you would set the Linear input box to 2. When you place dimensions in the drawing, AutoCAD LT multiplies the drawing distances by 2 to derive the dimension text value. By checking the Paper Space Only check box, you tell AutoCAD LT to apply the scale factor only when dimensioning in Paper Space. These two options in Alternate Units perform the same function for alternate dimension text. In Primary Units, the Scale options are controlled by the Dimlfac system variable. When Paper Space Only is enabled, Dimlfac becomes a negative value. For Alternate Units, the scale options are controlled by the Dimaltf system variable.

## The Tolerance Group

These options affect both primary and alternate units.

**Method**    sets the type of tolerance displayed in a dimension. Choose among the following: The Symmetrical option adds a single tolerance value with a plus-minus ($\pm$) sign; this is the same as Dimtol set to 1 and Dimlim set to 0. The Deviation option adds two stacked values, one a plus value and the other a minus value. The Limits option places two stacked dimension values, showing the allowable range for the dimension instead of the single dimension (this is the same as Dimtol set to 0 and Dimlim set to 1). The Basic option draws a box around the dimension text; the Dimgap system variable set to a negative value produces the same result.

**Upper Value**    sets the maximum tolerance limit. This is stored in the Dimtp system variable.

**Lower Value**    sets the minimum tolerance limit. This is stored in the Dimtm system variable.

**Justification**    sets the vertical location of stacked tolerance values.

**Height**    sets the height for tolerance values. This is stored in the Dimtfac system variable as a ratio of the tolerance height to the default text height used for dimension text.

### The Text Group

These options let you control the appearance of text in a dimension.

**Style (Dimtxsty)**    sets the text style used for dimension text.

**Height (Dimtxt)**    sets the current text height for dimension text.

**Gap (Dimgap)**    sets a margin around the dimension text, within which margin the dimension line is broken.

**Color (Dimclrt)**    sets the color of the dimension text.

**Round Off (Dimrnd)**    sets the amount that dimensions are rounded off to the nearest value. This setting works in conjunction with the Dimtol system variable.

## Importing Dimension Styles from Other Drawings

Dimension styles are saved within the current drawing file only. You don't have to recreate the dimension style for each new drawing, however. You can import a dimension style from another drawing by cutting and pasting across the Windows 95 clipboard.

To do this, in your source drawing select any dimension that uses the required dimension style. Copy the dimension to the Windows 95 clipboard (Ctrl-C). Then open your target drawing, and paste in the dimension from the clipboard (Ctrl-V). If you check in the Dimension Styles dialog box (type **Ddim** ↵), you will see that your copied dimension style is now available in the target drawing. You can now erase the copied dimension from the target drawing. The dimension style is still available in this drawing.

## Drawing Blocks for Your Own Dimension Arrows and Tick Marks

If you don't want to use the arrowheads supplied by AutoCAD LT for your dimension lines, you can create a block of the arrowheads or tick marks you like to be used in the Arrowheads group of the Dimension Styles/Geometry dialog box.

For example, say you want to have a tick mark that is thicker than the dimension lines and extensions. You can create a block of the tick mark on a layer you assign to a thick pen weight, and then assign that block to the Arrowhead setting.

1. Click on the Dimension Styles button on the Dimensioning toolbar to open the Dimension Styles dialog box, and then click on Geometry to open the required subdialog box.

2. Choose User Arrow from the first pull-down list in the Arrowheads group. At the User Arrow dialog box, enter the name of your arrow block.

When you draw the arrow block, make it one unit long. The block's insertion point will be used to determine the point of the arrow that meets the extension line, so make sure you place the insertion point at the tip of the arrow. Because the arrow on the right side of the dimension line will be inserted with a zero rotation value, create the arrow block so that it is pointing to the right (see Figure D.4). The arrow block is rotated 180° from the left side of the dimension line.

---

 **TIP**  If you have been using a custom arrowhead, and wish to return to the AutoCAD LT default arrowhead, enter **Dimblk** ↵, .(period) ↵.

---

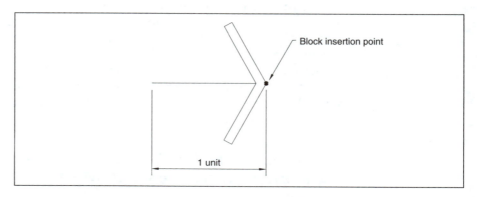

*Figure D.4:*    *The orientation and size of a block used in place of the default arrow*

To have a different type of arrow at both ends of the dimension line, create a block for each arrow. Then, in the Dimension Styles/Geometry dialog box, choose User in the pull-down list for the 1st arrowhead, and enter the name of one block. Then choose User in the pull-down list for the second arrowhead, and enter the name of the other block.

# Appendix E

# Standard AutoCAD LT Commands

**THIS** appendix provides a comprehensive list of all the standard AutoCAD LT commands. If many of these commands look foreign to you, it is probably because they were not discussed directly in the main part of this book. The tutorials and instructions in this book put emphasis on the toolbar and toolbar buttons. However, we do supply the command names next to the related toolbar button wherever possible in the main part of this book. For example, in a typical tutorial step, you might see:

1.  Click on Hatch from the Draw toolbar, or type **Bhatch** ↵ at the command prompt.

    In this example, the command name, Bhatch, is provided as an alternate.

    Be aware that many of the toolbar and toolbar icon buttons related to these commands automatically provide input for command options. For example, while there is only one Arc keyboard command, you will find seven buttons on the Arc flyout on the Draw toolbar. Each of these buttons supplies a different set of responses to the Arc commands options. The net result is a set of buttons, each providing a different way to draw an arc. As shown in *Chapter 2*, you can manually enter the Arc command and supply those options yourself. For a clearer understanding of how toolbars and toolbar buttons relate to the keyboard commands, see *Chapter 17*.

    Table E.1 briefly describes each command, and provides (where applicable) a keyboard shortcut for the command, and a listing of options and comments on its operation. A keyboard shortcut is an abbreviated version of the command: A for Arc; V for Viewtoolbar, and so on. These shortcuts are mapped in the ACLT.PGP file in your AutoCAD LT directory. ACLT.PGP is an ASCII file. Using a text editor, you can redefine any of the shortcuts to an alternative abbreviation, or add a shortcut of your own.

Some commands can be used "transparently," while AutoCAD LT is still executing another command. Transparent commands are indicated with an apostrophe preceding the command name.

*Table E.1:*   **AutoCAD LT Commands**

| Command Name | Description | Shortcut | Options/Operations |
|---|---|---|---|
| 3DPOLY | Draws a 3D polyline. | | 3D polylines allow 3D point selection; however, 3D polylines cannot have width or thickness. |
| ABOUT | Displays your serial number and a scrolling list box with the contents of the ACLT.MSG file. | AB | *NA* |
| ALIGN | Moves and rotates objects to align with other objects. | | After selecting objects, pick up to three sets of source and destination points. |
| APERTURE | Controls the size of the Object Snap cursor. | AP | Size of aperture is in pixels. |
| ARC | Draws arcs. | A | Pick points on screen or supply them at the command line. |

*Table E.1:*  **AutoCAD LT Commands (continued)**

| Command Name | Description | Shortcut | Options/Operations |
|---|---|---|---|
| AREA | Calculates area and perimeter of area defined by points, poly-line, circle, spline curve, and polygon. | AA | **A** = add mode, **S** = subtract mode, **O** = select object to find area and perimeter. |
| ARRAY | Constructs multiple copies in a matrix or circular pattern. | AR | **R** = rectangular, **P** = polar. |
| ATTDEF | Creates an attribute definition. | AD | **I** = visible/invisible, **C** = constant/variable, **V** = controls verify mode, **P** = controls preset, **Tag** = attribute "ID," **Prompt** = attribute prompt, **default** = attribute default value. |
| ´ATTDISP | Controls visibility of attributes. | AT | **On** = all are made visible; **Off** = all are made invisible; **N** = normal; only attributes set to invisible are not shown. |
| ATTEDIT | Edits attributes. | AE | You can edit attributes globally or one at a time. You can also change attribute text size, orientation, and locations. |

*Table E.1:*  **AutoCAD LT Commands (continued)**

| Command Name | Description | Shortcut | Options/Operations |
|---|---|---|---|
| ATTEXT | Extracts attribute data. | AX | **C** = comma-delimited format, **D** = DXF format, **S** = space-delimited format, **O** = extract from specific objects. |
| AUDIT | Audits drawing integrity. | | **Y** = fix errors, **N** = don't fix errors but produce report. |
| ´BASE | Changes insertion origin for the current drawing. | BA | Pick a point. |
| BHATCH | Fills an enclosed area with an associative hatch pattern. | H | Automatic boundary and island detection. Hatch preview offered. *See also* Boundary. |
| ´BLIPMODE | Controls blips. | BM | **On** = show blips, **Off** = don't show blips. |
| BLOCK | Defines a block from a set of objects. | | **?** = list existing blocks. |
| BMAKE | Defines a block using a dialog box. | B | All options are presented via dialog box rather than as command line prompts as with the Block command. |

*Table E.1:*   **AutoCAD LT Commands (continued)**

| Command Name | Description | Shortcut | Options/Operations |
|---|---|---|---|
| BMPOUT | Creates a bitmap image (.BMP file) of objects in your drawing. | | Allows you to select specific objects for inclusion. |
| BOUNDARY | Creates a poly-line from a closed area. | | Islands can be excluded; the boundary must be contiguous. |
| BREAK | Breaks objects into two parts. | BR | Select object, then second point of break; or **F** = pick first and second point. |
| CHAMFER | Joins two lines or surfaces in a chamfer. | CF | **D** = set chamfer distances, **P** = chamfer each vertex of a polyline, **A** = specify angle of chamfer, **T** = trim edges to chamfer-line endpoints, **M** = (select) method; either 2 distances or distance and an angle. |
| CHANGE | Modify an existing object's properties. | CH | **P** = change common properties, such as **C** = color, **E** = elevation, **LA** = layer, **LT** = line-type, **S** = linetype scaling, **T** = thickness. Also changes text height, style, angle, value, line endpoints, and circle radius. |

Table E.1:   AutoCAD LT Commands (continued)

| Command Name | Description | Shortcut | Options/Operations |
|---|---|---|---|
| CHPROP | Modifies common properties of objects. | CR | **C** = color, **LA** = layer, **LT** = linetype, **S** = linetype scaling, **T** = thickness. |
| CIRCLE | Draws circles. | C | **3P** = based on 3 points on circumference, **D** = enter diameter, **R** = enter radius, **TTR** = tangent to two objects and a radius. |
| ´COLOR | Sets default color for new objects. | | *Number* = color number, *Name* = color name for standard colors only, **Bylayer** = use layer color, **Byblock** = floating object color. |
| COPY | Copies objects. | CP, DUP | **M** = multiple copies. |
| COPYCLIP | Copies selected objects to the Windows clipboard for inclusion in other drawings and Windows applications. | CC | Selected objects are stored in both image and vector formats; if text-only is selected, it is stored in ASCII format. |
| COPYEMBED | Copies selected objects to the Windows clipboard for embedding in another program. | CE | Any changes made to the selected objects in AutoCAD LT will not be reflected in the target program. |

*Table E.1:*　**AutoCAD LT Commands (continued)**

| Command Name | Description | Shortcut | Options/Operations |
|---|---|---|---|
| COPYHIST | Copies the text in the command line history to the Windows clipboard. | | You may then paste the text into a Windows text processor. |
| COPYLINK | Copies the current view to the Windows clipboard for linking to other Windows OLE applications. | CL | Use the Pastespec command to paste and link the view into other documents. |
| CUTCLIP | Copies selected objects to the Windows clipboard and erases them from the drawing. | | Cutclip does not create links for use in OLE applications. |
| DDATTDEF | Dialog box to create attribute definition. | DAD | *See* Attdef. |
| DDATTE | Dialog box to edit attributes. | DE | Displays attribute prompt and value. Values are editable through input box. |
| DDATTEXT | Dialog box to extract attribute data. | DAX | *See* Attext. |

*Table E.1:*   **AutoCAD LT Commands (continued)**

| Command Name | Description | Shortcut | Options/Operations |
|---|---|---|---|
| DDCHPROP | Dialog box to change properties. | DC | *See* Chprop. |
| DDCOLOR | Dialog box to set color for new objects. | CO | *See* Color. |
| DDEDIT | Dialog box to edit text, paragraph text, and attribute definitions. | ED, TE | Displays text in an input box, allowing you to edit single lines. |
| ´DDE-MODES | Dialog box that sets defaults for new objects. | EM | Sets layer, linetype, linetype scaling, color, elevation, thickness, and text style. |
| ´DDGRIPS | Dialog box to set up the Grips feature. | GR | Turns grips on or off, and sets grip color and size. |
| DDIM | Controls dimensioning settings. | DM | Presents a series of dialog boxes for setting dimension styles and variables. *See Appendix D.* |
| DDINSERT | Dialog box for the Insert function. | I | Inserts a block or file and lets you define insertion point, scale, and rotation angle. |
| DDLMODES | Dialog box for controlling layers. | LD | Sets current layer, creates new layer, and controls visibility, color, linetype. |

*Table E.1:*    **AutoCAD LT Commands (continued)**

| Command Name | Description | Shortcut | Options/Operations |
|---|---|---|---|
| DDLTYPE | Dialog box for loading and setting linetypes. | LT | *See* Linetype. |
| DDMODIFY | Dialog box for editing object properties. | | Similar to Ddchprop, with additional options specific to the object selected. Unlike Ddchprop, you can only select one object. |
| ´DDOSNAP | Dialog box for Osnap settings. | OS | Controls default Osnap settings and size of Osnap cursor. *See* Osnap. |
| ´DDPTYPE | Dialog box for the selection of point styles. | | Lets you select a point style from a graphic. Point objects are then drawn in the style you select. |
| ´DDRE-NAME | Dialog box for renaming items. | DR | Renames blocks, line-types, layers, text styles, viewports, UCSs, and dimension styles. |
| ´DDR-MODES | Dialog box for setting standard modes. | DA | Sets grid, snap, groups, and other drawing modes. |
| ´DDSELECT | Dialog box for setting selection modes. | SL | Sets Noun/Verb Selection, shift-pick, click-drag, automatic window, and pickbox size. Also sets object sort method. |

*Table E.1:* **AutoCAD LT Commands (continued)**

| Command Name | Description | Shortcut | Options/Operations |
|---|---|---|---|
| ´DDSTYLE | Dialog box for modifying text styles. | ST | Modify Font and text effects via input boxes. |
| DDUCS | Dialog box for setting and recalling UCSs. | UC | Lets you save a UCS under a name or list a UCS's coordinates. |
| DDUCSP | Dialog box for selecting a pre-defined UCS. | UP | Lets you select a UCS from a predefined set of UCSs. |
| ´DDUNITS | Dialog box for unit style settings. | DU | Controls unit and angle style, as well as degree of precision for each. |
| DDVIEW | Dialog box for saving and restoring views. | V | **Views** lists currently available views. **Restore** restores the highlighted view. **New** opens New View dialog box that lets you save a view through standard methods (*see* View). **Delete** deletes a view from the list. **Description** displays information about the current view. |
| ´DELAY | In scripts, delays execution of next command. | | Place just after the command you want to pause in a script. Follow Delay with a value in milliseconds. |

*Table E.1:*    **AutoCAD LT Commands (continued)**

| Command Name | Description | Shortcut | Options/Operations |
|---|---|---|---|
| DIM | Starts the dimension mode. | D | While in dimension mode, you can only enter dimensioning commands. |
| DIM1 | Lets you enter a single dimension command. | D1 | After the first one, you can enter any number of dimension commands. |
| DIM-ALIGNED | Creates an aligned linear dimension. | DAL | Select extension line origins, or ↵ to select object. |
| DIM-ANGULAR | Creates an angular dimension. | DAN | Select objects, or ↵ to specify vertex and angle endpoints. |
| DIM-BASELINE | Continues a linear, angular, or ordinate dimension from baseline of previous or selected dimension. | | Baseline is first extension line of previous dimension, or extension line nearest the selection point. |
| DIM-CENTER | Creates a center mark, or the center lines of circles and arcs. | | Controlled by the value of the Dimcen dimensioning variable (*see Appendix D*). |

*Table E.1:* **AutoCAD LT Commands** *(continued)*

| Command Name | Description | Shortcut | Options/Operations |
|---|---|---|---|
| DIM-CONTINUE | Continues a linear, angular, or ordinate dimension from second dimension line of previous or selected dimension. | | Continuation is from second extension line of previous dimension, or extension line nearest the selection point. |
| DIM-DIAMETER | Creates diameter dimensions for circles or arcs. | DDI | Includes center marks and center lines as determined by value of the Dimcen dimensioning variable (*see Appendix D* for more on Dimcen). |
| DIMEDIT | Edits dimensions' text and extension lines. | | **H** = home text location, **N** = new dimension-line text, **R** = rotate text angle, **O** = oblique extension lines. |
| DIM-LINEAR | Creates horizontal, vertical or rotated linear dimensions. | DLI | Select extension-line origins, or ↵ to specify object. |
| DIM-ORDINATE | Creates ordinate point dimensions. | DOR | Second point determines X or Y datum, or you can specify explicitly. |

*Table E.1:*   **AutoCAD LT Commands (continued)**

| Command Name | Description | Shortcut | Options/Operations |
|---|---|---|---|
| DIM-OVERRIDE | Overrides dimension system variables for individual dimensions. | | Does not affect current dimension style. |
| DIM-RADIUS | Creates radial dimensions for circles or arcs. | DRA | Includes center marks and center lines by value of the Dimcen dimensioning variable. |
| DIM-STYLE | Creates and modifies dimension styles at the command line. | | Same as the dialog boxes with Ddim command. |
| DIM-TEDIT | Moves and rotates dimension text. | | **L** = left side, **R** = right side of dimension line, **H** = middle of dimension line, **R** = angle of rotation. |
| 'DIST | Finds the distance between points. | DI | Pick two points. |
| DIVIDE | Marks off an object in equal segments. | | Select an object, then specify number of segments you want. Uses point objects as markers by default, but you can use blocks. |

*Table E.1:*  **AutoCAD LT Commands (continued)**

| Command Name | Description | Shortcut | Options/Operations |
|---|---|---|---|
| DLINE | Draws a double line using line segments and arcs. | DL | **B** = break at intersection; **C** = cap on one or both ends; **O** = offset double line from specified point; **S** = snap start or end of double line to existing object. |
| DONUT | Draws a circle with thickness. | DO | Specify inside diameter and outside diameter of circle. For a solid circle, make inside diameter 0. |
| DTEXT | Draws text directly in graphic area. | DT, T | Select start point, style, or justification; then specify height if style height is set to 0, and rotation angle. You can enter several lines of text. Each ↵ drops cursor down one line. |
| DVSIEWER | Opens the Aerial View driver. | DS | Select from three menus: View menu controls Zoom in/out and global; Mode menu switches between Pan and Zoom; Options menu locates specific parts of the drawing and updates the drawing dynamically. |

*Table E.1:    AutoCAD LT Commands (continued)*

| Command Name | Description | Shortcut | Options/Operations |
|---|---|---|---|
| DVIEW | Controls view of 3D perspectives. | DV | **CA** = camera location, **CL** = set clip planes, **D** = camera-to-target distance and turns on perspective mode, **H** = hidden-line removal, **Off** = turns perspective off, **PA** = pan view, **PO** = allows selection of target and camera points, **TA** = allows selection of target point by view, **TW** = twist camera view, **U** = undo last option, **X** = eXit Dview, **Z** = zoom in/out or set camera focal length, **T** = toggle between setting angle from XY plane and x-axis of XY plane. |
| ELEV | Sets the default elevation and thickness for new objects. | EV | Can be set from Ddemodes dialog box. |
| ELLIPSE | Draws an ellipse or elliptical arc. | EL | **A** = arc, **C** = select center point. |
| END | Exits AutoCAD LT. | | If drawing has been changed, you are offered choice of saving file or discarding changes. |

*Table E.1:    AutoCAD LT Commands (continued)*

| Command Name | Description | Shortcut | Options/Operations |
|---|---|---|---|
| ERASE | Deletes objects. | E | Standard selection options. |
| EXPLODE | Reduces compound objects (blocks, polylines, dimensions, etc.) to basic objects. | EP, X | Nested blocks are not broken down. Spline polylines break down into line segments. |
| ´EXPORT | Saves objects to other file formats. | EXP | **.BMP** = Bitmap format; **.WMF** = Windows Metafile; **.EPS** = Encapsulated PostScript; **.DXF** = Drawing Exchange format; **.DXX** = DXX Extract. |
| EXTEND | Extends objects to meet other objects. | EX | You can select multiple objects to extend by using a Fence selection option. **P** = project based on UCS or view, **E** = to extended edge, **U** = undo last extend. |
| ´FILL | Controls visibility of filled objects. | FL | **On** = fill solids, traces, and wide polylines; **Off** = show outlines only. |
| FILLET | Rounds and fillets edges of objects. | F | **P** = fillet a polyline, **R** = set radius for fillet, **C** = chain, **E** = edge, **T** = trim lets you choose whether or not to trim lines to arc endpoints. |

**App. E**

Table E.1:    AutoCAD LT Commands (continued)

| Command Name | Description | Shortcut | Options/Operations |
|---|---|---|---|
| ´GRAPHSCR | Flips from text to graphics mode. | | Same as F2. |
| ´GRID | Sets grid settings. | G | **On** = turn on grid, **Off** = turn off grid, **S** = match snap spacing, **A** = set grid aspect ratio, *number* = set grid spacing to number specified, *numberx* = set grid spacing to be multiple of snap setting. |
| HATCH | Draws non-associative hatch patterns within existing entities or by picking points. | | *Name* = predefined pattern, *\*name* = predefined pattern exploded, **U** = simple line or cross-hatch (user specifies spacing and rotation), **?** = list predefined hatch patterns. *See* Bhatch. |
| HATCH-EDIT | Modifies an existing associative hatch block. | HE | **D** = disassociate into regular hatch, **I** = new internal calculation point, **P** = properties (name, scale, etc.) of hatch block. |
| ´HELP | Provides information on commands and operations. | | If used while in middle of a command, provides information regarding the current operation. |

Table E.1:    **AutoCAD LT Commands (continued)**

| Command Name | Description | Shortcut | Options/Operations |
|---|---|---|---|
| HIDE | Performs hidden-line removal. | HI | *NA* |
| ´ID | Displays coordinates of selected point. | | Asks you to select point, which becomes "last point" for reference with @. |
| IMPORT | Imports other file formats into AutoCAD LT. | IM | **.WMF** = Windows Metafile; **.DXF** = Drawing Exchange format. |
| INSERT | Imports file or inserts block. | IN | Use ***blockname*** = ***filename*** to redefine internal block; ★ means insert and explode; other options are independent X, Y, and Z scale, as well as rotation angle. *See also* Ddinsert. |
| INSERTOBJ | Allows you to open other Windows 95 applications from inside AutoCAD LT, create objects in the application format, and insert them into the current drawing. | | Size and position the object in AutoCAD LT using its Windows handles. To edit an inserted object, double-click on it to return to its native application. (*See* "Adding Sound, Motion, and Photos to Your Drawings" in *Chapter 14*.) |

*Table E.1:*   **AutoCAD LT Commands (continued)**

| Command Name | Description | Shortcut | Options/Operations |
|---|---|---|---|
| ´ISOPLANE | Selects plane of isometric grid. | IS | **L** = left, **R** = right, **T** = top, ↵ = toggles between planes (*see also* Ddrmodes). |
| ´LAYER | Provides command-line layer control. | LA | **C** = set layer color, **F** = freeze a layer, **L** = set layer linetype, **LO** = lock a layer, **M** = create a layer and make it current, **N** = create new layer, **On** = turn on layer, **Off** = turn off layer, **S** = set current layer, **T** = thaw layer, **?** = list layers, **U** = unlock layers. For **F, N, On, Off,** and **T,** you can provide multiple layer names by listing them with comma separators; wildcard characters are also allowed. |
| LEADER | Creates a line that connects to an associative annotation. | LE | Format can be **ST** = straight lines, **S** = spline curve, **A** = with arrowhead, and **N** = no arrowhead. Annotation can be **T** = geometric tolerances, **M** = multiline text, **C** = copy of existing annotation, **B** = block insert, **N** = no annotation. |

Table E.1: **AutoCAD LT Commands** (continued)

| Command Name | Description | Shortcut | Options/Operations |
|---|---|---|---|
| LENGTHEN | Changes the length of objects and included angle or arcs. | LEN | Change is by **DE** = delta increment, **P** = percentage of current length, or **T** = absolute total length; **DY** = enters dynamic drag mode. |
| ´LIMITS | Sets the drawing limits. | LM | Select two points to define boundaries of limits. **On** = limits checking on, **Off** = limits checking off (limits checking forces objects to be drawn inside limits). |
| LINE | Draws lines. | L | **C** = close series of lines, **U** = undo last line segment, ↵ = at Start Point prompt, starts line from last line or arc. |
| ´LINETYPE | Controls linetype settings. | | **?** = List the linetypes available from linetype file, **C** = create linetype definition, **L** = load linetype definition, **S** = set current default linetype for new objects. |
| LIST | Shows properties of objects. | LS | Uses standard selection options. |
| LOGFILE-OFF | Closes log file opened by Logfileon. | | *NA* |

*Table E.1:*    **AutoCAD LT Commands (continued)**

| Command Name | Description | Shortcut | Options/Operations |
|---|---|---|---|
| LOGFILE-ON | Writes text window to a log file. | | *NA* |
| LTSCALE | Sets linetype scale. | LC | *See* Ltscale and Celt-scale system variables in *Appendix D*. |
| MAKE-PREVIEW | Creates .BMP file to allow previewing of files created in a previous version of Auto-CAD LT. | | *NA* |
| MEASURE | Marks off specific intervals on objects. | | **B** = use a block to mark intervals. Default marking device is a point object. |
| MENU-LOAD | Loads partial menu files. | | Specify name of the menu file. |
| MENU-UNLOAD | Unloads partial menu files. | | Specify name of the menu group. |
| MIRROR | Creates a reflected copy. | MI | You can specify a copy, or just mirror an object without copying. |
| MOVE | Moves objects. | M | Standard selection options. |
| MSLIDE | Makes a slide. | | Specify filename. |

Table E.1: **AutoCAD LT Commands (continued)**

| Command Name | Description | Shortcut | Options/Operations |
|---|---|---|---|
| MSPACE | Switch to Model Space. | MS | Can only be used while in Paper Space. |
| MTEXT | Creates paragraph text. | MT | Fits within nonprinting text boundary; allows standard text justification, style, height, and rotation selections. |
| MULTIPLE | Repeats the next command. | MU | Command is repeated until user enters Esc. |
| MVIEW | Controls Paper Space viewports. | MV | **On/Off** = turns display of viewport on or off, **Hideplot** = causes hidden-line removal of viewport at plot time, **Fit** = fits new viewport in current view, **2/3/4** = creates two, three, or four viewports, **Restore** = restores viewport configurations saved with Vports command. |
| NEW | Creates new drawing. | N | Dialog box lets you choose a drawing template. |
| OFFSET | Creates parallel copies. | OF | **T** = select a point through which offset passes, **number** = offset distance. |

Table E.1:    AutoCAD LT Commands (continued)

| Command Name | Description | Shortcut | Options/Operations |
|---|---|---|---|
| OLELINKS | Updates, changes and deletes existing OLE links. | | Dialog box allows you to update any links in the current drawing or set them to update automatically. |
| OOPS | Restores last erasure. | OO | NA |
| OPEN | Opens a new file. | OP | Dialog box allows you to save or discard current drawing edits. |
| ´ORTHO | Forces lines to be vertical or horizontal. | OR | Toggle with F8 key or Ctrl-O. |
| ´OSNAP | Allows exact selection of object geometry. | OE | You can set object snaps to be the default by using Osnap and entering the Osnap mode you want. Use None to turn default Osnaps off. |
| PAINTER | Matches properties of selected objects. | PA | Allows matching of all properties or selected properties: color; layer; linetype; linetype scale; thickness and some dimensioning values. |
| ´PAN | Shifts the current display in a specified direction. | P | NA |

*Table E.1:* **AutoCAD LT Commands (continued)**

| Command Name | Description | Shortcut | Options/Operations |
|---|---|---|---|
| PASTECLIP | Allows you to paste AutoCAD LT objects, text and a variety of file formats into the current drawing. | PC | You are prompted for an insertion point, and scale. All objects are inserted in the upper left corner of the drawing area. Text objects become Mtext objects. |
| PASTESPEC | Allows you to insert data from the Windows clipboard. | | The Paste Special dialog box allows you to convert the clipboard data format, from the native application format. |
| PEDIT | Edits polylines, 3D polylines, and meshes. | PE | **C** = closes a polyline; **D** = decurves a curved polyline; **Edit** = edits polyline vertices; **F** = curves fitted polyline; **Join** = joins a polyline to other polylines, arcs, and lines; **L** = controls non-continuous linetype generation through vertices; **O** = opens a closed polyline; **S** = spline curve; **U** = undoes last option; **W** = sets overall width; **X** = exits Pedit. |
| PLAN | Changes to plan view of a UCS. | PV | **C** = current, **U** = specified UCS, **W** = world coordinate system. |

*Table E.1:    AutoCAD LT Commands (continued)*

| Command Name | Description | Shortcut | Options/Operations |
|---|---|---|---|
| PLINE | Draws a 2D polyline. | PL | **H** = sets half-width value, **U** = undoes last option, **W** = sets beginning and end width of current segment, **A** = switches to drawing arcs, **C** = closes a polyline, **L** = continues previous segment. While in the Arc mode, **A** = arc angle, **CE** = center point, **CL** = close poly-line with an arc, **D** = arc direction, **L** = switch to line-drawing mode, **S** = second point of a three point arc. |
| PLOT | Plot a drawing. | PP | Uses a dialog box to offer plotter settings. Can be disabled using Cmddia system variable (*see Appendix D*). |
| POINT | Draws a point object. | PT | Point objects can be changed using Pdmode and Pdsize system variables (*see Appendix D*). |
| POLYGON | Draws a polygon. | PG | **E** = draw a polygon by specifying one edge segment, **C** = circumscribe polygon around a circumference, **I** = inscribe a polygon around a circumference. |

*Table E.1:*   **AutoCAD LT Commands (continued)**

| Command Name | Description | Shortcut | Options/Operations |
|---|---|---|---|
| PREFER-ENCES | Customizes the AutoCAD LT settings. | PF | Controls the following environment settings: File system; Work Space; User (including measurement system); Color and Font. |
| PSOUT | Exports drawing to Encapsulated PostScript format. | PU | If PostScript fonts are used in the drawing, they will be used with the .EPS file. |
| PSPACE | Switch to Paper Space. | PS | Only valid in Paper Space when moving from a Model Space viewport. |
| PURGE | Deletes unused named items. | PR | Layers, blocks, text styles, linetypes, and dimension styles will be removed if not being used. |
| QSAVE | Saves drawing. | | File is saved, without any messages or requests to you from AutoCAD LT. |
| QTEXT | Displays text as rectangles. | QT | **On** = turn on Qtext, **Off** = turn off Qtext. Can also be set using Ddrmodes. |
| QUIT | Exits AutoCAD LT. | Q, ET | Dialog box appears, letting you save or discard changes to current drawing. |

Table E.1: **AutoCAD LT Commands (continued)**

| Command Name | Description | Shortcut | Options/Operations |
|---|---|---|---|
| RAY | Creates a semi-infinite line. | | Pick starting point and specify point(s) through which ray(s) will pass. |
| RECOVER | Repairs a damaged drawing. | | AutoCAD LT automatically attempts a recovery. |
| RECTANG | Draws a rectangle. | RC | Prompts you to select points defining two opposite corners of rectangle. Rectang then draws a closed rectangular polyline. |
| REDO | Reverses last Undo command. | RE | Can only be used to Redo one Undo. |
| ´REDRAW | Refreshes the display. | R | Only in current viewport or Model Space. |
| REGEN | Regenerates a drawing. | RG | Refreshes display to reflect latest changes. |
| REINIT | Reinitializes I/O devices. | RI | Also reinitializes the ACLT.PGP file. |
| RENAME | Renames named items. | RN | Layers, blocks, dimension styles, text styles, linetypes, UCSs, views, and viewports. |
| ´RESUME | Resumes a script. | | *See* ´Script. |

*Table E.1:*  **AutoCAD LT Commands** *(continued)*

| Command Name | Description | Shortcut | Options/Operations |
|---|---|---|---|
| REVDATE | Inserts revision time, date, filename, and username. | RD | You can change user-name in Preferences. |
| ROTATE | Rotates objects. | RO | **R** = rotate with respect to an angle. |
| SAVE | Saves a drawing. | SA | Dialog box lets you determine name of file and where to save it. |
| SAVEAS | Saves and renames a drawing. | SS | Same as Save, plus renames the current drawing. |
| SCALE | Changes size of objects. | SC | **R** = scale relative to another object. |
| ´SCRIPT | Runs a script file. | SR | Script files contain the exact keystrokes to perform a series of actions. Virtually no interaction is allowed; best suited for batch operations such as plotting. |
| SELECT | Selects objects. | SE | Lets you pre-select objects using standard selection options. |
| ´SETVAR | Controls and displays system variables. | | **?** = show status of all or selected system variables. |

*Table E.1:*   **AutoCAD LT Commands (continued)**

| Command Name | Description | Shortcut | Options/Operations |
|---|---|---|---|
| SHADE | Performs Z-buffer shading on 3D models. | | *See* Shadedge and Shadedif system variables (*Appendix D*). |
| ´SNAP | Controls Snap function. | SN | Snap forces cursor to move in exact increments. ***Number*** = snap increment, **On/Off** = turns snap feature on and off (same as F9 or Ctrl-B), **A** = allows differing X and Y snap increments, **R** = rotates snap grid, **S** = lets you select between standard and isometric snap grids. *See also* Snapang and Snapbase system variables (*Appendix D*) and the Ddrmodes command. |
| SOLID | Draws a 2D filled polygon. | SO | *See* the Fill command. |
| SPELL | Checks spelling in a drawing. | | Dictionaries can be added to and changed. |
| SPLINE | Creates a quadratic or cubic spline (NURBS) curve. | SP | **C** = close with tangent to starting point, **F** = fit tolerance through points chosen, **O** = convert 2D or 3D spline fit polylines. |

*Table E.1:* **AutoCAD LT Commands (continued)**

| Command Name | Description | Shortcut | Options/Operations |
|---|---|---|---|
| SPLINEDIT | Edits a spline object. | | **F** = fit data, which sets tangency, tolerances, vertex location, etc.; **C** = close an open spline; **O** = open a closed spline; **M** = move vertex; **R** = refine spline definition by adding, elevating, and changing weight of control points; **E** = rEverse direction; **U** = undo last Splinedit operation; **X** = eXit. |
| ´STRETCH | Stretches vertices. | S | Objects and vertices can be selected separately with careful use of selection options. Last window (i.e. window, crossing window, Wpolygon, or Cpolygon) determines which vertices are moved. The Wpolygon and Cpolygon selection options offer greatest flexibility with this command. |

*Table E.1:*  **AutoCAD LT Commands (continued)**

| Command Name | Description | Shortcut | Options/Operations |
|---|---|---|---|
| ´STYLE | Creates text styles. | | You can set text height, width, and obliqueing angles, as well as other orientations; you also specify what font file to use. |
| TABLET | Controls digitizer tablet alignment. | TA | **On/Off** = turns tablet calibration on or off once tablet is calibrated; **Cal** = calibrates a tablet to match coordinates in the draw space; **Cfg** = configures the tablet for use with a digitizer template. |
| TBCONFIG | Allows you to create and customize toolbars. | | Dialog box allows you to create new toolbars, edit and combine toolbars and flyouts, and delete toolbars, and to control the display of icon buttons and tooltips. |
| TEXT | Creates text. | TX | Select a start point, style, and justification; height if style height is set to 0; and rotation angle. Text does not appear in the drawing until you press ↵ at end of text line. |

*Table E.1:* **AutoCAD LT Commands (continued)**

| Command Name | Description | Shortcut | Options/Operations |
|---|---|---|---|
| 'TEXTSCR | Flips display to text mode. | | Same as F1. |
| 'TIME | Displays time values. | TI | Shows date the drawing was created, current time in drawing, and offers an elapsed timer. |
| TOLER-ANCE | Creates geometric tolerances. | TO | You choose feature control frames from dialog box interface. |
| TOOLBAR | Allows you to show, hide and position individual (or all) toolbars. | TL | You may specify whether the toolbar is to be docked (at Left/Right/Top/Bottom) or floating. |
| TRACKING | Locates a point relative to other points in a drawing. | | Is used while another command (such as Line) is active, to assist precise positioning of object(s). |

Table E.1: AutoCAD LT Commands (continued)

| Command Name | Description | Shortcut | Options/Operations |
|---|---|---|---|
| TRIM | Trims objects back to another object. | TR | Several objects can be selected, both for trimming and as objects to trim to. The Fence option offers a quick way to do multiple trims. **U** = undo last trim, **P** = project trim boundary based on UCS or view, **E** = controls whether the cutting edge is extended beyond its actual length in order to trim objects that do not actually cross the cutting edge object. |
| U | Undoes one command at a time. | | *See* Undo. |

*Table E.1:* **AutoCAD LT Commands (continued)**

| Command Name | Description | Shortcut | Options/Operations |
|---|---|---|---|
| UCS | Controls the user coordinate system function. | | **D** = delete UCS, **O** = move origin, **OB** = match object, **P** = restore previous UCS, **S** = save the current UCS, **V** = create a UCS aligned with current view, **W** = set current UCS to WCS, **X/Y/Z** = rotate UCS about the x-, y-, or z-axis, **ZA** = define z-axis using 2 points, **3** = define UCS using 3 points, **?** = list existing UCSs. *See also* Dducs. |
| UCSICON | Controls UCS icon. | UI | **On/Off** = turns display of icon on and off, **Or** = when possible, places icon at UCS origin. |

*Table E.1:* **AutoCAD LT Commands (continued)**

| Command Name | Description | Shortcut | Options/Operations |
|---|---|---|---|
| UNDO | Undoes one or a series of commands. | UN | *Number* = number of commands to undo, **A** = turns on or off the treatment of menu macros as single groups, **B** = undoes backward to mark placed with M option, **BE** = marks beginning of undo group, **C** = controls the Undo features. Options are All/None/One. All turns on all the features listed here. None turns off the Undo feature. One limits Undo to one Undo, **E** = marks end of undo group, **M** = places the mark used by the Back option. |
| ´UNITS | Selects the unit style. | UT | *See* Ddunits. |
| UNLOCK | Unlocks locked files. | UL | *NA* |
| ´VIEW | Saves and restores views. | | **D** = delete a view, **R** = restore a view, **S** = Save a view, **W** = save a windowed view, **?** = list saved views. |

*Table E.1:* **AutoCAD LT Commands (continued)**

| Command Name | Description | Shortcut | Options/Operations |
|---|---|---|---|
| VIEW-TOOLBAR | Turns on and off the display of selected toolbars from a dialog box. | V | *NA* |
| VPLAYER | Controls layer visibility in Paper Space viewports. | VL | **?** = lists frozen layers in a viewport, **F** = freezes a layer in a viewport, **T** = thaws a layer in a viewport, **R** = resets layer visibility to default settings, **N** = creates a new layer that is frozen in all viewports, **V** = sets default visibility of existing viewports. |
| VPOINT | Selects a viewpoint for 3D views. | VP | **R** = sets rotation angle in the XY plane, **X,Y,Z** = specifies a viewpoint coordinate, ↵ = uses tripod and compass to determine viewpoint. In all cases, entire drawing is target location. |

*Table E.1:* **AutoCAD LT Commands (continued)**

| Command Name | Description | Shortcut | Options/Operations |
|---|---|---|---|
| VPORTS | Divides the Model Space display into viewports. | VW | **D** = delete a saved viewport configuration, **J** = join two viewports, **R** = restore a viewport configuration, **S** = save the current viewport configuration, **SI** = change to a single viewport, **2/3/4** = divides the current viewport into 2, 3, or 4 viewports, **?** = lists current and saved viewport configurations. |
| VSLIDE | Displays slide files. | VS | ***filename** = preload *filename* for next Vslide. |
| WBLOCK | Saves portions of a file to disk. | W | Generally used to write a block to a file; can also be used to save portions of a drawing. At Block name prompt you can enter **name** = write block name to file, **=** = write block to file using same name as the file, **★** = write the entire current file to a file, ↵ = write selected objects; you then see object-selection prompt. The ★ option is a quick way to purge a drawing of all named elements at once. |

*Table E.1:* **AutoCAD LT Commands (continued)**

| Command Name | Description | Shortcut | Options/Operations |
|---|---|---|---|
| WMFIN | Imports Windows metafiles. | WI | At the Import File dialog box, enter a file-name or search for the required file. |
| WMFOPTS | Set the import options for metafile objects. | | In the dialog box, check to specify Wire Frame and/or Wide Line options. |
| WMFOUT | Saves selected AutoCAD LT objects in Windows Metafile format. | WO | *NA* |
| XBIND | Imports named elements from an Xref drawing. | XB | Block, dimension styles, layers, linetypes, and text styles can be imported. |
| XLINE | Creates an infinite line based on two input points. | XL | After picking a point, these options define line: **H** = horizontal through point, **V** = vertical through point, **A** = at specified angle, **B** = bisect angle determined by 3 points, **O** = offset from existing object. |

*Table E.1:*    **AutoCAD LT Commands (continued)**

| Command Name | Description | Shortcut | Options/Operations |
|---|---|---|---|
| XREF | References another drawing with the current one. | XR | You can scale, rotate, or mirror cross-referenced files. You can also use object snap modes and set their layers (*see* Visretain system variable). You cannot edit Xrefs, however. **A** = attach an Xref, **B** = bind or import an Xref to become a permanent part of current drawing, **D** = detach an Xref, **O** = overlay, ignoring nested Xrefs, **P** = allows you to view and edit file names that AutoCAD LT uses for cross-references, **R** = reload an Xref, **?** = displays a list of Xrefs. |

Table E.1:   **AutoCAD LT Commands (continued)**

| Command Name | Description | Shortcut | Options/Operations |
|---|---|---|---|
| ′ZOOM | Controls the display. | Z | ***Number*** = zoom factor relative to drawing limits, ***numberx*** = zoom factor relative to current view, **A** = displays limits of drawing, **C** = displays view based on center point and height, **E** = displays drawing extents, **P** = displays a previous view, **W** = displays an enlargement of a window. |

# Index

Page numbers in *italics* refer to figures or tables; page numbers in **bold** refer to primary discussions of the topic.

# W

# What's on the Companion CD?

## Time-Saving, Quality-Enhancing Software Available Only with This Book

The attached CD is packed with useful utilities, as well as the drawings you'll create while using this book. Together, the book and CD present a unique, performance-based platform for learning, or expanding your mastery of, AutoCAD LT Release 3 for Windows 95.

## What's on the Companion CD?

The following utilities will smooth your way to AutoCAD LT success:

1. On-Screen AEC, a set of macros and architectural symbols developed by the author, all integrated with a standard AutoCAD LT menu and a full set of toolbars. This package offers the basic tools you'll need to start architectural drawings. A $50 value!

2. A library of Complex Linetypes for use with AutoCAD LT. You can use the linetypes as supplied, or use the shapes contained in the complex linetypes to create your own custom linetypes.

You'll also find:

▶ All the drawings you'll work on in the course of the book, in various stages of completion, so you can load a drawing without having to start from scratch.

▶ The most up-to-date version of the *AutoCAD Resource Guide*, an on-line hypertext encyclopedia with complete information on thousands of third-party products designed for specialized uses of AutoCAD and AutoCAD LT. Many of these come with self-running demos.

For complete information on how to install and use the files included on the CD, refer to *Appendix C*.